Understanding National Accounts

SECOND EDITION

François Lequiller, Derek Blades

This work is published under the responsibility of the Secretary-General of the OECD. The opinions expressed and arguments employed herein do not necessarily reflect the official views of OECD member countries.

This document and any map included herein are without prejudice to the status of or sovereignty over any territory, to the delimitation of international frontiers and boundaries and to the name of any territory, city or area.

Please cite this publication as:
Lequiller, F. and D. Blades (2014), *Understanding National Accounts: Second Edition*, OECD Publishing.
http://dx.doi.org/10.1787/9789264214637-en

ISBN 978-92-64-21462-0 (print)
ISBN 978-92-64-21463-7 (PDF)

The statistical data for Israel are supplied by and under the responsibility of the relevant Israeli authorities. The use of such data by the OECD is without prejudice to the status of the Golan Heights, East Jerusalem and Israeli settlements in the West Bank under the terms of international law.

Foreword

T oday more than ever, national accounts remain at the core of a modern system of economic statistics. The global economic and financial crisis has further underlined the importance of a timely, reliable and comprehensive monitoring of economic activity and also pointed to directions for new developments and extensions in the accounts. National accounts provide the conceptual and actual tool to bring coherence to hundreds of statistical sources available in OECD countries. They deliver essential macro-economic indicators to guide policymaking.

The questions, however, are whether users are sufficiently aware of the richness of information contained in the national accounts and fully exploit their analytical and statistical potential. At the same time, how can we ensure that users fully grasp the complex concepts underpinning the national accounts, as well as their limitations? And what about issues around their international comparability? This second edition of "Understanding National Accounts" intends to provide answers to these questions, and to many more, in an easy and accessible, yet rigorous, way. It is an update of the previous edition published by the OECD in 2006, which was very well received by both people familiar with the world of economic statistics, and national accounts in particular, and non-specialist users. Indeed, at the time many readers wrote to the authors that "for the first time, they had come across a book on national accounts that was easy to understand and not boring!"

Since 2006, four key developments have occurred that have made an update of the previous edition a must. First, the financial crisis that hit OECD countries has highlighted the need to better explain how strong movements in economic activity are actually reflected in national accounts. Second, in 2008, the System of National Accounts (SNA) underwent a major round of modernisation. One example of the revisions to the accounting system has been to treat expenditure in R&D as investment in knowledge. Previously, it was simply considered as a current cost item. Third, the new emphasis put on "better lives", beyond the traditional objective of economic growth and GDP, has offered an opportunity to outline how the national accounts can also be a rich underlying source for tracking households' material well-being. Finally, new data on "trade in value added" are now being compiled in parallel to core national accounts, allowing to better understand the increased interconnectedness of our economies

This new, augmented, version of "Understanding National Accounts" reflects the four developments above. In particular, its publication has been scheduled to coincide with the time when most OECD countries will have moved to the new 2008 System of National Accounts.

I am confident that, like the previous one, this edition of the report will receive a similar warm welcome from all those, and they are numerous, whether young statisticians, students, journalists, economists, or citizens, who want to know more about the statistics that are at the heart of the measure of economic development in OECD economies.

Martine Durand
OECD Chief Statistician and Director,
Statistics Directorate

Table of contents

Acknowledgements

In memoriam: Derek Blades, the co-author of this book, died on 25 June 2014. All his life, Derek Blades was extremely active in the international network of national accountants, in particular within the OECD. His great professional competence, his pedagogical skills as well as his gift for social relations will be deeply missed. François Lequiller could not have drafted this manual without him.

The authors would like to thank:

Peter van de Ven, Head of the National Accounts Division in the Statistics Directorate of OECD, for having supervised the preparation of this new version of *Understanding National Accounts* and drafted the new Chapter 16 on "National accounts in a globalising world".

Brent Moulton, Associate Director for National Economics at the Bureau of Economic Analysis, for updating Chapter 12 on US national accounts and drafting the new Chapter 13 on "The 2007-2009 financial crisis and recession as reflected in the national accounts".

Marco Mira d'Ercole and Romina Boarini, respectively Heads of Division and Section of the Household Statistics and Progress Measurement Division in the Statistics Directorate of OECD, for having drafted the new Chapter 15 on "GDP and the welfare metric: the "Beyond GDP" agenda".

Pierre-Alain Pionnier, from OECD, for his contribution on the comparison of profit rates in Chapter 3.

Special thanks to Esther Bolton and Leonie Beisemann who have magnificently updated all the chapters with the appropriate new data and introduced many improvements; creating the StatLinks and updating the glossary, and reviewing the final edition. Without them, this new version of *Understanding National Accounts* would not have been possible. Special thanks for a thorough review of the updated manuscript to Luna Angelini Marinucci, Rachida Dkhissi, Michela Gamba, Catherine Girodet, György Gyomai, Eun Jung Kim, Pierre-Allain Pionnier, Jennifer Ribarsky, Catherine La Rosa-Elkaim, Isabelle Ynesta, all from the Statistics Directorate of OECD. Anne-Lise Faron assisted in preparing the manuscript for typesetting. The splendid format of the manual is due to Audrey Garrigoux and Kate Lancaster, from the Public Affairs and Communication Directorate.

Chapter 1

The essential macroeconomic aggregates

This chapter offers an initial definition of essential macroeconomic variables, taken from the May 2013 edition of OECD Economic Outlook. Germany is taken as the example country. The chapter first looks at GDP, before turning to the other principal indicators used by the OECD economists: private consumption, gross fixed capital formation, GDP deflator, household saving ratio and financial balance of general government.

I n this first chapter, our aim is to give an initial definition of the essential macroeconomic variables, listed in the table below, and taken from the *OECD Economic Outlook* May 2013 (OECD, 2013a).[1] We have chosen to illustrate this chapter using the example of Germany, but we might as well have chosen any other OECD country, since the structure of the country chapters in the *OECD Economic Outlook* is the same for all countries.

Each chapter of this book uses an example from a different country.

Table 1.1. **Main macroeconomic variables**
Germany,[a] 2005 euros, annual changes in percentage

	2010	2011	2012	2013	2014
Private final consumption	0.8	1.7	0.6	1.0	2.2
Gross capital formation	9.8	7.6	-4.9	-0.5	5.4
Gross domestic product	4.0	3.1	0.9	0.4	1.9
Imports	10.9	7.5	2.2	1.9	6.4
Exports	13.4	7.9	4.3	0.9	4.6
Household net saving ratio	10.9	10.4	10.3	10.3	10.1
GDP Deflator	0.9	0.8	1.3	1.2	1.7
Government net lending, as a percentage of GDP	-4.2	-0.8	0.2	-0.2	0.0

a) The *OECD Economic Outlook* dates from May 2013. At that time, the data for 2013 and 2014 were forecasts by the OECD economists. The data for 2010, 2011 and 2012 were actual observations by Destatis, the Federal Republic of Germany's statistical office.
Source: OECD (2013), "OECD Economic Outlook No. 93", OECD Economic Outlook: Statistics and Projections (database), doi: *http://dx.doi.org/10.1787/data-00655-en.*

StatLink ⬛⬛⬛ *http://dx.doi.org/10.1787/888933143526*

Comments made by OECD economists in May 2013 included the following:

"After decelerating throughout 2012 and turning negative in the fourth quarter, real GDP growth is expected to strengthen gradually during 2013 and reach 2% in 2014. While subdued activity in the euro area will hold back the recovery, the pick up of world trade is projected to increase export growth. Wage and employment gains as well as low interest rates will support domestic demand, narrowing the current account surplus to 6% of GDP. The unemployment rate is expected to fall somewhat further, while consumer price inflation may rise to 2% in 2014." (OECD, 2013a).

The OECD economists, commenting on the development of the German economy in May 2013, expected a stronger growth of the **gross domestic product** (commonly known as **GDP**) for 2014 thanks to a strengthened world trade and thus an increase in exports.

Definitions of terms appearing in bold are available in the glossary of this book.

In Germany, as in most OECD countries, 2009 was a terrible year: GDP decreased by 5.1%. The table shows the rebound of the GDP in 2010 (4.0%), the modest growth of the GDP in 2012 (0.9%) and 2013 (0.4%) and an expected positive growth of 1.9% in 2014. This last positive prospect, however, largely depended on further developments of the crisis in the euro area, which imposed a potential threat on the expected recovery. The deceleration of growth between 2012 and 2013 is of 0.5 percentage point. This may be seen very small, but it must never be forgotten that national accounts variables are measured in billions.

In practice, most OECD countries technically compile their national accounts in millions, and thus many tables published appear in millions. But this is far from meaning that the data are accurate at the level of millions. It is wise to round these data to billions.

In the case of Germany, 1% of GDP amounts to roughly 26 billion euros, and thus 0.5% to 13 billion euros, corresponding to roughly the total annual earnings of 400 000 employees, a substantial number.

In this chapter, we begin by defining GDP, before turning to the other principal indicators used by the OECD economists: private consumption, gross fixed capital formation, GDP deflator, **household** saving ratio, and financial balance of **general government**. For all the national accounts data discussed in this chapter, we refer the reader to the OECD web site for this book, or to the general OECD web site under the heading "quarterly national accounts" or "annual national accounts". The quarterly national accounts are more pertinent for those who wish to have the most recent figures.

1. Defining GDP

GDP, Gross Domestic Product, is the most frequently used indicator in the national accounts. It lies at the heart of the entire system of national accounts, and its definition is now internationally agreed upon (see Box 1.1 on "The reference manuals"). GDP combines in a single figure, and with no double counting, all the *output (or production)* carried out *by all the firms, non-profit* *institutions, government bodies and households* in a given country during a given period, regardless of the type of goods and services produced, provided that the production takes place within the country's economic territory. In most cases, it is calculated quarterly or annually, but it can also be calculated monthly.

Box 1.1. **The reference manuals and their implementation**

The standards governing national accounts are enshrined in two international reference manuals: the "System of National Accounts 2008" (SNA 2008), which is recognised globally, and its European version, called the "European System of Accounts 2010" (ESA 2010). The global manual (SNA 2008) is co-signed by the five major international economic organisations: the United Nations, the International Monetary Fund, the OECD, the World Bank and the European Commission. The European manual is totally compatible with the global manual and includes additional useful details. It also has a more legally binding character because, according to European regulations, EU member countries are obligated to implement it. These manuals have contributed substantially to improving the international comparability of data, although further progress still has to be made in this endeavor (see Chapter 3). The current complete versions of SNA 2008 and ESA 2010 are available online.

Warning: while the manuals date from 2008 or 2010, their implementation takes time because the process of production of national accounts statistics is quite heavy. The present book is published in 2014 just before the majority of OECD countries have implemented them. United States of America, Australia, Israel, Mexico and Canada have implemented it in 2013, Korea in March 2014. But European countries implemented the ESA 2010 only in October 2014, at the exact same moment as the publication of this book. The data illustrating the chapters of the present book are therefore sometimes extracted from the previous system. One should not however give too much importance on this limitation. Compared with the old system, the main change is that R&D expenditure is now counted as investment rather than intermediate consumption (see Chapter 14). In practice, this leads to an increase of the level of GDP by around +2.5% in the United States of America, and +1.9% in average in the European Union. It is important to note that this impact is "structural" in the sense that the increase affects more or less all years. In other words, the time-series of GDP is increased more or less by the same amount in all years, thus the growth rate of GDP, which is the main headline indicator, is only marginally affected. In order to illustrate the impact of the change for France, which published its new accounts in May 2014, see Chapter 14. For Germany, the statlink of Table 1.1 of this book contains a table illustrating the changes due to the implementation of ESA 2010 for the main indicators included in Table 1.1.

However, measuring a country's total output is not a simple matter (see boxes "Accuracy" and "Limitations and pitfalls" at the end of this chapter), and national accountants have therefore had to devise innovative methods of calculation.

The output of a single firm can be measured fairly easily. In the case of a firm making pasta, for example, it can be measured as tonnes of pasta made during the year, or, if we multiply the number of tonnes by the price of the pasta, by the amount of output valued in dollars (or in euros in the case of Germany, since this is the national currency). But we shall see that it makes little sense to add together the output measured in dollars from all firms to arrive at a macroeconomic figure. That is because the result of this calculation depends heavily on the way the firms are organised.

Take again the example of the pasta manufacturer and compare two different production scenarios in a given region. Suppose that in the first year there is only one firm, firm A, that makes both the pasta and the flour used to make the pasta. Its output amounts to 100 000 dollars, corresponding to 100 tonnes of pasta, with each tonne valued at 1 000 dollars. Now suppose that the following year, firm A is split into two, with firm A1 specialising in making flour and selling 30 000 dollars' worth to firm A2, which carries out the final production of pasta. Firm A2 makes the same quantity of pasta as in the first year, i.e. 100 tonnes, and at the same price, i.e. 1 000 dollars per ton.

Pasta industry

	Year 1	
	Firm A	
Output	$ 100 000	
	Year 2	
	Firm A1	Firm A2
Output	$ 30 000	$ 100 000

In the first year, the output in this region will be worth 100 000 dollars; in the second year, the value of total output could be the sum produced by firm A1, i.e. 30 000 dollars, and that of firm A2, i.e. 100 000 dollars, resulting in a total of 130 000 dollars. But it would clearly be absurd to use this total as our macroeconomic indicator of activity in the region. It shows an increase of 30% (130 000/100 000 = 1.30, often written as + 30 %, or more simply 30 %), when in fact no change at all took place at the strictly macroeconomic level. The same quantity of pasta was produced at the same price. All that changed was the legal and commercial organisation of the firms.

The above discrepancy generated the national accountants' innovative idea of calculating the contribution of each firm not as its output, but as its **value added**. This expression is profound since it consists of measuring *the value* that the firm *adds* to that of the firms that supply its inputs. Let us consider the pasta example again. Compared with the situation in the first year, when there was only firm A, the value added by firm A2 is not equal to 100 000 dollars. That is because firm A2 buys 30 000 dollars' worth of flour, whereas previously it had made this flour itself and did not count this as output. Therefore, the national accounts system proposes calculating the value added of firm A2 as 100 000 – 30 000 dollars. In other words, the value of the firm's output minus the value of the products used to carry out its production during the period.

The products consumed in the production process during the period are known as **intermediate consumption**. By deducting their value from that of output, one eliminates the *double counting* that occurred earlier when summing of the output of firms A1 and A2. In the second year, the output of flour was in fact counted twice: once in the value of the output of firm A1 (30 000 dollars) and a second time in the value of the output of firm A2 (whose 100 000 dollars in output in fact includes the value of the flour bought and used in the production process).

If one applies this same reasoning to all firms, calculating for each its value added, it is then possible to add together the value added of each firm, *without double counting*. The result will be an indicator that is independent of the way firms are organised. This is illustrated in the following table, which includes the farm that produced the wheat from which the flour was made. For the sake of simplicity, let us assume the farmer uses no intermediate consumption; he obtains his wheat solely from his labour and machinery, without buying seeds or fertilisers. As can be seen from the following diagram, the sum of the output of each unit changes, but the *sum of the value added of each unit* remains equal to 100 000 dollars, regardless of the pattern of organisation.

Year 1		
	Farmer	Firm A
Input	*Labour + machinery + wheat*	*Labour + machinery + wheat*
Output	$ 10 000	$ 100 000
Intermediate consumption	0	$ 10 000
Value Added	**$ 10 000**	**$ 90 000**

	Year 2		
	Farmer	Firm A 1	Firm A2
Input	*Labour + machinery*	*Labour + machinery + wheat*	*Labour + machinery + flour*
Output	$ 10 000	$ 30 000	$ 100 000
Intermediate consumption	0	$ 10 000	$ 30 000
Value Added	**$ 10 000**	**$ 20 000**	**$ 70 000**

This is why GDP is defined as being equal to the sum of the value added of each firm, government institution and producing household in a given country: **GDP = Σ Values Added**.

To be more precise, one should say "GDP = ΣGross Values Added, plus taxes minus subsidies on products". See Table 1.5.

Because each value added is itself equal to output minus intermediate consumption, the end result is: GDP = **Σ outputs – Σ intermediate consumptions**.

The composite formula for GDP (known as an **"aggregate"**) constitutes a macroeconomic indicator of output that is independent of the pattern of organisation and avoids double counting. It provides a good illustration of the three essential rules followed by national accountants when they move from the microeconomy to the macroeconomy:

● avoid double counting;

● devise aggregates that are economically significant (i.e. whose value is independent of non-economic factors); and

● create indicators that are measurable in practice.

GDP vs. other aggregates

Why the bizarre title "Gross Domestic Product", or GDP? It should be clear by now that "product" describes what one is trying to measure, i.e. the result of production. "Domestic" indicates that the output measured is produced within the economic territory of the country, or the group of countries, concerned. (It is in fact entirely possible to calculate GDP for a group of countries, such as that of the euro area.) "Gross" means the **consumption of fixed capital** is not deducted (see below).

"Domestic" is also in opposition to "National", as in **GNI** or **Gross National Income**, which is the current title of what was referred to as **GNP**, or **Gross National Product**, in previous systems of national accounts ("GNP" is still widely used out of habit). GDP measures the total *production* occurring within the territory, while GNI measures the total *income* (excluding capital gains and losses) of all economic agents residing within the territory (households, firms and government institutions).

To convert GDP into GNI, it is necessary to add the income received by resident units from abroad and deduct the income created by production in the country but transferred to units residing abroad. For example, the earnings of workers living in Germany but working in neighbouring parts of Switzerland or Luxembourg have to be added to the German GDP to obtain its GNI. Conversely, the earnings of the seasonal or regular workers living in France or Poland and working across the border in Germany have to be deducted from the German GDP to obtain the German GNI.

For large countries like Germany, the difference between GDP and GNI is small (2.4%, as seen in the following table). But it is larger for a small country like Luxembourg, which pays out a substantial percentage of its GDP as workers' earnings and other so-called "primary income" to the "**rest of the world**" (which is the term used by national accounts to signify "all countries other than Luxembourg", in this case). Primary income includes interest paid on money invested in Luxembourg. Luxembourg also receives substantial primary income from abroad, including interest. In the final analysis, the difference between GDP and GNI is around -31.9% for Luxembourg. Ireland is in a comparable situation to Luxembourg, since it pays out substantial dividends to the parent companies of the American multinational firms that have set up there, partly, but not entirely, for tax reasons. The result is that Ireland's GNI is 18.3% lower than its GDP. While for these two countries GNI is lower than GDP, the opposite also happens – Germany and Switzerland are a case in point.

Table 1.2. **Reconciliation of GDP and GNI for Germany,
Luxembourg and Ireland**

Million euros

Year 2012	Germany	Luxembourg	Ireland
B1_GS1: Gross domestic product	2 666 400	42 899	163 938
(+) D1_D4FRS2: Primary incomes receivable from the rest of the world	206 600	101 109	58 316
(-) D1_D4TOS2: Primary incomes payable to the rest of the world	142 930	114 784	88 390
B5_GS1: Gross national income at market prices	2 730 070	29 225	133 864
Difference between GDP and GNI (%)	2.4	-31.9	-18.3

Source: OECD (2013), "Aggregate National Accounts: Disposable income and net lending/borrowing", OECD National Accounts Statistics (database), *http://dx.doi.org/10.1787/data-00002-en.*

StatLink ⏩ *http://dx.doi.org/10.1787/888933143536*

A distinction is also made between GDP and **Net Domestic Product (NDP).** In order to produce goods and services ("the output") at least three factors are required: labour (the "labour force"), goods and services (intermediate consumption) and capital (machinery). These various factors represent the "inputs" in the production process.

In order to arrive at a genuine measurement of the *new wealth created during the period*, a deduction has to be made for the cost of using up capital (such as the "wear and tear" on machinery). This is known as **consumption of fixed capital**. When this consumption is deducted, the result is **net value added,** and NDP is the sum of these net values added: NDP = Σ Net Values Added. Although less widely used than GDP, NDP is, in theory, a better measure of the wealth produced since it deducts the cost of wearing out the machinery and other capital assets used in production. For similar reasons, in theory, Net National Income is a better measure than GNI of the income created because Net National Income deducts the cost of using up capital assets. However, OECD economists tend to prefer GDP or GNI (over NDP and NNI) for two reasons. First, methods for calculating consumption of fixed capital are complex and tend to differ between countries, thus creating doubts about the comparability of results. Second, when ranking countries or analysing growth, the differences between GDP and NDP are small and do not change the conclusions.

2. The first fundamental equation: Deriving GDP in volume

Let us go back to Table 1.1: "Main Macroeconomic Variables", shown at the very beginning of the chapter. Comments from OECD economists (shown below the table) indicate that they are not interested in GDP growth as such, but in the growth of "real" GDP. What does this expression mean?

Economists and journalists have acquired the unfortunate habit of using the general term "growth" instead of specifying "growth in real GDP". A typical sentence is: "growth is 2%" instead of "growth in real GDP is 2%". This lack of precision sometimes results in bizarre terminology, such as "negative growth", which is an oxymoron; it would be better to say "a decrease of GDP in volume". Incidentally, national accountants prefer the term "GDP in volume" to "real GDP" because inflation is just as real as growth.

The A-B-C of macroeconomics consists of distinguishing what part of the change in national accounts aggregates at current prices stems from a change in the quantities produced and what part stems from a change in prices. Let us suppose, for example, that the output of pasta is worth 100 000 dollars in the first year and 110 000 dollars in the second. The macroeconomist will immediately want to know if this 10% growth (which may be described as "nominal" or "in value" or, better still, "at current prices") is due to an increase in the quantity of pasta or to an increase in its price. An increase in quantity is good news, while an increase in prices ("inflation") tends to be bad news. Keeping in mind the aim of separating the good growth (the quantities) from the bad growth (inflation), national accountants have developed sophisticated methods for separating out movements in GDP "at current prices" into two components: (1) an indicator of the change in quantity (the "real GDP" or, preferably, "**GDP in volume**"); and (2) an indicator of the change in prices, called the "**GDP deflator**". These methods are described in detail in Chapter 2.

Recall that the 100 000 dollars' worth of pasta production mentioned earlier equals 100 tonnes of pasta (the quantity) multiplied by 1 000 dollars (the price per tonne). In almost the same way, the index of the growth rate of GDP at current prices is exactly equal to the index of the growth rate of GDP in volume multiplied by the index of the growth rate of the GDP deflator:

Fundamental equation (1)

[1 + the growth rate (divided by 100) of GDP at current prices] =
[1 + the growth rate (divided by 100) of GDP in volume] ×
[1 + the growth rate (divided by 100) of the GDP deflator]

This is a fundamental equation in the national accounts, and the term "deflator" stems directly from it. This is because one can derive from this fundamental equation the following equation:

[1 + (Growth rate of GDP in volume/100)] =
[1 + (Growth rate of GDP at current prices/100)] /
[1 + (Growth rate of the GDP deflator/100)]

In this way, starting with GDP growth at current prices, one "deflates" (i.e. divides) this by the price indicator (the GDP deflator) to obtain the volume indicator (GDP volume). Conversely, in the previous version of the equation, GDP growth in volume was "inflated" by the price indicator in order to obtain GDP growth at current prices. Note that these equations showing the breakdown into volume and price movements apply not only to GDP but also to some of the other key variables in the national accounts, notably investment and consumption. Note also that this equation also applies to absolute levels. Thus, GDP in volume at absolute levels (i.e. in millions of dollars of the "base" year) is equal to GDP at current prices at absolute levels (i.e. in millions of dollars) divided by the implicit deflator, expressed as a price index divided by 100. When this operation is done, the base year for GDP in volume corresponds to the year for which the price index is conventionally equal to 100.

Macroeconomists pay very little attention to the evolution of GDP at current prices. It does not even appear in the main OECD table for Germany (see Table 1.1). In contrast, its two main components – real GDP and the GDP deflator – feature prominently in the table, one of them being used to measure growth and the other to measure inflation. GDP at current prices is, however, used as the denominator to standardise many important aggregates, such as the public deficit, the balance of exports and imports, national savings, etc. Ratios calculated as percentages of GDP, with both numerator and denominator usually expressed in current prices, are used to make international comparisons of variables that would otherwise depend on the size of the country.

Figure 1.1 below illustrates for Germany the relationship between GDP at current prices, GDP in volume and the GDP deflator. Unlike the earlier OECD table, which shows growth rates, this figure contains "absolute amounts". In other words, the two aggregates – GDP at current prices and GDP in volume – are expressed in billions of euros.

Figure 1.1. **Gross domestic product, in value and in volume**

Germany, million euros

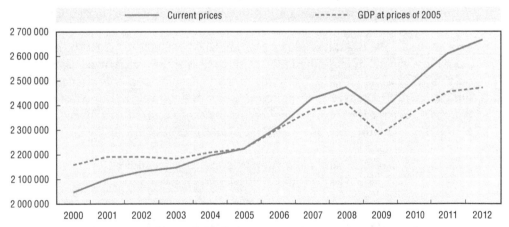

Source: OECD (2013), "Aggregate National Accounts: Gross domestic product", OECD National Accounts Statistics (database), http://dx.doi.org/10.1787/data-00001-en.

StatLink ᴍᴩ http://dx.doi.org/10.1787/888933143546

It can be seen that the Germany GDP at current prices was roughly 2 470 billion euros in 2008, while the German GDP in volume (i.e. constant prices, shown in the figures as "GDP at prices of 2005") was around 2 410 billion euros for the same year. The GDP deflator (inflation) cannot be calculated in billions of euros and therefore does not appear as a separate line on the figure.[2] However, the GDP deflator can be inferred as the gap between

GDP in volume and GDP at current prices. The widening of this gap after the year 2005 indicates, in principle, the existence of inflation.[3] This is indeed the case, as can be seen from the fact that after 2005, GDP at current prices (the dark line) increases much faster than GDP in volume (the dotted line).

Notice that the two lines coincide in the year 2005. That is because in this figure, GDP in volume for all the years has been calculated using the prices prevalent in the year 2005. It is for this reason that the legend for the dotted line refers to GDP "at prices of 2005". By definition, the two aggregates – GDP at current prices and GDP in volume – have to be equal for this particular year (known as the "base year" or the "reference year"). We shall come back to these questions in Chapter 2, but what one should infer from this example is that it is very important whether the aggregate is in volume or not. The choice of the base year is less important, especially when applied to growth rates, which is what economists focus on.

Table 1.3 shows the variations in Germany's GDP deflator. It can be seen that the years 2010 to 2012 were characterised by fairly low inflation, which remained near to 1%. For comparison, the table also shows the annual variation in the consumer price index (CPI).[4] This index is another indicator of inflation that is better known and more frequently used than the GDP deflator, mainly because it is available monthly and relates to the aggregate that is of most interest to people, namely consumption. The GDP deflator, also called "the implicit GDP price index" or, simply "implicit GDP deflator", is on the one hand more general in scope than the CPI, since it also covers capital goods. But on the other hand, it is less general because it measures only domestic inflation, with increases in import prices not directly taken into account. Moreover, except for the very few countries that compile their national accounts each month, the GDP deflator is available only quarterly.

Table 1.3. **GDP deflator and consumer price index**
Germany, annual growth rates in percentage

	2010	2011	2012	2013	2014
PGDP: Gross domestic product, deflator, market prices	0.9	0.8	1.3	1.2	1.7
CPIH: Consumer price index, harmonised	1.2	2.5	2.1	1.6	2.0

Source: OECD (2013), "OECD Economic Outlook No. 93", OECD Economic Outlook: Statistics and Projections (database), doi: http://dx.doi.org/10.1787/data-00655-en.

StatLink ⟨⟨⟩⟩ http://dx.doi.org/10.1787/888933143552

3. Defining demand: the role of investment and consumption

Let us return to Table 1.1 at the beginning of this chapter. The OECD economists had noted an upturn in investment by firms and households that can be seen in Table 1.1 by looking at the variable "Gross capital formation", which had declined 4.9% in 2012, 0.5% in 2013, but was expected to significantly rebound by 5.4% in 2014. Like real GDP, this variable is shown in Table 1.1 "at 2005 prices", in other words "in volume". For a macroeconomic aggregate, growth of more than 3% in volume is a good performance, even if China or India show even better performance. However, at the time of writing, this was still only a forecast waiting to be confirmed.

In the national accounts, investment, i.e. the purchase of machinery (including software) and buildings (offices, infrastructure, dwellings) and the constitution of stocks (inventories) is known as **gross capital formation (GCF)**. When stock-building (or **"changes in inventories"**) is excluded, leaving only the purchases of buildings and machinery, the result is known as **gross fixed capital formation (GFCF)**. This variable measures total expenditures on products intended to be used for future production. These types of products are collectively known as "fixed" capital".[5] Why not simply call them investment, as economists in fact often do? Because the word "investment" in everyday use applies as much to financial investment ("I invest in shares of the stock market") as it does to investment in machinery and buildings. So to make a clear distinction between the two applications, the national accountants use this somewhat peculiar terminology. Finally, the word "gross" indicates that the expenditure is measured without deducting the consumption of fixed capital (the wear and tear).

The OECD economists were counting to some extent on *"wage and employment gains to support domestic demand"*. "Private final consumption" is the main part of domestic demand and OECD economists expected a surge of private consumption of 2.2% in 2014. "Private consumption" is essentially what the national accountants call **household final consumption expenditure**.

Private consumption includes household consumption expenditure and also expenditure by "non-profit institutions serving households" (NPISHs). For the definition of "households" and "NPISHs", see Chapters 5 and 6.

This variable covers all purchases made by consumers: food, clothing, housing services (rents), energy, durable goods (notably cars), spending on health, on leisure and on miscellaneous services. Consumption expenditure does not, however, include households' purchases of dwellings, which are counted as household GFCF. The "consumption" variable is in contrast to "GFCF", with consumption intended to designate purchases that are consumed (in the sense of "used up" or "destroyed") during the period, while GFCF refers to purchases intended to be used for future production. However, this distinction is somewhat arbitrary, since purchases of cars by households (goods that are certainly intended to last) are classified as consumption (see box "Limitations and pitfalls"). Why "final" consumption? It is in contrast to intermediate consumption, referred to earlier.

After GDP, household final consumption is undoubtedly the most important variable in the national accounts, representing in general more than 60% of GDP. Indeed, the economic model providing the underlying framework for the national accounts is aimed at maximising this consumption, although today there is increasing concern that consumption should be sustainable in the longer term ("sustainable development").

4. Second fundamental equation: Reconciling global output and demand

Final consumption and investment are two of the main components of "final" macroeconomic demand. The great attraction of the national accounts is that they constitute a "reconciled" model of the economy, balancing supply and demand. In fact, the second fundamental equation of the national accounts can be written as follows:

Fundamental equation (2)

GDP = Sum of final demand aggregates

In order to grasp the origin of this essential accounting equation, let us return to the example of the pasta industry.

	Year 2		
	Farmer	Firm A1	Firm A2
Input	*Labour + machinery*	*Labour + machinery + wheat*	*Labour + machinery + flour*
Output	$ 10 000	$ 30 000	$ 100 000
Intermediate consumption	0	$ 10 000	$ 30 000
Value added	**$ 10 000**	**$ 20 000**	**$ 70 000**

Recall that GDP is equal to total value added or, equivalently, to total output minus total intermediate consumption. If one adds up the output, this means adding together the 10 000 dollars' worth of wheat, the 30 000 dollars' worth of flour and the 100 000 dollars' worth of pasta, resulting in a total of 140 000 dollars. If one now deducts the intermediate consumption, this means removing the 10 000 dollars' worth of wheat and the 30 000 dollars' worth of flour, leaving the 100 000 dollars' worth of pasta. If one simplifies matters by ignoring possible inventory accumulation in the factory and in the distribution circuit, the 100 000 dollars corresponds exactly to the purchases by households, in other words to household final consumption expenditure.

This example shows that GDP, the sum of all values added, is equal, *by definition*, to final demand, which, in this case, consists only of household demand for pasta.

Only a small amount of elaboration is needed to bring this example much closer to reality. If one introduces a firm that makes the machinery used to manufacture pasta, it can be verified that GDP equals exactly the consumption of pasta plus the purchase of the machinery used to make it, i.e. household consumption plus GCF. This opens the system up to GCF in addition to household consumption. In addition, if we assume that the economy is open to imports and that there is external demand reflected in exports, the equation is now supplemented with these additional flows:

GDP + Imports = Household consumption + GCF + Exports

The left-hand side of the equation consists of supply at the macroeconomic level, made up of domestic production (GDP) and external supply (imports). The right-hand side consists of final demand, broken down into domestic demand (household consumption and GCF) and external demand (exports). Macroeconomists often use this equation in another, mathematically equivalent form:

GDP = Household consumption + GCF + Net Exports

The left-hand side now consists solely of GDP, the principal indicator of economic activity. The right-hand side consists of the "final uses" that are the major components of domestic demand together with "net exports", which is simply the difference between exports and imports. This accounting equation is fundamental in analysing the economic condition. It provides a perfect illustration of the impact of demand on supply, according to Keynesian reasoning. It is no accident, in fact, that national accounting was developed during the 1940s, just after Keynes' major discoveries.

To be fully precise, the above equation has to be made slightly more complex, as shown in Table 1.4. The second fundamental equation in the national accounts can easily be verified by looking at this table. The addition of the rows in bold type (total final consumption, gross capital formation, external balance of goods and services) is equal to GDP, to the nearest million euros. This table introduces the concept of *final consumption of NPISHs* ("non-profit institutions serving households"), which accounts for only a tiny proportion of GDP (1.6 %),[6] so that economists often add it to household consumption, thus creating the "private consumption" aggregate.

A much more important introduction is that of *general government consumption* (19.3% of GDP), which exceeds GFCF (17.6%) but is substantially smaller than household consumption (55.9%). We shall return to the significance of this "general government consumption" variable in Chapter 5. The table also shows stock-building ("changes in inventories"). Although usually small in absolute terms, stock-building nevertheless plays an important role in the short term. In fact, inventories come into play as a "shock absorber" between production and final demand from households and firms. Note that unlike other variables, changes in inventories are not shown in macroeconomic tables as a percentage of GDP or as a growth rate, but as contributions to GDP growth (see Box 1.2: "Contributions to growth").

Table 1.4. **Germany, expenditure approach**
Germany, 2012

Codes[a]		Million euros	% of GDP
B1_GE	Gross domestic product (expenditure approach)	2 666 400	
P3	**Final consumption expenditure**	**2 048 220**	
	of which:		
P31S14	Final consumption expenditure of households	1 490 500	55.9
P31S15	Final consumption expenditure of non-profit institutions serving households	43 370	1.6
P3S13	Final consumption expenditure of general government	514 350	19.3
P5	**Gross capital formation**	**460 270**	
	of which:		
P51	Gross fixed capital formation	470 550	17.6
P52	Changes in inventories	-13 150	
B11	**External balance of goods and services**	**157 910**	
	of which:		
P6	Exports of goods and services	1 381 030	51.8
P7	Imports of goods and services	1 223 120	45.9

a) The table shows the official SNA codes, which the reader can find on the website accompanying this book. These codes facilitate the understanding and manipulation of the data.

Source: OECD (2013), "Aggregate National Accounts: Gross domestic product", OECD National Accounts Statistics (database), *http://dx.doi.org/10.1787/data-00001-en*.

StatLink ⟪⟫ *http://dx.doi.org/10.1787/888933143564*

Short-term macroeconomic analysis relies heavily on the equation set out on the previous page, but expressed in volume. The equation provides a mathematical explanation of GDP growth in terms of its various components. The value of national accounts is that the general macroeconomic concept of the influence of demand on supply in this way takes concrete form as an accounting equation.[7] This was the same equation underpinning the OECD economists' remark: "*While subdued activity in the euro area will hold back the recovery, the pick up of world trade is projected to increase export growth…and thus GDP*".

Box 1.2. **Contributions to growth**

In this box, the sign Δ will be used to express the difference between two years (or two quarters), so that ΔGDP_t signifies $GDP_t - GDP_{t-1}$, in other words the difference between GDP in year (quarter) t and GDP in year (quarter) t–1. Using this notation, $\Delta GDP_t / GDP_{t-1}$, will be equal to the GDP growth rate for year (or quarter) t compared with year (or quarter) t–1.

The starting point is a simplified volume equation: $GDP_t = C_t + I_t + X_t$ (where GDP = Final consumption + GFCF + Exports). For this simplified equation, we assume that there are no imports and no inventories. Mathematically, this results in the "difference" equation: $\Delta GDP_t = \Delta C_t + \Delta I_t + \Delta X_t$. Dividing both sides by GDP_{t-1} then results in equation (a):

$$\frac{\Delta GDP_t}{GDP_{t-1}} = \frac{\Delta C_t}{GDP_{t-1}} + \frac{\Delta I_t}{GDP_{t-1}} + \frac{\Delta GDP_t}{GDP_{t-1}}$$

Dividing and multiplying each term on the right-hand side by its value in t–1 and reorganising, one obtains equation (b):

$$\frac{\Delta GDP_t}{GDP_{t-1}} = \frac{C_{t-1}}{GDP_{t-1}} \frac{\Delta C_t}{C_{t-1}} + \frac{I_{t-1}}{GDP_{t-1}} \frac{\Delta I_t}{I_{t-1}} + \frac{X_{t-1}}{GDP_{t-1}} \frac{\Delta X_t}{X_{t-1}}$$

The verbal translation of this second equation is as follows: GDP growth breaks down exactly into the contribution of consumption plus the contribution of investment plus the contribution of exports. Each contribution is equal to the weight of the variable multiplied by the growth rate of the same variable in the current period. The weight of the variable is equal to its value in the previous period divided by the GDP of the previous period.

This breakdown of growth is widely used by macroeconomists. As can be seen, it is based on the second fundamental equation. Exercise 4, at the end of this chapter, will enable you to carry out a practical application. It involves the calculation of the contribution of changes in inventories and net exports. Since these variables can be positive or negative, it is necessary to use version (a) of the above equation to calculate their contributions to growth, and not version (b). In macroeconomic tables expressed in growth rates, changes in inventories and net exports are never shown in terms of percentage growth rates but solely as contributions to growth.

It is important to note that the calculation of contributions to growth basically relies on the accounting identity between GDP and final demand. Unfortunately, this mathematical link is no longer fully valid when using chain-linked volume measures because the results are not additive. Chapter 2 explains chain-linked volume accounts, their advantages and disadvantages, and shows how to compile contributions to growth in this new context.

5. Third fundamental equation: Reconciling global output and income

The previous section dealt with the first macroeconomic reconciliation, between global output (measured by the sum of the values added) and final demand. There is a second reconciliation, this time between global output and the income of economic agents. Any production activity generates income that is shared between the three "factors of production": labour, capital and intermediate consumption. Since value added is equal to output minus intermediate consumption, this second macroeconomic reconciliation can be written more simply by eliminating intermediate consumption and using value added as the global indicator of output. This means that there are now just two factors creating value added, namely labour and capital, which are compensated respectively by salaries and by the profits generated through production. It is these types of income that subsequently enable economic agents – households and firms – to consume and invest. For example, the 100 000 dollars of GDP of our now-familiar pasta industry are divided between the profits of the farmer, the two firms A1 and A2, and the salaries of the staff at firms A1 and A2.

In the end, our two macroeconomic reconciliations can be summarised in the following double fundamental equation:

Fundamental equation (3)

**Output (sum of the values added) =
Income (employees' salaries + company profits) =
Final demand (Consumption + GFC + Net exports)**

We shall be evaluating the way in which the national accounts record income in the chapters dealing with the accounts of households, enterprises and government sectors. For the moment, let us note simply the following fundamental result: GDP is also equal to total income. This is the third fundamental equation. Note also that in the national accounts one talks of **"compensation of employees"** rather than salaries, because the cost of labour includes social contributions paid by the employers, and that profits are known as **operating surplus** or, in some cases, as **mixed income**.[8] The operating surplus is described as "gross" when no deduction is made for the cost of the depreciation of capital, known as "consumption of fixed capital" in the national accounts. It is in fact preferable to analyse this surplus in "net" terms, in other words, after deducting consumption of fixed capital, as we shall see in Chapter 7.

Three ways to measure GDP

To summarise, there are three "approaches" to GDP: (1) the output approach (the sum of gross values added); (2) the final demand approach (consumption + investment + net exports); and (3) the income approach (compensation of employees + gross operating surplus + gross mixed income).[9]

Table 1.5 illustrates the equality of the three approaches for 1991 and 2012. The presentation is slightly more complicated than the double equation set out above, notably because of the introduction of **taxes net of subsidies**. For the time being, however, we will ignore this difficulty. Below, the reader can verify that the "three" GDPs are exactly equal, at 1 535 billion euros in 1991 and 2 666 billion euros in 2012.[10] Comparison between the two years illustrates certain fundamental changes that have taken place in Germany since reunification and the recent impact of the 2008 economic crisis. As Figure 1.2 shows, the share of employee compensation in GDP fell regularly from 56.0% in 1991 to 49.0% in 2007 but rebounded then to 51.6% in 2012. This rebound originates from the fact that it was the profits that bore the brunt of the shock of the crisis in 2008-09.

Table 1.5. **The three approaches to GDP**

Germany, billion euros

		1991	2012
GDP	Gross domestic product (output approach)	1 535	2 666
B1B	Gross value added at basic prices, excluding FISIM	1 393	2 387
D21_D31	+ Taxes less subsidies on products	141	280
GDP	Gross domestic product (expenditure approach)	1 535	2 666
P3	Final consumption expenditure	1 171	2 048
P5	+ Gross capital formation	369	460
P6	+ Exports of goods and services	394	1 381
P7	− Imports of goods and services	400	1 223
GDP	Gross domestic product (income approach)	1 535	2 666
D1	Compensation of employees	859	1 376
B2+B3	+ Gross operating surplus and gross mixed income	554	1 016
D2	+ Taxes less subsidies on production and imports	122	274

Source: OECD (2013), "Aggregate National Accounts: Gross domestic product", OECD National Accounts Statistics (database), *http://dx.doi.org/10.1787/data-00001-en.*

StatLink ᐩᕱᕱᕵ *http://dx.doi.org/10.1787/888933143571*

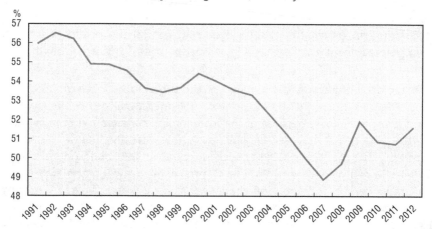

Figure 1.2. **Employee compensation**

As a percentage of GDP, Germany

Source: OECD (2013), "Aggregate National Accounts: Gross domestic product", OECD National Accounts Statistics (database), *http://dx.doi.org/10.1787/data-00001-en.*

StatLink ⬛🖼📲 *http://dx.doi.org/10.1787/888933143584*

Saving ratio and the general government financial balance

The principal macroeconomic indicators used by the OECD in Table 1.1. include two aggregates to which no reference has yet been made: the *household saving ratio* and the *general government financial balance.* They are shown again below.

Germany

Summary of recent results and forecasts

	2010	2011	2012	2013	2014
Household saving ratio[a]	10.9	10.4	10.3	10.3	10.1
General government financial balance[b]	-4.2	-0.8	0.2	-0.2	0.0

a) Net saving as % of net disposable income.
b) % of GDP.
Source: OECD (2013), "OECD Economic Outlook No. 93", OECD Economic Outlook: Statistics and Projections (database), doi: *http://dx.doi.org/10.1787/data-00655-en.*

The household saving ratio is equal to saving by households expressed as a percentage of their disposable income,[11] both these variables being expressed at current prices. The ratio represents the portion of household income that is not consumed. In 2012, the German household saving ratio was 10.3%. In other words, out of every thousand euros of household income (after tax), 103 euros were saved – for investment in housing, kept as cash or used to purchase financial products such as shares, bonds or life insurance. This variable is of great importance in macroeconomics, as its evolution determines the relationship between income and consumption.

The general government financial balance corresponds to what is commonly referred to as the public surplus or deficit.

"General government" includes the central government, local authorities, social security and the various organisations depending on them.
However, it does not cover enterprises such as railways, telephone companies or electricity firms, which are state-owned in some countries.
We shall be returning to these classifications in Chapters 7 and 9.

In the national accounts, it has the more complicated but fairly eloquent title "net lending/net borrowing of general government". This variable is equal to the difference between the sum of all general government revenues and the sum of general government expenditures, whether they be "current" (civil service salaries, interest on the public debt) or "capital" (investment). A negative difference shows that government has a borrowing requirement. That is because when revenue falls short of expenditure it will be necessary to find financing for the difference, mainly through borrowing and hence increasing the public debt. A positive difference shows the existence of a financing capacity. Since the 1991 unification, this has occurred three times, in 2000, 2007 and 2012, in Germany, and the budget is expected to be balanced in 2014.

It has become customary, especially for European countries since the signing of the Maastricht Treaty, to express "net lending/net borrowing of general government" as a percentage of GDP at current prices. This is one of the cases in which GDP at current prices is used in absolute terms as the denominator of a magnitude. This approach makes it possible to compare deficits between countries while automatically adjusting for the different size of their economies, and it underlies the "Maastricht criterion" stipulating that the public deficit must not exceed 3% of GDP. Following the recent financial and economic crisis, most governments of the European Union found themselves in "excessive deficit" because they had to increase their social expenses, in particular unemployment benefits, while, at the same time tax and social contributions revenues were lower because of recession or very slow growth. The European Commission has significantly increased the constraints of the Stability and Growth Pact during 2010-11 to face the increasing threat posed by the high debt level due to the accumulation of these deficits.

This completes our presentation of all the variables that appear in Table 1.1: "Main Macroeconomic Variables".

Notes

1. The *OECD Economic Outlook* contains the biannual macroeconomic forecasts for each OECD country and the OECD area as a whole. Each edition is numbered, with the edition for May 2013 being the 93rd in the series.

2. When not shown as a growth rate, the GDP deflator is shown, like all price indices, as a series of dimensionless numbers whose change represents changes in prices, with the value in a given base year equal to 100.

3. Strictly speaking, one should use a logarithmic scale for the vertical axis.

4. In fact, what we have here is the European version of this index, known as the "Harmonised index of consumer prices" (HICP) for Germany.

5. In contrast to "variable" capital, consisting of changes in inventories. These expressions go back to Karl Marx, who provided the far-distant inspiration for some of the ideas behind the national accounts.

6. Non-profit institutions may account for an appreciable part of GDP but most of them are recorded in a different sector in the national accounts. For example, mutual insurance institutions are included in the insurance sector. The NPISH sector covers only a small portion of all non-profit institutions, specifically those that are both financed and controlled by households.

7. Unfortunately, modern calculating methods mean that fundamental equation 2 no longer holds exactly in volume. We shall be returning to this problem of non-additivity in Chapter 2. For the time being, it is possible to ignore this difficulty.

8. "Mixed income" is the term applied to the gross operating surplus of "non-incorporated enterprises". Further light will be thrown on this point in Chapter 6.

9. One could also calculate the three approaches in terms of Net Domestic Product: the output approach (the sum of net values added); the final demand approach (consumption + net investment plus net exports); and the income approach (compensation of employees + net operating surplus + net mixed income).

10. This equation is not strictly verifiable for all countries, because of statistical discrepancies – notably in the case of the United States. See Chapters 10 and 12. Moreover, and this is a remark valid for the rest of the book (including exercises), the numbers shown in the tables are often rounded, so that totals do not match exactly the sum of their components. It may happen that there is a mistake, but more often it is simply that the sum of rounded numbers is not exactly equal to the rounding of the sum. This is the case in Table 1.5 with the value of 1 535 for the GDP (demand approach) for 1991. If one compiles P3 + P5 + P6 – P7, one obtains 1 534, and not 1 535. There is no mistake here. It is simply that the equality holds exactly when numbers are expressed in millions of euros, but does not when they are rounded into billions.

11. In this case, the saving and the disposable income are both net, meaning that consumption of fixed capital on dwellings owned by households is deducted from both aggregates. It is also possible to calculate the saving ratio on a gross basis.

References

European System of Accounts 2010 (ESA 2010), ISBN 978-92-79-31242-7 doi: *http://dx.doi.org/10.2785/16644.*

OECD (2013a), *OECD Economic Outlook*, Vol. 2013/1, OECD Publishing, doi: *http://dx.doi.org/10.1787/eco_outlook-v2013-1-en.*

OECD (2013b), "OECD Economic Outlook No. 93", OECD Economic Outlook: Statistics and Projections (database), doi: *http://dx.doi.org/10.1787/data-00655-en.*

OECD (2013c), "Aggregate National Accounts: Disposable income and net lending/borrowing", OECD National Accounts Statistics (database), *http://dx.doi.org/10.1787/data-00002-en.*

OECD (2013d), "Aggregate National Accounts: Gross domestic product", OECD National Accounts Statistics (database), *http://dx.doi.org/10.1787/data-00001-en.*

SNA 2008, European Commission, International Monetary Fund, Organisation for Economic Co-operation and Development, United Nations, World Bank, New York, 2009, System of National Accounts 2008, *http://unstats.un.org/unsd/nationalaccount/docs/SNA2008.pdf.*

Key points

- GDP is the sum of output within the country's territory minus the sum of intermediate consumption (increased by taxes net of subsidies on products).

- GDP is equal to the sum of the gross value added of each firm, non-profit institution, government body and household producing on the territory (increased by taxes net of subsidies on products).

- The change in GDP expressed in volume is the principal indicator of the change in macroeconomic activity.

- First fundamental equation: the index of the variation in GDP (or any other variable) at current prices breaks down precisely into the product of the index's variation in volume and the index's variation in prices, the latter being known as the "deflator" or the "implicit price index". The deflator can be used as a measure of inflation but differs from the consumer price index.

- Second fundamental equation: GDP is equal to the sum of the final demand aggregates.

- Third fundamental equation: GDP is equal to the sum of incomes (compensation of employees, gross operating surplus and gross mixed income of firms) increased by taxes net of subsidies on production.

- There are therefore three equivalent approaches to GDP: the output approach (sum of gross values added); the final demand approach (the sum of final consumption, GFCF, changes in inventories and net exports); and the income approach (sum of employee compensation, gross operating surplus and mixed income).

Going further

How are these figures obtained?

This is probably the most difficult question to answer in a short textbook on national accounts, but we shall attempt to do so. The illustrations will be taken from the French case, the one the authors know best. However, it will not be possible to give the reader precise answers, since many different methods are used, as is only natural in drawing up accounts covering all economic agents, including in the French case some 25 million households.

Despite their name, the national accounts bear only a partial similarity to the accounts of a company. The general frameworks are similar but the data sources are entirely different. The company accountant has at his disposal a ledger showing to the last cent all the transactions carried out by the firm during the period. The national accountant obviously has nothing similar for all agents, especially for households. For this reason, it is not unreasonable to speak of "national accounts statistics". The addition of the word "statistics" implies acceptance of the notions of approximation, estimation and revision, things in which the national accountants excel but which are anathema to company accountants.

In France, the principal methods for calculating the figures in the national accounts are based on the exploitation of the extremely comprehensive administrative sources available. These consist, on the one hand, of the database built up by Insee (the French public statistics office) on the basis of companies' tax declarations and, on the other, on the centralised information gathered by the public accounting system regarding government institutions. The tax source provides Insee with regular and virtually exhaustive information on more than 2 million French firms. Because these firms are obliged to submit fairly complete accounts drawn up according to precise rules (the "plan comptable general" or general accounting framework), it is possible to use these accounts to calculate the value added of each individual firm (in the case of the large firms) or for groups of firms (in the case of the small ones) and then to add them up. This covers the private sector (referred to as the "market" sector in the national accounts). As regards the "non-market" sector (central government, local authorities and tens of thousands of government institutions) the centralisation of their accounts is carried out by the "Direction de la Comptabilité Publique" (Public Accounts Directorate) in the Finance Ministry, making it possible to calculate fairly precisely the value added for the non-market sector.

There is no such direct source in the case of households, whose consumption represents 60% of GDP. The national households' account is often calculated indirectly by using statistics from other sources. For example, the compensation of employees received by households is calculated by adding up compensation of employees paid out by firms, non-profit institutions and public units. Another common method is to obtain estimates of household aggregates "by difference". Take dividends for example. The dividends paid out by firms are known and the receipts of these dividends by firms and public bodies are also known. The balance of payments provides estimates of the dividends paid to, and received from, the rest of the world, from which one can compile the net dividends received from abroad (dividends received from abroad less dividends paid to other countries). There is a macroeconomic "accounting identity" which states that: "Dividends paid by firms = Dividends received by general government and firms + Net dividends from abroad + Dividends received by households". Turning this equation around gives: "Dividends received by households = Dividends paid by firms – Dividends received by firms and by general government – Net dividends received from abroad". Dividends received by households can therefore be calculated in this way as a "balance", i.e. what is left over. National accountants readily admit that it would be better to have direct sources concerning households, since calculation as a balance has the drawback of concentrating all measurement errors on the single household item. However, it is out of the question to ask households to draw up accounts, and it is therefore necessary to make the best of what is available.

As for the measurement of changes, the sources differ between quarterly accounts (these being the first to be published) or annual accounts. Quarterly accounts use monthly indicators to extrapolate the value of the national accounts variables. These indicators may not correspond perfectly to the definition used in the national accounts but are rapidly available. For example, use is made of the monthly turnover statistics that Insee obtains using Value-Added Tax (VAT) declarations in order to extrapolate, as a growth rate, the "output at current prices" variable. The figure for turnover is admittedly not exactly equal to output, since there may have been changes in inventories between the two periods concerned, but it is the only reasonably similar variable readily available. These "provisional" figures are subsequently revised when Insee has at its disposal (one year later) first-hand information regarding companies' accounts, the result being the so-called "semi-definitive" and, (two years later) the "definitive" accounts based on quasi exhaustive companies' accounts. This term is in fact an overstatement, because these "definitive" accounts can themselves later be revised when a new "base" year is introduced. We shall be returning to these issues in Chapter 10.

Accuracy of national accounts

National accounts could better be called "national accounts statistics" because without this qualifier users may think they are as reliable as the business accounts of a company. This is not true. In particular, while GDP for technical reasons is often expressed in millions of units of the national currency, users should be aware that they are very, very far from being accurate at the level of millions. National accounts' quality is highly dependent on the quality of the statistical system that exists in a given country. And in all countries, at varying degrees, this system does not cover all units, leaving a significant number of adjustments to be made. National accounts data are therefore approximations. It is not even possible to give a summary figure of the accuracy of the GDP. Indeed, national accounts, and in particular GDP, are not the result of a single big survey for which one might compile a confidence interval. They are the result of combining a complex mix of data from many sources, many of which require adjustment to put them into a national accounts database and which are further adjusted to improve coherence, often using non-scientific methods.

It is useful to know that GDP levels can be revised by 1 to 3 percentage points when new benchmark data are introduced (excluding conceptual changes). It can even happen, although rarely, that some countries modify their estimate of GDP by more than 15% (Italy in 1987, China in 2005). In international comparisons, it is important to note that the quality of national accounts is not the same in all countries (see Chapter 3 on international comparisons). Overall, the OECD Statistics Directorate believes it may be misleading to establish a strict order of ranking countries based on GDP per capita at purchasing power parity in cases when countries are clustered around a narrow range of outcomes of less than 5 percentage points.

Limitations and pitfalls to be avoided

The results provided by the national accounts are now such a familiar part of everyday economic information that there is a tendency to forget how extremely ambitious the original project was and still is. It is no accident that the two major creators of modern national accounts (Simon Kuznets of the United States and Richard Stone of the United Kingdom) were both awarded Nobel prizes for economics (Kuznets in 1971 and Stone in 1984). However, it must be realized that, in order to achieve the aim of summarising a country's entire economic activity in a set of internally consistent tables, national accounts have to accept significant approximations and adopt conventions that are sometimes arbitrary. It is necessary to be well aware of these conventions in order to avoid certain pitfalls. The following are a few of them.

Households' internal production (cooking, cleaning, running errands) is not covered in the national accounts. The principal reason is that inclusion would involve making very bold estimates of market value. This leads to the familiar criticism of GDP that if a man marries his cook the result is a reduction in GDP – perfectly true, but the problem is nevertheless marginal.

On the other hand, the national accounts include an estimate of the production of services in the form of the accommodation house owners provide for themselves. This is called "imputed rents" and is fairly difficult to estimate, since there is no observable transaction involved. However, if one were not to make this estimate, the change in GDP could be affected by a change in the proportion of households owning their own dwelling.

GDP includes the value added of general government. However, part of the production of general government ought in fact to be counted as the intermediate consumption of other branches. The national accounts assume only households are users of the services of general government. But in reality, firms also use the services of the police and other collective services provided by government. However, since there is no means of measuring this intermediate consumption, it is ignored, and GDP can therefore be said to be correspondingly overestimated.

The underground economy is badly measured in the national accounts. While, in principle, illicit activities should be included in GDP, this is difficult in practice. However, statistical offices make adjustments to take into account "underground" employment or tax fraud. In the case of France, for example, these adjustments increase GDP by around 4%.

The current version of the international system of national accounts (SNA 2008) contains a recommendation that R&D (including software) be counted as GFCF (investment) and not as intermediate consumption (current expenditure), with the result that GDPs have been revised upwards, by between 1% and 4% depending on the country. This is because GFCF forms part of final demand and hence GDP (fundamental equation 2), whereas intermediate consumption does not.

Expenditure for the purchase of a house is recorded as GFCF, but expenditure on durable goods, cars in particular, is classified as consumption. And yet the services rendered by a car generally last a fairly long time, although obviously not as long as those of a house. However, it was necessary to draw a line somewhere between consumption and investment.

It may seem strange that GDP rises if there are more road accidents. This is partly because of greater activity by emergency services. On the contrary, one would intuitively like to see GDP diminishing in such circumstances. But this would be to confuse a measure of output (GDP) with a measure of welfare, which GDP is not (see Chapter 15). At most, GDP is a measure of the contribution of production to welfare. There are a great number of other dimensions to welfare that GDP does not claim to measure.

We shall be returning to these conventions throughout this book. They may be open to criticism, but it must not be overlooked that they have been the subject of lengthy discussions by national accountants and were often chosen for sound practical reasons. For example, we shall see in Chapter 10 that indirect taxes can be said to be counted twice over in GDP, but this was the only solution that met other criteria.

While the national accounts system has the above major limitations, it should not be criticised out of misunderstanding about its objectives and definitions. For example, many people fail to understand why GDP does not fall following major natural catastrophes (or terrorist attacks). This is because they misunderstand the definition of GDP, which, as we have seen, measures output during a given period. People tend to confuse GDP with the country's economic wealth. Undoubtedly, major calamities destroy part of the economic wealth (buildings, houses, roads and infrastructure*), but they do not, per se, constitute negative production and so do not directly contribute to a decline in GDP. Destruction can indirectly affect production in a negative or positive way. When a factory is destroyed it ceases production, but it also has to be rebuilt and this constitutes production. For this reason, paradoxically, it is possible for a natural catastrophe to have a positive impact (in the purely mathematical sense of the word "positive") on GDP.

The above remarks should also make it clear to the reader that GDP does not represent "the national wealth", as is sometimes said. National wealth is the stock of the nation's assets, while GDP is a flow of output. At the very most, GDP might be considered a measure of the change in national wealth. But even this is incorrect, since GDP does not contain the whole of this change because it excludes capital gains and losses. It is therefore preferable to speak of GDP simply as total output during a specific period.

Shortcuts

The national accounts are complicated and at the same time have important implications. For example, a major part of the EU Member countries' contributions to the budget of the European Commission depends

---

* Only a very few economic accounting systems, and not the national accounts, include an evaluation of human capital (see Chapter 15). This is why human losses do not appear in this list.

directly on their relative levels of GDP (GNI to be more precise). When methods are modified or figures are revised, it is useful for national accountants to know rapidly whether these modifications have "an impact on GDP", in their jargon. In order to find a quick answer to this question, the national accounts experts use certain "shortcuts". For example, they use this rule based on final demand: GDP is modified only if an element of final demand is modified.

Consider the following example. In 2012, the accounts for the year 2010 are recalculated using the database consisting of comprehensive company accounts. It then turns out, on the basis of these more reliable statistics, that the output of temporary employment services (in other words, the hiring of manpower) was substantially underestimated in the initial estimates. This leads to an appreciable increase in total output. Does this have an impact on GDP? The immediate answer is, no! The hiring of manpower is not part of household consumption; it is not investment; it does not enter foreign trade (or only to a very small extent). It therefore does not enter into final demand and is instead intermediate consumption. As a consequence, GDP is unaffected. This does not mean, however, that no modification has taken place. For one thing, the distribution of value added between the various branches has changed, with that of services increasing and that of manufacturing decreasing because of the increase in its intermediate consumption. However, the modification in total output is neutralised by an increase in intermediate consumption. See Exercise 7 for a practical application of this point.

This final demand rule works well in numerous cases. Take two other examples, R&D (Research and Development expenditure) and VAT (Value Added Tax, a type of sales tax). The new system of national accounts SNA 2008 introduced new rules for the treatment of R&D. Instead of being recorded as intermediate consumption, purchases of R&D were to be regarded as GFCF. Does this modification have an impact on GDP? The answer is, yes, because GFCF forms part of final demand, which is modified accordingly. Suppose the government decides to finance its expenditure by reducing income tax (which is unpopular) by 5 billion euros and by correspondingly increasing VAT (a less painful tax). This modification appears to be neutral at the macroeconomic level, since the deficit is unchanged. But that is not actually the case. Because final demand includes household consumption, which is measured at market prices and includes VAT, GDP will be increased by 5 billion euros (everything else remaining equal). It can therefore be shown that the precise origin of government financing (direct or indirect taxes) can affect the Maastricht public deficit criterion without any change in the deficit itself. This is because the denominator of the ratio on which the criterion is based is GDP. The ratio can therefore change even if the numerator, in this case the deficit, is unchanged. The national accounts are full of surprises.

On the other hand, GDP does not change if two elements of final demand are adjusted in opposite directions. For example, if the estimate for exports is reduced, and if this reduction is offset by an increase in final consumption, GDP remains unchanged.

Exercises for Chapter 1

Exercise 1: Observations and forecasts

Go to the OECD web site (*www.oecd.org*), find the most recent issue of the "Economic Outlook" and update Table 1.1 at the beginning of this chapter using the most recent figures. Comment on the differences between the new figures and the old. What has happened to bring about the change in the figures? In which direction did the OECD forecasters err?

Exercise 2: A simple calculation of GDP

Consider four firms: firm A, a mining enterprise, extracts iron ore; firm B, a steelmaker, uses iron to make steel sheets and ingots; firm C, a carmaker, makes automobiles using steel; firm D, a manufacturer of machinery and robots, also uses steel. Calculate the production, intermediate consumption and values added in millions of euros based on the following assumptions.

Firm A extracts 50 000 tonnes of ore, at 200 euros per tonne, its purchases during the period limited to the purchase of one machine made by firm D, costing 10 million euros. Firm B produces 15 000 tonnes of steel sheet at 3000 euros per tonne, having bought and used all the ore produced by firm A. Firm C has manufactured 5000 vehicles and sold them all to households for 15 000 euros each, having purchased 20 million euros' worth of steel sheet from firm B, but using only 18 million euros' worth in the manufacture of its cars. In addition, Firm C imported 5000 engines from a foreign subsidiary, each being valued at 4000 euros, and purchased domestically 2 robots made by firm D. Firm D sold one machine for 10 million euros and two robots, each worth 5 million euros, having used 10 million euros' worth of steel sheet from firm B.

Calculate the GDP of this economy. Calculate also the final demand of this economy, assuming that it has no exports. Verify that GDP is equal to final demand. (Remember that purchases of machinery are not intermediate consumption, but GFCF).

Exercise 3: Relationship between current prices, volume and deflator

The table below shows the series for GDP growth at current prices and the GDP deflator growth rate in the case of France. GDP at current prices in 2005 was equal to 1 718 047 million euros. Calculate the series for GDP in volume in millions of "2005 euros". Show how to calculate the series for GDP in volume directly from the growth rates, without using absolute amounts and without using division. Comment.

	2005	2006	2007	2008	2009
(1) Growth rate GDP	1.83	2.47	2.29	-0.08	-3.15
(2) Growth Rate Deflator	1.91	2.14	2.59	2.54	0.72

Exercise 4: Calculation of contributions to growth

The following table shows the French quarterly national accounts for Q2 2013, in volume, chained at previous year's prices, base 2005. Using the box earlier in the text, calculate to two decimal places the breakdown of growth in Q2 2013 for the contributions of domestic demand excluding inventories, changes in inventories and net exports. Comment.

Warning: in order to simplify the exercise, changes in inventories have been calculated for the sake of this exercise as the balancing item of the equation. This circumvents the difficulty raised by the chain linking process (see Chapter 2 for chain linked national accounts).

Quarterly national accounts
Volumes chained at previous year's prices, base 2005

	Q1 2013	Q2 2013
Change in inventories	-958	-274
Imports	131 850	134 137
Exports	125 297	127 769
Net exports	-6 553	-6 368
Total final domestic demand excluding inventories	458 369	459 839
Total gross domestic product	450 858	453 197

Exercise 5: The public deficit and the Maastricht criterion

On the basis of the following table, determine whether France meets the public deficit criterion (not more than 3% of GDP) during the period in question.

	2007	2008	2009	2010	2011	2012
Total expenditure	992.6	1 030.0	1 070.6	1 095.6	1 118.5	1 151.2
Total revenue	940.7	965.4	928.0	958.3	1 012.7	1 052.4
Gross domestic product	1 886.8	1 933.2	1 885.8	1 936.7	2 001.4	2 032.3

Exercise 6: Synonyms

There are a number of terms that are used in national accounts, but economists use a wide range of synonyms for them. Choose from the list in italics below all the correct synonyms for: (A) GDP at current prices; (B) GDP in volume; (C) GDP deflator; (D) public deficit. Beware that not all of them are synonyms for any of the above.

1. GNP, 2. GNI at current prices, 3. Nominal GDP, 4. Sum of output in euros, 5. GDP in quantities, 6. GDP in value, 7. GDP at constant prices, 8. Sum of gross values added in volume, 9. Deflated Net Domestic Product, 10. Real GDP, 11. GDP price index, 12. Consumer price index, 13. GDP at 1995 prices, 14. Sum of deflated incomes, 15. "Growth", 16. Financing capacity of public enterprises, 17. General government net borrowing.

Exercise 7: Impact of modifications to GDP

(Follow-up to Exercise 2 and application of the "Shortcuts" box.) In Exercise 2, you calculated the GDP of this economy. Let us now suppose that we omitted to mention that firm C, the car maker, hired manpower from firm E, the temporary employment agency, for the sum of 15 million euros. Has the GDP of the economy been modified by this fresh information? Confirm your reply by reconstituting the table for the different industries, with comments.

Exercise 8: Deflators and growth

There has been in the first decade of this century controversy regarding the comparability of growth as measured in Europe and in the United States. More particularly, this concerns the deflator for firms' investment in computers, now a very large item of expenditure. The statistical methods used in the United States mean that the relevant deflator falls faster than in Europe (see box in Section 3 of Chapter 2). First, show why for the same growth in purchases of computers at current prices, this difference in statistical method leads to a difference in GDP growth in volume. Go on to explain why this difference in GDP diminishes (to a vanishing point) if European countries produce few computers (or none).

The solutions to these exercises are available at:
http://dx.doi.org/10.1787/9789264214637-19-en

Chapter 2

Distinguishing between volume and price increases

This chapter considers growth, the overall change in the quantity of goods and services produced and made available to consumers and investors, as measured by changes in volume. The main task of national accounts is to separate out, within the change in the observed monetary aggregates, the part of growth that comes from a change in quantities from the part of growth due to a change in prices. The chapter explains in detail how statisticians set about distinguishing these changes through what is known as the volume/price breakdown.

Everyone wants the maximum possible growth, although today the preference is for "durable" or "sustainable" growth. The generic term "growth" indicates the overall change in the quantity of goods and services produced and made available to consumers and investors. The prime task of national accounts is to separate out, within the change in the observed monetary aggregates, the part of growth that stems from a change in quantities from the part that is due to a change in prices. An increase in quantities or, as the national accountants would say in "volumes", is generally a good thing. A rise in prices, known as inflation, is not generally good news. A change in a monetary aggregate has accordingly very limited interest in the national accounts. However, it takes on economic significance when, to use the national accountants' jargon, one carries out its "volume/price breakdown". This is why this highly technical chapter comes first, even before those on output and final uses.

1. A word of caution: Compare volumes

The following table, taken from the OECD national accounts database, compares GDP growth for the Netherlands, Mexico and Turkey between 1980 and 2012. Looking at this table, one might get the impression that Mexico and Turkey posted formidable growth compared with the Netherlands. Indeed, while the Netherlands is reported to have annual average growth of 6.1%, Mexico was bounding along at 43.8% and was itself outstripped by Turkey, with 74.2%. This conclusion, however, contains a huge trap. It only takes a glance at the second line of the table's title to see the words "current prices", meaning that the table is comparing amounts calculated at the average prices of each year. Consequently, these amounts reflect the full impact of the rise in prices, or the inflation occurring between 1980 and 2012. As it happens, Mexico and Turkey are two countries that continued to suffer from galloping inflation during this period, whereas the Netherlands experienced significantly lower inflation starting at the end of the 1980s.

Average annual % GDP growth, 1980-2012
Current prices

Netherlands	6.1
Mexico	43.8
Turkey	74.2

The above international comparison is therefore not meaningful. It is necessary to separate the wheat (the growth, understood as being "in volume") from the chaff (the inflation, or the change in prices). Accordingly, the next table shows the figures in volume, accompanied by those for the changes in prices. The performance of the Netherlands then turns out to be much better: its volume growth is only slightly lower than those of the other two countries, while its inflation is dramatically lower.

Table 2.1. **GDP, volume and price indices**
Annual growth rate, 1980-2012

	Volume	Prices
Netherlands	3.1	2.9
Mexico	3.6	38.8
Turkey	6.3	63.8

Source: OECD (2013), "Aggregate National Accounts: Gross domestic product", OECD National Accounts Statistics (database), *http://dx.doi.org/10.1787/data-00001-en.*

StatLink ⚙️ *http://dx.doi.org/10.1787/888933143598*

If, in addition, the volume growth is adjusted for population growth, the Netherlands performance comes out even better, with volume growth per head of 1.7% a year over the same period, compared with 0.5 % for Mexico and 1.7% for Turkey.

The aim of this chapter is to explain in detail how statisticians set about distinguishing changes in volume from changes in prices, in other words arriving at what is known as the *volume/price breakdown*.

But even if this second international comparison is correct, it still lacks something, since it provides information only on the changes and says nothing about the comparative *level* of each country's GDP. Filling this gap seems like a simple matter. One takes GDP at current prices and then makes two modifications. First, divide by the number of inhabitants to obtain GDP per head, so as to avoid comparing things that are not strictly comparable. Second, use the same currency in all cases. OECD practice is to express all amounts in United States dollars, but one could just as well have used the euro or the Mexican peso; the essential thing is to use one single unit of account. The following table shows the level of GDP per head for these three countries, expressed in US dollars. What does it tell us? That the inhabitants of the Netherlands have an annual average income well above those of the other two countries: if the figure for the Netherlands is conventionally equal to 100, that of Turkey is 22.9 and that of Mexico is 23.2. But are we comparing things that are genuinely comparable?

Table 2.2. **GDP per capita**

2012

	Per head, USD	Netherlands = 100
Netherlands	45 970	100.0
Mexico	10 648	23.2
Turkey	10 525	22.9

Source: OECD (2013), "Aggregate National Accounts: Gross domestic product", OECD National Accounts Statistics (database), *http://dx.doi.org/10.1787/data-00001-en.*

StatLink ᵐˢᵖ *http://dx.doi.org/10.1787/888933143612*

The answer is not really, since even when the figures are expressed in a common unit of account, they fail to obey our watchword of only comparing volumes. Prices of certain goods and services can be very different from one country to another. For example, the price of renting a 100 m^2 apartment may be 2000 euros in Amsterdam (the Netherlands), while for the same money one can rent a 300 m^2 apartment in Istanbul (Turkey) or Mexico City. One therefore has to go further and eliminate differences in price levels so as to be able to compare solely the *volumes* produced in each country and not figures that are affected by differences in price levels. The OECD makes this adjustment by using "purchasing power parity". The next table, based on this adjustment, provides the proper comparison for volume among the three countries. While it confirms that the standard of living in the Netherlands is much higher, it raises the levels of GDP per head for Turkey and Mexico. This international comparison of absolute levels in the national accounts uses what the statisticians describe as the *spatial volume/price breakdown*. This technique will be described in more detail in Chapter 3. The present chapter will focus on *temporal volume/price breakdown*.

Table 2.3. **GDP per capita using purchasing power parities**

2012

	In US dollars, adjusted for purchasing power parity	Netherlands = 100
Netherlands	43 146	100.0
Mexico	18 288	42.4
Turkey	18 114	42.0

Source: OECD (2013), "Aggregate National Accounts: Gross domestic product", OECD National Accounts Statistics (database), *http://dx.doi.org/10.1787/data-00001-en.*

StatLink ᵐˢᵖ *http://dx.doi.org/10.1787/888933143620*

2. The volume/price breakdown applied to changes over time

To respect the watchword "compare volumes", it is necessary to calculate national accounts aggregates in volume. To do this, the first step is to take detailed statistics, product by product, each one expressed in volume. Then, in a second step, aggregate them, or calculate their total.

Generally speaking, the detailed statistics typically available to national accountants are of three types: (a) statistics expressed in quantities, such as the number of tonnes of steel produced; (b) statistics expressed in current prices (also called "in value" or "nominal"), such as figures taken from company accounts; and (c) price indices, such as the numerous components of the household consumer price index (CPI). Statistics of type (a) are used directly by national accountants to calculate the change in volume within the detailed classifications. The variation in the output volume of a specific type of steel, as measured in the national accounts, will then equal the variation in the tonnage produced of this steel.

If statistics expressed in quantities are not available, national accountants combine statistics of types (b) and (c) to obtain an indicator of volume. As we saw in the first fundamental equation in Chapter 1, if one divides the change in magnitude expressed in current prices by the change in the price of the corresponding products, one obtains a measure of the change in volume. This is what national accountants call "deflation". Exercise 1, at the end of this chapter, illustrates a very simple case of "deflation".

To calculate macroeconomic growth, national accountants use hundreds of statistical series that are either directly expressed in quantity or derived via this process of deflation. In the case of France – and the figures are probably similar in other countries – almost 85% (in terms of value added) of the detailed series of output in volume in the national accounts are derived from the deflation of a series at current prices by an appropriate price index. In order for the deflation approach to work well, it is necessary to have good figures for sales or corresponding monetary flows (at current prices) and suitable price indices. National statistical offices in the OECD countries construct indicators of this kind, the best-known being the indices of turnover, of consumer prices and producer prices. These indicators are essential for the national accounts, but to enumerate them would go beyond the scope of this textbook. In the remainder of this chapter, we shall deal only with the problem – quite difficult in itself – of how to combine (i.e. aggregate) these detailed statistics in volume.

3. The difficulties of aggregation

If we had a very simple economy that produced and consumed just one product, there would be no difficulty in measuring the macroeconomic growth in volume. One would simply have to calculate the number of tonnes (or, more generally, any physical units) of this single product. However, the economy is made up of a multitude of products, goods and services, very different from each other. How can one add these together in order to obtain a macroeconomic indicator? First, we need a common unit of measurement.

One could, for example, add the physical units expressed in tonnes. But how meaningful would it be to add tonnes of apples to tonnes of clothes and to tonnes of battle tanks? The result might possibly be useful for the logistic management of an army on the move, but it obviously has little macroeconomic meaning. Is it even legitimate to add, one by one, all the cars produced in a country in order to create a macroeconomic indicator? Not really, since adding a small cheap car to a luxury car would give a false picture of the total output: a large car "counts" for more in economic terms than a small one. Therefore, we have a problem of "aggregation" that is fundamental to macroeconomic measurement.

The answer to this problem is fairly obvious to economists. It consists of relying on the price structure. Once products are expressed in monetary units, it becomes legitimate to add them together. Therefore, adding the number of small cars multiplied by their price to the number of luxury cars multiplied by their price will equal the total turnover of the carmakers, and it will also equal the total value of cars bought by households. These aggregate figures, in which units are "weighted" by their prices, are additive and have a macroeconomic meaning. The relative price of products provides a good economic weighting system for physical quantities because it represents the relative cost of manufacturing the products and/or the relative utilities attributed to them by consumers. Clearly, prices are not always set by the relative costs or the relative utilities, and they might be influenced by monopolistic behaviour or by distortions due to taxation. Even so, broadly speaking, the structure of relative prices provides a valid weighting system.

To calculate volumes, national accountants therefore rely on the summation of physical units weighted by the prices of these units. This still leaves one problem, however. Since the aim is to measure the change in volume, one wants to compare several different periods. Unfortunately, prices vary at the same time as the physical quantities. It will therefore be necessary to "freeze" the variation in prices. To calculate the evolution in volume between two periods, national accountants compare the sum of the physical units in the first period, weighted by a given price structure, with the sum of the physical units in the second period, weighted by the *same* price structure. An example will make this easier to grasp.

Let us suppose that there are two types of cars, small cars, which we shall call "s" and large cars, which we shall call "l". We shall denote the number of units of the small cars by Q_s and the number of units of the large cars by Q_l. We shall add to these variables a subscript t to signify that this is the value of the variable in period t. For example, $Q_{s,t}$ signifies the number of units of small cars produced (or purchased) in period t. P_s denotes the price of the small car and P_l that of the large. In order to calculate the evolution in volume between period t and period t', national accountants compare the amount $(Q_{s,t} \times P_s) + (Q_{l,t} \times P_l)$, which is the volume in period t, with the amount $(Q_{s,t'} \times P_s) + (Q_{l,t'} \times P_l)$, which is the volume in period t'. It can be seen that prices remain constant in this comparison, with P_s and P_l used for both periods. It is in fact possible to choose different price pairs: those of period t, those of period t', or a combination of the two. However, regardless of the choice, the pairing will be the same for the two periods. Hence the terminology used to describe this system of calculating volumes, namely **constant-price accounting**. Exercise 2, at the end of this chapter, provides an example of constant-price accounting.

The manipulation of volumes can produce certain surprises for those unfamiliar with the system. Let us suppose that the price of the large cars is twice that of the small ones. Let us also suppose that the carmaker produces exactly the same total number of cars (say, 100) in both years but that the proportion of the large cars rises from 50% to 80%. Let us calculate the variation in volume using the previous formula. This equals $(80 \times 2) + (20 \times 1)$, which is the volume of cars produced in the second year, divided by $(50 \times 2) + (50 \times 1)$, which is the volume of cars produced in the first. The result of this calculation is 1.2, signifying an increase of 20%.

This example shows that to measure the change in volume there is no need to know the absolute price of the small or large cars. All that matters is their relative pricing.

This means that, despite the fact that the total number of cars expressed in units has remained unchanged, the national accounts record a growth of 20%. Is this really a surprise? No, because the volume in the national accounts measures not the increase in the number of cars, but the utility derived by the consumers. This utility has indeed increased by 20% when measured using the yardstick of relative prices. This is not surprising, since the utility of a luxury car is greater than that of a small car. It is essential to fully understand the difference between an increase in quantities and an increase in volume in order to grasp the measurement of growth as recorded in the national accounts.

In particular, volume takes into account all kinds of differences in quality. For example, the national accounts do not add together tonnes of top-grade petrol and tonnes of second-grade petrol, since the two products are not entirely substitutes for each other, despite their similarity. The national accountants also consider the type of sales outlet involved (small local store or supermarket), since this is one of the characteristics of the product, and in principle will not add together two identical products distributed through different retailing circuits. The impact of taking into account these differences in quality is most striking in the case of computers (see Box 2.1). This case illustrates another essential difficulty of measuring volume and prices when new products are introduced into the market. In this case, constant-price accounting is an inadequate instrument, because it presupposes that all products existed in the first period of comparison, which, by definition, cannot be true for entirely new products (mobile telephones, for example, in the middle 1990s).

Box 2.1. **Measured in the national accounts, the volume of computers rises very sharply**

Let us suppose that in year A, 1000 computers of type X were sold, having a power of P_x and a clock speed of V_x. Let us now suppose that in year A + 1, 1000 computers were again sold, this time of type Y, having a power of P_y and a clock speed of V_y, for the same unit price. The spectacular advance in microprocessor technology means that P_y and V_y are considerably greater than P_x and V_x.

The national accounts are not going to say that the volume of computers is equal to the number of computers. Account will be taken of the quality of each computer and these qualities will be weighted by their prices. In most cases, however, the computer of type Y did not even exist in the previous period A so that no price is available to provide the weighting. The statisticians then carry out econometric (also known as "hedonic") studies of the relationship between the prices of computers and their key characteristics, such as their power and their speed, the purpose being to determine what value purchasers of computers put on improvements to each of these characteristics. Using these relationships, they estimate what the computer type Y would have cost in year A, had it existed. Let us suppose, for example, that the price of the new computer type Y is estimated to be 20% higher than that of the computer of type X in year A. This means that the price of Y has decreased by 20% since year A. It is a realistic hypothesis, as it is well known that PC prices fall very rapidly even when their power is increasing. The volume of computers in the national accounts for year A + 1 will therefore be calculated "at year A prices", i.e. at prices that are 20% higher than those of year A. The volume of computers as measured in the national accounts therefore rises much faster than the number of computers bought. It is indeed this phenomenon that explains why the national accounts now make use of chained accounts rather than constant-price accounts (see following boxes).

The same phenomenon would be observed in cars if the prices of Mercedes fell to become closer to those of Fiats. The public would buy Mercedes instead of Fiats, and the national accounts would record a sharp increase in volume, even though the number of cars sold remained unchanged. Unfortunately, this phenomenon does not occur in cars.

---

4. Volume indices and price indices

At this point, it is necessary to take a fairly long mathematical digression to explain the notions of *volume index* and *price index* so that the reader can fully understand how volume is measured in the national accounts. A **volume index** is a weighted average of the changes between two periods in the quantities of a given set of goods or services. Traditionally, these indices are given a standard value of 100 for a given period, although in this text the indices are implicitly standardised as 1, and not 100. This is of little importance, however, since both volume and price indices are numbers that can be interpreted only in terms of change. By convention, the time period used as the starting point will be denoted as being period 0 and the period being compared with it as period t. The two time periods can be consecutive or non-consecutive.

The ratios of the quantity or the price of a given product in period t to the quantity or the price of the same product in period 0, i.e. $\frac{q_t}{q_0}$ or $\frac{p_t}{p_0}$, are known as the quantity ratio and the price ratio, respectively. The quantity and price ratios are independent of the units in which the quantities and prices are measured. Most of the indices can be expressed in the form of weighted averages of these price or quantity ratios, or can be derived from them. The various formulae differ mainly in the weighting attached to the individual price or quantity ratios and in the particular type of mean used – arithmetic, geometric, harmonic, etc.

The two most commonly used indices are those of Laspeyres and Paasche, named after two 19th-century statisticians. Most national accounts systems (and in particular the European systems) use Laspeyres indices to calculate volumes and Paasche indices to calculate changes in prices. Both the Laspeyres and Paasche indices can be defined as weighted averages of price or quantity ratios, the weights being the values at current prices of goods or services in one or other of the two periods being compared.

Let $v_{ij} = p_{ij}\, q_{ij}$ be the value at current prices of product i in period j. The Laspeyres volume index (L_q) is a weighted average of the quantity ratios:

$$L_q = \sum_i \frac{v_{i0}(q_{it} \div q_{i0})}{\sum_i v_{i0}} \tag{1}$$

The period providing the weights for the index is known as the "base" period. It typically (but not always) coincides with the "reference" period for which the index has a standardised value of 100. Since the summation always involves the same set of goods and services, it is possible to dispense with the subscript i in expressions of type (1). And since by definition v_j is equal to $p_j q_j$, it is also possible to replace it in (1) to obtain (2):

$$L_q = \frac{\sum p_0 q_t}{\sum p_0 q_0}$$

(2)

Algebraically, expressions (1) and (2) are identical. This means that the change in volume at constant prices can be calculated in two ways with the same result: either as the average of the *changes* in quantity of the various products weighted by the values at current prices in the base year; or, as the amount of quantities in period t multiplied by the prices in the base year divided by the value at current prices in the base year. Exercise 3, at the end of this chapter, illustrates this result using the example given earlier of the small and large cars.

The Paasche price index can be defined in reciprocal fashion to the Laspeyres index, applying the values at current prices in period t as weights and using a harmonic mean of the price and ratio quantities instead of an arithmetic mean.

The Paasche price index P_p is defined as follows:

$$P_p = \frac{\sum v_t}{\sum v_t (p_0 \div p_t)} = \frac{\sum p_t q_t}{\sum p_0 q_t}$$

(3)

It will be seen from this formula that what we have is indeed a price index, since in this case it is the prices that vary and the quantities that remain fixed, in contrast to the volume indices we saw earlier. The Paasche index can be interpreted as the reciprocal of a Laspeyres index "turned backwards", in other words the inverse of a Laspeyres index for period 0, with period t as the base period. The reciprocity between the Laspeyres and Paasche indices leads to numerous symmetries that can be exploited in calculations.

In particular, the product of a Laspeyres *volume* index and the corresponding Paasche *price* index is equal to the change in the value, at current prices, of the goods or services between period 0 and t, i.e.

$$L_q P_p = \frac{\sum p_0 q_t}{\sum p_0 q_0} \frac{\sum p_t q_t}{\sum p_0 q_t} = \frac{\sum v_t}{\sum v_0}$$

(4)

Relationship (4) is fundamental in national accounts. Reading it from right to left, it shows that the variation of an aggregate at current prices is equal to the product of the volume index and the price index. It expresses mathematically what we called the "first fundamental equation" in Chapter 1.

This equation is constantly exploited in national accounts. For example, it is used to obtain indirectly the volume index by dividing the relative variation in values by the Paasche price index, in a method discussed earlier and known as "deflation", as shown by:

$$L_q = \frac{\dfrac{\sum v_t}{\sum v_0}}{P_p} \tag{5}$$

Because it is generally easier, and less costly, to calculate price indices than volume indices, it is the usual practice in economic statistics to calculate volumes using deflation. This practice is constantly applied in national accounts (see Exercise 4).

5. Constant prices

Let us now consider a chronological series of Laspeyres volume indices, i.e.:

$$\frac{\sum p_0 q_0}{\sum p_0 q_0}, \frac{\sum p_0 q_1}{\sum p_0 q_0}, \ldots, \frac{\sum p_0 q_t}{\sum p_0 q_0} \tag{6}$$

If one multiplies all the items in the series by the common denominator $\sum p_0 q_0$, one obtains the so-called "constant-price" series, of which we saw an example earlier, in the case of the small and large cars:

$$\sum p_0 q_0, \sum p_0 q_1, \ldots, \sum p_0 q_t \tag{7}$$

The relative movements of this series, from one period to another, are identical to those of the corresponding Laspeyres indices given by (6), since the two series differ only by a scalar equal to the first term of the second series. The term "constant prices" is justified by the fact that these aggregates use the price structure of a fixed period, in this case period 0.

This system of accounts at constant prices was widely used by national accountants since it has one very useful property, namely that the aggregates obtained are additive; in other words, it is legitimate to add or subtract "bits" of these accounts. For example, the volume of output for cars plus trucks is exactly equal to the volume of output of the two together. It will be seen later that this property of additivity is lost when this system is abandoned in favour of the more complicated volume indicators recommended in the current version of the international manual SNA 2008, and now applied by all OECD countries.

The units in which these accounts at constant prices are expressed nevertheless remain artificial. Given that what is involved is the multiplication of a dimensionless series (the series of indices in (6)) by a value in the current prices of the base year ($\Sigma p_0 q_0$), one might conclude that the result is a series expressed in the current monetary unit (billions of euros, example). However, since the prices are those of a past year and not current prices, the terminology "accounts in [base year] [monetary units]" is used – for example "in 2005 euros" for the euro area. Although this terminology is widely used, it does have an inherent weakness: there are as many values of the "2005 euro" as there are transactions in the national accounts. The series for household consumption in volume uses a value of the "2005 euro" equal to that deflated by the household consumer price indicator, whereas the series for GFCF uses a value deflated by the price index for GFCF, and so on.

Therefore, when the national accounts are calculated at constant prices and the base period is 2005, one speaks of aggregates "at 2005 prices". But, national accounts in volume are not strictly calculated at constant prices, but are obtained through a chaining process of constant prices for the previous year. It is this complication that we are now going to tackle below.

6. "Chained" accounts and the loss of additivity

Without going into the detailed problems of volume indices, it is relatively easy to explain why constant prices are not fully satisfactory for economic analysis. The choice of a fixed year means that one is using price structures that become more and more remote from the current structure, the further one moves away from the base year. Take the French case, for example. Prior to recent reforms of the French national accounts, the pattern of relative prices used in France for calculating changes in volume in the current year dated as far back as 18 years, because the French national accounts continued using the old "base 1980" until 1998. The increasing remoteness from the base period can clearly lead to measurement distortions. For example, the "quantities" of computers bought towards the end of the 1990s were rising steeply from year to year. It was hardly reasonable to weight these increases using the price structure of the year 1980, when the relative prices of computers were very high. On the contrary, it was precisely because the relative prices of computers fell sharply that the market for computers boomed. Weighting this increase using the old price structures led to changes in volume being overstated and the decrease in prices being understated in the more recent periods, thus distorting the historical picture (see Box 2.2 below).

It is for this reason that the national accounts use what is now called the "chain-linking method". The most widely used method involves three stages. In the first stage, the accounts are calculated at the prices of the previous period. The price structure of the previous period is valid for weighting the changes in quantity in the current period. In this way, one obtains the change

Box 2.2. **An example of distortion due to the use of constant prices**

The use of constant prices taken from a distant base year leads to distortions in the evolution of volume, which become all the more significant when there are substantial variations in relative prices. The best-known example is that of computers. Using the case of France, let us calculate the volume of equipment GFCF, including traditional types of machinery as well as computers (excluding transport). Between 1980 and 2000, the price index for computers, with 1980 = 100, plummeted to 8.7. In the same period, the price index for other types of equipment rose, reaching 136.1 at the end of the period. Now let us compare the volume of the aggregate formed by computers plus the other types of equipment. When one uses the constant prices of the year 1980, this combination shows a rise of 316% between the two dates. When one uses the constant prices of the previous year and then chains them, the figure is only 143%, and this is the correct figure. The first figure, based on the structure of relative prices in 1980 overstates the increases in investment in computers, increases that are explained in large part precisely because the relative prices of computers have fallen.

Figure 2.1. **Difference between constant 1980 prices and chained prices**
France, computers and other materials

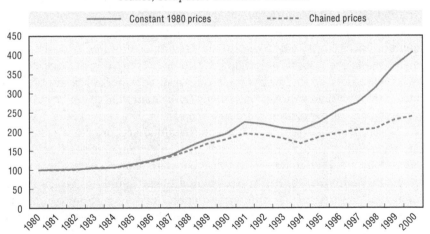

Source: OECD (2013), "Aggregate National Accounts: Gross domestic product", OECD National Accounts Statistics (database), *http://dx.doi.org/10.1787/data-00001-en.*
StatLink ⋙ *http://dx.doi.org/10.1787/888933143602*

in the aggregates between the preceding and the current period, referred to in the case of annual accounts, as "accounts at previous year's prices". Next, these changes are chained (i.e. multiplied each one with the subsequent one), aggregate by aggregate. In this way, one obtains a series of growth rates each of which uses the price structure of the previous period. Finally, in order to provide volume series in levels, this series is multiplied by the value of the accounts at the current prices of the reference year, currently, for many countries, the year 2005 (but this changes every five years).

The advantage of the chain-linking method is that the previous period's price structure is more relevant than the price structure of a fixed period from further into the past. It can be shown, however, that in theory an even better measure of volume changes is obtained when the average price structure of the previous and current period is used. Chained volumes using the previous year's structure are usually described as "Laspeyres chains"; indices that use the average of the previous and the current period are described as "Fisher chains". For practical reasons, most countries use Laspeyres chains, although both Canada and the United States are now using Fisher chains (see Box 2.3 below). The differences between the two are generally very small. Fisher chains are well-suited to the method used to produce national accounts in the United States. But Fischer chains are considered too complicated by other countries in particular because they are entirely non additive. These countries indeed use production processes for their national accounts that require the use of accounting identities, thus necessitating at least additive accounts in prices of the previous year.

Presentation of the accounts based on Laspeyres chained volumes should be called "accounts at previous year's prices, chained, reference 2005". However, in practice, countries and economists continue to use the term "constant prices" or even describe the series as "in 2005 euros". (Exercise 5, at the end of this chapter, shows a chained-volume presentation in three stages.) The advantage of chained accounts compared with accounts at constant prices is that they avoid distortions arising from changes in the price structure over time and the overstatement discussed earlier. The United States, whose statistical office was the first to introduce chained accounts, has calculated that the use of a fixed 1996 base rather than the chained index would have increased by 1.6% the growth of US GDP between 2001 and 2003: instead of being 2.7% annually, US GDP growth would have been 4.3%, which seems unrealistic. The bulk of the difference comes, once more, from computers, whose large quantity increases in 2001-03 would have been overestimated had the pricing of 1996 been used.

The great disadvantage of the chain-linking method is that additivity of the chain-linked volume levels is no longer possible. In particular, and this is of fundamental importance, it is no longer possible to derive one aggregate in volume by taking a combination (sum of or difference between) other aggregates also expressed in volume. For example, an item in a less detailed classification is not exactly equal to the sum of the corresponding items in a more detailed one. Exercise 6, at the end of this chapter, shows how it is possible to calculate with all due rigour an aggregate that is not supplied by a statistical institute. The box "Limitations of the national accounts" shows that this problem also affects the calculation of contributions to growth.

Box 2.3. How volumes are obtained in the United States national accounts

The volume series of the US national accounts (NIPAs, see Chapter 12) are obtained using chained Fisher volume indices that are currently "referenced" to year 2009 (in the United States, the term "reference" is preferred to the term "base"). These series are entitled "chained (2009) dollars", or sometimes, simply "chained dollars". The volume change of each quarter is compiled as a Fisher volume index, which is the geometric mean of a Laspeyres volume index and a Paasche volume index. This index number has the advantage of using price weights that are representative of both periods for which the change is calculated. These quarterly links are then chained (multiplied each one to the other) to form an index number time series, which is conventionally given the value of 100 for the reference year, currently the year 2009. This reference year changes every four or five years, on the occasion of a comprehensive revision of the NIPAs. This time series is then multiplied by the value at current prices of the given aggregate for the year 2009. Thus, users obtain time series expressed in "billion dollars of year 2009". As with all chained series, these aggregates are not additive. Exercise 7, at the end of this chapter, illustrates how to manipulate forecasts of the US data, taking into account these complex chained series.

---

7. Unpleasant practical consequences of chain linking

Chain linking has now been adopted by nearly all OECD countries, both for annual and quarterly accounts. As explained above, it has a substantial advantage compared to the use of pricing in a fixed year because it gives more accurate aggregate volume *growth rates*. It has, however, a major practical drawback because given the loss in additivity in chain-linked levels, users cannot easily make simple calculations based on accounting identities, a situation that makes the life of macroeconomists quite miserable. For example, now that almost all OECD countries have adopted chain linking, it is not possible for a scrupulous economist to derive a simple total, such as the volume time series of total final demand based on the sum of internal plus external final demand. More generally, the second fundamental equation of Chapter 1, $GDP = C + GFC + X - M$, does not hold mathematically for volume time series expressed in chain-linked levels because there is an additional residual term between the two elements of this equality. This residual term has no economic interpretation.

In practice, economists regularly use totals, sub-totals or differences to make their economic models function. The less scrupulous (or those in a hurry) simply ignore the problem of non-additivity and continue to use these identities as if they were still valid. As the residual term is often small, this remains acceptable in many cases. However, it becomes imprudent when manipulating aggregates containing time series with significant differences in relative pricing over time, such as the pricing of computers compared to other machinery.

In the OECD, the main forecasting model of the Economics Department ("Interlink") functions, like others, with sums and differences. However, because the OECD wants to obtain exactly what OECD countries publish, it is obligated to be as scrupulous as possible. Thus, all totals, sub-totals or differences are obtained through a two-steps process that replicates almost exactly the chain-linking calculation made by the national accounts of each country. For example, total final demand, as in our example above, is not compiled directly but in two steps. First, one calculates separately internal demand and external demand in volume terms expressed in prices of the preceding period. This is obtained via the application of the growth rate of each of these variables to the current price level of the preceding year. Second, the sum of the two amounts will be calculated, and the corresponding correct growth rate can be derived from it. This is a valid process because volumes expressed in prices of the preceding year are additive, at least for countries that use chained Laspeyres indices (most OECD countries). It is a very good approximation for the few countries that use Fisher indices (USA, Canada).

An interesting feature of this scrupulous approach is that it does not use any of the volume levels expressed in chain-linked terms. Only growth rates and levels at current prices are used. The question is therefore raised: why do statistical offices continue to publish volume time series in chained-linked levels? The answer seems to be that it is by force of habit, since volume time series in chain-linked levels are of no real use; they cannot be used in accounting identities, and they cannot be used to compile shares. They can only be used to derive growth rates. But then why not simply publish growth rates? This is typically why the US Bureau of Economic Analysis (BEA) stopped publishing some volume series expressed as chained-linked levels (i.e. "in 2009 dollars"), since these results were likely to be misinterpreted by users.

Last, but not least, we should consider the treatment of two variables that, by definition, have no meaning when expressed in terms of growth rates: the volume of changes in inventories and the volume of changes in net exports. These two variables appear in the main aggregate table for each OECD country in the OECD Economic Outlook (OECD, 2013). They are not expressed in terms of growth rates (as all other variables) but in terms of contributions to GDP growth. This is because growth rates have no meaning for these variables since they can be negative in one period and positive in the next, or conversely. These variables are therefore shown in terms of their contributions to GDP growth. If it is deemed essential to present them in terms of chain-linked *levels*, one simple solution is to calculate these levels so that they correspond to the level which would generate the exact contribution to growth as if the data were additive (see Box 2.5: "Contributions and additivity").

At present, many OECD countries calculate the level of chained net exports simply as the difference between chain-linked imports and chain-linked exports. But this approach does not result in an exact amount for the contribution of net exports to GDP.

This may seem complicated, but it is in fact simple and is illustrated in Exercise 7. See also the section "Going further: Chain-linked levels of changes in inventories and other similar variables", at the end of this chapter.

Overall, the rationale of this subsection has been to show that because of the loss of additivity due to chain-linking, volume series of national accounts expressed as chain-linked levels should be replaced by growth rates and/or contributions to growth. In particular, tables of contributions to growth are the only tables in volume that remain additive (at least for annual data* and when they are compiled correctly using additive accounts), regardless of whether Laspeyres or Fisher indices are used. Thus, it is more than probable that econometric models will increasingly use contributions to growth, and statistical offices should give these a high priority.

8. The special cases

Since the national accounts cover the entire economy, they include certain products for which the notion of quantity is not always clear. The first case is that of unique products. For example, it is very difficult to calculate the change in volume for the output of shipyards because it is practically never the same ship that is built in successive years. Each ship is a unique product made up of a multitude of variable elements. In that case, how is one to make a comparison between the two years?

A second example is that of services provided between firms, such as software maintenance, or the services of business-law firms. How is the quantity of these services to be defined? One possibility is to rely on ancillary indicators like the number of hours worked. For example, the quantity of software maintenance could be regarded as equal to the number of hours worked by the computer experts. A very similar result could be obtained by

---

* Quarterly contributions are generally not totally additive.

using a volume indicator derived by deflating the turnover of the maintenance firms by an hourly wage index. This is what the national accountants often do in practice. However, the result is open to dispute. For one thing, this indicator implicitly assumes that there is no productivity gain affecting these software experts, which is not a realistic hypothesis. Fortunately, the measurement of the volume of these services does not affect GDP because they are intermediate consumption, and only elements contributing to final demand affect GDP (see box "Shortcuts" in Chapter 1). How such services are measured nevertheless affects the allocation of GDP among sectors.

This difficulty crops up especially when measuring the volume of output for public services, which account for a very substantial part of GDP, since they include education and public health care, defence, law and order and general administration, all of which are elements of final demand. In these cases, there is simply no price available, since by definition this output is not offered for sale. In principle, therefore, one cannot even use deflation. Nevertheless, these services have a cost, consisting mainly of the pay received by the public employees, plus various types of intermediate consumption (for example, electricity, telecommunications, stationery and other office supplies) and also of consumption of fixed capital (wear and tear, for example, on school and hospital buildings). In order to calculate the volume of output, these costs will have to be deflated and then added together. For example, salaries can be deflated by a salary index for teachers, public hospital staff, military personnel and other government workers. As with the example of the software-service providers, this method implies constant productivity for these categories of personnel, which is disputable to say the least.

For this reason, many statistical offices are considering introducing direct indicators of volume, known as "output indicators". For example, in the case of education, the direct indicator might be the number of pupils successfully completing their schooling, although this indicator has the defect of considering all pupils as identical and assuming that the standard of examinations remains constant. In the case of public hospital services, the indicator could be the number of patients weighted by the cost of treatment, with a careful distinction being made between the different types of treatment. This is a highly promising indicator.

Unfortunately, it is not easy to find suitable indicators for the output of other services rendered by general government. For example, how is one to assess the output of tax inspectors, firemen or members of the armed forces? For these branches of general government, one is reduced to deflating the costs – and in particular, deflating wages paid by an index of salaries. The usual practice is to deflate wages paid by the increase in basic wage rates agreed upon by the government and employee representatives. However, the government's wage bill will change not only because of these agreed upon changes to the basic wage but also because of changes in the composition of the labour force: if there are more staff in higher grades this year compared to last year, then the government wage bill will rise. In addition, in most countries the wage scales for government employees provide for regular increases based on years of service. Note that a deflation process that depends only on agreed upon changes to the **basic wage** will mean that increases in the government wage bill that arise either because more staff are being hired in senior grades or because the government labour force is ageing (and presumably becoming more productive) will count as increases in the volume of output. There is, however, not much empirical evidence to show that the output of government increases either because more high-grade civil servants are employed or because the average length of service is increasing. It may or may not be true, but this is the best that national accountants can do at the present time.

The volume/price breakdown is even more difficult in the case of industries such as banking and insurance. We shall see in Chapter 4 that national accountants measure the output of these activities "by difference": the difference between interest receipts and payments in the case of the banks, and the difference between insurance premiums received and insurance indemnities paid out in the case of insurance. This way of measuring current price output provides no clear indication of how to allocate output between volume and price. The definition of volume in the case of these services therefore remains somewhat vague, and countries use different methods.

Other special cases relate to trade and transport margins and to taxes on products. Many countries estimate their national accounts using what is known as a **supply and use balance** (see Chapter 10) using the following equation:

Production + Imports + Trade and transport margins
+ Taxes on products – Subsidies on products = Intermediate consumption
+ Final uses excluding inventories + Change in inventories.

In order to establish this equilibrium in volume, "taxes and subsidies in volume" and "margins in volume" must be estimated. These are strange concepts, to say the least, since they relate to prices and comprise no element of quantity.

The convention adopted is as follows: the volumes are seen as equal to the tax (or marginal tax rate) of the base year (which is the previous year when using chain-linked Laspeyres) applied to the tax base of the current year, itself valued in volume terms. For example, the Value Added Tax (VAT) at 2012 prices on the consumption of cars in year 2013 would equal the VAT rate for the year 2012 applied to the consumption of cars in the year 2013, at 2012 prices. In the case of a basic product, the VAT in volume will therefore move exactly in line with the tax base in volume. Exactly the same will be true of the subsidies and margins in volume at the basic level (see Box 2.4 below for an exception). National accountants attempt to present taxes and margins in volume, and – stranger still – create price indices for taxes and margins, only because they want to provide the same presentation for accounts in volume as for accounts at current prices.

Box 2.4. **The case of margins on computers**

As explained above, the volume trade margin on sales of computers evolves, by definition, in line with the volume of computer purchases. However, in many countries national accountants measure the volume of computer purchases not by the number of computers sold, but, to simplify, by their calculating power, and this power evolves much more rapidly than the number of computers sold. Is it then reasonable to think that the trade margin in volume on computers evolves in line with computer purchases in volume? This is tantamount to saying that the volume of the commercial service produced by a seller of computers in a retail outlet (or on the Internet) is proportional to the power of the computer – not a very convincing assumption. In fact, the volume of the commercial service is the same for a powerful computer as for a not-so-powerful one. To this extent, it would seem that the national accounts overstate the volume of output of the commercial service in the case of computers. Fortunately, the amounts involved are small and do not affect GDP, only the distribution of value added between industry and services.

---

9. And what about the price indices?

So far, not much has been said about price indices because we preferred to concentrate on the estimation of volumes. In practice, however, once one has defined the method for calculating volumes, the method for calculating price indices is also entirely determined, because of the first fundamental equation set out in Chapter 1: *The variation in a variable at current prices breaks down exactly into its variation in volume and its variation in price.* This principle has been confirmed by formula (4) in the present chapter. Since the variation in current prices is a simple and self-evident notion, and since we have defined above the variations in volume, there is nothing to add on price indices apart from saying that the variation in prices is obtained by dividing an index at current prices by a volume index. Remember that when volume is expressed via a Laspeyres index, the result of this division is – by definition – a Paasche index (chained, in the case of chained accounts), and not a Laspeyres index.

In fact, macroeconomists make less use of price indices in the national accounts (which they often refer to as "implicit price indices" or "implicit deflators") than they do of volumes. In order to monitor inflation, they often prefer to use the Consumer Price Index (CPI) rather than the deflator of household consumption. For one thing, the CPI is available monthly and the household-consumption deflator quarterly at best. In the United States, however, macroeconomists are increasingly using the deflator of household consumption (called "Personal Consumption Expenditure (PCE) Implicit Price Index", see Chapter 12). In the national accounts, the price index of household consumption is also widely used to calculate the **purchasing power of household gross disposable income** (see Chapter 6).

Box 2.5. **Contributions and additivity**

The problem of non-additivity in chained accounts also affects the calculation of contributions to growth. Let us recall first the method used for calculating a contribution. Using a simplified example, let us assume there are only two aggregates in GDP: household consumption, denoted by C_t, and exports, denoted by X_t. GDP_t will denote GDP in year t. Δ will be used to indicate the variation in an aggregate, so that ΔGDP will signify the variation of GDP between t and t+1. Using this notation, the GDP growth rate can be written as $\Delta GDP \div GDP_t$.

Taking as starting point the equation $GDP_t = C_t + X_t$, it is possible to write $GDP_{t+1} - GDP_t = C_{t+1} - C_t + X_{t+1} - X_t$, which in turn gives, using our notations, $\Delta GDP = \Delta C + \Delta X$, or, dividing through by GDP_t:

$$\frac{\Delta GDP}{GDP_t} = \frac{\Delta C}{GDP_t} + \frac{\Delta X}{GDP_t}$$

This last equation can also be rewritten if we multiply and divide both terms on the right-hand side by the same term (either C or X), as follows:

$$\frac{\Delta GDP}{GDP_t} = \frac{C_t}{GDP_t} \times \frac{\Delta C}{C_t} + \frac{X_t}{GDP_t} \frac{\Delta X}{X_t}$$

We therefore have the following result: the GDP growth rate is equal to the growth rate for consumption, weighted by the share of consumption in the previous year's GDP, plus the growth rate for exports weighted by the share of exports in the previous year's GDP. The two terms on the right-hand side of the equation are known as "contributions to the GDP growth rate" from consumption and exports, respectively. The sum of the two together is equal to the GDP growth rate.

> ### Box 2.5. **Contributions and additivity** (cont.)
>
> As can be seen, the above result stems from the equation $GDP_t = C_t + X_t$. With chain-linked data, however, this equation no longer strictly holds, since chain-linked accounts are not additive. Therefore, in order to calculate the precise contributions it is necessary to revert to additive accounts (see Exercise 6 at the end of this chapter), and then make the calculations. It is only by using additive accounts that contributions to growth can be correctly calculated. It is indeed this method that is used by statistical offices when they publish tables of contributions to growth. And it is important to note that the tables on contributions to growth published by statistical offices have not been calculated from the chained volume levels disseminated in traditional tables, but from additive accounts that are not easily available to users. One advantage of using the correct tables for contributions to growth is that because they are derived from additive accounts, they are themselves additive. Economists can therefore use these tables to calculate sums and differences in various types of contributions, including changes in inventories and net exports, as illustrated in Exercise 7.

References

OECD (2013a), "OECD Economic Outlook No. 93", OECD Economic Outlook: Statistics and Projections (database), doi: *http://dx.doi.org/10.1787/data-00655-en.*

OECD (2013b), "Aggregate National Accounts: Gross domestic product", OECD National Accounts Statistics (database), *http://dx.doi.org/10.1787/data-00001-en.*

Key points

- To compare growth rates, use only the volume series and not the current price series.

- Detailed volume indices in the national accounts are commonly derived by deflating figures at current prices using the appropriate price indices.

- For aggregating quantities, national accountants use a fixed price structure. The volumes obtained in this way are known as constant-price accounts. The year corresponding to the fixed price structure is known as the base year.

- A change in volume is not the same thing as a change in quantity, since volume takes into account differences in quality and in the price levels of products.

- The Laspeyres volume index is the most widely used formula for calculating aggregated volume indices for national accounts.

- A Laspeyres volume index is a weighted average of changes in quantities, weighted by the values at current prices in the base year.

- The Paasche price index is the most widely used formula for calculating aggregated price indices in the national accounts.

- The product of the Laspeyres volume index and the Paasche price index is equal to the index of current prices.

- In most OECD countries, the national accounts in volume are calculated at the prices of the previous year, and then chained. The chained accounts use as weights the prices of the previous year and are therefore suitable for measuring changes in volume. Their drawback is their non-additivity.

- In North America, national accounts in volume also use the chaining principle, but they are based on Fisher volume and price indices. Their levels are not additive either.

- It is recommended that growth and contributions to growth figures are used to represent volume growth. Contributions to growth are additive when calculated from additive accounts.

Going further

Chain-linked levels of changes in inventories and other similar variables

The compilation of chain-linked changes in inventories is a problem. Let us use CI(Y) for the changes in inventories of year Y. In principle, if one applies the general formula for chain-linked volumes expressed at previous year prices, then CI(Y)chain – linked = CI(Y – 1)chain – linked × [CI(Y)in previous year's price ÷ CI(Y – 1)at current prices].

But experience shows that the above multiplication formula in not applicable to changes in inventories. Indeed, it results in extreme values for chain-linked changes in inventories (for reasons discussed at the end of the section). These extreme values cannot be used to calculate contributions to GDP growth, although, as explained in the main text, economists report volume changes in inventories exclusively as "contributions to growth of GDP". What is to be done? As discussed in the main text, one solution is to avoid presenting these series in terms of chain-linked levels. However, many statisticians still want to present these series in such a format. One proposal is interesting: it is based on the fact that the above multiplication formula is mathematically equivalent to the following additive formula: CI(Y) chain – linked = CI(Y – 1) chain – linked + [CI(Y) in previous year prices – CI(Y – 1) at current prices] ÷ Chain – linked price index of CI(Y – 1). However, this formula remains unusable because the chain-linked price index of CI(Y) can also take extreme values.

Another possibility is to substitute in the above additive formula a reasonable chain-linked price index instead of one liable to take extreme values. One could use the producer price index for the goods for which the changes in inventories are compiled, or, at the level of total changes in inventories, the chain-linked price index of GDP. It can be shown that if one uses the chain-linked price index for GDP, the formula ensures that the contribution to GDP obtained using the chain-linked CI(Y) is the correct one. Let us prove that. The starting formula, which we shall call F, is

CI(Y)chain – linked = CI(Y – 1)chain – linked + [CI(Y)in previous year prices
– CI(Y – 1)at current prices] ÷ Price index of GDP(Y – 1).

This is equivalent to: CI(Y)chain – linked = CI(Y – 1)chain – linked + [CI(Y)in *previous year prices – CI(Y – 1)at current prices] ÷ [GDP(Y – 1)at current prices ÷ GDP(Y – 1)chain – linked].*

From this, one can derive: [CI(Y)chain – linked – CI(Y – 1)chain – linked] ÷ GDP(Y – 1)chain – linked = [CI(Y)in previous year prices – CI(Y – 1)at current prices] ÷ [GDP(Y – 1)at current prices].

The second term of the above equation is precisely the correct formula for calculating the contribution to GDP growth of CI(Y), because accounts in previous year prices are additive. Thus, formula F (applied as if the volume series were additive) ensures that the chain-linked series CI(Y) can be used to derive easily the correct contribution to growth. It is interesting to note that formula F shows that chain-linked changes in inventories can be compiled as the accumulation of change in inventory changes expressed in previous year prices, with each link being deflated by the chain-linked price index of GDP. This presentation of the chain-linked series of changes in inventories is intellectually satisfying because it presents a sensible relation between the change in the volume of changes in inventories expressed at previous year's prices and the change in inventory changes expressed in chain-linked volume level.

Formula F can be used as an alternative to the one illustrated in Exercise 7. In fact, the two are exactly equivalent and both give a time series from which one can derive the correct contribution to growth. Two final points before we close this box. First, formula F can be used for variables other than changes in inventories, for example net exports. Second, there are reasons why the first formula in this box gives extreme results. Mathematically, the reason is that because changes in inventories can be positive or negative and also very close to zero, the second term of the first equation can be massively positive or negative and extremely sensitive to minuscule revisions. Statistically, the reason is that chain-linking is not suitable for measuring changes in inventories in volume terms. Indeed, it can be proven that chain-linking should only be used when the price structure is changing regularly among the different goods or services being aggregated. A good example of this is the regular price decreases in computer prices relative to the pricing of other machinery. However, because inventories can comprise extremely heterogeneous goods from one period to another, they are not suitable for chain- linking.

Exercises for Chapter 2

Exercise 1. Using deflation to derive volume

Deflation is a fairly easy concept to apply. Let us suppose that a seller of lollipops has a turnover of EUR 1 200 in October. He raises the prices of his lollipops by 12% on 1 November. His turnover in November is EUR 1 680. Calculate via deflation the increase in lollipop sales volume. Check your result using quantities, given that the price of a lollipop before the increase was EUR 1.25. Now suppose that instead of increasing his price by 12% he in fact reduced it by 12%, while maintaining the same turnover. What will the increase in volume be now?

Exercise 2. Calculation of volume at various price levels

Let us take three products, A, B and C, with the following series of quantities and prices in each of three periods:

	Period 1		Period 2		Period 3	
	Quantity	Price	Quantity	Price	Quantity	Price
A	20	5	40	3	60	2
B	150	0.2	145	0.25	160	0.25
C	12	25	6	40	5	35

Calculate, for each period, the amount at current prices, the volume at constant period 1 prices, the volume at constant period 2 prices and the growth rates 2/1 and 3/2 of the aggregate constituted by the totality of the three products. Comment on the results.

Exercise 3. Calculation of a Laspeyres index and equivalence of calculation methods

The aim of this exercise is to show the equivalence between the two Laspeyres formulas presented in Section 4 of this chapter. Formula (1) corresponds to the calculation of a weighted index; formula (2) corresponds to the calculation of growth rates for accounts at constant prices.

Take the case of two types of car, small and large, and the respective quantities sold in two periods at various prices, as shown in the following table. First, use Formula (2) to calculate the volume growth rate for all the cars at constant prices, and then use Formula (1), to calculate a weighted quantity index. Check against the theoretical result.

	Period 1		Period 2	
	Quantity	Price	Quantity	Price
Small cars	1 000	10.0	600	10.5
Large cars	200	20.0	600	21.0

Exercise 4. Calculation of Laspeyres indices, Paasche indices and deflation

Let us again consider at the table used in Exercise 3. Calculate the index for the change in current prices. Calculate the Paasche price index. Obtain the Laspeyres volume index by deflation. Verify that the result is the same as that given by Exercise 3.

Exercise 5. Calculation of " chained accounts " (chained Laspeyres indices)

The following table gives a sequence of prices and quantities for three products A, B and C. The aim of this exercise is to calculate the volume for the aggregate consisting of the set A + B + C adopting the method used in the French national accounts known as "accounts at previous year's prices, chained, base 2010". For this purpose, use the structure of the following table. First, calculate the account for A + B + C at current prices for all four years. Then calculate the volumes of the last three years at the previous years' prices. After that, calculate the growth rates of these volumes (watch out for the trap). Finally, chain these growth rates using the year 2010 as base. The result is the accounts at previous year's prices, chained, base 2010. Is there a difference between the growth rates in this series and the growth rates in volume at previous year's prices?

Next, compare these results with those obtained by using constant prices (i.e. "accounts at 2010 prices") to derive absolute levels and growth rates.

	2009		2010		2011		2012	
	Quantity	Price	Quantity	Price	Quantity	Price	Quantity	Price
A	20.00	5.00	40.00	4.00	60.00	2.00	90.00	1.00
B	150.00	0.20	145.00	0.25	160.00	0.25	175.00	0.30
C	12.00	25.00	6.00	40.00	5.00	40.00	7.00	36.00

Aggregate A +B + C	2009	2010	2011	2012
Accounts at current prices				
Accounts at previous year's prices				
Growth rates				
Accounts at previous year's prices, chained, base 2010				
Accounts at 2010 prices				
Growth rates				

Exercise 6. Chained accounts and the loss of additivity

The table below is an old one taken from the French national accounts in SNA 1993, listing annual GDP in volume (at previous year's prices, chained, base 2005), imports and the sum of the two, known as total resources.

For each of the aggregates below, the year-to-year changes are also shown, with a high degree of precision (three decimal places). Make your own calculation of total resources by summing GDP and imports and comparing the result with the total given by INSEE, the French statistical office. Do you conclude that INSEE is no longer capable of simple addition? If not, where does the problem lie? Try to reconstitute the INSEE growth rate for between 2011 and 2012, using the accounts at the previous year's prices and knowing that for 2011, at current prices GDP = 2 001.4 and imports = 597.6. What are your conclusions?

(billion 2005 euro)	2009	2010	2011	2012
Gross domestic product	1 742.58	1 772.64	1 808.57	1 808.82
Evolution in %		1.725	2.027	0.014
Imports	468.75	510.48	536.68	531.02
Evolution in %		8.902	5.132	-1.053
Total Resources	2 211.28	2 281.36	2 343.01	2 337.59
Evolution in %		3.169	2.702	-0.232

Source: Insee: National Accounts: Gross domestic product and main economic aggregates: Gross domestic product and its components in volume at chained prices (Billions of 2005 Euros)

Exercise 7. Volume changes in inventories: levels or contributions to GDP?

Let us suppose GDP is broken down as final demand minus changes in inventories (FDLI) and changes in inventories (I). Here are the accounts, expressed in prices of year 1:

At prices of year 1	Year 1	Year 2
FDLI	1 430	1 468
I	-43	69
GDP	1387	1537

Is it correct to say that the accounts of year 1 are in current prices? Is it correct to say that the accounts for year 2 are in volume terms? Why are these accounts additive (e.g. GDP = FDLI + I)? Calculate growth rates for year 2. Why is it not possible to calculate a growth rate for I? Calculate contributions to change in GDP for both FDLI and I.

Below are the volume accounts for year 3, expressed in prices of year 2. Calculate growth rates and contributions to GDP growth.

At prices of year 2	Year 2	Year 3
FDLI	1 490	1 363
I	123	148
GDP	1 613	1 511

How would the OECD economics department present a table including the three years? Explain why it is not possible, because of changes in inventories, to easily present the same table but with all variables expressed in chain-linked levels (i.e. where year 1 is the reference year). Propose a solution whereby the levels of changes in inventories correspond exactly to those from which one can derive exact contributions to change of GDP.

Exercise 8. The US approach: forecasting using chained accounts

As explained in this chapter, the disadvantage of using chain-linked volume numbers is their lack of additivity, a feature that makes the life of forecasters quite uncomfortable. This exercise, largely inspired from a paper by the US Bureau of Economic Analysis (BEA), proposes a simple way to derive a very good approximation of BEA results, which are based on sophisticated chained Fisher indices. The simplified approach uses additive accounts at prices of the "previous quarter".

The table below shows the situation in the beginning of 2002. The first two columns are data published by the BEA at that time. The first column contains data at current prices ("current dollar level"). The second column contains data in "chained-dollar levels". The third column shows a set of forecasts by an unknown forecaster for the second quarter of 2002 (2002 Q2). These forecasts are expressed as growth rates (of course in volume terms). *Important notice:* in US accounts, quarterly growth is traditionally expressed at "annual rates". This means that quarter-to-quarter growth is raised by an exponent of 4. For example, 2.0 is the forecast growth rate for durable goods in the second quarter. In fact, this means the quarter-to-quarter growth is equal to $(1 - (1 + 0.02)^{(1/4)}) = +0.496\%$. Only these quarter-to-quarter growth rates should be applied to previous quarter's levels.

Using the data of the first three columns, calculate GDP growth for 2002 Q2 at an annual rate in two ways. First, using the correct approach, apply quarter-to-quarter growth to each component of GDP in 2002 Q1 *at current dollar levels* to obtain the fourth column, which will therefore be in billions of dollars at prices of 2002 Q1, or "2002 Q1 dollar levels". You can now sum up these numbers to obtain GDP, from which the annual growth rate can be compiled. Indeed, because they represent accounts at prices of the preceding period, they are additive. The result should be forecasted GDP growth of 1.3% at an annual rate. Second, using the incorrect solution, apply quarter-to-quarter growth to each component of GDP in 2002 Q1 at chained dollar levels. Obtain GDP growth using these data. Comment on the difference between the two ways to measure GDP. How can we then create a forecast for 2002 Q3?

	2002 Q1		Correct solution 2002 Q2	Wrong solution	
	Current dollar level	Chained dollar levels	Forecasted growth at annual rate	"2002 Q1 dollars" levels	Chained dollars levels
Personal consumption expenditures					
Durable goods	859	976	2.0	?	?
Nondurable goods	2 085	1 921	-0.1	?	?
Services	4 230	3 642	2.7	?	?
Gross private domestic investment	1 559	1 551	7.9	?	?
Fixed investment					
Non residential					
Structures	288	243	-17.6	?	?
Equipment and software	838	954	3.3	?	?
Residential	463	384	2.7	?	?
Change in private inventories		-29		?	?
Net export of goods and services					
Exports					
Goods	680	738	15.9	?	?
Services	298	292	10.7	?	?
Imports					
Goods	1 102	1 250	27.9	?	?
Services	235	226	-2.1	?	?
Government consumption and investment					
Federal	672	598	7.5	?	?
State and local	1 267	1 099	-1.7	?	?
Gross domestic product before residual		9 343			?
Residual		20			?
Gross domestic product	10 313	9 363		?	?
Forecasted growth				??	??

The solutions to these exercises are available at:
http://dx.doi.org/10.1787/9789264214637-20-en

Chapter 3

International comparisons

This chapter examines the comparison of national accounts data among several countries. Cross-country comparisons are more difficult because: the statistical methods for estimating national accounts variables can vary from one country to another; countries' national institutions may be different; and countries do not have the same currency and the same price levels. Nevertheless, such comparisons can be made, even if in some cases adjustments are to be made. They are achieved by comparing: the growth rates of certain variables (such as GDP in volume), certain ratios (such as the profit rate or the public debt ratio) and the absolute levels of certain national variables among several countries (such as the level of GDP per capita).

In Chapter 2, we examined the comparability of data over time for the national accounts *of a given country*. We saw how to separate changes in volume from changes in prices. In this chapter, we shall examine the comparison of data *among several countries*. Inter-country comparisons are more difficult for at least three reasons: (1) despite the efforts to achieve international synchronization, the statistical methods for estimating national accounts variables can vary from one country to another; (2) individual countries' institutions can be different; and (3) countries do not have the same currency and the same price levels.

Despite these difficulties, it is part of the OECD mission to make international comparisons in order to be able to recommend economic policies that have been successful. These international comparisons take place at three levels. The first and simplest consists of comparing the growth rates of certain variables, such as GDP in volume. In this case, the fact that countries have different currencies or institutions is not of great concern. The second level, to be examined in the second section, consists of the inter-country comparison of ratios, for example the profit rate or the public debt. In these cases, differences in statistical methods as well as in institutions can have a negative effect on comparisons, but the existence of different currencies still has no effect. The third level consists of comparing the absolute levels of certain national variables among several countries, such as the level of GDP per head or the level of household consumption per head. This final type of comparison is the most problematic. That is because on top of the two factors already mentioned, there is the added problem of currency conversion, which has to be solved by using "**purchasing power parities**". These allow for a *spatial* volume/price breakdown (i.e. a volume/price breakdown among countries for a given point in time rather than a breakdown between different time periods for a given country).

1. Comparison of growth rates

The *OECD Economic Outlook* (OECD, 2013), a biannual survey of OECD countries, opens with the following table comparing GDP growth rates in volume for three major countries or areas.

Table 3.1. **GDP annual growth rate in percentage**

	1995-2012 average	2008	2009	2010	2011	2012
Japan	0.8	-1.0	-5.5	4.7	-0.6	2.0
United States	2.5	-0.3	-2.8	2.5	1.8	2.8
Euro area (17 countries)	1.5	0.4	-4.4	2.0	1.6	-0.7

Source: OECD (2013), OECD Economic Outlook, Vol. 2013/2, OECD Publishing, doi: http://dx.doi.org/10.1787/eco_outlook-v2013-2-en.

StatLink ⇒ http://dx.doi.org/10.1787/888933143638

Table 3.1 shows what appears to be a quasi-structural difference in growth for these three major areas. Between 1995 and 2012, average annual growth in the United States was 1.7 percentage points higher than Japanese annual average growth and 1.0 percentage points higher than that of the euro area. A difference of as little as one point, if it were to persist systematically in the future, would result in the relative economic power of the United States rapidly becoming even more substantial than it already is. In the space of 10 years, the United States would outstrip the others by 1.01^{10}, i.e. +10.5 points! This is an enormous difference and should be cause for serious reflection by the other countries.

The above international comparison is not completely convincing, however. There is in fact a fundamental difference between the United States, Europe and Japan that is often overlooked. That is because the population of the United States is structurally more dynamic, rising by 1.0% a year, compared with only around 0.1% growth for Japan and 0.4% for the euro area. This means that it is better to compare growth in GDP per inhabitant rather than in GDP itself, if valid long-term conclusions are to be drawn. Using this adjusted yardstick, the difference between the growth rates per head was only 0.8 points in the case of Japan (instead of 1.7), and 0.4 points for the euro area (instead of 1.0 points).

Table 3.2. **Growth in real GDP and real GDP per inhabitant**
1995-2012, average annual growth rate in percentage

	Real GDP	Difference vis-à-vis the United States of America	Real GDP per inhabitant	Difference vis-à-vis the United States of America
Japan	0.8	-1.7	0.7	-0.8
United States	2.5	0.0	1.5	0.0
Euro area (17 countries)	1.5	-1.0	1.1	-0.4

Source: OECD (2013), "Aggregate National Accounts: Gross domestic product", OECD National Accounts Statistics (database), http://dx.doi.org/10.1787/data-00001-en.

StatLink ⇒ http://dx.doi.org/10.1787/888933143647

The differences remain appreciable, nevertheless, especially for Japan. For the euro area, the difference appears to be smaller, but this masks more substantial disparities within the area itself. The OECD's principal concern at the present time is therefore to use these results to persuade the less dynamic countries to carry out structural reform in order to re-stimulate their growth and reduce their unemployment rates.

But is this comparison of GDP growth rates statistically valid? It is to the extent that through the adoption of international manuals for statistics and national accounts, the international community of statisticians uses definitions and conventions common to all countries. In the case of national accounts, the basic reference manual is the 2008 version of the System of National Accounts (SNA 2008). Its European counterpart, the 2010 version of the European System of Accounts (ESA 2010) has the weight of European law that EU members are obligated to apply.

See Box 1.1: "The reference manuals" in Chapter 1 and also Chapter 14.

This is therefore reassuring for users. As a first approximation, there is indeed a high degree of comparability between OECD countries in regard to definitions and conventions. This is what enables the OECD to compile an international database of national accounts that constitutes the best source for making inter-country comparisons (see Box 3.1: "The OECD's international database").

Box 3.1. **The OECD international databases**

The OECD collects from each of its member countries several thousand series relating to annual and quarterly national accounts:

- Every quarter: Quarterly National Accounts
- Once a year (February and July): "National Accounts of OECD Countries", Issue 1: *Main Aggregates*; "National Accounts of OECD Countries", Issue 2: *Detailed Tables.*
- Once a year (December): "National Accounts of OECD Countries", *Financial Accounts*; "National Accounts of OECD Countries", *Financial Balance Sheets*; "National Accounts of OECD Countries", *General Government.*

The OECD's forecasting database disseminated twice a year, as the *Economic Outlook* Statistical Annex Tables, published at the same time as the *OECD Economic Outlook.*

All OECD databases are available at *www.oecd-ilibrary.org/.*

---

2. Comparison of ratios: The example of the saving ratio, the profit rate and the public debt ratio

The household **saving ratio** is one of the key variables in the national accounts (see Chapter 1). It equals saving divided by disposable income (and multiplied by 100), and it represents the allocation of income between consumption and saving, an essential item of information in economic analysis. It turns out that the saving ratio is very significantly lower in Japan and in the United States than in other countries like Australia or Germany.

Table 3.3. **Household saving ratio in percentage**

Net saving, unless otherwise indicated

	2009	2010	2011	2012
Australia	9.8	11.0	11.7	10.5
Finland	4.2	3.6	1.3	0.9
Germany	10.9	10.9	10.4	10.3
Italy	7.1	4.9	4.3	3.6
Japan	2.3	2.1	2.6	1.5
United Kingdom*	7.0	7.3	6.7	7.2
United States	6.4	5.9	5.9	5.8

* Gross saving.

Source: OECD (2013), "Detailed National Accounts: Non-financial accounts by sectors, annual", OECD National Accounts Statistics (database), doi: http://dx.doi.org/10.1787/data-00034-en.

StatLink ⬛ http://dx.doi.org/10.1787/888933143659

If Table 3.3. showed saving rates of US households before the financial and economic crisis of 2008, it would have shown that US households hardly saved at all, allocating almost their entire incomes to consumption. Before the 2008 crisis, nearly 0% of net disposable income was saved. This demonstrated, on the one hand, the strong confidence in the future shown by US households and, on the other, their lack of concern regarding the financing of their country's investment. In fact, it is not US households that financed this investment but foreign investors who, having confidence in the US economy, continue to buy large amounts of US Treasury bonds. However, the economic crisis changed the picture. With dramatically rising and persisting unemployment, the confidence in the future of US households has dwindled, and this is now reflected by higher saving rates, which remain however lower than in Europe. Some people worry about the dramatic impact on the world economy that could result from erosion of foreign investor confidence in the US, while others think that this imbalance will gradually be reabsorbed without producing a new crisis.

In contrast, it is striking to note the very different behaviour of German households, who save more than 10% of their net incomes. Many economists, in the OECD and elsewhere, are trying to find explanations for such wide differences among countries that are basically quite similar. Some economists believe that when households lack confidence in the ability of their economy to guarantee them a job and a good pension, the saving rate falls. But is it the case for Germany? The case of Italy is also strange as this country is confronted to a serious crisis. The OECD economists have tried to explain the decrease of the saving rate as the result of the 2008 crisis which led to the fall in Italian disposable incomes.

One source of non-comparability relates to the calculation of the saving ratio, which can be calculated in two different ways: (1) the "net" approach, in which one deducts households' consumption of fixed capital (CFC) from both the numerator (saving, denoted as S) and also from the denominator (disposable income, denoted as DI); or (2) the "gross" approach, in which the consumption of fixed capital is not deducted from neither the numerator nor the denominator. The first approach gives a "net" saving ratio equal to: $(S - CFC)/(DI - CFC)$; the second gives a "gross" ratio: S/DI. The first result is mathematically lower than the second. Table 3.3 above shows "net" ratios except for the United Kingdom, as is the case of the table included in the *Economic Outlook*.

While many countries publish "net" ratios, which are preferred by the OECD, the United Kingdom and some others have opted for the "gross" saving ratio. There are reasons for preferring a gross ratio. First, it corresponds more closely to the observed financial flows, whereas the net ratio is artificial in that it incorporates an imputed flow, i.e. the consumption of fixed capital. Second, it is probable that net ratios are less comparable between countries than gross ratios because of the differing methods used to calculate the consumption of fixed capital. In all cases, however, one must avoid improper comparison of a gross ratio with a net ratio. By looking at Table 3.3, this error might nevertheless be made, since in that table (as indicated in the footnote), the ratio for the United Kingdom is gross while for the other countries it is net.

Table 3.4 below rectifies this error by showing net ratios for all countries, including the United Kingdom. As can be seen from this corrected table, saving behaviour in the United Kingdom turns out in to be even lower than that of the United States, and not, as Table 3.3 incorrectly indicated, somewhere in between that of the United States and Germany. The first lesson here is that when presented with international comparisons it is necessary to look closely at all the footnotes in order to avoid rough errors.

Comparability of ratios is even more complex in the domain of profit rates. As will be seen in Chapter 7, economists use a ratio calculated as gross (or net) operating surplus divided by gross (or net) value added to derive an indicator of the profit rate of businesses. Based on the gross definition, and using as the basis of comparison the sector of "non-financial corporations", Figure 3.1 below shows a substantial (and surprising) difference in the level of profit rate

Table 3.4. **Household net saving ratio in percentage**

	2009	2010	2011	2012
Australia	9.8	11.0	11.7	10.5
Finland	4.2	3.6	1.3	0.9
Germany	10.9	10.9	10.4	10.3
Italy	7.1	4.9	4.3	3.6
Japan	2.3	2.1	2.6	1.5
United Kingdom	2.3	2.9	2.2	2.8
United States	6.4	5.9	5.9	5.8

Source: OECD (2013), "Detailed National Accounts: Non-financial accounts by sectors, annual", OECD National Accounts Statistics (database), doi: *http://dx.doi.org/10.1787/data-00034-en.*

StatLink ᴍᴤ▇ *http://dx.doi.org/10.1787/888933143663*

between three major European economic partners: France, Germany and Italy. Apparently, the profit rate of Italian non-financial corporations, while decreasing, has been systematically substantially higher than in Germany, and even more, France.

Figure 3.1. **Profit rate for non-financial corporations**
Gross operating surplus/gross value added, in %

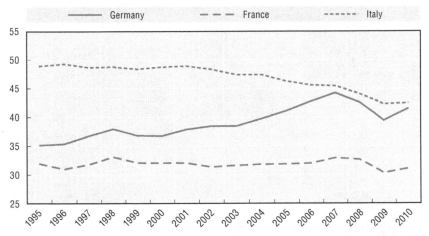

Source: OECD (2014) "Detailed National Accounts: Non-financial accounts by sectors, annual", OECD National Accounts Statistics (database), doi: *http://dx.doi.org/10.1787/data-00034-en.* OECD calculations.

StatLink ᴍᴤ▇ *http://dx.doi.org/10.1787/888933143671*

However, this comparison is biased, because the composition of the sector "non-financial corporations" is different between these three countries. Contrary to France, Germany and Italy both classify a significant number of "quasi-corporations" inside their non-financial corporation sector. They are small units close to sole proprietorships, with many non-salaried workers. The labour remuneration of these non-salaried workers is, by definition, included in operating surplus. Thus the average profit rate in Germany and Italy is inflated compared to France, where there are no non-salaried workers classified in the non-financial corporation sector. Figure 3.2 shows an adjusted profit rate for Italy, compiled excluding the estimated amount of the remuneration of non-salaried workers. As can be seen, the comparable profit rate for Italy becomes much closer to the French one. Such an adjustment necessitates having an estimate of the number of non-salaried workers classified in the sector non-financial corporations. This was not possible for Germany. But, if that were possible, the curb for Germany would have also been adjusted downwards.

Figure 3.2. **Adjusted profit rate for non-financial corporations**

Gross operating surplus/gross value added, non-financial corporations, in %

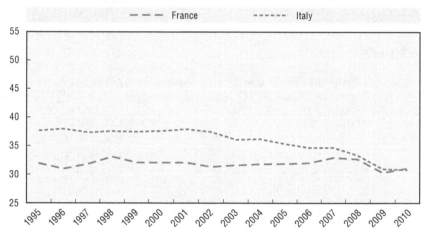

Source: OECD (2013), "Detailed National Accounts: Non-financial accounts by sectors, annual", OECD National Accounts Statistics (database), doi: *http://dx.doi.org/10.1787/data-00034-en*. OECD calculations.

StatLink ⬛ *http://dx.doi.org/10.1787/888933143681*

International comparisons of the ratios of "public debt" (i.e. debt/GDP) are also not so straightforward, even if this is one of the major headline macroeconomic indicators. First, the definition of "public" might differ from one country to another. In Europe, it is strictly based on the concept of general government (see Chapter 9). Outside Europe, the headline public debt ratio is sometimes based on an extended concept, which includes market oriented public corporations controlled by the general government. Other compilation conventions, such as consolidation, netting, and the coverage of debt instruments might affect the international comparability of this ratio, as explained in Box 13.3 of Chapter 13.

3. Comparison of levels of variables: GDP per head in volume

The figure below is very simple but telling. It shows the evolution in the volume levels of GDP per head for Japan, the euro area and the United Kingdom relative to the United States, which has been set to equal 100. The figure shows that GDP per capita in Japan and the euro area, as well as the United Kingdom, ranges between 70% to 80% of GDP per capita in the United States. It also reveals that around 1995 the relative levels of GDP per head for the euro area and the United Kingdom were roughly equal at 71.0%, and those for Japan were at 80.0% of the United States level.

Figure 3.3. Real GDP per head relative to the United States

Indices, based on 2005 PPPs and 2005 prices (USA = 100)

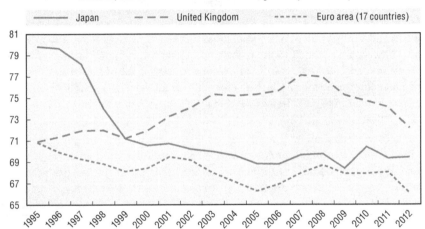

Source: OECD (2013), "Aggregate National Accounts: Gross domestic product", OECD National Accounts Statistics (database), *http://dx.doi.org/10.1787/data-00001-en.*

StatLink ᴍᴥ *http://dx.doi.org/10.1787/888933143694*

While not shown on the graph, between 1980 and 1994, Japan's economic growth was much faster than that of the United States, and, as a consequence, its GDP per head tended to approach that of the United States. However, its relative level peaked in 1994, at roughly 82%. From then on, Japan suffered a period of severe "deflation" (economic stagnation and falling prices) and lost in 10 years what it had gained vis-à-vis the United States in the previous 10. Therefore, between 1995 and 2012 Japan lost 10 percentage points in relation to the United States.

Prior to 1980, the euro area had also shown some relative growth compared with the United States, and this had raised hopes of convergence at some point. But the euro area also started to stagnate by comparison between 1980 and 1994 and then to show a relative decline. In relation to the United

Box 3.2. **GDP and the measurement of welfare**

Criticisms are often voiced concerning the shortcomings of GDP per head as a measure of welfare, as more or less implied by this international comparison of GDP per head. In a way, these criticisms are justified. But GDP per head is not a measure of economic and social "welfare" (see Chapter 15). It is not even a measure of wealth. It is merely an overall measure of the production of goods and services. However, it should not be forgotten that this production is itself an important dimension of welfare. We are all consumers of goods and services, and we are all glad to have more of both. Strong GDP growth also goes along with a decline in unemployment. However, it is indisputable that there are dimensions of welfare that are not reflected in GDP, such as choice of leisure activities, social inequality, security of goods and persons, and quality of the environment. It is therefore reasonable to raise probing questions as to how best to guide economic development so that it serves human development and welfare.

How can these alternative factors be considered? Official statisticians (in national statistical offices) are inclined to tell users that instead of trying to say everything via a single indicator, such as GDP, they might consider using a set of indicators that enable them to make inter-country comparisons for some or all these factors, GDP merely being one of these indicators. This is in fact what the OECD does, for example by publishing the Better Life Index.*

However, some economists (mainly in universities) advocate the construction of a single indicator, a sort of super-GDP, covering not only the production of goods and services but also social and environmental factors. This indicator, for example, would show a decline given deterioration in the environment, an increase in violence or a widening of socio-economic inequalities. It would then be a simple matter to rank countries according to their success at all these levels. Some organisations have created an index of this type, an example being the United Nations' "human development index", which has three components: standard of living, level of education and health standard. Many economists have also proposed indicators of this kind.

But the problem with a "super-GDP" indicator is that it is not clear how to combine social and environmental dimensions with the production of goods and services. In other words, what "prices" can be used to weight the environment or social inequalities, in relation to the production of milk or machinery? The weights being proposed remain fairly arbitrary, and this diminishes the credibility of such indices. In fact, it can be shown that varying the weights for the hard-to-quantify factors leads to a substantial change in country rankings. Therefore, until a genuine consensus is reached regarding the method of calculation, there is little chance that a "super-GDP index" will be calculated by official statisticians. Chapter 15 discusses thoroughly these issues.

* Readers interested in the Better Life Index can visit the website: *www.oecdbetterlifeindex.org/*.

States, the euro area's level of GDP per head for 2012 was 5 percentage points below what it had been in 1995. This was caused mainly by the large continental countries (Germany, France, and Italy) and not the smaller ones. Results for the United Kingdom, which is not part of the euro area, shows that this dismal picture was not true of all European countries. On the contrary, the United Kingdom, which had shown a relative decline in the 1970s, rebounded strongly in the early 1980s and has gained several percentage points in relative terms over the past 25 years. However, in the last period of crisis, it has lost substantial relative GDP per head compared to the United States. During the recent great recession, it appears that the United States has maintained its relative GDP per head compared to Japan and the Euro zone.

In purely statistical terms, Figure 3.3 is an ingenious comparison of absolute levels of GDP per head in certain countries with that of the United States, as well as a comparison of growth rates in GDP per head over time. It is important to understand that what is being compared here is *volumes* of GDP per head, and not monetary values of GDP per head. To compare GDP in volume for countries with different currencies – and different purchasing power for those currencies – it is necessary to calculate a spatial volume/price breakdown using a method known as "purchasing power parities" (PPP).

4. The spatial volume/price breakdown: Purchasing power parities*

The objective here is to compare *absolute levels* of GDP per head (or other variables such as consumption) among different countries or regions *in volume*, for a given period (usually one year). Why in volume? Because the aim is to compare the quantities of goods and services produced in each country and not the monetary value of this output. The monetary value will in fact be affected by the differences among price levels. How can this spatial (i.e. among countries, regions or zones) comparison in volume be done?

Recall that when analysing growth over time for a given country, GDP in volume is calculated by dividing GDP at current prices by a price index that is equal to 100 for a set base period. Exactly the same approach is used for spatial comparisons. A figure for GDP in volume is obtained by dividing GDP at current prices by a "purchasing power parity" index, set to equal 100 for a given country. Thus, as in the case of a temporal price index, there is a "base" used as reference (and for which the index value is 100), but in the case of a spatial index the base is a country or a region, and not a time period. For the base in spatial comparisons, the OECD usually uses either the average level of prices for OECD countries, or more simply, the level of prices in the United

---

* For a complete presentation, readers should refer to: Purchasing Power Parities and Real Expenditures 2007, 2005 Benchmark Year (2008 Edition), OECD and Eurostat.

States. For this reason, "purchasing power parities" presented by the OECD have USA = 1 (or 100).

For a simplified illustration of the purchasing power parities (PPP) method, let us consider first the case of countries with the same currency, thus avoiding having to manipulate exchange rates. Also for simplicity, there is only a single product – the hamburger. Let us suppose that the GDPs are expressed at current prices in the same currency (for example the euro) and equal to 1000 for country A and 1200 for country B during the specified period. This can be written as $GDP_a = 1\,000$, $GDP_b = 1\,200$. Furthermore, since there is only one product, the hamburger, the respective GDPs can be written as $P_a{}^*H_a$ and $P_b{}^*H_b$, where P_a is the price in euros of a hamburger in country A, and H_a is the number of hamburgers produced in country A (similarly for country B).

Our objective is to compare the volumes, i.e. the quantities H_a and H_b. To do this, we shall calculate the price ratio PPP, called "the purchasing power parity of B with respect to A", as: $PPP = P_b \div P_a$. By deflating the GDP of B by this PPP, in other words dividing GDP_b by PPP, we obtain $P_a \times H_b$. This results in the GDP in volume of country B expressed "in country A prices". By then dividing this volume by GDP_a, we obtain $H_b \div H_a$, which is exactly the relative valuation in volume that we are after. It can be seen that: (1) PPP is a ratio of the price levels of identical products in the two countries; (2) the volume obtained by deflating a country's GDP by its PPP is a valuation of its GDP *at the base country's prices*, thus eliminating the difference between *price levels* in the two countries; and (3) the value of this GDP in volume in relation to the GDP at current prices of the base country gives a comparison *in volume*, which is our aim.

Now suppose the two countries do not have the same currency. Country A (the United States, for example) has the dollar, while country B has the euro. If the price of a hamburger in country A is Pa, in dollars, and the price of a hamburger in country B is P_b, in euros, the PPP of a hamburger between country A and country B will still be equal to $P_b \div P_a$. In this case, however, the PPP is expressed as a currency ratio, since it equates to an amount in euros per dollar. How should it then be interpreted? It is the amount in euros that has to be spent in country B to obtain the same quantity of hamburgers that can be bought with a dollar in country A. The PPP is therefore equal to the conversion rate that equalises the purchasing power of the two currencies. When we divide the GDP of country B by the PPP, we kill two birds with one stone: we eliminate the differences between the price levels in the two countries; and we express the two amounts in the same currency unit, that of the base country.

Why not simply use the actual exchange rate seen on the currency markets? Because the market rate does not properly adjust for the difference in price levels between two countries and therefore does not provide a true comparison of the volume of goods and services produced per head. Let us try to compare GDP per head in Sweden and in the United States using just the exchange rate. First, divide GDP per head in Sweden expressed in Swedish crowns by the crown/dollar exchange rate. What we get is the Swedish GDP per head expressed in dollars. For a direct comparison with United States GDP, this magnitude (now expressed in dollars) is divided by the GDP per head in dollars of the United States (and multiplied by 100). This gives the dotted curve in Figure 3.4, which is a percentage index giving the size of Swedish GDP per head relative to that of the United States (which, by convention, is equal to 100). The value of this index can be read on the left hand axis of the figure.

Figure 3.4. **GDP per capita using exchange rates**

Sweden GDP per capita as a percentage of United States GDP per capita and US dollar per Swedish krona

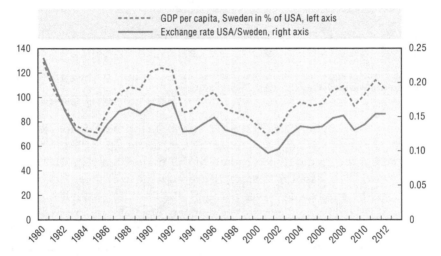

Source: OECD (2013), "Aggregate National Accounts: Gross domestic product", OECD National Accounts Statistics (database), *http://dx.doi.org/10.1787/data-00001-en.*

StatLink ㎳🔗 *http://dx.doi.org/10.1787/888933143707*

The shape of the curve clearly shows that this calculation is not a proper indicator of relative GDP in volume. It is definitely not true that the Swedish GDP per capita in volume (dotted line) was 120% of the one of the United States in 1990, and then fell down to 71% ten years later only to steadily climb up and reach the 1990 level in 2011 again. This volatility can be linked to the movement of the exchange rate of the US dollar and the Swedish crown (solid line). The graph visualizes this correlation between the two variables: it is very obvious that both curves always move in the same direction. Thus, the currency exchange rate is not a good relative deflator.

So it is not possible to use market exchange rates. Instead, it is necessary to construct specific indices for the spatial volume/price breakdown, or

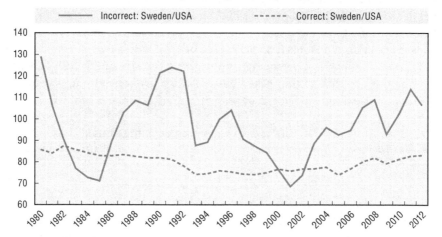

Figure 3.5. **Correct and incorrect GDP per capita**

Sweden GDP per capita as a percentage of United States GDP per capita,
deflated by exchange rates and PPPs

Source: OECD (2013), "Aggregate National Accounts: Gross domestic product", OECD National Accounts
Statistics (database), *http://dx.doi.org/10.1787/data-00001-en.*

StatLink ᴍᴀᴘ *http://dx.doi.org/10.1787/888933143712*

purchasing power parity (PPP). These PPP indices are price ratios for identical
products, the basic building block being the ratio discussed earlier. Indices of
this kind can be calculated for each of the major items in GDP (final
consumption, GFCF, exports, imports). The overall mean of these PPP indices
constitutes the purchasing power parity of GDP. Therefore, PPP is a spatial
deflator of GDP, making it possible to compare absolute volumes between
countries by eliminating the difference in national price levels. As we have
seen, such a deflator is not restricted to countries with different currencies. It
is equally valid for use between countries with the same currency (for
example between countries in the euro area) or even between regions within
a country, quite simply because price levels can differ appreciably between
geographic regions, even if they have the same currency unit. To take the case
of France, the same wage in euros is worth more in the French provinces than
in Paris, simply because the cost of housing is much higher in Paris.

Figure 3.5 shows the Swedish GDP per head in relation to that of the
United States using two different methods. The first, shown by the continuous
line, is the one already seen in Figure 3.4. This is the incorrect method,
consisting of dividing Swedish GDP per head by the exchange rate. The
second, shown by the broken line, consists of dividing the same figures by the
PPP for Swedish GDP, with USA = 1. This method – the correct one – makes it
possible to conclude that the Swedish GDP per head in volume has remained

quite stable at around 80% of that of the United States, showing a slight decline between 1980 and 2004, and showing a small upward trend since 2005.

The question might be asked: what is the relationship between the PPP and the exchange rate? In Figure 3.6 below, Sweden's PPP relative to the United States is shown by the broken line, and the exchange rate between the US dollar and the Swedish Crown by the continuous line.

Figure 3.6. **PPPs and exchange rates**

Swedish kronor per US dollar using PPPs and exchange rates

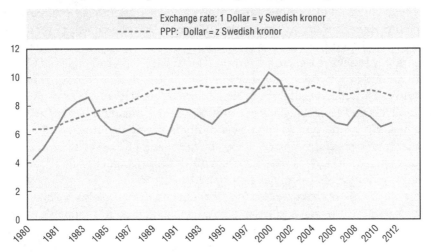

Source: OECD (2014), "Aggregate National Accounts: PPPs and exchange rates", OECD National Accounts Statistics (database), doi: http://dx.doi.org/10.1787/data-00004-en.

StatLink 🔗 http://dx.doi.org/10.1787/888933143726

The exchange rates shown in Figure 3.6 are the inverse (1/×) of those in Figure 3.4.

Both are expressed in the same unit, i.e. an amount of Swedish crowns per United States dollar. However, the PPP represents the amount in crowns that has to be spent in Sweden to obtain the same quantity of goods and services that a dollar will obtain in the United States, whereas the exchange rate is the result of supply and demand between Swedish crowns and dollars on the currency market. It has been sometimes argued that the PPP is a sort of equilibrium exchange rate. One could even say that if the exchange rate seen on the currency markets is below the PPP, the exchange rate can be expected to rise (and vice versa), since in that case holders of dollars would have an interest in going and spending them in Sweden, or vice versa.

However, even though the graph shows that the exchange rate has been fluctuating around the PPP, it is necessary to guard against a simplistic interpretation of this comparison. Fluctuations on currency markets depend on many other factors. It would therefore be most imprudent to speculate ("take a position") on a currency solely on the basis of its comparison with the PPP calculated by the OECD. Furthermore, trade in currencies is dominated by exports and imports and capital movements, whereas the PPP is calculated for all goods and services, including those that are neither imported nor exported.

In real life, calculating PPP is a complex matter. It is initially based on surveys to ascertain prices for a representative sample of comparable products in each country. The main difficulty lies in the choice of products. They must be both comparable and representative (i.e. the kind that are commonly purchased in each country). This is easy for hamburgers but more difficult for other goods and services, which are often different from one country to another. Next, price ratios have to be compiled for a large number of products and several regions or countries. If there are multiple products and regions, the overall purchasing power parity is a weighted mean of the price ratios among several countries (zones or regions) for a basket of comparable goods and services. This basket covers all the components of final demand (consumption, investment, net exports). Also, the formula for deriving PPP is more complex than that used to calculate the volume/price breakdown over time. That is because one wants to arrive at a measure that is both "symmetrical" and "transitive". Symmetrical means the relative volume for country B with respect to country A equals the inverse: that of country A with respect to B. Transitivity means that if country C is equivalent to 80% of B, and B is 75% of A, one should be able to calculate directly that C is equal to $(0.8 \times 0.75) \times A$.

Despite the complexity of deriving PPP, we can ascertain the following general principles extrapolating from the earlier example of the single hamburger: (1) PPP is a price ratio; (2) PPP is the exchange rate that equalises the price of the selected basket of goods and services; (3) to derive PPP, one always uses a reference country or group of countries, and magnitudes expressed in PPP are therefore always relative magnitudes. For PPP calculations, the OECD often uses the United States as the reference country, and this is why in OECD tables one often sees "United States = 100". But this should not be interpreted as anything but a simple choice for purposes of presentation. Indeed, OECD tables sometimes use the OECD average as the reference, setting it equal to 100. Once again, it must be stressed that like any figure in volume, the level of the variable expressed in PPP has no meaning in and of itself. Only the *relative* levels are meaningful, and the relative levels do not depend on the choice of reference country. Whether one sets the United States as equal to 100, or the OECD average to 100, makes no difference to the relative levels.

Figure 3.7 below illustrates the difference between GDPs expressed at current exchange rates and GDPs expressed in purchasing power parities for a group of OECD countries for the year 2012. It can be seen that the main effect of using PPPs rather than exchange rates is to increase the relative GDPs of poorer countries like Hungary, Mexico, Poland and Turkey. Why is this? Because the relative level of prices in poorer countries is below that in rich countries, and this difference is not fully incorporated into market exchange rates. Another factor is that PPP covers all goods, including those that are not internationally traded, such as housing. And housing in poor countries is cheaper than in rich countries. Using PPP as the deflator therefore gives a better picture of each country's actual income, especially in the case of the poorer countries.

Figure 3.7. **GDP per capita using exchange rates and PPPs**
As a percentage of US GDP per capita, 2012

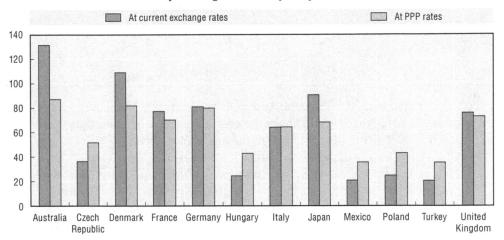

Source: OECD (2013), "Aggregate National Accounts: Gross domestic product", OECD National Accounts Statistics (database), http://dx.doi.org/10.1787/data-00001-en.

StatLink 📊 http://dx.doi.org/10.1787/888933143738

Although PPPs are more suitable than exchange rates for purposes of international volume comparison, they are a statistical construct rather than a precise measure. In particular, it is more difficult to calculate PPP than to calculate price indices over time. It is relatively easy to calculate rent increases over time, but how is one to compare the rent of an apartment in London with that of apartments in Warsaw or Madrid? Another difficulty is that the budgets allocated to the price inquiries needed for PPP calculations are limited, with the result that the number of observations is small compared with those done for the calculation of a price index over time. Generally speaking, the variance from one year to another in the PPP calculations is quite large. Therefore, for temporal comparisons of volume GDP, the OECD recommends not deflating the GDP per head series by the "current" PPP series. The results lack homogeneity over time, even though theoretically they have the advantage of using a price structure that is constantly updated.

It is better to use the national series for GDP in volume at the prices of a common base year (for example 2005) and to deflate these by the PPP for a fixed year (for example 2005), although it is not necessary to use the same year. In this way, one obtains series that relate to two kinds of comparisons in volume: volume over time and spatial volume. These have the precise advantage of presenting the volume growth of GDP per head in each country, while at the same time making it possible to make inter-country comparisons of volume levels.

On the other hand, they have the disadvantage of using fixed price indices. For example, they overstate the most recent relative GDP in volume of countries that are large producers of computers, whose prices tend to fall over time. By relying on price indices based on a time period in the past, they therefore tend to attribute a larger weighting to computers than the use of more recent time periods does.

It is this method, sometimes known as "constant PPP", which is used in Figure 3.3 of this chapter, and hence the title of the figure includes the phrase "based on 2005 PPPs". In fact, although the figure shows the series for GDP per head relative to that of the United States for the period from 1995 to 2012, the PPP used is only for the year 2005. The figure for other years is obtained by applying to the levels for 2005 the changes in GDP per head in volume for the country concerned. Exercise 1, at the end of this chapter, explains how to use this method. More details can be found in the following documents: *www.oecd.org/std/47359870.pdf* or *www.oecd.org/dataoecd/50/27/1961296.pdf*.

5. Comparison of variables in absolute terms: Household consumption

In addition to the problem of finding a suitable spatial price index to use as a deflator, the inter-country comparison of absolute levels of variables poses other difficulties, related to institutional differences between countries. For example, inter-country comparisons of absolute levels of household consumption contain a trap into which it is all too easy to fall. As explained in Chapter 5, there are two possible definitions of household consumption in national accounts:

- **Household final consumption expenditure** corresponds to the purchase of goods and services by households.

- **Household actual individual consumption.** This equals household consumption expenditure (above) plus "individual consumption," which is the amount spent by general government and the NPISHs (non-profit institutions serving households) on things that directly benefit households, such as healthcare and education. Households do not pay directly for these services (they pay for them indirectly through taxes), but they benefit from them.

International comparisons of consumption per head are meaningful only if based on actual individual consumption and not consumption expenditure. This is because there are significant differences between countries regarding the proportion of expenditure carried out directly by households for healthcare and education and the proportion carried out on their behalf by government. If one uses expenditure and not actual consumption, one falls into the trap of understating consumption per head in countries that "socialise" this type of expenditure to a greater extent (the countries of western Europe in particular) compared with countries that leave this expenditure more to the private sector (United States). This is why in its volume series in national accounts, the OECD publishes a comparative series of *actual individual consumption* per head deflated by a suitable PPP.

Figure 3.8 shows the percentage of GDP accounted for by consumption expenditure and actual individual consumption for 10 countries in 2012 (current prices, in national currencies). For these 10 countries, household final consumption expenditure ranges from 45% to 65% of GDP, whereas actual individual consumption is roughly 70%. The largest differences are for France and Denmark, two countries that have to a greater extent "socialised" their expenditure on healthcare and education.

Generally speaking, therefore, international comparisons of absolute levels of variables in the national accounts are problematic. For one thing, countries do not all use exactly the same conventions. As was shown in the first section, this has little impact on comparisons of growth rates but can affect comparisons of absolute levels to the tune of several GDP percentage points. In addition to these differences, there are wide variations in the quality of the underlying statistical systems. Some statistical offices have very comprehensive listings of firms and/or access to exhaustive tax declarations by firms (by agreement with their tax authorities). These statistical offices therefore have statistics covering most parts of their economies. Other countries, by contrast, do not have such exhaustive basic data at their disposal. In principle, countries are expected to adjust their GDPs to take account of this **"non-observed"** or **"underground"** economy (see Chapter 4). However, it would be pretentious to claim that these adjustments are based on exactly the same methods in each country. All things considered, it would be

Figure 3.8. **Household: final consumption expenditure versus actual individual consumption**

As a percentage of GDP, 2012

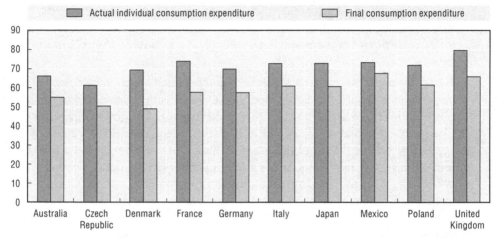

Source: OECD (2013), "Aggregate National Accounts: Gross domestic product", OECD National Accounts Statistics (database), *http://dx.doi.org/10.1787/data-00001-en.*

StatLink ᵐᵍᵖ *http://dx.doi.org/10.1787/888933143743*

an illusion to think that the degree of precision regarding GDP levels is less than several percentage points.

In addition to these problems, when one takes into account the lack of precision in the calculation of purchasing power parities, the conclusion is that it is not possible to have unlimited confidence in comparisons of absolute levels. At the OECD, for example, a difference of less than 5% between the GDP per head of two different countries is not considered really significant. Remember, however, that a difference between *growth rates in volume* of 0.2%, for its part, is indeed significant. One often sees journalists making great play of the fact that a given country's GDP per head has exceeded that of another by even less than a single percentage point. Information of this kind has to be treated with caution, and if the difference remains very small, one should check whether the volume growth trends confirm this result. If they do not, it would be more reasonable to say that the GDPs per head of the two countries are "approximately the same".

References

OECD (2014), "Aggregate National Accounts: PPPs and exchange rates", OECD National Accounts Statistics (database), doi: *http://dx.doi.org/10.1787/data-00004-en*.

OECD (2013a), *OECD Economic Outlook*, Vol. 2013/2, OECD Publishing, doi: *http://dx.doi.org/10.1787/eco_outlook-v2013-2-en*.

OECD (2013b), "Aggregate National Accounts: Gross domestic product", OECD National Accounts Statistics (database), *http://dx.doi.org/10.1787/data-00001-en*.

OECD (2013c), "Aggregate National Accounts: Population and employment by main activity", OECD National Accounts Statistics (database), doi: *http://dx.doi.org/10.1787/data-00003-en*.

OECD (2013), "Detailed National Accounts: Non-financial accounts by sectors, annual", OECD National Accounts Statistics (database), doi: *http://dx.doi.org/10.1787/data-00034-en*.

Key points

- The definitions and conventions used in national accounts are international. In principle, therefore, it is possible to compare national accounts data among countries.

- In practice, the methods used are not exactly the same and countries' institutions are different. In the final analysis, the growth rates of the variables in national accounts are more comparable than their absolute levels.

- It is necessary in the case of certain variables to carry out appropriate transformations: for example, dividing by the size of the population (resulting in aggregates "per head") or taking institutional differences into account.

- In order to compare levels of GDP per head among several countries or regions in volume, it is essential to deflate them by the purchasing power parities (PPP) for GDP, and not by actual market exchange rates.

- By dividing GDP (or another variable) by the suitable PPP, one eliminates differences in price levels between two countries, making it possible to compare the variables in volume.

- PPP is also calculated between different countries with the same currency (or between regions in the same country), since the same currency does not necessarily have the same purchasing power in different geographical regions.

Exercises for Chapter 3

Exercise 1. Calculations of GDP per head in constant PPP and comparison with current PPP

Question 1: Table 1 below shows PPP for the United States, Sweden and Japan; Table 2 shows GDP in volume (at 2005 prices) for the same countries; and Table 3 shows their populations. Using data from these three tables, create a new table of relative indices of *GDP per head in volume (USA =100)*, *at constant 2005 PPP*. Based on the results, draw a figure similar to Figure 3.3 in this chapter.

Question 2: Table 4 presents the GDP of these same countries but this time at current prices. Calculate a series for GDP per head deflated by *current PPP*. Compare the results with the table you created to Question 1. Comment on the differences.

Table 1. **Purchasing Power Parities for GDP**

	2000	2001	2002	2003	2004	2005	2006	2007	2008	2009	2010
Japan	155.11	149.86	143.77	139.82	134.16	129.55	124.86	120.22	116.85	116.35	112.42
Sweden	9.14	9.35	9.35	9.34	9.11	9.38	9.09	8.89	8.77	8.96	9.07
United States	1.00	1.00	1.00	1.00	1.00	1.00	1.00	1.00	1.00	1.00	1.00

Table 2. **GDP in volume, at 2005 prices, billions of units in national currency**

	2000	2001	2002	2003	2004	2005	2006	2007	2008	2009	2010
Japan	474 830.2	476 518.1	477 897.8	485 950.9	497 422.9	503 903.0	512 433.6	523 667.1	518 212.4	489 570.9	512 346.3
Sweden	2 425.1	2 455.7	2 516.7	2 575.5	2 684.5	2 769.4	2 888.4	2 984.1	2 965.8	2 816.7	3 001.4
United States	11 558.8	11 668.4	11 875.7	12 207.1	12 670.8	13 095.4	13 444.6	13 685.2	13 645.5	13 263.1	13 595.6

Table 3. **Population, in thousand**

	2000	2001	2002	2003	2004	2005	2006	2007	2008	2009	2010
Japan	126 926	127 133	127 401	127 635	127 734	127 755	127 839	127 980	128 046	128 034	128 043
Sweden	8 872	8 896	8 925	8 958	8 994	9 030	9 081	9 148	9 220	9 299	9 379
United States	282 398	285 225	287 955	290 626	293 262	295 993	298 818	301 696	304 543	307 240	309 776

Table 4. **GDP at current prices, billions of units of national currency**

	2000	2001	2002	2003	2004	2005	2006	2007	2008	2009	2010
Japan	509 860.0	505 543.2	499 147.0	498 854.8	503 725.3	503 903.0	506 687.0	512 975.2	501 209.3	471 138.7	482 384.4
Sweden	2 265.4	2 348.4	2 443.6	2 544.9	2 661.0	2 769.4	2 944.5	3 126.0	3 204.3	3 105.8	3 337.5
United States	10 289.7	10 625.3	10 980.2	11 512.2	12 277.0	13 095.4	13 857.9	14 480.3	14 720.3	14 417.9	14 958.3

The solutions to these exercises are available at:

http://dx.doi.org/10.1787/9789264214637-21-en

Chapter 4

Production: What it includes and excludes

This chapter looks at measuring production. Broadly, production leads to an "output" of goods and services, creating jobs, and generating income. Output is a central concept for national accounts, but what does output cover precisely? This chapter traces the "production frontier", looking at how economists decide what to include in GDP and what to exclude. It considers the relation of the illegal and underground economies to this frontier, and it also looks at the measurement of output and of value added.

Production is what leads to "output" (as it is termed in the national accounts), creating jobs, generating income for workers and owners of capital, and resulting in the goods and services found in our stores. Output is a central concept in economics. It is essentially used by economists *in volume* terms (i.e. not at current prices).

Output results from the three *factors of production*: labour, capital and intermediate consumption (inputs). Standard macroeconomic presentations often use a measure based on value added (rather than output) making it possible to dispense with intermediate consumption and hence show only labour and capital as the factors of production. When modelling the growth of output in volume (or, rather, the growth of value added when intermediate consumption has been deducted from both sides of the equation), OECD economists use the following formula:

$$Y' = [f(L,K) \times MFP]'$$

Y' is the growth rate of value added; L stands for labour and K for capital; f is the production function; and the sign ' means the derivative. The term "MFP" stands for "multifactor productivity", which is that part of the change in value added that cannot be attributed to changes in the volume of labour or to capital inputs in production. Its rate of change represents the contribution to value added growth of a more productive combination of labour and capital (for example, improved organisation of work or new techniques). MFP is sometimes called "disembodied technological progress", since it is the result of technical progress that is not reflected in the measurement of capital and labour. MFP is not directly measurable and can only be obtained as a residual from the above formula. Despite its elusive nature, MFP provides the main driving force behind long-term increases in the standard of living. In recent years, numerous studies have shown that MFP has been growing faster in the United States, Canada, Australia and Nordic European countries compared with France, Germany and Italy. Within continental Europe, this has triggered an awareness of the need to invest in new technologies and R&D and to carry out structural reforms.

OECD economists also use output (value added) statistics, again in volume terms, to estimate the "output gap". They do so as part of the regular monitoring of the economic situation in member countries. The basic idea is simple. Given the quantity of labour and capital available at a given moment, what is the maximum growth rate of GDP in volume that can be obtained without fuelling inflation? The corresponding level is known as "potential GDP". Potential GDP is compared with observed GDP. If observed GDP is lower than potential GDP, there is said to be a "negative output gap". In this situation, governments often resort to stimulating demand, either by tax cuts or by additional public spending (major infrastructure projects, and/or recruitment of civil servants, for example). The Central Bank, for its part, may decide to reduce its key interest rates. If there is a "positive output gap" – actual growth exceeds potential growth – it may then be difficult to raise public spending or lower taxes without automatically generating inflation, and the most common response is for the Central Bank to raise its key interest rates.

Although the idea itself is simple, the calculation of potential GDP is a complex matter, since it requires measuring the stock of capital and the value of the services provided by this capital, as well as measuring the labour factor. The latter is not simply the number of workers but rather the number of hours worked, adjusted for the qualitative composition (skill levels) of the workforce. Next, it is necessary to estimate the macroeconomic production function that relates these production factors to output. Despite these difficulties, the OECD evaluates the potential GDP growth rate for its members and regularly publishes the resulting "output gaps". For example, in 2013 OECD economists thought that the Japanese output gap is nil (meaning that growth was at its potential level), whereas it was negative in the United States (-3.1), Germany (-0.8) and France (-2.4) (OECD, 2013). These figures vary according to the phases of the economic cycle.

Economic growth is not steady but follows "economic cycles".
Following a recession (a lower increase or even a decline in GDP),
the economy driven by increasing demands (e.g. corporate investment)
picks up again, reaches a peak and then declines, falling back again
into a recession. The whole cycle usually lasts between 6 to 10 years.
And then a new cycle starts again.

Non-inflationary growth above potential GDP can only be obtained by increasing the apparent productivity of capital and labour (see Box 4.1), and one of the ways to achieve this is via structural reforms.

Studies published by the OECD systematically include major sections on the progress made by member countries in regard to "structural reforms". This expression often arouses suspicion on the part of the trade unions, which see it as a code word for attacks on acquired social rights, such as guaranteed minimum wages, employment-protection legislation and the entitlement to unemployment benefits following the loss of a job. However, this is a one-sided view of the matter, since structural reform involves deregulating

---

Box 4.1. **Apparent labour productivity**

Apparent labour productivity is defined as the ratio of output to labour. If Y denotes the volume of output and L the volume of labour, labour productivity is equal to Y/L, i.e. the quantity of output per unit of labour. For macroeconomic work, economists prefer to use value added in volume (i.e. GDP) as the numerator rather than output. The denominator used is the volume of labour, measured by the number of workers multiplied by average working hours (ideally adjusted for the skill level). In practice, one is usually more interested in growth in labour productivity than in its absolute level. This means calculating $Y' - L'$ (rather than Y/L), where Y' is the growth in volume of value added, and L' is the growth in the volume of labour.

---

markets for goods and services in addition to the labour market. Structural reform of product markets involves increased competition between producers through, for example, the opening up of markets to foreign competitors, the abolition of cartels and other anti-competitive arrangements, and the abandonment of state monopolies, especially in such fields as rail and air transport, telecommunications, electricity, gas and water.

In order to identify which sectors of the economy are particularly in need of structural reform, OECD economists compare the productivity of various industries in different member countries. They pay particular attention to the growth of certain sectors, such as carmakers, airlines and electricity companies. They then try to identify the institutional structures in countries with the fastest growth. What apparently works in these countries can be tried in others. All these analyses are largely based on the data for output, or value added in volume, provided by national accounts.

1. The production frontier

As it may have become clear from the above, **output** is a central concept for national accountants aiming to compile useful data.

But the concept of "output" is foreign to business accounting, which focuses exclusively on "sales".

But it remains to be seen precisely what output covers. To do that, we need to trace the "production frontier", deciding what to *include* in GDP and what to *exclude*. Most of what to include in GDP is non-controversial. For a start, output as measured in the national accounts includes what creates the goods and services that households buy for their everyday needs, and that firms buy to be able to produce these goods and services. The important word in this last sentence is "buy", implying that all transactions that are "monetised" are included in GDP. But what about the activity of civil servants and members of the armed forces? Nobody buys the output of ministries or of the army. Another grey area is that of household services rendered free of charge. If one person pays another to clean his windows, this is output, since a service has been sold. But what if people clean their own windows? Does this lie within the production frontier?

As we shall see later, there is general consensus favouring the inclusion in GDP of the services provided by general government. Although these services are not sold, they are included as output (value added) in the national accounts and are called non-market services produced by general government. This value added is very substantial, since it represents roughly 15% to 20% of GDP, depending on the OECD country concerned. By contrast, the "non-traded output" of households – cooking, cleaning, child care, etc. – is, with one exception, not included in the national accounts. The exception consists of the housing that homeowners implicitly provide for themselves. The national accounts act *as if* the owner-occupiers provided housing services (a dwelling to live in) to themselves. These notional, or in national accounts jargon "imputed" transactions, are estimated to be equal to the rents that homeowners would have paid to live in dwellings of the same type, in the same district and with the same service facilities. These imputed rents are added to actual rents to calculate the total output of "housing services".

Imputations are carried out only when they are absolutely necessary for the analysis of changes over time in macroeconomic aggregates or for comparisons between several countries. This is the case for these imputed rents of owner-occupiers. If this output were not included by imputation, the result would be a structural decline over time in GDP, because the long-term upwards trend in home ownership would automatically produce a downward trend in the total value of actual rents (and thus in GDP, all things being equal). It would also make it difficult to compare the GDPs of different countries because the rate of home ownership varies markedly among countries.

Another example of imputation in national accounts is that of goods (mainly food) that some households produce for their own consumption. This represents only a very small part of output in OECD countries, but in developing countries, where farmers consume much of their own production, the proportion of this production for own consumption is much higher. In some countries, farmers and other households even produce their tools, houses, outbuildings or their own clothes. As a result, the convention adopted in national accounts has been to impute in the calculation of GDP the output of all **goods** going into households' own consumption, attributing to them the market price of an identical good. On the other hand, as we saw earlier, the

services households produce for themselves are not imputed in the national accounts, with the notable exception of housing services in the case of owner-occupiers. Nor is any account taken of the services some households provide to others free of charge (repairing a neighbour's dripping tap for nothing).

When services are provided for payment, attempts are made to include them in output by estimating, for example, the value of paid lessons or paid baby-sitting services.

Such exclusions may seem arbitrary, but they at least have the merit of avoiding having to make too many imputations, some of them extremely hazardous (see box "Household Services" at the end of this chapter).

In conclusion, national accounts define output as the result of the utilisation of one, or more, of the three factors of production: labour, capital and intermediate consumption (material inputs). This necessary condition leads to a very broad definition of output. However, this is later narrowed down by the imposition of other criteria, as the following "decision tree" shows (start reading the diagram from the top left-hand corner). The most important arrow in the diagram, which one could regard as the heart of national accounts, is in the top right-hand corner. It indicates that output consists essentially of the value of goods and services produced by certain economic agents *for sale* to other economic agents (monetary exchange, or in exceptional cases, barter). In the economies of the OECD countries, this constitutes the bulk of output. However, one must not overlook the non-market services produced by general government and the imputed housing services enjoyed by owner-occupiers.

The production decision tree

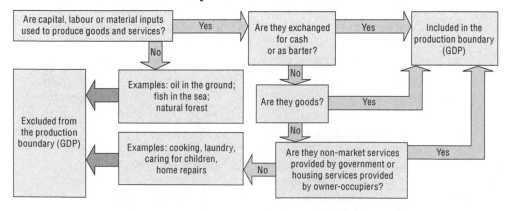

Before going into more detail, it is important to note that output in the national accounts is the output of productive activity *during* a period, which can be a year or a quarter. It is described as a "flow variable" as opposed to a "stock variable", which measures a stock, such as the stock of finished products on the 31 December of a given year. Flow variables can be summed; in other words the output for a given year is the sum of the output of the individual quarters. This is not true of stock variables.

2. The illegal economy and the underground economy

In the diagram shown above, there is no distinction made between legal and illegal production. One can therefore conclude that illegal activities are within the production frontier and are hence included in GDP. Such activities are of two types: (1) illegal, such as trading in stolen goods, organised prostitution (in countries where it is illegal) and drug production and drug-dealing; and (2) legal but illegally conducted, such as plumbing or repair work paid in cash and not declared to the tax authorities.

In the OECD countries, illegal activities are marginal in macroeconomic terms. Most estimates have put them at less than 1% of GDP. Although theoretically included in GDP, in practice they are not estimated and can therefore be considered not to figure in GDP.* On the other hand, legal activities carried out illegally (in order to avoid paying taxes and social contributions) constitute what is known as the "black" or "hidden" economy and are estimated to be anywhere from 2% to 15% of GDP in OECD countries. This proportion is so large that national accountants have had to develop special techniques to ensure they are included in GDP estimates. Figure 4.1 shows the share of GDP generated by hidden or underground activities. In the figure, these are referred to as the "non-observed" economy because they cannot be observed by the usual types of surveys. In Spain, for example, the non-observed economy represented at that time 11.2% of official GDP. This is the share of value added that has been added to the official statistical sources using these special techniques. It is therefore not true to say that the national accounts do not include the "underground" economy. For a concrete example of how this is done, see the box entitled "The adjustments for the underground economy in the case of France" in the section Going further.

---

* It can be noted, however, that more and more countries are trying to capture illegal activities as well. In the European Union, with the introduction of the new standards, it has become mandatory as per the end of 2014 to also include an estimate of these activities.

Figure 4.1. **Non-observed activities included in the GDP (selected countries)**
Adjustment for non-observed actitivies, in %, years around 2002

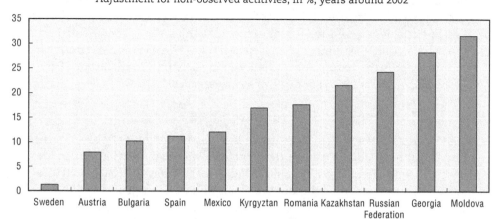

Source: United Nations Economic Commission for Europe: Non-observed economy in national accounts, Survey of country practices (2008)

StatLink 📈 *http://dx.doi.org/10.1787/888933143750*

3. Measurement of output and of value added: The general case

As we saw earlier, output in the national accounts mainly consists of the value of goods and services produced in order to be *sold* to other agents (output not intended for sale is not recorded, with certain exceptions). As pointed out in Chapter 1, this poses a problem of aggregation, in that the sum of output measured in this way can change over time, not because more goods and services are produced but because firms are able to outsource certain activities previously carried out in-house (see Box 4.2: "The trap of internalisation and externalisation"). National accountants have therefore created the concept of **value added**. We shall be returning to this later.

However, even if value added is preferred to output, the concept of **output** is widely used in national accounts. How is it measured? Output at current prices is generally measured by sales. But an adjustment is necessary. In the case of goods, at least part of the output produced in the designated period may not be sold, and so it is stocked as inventory. Similarly, some of the goods sold in the current period may have come out of inventory (and not produced during the period). Finally, part of the output during the period may not have been completely finished and is stocked as "work in progress". In the end, output at current prices is measured as: sales plus the change (positive or negative) in inventories of finished products or work in progress. This formula is regularly used to calculate output, since the data required exist in company accounts, albeit not always in easily usable form (see Box 4.3).

Box 4.2. **The trap of internalisation and externalisation**

In the measurement of output, national accounts do not include "own-account" production – that is, the intermediate goods and services produced and consumed by companies internally. National accounts record own-account production of firms only when the goods are intended for investment. For example, if a company makes cars, the national accounts will not record the production of the engines that power these cars if they are manufactured by the same company. Similarly, national accounts will not include the personnel services of this carmaker, if these services are provided internally. Recording the "own-account" output of intermediate goods and services would result in unduly inflating the figure for total output. On the other hand, if personnel services and the manufacture of engines are outsourced, in other words if the carmaker purchases these goods and services from another company, then this output will be recorded. A move from one form of organisation to another will therefore inflate total output, although in reality no new good or service has been created. Hence the attraction of the concept of value added (see Chapter 1), whose total is independent of a change in how firms are organised.

It is important to note that own-account output of capital goods, such as machines or software, is recorded in the national accounts. But why is own-account output of intermediate goods not recorded? It is not recorded, because intermediate goods and services have no impact on GDP, since by definition they will be consumed during the production process. Capital goods, on the other hand, are used over longer periods of time.

Box 4.3. **The problem of changes in the value of inventories**

One might think it is a simple matter to use data in company accounts to determine inventory changes. However, in practice it is not so easy, because inventories generate holding gains when prices are rising and holding losses when they are falling. It is a fundamental principle of national accounts to exclude holding gains and losses in the measurement of output. Indeed, if a firm makes a holding gain by merely keeping products in inventories, this does not constitute a productive process and therefore cannot be included in GDP. As a result, it is necessary to adjust the figures for inventory changes obtained from company accounts in order to eliminate holding gains and losses on inventories.

As for the prices at which output is measured, these are the "basic prices" corresponding to the revenue per unit of products sold that remain in the hands of the producer.

An exception among OECD countries is the USA, which calculates its output and value added at market prices (i.e. including taxes on products). See Chapter 12.

Basic price therefore does not include taxes on products (for example, value-added taxes or special taxes on petroleum products or alcoholic beverages), because these amounts do not remain with the producer but are forwarded to the tax authorities. On the other hand, the basic price includes the subsidies received on products. Therefore, in the national accounts, the prices for exported agricultural products are not the low prices made possible by the export subsidies granted to farmers of OECD countries but the actual sales prices plus the subsidies, thus a price that is closer to the real costs of production. Finally, output in volume is compiled as output at current prices deflated by the appropriate price index.

Intermediate consumption represents the value of the basic materials, components and semi-manufactured goods going into the product, as well as the value of the electricity, the cost of rents, IT services, insurance, legal and accounting services, etc., used in the production of a good or a service. In short, intermediate consumption consists of everything needed to produce other goods and services intended for sale, other than the labour of the internal workforce and the services provided by plant and machinery, offices and factory buildings.

Just as output is not equal to sales, intermediate consumption is not equal to the purchases of goods and services intended to be intermediately consumed. This is because certain intermediate goods used in the production during the period may have been bought and stocked in a previous period. Similarly, some purchases during the period may be consumed after it has ended, having been stocked in the meantime. In the end, intermediate consumption is equal to the purchases during the period *minus* the change (positive or negative) in the value of the inventories of goods and services for intermediate consumption. Firms often refer to these inventories as "materials inventories". Like output, intermediate consumption is a flow, corresponding to what has been consumed *during* a period (a year or a quarter). This leads to the exclusion from the definition of intermediate consumption of the goods used for production but not entirely consumed during the period, such as machinery or software. These capital goods are classified as "gross fixed capital formation" or GFCF.

Value added, as its name implies, measures the value the firm adds to the products used to manufacture the output and is equal to: output *minus* intermediate consumption. It can be deduced, using the definitions given earlier for the measurement of output and intermediate consumption, that value added at current prices is equal to: sales *minus* purchases *plus* total inventory changes (finished products, work in progress and materials). Value added is a central concept in national accounts. However, because it is defined as a difference between two monetary values (output minus intermediate consumption), it is not clear at first sight exactly what it represents. A useful way of defining valued added at current prices is to consider it as the amount of money generated by production that remains available to pay:

● wages and salaries and social contributions (*compensation of employees*);

● production taxes (other than that on products) net of operating subsidies;

● replacement of equipment gradually worn out during production (*consumption of fixed capital*);

● interest payments on loans;

● dividends paid to shareholders;

● purchase of new equipment; and

● financial saving – or the firms' investment in financial products.

It is sometimes this approach that is used in practice to measure firms' value added at current prices in the national accounts (see box "The data sources for the value added of non-financial enterprises in France" at the end of chapter). Value added in volume is the difference between output in volume and intermediate consumption in volume.

4. The measurement of output and of value added: Special cases

The definition of output at current prices as equal to sales plus changes in inventories of finished products and work in progress is applicable to virtually the totality of the business sector in the national accounts. This sector is also known as the **market sector**, for which there exists a market with recorded sales, transactions and prices that permit the direct measurement of output. Note however that, even in the market sector, there are activities whose output is difficult to measure or even identify such as banks, insurance companies and retail distributors for which the definition of output based on sales does not work very well. They are all market activities, but their output is mainly purchased indirectly. Therefore an alternative measure of output is needed. Furthermore, there are large activities for which the notion of sales is non-existent, and these constitute the **non-market sector**, covering mainly services provided by general government. The organizations concerned do not sell their services, and it is therefore necessary to find a different measure of their output.

Non-market producers are those that provide services, and in some cases goods, either free of charge or at prices that are not economically significant, meaning in practice prices that cover less than half the cost of production. General government bodies constitute the bulk of the non-market producers, but there are others, like the non-profit institutions (see Chapter 5). Most of the services provided by general government – defence, economic policy, foreign policy, public education and public health care – are provided to the general public without charge. These services are obviously financed through taxation and social contributions, but there is no direct link between the payment of the tax and the level of services received. Citizens or firms are not entitled, for example, to vary their taxes based on the amount of defence or policing they want to consume. A tax is a compulsory transfer to general government and is not the price of a public service.

Certain services provided by general government, like education and healthcare, are provided to households on an individualised basis, meaning that it is possible to know who consumes them. For instance, a family sends its children to the state school, and one therefore knows that it is a consumer of these services. Other services are provided only on a collective basis, meaning it is impossible to know who consumes what. An example is policing: all economic agents, households and firms consume part of the services of the police, but it is impossible to know how much each consumes. In the case of the individualised services, government can sometimes charge part of the price to the consumer (for example, the contribution to the cost of a hospital bed), but this price is usually well below the production costs of the services consumed, and the services are therefore considered non-market.

Whether individual or collective, as there are practically no sales, non-market output at current prices is conventionally measured as equal to the sum of its production costs, including: (a) the intermediate consumption; (b) the compensation of employees; (c) the consumption of fixed capital, which is the utilisation cost of the equipment used by non-market producers (see following Box 4.4); and, in rare cases (d) the other taxes paid on production. Exercise 4, at the end of this chapter, shows that measurement of non-market output in the national accounts basically assumes that these are non-profit activities, a very reasonable assumption.

The general formula for measuring output from sales cannot be used to measure the **output of banks,** because banks invoice directly only a very limited portion of their services (for example, foreign exchange commissions, cheque-handling fees, stock-market transaction fees, separately-charged financial advice), but not the bulk of their service, which is making loans.

114

> ### Box 4.4. **Is the output of general government understated?**
>
> Before a firm decides to buy capital goods, it calculates the return, or yield, on the funds it will be investing. This return must be sufficient to cover wear and tear (the consumption of fixed capital) plus a net income that is at least equal to the interest that could be obtained by investing the funds in financial products (bonds, for example). If the return is not sufficient to cover these two elements, a rational entrepreneur will buy the financial products rather than the physical capital. The sum of the consumption of fixed capital and this net return is known as services from capital.
>
> In the case of general government, the production costs used to evaluate output include consumption of fixed capital, but they omit the net return. For a firm, the net return is close to its net operating surplus (see Chapter 7). Because government services are not sold (or only to a marginal extent), it is not possible to calculate the net operating surplus, but the net return could be estimated by applying an appropriate rate of interest to the value of the general government's capital. Views may differ regarding the appropriate interest rate, but it can be said that the present method of valuing non-market output significantly understates the contribution of general government to GDP. For example, the present method implies that scanners or x-ray machines produce no net return when they are used in a public hospital but do so when used in a private clinic.

Measurement using the general formula would result in their value added being very small, if not negative; in other words, their intermediate consumption would be greater than their sales! Because banks are obviously profit-making enterprises, there is something wrong here. The fact is that banks make the bulk of their profits by borrowing at low interest rates from depositors and then lending the proceeds to other borrowers at a higher interest rate. The difference between these two interest rates, which provides the essential part of banks' remuneration, is interpreted in national accounts as their **financial intermediation** service. The banks are in fact intermediaries between those who want to save – mainly households – and those who want to borrow – mainly firms. Without the banks, these agents would have greater difficulty in coming together. The national accounts therefore measure the output at current prices of banks as the sum of their sales *plus*, approximately, the difference between the interest received from borrowers and the interest paid to lenders. This difference, which forms the bulk of the total, is known as **financial intermediation services indirectly measured** or FISIM (see Going Further).

Measuring the output of **insurance companies** is even more problematic than in the case of banks. For the sake of simplicity, we shall deal here only with non-life (property) insurance (automobile insurance, home insurance, etc.). The money received by these non-life insurers in the form of premiums does not constitute payment for an insurance service but instead mainly goes into a fund from which indemnities will be paid in the event of claims. This being said, insurance premiums cover these indemnities *plus* claim management expenses *plus* the profits of insurance firms. The output at current prices of insurance companies corresponds to these two last items: management expenses and profits. The output will therefore be measured in the national accounts as the *difference between premiums received and indemnities paid out*, this being mathematically equal to management expenses plus profits. Things are in fact slightly more complicated than this, because insurance companies immediately invest the premiums received and leave them invested until such time as they are paid out in the form of indemnities. They therefore derive incomes which, economically speaking, belong to the insured and not to the insurance companies. Therefore, the national accountants impute a repayment of this income from the insurance companies to the insured (households or firms), which then pay them back to the insurance companies, the sums involved still being imputed. It is as if households paid not only premiums but also the investment income. In the end, the output at current prices of insurance companies is equal to the premiums *plus* the investment income *minus* the indemnities.

When measuring output for the national accounts, **distribution** (both wholesale and retail) also constitutes a special category. This is because if the general formula were applied the results would significantly overestimate total output, since sales in the distribution channel are already recorded as the value of the goods created by the actual producers. Therefore, the output for distribution is measured as the margin obtained on the products sold. So the output at current prices of distributors is equal to the value of their sales minus the value of the products bought for resale.

This is made on the assumption that inflation is low and hence that there are no significant rises in market prices between the time of purchase and the time of resale. If this assumption does not hold, the rises must be taken into account and the sums involved deducted from the margin. Remember that holding gains or losses are not included in the measure of output in national accounts.

This is known as their distribution margin. The intermediate consumption of distributors therefore excludes their purchases for resale; it consists only of rent, electricity, advertising, packaging and other operating expenses. Their value added is calculated in the usual way, by deducting their intermediate consumption from their output.

5. Nomenclatures and classifications

The broad nature of the production frontier used in national accounts has several advantages. It provides a useful, albeit approximate, measure of total production (or rather total value added) that is reasonably comparable between countries and over time. However, it is too global for certain economists, who would prefer to concentrate on more narrowly defined parts of the economy. For example, studies of productivity normally concentrate solely on the market sector, excluding the output of general government and eliminating imputations such as the output of housing services by owner-occupiers. In other cases, the economic researcher will want to focus on, for example, agriculture, the metalworking industries or business services.

To meet these specific needs, national accountants have compiled classifications (sometimes known as nomenclatures) of *industries* (also called *branches*). A branch of activity is defined as a grouping of homogeneous production units. Branches are identified by reference to a product classification, so that a branch produces only the goods or services described under a given heading of the product classification. The international reference classification for branches is the ISIC Revision 4.

The international reference classification for products is the CPC (Central Product Classification) and is described in Chapter 11.

Table 4.1 shows percentages of total value added for major branches in four OECD countries. The classification used is the international industry classification in the national accounts (which is based on the ISIC) at the so-called A10 level (10 major branches shown in bold type in the table), and is divided into 21 sections (the branches lettered from A to U). For example, the A10 level 2 "Manufacturing, mining and quarrying and other industrial activities" is broken down into four sections, B Mining and quarrying, C Manufacturing, D Electricity, gas, steam and air conditioning supply and E Water supply, sewerage, waste management and remediation activities. Firms often operate in several branches, since many of them are diversified. In this case, they are broken down into virtual units producing a homogeneous good. For example, the "Manufacturing" branch includes all productive units producing industrial goods, whether these units are entire firms or parts of firms, known as "establishments". Differences in structure can be seen between highly developed countries, such as the United States and France, where services are very substantial, and less advanced countries like Korea where industry is still very important. Note that the total of values added is not called GDP in the table. This is not an omission; GDP is not equal to the sum of gross values added. GDP is equal to the sum of gross value added plus taxes net of subsidies on products (see Chapters 1 and 10).

Table 4.1. **Value added by industry at current prices**

As a percentage of total value added, 2010

	Industry	France	Korea	Italy	United States
A	**Agriculture, forestry and fishing**	**1.8**	**2.6**	**1.9**	**1.1**
	Manufacturing, mining and quarrying and other industrial activities	**12.8**	**33.1**	**19.0**	**15.5**
B	Mining and quarrying	0.1	0.2	0.3	1.6
C	Manufacturing	10.3	30.3	16.1	11.7
D	Electricity, gas, steam and air conditioning supply	1.6	1.8	1.7	1.8
E	Water supply; sewerage, waste management and remediation activities	0.8	0.8	0.8	0.3
F	**Construction**	**6.1**	**6.3**	**6.1**	**3.5**
	Wholesale and retail trade, transportation and storage, accommodation and food service activities	**18.4**	**15.4**	**20.4**	**17.6**
G	Wholesale and retail trade, repair of motor vehicles and motorcycles	11.0	8.9	10.7	11.6
H	Transportation and storage	4.8	4.2	5.6	3.2
I	Accommodation and food service activities	2.5	2.3	4.1	2.9
J	**Information and communication**	**5.0**	**4.0**	**4.5**	**5.6**
K	**Financial and insurance activities**	**4.8**	**6.8**	**5.3**	**8.5**
L	**Real Estate Activities**	**13.2**	**7.1**	**13.4**	**10.8**
	Professional, scientific, technical, administrative and support service activities	**12.0**	**5.4**	**8.4**	**12.1**
M	Professional, scientific and technical activities	6.4	3.2	6.0	8.1
N	Administrative and support service activities	5.6	2.1	2.5	4.0
	Public administration and defence, education, human health and social work activities	**22.6**	**16.8**	**17.4**	**21.9**
O	Public administration and defence; compulsory social security	7.8	6.2	6.8	8.8
P	Education	5.7	6.2	4.7	5.5
Q	Human health and social work activities	9.1	4.5	5.9	7.6
	Other service activities	**3.4**	**2.4**	**3.5**	**3.4**
R	Arts, entertainment and recreation	1.5	1.4	1.0	1.0
S	Other service activities	1.6	1.1	1.4	2.3
T	Activities of households as employers; undifferentiated goods and services producing activities of households for own use	0.4	0.0	1.1	0.1
U	Activities of extraterritorial organizations and bodies	0.0	0.0	0.0	0.0
	Total value added	**100.0**	**100.0**	**100.0**	**100.0**

Source: OECD (2013), "STAN Industry Rev. 4", STAN: OECD Structural Analysis Statistics (database), doi: *http://dx.doi.org/10.1787/data-00649-en*.

StatLink ⟐ *http://dx.doi.org/10.1787/888933143775*

For a yet more detailed picture, look at Table 4.2, based on the "A38" level of the international classification. This gives output, intermediate consumption and value added for Belgium in 2010, broken down by sub-branches of manufacturing.

Table 4.2. **Output, intermediate consumption and value added of manufacturing branches**

Belgium, 2010, million euros

Industry code and title		Output	Intermediate consumption	Gross value added
C	Manufacturing	198 876	155 126	43 751
CA	Manufacture of food products, beverages and tobacco products	32 685	26 069	6 616
CB	Manufacture of textiles, wearing apparel, leather and related products	5 648	4 145	1 502
CC	Manufacture of wood and paper products; printing and reproduction of recorded media	10 527	7 642	2 884
CD	Manufacture of Coke and refined petroleum products	30 397	29 048	1 349
CE	Manufacture of chemicals and chemical products	26 857	20 603	6 254
CF	Manufacture of basic pharmaceutical products and pharmaceutical preparations	9 364	5 270	4 095
CG	Manufacture of rubber and plastics products, and other non-metallic mineral products	12 544	8 618	3 927
CH	Manufacture of basic metals and fabricated metal products, except machinery and equipment	33 057	26 571	6 486
CI	Manufacture of computers and peripheral equipment	3 559	2 302	1 257
CJ	Manufacture of electrical equipment	3 506	2 116	1 390
CK	Manufacture of machinery and equipment n.e.c.	8 070	5 131	2 939
CL	Manufacture of transport equipment	17 096	14 016	3 080
CM	Other manufacturing; repair and installation of machinery and equipment	5 567	3 595	1 971

Source: OECD (2013), "STAN Industry Rev. 4", STAN: OECD Structural Analysis Statistics (database), doi: *http://dx.doi.org/10.1787/data-00649-en.*

StatLink ᴍᴤᴪ *http://dx.doi.org/10.1787/888933143785*

References

Ahmad, N. and S. Koh (2011), "Incorporating Estimates of Household Production of Non-Market Services into International Comparisons of Material Well-Being", *OECD Statistics Working Papers*, No. 2011/07, OECD Publishing, doi: *http://dx.doi.org/10.1787/5kg3h0jgk87g-en.*

OECD (2013a), *OECD Economic Outlook*, Vol. 2013/1, OECD Publishing, doi: *http://dx.doi.org/10.1787/eco_outlook-v2013-1-en.*

OECD (2013b), "STAN Industry Rev. 4", STAN: OECD Structural Analysis Statistics (database), doi: *http://dx.doi.org/10.1787/data-00649-en.*

United Nations Economic Commission for Europe: Non-observed economy in national accounts, Survey of country practices (2008), UNITED NATIONS PUBLICATION Sales No. E.08.II.E.8- ISBN 978-92-1-116987-4 -ISSN 0069-8458.

Key points

- The production frontier used for national accounts includes:
  - ❖ the production of goods and services intended to be sold, known as market output;
  - ❖ the unsold production, known as non-market output, of general government and non-profit institutions;
  - ❖ the production of goods by households for their own consumption, and the own-account production of capital goods by businesses;
  - ❖ the housing services (imputed rents) of homeowner-occupiers, not including the other services produced by households for their own account.
- Market output at current prices is measured as: sales plus changes in inventories of finished products and work in progress.
- Output is measured at the basic price, which equals the per-unit revenue received by the producer, excluding taxes on products but including subsidies on products.
- Non-market output (that of general government and non-profit organizations) is measured by the sum of its costs, including intermediate consumption, compensation of employees, consumption of fixed capital and other taxes on production.
- Housing services provided by homeowner-occupiers are imputed as being equal to the rents they would have paid for comparable housing.
- The output of banks is measured, for simplification, as the difference between interest received and interest paid, plus the sales of directly invoiced services.
- The output of insurance companies is measured as the difference between premiums and indemnities, plus investment income.
- The output of the distribution sector is measured by the distribution margin.

Going further

Household Services

Official national accounts do not include the domestic and personal services provided by members of a household for their own consumption. This means that activities like cooking, housecleaning, washing clothes and looking after children or elderly people are excluded from GDP unless these activities are carried out by people paid for doing so. This had led John Hicks, the famous economist and national accounts pioneer, to remark that it was possible to reduce GDP by marrying one's cook.

National accountants have rejected the idea of including these services in GDP for practical reasons: the difficulty of imputing values to such services, and to the consequences this would have for the analysis of variations in GDP, which would then contain a substantial portion that is completely "invented". How indeed can one value the service provided by a mother making meals for her family? At the price of an employee in a fast-food preparing a hamburger or at the price of a chef in a three-star restaurant? This method is referred to as "replacement costs". On the other hand, some people have suggested estimating the price of the imputed salary at its "opportunity costs", in other words what the mother would have earned had she been working outside the household. This estimation method would produce widely differing results. For example, if the mother is a senior executive, the opportunity cost will be much higher than if she is a cashier in a supermarket. Another difficulty is how to distinguish between activities when there is joint production. A father is simultaneously peeling vegetables for the family meal, keeping an eye on the baby and helping another child with homework. How much time should one allocate to the cooking, to looking after the baby and to the education of the other child? Should the value of these activities be reduced because they are being carried out at the same time?

The *OECD Working Paper* "Incorporating Estimates of Household Production of Non-Market Services into International Comparisons of Material Well-Being" (Ahmad and al., 2011) discusses the differences of the two approaches, which are illustrated in the figure below. The example of the UK shows the valuation issue very well. While household production of non-market services calculated according to the replacement costs approach are equal to 26.0% of GDP, the opportunity costs approach suggests that these services are as high as 68.0% of GDP.

Figure 4.2. **Household production of non-market services**
Percentage of GDP

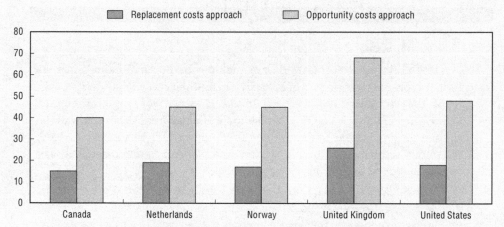

Source: Ahmad, N. and S. Koh (2011), "Incorporating Estimates of Household Production of Non-Market Services into International Comparisons of Material Well-Being", OECD Statistics Working Papers, No. 2011/07, OECD Publishing, doi: http://dx.doi.org/10.1787/5kg3h0jgk87g-en.

StatLink ﹅﹅ http://dx.doi.org/10.1787/888933143768

The decision to place unpaid domestic services outside the production frontier of the national accounts has been quasi-controversial. In most countries, these unpaid services are mainly carried out by women and are manifestly just as important for the general welfare as many of the paid services that are within the production frontier. It is mainly for practical reasons that the activities are excluded. Moreover, one has to realise that including these activities in the system of national accounts would also change the meaning of a whole range of other indicators, such as household disposable income and final consumption expenditure. Both would also increase with the value of the unpaid activities. As a consequence, someone becoming unemployed could very well see his/her income increasing, because the value of the additional unpaid activities could well be higher than the loss of cash income. However, in order to provide the public with better information, several statistical offices compile so-called satellite accounts containing an estimate of this unpaid domestic work. These statistics, forming an annex to the national accounts, show what GDP would have been had unpaid domestic work been included.

The adjustments for the underground economy in the case of France

To account for the underground economy, all OECD countries make substantial adjustments to the officially obtained GDP. In the case of France, this adjustment amounts to around 4%. It must be made clear, however, that this figure is just an approximation. What INSEE (the French statistical office) calls the underground economy comprises three sub-groupings: illegal activities (drug dealing, organised prostitution, etc); black labour (clandestine enterprises); and tax fraud. INSEE, like other statistical institutes, does not try to evaluate illicit activities. To account for black labour, it adjusts GDP by roughly 1%. The approach adopted is highly empirical: on the basis of official investigations and socio-economic research, INSEE has picked out sectors where there is a strong presumption of underground work and then estimated, very crudely, sector by sector, the scale of this activity, based on expert opinion.

In the case of tax fraud and tax evasion, INSEE adjusts the accounts by around 3%, of which 2.5% is for dissimulation of receipts and 0.5% for unpaid VAT (Value-Added Tax). As regards the dissimulation of receipts, the sources used are official figures from the tax authorities compiled on the basis of sample tax investigations. For VAT, the source is a comparison between the theoretical VAT amount calculated on recorded taxable transactions, and the VAT actually recovered by the government, together with several minor adjustments. In addition to these adjustments, there are accounting adjustments for undeclared gratuities and benefits in kind. Each of these represents roughly 0.5% of GDP.

Data sources for the value added of non-financial enterprises: The example of France

One of the drivers that enhance the quality of national accounts is that they are based on the extensive aggregation of individual firms' accounts. In the case of France (but this is applicable to other countries too), INSEE (the French statistical office) has access, albeit after a certain delay, to all the accounts sent by firms to the tax authorities as part of their declarations for profits tax. This source is virtually exhaustive as regards firms and individual entrepreneurships. It is therefore from this source that the largest part of GDP is estimated. Sales of non-financial enterprises as shown in company accounts constitute an essential source for the calculation of the output of the non-financial market sector in the national accounts. However, this is not as simple as it might seem, since there are numerous adjustments to be made to the company accounts, which do not use exactly the same definitions as the national accounts. Adjustments also have to be made to allow for the underground economy and to take into account other sources of an even more reliable nature, such as those derived from the government budget. For example, the national accountants have to make sure that the taxes paid by enterprises, as included in the company accounts, are equal to the relevant taxes received by the authorities. When this is not the case, it is the government accounts that are considered as taking precedence and the data from the company accounts are altered accordingly. This adjustment clearly modifies the measurement of company profits (the gross operating surplus). Onto these figures have to be added the results of INSEE's direct surveys of enterprises (the EAE, or Enquête Annuelle d'Entreprise), whose results are mainly used to make a detailed breakdown of sales by branch.

FISIM

FISIM (financial intermediation services indirectly measured) is the term used to describe the services that banks provide to their customers but which are not invoiced. For bank depositors, these services generally include the management of current accounts, the sending out of bank statements and fund transfers between accounts. Instead of directly invoicing these services, the banks reduce the interest paid to depositors. This interest is in fact lower than the one customer could have obtained by lending their money directly to borrowers. For bank borrowers, these services include the monitoring of their creditworthiness, financial advice, the smoothing over time of repayments and the recording of these repayments for accounting purposes. The cost of these services is an inseparable part of the interest rate that the bank charges to these borrowers.

FISIM at current prices is calculated using the following (simplified) formula:

$$(rl - rr) \times L + (rr - rd) \times D$$

In the formula above, rl is the observed interest rate on loans, rr is the so-called reference rate, rd is the observed rate of deposits, L is the amount of loans, and D is the amount of deposits. The reference rate rr is an estimate of a pure interest rate, involving no risk element, thus corresponding to economics agents' preference for the present. The difference between the interest rate paid by borrowers (rl) and the reference interest rate (rr) is used to measure the price of FISIM for the borrowers. The difference between the reference interest rate (rr) and the rate of interest received on bank deposits (rd) is used as the price of FISIM for depositors. These prices are then multiplied by total borrowing, and by total deposits, in order to arrive at the total FISIM consumed by the various economic agents.

The logic of national accounts requires that if FISIM is counted in the measurement of output it must also be recorded as consumption on the part

124

of those using these services. For a firm borrowing from a bank, FISIM will therefore be intermediate consumption. For a household depositing money with a bank or obtaining a loan from a bank, FISIM will be an element in final consumption expenditure. For a long time, national accountants had found no convincing way of allocating this output to consumers and, except in the United States, Canada and Australia, FISIM was conventionally regarded as intermediate consumption at the level of the economy as a whole. Fortunately, a solution has been found in 2005 and adopted by all OECD countries. This still leaves the problem of the choice of reference interest rate. European countries have chosen a rate that is an average of the short-term inter-bank rate and certain longer-term rates, while the United States has chosen the rate on US Treasury Bonds. The allocation between households and enterprises is made pro rata, based on the respective shares of loans and deposits of these two groups.

The financial crisis of 2007-09 (see Chapter 13) has attracted the attention on the role of banks in the economy and on the measurement of their output in the national accounts. Some commentators went to say that banks should not have any positive output in the national accounts, as they were, in the end, responsible for the great recession of 2007-09. Without going so far, others commented that the national accounts were inappropriate as they showed an increase of the output of banks during the recession, which is counter-intuitive. Such statements should be corrected. Even if one has to recognise that national accountants still have difficulties to obtain a convincing measure of the volume of the banking output, it is to be reminded that the important measure for national accounts is the volume measure and not the current price measure. In this context, any increase in the spread between rl, rd and rr is to be interpreted as a change in the price of FISIM and not in the volume of FISIM. In other terms, a change in the risk premium is a change in the price of intermediation services. In any case, the output of the financial sector in the United States national accounts does not increase during the crisis period of 2007-12. On the contrary, it decreases both in current prices and in volume.

Exercises for Chapter 4

Exercise 1. Change in the structure of production

This exercise is based on the table in next page taken from Austrian national accounts at current prices. Show that the Austrian economy has increasingly become a service economy. Illustrate the result by a graph. In which branches are non-market activities to be found? Which branch contains the imputation of rents for homeowner/occupiers? What difference is there between the sum of the values added in this table and GDP? Which of the large branches has grown most since 1980? Express the result as an annual average growth rate. Which of the large branches has grown the least? Is this result in current prices totally convincing?

Exercise 2. Branches and products

Table 4.2 in this chapter shows output, intermediate consumption and value added of the manufacturing branch for Belgium. Using examples from this table, reconstitute the fundamental relationship linking these three magnitudes. Illustrate for certain branches the differences in their so-called outsourcing rates (externalisation rates). What differences would have been made to this table if one had wanted to present the data by product, and not by branch?

Exercise 3. Calculation of output

The following are the simplified data for a firm producing cars. Sales of cars: 1 353 500. Purchases: raw materials: 540 000; temporary employment services: 350 500; machine tools: 264 000. Inventories of finished products at the start of the period: 245 000; at the end of the period: 346 700. Inventories of raw materials at the beginning of the period: 73 200; at the end of the period: 43 000. Calculate the output, the intermediate consumption and the value added at current prices, assuming no change in prices during the period. Why is this last condition important?

Exercise 4. Calculation of output: the non-market case

The following are simplified data for a unit of general government. Civil servants' gross wages and salaries: 562 980; employers' social contributions:

Austria: gross value added by branch

	1980	1995	2011
Agriculture, forestry and fishing	**3 400**	**3 883**	**4 494**
Manufacturing, mining and quarrying and other industrial activities	**19 139**	**37 199**	**61 376**
Mining and quarrying	921	543	1 389
Manufacturing	15 819	30 581	50 925
Electricity, gas, steam and air conditioning supply	1 899	4 192	6 082
Water supply; sewerage, waste management and remediation activities	500	1 883	2 980
Construction	**5 755**	**12 758**	**18 499**
Wholesale and retail trade, transportation and storage, accommodation and food service activities	**16 458**	**35 210**	**61 080**
Wholesale and retail trade, repair of motor vehicles and motorcycles	9 931	20 478	34 911
Transportation and storage	3 854	8 531	12 819
Accommodation and food service activities	2 673	6 201	13 350
Information and communication	**1 746**	**5 240**	**8 278**
Financial and insurance activities	**3 532**	**8 997**	**13 876**
Real Estate Activities	**3 011**	**12 013**	**26 050**
Professional, scientific, technical, administrative and support service activities	**2 225**	**9 023**	**24 043**
Professional, scientific and technical activities	1 318	5 154	12 642
Administrative and support service activities	907	3 869	11 401
Public administration and defence, education, human health and social work activities	**11 024**	**28 754**	**47 219**
Public administration and defence; compulsory social security	3 940	10 632	15 545
Education	3 765	8 782	14 774
Human health and social work activities	3 319	9 339	16 900
Other service activities	**1 642**	**4 295**	**7 617**
Arts, entertainment and recreation	441	1 600	3 374
Other service activities	1 149	2 630	4 136
Activities of households as employers; undifferentiated goods and services producing activities of households for own use	52	64	107
Total value added	**67 931**	**157 371**	**272 532**
GDP	76 359	174 794	299 240

65 450; purchases of materials: 85 340; tax revenue: 485 770; depreciation: 124 320. Calculate output, intermediate consumption and value added. Verify that the measure of output corresponds to the assumption that this administrative body is non-profit.

Exercise 5. Calculation of output: the case of banks

The following are the simplified data for a bank: foreign exchange commissions: 32 980; stock-market trading commissions: 23 430; interest received: 357 850; interest paid: 204 650; purchases of materials: 34 520; purchases of IT consultancy services: 32 890; purchases of software: 12 590; inventory of materials at the start of the period: 7 420; inventory of materials at the end of the period: 3 860. Calculate the output, the intermediate consumption and the value added. Assume the figure for FISIM is interest received minus interest paid.

Exercise 6. Calculation of output: the case of distributors

The following are the simplified data for a retail chain: sales: 4 567 800; total purchases: 4 120 500 (of which, goods for resale: 3 987 350); inventories of goods for resale at start of period: 476 000; at end of period: 548 400; inventories of materials at start of period: 120; at end of period: 3 250. Calculate the output, the intermediate consumption and the value added. Inflation is assumed to be negligible.

Exercise 7. Calculation of output: the case of insurance companies

The following are the simplified data for an insurance company: premiums received: 210 400; indemnities paid out on claims: 187 500; income from the investment of reserves: 34 270; purchases of consumables: 24 320; inventories of materials at the start of the period: 5 630; at the end of the period: 20. Calculate the output, the intermediate consumption and the value added. Now suppose that an exceptional claim raises the amount of indemnities for this same period to 245 000. Recalculate the output. How is this result to be interpreted?

The solutions to these exercises are available at:
http://dx.doi.org/10.1787/9789264214637-22-en

Chapter 5

Defining final uses of GDP

Changes in the final uses of GDP, or demand, determine the growth of real GDP in the short term. Governments generally try to influence three variables in order to maintain growth at a rate that keeps inflation and employment at the desired levels: demand from households, public consumption and investment. Together, these variables are known as domestic demand. Economists look at this demand, as well as at external demand and net exports, when trying to predict future economic developments. This chapter looks at measuring and shaping demand and at what is contained in each of the components of final uses.

Changes in the **final uses** of GDP, or **demand** to use the economists' term, determine the growth of real GDP in the short term. This chapter gives the definition of the components of this demand.

The authors of the *OECD Economic Outlook* for 2013, commenting on recent economic developments in the United Kingdom (the country chosen for illustration in this chapter), wrote:

"Continuing weakness of euro area trading partners, slow real income growth and necessary public and private sector deleveraging are generating strong headwinds for the economy. Growth is expected to pick up gradually through 2013 and 2014 as gross fixed investment and exports gain momentum. Inflation expectations are above the inflation target, but inflation is projected to decelerate owing to persistent economic slack (...). The muted global recovery, especially in Europe, and the necessary adjustment of still-impaired public and private sector balance sheets continue to weigh on growth. Despite a resilient labour market, private consumption is held back by weak average real earnings, fragile confidence and household deleveraging. Private investment is restrained by weak aggregate demand and high uncertainty. Exchange rate depreciation over recent years has not led to a major boost in exports, hampered by subdued demand. Yet exports have also underperformed the growth in UK's overseas markets, pointing to supply-side impediments, notably in financial services exports and oil". (OECD, 2013a)

There are three target variables that governments try to influence in order to maintain growth at a rate that keeps inflation and employment at the desired levels: (1) demand from households (or, in the national accounts terminology, "households' consumption expenditure"); (2) public consumption (or "general government consumption expenditure"); and (3) investment (or "gross fixed capital formation"). To influence these variables, governments use fiscal and monetary policy instruments (see section "Going further: How do monetary and fiscal policies operate?").

The total of these three variables is known as **domestic demand**. Exports are also a major component of final demand, but in this case **external demand**. It is conventional to show external demand as being equal to exports *minus* imports, the result being known as **net exports**.

These are the variables that economists look at when trying to predict future economic developments. At first, macroeconomic forecasts are made by estimating final uses based on their recent movements, taking into account recent and expected changes in monetary and fiscal policy. Once these forecasts have been prepared for each member country, the OECD economists then exploit their knowledge of the financial and trading links between OECD countries to see whether the forecasts for each country are consistent for the OECD area as a whole. This leads to an iterative process in which the individual country forecasts are adjusted to produce a consistent set of forecasts taking into account the probable impact of the monetary and fiscal policies of each country on all the others.

This chapter will look at what is contained in each of the components of final uses. It is essential to bear in mind throughout the chapter, even though we do not always repeat the point, that economists are mostly interested in the variation in volume of these variables, and not in their movements at current prices. Some tables in this chapter use data at current prices but the proper definition of the variable in the context of macroeconomic forecasting is the corresponding variable in volume (i.e. after deflation of the variable in current prices by the appropriate price index). Exercise 1 at the end of this chapter illustrates how a table of final uses at current prices is converted into volume terms.

1. Final uses in the national accounts

Table 5.1 shows the principal components of final uses and their importance in relation to GDP for the United Kingdom. An obvious feature is the importance of the item "households' final consumption expenditure". This accounts now for more than 60% of GDP in the United Kingdom, and the percentage is similar in other OECD countries.

What does "final uses" mean?

First of all, why "uses"? Quite simply because we are dealing with the use of resources placed on the market, these resources being output, imports and withdrawals from inventories. In large part, these uses consist of *purchases* by economic agents, and this is why one speaks of *final expenditures* as well as *final uses*: these two terms mean the same thing.

And then, why "final"? In the national accounts, the uses of resources are described either as *intermediate* or *final*. Intermediate uses consist of goods and services that are consumed (one could also say used-up or transformed) in a production process within the economic territory and during the accounting period (one year); final uses comprises all other goods and services. Note that it is not the nature of the good or service that determines whether it is intermediate or final. A steak bought by household is "final", but if a restaurant buys the same steak, it is "intermediate". Similarly, a steel sheet will generally be

Table 5.1. **United Kingdom: Share of final uses in GDP**

Current prices, percentage of GDP

SNA code		1980	1990	2000	2005	2012
P31S14	Final consumption expenditure of households	57.7	60.0	63.2	62.2	63.3
P31S15	Final consumption expenditure of non-profit institutions serving households	1.4	2.0	2.4	2.4	2.5
P3S13	Final consumption expenditure of general government	21.9	19.6	18.3	21.0	21.8
P51	Gross fixed capital formation	19.2	20.4	17.4	16.8	14.3
P52	Changes in inventories	-1.1	-0.3	0.5	0.4	0.3
P53	Acquisitions less disposals of valuables	0.0	0.0	0.0	0.0	0.1
P6	Exports of goods and services	27.1	24.2	27.3	26.6	31.6
P7	Imports of goods and services	-24.7	-25.9	-29.2	-29.4	-33.8
DB1_GE	Statistical discrepancy	0.0	0.0	0.0	0.0	-0.2
B1_GE	Gross domestic product (expenditure approach)	100.0	100.0	100.0	100.0	100.0

Source: OECD (2013), "Aggregate National Accounts: Gross domestic product", OECD National Accounts Statistics (database), http://dx.doi.org/10.1787/data-00001-en.

StatLink ᵇᵉᵖᵃ http://dx.doi.org/10.1787/888933143804

an intermediate good, but it can also become final if it is stocked during the current period to be consumed in a later period, or if it is exported. "Final" therefore simply refers to all the goods and services used during the period, that are not entirely consumed (used-up or transformed) in a production process in the course of that same accounting period. It will be shown later that several conventions have had to be introduced in order to distinguish "final" from "intermediate" in practice.

In the case of households, apart from their activities as sole proprietorships and excluding the special case of dwellings, all the goods and services they buy are final, because despite the fact that they are in large part consumed during the accounting period, they are not used in a production process. It is necessary to remember the definition of output given in Chapter 4: preparing meals and washing clothes in the home are not considered as output in the national accounts. As a result, a raw steak is not considered as intermediate consumption in the production of a meal by a member of a household. The objection can be raised that certain goods purchased by households are not entirely consumed during the accounting period: wine and tinned preserves, for example, can be stocked for several years, while durable goods like cars, computers and household electronics provide services for their owners over many years. The response to these objections is that, by convention, all goods and services apart from dwellings are considered to have been entirely consumed once they have been acquired by households.

Another important point is that expenditure by general government and non-profit institutions is classified by convention as final, either as final consumption expenditure or as gross capital formation (GCF). It may be asked whether some of these services should not be treated as intermediate. While there is little difficulty in accepting that education and healthcare are of a "final" nature, many public services – ranging from defence and policing to street lighting and road maintenance – have some of the characteristics of the "intermediate" category. They clearly contribute to production, since there would be much less output if the government failed to defend the country against a foreign invasion, to maintain law and order and to keep the road system in good condition. Indeed, the absence of such services can lead to catastrophic slumps in output, as the experience of numerous developing countries can testify.

The problem is that it is not possible to say just how much of these services provided by general government contribute to the output of firms and how much to the general well-being of the population. Both households and firms benefit from public security, the road network and the many other contributions to civilised living provided by general government. And even if it were possible to separate out that part of general government services that contributes to production, one would then be obliged to allocate the production costs in a very arbitrary fashion among the producers. These are the reasons that have led national accountants to treat all services provided by general government as "final".

Conversely, all spending by firms on goods and services is "intermediate" apart from investment (GFCF) and changes in inventories. Purchases of investment goods are recorded as *final* and not intermediate expenditure because the consumption of these goods (referred to as *consumption of fixed capital* by the national accountants and as *depreciation* by economists) takes place over a period of more than one year. Changes in inventories also form part of final uses because the relevant goods are not used in the same accounting period.

Exports – the goods or services sold abroad – are considered as "final" (even though they may be used in a production process by the importing country) because they are final sales from the point of view of the exporting country. From the point of view of the importing country, the value of these imported goods and services is included either in final goods and services or in intermediate goods and services and has to be subtracted from the total of final goods and services to obtain Gross *Domestic* Product. This is why imports carry a negative sign in Table 5.1.

To sum up, the definition of "final" goods and services is based on several conventions. Purists may find this unsatisfactory since a different set of conventions would give a different set of national accounts. However, it can definitely be said of the current conventions that they result in a set of statistics that have, over many years, proved useful in describing and managing countries' economies.

2. Households' final consumption expenditure

Households' final consumption expenditure is the largest component of final uses. It includes:

1. *Purchases of the goods and services used by households to meet their everyday needs:* clothing, household durables, rent, transport, personal services and so on. These purchases represent by far the largest part of household consumption expenditure. There are three points to note:

   - Some of these purchases are made on credit. In this case, the national accountant has to break the transaction down into three parts: the price of the good itself (for example, a car); the administrative expenses of the financial company making the loan; and the payment of interest. The first part is assigned to household expenditure in the "cars" category; the second to household expenditure in the "financial services" category, but the third is excluded from household consumption expenditure and counted as an interest payment[1] in the household primary income account (see Chapter 6 which deals with the household account). Note that the expenditure on cars is recorded in its entirety the moment the purchasers take possession of them, and not according to the timing of the loan repayments, even when the purchase is made under a financial lease or hire-purchase arrangement.

   - Purchases of dwellings are final uses but are included, not in consumption expenditure, but in gross fixed capital formation. National accountants regard the owners of dwellings as producing housing services either for themselves or for tenants. These households invest (by buying the house) and carry out intermediate expenditure, for example on the purchase of building materials or of services of plumbers and electricians needed to keep the dwelling in good condition.[2] Both the purchase of the dwelling (capital formation) and expenditures for repair and maintenance (intermediate consumption) are excluded from households' final consumption expenditure. The former remains a final use, while the latter is an intermediate use.

   - In the national accounts, the household sector includes sole proprietorships, also called unincorporated enterprises (see Chapter 6). Accordingly, spending by households on goods and services intended for consumption in the production process of the enterprise does not form part of households' final consumption but is considered intermediate consumption by the unincorporated enterprise.

2. *Partial payments for goods and services provided by general government.* This covers cases in which the households have to pay a part of the public services provided – for example, a ticket for entry to a public museum, the price of which covers only a small part of the services provided. If

prescription medicines and medical services are partly reimbursed by government, the part actually paid by households is included here.[3] The portion that is reimbursed forms part of expenditure by general government, and of households' *actual* consumption, as will be shown later.

3. *Payments to general government for various types of licences and permits (when these are made in exchange for a genuine service)*. Compulsory payments designed merely to produce income for general government are treated as taxes and therefore excluded from households' consumption expenditure. The borderline between the two categories is somewhat arbitrary: licences for owning vehicles, boats or aircraft are treated as taxes, while fees for issuing passports and driving licenses are usually regarded as payments for services. In some countries, licence fees for public service television are treated as household final consumption expenditure, but in the United Kingdom the television licence fee is recorded as a tax. (See box "Limitations of national accounts: consumption of television and of free Internet services").

Households' consumption expenditure also includes a certain number of **imputed expenditures**. These are items of expenditure that have not really taken place but for which values are assigned – or "imputed" – in order to improve comparability over time and between countries. The main imputed items of expenditure are:

● *Owner-occupiers' imputed rents*. People living in dwellings they own are considered to be selling housing services to themselves. The rents recorded in the national accounts therefore include both the actual rents paid by tenants and imputed rents in the case of owner-occupiers. In most countries, this is the largest imputed item in households' individual consumption. The amount of the imputed rent is measured by the rents paid for comparable housing in a similar part of the country.

● *Own-account consumption*. Consumption expenditure includes the value (estimated using the corresponding market prices) of the consumption of goods produced by people for themselves. The most important examples are agricultural products produced by farmers for themselves and their families. Note that imputations are made only for goods. With the exception of the housing services of owner-occupiers, no imputation is made for other services such as cooking, looking after children and cleaning when these are produced and consumed within households.

● *Income in kind*. Employees may receive goods and services either free of charge or at very low prices as part of their wages. For example, railway employees are often entitled to travel by train more or less free of charge, members of the armed forces frequently obtain free meals, etc. In the national accounts, these benefits in kind are valued at their cost to the employer. They are then added to compensation of employees and also appear in households' consumption expenditure.

- *Financial intermediation services indirectly measured (FISIM).* Banks commonly provide their customers with certain services free of charge or at prices that are below the cost of production. They cover their production costs by charging higher interest rates on the loans they make than on the deposits they receive. FISIM (see Chapter 4) on loans from banks is essentially measured by the difference between the interest received and a reference rate (usually somewhere in between the debit interest rate and the credit interest rate). FISIM on deposits on the other hand is calculated as the difference between the reference rate and the interest paid on deposits. Some of this FISIM is consumed by households and so must be included in household final consumption expenditure, or, in the case of mortgage loans for example, as intermediate consumption related to the production of housing services.

Consumption made outside the home territory

Households' final consumption expenditure must include all consumption expenditure made by households resident in the United Kingdom (to take the country illustrated in this chapter), whether this expenditure takes place on UK territory or elsewhere.

For the definitions of "residence" and "economic territory", see Section 9 of this chapter.

This means having to add to the consumption carried out on home territory the consumption by UK tourists abroad. Since the national accountants do not know what products tourists have consumed abroad, they record a total amount under "expenditures by resident households abroad", which is recorded as an import and added to consumption on home territory (which for its part is available in great detail). Conversely, the consumption recorded on home territory must be reduced by the value of purchases by foreign tourists (non-resident households) in the United Kingdom.

The price system applied to final uses

The general rule applied in national accounts is that final uses are valued at the prices agreed to by the parties to the transaction. These prices are described as *market prices* or *acquisition prices*. In the case of payments by households, they correspond to the price paid in stores. Points to note:

- The prices of final uses include non-deductible VAT and other taxes on products, such as sales taxes, specific duties on tobacco, alcoholic beverages or motor fuels. The box entitled "Typology of taxes" explains the distinction between *taxes on products*, such as sales taxes and VAT, which are included in household consumption expenditure, and *current taxes on income and wealth*, which are excluded.

● The prices of final uses include transport and marketing costs.

● The prices of final uses are net of rebates, meaning that they can be lower than the stated prices (or the "catalogue prices"), whether the reduction was obtained by bargaining or having been spontaneously offered by the seller in order to encourage sales.

● The prices of final uses include the tips paid over and above the stated prices. The most common examples are the tips paid in restaurants, taxis and hairdressers.

Box 5.1. **Typology of taxes**

National accountants separate the taxes paid by households and other agents into four groups: taxes on products (D21); current taxes on income and wealth (D5); other taxes on production (D29); and capital taxes (D91). Only the first two groups, which are the largest, will be dealt with here. Taxes in the first group are often called "indirect taxes" and those in the second "direct taxes".

In the OECD countries, taxes on products mainly consist of VAT, sales taxes and other specific taxes such as duties on petroleum products, tobacco or alcoholic beverages. To these one can add certain other minor taxes and customs duties. These taxes are collected at the time of the sale of the goods and services concerned and are therefore an integral part of the prices the buyer has to pay to acquire them. Prices "including taxes on products" are the most appropriate from the point of view of the economic analysis of consumption and are therefore the ones used by the national accounts. Sales to foreign tourists that are made free of VAT or sales taxes are recorded excluding these taxes, even if the purchaser initially pays them and is subsequently reimbursed. These taxes are said to be "deductible". Only non-deductible taxes are included in the prices used in the national accounts.

Current taxes on income and wealth for households mainly consist of taxes on incomes from employment and the like, and on profits of unincorporated enterprises, but also include local taxes, property taxes, other wealth taxes and some less important taxes. These "direct" taxes are not included in consumption expenditure but are treated as transfers, i.e. a payment for which nothing is directly received in return. These taxes are recorded in the secondary income distribution account, as explained in Chapter 6 on the household account.

Classification of household expenditure

The main classification used for household expenditure is described as a classification according to *purpose* and is known as COICOP – *Classification of Individual Consumption by Purpose*. In this case, the products are classified under major headings that are better suited to the analysis of consumption than the standard classification of products, which is more aligned to the analysis of production. Table 5.2 illustrates the changes in consumption expenditure in the United Kingdom on the basis of this classification by purpose. It shows the spectacular decline in just 25 years in the share of expenditure allocated to everyday purposes (food, alcoholic beverages and tobacco, clothing) in favour of leisure and services in general. This phenomenon is true for all countries where real incomes have been increasing. Economists say that "the income elasticity of the demand for basic goods tends to be lower than the income elasticity of the demand for services". The **elasticity** of one variable in relation to another is measured by the ratio between the index of the growth rate of the first and the index of the growth rate of the second. In this case, the elasticity of the demand for services in relation to income is therefore equal to: (100 + *the growth in the demand for services*) ÷ (100 + *the growth rate in income*).

This table also illustrates a major problem in looking only at expenditures made directly by households. The shares of healthcare (row CP060) and education (row CP100) are very small, since what we have here is only the portions of these services that are directly paid by households. In fact, the bulk of these services are free of charge, albeit financed indirectly by taxes or social contributions. The true consumption by households of health and education services is therefore much larger, but the part provided by government is recorded as *individual consumption of general government* and not as *household consumption expenditure*. We shall return to this point in Section 5.

A final point to note in this table is that the second and third row from the bottom concern tourist expenditure. As explained earlier, it is necessary to add to consumption on home territory the consumption by UK residents abroad, and deduct the consumption of non-resident households in the United Kingdom (hence the negative sign in this line) in order to obtain the final consumption expenditure by resident households.

3. Final consumption expenditure by general government

This is the second largest final use after household consumption. Expenditures by general government are considered *by convention* as forming part of the final uses (final consumption or gross fixed capital formation, GFCF) of general government itself. For example, current expenditure on

Table 5.2. **United Kingdom: Share of households' expenditure in classification by purpose**

At current prices, percentage of total final consumption expenditure

		1980	1995	2012
P31CP010	Food and non-alcoholic beverages	17.8	10.7	9.1
P31CP020	Alcoholic beverages, tobacco and narcotics	5.7	4.1	3.6
P31CP030	Clothing and footwear	7.7	6.1	5.8
P31CP040	Housing, water, electricity, gas and other fuels	16.0	18.8	25.8
P31CP050	Furnishings, households equipment and routine maintenance of the house	6.9	5.9	4.9
P31CP060	Health	0.9	1.5	1.6
P31CP070	Transport	15.0	13.8	14.3
P31CP080	Communications	1.7	2.1	2.1
P31CP090	Recreation and culture	9.9	11.2	10.5
P31CP100	Education	0.9	1.3	1.5
P31CP110	Restaurants and hotels	10.7	11.0	9.8
P31CP120	Miscellaneous goods and services	7.4	13.3	10.4
P33	Final consumption expenditure of resident households abroad	2.0	3.0	2.9
P34	Final consumption expenditure of non-resident households on the territory	-2.6	-2.9	-2.4
P31NC	Total final consumption expenditure of households	100.0	100.0	100.0

Source: OECD (2014), "Detailed National Accounts: Non-financial accounts by sectors, annual", OECD National Accounts Statistics (database), doi: *http://dx.doi.org/10.1787/data-00034-en.*

StatLink ⟨⟨⟨⟨ *http://dx.doi.org/10.1787/888933143812*

police and education is regarded as consumption by general government. What lies behind this strange convention, given that these services benefit households and enterprises? Essentially, it is because no one knows how to attribute this expenditure precisely to the beneficiaries, since they do not buy them, even though they pay the taxes that finance them. It has therefore been agreed not to attempt to allocate these expenditures to their beneficiaries but to attribute all these expenditures to general government itself, by convention. Among other advantages, this makes it possible to remain closer to the actual monetary flows.

In accounting terms, final consumption expenditure by government is equal to its cost, defined by the following sum:

● compensation of employees of the government;

● *plus* purchases by government of materials and other intermediate consumption items,;

● *plus* consumption of government fixed capital;

- *plus* purchases of goods and services by the government for the benefit of households (for example, reimbursement of healthcare services, housing allowances, etc.);

- *plus* other taxes on production paid (a very small item for government);

- *minus* partial payments by households or firms for services provided by government (entry to museums, sales of government publications, etc.);

- *minus* own account production of gross fixed capital formation.

Although this expenditure is all recorded as final consumption by general government in the standard national accounts tables, national accountants distinguish, within general government consumption expenditure, the part that is "collective" from the part that is "individual". *Individual consumption expenditure* is expenditure that is clearly carried out for the benefit of individual households. Table 5.3 shows that individual expenditure now represents more than 60% of total expenditure in the UK, following an appreciable rise in this percentage in the past 30-35 years. This expenditure mainly covers public education and public healthcare. It is this expenditure that was missing from Table 5.2 but which is required in order to show the true picture of the goods and services consumed by households. Individual expenditure of government also includes spending on aid for social housing, the operating expenses of museums and other government services to households.

Collective consumption expenditure comprises expenditure related to the activities of general government that are not attributable uniquely to individual households and also benefit enterprises. This includes expenditure on Congress, National Assemblies, Parliaments, etc., on ministries of foreign affairs, safety and order, defence, home affairs, economic affairs and the protection of the environment, as well as government R&D activities.

There is an important economic distinction between these two categories of expenditure. In the case of individual consumption expenditure, the cost to general government of supplying the services depends more or less directly on the number of households making use of the services. It will cost almost twice as much to teach 10 000 children as 5 000. The cost of collective services, on the other hand, depends much less on the number of "customers". Defence services are available to anyone living in the country. Large countries may need to have larger armies than small countries but there is no direct link between the number of people benefiting from collective services and the cost of supplying them.

Table 5.3. **United Kingdom: Breakdown of final consumption expenditure of general government**

	1980	2000	2012
P31S13 Individual consumption expenditure of general government	47.9	57.2	63.3
P32S13 Collective consumption expenditure of general government	53.6	42.8	36.7
P3S13 Final consumption expenditure of general government	100.0	100.0	100.0

Source: OECD (2013), "Aggregate National Accounts: Gross domestic product", OECD National Accounts Statistics (database), http://dx.doi.org/10.1787/data-00001-en.

StatLink ⬛🖳 http://dx.doi.org/10.1787/888933143828

4. Final consumption expenditure of the NPISHs

Non-profit institutions serving households (NPISHs) are units formed by groups of households in order to supply services to themselves or to other households on a non-commercial basis. NPISHs include political parties, trade unions, religious organisations, sports clubs, cultural associations, charities and associations with philanthropic aims (Red Cross etc.), and certain charitable foundations. In some countries, a number of universities are also classified in this sector. It has to be noted, however, that NPISHs do not include all institutions with non-commercial aims – far from it. This is because in order to be defined as NPISHs they have to be mainly financed by households' donations or regular subscriptions. Those non-profit institutions that are not directly financed by households but are, for example, controlled or financed by enterprises (Chambers of Commerce, professional associations, mutual insurance companies, etc.) are classified as being in the enterprise sector. Those controlled or financed by general government are classified in the general government sector. In the end, the NPISHs constitute only a small sector in the national accounts.

Like general government, the NPISHs provide "non-market" services. For this reason, their treatment in the accounts is similar to that of general government. The output of services by NPISHs is valued at cost, and by convention the NPISHs "consume" the services they produce. Final consumption expenditure of the NPISHs is therefore equal to their operating costs. Note that donations to charitable organisations are not payments for services. They are regarded as transfers and are recorded in the household account in the secondary distribution of income account (see Chapter 6).

We saw earlier how the consumption expenditure of general government was divided between individual expenditure and collective expenditure. This distinction does not have to be made for the NPISHs, since these organisations are at the service of individual households and all their expenditure is therefore considered as individual.

5. Moving from consumption expenditure to actual consumption

To improve the analysis of households' consumption by incorporating the individual consumption financed by general government or the NPISHs, the national accountants have invented the concept of **actual consumption**. Households' actual consumption is equal to households' consumption expenditure plus the *individual consumption expenditure* of general government and NPISHs. This individual consumption expenditure is also known as "transfers in kind". Table 5.4 illustrates this move from the notion of "who spends" to that of "who consumes".

Table 5.4. **United Kingdom: Moving from "who spends" to "who consumes"**
2012, billions, national currency

	(P3) Final consumption expenditure (Who spends?)		(P4) Actual final consumption (Who consumes?)	
Household (S14)	Final consumption expenditure of households (P31S14)	991.0	(P4S14)	1 245.8
			Final consumption expenditure of households (P31S14)	991.0
			Final consumption expenditure of NPISH (P31S15)	38.8
			Individual consumption expenditure of general government (P31S13)	216.0
NPISH (S15)	Final consumption expenditure of NPISH (P31S15)	38.8		None (0)
General Government (S13)	Final consumption expenditure of general government (P3S13)	341.2		
	Individual consumption expenditure of general government (P31S13)	216.0	Collective consumption expenditure of general government (P32S13)	125.2
	Collective consumption expenditure of general government (P32S13)	125.2		

Source: OECD (2013), "Aggregate National Accounts: Gross domestic product", OECD National Accounts Statistics (database), *http://dx.doi.org/10.1787/data-00001-en.*

StatLink ᴍᴤᴘ *http://dx.doi.org/10.1787/888933143836*

Statistics of **actual consumption** have two analytical advantages. First, it is a measure that comes closer to households' welfare (see Chapter 15). To analyse the consumption of healthcare and education, it is not sufficient to use only the *direct* expenditure of households on healthcare or education and omit the expenditure for these purposes made by government for the benefit of households. The use of *actual final consumption by households* makes it possible to circumvent this omission. The second advantage is that international comparisons of households' consumption are meaningful only when they are based on *actual* consumption and not on consumption *expenditures*, as was shown in Chapter 3.

6. Gross fixed capital formation

Investment, or to be more precise, gross fixed capital formation (GFCF), is an essential variable for the purpose of economic analysis of demand. The GFCF of "pure" households (in other words, excluding unincorporated enterprises) consists of the purchase of dwellings. This is a good indicator of households' confidence in the future and can be used to predict movements in consumption expenditure. The GFCF of general government consists mainly of transport infrastructure, investments in military defence systems (including weapons systems), office buildings, schools, hospitals, etc.

However, what economists are mainly interested in is the gross fixed capital formation of the business sector (non-financial and financial corporations and unincorporated enterprises). This is the largest single component of investment and its movements often trigger off the beginning and the end of economic cycles. It also determines the growth in apparent labour productivity.

Gross fixed capital formation is precisely defined in the national accounts as the **net acquisition of produced fixed assets**, i.e. assets intended for use in the production of other goods and services for a period of more than one year: machinery, vehicles, offices, industrial buildings, software, R&D, etc. Some clarification is needed regarding the wording of this definition:

The term "fixed" was chosen in contrast to "variable" capital, which consists of inventories. These expressions probably date as far back as Karl Marx, one of the distant sources of inspiration for several of the ideas in the national accounts.

- The word *fixed* is used to indicate that additions to inventories are not included in GFCF. It does not mean that the equipment in question cannot move.

  For example, transport equipment (cars, trucks, ships, aircraft) are not "fixed" in the normal meaning of the word, but they are nevertheless included in GFCF. The same is true of livestock (notably milking cows), which are also included in GFCF.

- *Net acquisitions* signifies that GFCF records the *purchases* of fixed assets after deduction of *sales* of fixed assets on the second-hand market. It is therefore not impossible, theoretically, for GFCF to be negative. For example, car rental firms "turn over" their fleets very rapidly. They buy large numbers of cars, making a positive contribution to GFCF, but at the same time they sell them very rapidly, thus making a negative contribution. For a given period, therefore, it is quite possible that the value of their purchases is smaller than that of their sales. However, such a situation is very unlikely to occur at the macroeconomic level, because one firm's sales of second-hand equipment are often another firm's purchases.

This example illustrates the fact that GFCF includes used capital goods. For some developing countries, most GFCF in the form or machinery and equipment may consist of second-hand equipment imported from developed countries.

- The term *"produced assets"* signifies that only those assets are included in GFCF that are the result of a production process recognised by the national accounts. The national accounts also record transactions in *non-produced* assets such as land, primary forests and oil and mineral reserves. These *non-produced* assets are also included in the balance sheet accounts but are not included in GFCF because they have been produced by nature and not by human activity. Nature is not a producer in the eyes of national accountants.

Box 5.2. **A special case: financial leasing**

Rather than buying a capital good outright, some firms prefer to use financial leasing arrangements, consisting of regular rental payments followed by a purchase at the end of the rental period. For example, many airlines acquire their aircraft through financial leases. There are financial companies specialising in this type of arrangement. These companies are the legal owners of numerous capital goods that they do not actually use but make available for others to operate. Economically speaking, it makes more sense to treat the airlines as owners of these assets even though this is not legally true. National accountants, who systematically give economic aspects precedence over legal aspects, record these assets as being on the books of the non-financial corporations that are the actual users, i.e. the airlines in this example.

The GFCF borderline

Economists, national accountants and company accountants have spent considerable time discussing the definition of fixed assets, because GFCF determines the measurement of their stock of capital (see Chapter 8), which in turn determines growth. In principle, the more capital there is, the greater the growth can be.

There is general agreement concerning most kinds of capital goods. Transport equipment, machinery, offices, warehouses, factories and major civil engineering works are clearly fixed assets. But there is still disagreement regarding certain types of expenditure (software, R&D, trademarks) that are in the "grey area" between GFCF and intermediate consumption. In principle, the difference between these two factors of production is the fact that the former is not entirely consumed in the annual process of production, while the latter is. Where exactly does the borderline run?

Traditionally, only material goods (also called "physical" or "tangible" goods) were considered as fixed assets. These are the items listed at the beginning of the previous paragraph. However, more and more accountants and economists recognise that several expenditures that do not take material form are not entirely consumed in the productive process during the year. Thus, these expenditures should be "capitalised" and are known as "intangible assets" or "intellectual property products".

Expenditure on mineral exploration is an example. Although accountants in mining firms have long regarded this expenditure as capital (GFCF) rather than current expenditure (intermediate consumption), it is not that long ago that national accountants have agreed to do the same. Their reluctance stemmed from the fact that mineral exploration is entirely an acquisition of knowledge (Is there ore in a given geographic area or not?). This change was undertaken, however, in the SNA 1993 and now all expenditure on mineral exploration is regarded as GFCF, *even when the search is unfruitful*. This last point is not as strange as it might seem, because modern exploration technology more or less guarantees a constant success rate: for a given outlay on mineral prospecting, the companies know from experience what percentage will result in exploitable discoveries.

Some other types of intangible asset are also included in GFCF in the national accounts. These are *software, databases* and *entertainment, literary and artistic originals*.[4] The purchase or creation of software is expenditure that is not consumed in the period in which it takes place, since a programme is used for a period of several years. These expenditures, whether on an "in-house" software programme (such as a reservation system for an airline) or original software designed to be reproduced (such as Windows, owned by Microsoft), or reproductions (the rights to use Windows over a longer period that firms buy from Microsoft) are all included in GFCF.

A further step forwards has been taken with the introduction of the SNA 2008, according to which also R&D expenditure is recognised as part of GFCF. Clearly, one can see substantial investments in R&D to develop new or improved products, without which future income streams from productive activities may stagnate. The pharmaceutical industry and enterprises involved in ICT technologies and products are the obvious examples. There was some discussion on the inclusion of freely available knowledge, produced by R&D expenditures of government, but in the end it was decided to also capitalise these expenditures, as they may provide benefits for the society as a whole (similar to transport infrastructure).

The difficulty from the point of view of national accounts is less a question of principle but of practicality, given that they have now diverged from the conventions used in business accounts. In their own accounts, firms treat the purchase or creation of software or R&D only partially as capital expenditure, and the firms' accounts are a common statistical source for the national accounts. Why is this? First, because of the application of the cautionary principle by company accountants: when it is not certain that the result of R&D or a computer programme will have real value on the market, accounting standards recommend considering the expenditure as intermediate consumption and not as investment in fixed assets. For this reason, software-producing firms like Microsoft include no software among the assets on their balance sheets. Second, because firms often have an interest in treating software or R&D as a current expenditure so that it can be deducted immediately from their profits, thus reducing immediately their taxes. In the end, national accountants are left with no satisfactory statistical sources for valuing capital investment in software and are obligated to find substitute sources that are fairly approximate.

The GFCF classification

In the national accounts, data on GFCF are presented in several ways. First, GFCF can be broken down by the nature of the product, using the standard product classification. However, this is not the most useful classification, since it is better suited to analysing output than investment. Second, it can be broken down according to the industry or sector making the investment. For example, in the case of the United Kingdom, GFCF is shown by investing industry in Table 5.5. As can be seen, manufacturing is far from being the largest investing industry; investment by business services, transport and storage firms, as well as by real estate activities were substantially higher in 2012. To be noted is the "dis-investment "of 31 953 millions in the activity "Public administration". In fact, this figure does not correspond to effective dis-investments of the UK government but to overall negative transfer costs that have been classified by convention in this line by the UK national accountants.

But it is also possible to show a matrix combining two categories: by nature of product and by investing sector. Table 5.6 shows United Kingdom

Table 5.5. **United Kingdom: Gross fixed capital formation (P51) by industry**
Millions of pound sterling, current prices, 2012

Agriculture, forestry and fishing	3 262
Mining and quarrying	17 556
Manufacturing	18 707
Electricity, gas, steam and air conditioning	16 988
Water supply, sewage, waste management and remediation activities	12 144
Construction	8 547
Wholesale and retail trade, repair of motor vehicles and motor cycles	15 150
Transportation and storage	30 646
Accommodation and food service activities	8 019
Information and communication	18 732
Financial and insurance activities	11 934
Real estate activities	72 223
Professional, scientific and technical activities	6 271
Administrative and support service activities	1 736
Public administration and defence, compulsory and social security	-31 953
Education	2 543
Human health and social work activities	2 476
Arts, entertainment and recreation	7 397
Other service activities	1 874
Total activity	224 252

Source: OECD (2014), "Detailed National Accounts: Capital formation by activity", OECD National Accounts Statistics (database), doi: *http://dx.doi.org/10.1787/data-00008-en.*

StatLink ᴍᴴᴱ︎ *http://dx.doi.org/10.1787/888933143845*

GFCF broken down by institutional sector and by type of asset for the year 2012, using a classification suited to assets and distinguishing between:

● Material fixed assets:

1. Dwellings (excluding land).

2. Other buildings and structures.

3. Transport equipment.

4. Other machinery and equipment.

● Intangible fixed assets, including:[5]

1. Mineral exploration – spending on the search for oil or mineral deposits.

2. Software – standard or developed in-house, originals or copies of originals.

3. Literary and artistic originals, such as films, novels or music. These assets earn royalties.

It is important to note that GFCF in dwellings and other buildings does not include the value of the land on which they are situated. This is because land is not a produced asset. While *non-produced assets* are excluded from

Table 5.6. **United Kingdom: Gross fixed capital formation by type of asset and institutional sector**

	Public non-financial corporations	Private non-financial corporations	Financial corporations	Central government	Local government	Households and NPISH	Total
Dwellings, excluding land	3 017	1 011	0	94	0	47 012	51 135
Other buildings and structures	335	42 795	1 065	9 606	13 984	2 156	69 942
Transport equipment	223	5 054	41	36	420	270	6 043
Other machinery and equipment	999	33 114	3 238	3 862	1 209	2 174	44 595
Intangible fixed assets	1 987	28 188	3 539	575	288	1 843	36 421
Costs associated with the transfer of ownership of non-produced assets	-378	4 365	-884	1 393	8 769	8 769	16 116
Gross fixed capital formation	6 185	114 526	6 999	15 568	18 753	62 221	224 252

Source: Office for National Statistics (2013): United Kingdom National Accounts, The Blue Book, *United Kingdom National Accounts – The Blue Book, 2013 Edition.*

StatLink ▧ *http://dx.doi.org/10.1787/888933143854*

GFCF, the costs associated with the transfer of ownership of *non-produced* assets (transport and installation costs), as well as administrative expenses (lawyers' fees or taxes related to the purchase of these goods) are included in GFCF, as a separate category in the national accounts of the United Kingdom. In the case of *produced* assets, these expenses are included in the prices of the assets themselves.

The price system used

Like all final uses, *Gross Fixed Capital Formation* is valued at acquisition prices. In most cases, this amounts to recording it excluding VAT, since VAT is generally entirely deductible in the case of firms' investments. However, the acquisition prices of capital goods include transport and installation charges, as well as all specific taxes associated with the purchase of these goods. For example, lawyers' fees are included in the value of the purchase of a dwelling (but not the value of the land on which it is built).

7. Changes in inventories

The next item appearing in the final uses table is the *change in inventories*, i.e. the difference between additions to and withdrawals from inventories. In common economic parlance, one might use the terms "stock building" or "changes in stocks" for this entry, but the official name in the national accounts is "changes in inventories". In principle, only the additions to inventories should be part of final uses, and withdrawals from inventories should be classified as resources. However, in order to have accounts that are more compact, it was decided to count withdrawals from inventories as negative contributions to inventories and to combine the two flows.

First, inventories consist of the stocks of inputs intended to be used later as intermediate consumption in a production process (in companies' accounts these are known as "material inventories"). Second, they include stocks of finished goods that have not yet been sold. Third, they include stocks of merchandise purchased for resale, these being found mainly in wholesale and retail distribution. Fourth, they also comprise the strategic stocks (food, oil, stocks for intervention on agricultural markets) managed by government authorities. Lastly, they can also be "work in progress", which consists of goods being processed but which cannot yet be delivered to the user at the end of the accounting period. The value of these goods is therefore included in inventories. An important component of work in progress are goods such as ships, oil-drilling platforms and buildings that may take several months or even years to complete.[6]

One might think it would be an easy matter to calculate changes in inventories by taking the value of inventories at the end of the accounting period and subtracting the value at the beginning, this information being available in companies' accounts. In practice, however, evaluating changes in inventories on the basis of companies' accounting data is difficult because inventories generate holding gains or losses as the market prices of the goods held in stock rise or fall. These gains or losses are not the result of a production process and thus cannot contribute to GDP, which is fundamentally an indicator of production.

The fact that these holding gains and losses are eliminated from GDP does not mean that they are ignored in the national accounts. They may have an important impact on incomes when the prices of goods rise or fall. Expectations of holding gains or losses and their realization can have a substantial impact on the behaviour of producers and consumers. However, national accountants record them, not as elements of GDP, but instead in a "re-evaluation account" (see Chapter 8).

Let us suppose that prices are rising and that the change in inventories is calculated by taking the value of inventories at the end of the period minus the value at the beginning. The value obtained in this way will include a capital gain ("stock appreciation") that has to be eliminated in order to obtain the correct valuation of the changes in inventories for the purpose of the national accounts.

This paragraph illustrates the case of an increase in the price of inventories, but there are of course quite common cases of decreases in the price of inventories, which should be treated symmetrically. In this case, it would be more accurate to refer to "holding losses on inventories" and "stock depreciation".

If the inventories at the end of the period consisted only of products that were already in inventory at the beginning of the period, in other words, if no new article had been added to the inventories during the period and no article withdrawn, it would be easy to eliminate the holding gain, since it would be equal to the inflation rate times the opening value of the inventory. In reality, goods enter and are withdrawn from inventories at different moments in the accounting period, and it is quite possible that at the end of the period none of the original articles are still present.

When prices change and when products are continually being put into and withdrawn from inventory, there are three ways of evaluating the changes in inventories in the national accounts. The first is theoretically correct but impossible to apply in practice. The second is widely used, although it is in fact a very imperfect approximation. The third is easy, but very indirect and hence should be used with caution.

● The theoretically correct method consists of evaluating the goods coming into inventories at the market prices prevalent at the time of entry, and evaluating the withdrawals from inventories at the market prices ruling at the time of withdrawal. The algebraic sum of these entry and withdrawal values then gives the correct measure of the changes in inventories for the purposes of the national accounts. Unfortunately, this information is simply not available in practice.

● As a result, this theoretical method is replaced by an approximate method consisting of evaluating the value of the changes in inventories by applying to the quantities held at the beginning and at the end of the period either the average prices for the period or the mid-period prices (see Exercise 3).

● The third method is very indirect, consisting of calculating all the other items in supply-use accounts (see Chapter 10) and arriving at the changes in inventories as a residual of this accounting equation. This method is theoretically exact, but it leads to the incorporation into the "changes in inventories" item of all the errors contained in the other items.

The economic analysis of changes in inventories

Changes in inventories constitute a highly important indicator of possible changes in the growth rate. Nevertheless, the overall change in inventories remains difficult to interpret, because it includes two different types of goods: inputs and finished products. A positive change in inventories of inputs is a good sign since it signifies that producers are expecting an increase in future production. Conversely, an increase in inventories of finished products may indicate that the producers are having difficulty in selling their output and may therefore be about to cut back production and lay off staff. The interpretation of these figures can usefully be complemented by other information, such as industrial business surveys.

8. Net acquisitions of valuables

This item is very small (see Table 5.1) and is therefore no more than a curiosity for the macroeconomist. Valuables are goods that are bought not to be consumed or used in production, but in the expectation that they will increase (or at least retain) their value over time. Examples include gem-stones, precious metals and paintings by old masters. In general, transactions in these objects take place between households and are therefore consolidated (in other words, cancel out) in the national accounts, except in cases where the goods cross frontiers. In certain countries – notably the United Kingdom and Hong Kong – commercial banks invest in precious metals and these are also classified as valuables. Note, though, that gold stocks held by central banks are classified as "monetary gold" and are shown as financial assets and not as valuables.

9. Exports and imports of goods and services

Exports and imports are key aggregates in the analysis of a country's economic situation. In today's extremely globalized world, whenever the United States (the world's largest national economy, accounting for more than 20% of world GDP) slows down or accelerates, all other economies are affected (see Chapter 16). The same relationship applies to all other countries because they are all exchanging an increasing amount of goods and services. Exchange rates play an important role here. If the pound sterling or the euro appreciates versus the dollar, exports from the United Kingdom or the euro area to the dollar countries suffer as a result. (Note however, that the price of their oil imports will decline, since oil is priced in dollars.) As can be seen in Figure 5.1, the United Kingdom's "degree of openness" is 65%, but this is still low compared with that of a smaller European country such as Belgium, which is even more open to exports and imports. The "degree of openness" is usually calculated as the following ratio: [(*Exports + Imports*)/*GDP*] × 100. It measures the extent to which a country is dependent on trade flows with its trading partners. The evolution in the degree of openness in the case of Belgium is a clear reflection of the country's growing openness to foreign trade, especially after 1993, when the single European Market was put in place.

Figure 5.1. **Belgium and United Kingdom: Degree of openness**
Imports plus exports as percentage of GDP

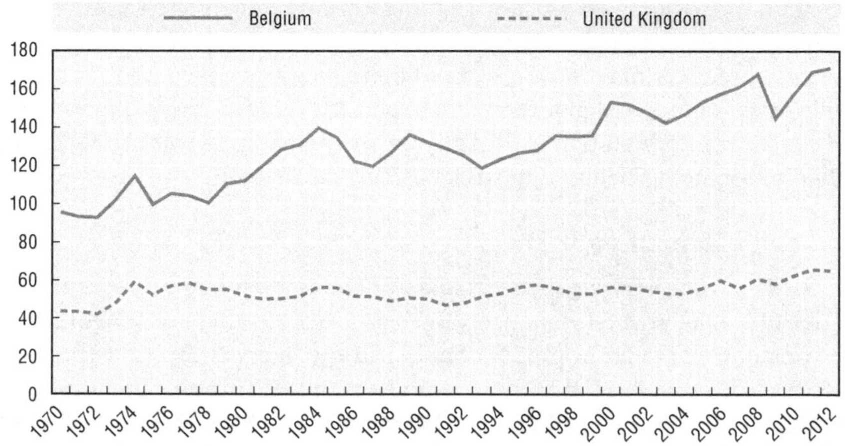

Source: OECD (2013), "Aggregate National Accounts: Gross domestic product", OECD National Accounts Statistics (database), http://dx.doi.org/10.1787/data-00001-en.

StatLink ᵐᵖ http://dx.doi.org/10.1787/888933143796

In the national accounts, "foreign trade" means foreign trade in goods and services. However, since figures for foreign trade in goods are available long before figures for foreign trade in services, a tradition – disputable, admittedly – has been built up of sometimes applying the term "foreign trade" solely to trade in goods. Caution is therefore needed. Customs statistics generally do not cover services and therefore foreign trade on a customs basis may only cover goods; external trade figures in the balance of payments or the national accounts include both goods and services.

All these remarks point to the analytical importance of exports and imports for users of the national accounts (see Chapter 16 for more). These flows are traditionally broken down into four parts: foreign trade in goods; foreign trade in services; direct purchases by non-residents in the economic territory (considered as exports of services); and direct purchases by residents in the rest of the world (considered as imports of services). These two latter items in fact cover, if we continue to use United Kingdom as an illustration, spending by foreign tourists in the UK as well as by UK tourists in foreign countries, as discussed in Section 2 of this chapter. We shall not return to the calculation of exports/imports, but we do need to define three important concepts: *economic territory*, *residence* and the *rest of the world*. These concepts are necessary to a precise definition of exports and imports.

A country's **economic territory** is the geographic area corresponding to the nation state. It includes its air space, its territorial waters, its territorial enclaves in the rest of the world (UK embassies in foreign countries, to take our current example) and free zones. Conversely, it excludes foreign embassies located in the UK. The definition of economic territory is important because only output taking place within the economic territory is recorded in the national accounts. A foreign subsidiary of a UK multinational is not productive in the sense used to draw up the UK national accounts, and its output is included in the national accounts of the country in which the subsidiary is located.

There have been changes in the economic territory covered in certain national accounts. For example, it is not that long ago (in 1999) that the French national accounts have included the overseas departments in French economic territory. Previously, the economic territory in the French national accounts had been limited to metropolitan France. Because these departments were not included in the territory, the national accounts did not include the output of firms situated in these departments, and therefore recorded exports and imports to and from these overseas departments. Now that these departments are included, the French national accounts include the output of firms located in these departments; therefore, they do not record transactions between these departments and metropolitan France as exports and imports. This type of mismatch between the official definition of a country and its economic definition in the national accounts is not so infrequent; for example, the US national accounts do not include Puerto Rico. Generally, however, the quantitative impact on the accounts is negligible.

The concept of residence is associated with that of economic territory in the national accounts. A unit is said to be resident in a country when its "centre of economic interest" is situated in that country's economic territory. This is usually taken to mean that the unit has carried out economic activity there for more than one year. Only resident units are included in the institutional sectors of the national accounts. Most firms, including unincorporated enterprises that have an activity in the territory, are regarded as resident. For households, the test is where they spend their income. Only those households that live for more than one year and make most of their consumption expenditures on the territory are regarded as resident. Households whose members work in the country but live and make most of their consumption expenditures abroad are excluded. This means, for example, that seasonal workers coming from another country to work for a few months a year in the United Kingdom are not regarded as resident, and their disposable income is not included in household disposable income in the UK national accounts. Conversely, certain British workers living and consuming in the United Kingdom while working in Ireland or another country are included as resident households. Foreign tourists who consume in the United Kingdom only for a short period (generally a few weeks) are not counted as resident.

The rest of the world is composed of all non-resident units carrying out transactions with the country under review, here the United Kingdom. The rest of the world therefore comprises all non-resident units that sell their products to UK resident units (these sales being imports, seen from the United Kingdom) and all non-resident units that buy products manufactured in the United Kingdom (these purchases being exports, seen from the United Kingdom). Exports and imports of goods and services constitute the principal transactions with the rest of the world, but there are many other categories: payment of wages and salaries to non-resident households; transfers by immigrant workers resident in the United Kingdom of part of their income to their families remaining abroad; subsidies paid to the United Kingdom by Europe; VAT paid by the United Kingdom to Europe, etc. The totality of these transactions appears in the rest of the world account included in the "integrated account" (see Chapter 10). The balance of payments statistics are the main statistical source for the rest of the world account.

It should be noted that in the most recently adopted standards for the system of national accounts (SNA 2008), exports and imports are purely recorded on the basis of change in (economic) ownership between residents and non-residents. In this respect, they deviate from the so-called "merchandise trade statistics" which typically register the exports and imports of goods on the basis of the goods crossing the national borders. The difference between the two ways of recording can be quite substantial, especially in a world with growing global production arrangements. To give two examples, "merchanting" concerns the purchase by a wholesale trader in say country A of goods in country B which are subsequently resold in country C. In the national accounts, these goods will be treated as imports (actually negative exports) and exports of country A, although they most of the time will not have crossed the borders of country A. Another example relates to "goods for processing", in which an enterprise in country A may decide to send semi-manufactured goods to an enterprise in country B for further processing (e.g. assemblage). Subsequently, the finished products are sent back to the owner in country A. In this case, one can observe flows of goods crossing borders, without any change in ownership. In the national accounts, the fee paid by the principal to the processing enterprise will be recorded as an import of services, and no imports and exports of goods will be registered.

Although flows of services are increasing, merchandise trade data continue to constitute the core of trade relations between a country and the rest of the world. Statistics of exports and imports of goods were for a long time the best statistics available for compiling national accounts because custom authorities needed them for the collection of duties and the monitoring of trade in goods. The quality of these statistics has deteriorated in Europe as a result of the introduction of the single market, because there is no longer any legal control by custom authorities over merchandise moving within the European Union. However, the statistical services or the custom authorities of individual European countries have introduced surveys of the major exporters and importers in order to be able to continue to monitor these movements. In the absence of these surveys, it would no longer be possible to compile the national accounts.

Customs statistics not only show the amounts of exports and imports but also give information on the quantities traded – tonnage, number of units, etc. – for a highly detailed list of products (customs classifications typically contain several thousand items). This information is used by national accountants to calculate export and import prices by dividing the values by quantities. These price indices are known as "unit value indices". This procedure is sometimes criticised because, despite being based on quite detailed statistics, it mixes together prices of products of different qualities. In practice, the result is that unit value indices can vary considerably from one period to another, so that the national accountants must apply a smoothing process to make them intelligible. Some countries have developed special price surveys covering exporters and importers to replace these imperfect "unit value indices".

In the national accounts, detailed figures for imports of goods are valued at "cif" prices, meaning that the prices of the goods include "cost, insurance, freight" when they enter the frontier of the United Kingdom. Exports, for their part, are valued at "fob" prices, a maritime term that stands for "free on board", signifying that the prices of the goods include transport and insurance costs when they arrive at the exporting country's frontier but not the transport and insurance costs further to the importing country's frontier. This is why one frequently sees in the national accounts tables that specify "imports cif" or "exports fob". To complicate things further, total imports in the national accounts are calculated at fob prices, in other words excluding the cost of transport to the frontier. The conversion to fob prices facilitates comparison with the balance of payments and results in an item called "cif-fob adjustment", which is explained in Chapter 10.

Differences in the movements of import and export prices are used to calculate **terms of trade indices**. The terms of trade are defined as the ratio between the index of export prices and the index of import prices. Exercise 4 gives an example of how these indices are calculated.

The amounts involved in *foreign trade in services* are much smaller than for trade in goods. However, these flows are rising sharply as the result of the increasing outsourcing of service activities. Until recently, exports and imports of services mainly consisted of transport services (sea, air) and insurance (reinsurance is frequently outsourced). It should also be remembered that, conventionally, expenditure by non-resident households on the domestic economic territory is classified as trade in "tourist services". However, there is now increasing overseas outsourcing of services to businesses and individuals (processing of goods, "call centres", trade in software, data processing). "Medical tourism" is also expanding, with people travelling abroad to receive treatment that is illegal or too expensive in their home countries.

The statistical sources for trade in services are usually of lesser quality because this trade is difficult to identify. A very long time ago, the principal source was based on declarations made by banks to their central banks, which monitored all transactions made with the rest of the world in order to keep a check on the country's foreign-currency reserves situation. However, these declarations have been discarded in many countries and it is now necessary to carry out surveys of the principal operators dealing with the rest of the world. Monitoring external trade in services in an increasingly globalized world is a challenge that national accountants will have to face in coming decades, which is dwelt upon in more detail in Chapter 16.

Notes

1. Here, we disregard the part of interest that is recorded as financial intermediation services indirectly measured (FISIM, see Chapter 4), which is treated as either intermediate consumption or as final consumption expenditure.

2. Here, it should be noted that major renovations to a dwelling are also considered as GFCF.

3. The portion reimbursed by mutual institutions or private insurance companies is also included in households' consumption expenditure.

4. *Entertainment originals* take material form as hard-copy novels, films, CD-ROMs or tapes. But these forms have economic value only when protected by copyright. It is this protection that gives them their value and explains their classification as intangible assets. The evaluation of these assets by the national accountants can be quite problematical in practice.

5. Please note that these data are still according to SNA 1993, and as such do not yet include R&D-investments.

6. The only exceptions to recording incomplete work as work-in-progress are for partially completed projects for which the ultimate owner is deemed to have taken responsibility, either because the production is for own final use or as evidenced by the existence of a contract of sale or purchase.

References

Insee Databases (2013), Statistical indices and series: Macroeconomic Database: National Accounts, *www.bdm.insee.fr/bdm2/index?request_locale=en*.

OECD (2014), "Detailed National Accounts: Capital formation by activity", OECD National Accounts Statistics (database), doi: *http://dx.doi.org/10.1787/data-00008-en*.

OECD (2014), "Detailed National Accounts: Non-financial accounts by sectors, annual", OECD National Accounts Statistics (database), doi: *http://dx.doi.org/10.1787/data-00034-en*.

OECD (2013a), OECD *Economic Outlook*, Vol. 2013/1, OECD Publishing, doi: *http://dx.doi.org/10.1787/eco_outlook-v2013-1-en*.

OECD (2013b), "Aggregate National Accounts: Gross domestic product", OECD National Accounts Statistics (database), *http://dx.doi.org/10.1787/data-00001-en*.

Office for National Statistics (2013), United Kingdom National Accounts, The Blue Book, *United Kingdom National Accounts – The Blue Book, 2013 Edition*.

System of National Accounts 2008, European Commission, International Monetary Fund, Organisation for Economic Co-operation and Development, United Nations, World Bank, New York, 2009, *http://unstats.un.org/unsd/nationalaccount/docs/SNA2008.pdf*.

Vanoli, A. (2005), "A history of national accounts", IOS press.

Key points

- Economists use the word "demand" to cover what are known as final uses in the national accounts: consumption expenditure by households and general government; investment (GFCF); changes in inventories; and net exports (exports minus imports).

- In the case of producing units, uses may be "final" or "intermediate". Final refers to goods and services that are not entirely consumed during the period in a production process – i.e. GFCF and changes in inventories. Intermediate refers to goods and services that are entirely consumed in a production process during the period.

- By convention, all goods and services bought by households other than those directly related to dwellings are considered as final consumption, even if they are durable goods and are not entirely consumed during the period. Purchases of dwellings (including major renovations to the dwellings) by households are GFCF.

- By convention, general government is considered to consume the services it produces. Final consumption expenditure by general government is equal to the compensation of employees, *plus* intermediate consumption, *plus* consumption of fixed capital, *plus* expenditure on market goods and services by general government on the behalf of households, plus other taxes on productions paid, *minus* partial payments, *minus* own account production of gross fixed capital formation.

- The price applied in the case of final uses is the market (or acquisition) price, including trade and transport margins and also non-deductible VAT and taxes on products.

- Actual individual consumption is equal to households' consumption expenditure *plus* the individual portion of the consumption expenditures of general government and NPISHs.

- Gross fixed capital formation, often known more briefly as investment, is defined as net purchases of produced fixed assets.

- Changes in inventories are equal to additions to inventories *minus* withdrawals from inventories. Evaluating these variations on the basis of the inventories at the beginning and at the end of firms' accounting periods is problematical because of the existence of holding gains or losses on the inventories. These have to be excluded from the change in inventories.

- A distinction is often made between the exports and imports of goods and the exports and imports of services. Detailed imports are valued "cif" and detailed exports are valued "fob". Both, total imports and detailed exports, are valued "fob".

Going further

How do monetary and fiscal policies operate?

Monetary policy consists of the central bank influencing interest rates, either directly or by affecting the money supply. Fiscal policy consists of the government modifying tax rates and increasing or reducing public expenditure.

Concerning monetary policy, a rise in interest rates will tend to reduce consumption expenditure by households because it increases the cost of consumer borrowing and makes saving more attractive. It will also tend to reduce gross fixed capital formation, first because the reduction in household spending reduces firms' incentive to invest in new plant and equipment, and second because it increases their borrowing costs. For equivalent reasons, a decline in interest rates will stimulate household spending and corporate investment.

In the past, many governments tried to encourage exports and reduce imports by means of a different instrument of monetary policy, namely manipulation of exchange rates. More recently, however, most OECD governments have tried to hold their exchange rates stable versus their trading partners, with the Euro Area countries going so far as to fix exchange rates with each other.

Fiscal policy operates through two channels: increasing or reducing revenue and increasing or reducing expenditure. Cutting income tax rates has an immediate impact on household income and indirectly on spending. The increased spending has a secondary impact on capital formation (with firms investing more to meet the higher demand). Cutting taxes on profits encourages producers to increase output either by more investment or by higher utilisation of existing capacity.

General government makes both current expenditures (mainly civil service salaries) and expenditures on capital formation (roads, railways, urban development, etc.). Raising these two types of expenditure automatically increases GDP and also produces secondary effects inasmuch as a higher government wage bill will increase household consumption expenditure, and the demand for construction materials stimulates activity in the industries supplying them.

The Euro Area countries now have much less freedom in regard to monetary and fiscal policy. They no longer have any possibility of modifying their exchange rates and have very little control over the exchange rate of the euro. Interest rates are set uniquely by the European Central Bank. While fiscal policy is somewhat less restricted, the European Stability and Growth Pact limits the possibilities in this respect by setting a ceiling of 3% of GDP on the difference between revenue and expenditure, although during the economic and financial crisis which started in 2008, these goals could not be realised. Governments can reduce taxes but are then obliged to make corresponding cuts in expenditure, hence cancelling out the global impact on the economy.

The limitations of the national accounts: Consumption of television or of Internet services financed by advertising

In most countries, consumption of television services in terms of viewing hours is large – especially in households with young children. However, this is very poorly reflected in national accounts statistics on household consumption. These statistics only show the payments made by households for access to cable TV networks, and in some countries, charges levied by government to finance public broadcasting. "Consumption" of television by households in the national accounts does not reflect television services that are financed by advertising. It is true that the cost of advertising is included in the price of the goods or services advertised and thus will "appear" as part of final consumption in the national accounts but not as consumption of television, and especially not in volume terms. In the national accounts, commercial television stations are regarded solely as sellers of advertising media (some cynics would maintain that this is fairly close to reality...).

The picture is complicated as regards the fees levied by some governments to finance public television services. France regards these fees as a payment for services, and so they are included in households' consumption expenditure. The UK, on the other hand, regards them as a direct tax and so they are excluded from households' consumption expenditure. In countries, such as France, where governments levy charges for public television, an interesting paradox would occur if the government were to abolish the charge and either replace it by budgetary financing or privatise the public channels. Household consumption of television, and hence GDP, would be reduced despite the fact that the only thing that had changed was the source of finance. To solve the problem of this lack of recording of free television services, it would be necessary to impute a value to the "free" services and include this in household final consumption expenditure. However, national accountants have not gone as far as this, despite the fact that practical solutions have been proposed (see Box 28 of the monumental Vanoli, 2005). The bigger and bigger issue for national accounts is that this type of free service to households, but essentially financed by advertising, is formidably expanding, notably in the form of Internet services (Google, Facebook, Wikipedia, etc...)! Some economists have estimated that there are therefore billions excluded from the measure of final consumption, and hence GDP.

Data sources: How are the figures obtained?

As in the other chapters, the French annual accounts are used as an example of the kinds of sources and methods used to estimate final uses of the GDP. We will start with the easiest case and then go on to the more difficult areas.

The statistics for foreign trade (from the customs service) and for the balance of payments (from the Banque de France, the French Central Bank) provide information not only on exports and imports of goods but also on exports and imports of services. Through their traditional function of controlling all movements of goods at the frontier, the French Customs Service had an excellent information system that was ideal for the national accounts. However, as noted earlier, the introduction of the single European market in 1993 abolished the obligation to declare trade flows within Europe.

In its place a quasi-exhaustive survey is carried out by the customs services of exporting and importing countries. At the European level, a significant "asymmetry" has opened up in the case of trade within the region, in that total recorded exports are now roughly 2.5% higher than total recorded imports. It has been deduced from this that certain countries must be overstating their exports and/or understating their imports. Some observers have evoked the possibility of export fraud (inflation of export declarations, since exports are not subject to VAT). While the result has been to cast doubt on this source, national accountants continue to rely on it, as it is all that is available, and despite its shortcomings it remains one of the best sources for the national accounts.

Until the first decade of the 21st century, the balance of payments data published by the Banque de France included all transactions with the rest of the world made by the commercial banks and the largest industrial firms. The compulsory collection of this data made it possible to have quasi-exhaustive coverage of all monetary transactions with the rest of the world. By then sorting these transactions by type, it was possible to provide statistics on purchases and sales of services, particularly international transport and insurance. Nowadays, in many EU-countries, this system based on cash settlements has been replaced by a direct survey among residents having transactions with the rest of the world.

The Banque de France also calculates the tourist balance, i.e., spending by French tourists abroad and by foreign tourists in France. However, also in this case, the information system has been somewhat destabilised by the ending of the compulsory declaration by banks of intra-European flows and by the introduction of the euro, which eliminated one of the sources used for the evaluation of the tourist balance – namely statistics on purchases of foreign currencies for francs (the former French national currency) and vice versa. Like the Customs Service, the Banque de France has introduced surveys making it possible to ensure the continuity of the data on which national accountants continue to rely, although they also use other sources where they are available.

This shows that it will be increasingly difficult to compile national accounts in a Europe that has become more and more unified and multinational. One day perhaps, the national accounts of each European country will become the regional accounts of the national accounts of a United Europe. But this day is a long way off. In the meantime, the present national accounts will continue to be published, most probably at the cost of a gradual deterioration in their quality, particularly in regard to transactions with the rest of the world.

Consumption expenditure by general government is measured on the basis of government accounts. These accounts are very complete and of high quality (see Chapter 9). They provide a very good picture of wages and salaries, intermediate consumption and transfers in kind. The value of the consumption of fixed capital of general government, which is an imputed component of government final consumption expenditure, is made using estimates of the stock of government capital to which depreciation rules are applied taking into account the expected lifetimes of these assets. It is obviously much more of an approximation.

The principal source for gross fixed capital formation is additions to fixed capital, minus disposals, reported by firms in their tax declarations. As we saw earlier, Insee (the French statistical office) has access to nearly all tax declarations by firms and these cover the variables required. The source is therefore a good one. However, it has its limitations in the case of intellectual property products such as software and R&D, for which firms do not follow the requirements of the national accounts.

The same source is used for changes in inventories. However, the problem of "stock appreciation" makes its use somewhat problematical.

In the case of household consumption expenditure, the source is rather indirect. For most goods the starting point is retail sales, from which are deducted, often using somewhat bold assumptions, the portion of sales that go to firms. These will be either intermediate consumption or GFCF. For other products, use is made of various corporate and government sources, such as car registrations, tax data on sales of tobacco and alcoholic beverages, sales by the EDF-GDF partially state-owned companies for gas and electricity, and sales figures for the transport companies. Relatively little use is made of Insee's survey of households' budget. As other national statistical offices, Insee has been obliged to reduce the frequency and the sample size of this survey of household income and expenditure, which is extremely costly and not very well received by the respondent households.

These various sources of information are compared with each other in the supply and use tables which reconcile the total supply of goods and services with their final and intermediate uses. This estimation mechanism is described in Chapter 10.

Exercises for Chapter 5

Exercise 1. Final uses in volume (this exercise uses the knowledge gained in Chapter 2)

The following table is the French version in billion euros at current prices, of Table 5.1 in the present Chapter. The second table shows the corresponding price indices. For the analysis of growth, why must preference be given to accounts in volume rather than at current prices?

On the basis of these two tables, calculate the table of final uses in volume at 2005 prices. The sum of final uses in volume in 2005 and 2006 is equal to GDP in volume for 2005 and 2006, but why is this not precisely the case for 2007?

In the remainder of the exercise, the assumption will be made that volumes are additive. Using this assumption, calculate domestic demand and external demand. Calculate the contribution to GDP growth made by final domestic demand and final external demand in 2006 and then in 2007.

Final uses, in billions of euros, at current prices

		2005	2006	2007
P31S14	Final consumption expenditure of households	946.12	986.59	1 030.45
P31S15	Final consumption expenditure of non-profit institutions serving households	31.57	33.44	35.48
P3S13	Final consumption expenditure of general government	408.15	421.74	435.65
P51	Gross fixed capital formation	332.32	360.38	394.62
P52	Changes in inventories	9.81	13.73	18.74
P53	Acquisitions less disposals of valuables	0.97	1.03	1.05
P6	Exports of goods and services	452.87	485.91	506.72
P7	Imports of goods and services	463.75	504.71	535.94
B1_GE	Gross domestic product (expenditure approach)	1 718.05	1 798.12	1 886.79

Prices indices of final uses (2005 = 100)

		2005	2006	2007
P31S14	Final consumption expenditure of households	100.00	102.02	104.13
P31S15	Final consumption expenditure of non-profit institutions serving households	100.00	103.69	105.63
P3S13	Final consumption expenditure of general government	100.00	101.92	103.72
P51	Gross fixed capital formation	100.00	104.32	107.43
P52	Changes in inventories	100.00	116.56	119.47
P53	Acquisitions less disposals of valuables	100.00	114.83	116.54
P6	Exports of goods and services	100.00	102.01	103.95
P7	Imports of goods and services	100.00	103.60	104.27
B1_GE	Gross domestic product (expenditure approach)	100.00	102.14	104.78

Exercise 2. True, false or choose from the list

a) Which of the following are included in household consumption expenditures: fees levied by government for the public television service; the purchase of apartments; interest paid on loans; parking fines; driving licence fees?

b) A farmer produces 300 litres of wine each year. He sells 160 litres to his neighbours and stocks 140 litres for his own consumption. Which figure should be included in household consumption: 160 litres or 300 litres?

c) Total consumption expenditure by households includes expenditure by foreign tourists in France. True or false?

d) Actual household consumption is equal to household consumption expenditure plus that of general government. True or false?

e) Actual consumption of general government is equal to its collective consumption expenditure. True or false?

f) Which of the following items of expenditure are "collective" and which are "individual": primary education; medical research; reimbursement of medicines; police and fire brigades; operating costs of pension funds; cost of free concerts in municipal parks; expenses of troops serving with United Nations forces.

g) Fixed capital formation excludes transport equipment and live cattle. True or false?

Exercise 3. Valuation of changes in inventories excluding stock appreciation

The first row of the following table shows the price of an item held in inventories in each of six sub-periods. The following rows show the quantities. Fill in the shaded cells/rows, remembering that the *correct method* consists of valuing each addition to, and withdrawal from, inventories at the price of the sub-period concerned. The *approximate method* consists of using the average price for the totality of the sub-periods and applying this to the changes in inventories expressed in quantities. The *wrong method* consists of calculating the difference between the values at the end and beginning of the whole period. Comment on the differences. Calculate the "stock appreciation".

Sub-period	1	2	3	4	5	6
Price	4	5	5	7	6	9
Quantities:						
Inventory at the beginning of the sub-period	10					
Additions to inventories during the sub-period (+)	3			1	6	3
Withdrawals from inventories during the sub-period (-)		2	7	4		
Inventory at the end of the sub-period						
Value of additions (prices x quantities)						
Value of withdrawals (prices x quantities)						
Average price over the totality of the sub-periods:						
Wrong method						
a) Value of inventory at the beginning of the period in current prices:						
b) Value of inventory at the end of the period in current prices:						
c) Difference (b) – (a), including stock appreciation:						
Correct method						
a) Total value of additions:						
b) Total value of withdrawals:						
c) Correct measurement of the changes in inventories (excluding stock appreciation):						
Approximate method						
a) Quantity at the beginning of the period:						
b) Quantity at the end of the period:						
c) Approximate measure of the change in inventories (excluding stock appreciation)						

Exercise 4. The terms of trade

Using the following tables (showing French imports and exports of goods and services at current prices and in volume), you are asked to:

a) Derive the export price index for the period 2005-12.

b) Derive the import price index for the period 2005-12.

c) From these, deduce the terms of trade for the period.

Imports and exports at current prices
billions of euro

	2005	2006	2007	2008	2009	2010	2011	2012
Imports	463.8	504.7	535.9	561.7	475.1	538.3	597.6	602.6
Exports	452.9	485.9	506.7	521.0	440.7	494.5	538.3	557.6

Imports and exports in volume
billions of euro

	2005	2006	2007	2008	2009	2010	2011	2012
Imports	463.8	487.2	514.0	518.7	468.7	510.5	536.7	531.0
Exports	452.9	476.3	487.5	485.9	427.1	467.6	492.8	504.6

Source: Insee Databases (2013): Statistical indices and series: Macroeconomic Database: National Accounts *www.bdm.insee.fr/bdm2/index?request_locale=en*.

The solutions to these exercises are available at:
http://dx.doi.org/10.1787/9789264214637-23-en

Chapter 6

The household account

This chapter defines the three key indicators in the household account: household final consumption expenditure, household disposable income, and saving. It next looks at how these three indicators are identified and presented in the household sector accounts. Finally, the chapter considers an alternative way to measure household disposable income and consumption proposed by SNA 2008.

A **household** is a group of people collectively taking responsibility to feed and house themselves. A household can consist of a single person or of two or more people living under the same roof, these people generally being linked by family ties. However, there are also "institutional households" consisting of, for example, members of the armed forces living in a barracks or on board a ship, people detained in prison, or nuns living in a convent. National accounts make no distinction between these different categories of "household", and they are all lumped together in what is known as the *"household sector"*, carrying the code S14. In practice, however, the bulk of the household sector consists of families.

The other sectors described in the national accounts – *corporations, general government* and *non-profit institutions* – pursue a single goal, namely the production of goods and services. For households, on the other hand, things are more complicated. Members of a household, if they are employed, earn an income that they use to buy everyday goods and services or for investing in financial assets. However, members of a household can also, as is frequently the case, run a family business such as a shop, a cafe, a taxi firm or a farm. In the national accounts, these various enterprises are described by the term *unincorporated enterprises*; they have no shareholders and their responsibility is not limited in the case of payment default (see Chapter 7 on the business sector). Households also produce housing services (real or imputed).

As a consequence, the accounts of the household sector cover two quite different functions: the output of goods and services, on the one hand, and the allocation of an income to consumption and to saving, on the other. It is partly for statistical reasons that no distinction is made between these two functions. It is in fact generally possible to separate out transactions (relating to production, intermediate consumption, compensation and taxes on production) between "pure" households and unincorporated enterprises. Indeed, in certain countries (France, United States), a partial account of this kind is published for unincorporated enterprises. Nevertheless, it is impossible in practice to distinguish other transactions, meaning that there are no complete accounts for unincorporated enterprises nor are there complete accounts for "pure" households.

Certain other OECD countries publish accounts bringing together households and non-profit institutions serving households (NPISHs). This aggregation is based on the notion that, because these institutions are largely financed by households and because their purpose is to serve households, their accounts can be assimilated to those of households. Moreover, the NPISHs constitute a small sector, and their inclusion in the household account makes little difference to the final result. In the end, even though the international system of national accounts recommends that NPISHs should be shown separately from households, in practice users of national accounts who want to make international comparisons will often have to compare "households + NPISHs" (i.e., S14 + S15) rather than the S14 sector alone.

For economists, the "consumer" function of the household sector is of particular interest in that economic growth is influenced directly and immediately by growth in *household final consumption expenditure*, which in turn is determined by *household disposable income* and by the way in which this income is divided between consumption and *saving*. The expressions in italics in this last sentence identify the three key indicators in the household account that we shall be defining in this chapter.

1. The three key indicators in the household account

Table 6.1. shows, as percentages of GDP, the corresponding expenditure items in the case of Japan, the main ones being: *household final consumption expenditure*; *government final consumption expenditure*; *gross capital formation*; and, lastly, *exports*. An increase or decrease in GDP can be a consequence of variations in one or other of these components. In describing the evolution in the Japanese economy, economists have at various times been able to say that growth has been "driven by exports", "driven" or "slowed down" by consumption, or even sometimes that it was influenced or not by a combination of these factors. Table 6.1 nevertheless clearly brings out the predominant role played by household final consumption expenditure. Given that this expenditure contributes around 60% of GDP, a change in this aggregate is bound to have a major influence on GDP growth.

Obviously, all kinds of reasons may prompt a household to increase or reduce its consumption. In the first place, there are the variations in income, or the realisation of holding gains or losses on financial or real estate investments. However, the level of consumption is also influenced by the way in which the household sees its immediate future: likelihood of an increase or decrease in income; perception of the risk of unemployment; expectations regarding inflation. The influence of consumer behaviour on GDP leads economists to keep a close eye on indicators of "household morale" derived from opinion surveys in which consumers are asked questions such as whether they have confidence in the future, whether they expect to make major purchases soon and whether they think their financial situation has improved or deteriorated over the recent past.

Table 6.1. **Japan: final uses**
As a percentage of GDP

Code		2010	2011	2012
B1_G	Gross domestic product	100.0	100.0	100.0
P31S14	Final consumption expenditure of households	58.0	59.1	59.5
P31S15	Final consumption expenditure of non-profit institutions serving households	1.2	1.4	1.5
P3S13	Final consumption expenditure of general government	19.7	20.4	20.5
P5	Gross capital formation	19.8	20.0	20.6
P6	Exports of goods and services	15.2	15.1	14.7
P7	(-) Imports of goods and services	14.0	16.1	16.6

Source: OECD (2013), "Aggregate National Accounts: Gross domestic product", OECD National Accounts Statistics (database), *http://dx.doi.org/10.1787/data-00001-en.*

StatLink ▄▇▉▊ *http://dx.doi.org/10.1787/888933143862*

A second notable feature is the importance of gross capital formation. A substantial part of this is directly related to households, since it consists of purchases of housing, which are counted as household GFCF (gross fixed capital formation). This investment is partly financed by household saving.

Household **saving**, the second key indicator, accounts for a large proportion (more than 50%) of total saving in the OECD economies. Table 6.2 shows for Japan the proportion of total saving originating with households (and NPISHs). This proportion has already been traditionally high in Japan but reached about 75% in 2010. This reflects a post crisis situation where the deficit (negative saving) of the government has reached unprecedented levels, as well as the surplus (positive saving) of corporations. The sums saved by households are available to finance the gross fixed capital formation of other sectors (machinery, factories, transport equipment, roads, railways, communication networks, etc.) and also, in part, the GFCF of households themselves (purchases of housing). Since the end of World War II, there has been a noticeable causal link between the level of household saving and the size of the rise in GDP.

The United States is an exception. Since the end of World War II, the United States household saving ratio has been relatively low, in contrast to the high GFCF rate that has enabled GDP to grow more or less constantly throughout this period. This situation is explained by the powerful attraction the American economy holds for foreign investors. In other words, the United States has been able to finance its investment with the savings of foreign households.

At the microeconomic level, saving is also important in that it provides families with financial security in the event of job loss or illness, and it also

Table 6.2. **Japan: Breakdown of total net saving in the domestic economy by sector**

As a percentage of total net saving

		1980	1990	2000	2010
B8N-S1	Total economy	100.0	100.0	100.0	100.0
B8N-S11_S12	Corporations	28.3	14.7	61.3	504.9
B8N-S13	General government	10.1	34.8	-29.0	-479.7
B8N-S14_S15	Households and NPISHs	61.5	50.5	67.7	74.8

Source: OECD (2013), "Detailed National Accounts: Non-financial accounts by sectors, annual", OECD National Accounts Statistics (database), doi: *http://dx.doi.org/10.1787/data-00034-en*.

StatLink ᵐˢᵖ *http://dx.doi.org/10.1787/888933143871*

covers part of the retirement pension. The social security systems that had previously managed to provide adequate protection against these risks are now, because of the ageing of the population, in a difficult financial situation in many OECD countries. In recent years, OECD economists in the various Economic Surveys of countries have been recommending that the authorities offer incentives to households to save more and thus finance more of their retirement requirements themselves.

The third key indicator, **household disposable income,** is the sum of *household final consumption expenditure* and *saving*. As we have seen, rises in these two components are desirable for several reasons: an increase in household final consumption expenditure stimulates GDP growth, while an increase in saving permits the partial financing of investment and at the same time eases the burden on the social security system. It seems evident that this result can only be achieved if household income increases, and this increase is largely a function of the economy's capacity to achieve productivity gains through more efficient use of the labour and capital factors of production.

2. The household sector accounts

These three indicators are explicitly identified in the household sector accounts. It is essential to bear in mind that from now on in this textbook, these accounts and these indicators are expressed at current prices and not in volume.

The sequence of accounts for households is divided into "non-financial" and "financial" accounts. The financial accounts are examined in Chapter 8. At this stage, we shall look only at the sequence of non-financial accounts, starting with the *production account* and ending with the *capital account*. The accounts we shall show here are in T-account form, the "T" referring to their aspect. This is in fact the presentation adopted by most households in keeping track of their receipts and expenditure:

Expenditure	Receipts
1.	a)
2.	b)
3., etc.	c) Etc.

In the national accounts, the receipts are known as "*resources*" and are set out in the right-hand column. Expenditure is known as *use* and is set out in the left-hand column. The final item in the *uses* column is a "balancing item". This is the amount needed to bring *uses* and *resources* into balance. The balancing items of the various accounts (*value added, operating surplus, disposable income, saving* and *net lending/net borrowing*) are particularly interesting aggregates for the purpose of analysis. In the presentation of accounts adopted hereafter, these balancing items are shown in bold type.

Note that the only way to fully understand what is contained in any given balancing item is to examine the sequence of accounts leading up to it. For example, in order to reply to the question "what is household saving?" it is imperative to examine the series of items that have been added to, or deducted, from the value of the initial item in the sequence of accounts. This notion will become clearer as we progress with the examination of the household sector accounts.

To give an idea of the relative importance of the various items, we have chosen the example of the accounts of Italian households in 2012 (in billion euros, at current prices). The tables give the code of each transaction (for example, P1 for output). These are the codes used in international manuals (SNA 2008 and ESA 2010).

*The initial letter of each code is based on "Eurospeak" terminology: "**P**" indicates products; "**D**" redistribution transactions; "**F**" financial transactions; "**B**" balancing items; and "**K**" (for the German word "Kapital") indicates capital accumulation items. These short and precisely defined codes are very useful.*

The production account

The first account in the sequence is the *production account*. This very summary account initially consists of three items: *output, intermediate consumption* and the first balancing item, *gross value added*, which is the difference between the other two items. In the first table below, we have used the combined grouping "Households plus NPISHs" to illustrate the fact that certain countries publish accounts for these two sectors only in aggregate. A possible variation is the inclusion of "net value added", which is equal to gross value added minus the consumption of fixed capital.

Table 6.3. **Italy: Production account for households and NPISHs (S14 + S15)**
Billion euros, 2012

Uses		Resources	
P2. Intermediate consumption	136.6	P1. Output	543.7
B1G. Gross value added	407.1		
K1. Consumption of fixed capital	89.6		
B1N. Net value added	317.5		

Source: I.stat Statistics (2013): National Accounts: Annual sector accounts, http://dati.istat.it/
Index.aspx?DataSetCode=DCCN_SEQCONTIASA&Lang=.

StatLink ━━ http://dx.doi.org/10.1787/888933143886

If one excludes the NPISHs and looks at the production account of households on their own (S14), the following production account is obtained. It can be verified, by difference, that the share of NPISHs is very small, and therefore they will be ignored from now on.

Table 6.4. **Italy: Production account for households (S14)**
Billion euros, 2012

Uses		Resources	
P2. Intermediate consumption	133.4	P1. Output	536.2
B1G. Gross value added	402.9		
K1P1. Consumption of fixed capital	89.3		
B1N. Net value added	313.6		

Source: I.stat Statistics (2013): National Accounts: Annual sector accounts, http://dati.istat.it/
Index.aspx?DataSetCode=DCCN_SEQCONTIASA&Lang=.

StatLink ━━ http://dx.doi.org/10.1787/888933143896

The headings in this production account for households show the activities of unincorporated enterprises: farms, retail outlets, taxi firms, beauty parlours, etc. But they also include own-account production of goods by households, and the housing services "produced" by people who rent accommodation to others, or who own their accommodation (apartments or houses). As a consequence, the *output* item on the right hand side of the account includes the imputed rents of these "homeowner-occupiers", while the intermediate consumption in the left hand side includes (in addition to the intermediate consumption of unincorporated enterprises) the expenditure these owners have to make for the upkeep of their accommodation.

Generation of income account

The next account in the sequence is the *generation of income account*, which shows how the value added is distributed between remuneration of the labour and capital factors of production.

It starts by showing on the right-hand side, in the resources column, the balancing item from the previous account, in this case, the net value added.

Table 6.5. **Italy: Generation of income account for households (S14)**
Billion euros, 2012

Uses		Resources	
D1. Compensation of employees	50.1	**B1N. Net value added**	313.6
D11. Wages and salaries	40.9		
D12. Employers' social contributions	9.2		
D2. Taxes on production and importas, payable	20.7		
D3. (-) Subsidies, receivable	3.8		
B2N. Operating surplus, net	72.9		
B3N. Mixed income, net	173.7		

Source: I.stat Statistics (2013): National Accounts: Annual sector accounts, *http://dati.istat.it/Index.aspx?DataSetCode=DCCN_SEQCONTIASA&Lang=.*

StatLink ⬛🔗 *http://dx.doi.org/10.1787/888933143907*

The *uses* column contains two main items: *"compensation of employees"* and *"net taxes on production"*. When the value of these is deducted from *value added*, we have two balancing items, namely the **net operating surplus** and the **net mixed income**.

The *compensation of employees* item in this case covers only the employees of the unincorporated enterprises. Compensation consists of wages and salaries in cash, income in kind (free board and lodging, for instance) and the social contributions paid by the owners of unincorporated enterprises on behalf of their employees. It can therefore be seen that compensation of employees is not merely wages and salaries but represents the total cost of labour.

The *net taxes on production* item consists of the taxes payable for the ownership or utilisation of factors of production (labour and capital) – for example, the property taxes paid by owners of dwellings. The word "net" signifies that subsidies on production have been deducted. The subsidies obviously result in an increase in the size of the balancing items, *mixed income* and *operating surplus*. In the *generation of income account* for households, the subsidies are mainly those paid to farmers.

For the financial and non-financial corporate sectors, the balancing item of the account consists entirely of the **net operating surplus**, which measures the remuneration of the capital used in the production process or, in other words, the principal measure of "profit" in the national accounts (see Chapter 7). However, the situation is more complicated for the unincorporated enterprises sector, for which it is often impossible to separate out the remuneration of capital and the remuneration of labour. Take the example of a family retail business or a family taxi firm: once the value added has been reduced by the compensation of employees and by the net taxes on production, what remains is both the remuneration of the capital invested (in this case, the premises, equipment and stock or the vehicles) and also the remuneration of the work done by the owners of the enterprises and their families. Unlike the owners of financial and non-financial corporations, the owners of family firms are not obligated to show in their balance sheet the value of the fixed capital used – and it would in fact be virtually impossible to force them to do so. A taxi can be used as a family car when not needed for professional purposes, just as business premises can also provide accommodation for the family.

This explains why, when it is not possible to distinguish between income from capital and income from labour, the remuneration is described as "mixed" and the balancing item in the *production account* is entitled **net mixed income**. This is what we find recorded as EUR 173.7 billion in the above *generation of income account*. However, there is one case in which there is no doubt that what we have is income from capital and is therefore a balancing item that can be called **operating surplus, net**. This is the activity imputed to homeowner-occupiers consisting of providing housing services to themselves as occupiers of the accommodation concerned. This accounts for the bulk of the EUR 72.9 billion shown above.

Within mixed income, macroeconomists sometimes need to clearly distinguish between remuneration of the capital used in production and remuneration of the labour used in production. There exist at least two methods for doing this (see section "Going further: the breakdown of gross mixed income").

Distribution of primary income account

The next account in the sequence is the *distribution of primary income account*. "Primary" income means the income generated by a production process itself or by a closely related process. By contrast, "secondary" income consists of money transferred to, or from, households without being related to a productive activity.

Table 6.6. **Italy: Primary income account for households (S14)**
Billion euros, 2012

Uses		Resources	
D4. Property income	15.0	**B2N. Operating surplus, net**	72.9
D41. Interest	10.6	**B3N. Mixed income, net**	173.7
D45. Rents	4.4	D1. Compensation of employees	672.6
		D11. Wages and salaries	490.8
		D12. Employers' social contribution	181.8
		D4. Property income	196.8
		D41. Interest	52.1
		D42. Distributed income of corporations	124.6
		D43. Reinvested earnings on FDI	0.0
		D44. Property income attributed to policy insurance holders	17.9
B5N. Balance of primary incomes, net	1 100.9	D45. Rents	2.1

Source: I.stat Statistics (2013): National Accounts: Annual sector accounts, *http://dati.istat.it/Index.aspx?DataSetCode=DCCN_SEQCONTIASA&Lang=.*

StatLink ⟨᠍᠍⟩ *http://dx.doi.org/10.1787/888933143916*

Starting as usual on the side of resources, we have at the top of the column the balancing item from the previous account, **net mixed income/net operating surplus**.

Under resources, the *compensation of employees* item is much larger than the corresponding item in the previous account. This is because in this case it covers the compensation received by all employees in all firms, in general government or in non-profit institutions – and not merely those in unincorporated enterprises. This is the largest item of household income. As seen earlier, compensation of employees represents the total cost of labour and includes the social contributions paid by employers on behalf of their employees and even the "imputed" contributions. It may seem strange to record social contributions as being received by households. To understand the reasons, the reader is referred to the section "Going further: actual and imputed social contributions".

The "interest" item (D41) in the resources column for households includes the interest received on households' financial investments. The item D42 corresponds to the dividends paid by companies to households and to the "withdrawals from income of quasi-corporations" (D422) by households. This latter item is in principle reserved for recording payments to the owners of units known as "quasi-corporations", which are not corporations in the legal sense (and therefore pay no dividends in the legal sense, either) but which have similarities with corporations. This item is normally very small because quasi-corporations are fairly rare. However, the Italian national accounts are unusual, in that unincorporated enterprises with more than five employees are considered as "quasi-corporations" and are therefore classified in the corporate sector. Item D422 in the Italian case therefore refers to the gross mixed income of a very substantial group of small individual enterprises that in other countries are classified in the household account.*

Item D44 consists of imputed interest received by households on their life insurance policies, even though (unlike the interest earned on bonds or savings accounts) they are not able to use the interest freely. The section "Going further: insurance" explains the way in which life insurance and other types of insurance are treated. Finally, item D45 is composed of rents received for land or sub-soil assets (deposits of coal or other ores, for example). If the owners of this land or these deposits decide to allow them to be used by others in a production process, they are regarded as beneficiaries of a primary income. On the other hand, rents received for making a dwelling available (or for the temporary use of some other type of fixed capital, such as personal goods or vehicle) are considered as payments for the purchase of services. Therefore, they are included as output in the *production account*, and do not appear in item D45.

The *uses* column of the account includes item D4 "property income" paid by households. Note that the *interest* sub-item includes both the interest paid by households when they take out consumer or housing loans and the interest paid by unincorporated enterprises on their borrowings, notably for the acquisition of machinery or premises.

When the uses are subtracted from the resources, the result is the next balancing item: **balance of primary incomes**. This item is then carried to the top of the resources column in the fourth account, entitled *secondary distribution of income account*.

Secondary distribution of income account

The *secondary distribution of income* account traces the various transfers that take place subsequent to the distribution of primary income, with these transfers mainly aimed at correcting social inequalities. One could equally call this the *"redistribution account"*. The most important of these transfers result when government policies redistribute income from well-off households to poorer households, but the transfers appearing in this account can also include private initiatives, notably gifts to charities and repatriation of funds by immigrant workers from poorer countries to their families.

The transfers recorded here are called "current" (as opposed to "capital" transfers), either because they are taken out of income (and not out of capital) or because the beneficiaries regard them as part of current income.

---

* The same is true for Germany. See Chapter 3 for consequences on the comparability of profit rates.

Table 6.7. **Italy: Secondary distribution of income account for households (S14)**

Billion euros, 2012

Uses		Resources	
D5. Current taxes on income, wealth, etc.	199.7	**B5N. Balance of primary incomes, net**	1 100.9
D61. Social contributions	252.3	D61. Social contributions	2.5
D6111. Employers' actual social contributions	167.5	D62. Social benefits other than social transfers in kind	345.1
D6112. Employees' social contributions	40.4	D7. Other current transfers	25.9
D6113. Social contributions by self- and non-employed persons	30.1	D72. Non-life insurance claims	17.6
D612. Imputed social contributions	14.3	D75. Miscellaneous current transfers	8.3
D62. Social benefits other than social transfers in kind	1.9		
D7. Other current transfers	40.2		
D71. Net non-life insurance premiums	16.7		
D75. Miscellaneous current transfers	23.4		
= **B6N. Disposable income, net**	980.4		
+ K1. Consumption of fixed capital	89.3		
B6G. Disposable income, gross	1 069.7		

Source: I.stat Statistics (2013): National Accounts: Annual sector accounts, *http://dati.istat.it/ Index.aspx?DataSetCode=DCCN_SEQCONTIASA&Lang=.*

StatLink ᵃᵐˢᵖ *http://dx.doi.org/10.1787/888933143920*

The third item in the resources column is D62 *Social benefits other than social transfers in kind*. These are current social transfers benefiting households (retirement pensions, unemployment allowances, family and maternity allowances, sick-leave per diem allowances). Note that these transfers include neither the reimbursement of medicines and medical services nor housing allowances, which are considered as social transfers in kind and recorded in a different account as part of adjusted disposable income. We shall return to this latter concept at the end of the chapter.

Social benefits (D62) break down into "social insurance benefits" and "social assistance benefits". Social insurance benefits are paid out by social security plans organised by government and by private pension plans in return for prior contributions. Social assistance benefits may also meet the same types of needs as the social security benefits, but the recipients have not paid contributions, and these benefits are not provided as a matter of right. Certain subsistence allowances paid to asylum-seekers or minimum incomes provided to very poor people are examples of social assistance benefits.

The final two items in the resources column of this account fall under the heading *other current transfers*. These transfers are of two types: settlements of accident insurance claims by households (fire, theft, road accidents, etc.) and miscellaneous current transfers (money sent by relatives living abroad, grants by non-profit institutions to handicapped people or to disadvantaged families, aid given by the government to households that are victims of floods or other natural catastrophes).

In the uses column of this account, the first item is titled *D5 current taxes on income and wealth*. Current taxes on income include personal income tax and taxes paid on the "mixed income" of unincorporated enterprises. Current taxes on wealth cover the regular tax payments (usually annual) paid on household net wealth (in the French case, for example, the *"impôt de solidarité sur la fortune"*). Note that inheritance taxes are not included, being exceptional payments and therefore treated as capital transfers.

The next item in the uses column is titled *social contributions*. As explained in the section at the end of the chapter ("Going further: actual and imputed social contributions"), this item covers the contributions to a social security fund paid by employers on behalf of their employees, the contributions paid by the employees themselves, the imputed social contributions and the contributions paid by the owners of unincorporated enterprises (also called "self-employed").

The last item in the uses column is *other current transfers*. The net non-life insurance premiums are the premiums paid on non-life insurance policies, minus the estimated remuneration that the insured pay for the management services of the insurance company (for more details, see the box "insurance" at end of this chapter). The *miscellaneous current transfers* item covers the financial transfers made by migrant workers to their families in their home countries, gifts to non-profit institutions and parking and other fines.

The difference between uses and resources is equal to **net disposable income (NDI)**, a key indicator that represents the amount left at the disposal of households for either consumption or saving, over and above the replacement of the existing capital stock. It is called "net" because the amounts needed for the replacement of capital assets (dwellings and equipment of unincorporated enterprises) have already been deducted. However, certain analysts prefer to use the *gross disposable income* (GDI), which is equal to the previous figure plus the consumption of fixed capital. One reason is because there is uncertainty in the calculation of consumption of fixed capital and, in particular, on the international comparability of this calculation. Another reason to prefer GDI is that it can be better analysed than NDI in terms of purchasing power and correlated to final consumption in volume. The *purchasing power of GDI* is equal to GDI deflated by the price index of household consumption expenditure. If the purchasing power of GDI increases, this means that GDI is rising faster than inflation, and therefore there is a chance that households will consume more in real terms.

Another thing to note about NDI is that this household income aggregate includes sub-items that are already earmarked for particular uses and are therefore not open to a trade-off by households between consumption and saving. For example:

● The *output* item in the *production account* includes agricultural products held back by their producers for their own consumption and the imputed rents of homeowner-occupiers. As a result, the value added derived from these activities, which eventually becomes an element in disposable income, can clearly not be allocated to uses other than the consumption of the farm products and of housing services, respectively. In the OECD countries, own-account consumption of agricultural products is fairly negligible, but the imputed rents represent very substantial sums.

● The *compensation of employees* item in the *primary income distribution account* includes income in kind, but this income has already been "spent" on the corresponding goods and services provided to the employees.

● One part of the *property income interest* (D41) in the *Primary income distribution account* covers imputed interest on the reserves managed by the non-life insurance companies on behalf of policy holders. This imputed interest is earmarked as part of consumption of services provided by the non-life insurance companies.

The final point to note about NDI is that the concept of disposable income used in the national accounts is different from the theoretical concept as defined by certain economists (see "Income in national accounts and economic theory" in Going further). In particular, it does not include the holding gains or losses on shares or on real estate.

Use of disposable income account

The balancing item **net disposable income** is shown at the top of the resources column in the following account, the *use of disposable income account*.

Table 6.8. **Italy: Use of income account for households (S14)**

Billion euros, 2012

Uses		Resources	
P3. Final consumption expenditure	947.1	**B6N. Disposable income, net**	980.4
D8. Adjustment for the change in pension entitlements	0.6	D8. Adjustment for the change in pension entitlements	3.4
B8N. Net saving	36.2		

Source: I.stat Statistics (2013): National Accounts: Annual sector accounts, *http://dati.istat.it/ Index.aspx?DataSetCode=DCCN_SEQCONTIASA&Lang=.*

StatLink 🔗 *http://dx.doi.org/10.1787/888933143939*

The adjustment required in the second item of the resources column (coded D8) is necessary because of the way contributions paid to pension funds, as well as the pensions paid out by these funds, are treated in the *secondary distribution of income account*. They are in fact assimilated as contributions to, and benefits from, the social security system, even though they should be treated in the same way as transactions with the life insurance companies. This special treatment has been adopted because contributions paid to pension funds (and the pensions paid out by these funds) are generally regarded by households as similar to the contributions paid to social security funds and the benefits paid by these funds. If one regards them as having the same impact on consumer behaviour, it seems logical to apply the same treatment. However, transactions with pension funds are also recorded in the financial accounts (see Chapter 8). Therefore, it is necessary to make an adjustment in the non-financial account so that the value of the balancing item *(saving)* carried forward into the financial accounts is correct. The adjustment equals the change in pension entitlements, thus its name. When calculating the household saving ratio, it is important to recall that item D8 should be added to the denominator of this ratio (disposable income) since it is included in the numerator (saving).

The uses column within the "use of disposable income" account contains only two important items, namely *final consumption expenditure* and the balancing item **net saving**. A complete definition of household final consumption expenditure was already given in Chapter 5, but it is worthwhile recalling that household final consumption expenditure consists mainly of purchases of everyday goods and services (clothing, food, durable consumer goods, rents, transport, personal services, etc.) *plus*:

● the imputed rents "paid" by homeowner-occupiers;

● the estimated value of in-household output of goods, especially crops and livestock consumed by households owning an agricultural holding;

● the estimated value of goods and services received by employees by way of remuneration in kind;

On the other hand, household final consumption expenditure does not include:

● purchases of housing – dwellings. They are fixed assets used to produce the provision of housing services: they are therefore recorded in the capital account (GFCF) and are not considered consumption;

● purchases of other types of buildings and equipment used mainly for production by family enterprises are also GFCF (agricultural equipment, business premises, taxis, goods vehicles, etc.);

- purchases by family firms of intermediate consumption goods (seeds and fertilisers in the case of farmers, paint and brushes in the case of decorators, fuels and maintenance for taxi drivers, etc.) are intermediate consumption and not final consumption;

- purchases (less sales) of "valuables" – including gold coins, antiques, rare stamps and works of art – purchased to serve as "stores of value", are regarded as investments by the purchasers who hope their value will increase over time (or, at the very least, not diminish).

The balancing item, **net saving**, is the difference between NDI and consumption. This is our third key indicator. Because it is obtained as the difference between two very large aggregates, it is almost invariably tainted by errors. Even a relatively small adjustment in one or the other of the two contributing aggregates – disposable income and household final consumption expenditure – automatically leads to a relatively substantial adjustment in the balance. As a consequence, it is necessary to be wary of the initial published estimates of saving, as these will certainly be substantially readjusted in the following two or three years.

In practice, analysts are not interested in the level of household saving as much as in the household saving ratio, which is the ratio of household saving to disposable income (to which is added households' receipts of adjustment D8). For the purpose of international comparison, it is essential to use the same definitions. The method preferred by the OECD is to take the *net* saving ratio. The following table shows the household saving ratio in Italy and in other industrialised countries in recent years.

Table 6.9. **Net household saving ratio**

As percentage of disposable income

	2006	2007	2008	2009	2010	2011	2012
France	11.2	11.7	11.7	12.6	12.1	12.2	
Germany	10.8	11.0	11.5	10.9	10.9	10.4	10.3
Italy	9.5	8.9	8.5	7.1	4.9	4.3	3.6
Japan	1.3	1.1	0.6	2.3	2.1	2.3	
United States	3.5	3.2	5.2	6.4	5.9	5.9	5.8

Source: OECD (2014), "Detailed National Accounts: Non-financial accounts by sectors, annual", OECD National Accounts Statistics (database).

StatLink ⬛🖻🖥 *http://dx.doi.org/10.1787/888933143946*

Capital account

The balancing item **net saving** is forwarded to the top of the resources column in the *capital accumulation account*, which is the last non-financial account in the sequence. Because of the presence of "gross fixed capital formation" under the uses, it is preferable that this account be on a gross basis. This is why we have also included **gross saving** under resources, this aggregate being equal to net saving plus consumption of fixed capital.

Table 6.10. **Italy: Capital accumulation account for households (S14)**
Billion euros, 2012

Uses		Resources	
P51. Gross fixed capital formation	102.0	**B8N. Net saving**	36.2
P52. Changes in inventories	0.8	K1. Consumption of fixed capital	89.3
P53. Acquisitions less disposals of valuables	2.3	**B8. Gross saving**	125.5
K2. Acquisitions less disposals of non-produced non-financial assets	0.1	D9. Net capital transfers received	-0.1
B9. Net lending (+)/Net borrowing (-)	20.1		

Source: I.stat Statistics (2013): National Accounts: Annual sector accounts, *http://dati.istat.it/ Index.aspx?DataSetCode=DCCN_SEQCONTIASA&Lang=.*

StatLink 🔗 *http://dx.doi.org/10.1787/888933143956*

The only other item in the resources column is *D9 net capital transfers received*. The use of the word "net" refers to the fact that capital transfers paid have been deducted from the capital transfers received. The receipts include investment aids. The payments mainly consist of inheritance tax. In some countries, capital transfers received also include an adjustment between taxes and social contributions due and taxes and social contributions paid.

Gross saving is used to acquire financial and non-financial assets. The first four items in the uses column correspond to the acquisition of non-financial assets. The first of these, *gross fixed capital formation*, includes purchases of housing or of equipment (by unincorporated enterprises) and the planting of orchards, vineyards or forests, among other things. The *change in inventories* item covers stocks of finished products and intermediate consumption goods held by unincorporated enterprises. *Valuables* are objects such as precious metals, antiques and works of art purchased to serve as stores of value, and their purchase is considered as "investment", being often made with the intent to resell. The *non-produced non-financial assets* cover patents, copyrights, leaseholds and other assignable contracts entitling the holder to use land, buildings or mineral deposits.

The balancing item **B9 Net lending(+)/net borrowing(–)** is the amount available for the purchase of financial assets (for example, to be deposited in a savings account) or for debt repayment (paying off a car loan or a house mortgage, for example) and is almost always positive for the household sector as a whole. However, in some cases, such as Ireland and Spain in the recent years, households have become temporarily net borrowers, because of the housing boom. The "net lending" is also sometimes called "financial saving". Some countries publish a "financial saving ratio", which is equal to net lending divided by gross disposable income of households (and multiplied by 100).

3. An alternative way to measure household disposable income and consumption

The international system of national accounts SNA 2008 proposes an alternative method of measuring household disposable income and consumption that takes into account spending by general government and NPISHs for the benefit of households.

The underlying idea is that final consumption expenditure by general government and by NPISHs finances are quite different categories of services: collective services intended to benefit society as a whole, and services used by members of household on an individual basis. Examples of *collective services* are defence, law and order, tax collection, control of public spending, supervision of air quality and water pollution, drafting and promulgation of legislation, and public management in general. In theory, it is society as a whole that benefits from these services, and it is impossible to calculate the extent to which an individual household uses them.

The "individual services" supplied by general government include healthcare, education, social services, housing services, recreational and cultural services. In these cases, it is possible in principle to calculate the extent to which any individual household makes use of them. Households use these services to differing degrees, depending on their situation. For example, childless households will not make great use of education services, in contrast to families with numerous children. Similarly, the consumption of healthcare services depends on the frequency with which members of a household fall ill.

SNA 2008 includes these individual services, along with other transfers, in an alternative household income account titled *redistribution of income in kind account*. In this account, they are recorded in the resources column under the title *social transfers in kind*.

Social transfers in kind include the expenditure by general government and NPISHs on the provision of the various individual services mentioned above (healthcare, education, etc.), but also the reimbursement of purchases of goods and services, such as medical consultations and medicines, as well as housing allowances. The balancing item **net adjusted disposable income** is equal to disposable income, as usually measured, plus the social transfers in kind.

Table 6.11. **Italy: Redistribution of income in kind for households (S14)**

Billion euros, 2012

Uses		Resources	
		B6N. Net disposable income	980.4
B7N. Net adjusted disposable income	1 173.3	D63. Social transfers in kind	192.8

Source: I.stat Statistics (2013): National Accounts: Annual sector accounts, *http://dati.istat.it/ Index.aspx?DataSetCode=DCCN_SEQCONTIASA&Lang=.*

StatLink 📊 *http://dx.doi.org/10.1787/888933143962*

Given the existence of this alternative method of measuring disposable income, it was only logical that a new account be created illustrating the use of this new measure of income. This new account is called the *use of adjusted disposable income account.*

Table 6.12. **Italy: Use of adjusted disposable income account for households (S14)**

Billion euros, 2012

Uses		Resources	
P41. Actual individual consumption	1 139.9	**B7N. Net adjusted disposable income**	1 173.3
D8. Adjustment for the change in pension entitlements	0.6	D8. Adjustment for the change in pension entitlements	3.4
B8N. Net saving	36.2		

Source: I.stat Statistics (2013): National Accounts: Annual sector accounts, *http://dati.istat.it/ Index.aspx?DataSetCode=DCCN_SEQCONTIASA&Lang=.*

StatLink 📊 *http://dx.doi.org/10.1787/888933143974*

The first item in the uses column is *actual individual consumption*. Note that there is now no mention of "expenditure". Actual individual consumption measures the value of the goods and services actually consumed by households, including the goods and services financed by general government or NPISHs. This additional value is equal to the part of consumption of general government and NPISHs that can be considered "individual" as described in previous chapters.

It is important to note that the balancing item of this alternative account, **net saving**, remains strictly identical to the balancing item in the traditional presentation of the household accounts. This is because *adjusted disposable income* and *actual final consumption* have both been increased by the same amount (the value of social transfers in kind) so that the difference between the two, i.e., **saving**, remains unchanged. As mentioned in Chapter 3, the concepts of *adjusted disposable income* and *actual individual consumption* are mainly of interest in international comparisons.

References

I.stat Statistics (2013), National Accounts: Annual sector accounts, *http://dati.istat.it/ Index.aspx?DataSetCode=DCCN_SEQCONTIASA&Lang=*.

OECD (2013), "Aggregate National Accounts: Gross domestic product", OECD National Accounts Statistics (database), *http://dx.doi.org/10.1787/data-00001-en*.

OECD (2014), "Detailed National Accounts: Non-financial accounts by sectors, annual", OECD National Accounts Statistics (database), doi: *http://dx.doi.org/10.1787/data-00034-en*.

System of National Accounts 2008, European Commission, International Monetary Fund, Organisation for Economic Co-operation and Development, United Nations, World Bank, New York, 2009, *http://unstats.un.org/unsd/nationalaccount/docs/ SNA2008.pdf*.

Key points

- A household is a group of people who collectively take responsibility for feeding and housing themselves. A household can consist of a single person or two or more people living under the same roof, these people generally being linked by family ties.

- The principal function of the household sector is consumption, but it also has a productive function.

- The output of the household sector includes that of unincorporated enterprises and households producing housing services for themselves (homeowner-occupiers).

- "Gross disposable income" and "net disposable income" (GDI and NDI) are the most important balances for analysing the situation of households, measuring the sum available for consumption and saving.

- Changes in the purchasing power of gross disposable income are the main factor determining the change in the volume of goods and services consumed by households.

- Saving is equal to disposable income minus consumption expenditure; or, alternatively, adjusted disposable income minus actual individual consumption. Financial saving is the same thing as the net lending of households.

- The gross saving ratio is equal to gross saving divided by GDI (plus item D8). The net saving rate is equal to net saving divided by net disposable income (plus item D8).

- Social transfers in kind are equal to the "individual" consumption of general government and the NPISHs.

Going further

The breakdown of gross mixed income

Economists rely on national accounts to measure changes in the share of value added between wages and profits and, also, to measure changes in productivity over time and among countries (see introduction to Chapter 4). Economists find it hard to make their analyses unless they are able to distinguish in the national accounts between the returns to these two factors of production both for unincorporated enterprises as well as for corporations. This is why they usually try to break mixed income down into its two components: the implicit salary of the owner(s) and the return to capital.

There are two ways of doing this for unincorporated enterprises. The first consists of estimating the compensation of employees and of family helpers in the case of unincorporated enterprises. The return to capital is then the difference between the mixed income and this figure. The second method consists of estimating the return to capital and assuming that the rest of mixed income is the return to labour. The first method is generally based on the number of independent workers as reported in surveys of family employees or in the population census, on the assumption that they receive the same average compensation as dependent workers employed in similar activities. The second method takes as its starting point an estimate of the stock of fixed capital used by unincorporated enterprises, sometimes adjusting this stock downward to allow for the fact that this capital can also be used for private purposes. The observed average rates of return for similar assets in corporate enterprises are then applied to the assets of unincorporated enterprises to get the return to capital.

While in theory these two methods are equally valid, in practice it is the first that is mainly used, probably because the data needed are easier to obtain. These two methods can obviously be used simultaneously, but in this case the total obtained is often larger – sometimes considerably larger – than the mixed income recorded in the accounts. One possible explanation is that the owners of unincorporated enterprises earn a "psychological income" in the form of satisfaction at being their own masters and so accept lower remuneration for their labour and capital investment than would be true of a corporation.

Actual and imputed social contributions

"Compensation of employees" is defined in the national accounts in a way that shows explicitly the full cost of labour as a factor of production. For example, whereas in the real world social contributions are paid directly by the employers to the social funds and are never seen by the employees, the national accounts treat them as part of wages paid to households. As a result, the "compensation of employees" item includes all contributions, including imputed contributions (see below), and therefore reflects the total cost of labour. So that things should come out right in the end, the "secondary distribution of income account" contains another fictitious flow, this time from households to the social funds. What we then have is the following fictitious circuit for social contributions: Employer –> Households –> Social insurance funds. It is essential to keep this circuit in mind when interpreting the household account.

In most countries, employees and employers are obliged to make regular contributions to a social security plan that usually reimburses employees for medical costs, pays out unemployment benefits and provides retirement pensions. However, certain employers pay social security benefits directly to their employees without going through a social security fund. In this situation, national accountants consider that these employees and employers pay an "imputed" social contribution. They estimate the sum the workers would have had to pay to receive the social benefits paid to them, and these imputed contributions are included in "compensation of employees". Thus, the full cost of labour can be recorded in the accounts. The benefits they receive are recorded in the resources column of the "secondary distribution of income account" alongside the other social benefits. Because it is difficult to estimate the hypothetical contributions that these workers would have had to pay to receive benefits, national accountants often start from the principle that the imputed social contributions are equivalent to the benefits actually received. However, more and more national accounts estimate the social contributions regarding unfunded or underfunded defined benefit pension schemes based on actuarial calculations of the cost of future pensions and not on effective contributions, thus incorporating an additional element of imputation.

Pension funds and social security plans

One difficult issue, especially for international comparisons, is the recording of pension contributions and pension benefits of employees. One can distinguish two main types of pension systems: those functioning as "savings plans" (also called "by capitalisation") and those functioning as "transfer plans" (also called "by repartition" or "pay-as-you-go"). If the pension plan is a saving plan (often called a "pension fund"), each employee contributes to a fund from which his or her future pension benefit will be paid. Thus, the national accounts record all the contributions to the plan (both those of employers and of employees) as a form of saving (i.e. an increase in the pension asset of employees) and pension benefits as "dis-saving" (i.e. a decrease of the pension asset of retirees).

By contrast, a pension plan is a transfer plan (rather than a saving plan) when the pension contributions of current employees are used to pay the pension benefits of current retirees. In this case (which is typical of social security pension systems), the national accounts deduct pension contributions from income (and thus they are also deducted from saving), and pension benefits are considered part of income (and thus included in saving). Thus, there is a significant difference in impact on income between these two methods of financing the retirement of employees. To harmonise the measure of income, the SNA 2008 recommends recording also (in parallel) the pension contributions and benefits of saving plans (i.e. pension funds) as if they were transfer plans (i.e. social security). However, this creates a dissymmetry in the accounts, which has to be corrected by item "D8 adjustment for the change in pension entitlements" in the "use of disposable income account." It is interesting to note, however, that the United States, Canada and Australia – three major countries with pension funds – do not record this item because they do not use the parallel accounting that generates it.

Because of the dramatic financing problem caused by the forthcoming retirement of the "baby-boom" generation (those born between 1945 and 1960), significant reforms of pension systems are under way in many countries. These reforms are in two directions: first, reduce the pension promises and/or raise contributions; second, transform "defined benefits plans" in "defined contribution plans". This last sentence needs some explanation.

- A **defined benefit** plan is a pension plan for which the pension benefit is calculated in terms of a percentage of salary. In this type of plan, it is the sponsor of the plan, often the employer, who bears the financial risk of the pension benefit. Defined benefit plans are often "pay as you go" and thus unfunded. Typically, the social security retirement systems of continental European countries are unfunded defined-benefit plans.

- On contrary, **defined contribution** plans are saving plans: the pension benefit is the result of the accumulated contributions of the employee and the employer on behalf the employee. Thus, the employer does not bear the financial risk of the pension promise. Defined contribution plans are, by definition, funded, meaning that they hold a reserve of non-financial or financial assets that results from the investment of the accumulated contributions. It is from this reserve that the pension benefits are paid.

The SNA 2008 remains flexible about how to record unfunded pension plans, resulting in differences between OECD countries. Some countries, in line with business accounting recommendations, record all unfunded employer-defined benefit plans as if they are saving plans, including government plans for their employees. This requires the calculation of a pension liability for these plans (and thus a pension asset for the employees) using what is called actuarial methods. Actuarial methods for pension accounting consist in estimating the pension liability of defined benefit plans based on employee demographics and calculating from that the employer's expected outflows for pension payments. These outflows are transformed into a current liability and discounted using a discount rate. Some countries (essentially continental Europe) will continue to record unfunded pension plans as "pay-as-you-go" schemes. As a result, there is no full comparability for pension flows and stocks data between OECD countries. SNA 2008 urges OECD countries to produce an additional table where all pension flows and stocks are presented in a comparable way. It is premature to conclude today that this very useful table will be available for all OECD countries. EU countries have the obligation under the compulsory transmission program of ESA 2010 to produce this table for 2017. Hopefully, if other OECD countries achieve the same, it will be finally possible to have full comparability for pension flows and stocks.

Insurance

A distinction is made between two types of insurance: non-life (often described as accident insurance) and life insurance. With non-life insurance, the policyholder is compensated for theft, road accidents, fire, natural catastrophes, bodily injury, income loss, etc. Non-life insurance also covers a type of "life" insurance that would be more appropriately called "death" insurance. This is an insurance policy in which the insurance company agrees to pay the beneficiaries named by the insured person a predetermined sum in the event of his/her death (before a predetermined age in the case of "term" life insurance and at any date in the case of "whole life insurance"). Term life insurance is simply a wager between the policyholder and the insurance company. If the policyholder dies before the pre-agreed age, he "wins" in the sense that the insurance company will be obligated to pay a certain capital to the beneficiaries. On the other hand, if the policyholder is still alive at the predetermined age, it is the insurance company that "wins" since it will not have to pay out the premiums paid in by the policyholder during the duration of the policy. This insurance functions in a similar manner to non-life insurance and is quite different from life insurance as described below.

In the case of non-life insurance, national accountants divide the premium paid by the policyholder into two parts: the remuneration for the service provided, and the net premium, i.e., the remainder. The remuneration for the service corresponds to the estimated payment by the policyholder to the insurance company for the management of the funds collected in the form of premiums, the processing of claims, advisory services, publicity and other current expenditures. By assumption, the amount of the remuneration for the service is equal to the difference between the premiums received and the claims paid out plus what is known as the "premium supplement". This supplement corresponds to the property income received by the insurance company from investing the premiums in financial and other assets. National accountants regard this income as belonging to the policyholders. They therefore show it as "received" by the policyholders (in the resources column of the distribution of primary income account) before being "paid back" to the insurance company when they remunerate it for its services. Remuneration for the service is part of household final consumption expenditure. The net premiums (premiums minus remuneration for the service) are treated as a transfer between the policyholders paying the premiums and the policyholders eligible for receipt of claims. The net premiums are recorded in the "other current transfers" item in the uses column of the secondary distribution of income account, while the repaid claims are recorded in the "other current transfers" item in the resources column of the same account.

Life insurance works very differently from non-life insurance. A life insurance policy, or contract, is one of many ways in which a person can build up capital that will be repaid at a pre-agreed date, increased by the interest earned on invested premiums. A life insurance policy usually involves the regular payment of premiums or contributions. Life insurance defined here is thus a saving plan as defined in the previous box and is thus similar to any other financial investment (a savings account, share purchases, stuffing gold coins in the mattress, for example).

The contributions and the withdrawals made when the policy/contract matures are financial transactions and recorded in the financial accounts (see Chapter 8). Life insurance nevertheless requires two non-financial transactions that must be recorded in the non-financial accounts. First, as in the case of non-life insurance, the policyholder has to pay the insurance company for the service rendered in managing the funds collected. Most of the time, insurance companies record this remuneration for service separately, and it is therefore unnecessary to make estimates of the amount concerned. It is included in household final consumption expenditure as remuneration for services. Second, even though the insurance companies retain the interest received from investing the insurance premiums, and even though policyholders have no access to this interest before the policy matures, this interest, legally speaking, is the "property" of the policyholders. For this reason, it is recorded in the "property income" item in the resources column of the primary distribution of income account. This manner of proceeding has a legal justification but also an economic one. When a life insurance policy/contract offers a higher yield than usual, the policyholder feels richer and increases his consumption (the so-called "wealth effect"), even though the money will not be received before the pre-determined date. If the yield offered is lower than usual, he or she will be inclined to reduce consumption.

Income in national accounts and in economic theory

The national accounts define income as the flow of net resources arising directly, or through redistribution, from normal productive activities and potentially available for consumption. On the other hand, some economists define income as the maximum sum that can be consumed in a given period without reducing a household's real net worth (net worth is the difference between assets and liabilities; real net worth is this difference deflated by the price index for final consumption). It is therefore important to have a clear understanding of the differences that exist between the two definitions:

- Capital gains and losses, known as "holding gains/losses" in the national accounts, are related to changes in the prices either of fixed assets (notably housing) or of financial assets (notably shares). Households in OECD countries have on several occasions in the recent past benefited from rises, or suffered from falls, in the prices of these two types of assets. One remembers in particular the stock market bubble toward the end of the 1990s, and the steep drop in stock prices starting in 2000. More recently, the consequences of the burst of the housing price bubble in 2007-09, in the United States, and later in Ireland and Spain, have been catastrophic, leading to an unprecedented great recession since World War II. When the price changes are positive, the holding gains enable households to consume far more than their disposable income without eating into their net worth. Conversely, negative holding gains (i.e., losses) prompt households to consume distinctly less than their disposable income to compensate for the decline in their net worth. These amounts may therefore be included in the economists' definition of income, but they are not included in the national accounts definition of income.

- A second difference is that theoretical income (the economists' definition) includes capital transfers. But in the national accounts, only current transfers are included in the calculation of disposable income.

- Lastly, a household's net worth can be affected by events totally unrelated to the economic activities that constitute the principal subject of the national accounts. Floods, forest fires, gales and earthquakes reduce net worth by destroying buildings or other types of property. Conversely, net worth takes on increased value when, for example, a farmer finds oil on his land. The changes in asset values following events of this type are recorded under "other changes" in the volume of assets account, but they are not considered income in the national accounts.

However, by combining several different accounts, the national accounts system allows for the calculation of household net worth based on the theoretical concept of income, rather than disposable income.

Exercises for Chapter 6

Exercise 1. True or False?

a) When share prices rise:

　i) household disposable income increases;

　ii) household saving declines.

b) When a tenant buys the apartment he/she had previously been renting, GDP increases because it now includes an imputed rental income of homeowner-occupiers.

c) When, in a given year, the number of road accidents is higher than usual, household *disposable income* also tends to be higher than usual.

d) A rise in the rate of income tax automatically leads to a decline in household disposable income.

e) A farmer whose olive plantation is destroyed in a storm automatically suffers a decline in his disposable income.

f) A cut in the rate of inheritance tax automatically leads to a decline in household saving.

g) A cut in the rate of reimbursement of dental care leads to:

　i) a rise in GDP;

　ii) a decline in household disposable income.

Exercise 2. Test your knowledge of the household account

Enter the transactions described below in the sequence of accounts starting with the *production account* and going through to the *utilisation of disposable income account*.

The Devant household consists of Jacques, his wife Monique, their daughter Nicole, Monique's mother Simone, and Jacques' brother Xavier. During the year:

● Jacques receives a salary of 2 000 for his job as store manager. His employer pays 20 in social contributions. Jacques pays 25 in income tax and 15 in social contributions. He spends 100 on meals and transport and 280 to buy a new car. He finances this purchase with a loan and pays 5 in interest during the year as a whole. He hands over the rest of his salary to Monique, who is responsible for the household's accounts.

- Monique is unemployed throughout the year, receiving 350 in unemployment benefit. She spends 1 900 on food, 120 on rent and 15 on household insurance. (Even though Monique is unaware of this, 5 out of this 15 corresponds to remuneration for the service provided by the insurance company).

- Simone receives 45 from a pension fund to which her late husband was affiliated, as well as 265 in the form of a social security pension. She spends 130 on clothes and gives Nicole 25 in pocket money.

- Nicole spends all the pocket money received from her grandmother on sweets. She also receives 30 in pocket money from her parents but saves this in order to buy a bicycle.

- Xavier has no fixed employment, but carries out undeclared painting jobs for neighbours. This brings him 1 500 during the year, but he spends 400 of this on paint and brushes. He occasionally calls on a friend to help him and pays him 40. Once when on a worksite, he parked in an unauthorised space and his van was clamped, costing him 20 to have the clamp removed. He spends 450 on cigarettes, beer and football match tickets. He pays 60 in alimony to his ex-wife.

Production account

Uses	Resources
Intermediate consumption Value added	Gross output

Primary distribution of income account

Uses	Resources
Compensation of employees Wages and salaries Employers' social contributions Net taxes on production Mixed income/operating surplus	Value added

Allocation of primary income account

Uses	Resources
Property income	Mixed income/operating surplus
Interest	Compensation of employees
Rents	Wages and salaries
	Employers' social contributions
	Property income
	Interest and dividends
	Rents
Balance of primary incomes	

Secondary distribution of income account

Uses	Resources
Current taxes on income and wealth, etc.	**Balance of primary incomes**
Social contributions	Social benefits other than social transfers in kind
Employers' social contributions	Social security benefits in cash
Employees' social contributions	Social assistance benefits in cash
Social contributions by self-employed persons	
Other current transfers	Other current transfers
Net non-life insurance premiums	Non-life insurance claims
Miscellaneous current transfers	Miscellaneous current transfers
Disposable income	

Use of disposable income account

Uses	Resources
Household final consumption expenditure	**Disposable income**
	Adjustment for the change in pension entitlements
Saving	

The solutions to these exercises are available at:

http://dx.doi.org/10.1787/9789264214637-24-en

Understanding National Accounts
Second Edition
© OECD 2014

Chapter 7

Business accounts

The institutional framework in which firms operate matters for national accounts. In national accounts, they are divided into two groups: corporations and "unincorporated enterprises". The latter are small and do not have corporate status or complete sets of accounts, but may make a significant contribution to total value added. This chapter first examines the accounts of non-financial corporations and then returns to those of unincorporated enterprises.

O ECD economists are particularly interested in the institutional framework in which enterprises (firms) operate, in order to identify how to improve firms' performance and generate an increase in employment, among other benefits. In recent OECD reports on France, the authors have suggested a certain number of structural reforms intended to improve the performance of French firms. For example:

- Reduce the protection of permanent contracts (extend the trial period, broaden the definition of economic redundancy, shorten layoff and judicial procedures, reduce redeployment obligations) while reinforcing the link between benefits, job search and participation in enhanced active measures. Reform unemployment benefits to ensure they are generous in the short term, and less so later in the spell and for the older unemployed, while improving professional training.

- Allow the minimum cost of labour to fall relative to the median, especially for youth. In the medium term, reduce social security contributions further while cutting public spending and inefficient tax expenditures, and increasing environmental, real property and inheritance taxes.

- Reduce the regulations of professional services that go beyond the strict protection of users. Ease restrictions to price competition and to setting up of new stores in the retail sector. Remove regulatory entry barriers in potentially competitive segments of network industries.

In the national accounts, firms are classified into two groups: corporations and "unincorporated enterprises" (or "sole proprietorships"). Sole proprietorships are firms small in size that do not have corporate status or complete sets of accounts. They are themselves most often grouped with households, and in many cases transactions of the enterprise cannot be disentangled from the transactions of the relevant household as a consumer. The fact that they are grouped with households means that economic analysis often has to be confined to corporations, despite the fact that unincorporated enterprises also make a significant contribution to total value added. The following table shows the importance in terms of value added of the different institutional sectors in certain OECD countries.

As can be seen from these few examples, the corporate sector is the largest contributor to value added, far ahead of general government. Also value added generated by households is substantial, with much of this stemming from the imputation of output (imputed rents) for owner-occupied

Table 7.1. **Breakdown of gross value added by sector**

As a percentage of total gross value added, 2011

		France	Greece	Netherlands	Switzerland
S11-S12	Corporations	61.1	44.1	70.7	75.4
S13	General government	18.2	17.4	14.0	10.2
S14-S15	Households[a]	20.6	38.6	15.2	14.4
S1	Total economy	100.0	100.0	100.0	100.0

a) Including unincorporated enterprises and NPISHs (S15)

Source: OECD (2014), "Detailed National Accounts: Non-financial accounts by sectors, annual", OECD National Accounts Statistics (database), doi: http://dx.doi.org/10.1787/data-00034-en.

StatLink ⋙ http://dx.doi.org/10.1787/888933143982

housing. However, a further appreciable portion is in the form of value added of unincorporated enterprises. In particular, the fact that in Greece household value added accounts for almost 40% of total value added can be explained by the very large number of firms that do not have a corporate status and are thus grouped with households in the national accounts.

As for the corporations themselves, the national accounts break them down into two main sub-categories: non-financial corporations (S11) and financial corporations (S12). Financial corporations (banks, insurance companies) play a key role in the economy, but their accounts are not as easy to analyse as those of non-financial corporations, and it is amongst others for this reason that the national accounts show them separately. The definition of financial corporations can be found in Chapter 10.

Table 7.2. **France: breakdown of gross value added by sector**

As a percentage of total gross value added, 2011

S11	Non-financial corporations	56.1
S12	Financial corporations	5.0
S13	General government	18.2
S14	Households	18.9
S14AA	Non-financial sole proprietorships	7.6
S14A	"Pure" Households	11.3
S15	Nonprofit institutions serving households	1.7
S1	Total economy	100.0

Source: Insee Databases (2013): Statistical indices and series: Macroeconomic Database: National Accounts www.bdm.insee.fr/bdm2/index?request_locale=en.

StatLink ⋙ http://dx.doi.org/10.1787/888933143993

This table also shows that 7.6% of gross value added was accounted for by unincorporated enterprises, a larger figure even than that for financial corporations. Decision-makers have always paid great attention to the small and medium-sized enterprises (SMEs). Some SMEs are not corporations as legally defined, and, in many countries, they are therefore not classified in the corporate sector (S11) but rather as unincorporated enterprises inside the household sector (S14). These small units play a very important role in agriculture and the liberal professions and sometimes as "start-ups" in industry (after all, even Microsoft® began life as an unincorporated enterprise). However, their contribution to total value added remains limited by the fact that as they expand, small firms tend to be transformed into corporations. It is therefore the corporate sector, particularly the non-financial corporations, that provides the backbone of economic growth in most developed countries. This chapter will look first at the accounts of non-financial corporations and then return to the accounts of unincorporated enterprises.

1. The relationship between the firm (enterprise) and the corporation

For the national accounts, an enterprise is an **institutional unit**, in other words an economic agent having independent economic decision-making power and whose aim is to **produce market goods and services.** The word "market" is very important; it means that the products are sold on the market at *economically significant prices.* One of the criteria used by national accountants to determine whether a firm sells its products at an economically significant price is to see whether the value of its sales is equivalent on a lasting basis to more than 50% of its production costs. This definition therefore excludes, for example, general government units that provide free or almost free, products. Although it is far from being based on "profit-seeking" (if a firm's sales cover only 51% of its costs, it will have to be heavily subsidised to continue existing), this definition nevertheless implies that the behaviour of the firm as viewed by the national accounts is not based on altruism, in contrast to general government and NPISHs.

A **corporation** is a form of enterprise having a legal identity separate from that of its owners. This separation gives the owners the important advantage that in the event of failure of the business their responsibility toward those to whom the firm owes money is limited to the amounts they have invested in the business and does not extend to their personal assets (except in the case of an offence such as embezzlement). In the case of unincorporated enterprises, there is no legal distinction between the firm and its owners, and the latter are personally responsible for all debts in the event of business failure. In order to become a *corporation*, a firm has to comply with a certain number of legal conditions, some of which are costly, and this explains why owners of very small firms do not apply for these advantages.

One of the major legal requirements for corporations is the publication of a complete set of accounts recording the value of the financial and non-financial wealth at the start of the period ("opening balance sheet") and at the end of the period ("closing balance sheet"), as well as the receipts and payments made between these two dates. The period is generally one year and often corresponds to the calendar year. These accounts are an important source enabling national accountants to calculate the macroeconomic accounts of the corporate sector.

By contrast, most of the unincorporated enterprises do not have complete sets of accounts. Some of the transactions cannot be separated from those of their owners in their capacity as households. It is for this reason that, in general, the national accounts include them in the household sector. Two points to note:

- Certain non-financial corporations can be wholly or partially owned by the State (or other parts of general government). These are known as "public" enterprises. Even so, they are not classified under general government, since they sell their products at economically significant prices. There is, however, a problem for analysts because such firms can sometimes behave differently from private corporations. For example, certain public enterprises have a so-called public service function that often prevents them from charging their customers on the basis of actual marginal cost. Since some public enterprises do not therefore carry out their production according to quite the same rules as private corporations, the SNA recommends that national accountants draw up a special account in their case. In practice, however, very few OECD countries do so (e.g. United Kingdom).

- In principle, the crucial distinction between corporations and unincorporated enterprises as far as the national accountants are concerned is not so much about their legal status but as to whether or not they publish a complete set of accounts. A certain number of large units (for example NGOs, large legal firms, medical practices or co-operatives) are not legally constituted as corporations but nevertheless publish accounts showing their balance sheet and their transactions. These units are sometimes described as "quasi-corporations" and are then classified within the corporate sector. Some countries (Italy, Germany) extend this notion of "quasi-corporations" to a wide subset of unincorporated enterprises, thus modifying the interpretation of the profit share ratio (see Chapter 3).

2. The structure of corporate-sector accounts

As with all institutional units, the sequence of national accounts for the corporate sector is divided into *non-financial accounts* and *financial accounts*. The financial accounts will be described in Chapter 8. Here, we shall look only at the sequence of non-financial accounts, starting with the *production account* and ending with the *capital account*. These accounts show the following: how the income derived from production is divided between the factors of production (labour and capital); the amount by which this income is increased or reduced by "property income" or by various kinds of transfer (mainly taxes); and finally, how much is left to the firm for the acquisition of non-financial or financial assets. All this information is valued at current prices.

In the presentations of the production and income accounts, the receipts, designated as *resources*, are shown in the right-hand column of each account. The expenditure items are designated as *uses* and shown in the left-hand column. The capital account shows how capital formation is financed, so the *changes in assets* are shown on the left-hand side and *changes in liabilities and net worth* are shown on the right-hand side. The last item on the left-hand side is known as the *accounting balance* and is equal to the difference between total resources (or changes in liabilities and net worth) and total uses (or changes in assets). The accounts are designed to produce accounting balances such as *value added, operating surplus, saving* or *net lending/net borrowing*, aggregates that are of particular interest for economic analysis. In the accounts set out below, the accounting balances are shown in bold type. In order to give an idea of the relative importance of the different items, their values in billions of euros or dollars are shown for the year 2011. We have chosen to illustrate this chapter by taking first the non-financial corporation sector for France and then continuing with the non-financial corporate sector for Australia.

The corporate sector production account

The first account in the sequence is the *production account*. This contains just three items: *output* on the right (in other words under *resources*); *intermediate consumption* on the left (under *uses*); and the accounting balance (on the left, equal to the difference between the other two items) resulting in the *gross value added*.

The output of non-financial corporations amounted to 2 548.7 billion euros in France in 2011, a figure much higher than French GDP (2 001.4 billion euros). This should no longer come as a surprise at this point in the textbook, because it is clear by now that this output includes substantial double counting since the output of one firm may be the intermediate consumption of others. This figure for total output is therefore not a macroeconomic aggregate to be used for most analytical purposes. Instead, use is generally made of the gross value added of non-financial corporations, which is equal to 1 006.5 billion euros.

The output of firms is divided into market output and output for own final use. With the exception of certain service industries (e.g. retail trade) for which special conventions apply, market output, which constitutes the bulk of the total, is measured as the sum of sales and the changes in inventories of finished products and work in progress. For non-financial corporations, the output for own final use consists of the value of the non-financial assets made by the firm for its own use (for example in-house software). The amount involved is very small (roughly 1% of total output).[1] Intermediate consumption is measured as the difference between the purchases of goods and services needed for production and the change in inventories of these products.

Table 7.3. **France: production account for non-financial corporations (S11)**

Billion euros, 2011

Uses		Resources	
P2. Intermediate consumption	1 542.1	P1 Output	2 548.7
B1. Gross value added	**1 006.5**		
K1. Consumption of fixed capital	160.1		
B1N. Net value added	**844.0**		

Source: OECD (2014), "Detailed National Accounts: Non-financial accounts by sectors, annual", OECD National Accounts Statistics (database), doi: *http://dx.doi.org/10.1787/data-00034-en*.

StatLink ᘖᓔᔭᡂ *http://dx.doi.org/10.1787/888933144005*

Note that it is also necessary to take into account, among uses, the depreciation of the capital used (*consumption of fixed capital* in national accounts terminology). The consumption of fixed capital is the reduction in the value of produced capital (other than inventories) due to wear and tear and obsolescence. It is a production cost and its amount therefore appears in the left-hand column (in the same way as intermediate consumption), as a deduction from output to obtain the "true" figure for corporate value added, known as *net value added*. It is probably because of the difficulty of estimating the consumption of fixed capital (see "Going further") that statistical offices prefer to publish "gross" rather than "net" figures in the corporate sector accounts. However, from the point of view of analysing firms, it is the net accounting balance that is more suitable. Exercise 1 at the end of this chapter shows how one can easily move from the gross balances and accounting ratios to the net equivalents.

The corporate sector's generation of income account

The next account in the sequence is the generation of income account. This shows how the value added that has been created is distributed between the two factors of production: the labour factor (compensation of employees) and the capital factor (gross operating surplus). The account begins on the right with the gross value added (this is often the case, but one could also use *net* value added). Under *uses*, one finds compensation of employees, itself broken down between wages and salaries and employers' social contributions.

One should note that wages and salaries include employees' contributions and income tax withheld at source. Similarly, although employees do not in practice receive the employers' social contributions (which, like the employees' contributions, are paid directly to social insurance plans, tax authorities, etc.), the national accounts treat them *as if* employees did receive them, in such a way as to show the total cost of the labour factor to the employers. The contributions included comprise both those actually paid by the employers and the so-called imputed contributions. The contribution circuit is explained in detail in Chapter 6.

Table 7.4. **France: Generation of income account for non-financial corporations**

Billion euros, 2011

Uses		Resources	
D1. Compensation of employees	676.5	**B1. Gross value added**	1 006.5
D11. Wages and salaries	511.0		
D12. Employers' social contributions	165.5		
D29. Other taxes on production	53.2		
D39. Other subsidies on production	16.3		
B2. Operating surplus, gross	293.2		
K1. Consumption of fixed capital	160.1		
B2N. Operating surplus, net	133.0		

Source: OECD (2014), "Detailed National Accounts: Non-financial accounts by sectors, annual", OECD National Accounts Statistics (database), doi: *http://dx.doi.org/10.1787/data-00034-en*.

StatLink ⬛🖘 *http://dx.doi.org/10.1787/888933144010*

The **other taxes** and **other subsidies on production** (D29 and D39) are the difference between total taxes and subsidies on production **less** taxes and subsidies on products (D21 and D31), respectively. The latter, (which include VAT) do not appear in the accounts for corporations even if corporations are, in practice, collecting these taxes, because production in the national accounts is valued at basic prices, i.e. excluding taxes on products and including subsidies on products.

Before arriving at the gross operating surplus, which represents the remuneration of the capital factor, other taxes on production (D29) and other subsidies on production (D39) need to be looked closely. These taxes on production are made up of taxes on wages or capital paid by firms (in France, consisting of the territorial economic contribution, which replaced the "*taxe professionnelle*" since 2010, taxes on land and buildings, and solidarity contributions of companies). The subsidies on production in the case of firms are small subsidies paid by the government to help firms in boosting their production. The main subsidies on production in France are in fact paid to farmers, who are for the most part not classified as corporations but as unincorporated enterprises. Notice that the minds of national accountants sometimes work in a complicated fashion. In this case, subsidies are not shown as receipts but as negative uses.

*An advantage of this way of recording is that **other taxes** and **subsidies** can be combined in one item such as, i.e. "other taxes **less** subsidies on production".*

The **gross operating surplus** (or, after deduction of the consumption of fixed capital, the **net operating surplus**) is the principal measure of firms' performance in terms of operating profits. This measure differs from profits as calculated in company accounts, as explained in Going further toward the end of this chapter. This explains why the national accountants have chosen to give this item a name other than "profit".

It is possible to calculate from these results a *profit share* (also called sometimes in France, "margin rate" – *taux de marge*), equal to the gross operating surplus as a percentage of gross value added. This is a key indicator of firms' performance in the national accounts. In line with what stated earlier, it is preferable to use a net profit share, i.e. the net operating surplus divided by the net value added. The following graph shows the evolution in French net and gross profit share since 1990. The two move virtually parallel, although the net share declined more strongly than the gross share during the recent crisis. The choice between gross and net profit shares is therefore of primary importance in international comparisons when comparing variable levels, rather than changes. Also it is important for international comparisons to adjust possible different definitions of the sector "non-financial corporations". As indicated in Chapter 3, some countries (Germany, Italy) include in this sector "quasi-corporations" with a substantial number of non-salaried workers, thus including in their gross operation surplus elements of mixed income. However, looking at an individual country, the change in the profit share becomes the focus of interest. On either a gross or a net basis, the profit share for non-financial corporations in France rose between 1996 and 1998. After 1998, the share remained relatively stable until the economic and financial crisis showing a marked decline. Among the quarterly national accounts tables published for France, two are of particular interest as they focus on the origin of change in profit shares. These tables are the subject of exercises 4 and 5 (since these are difficult exercises, it is advised to look directly at the answers).

Figure 7.1. **France: Net and gross profit share, non-financial corporations**

As a percentage of gross value added

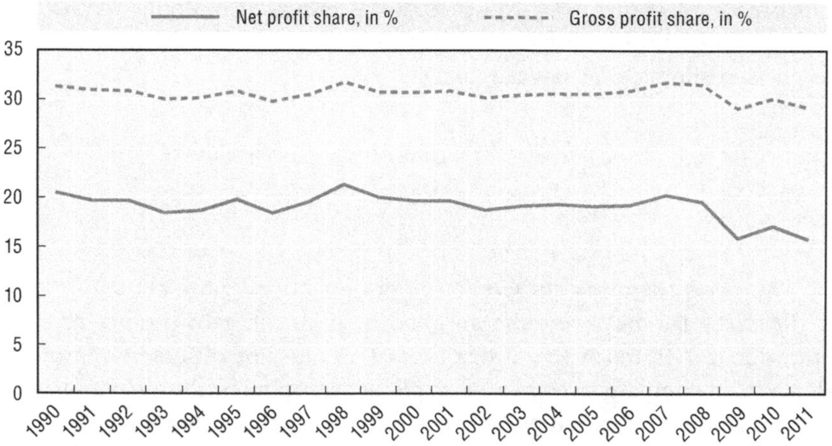

Source: OECD (2014), "Detailed National Accounts: Non-financial accounts by sectors, annual", OECD National Accounts Statistics (database), doi: *http://dx.doi.org/10.1787/data-00034-en.*

StatLink ⬛ *http://dx.doi.org/10.1787/888933144036*

Distribution of income account

Leaving France aside, let us continue to explore the accounts of the corporate sector in Australia. Although situated at the antipodes, the two countries use the same system of national accounts. However, Australia does not calculate the production account and the generation of income account for corporations; instead, it starts calculating the accounts of the corporate sector only at the third stage, the one known as the *distribution of income account*. This distribution of income account starts with the operating surplus. It then shows all the current transfers carried out by corporations either as uses or as resources.

Table 7.5. **Australia: distribution of income account for non-financial corporations (S11)**[*]

Billions of Australian dollars, 2012

Uses		Resources	
D4. Property income, paid	130.2	B2N. Net operating surplus	192.1
D5. Current taxes on income, wealth, etc.	47.1	D4. Total property income, receivable	36.0
D62. Social benefits		D61. Social contributions	
D7. Other current transfers, total	9.8	D7. Other current transfers	4.4
B6N. Net disposable income = B8N. Net Saving	**45.4**		

[*] Fiscal year beginning on 1 July 2012 and ending on 30 June 2013.

Source: Australian bureau of statistics (2013), Australian system of National Accounts: Table 17. Non-Financial Corporations Income Account, *www.abs.gov.au/AUSSTATS/abs@.nsf/DetailsPage/5204.02012-13?OpenDocument.*

StatLink ⬛ *http://dx.doi.org/10.1787/888933144028*

These transfers include, in the first place, **property income**. While only the total (D4) appears in the above table, there are five types of property income: interest (D41); distributed income of corporations (D42); reinvested earnings on direct foreign investment (D43); investment income disbursements (among which property income attributed to insurance policyholders) (D44); and rents on land and sub-soil assets (D45). Most of these are liable to appear both in corporations' resources (when the amount is receivable) and in their uses (when the amount is due). To analyse these items, it is important to note that the corporation accounts are not "consolidated" in the national accounts. When aggregating the accounts of the many units of the sector, "consolidation" means eliminating the transactions between units of the same sector being aggregated. This therefore leaves only transactions between units of the sector in question with units of *other* sectors. On the contrary, not consolidating means not carrying out this elimination, in other words simply summing up all transactions, whether internal or external to the sector in question.

In these non-consolidated accounts, the amount of 36.0 billion Australian dollars of property income receivable by Australian non-financial corporations in 2012 includes, for example, the dividends payable, being part of distributed income, by certain corporations *to other corporations*. It is in fact very difficult to consolidate the accounts of corporations because, while one knows whether a corporation is the payer or the recipient, one often does not know to whom this amount is paid, or from whom it is received. Thus, in the non-consolidated non-financial corporate accounts for Australia, the property income payable by non-financial corporations (130.2 billion Australian dollars) is not payable solely to agents other than non-financial corporations (i.e., financial corporations, households, general government and the rest of the world). Much of this property income is also payable to other non-financial corporations, and this may explain the size of the item for property income receivable (36.0 billion Australian dollars). To obtain the approximate amount of net property income receivable by other agents (financial corporations, households, general government, rest of the world) it is necessary to calculate the difference between the property income payable (130.2) and the property income receivable (36.0), i.e. 94.2 billion Australian dollars.

- D41 – *Interest*. This is, for example, the interest paid on loans obtained by non-financial corporations from banks (financial corporations). It can also relate to interest paid on issued bonds.

- D42 – *Distributed income of corporations*. These are the portions of profits paid out by firms to their shareholders, mainly in the form of dividends. At the same time, corporations receive dividends on their holdings in other corporations. "Distributed income" in this case includes all types of methods used by corporations to distribute part of their profits, including the issuance of new shares. It also includes income that owners may withdraw from their quasi-corporations.

Note for experts: the counterpart of this flow appears in item F5 of the financial accounts (shares and other equities).

- D43 – *Reinvested earnings on direct foreign investment.* This item is interesting in that it reflects an imputation in the national accounts, in this case stemming from taking into account the phenomenon of *control* by certain multinational firms (known as parent companies) on other firms (known as subsidiaries) located abroad. A firm is deemed to control another when it is capable of significantly influencing the decisions of the latter, notably as regards to the distribution of income. In this case, the parent company has a completely free choice of whether to have a dividend for itself or to assign it to its subsidiary. To reflect the genuine degree of enrichment (or impoverishment, if the subsidiary is making losses), what is recorded in this row is the amount of profits that is not redistributed in the form of dividends but retained in the subsidiary.

  Despite being described as "reinvested profits", this item can be negative when the subsidiary is making losses. It is to be found in both "resources" and "uses". In "resources", the amount is the profits reinvested by Australian multinational corporations in their overseas subsidiaries; in "uses", the amount represents the profits reinvested by foreign multinational corporations in their Australian subsidiaries. This item, despite being of interest, may be difficult to capture, since information on foreign subsidiaries of multinational corporations can be of mediocre quality. This is further complicated by the growing globalisation and the set-up of "special purpose entities" to minimise total payments of taxes. Another special feature of the item is that the reasoning is applied only to multinational corporations (and investment funds, see below): national accountants do not apply it between Australian parent companies and Australian subsidiaries.

- D44 – *Investment income disbursements.* This transaction category consists of three items: property income attributed to insurance policyholders, investment income payable on pension entitlements, and investment income attributable to collective investment fund shareholders. The first item is an imputed flow corresponding to the property income obtained by insurance companies investing their technical reserves. Since these technical reserves belong not to the insurance companies but to the policyholders (in this case, the policyholders are the non-financial corporations), the national accounts are compiled as if the property income was paid back to the policyholders and then paid out again in the form of consumption of insurance services. The second item is also an imputed flow, and relates to the investment income attributed to pension entitlements.[2] The third item concerns the undistributed income of investment funds which, similar to the reinvested earnings on foreign direct investment, are treated as being distributed and subsequently reinvested.

- D45 – *Rents on land and sub-soil assets*. This fifth type of property income consists of rent received by owners of land or sub-soil assets (oil, coal, mineral deposits) in cases where the exploitation is entrusted to others. Note that this item does not include rentals from office buildings or from rental cars used by corporations, which are purchases of services recorded as intermediate consumption in the production account.

The next item in the "uses" part of the distribution of income account is current taxes on income (D5). This item mainly consists of corporation tax, which amounted to 47.1 billion Australian dollars in 2012. The distribution of income account also includes social contributions received (D61) and social benefits paid (D62). This may seem surprising, given that most social contributions are paid to social insurance plans, and that the benefits are received from the same plans, although they are not classified in the corporate sector. The reason for the existence of such flows is that large firms sometimes set up their own system of pensions or social insurance. In this case, the benefits are paid directly by the firm to current or former employees. However, the national accounts act as if the imputed contributions corresponding to these benefits were paid to employees as part of their compensation (in the generation of income account) and then paid back by these same employees to these same corporations, which then use them to pay out the social benefits. As we have already seen, this complicated system is aimed at bringing out the totality of the cost of labour in the generation of income account. However, Australia does not follow the 2008 SNA in this regard. While its national accounts act as if the imputed contributions by employers were paid to employees, it does not show them being paid back to the employers. Hence, there are no entries to be made for social benefits (D61 and D62). Australia is not alone in deviating from the international standards in this respect.

The other items in this account are "other current transfers" (D7). In particular, these consist of flows related to corporations' non-life insurance policies. Corporations receive compensation for non-life claims and pay net non-life insurance premiums. Since the national accounts are based on the accrual accounting principle (see Chapter 10), it is not the claims *paid* to the corporations during the period that are recorded but rather the claims *due* during the period. And why is the word "net" attached to the insurance premiums? The answer is because the national accounts distinguish three elements in the payment of an insurance premium: (1) the payment for an insurance management service; (2) the participation of each policyholder in the claims paid out; (3) the VAT and the specific taxes payable on insurance. The net premium corresponds only to the second element, the first being treated as intermediate consumption of insurance services in the production account of non-financial corporations. The third element is collected by the insurance companies but does not appear in their accounts for national accounts purposes; instead, it is recorded as being received directly by government, without showing who the payer is. For a better understanding of the recording of insurance-related flows, the reader is referred to the section "Going further – Insurance: are net premiums equal to the claims paid out?"

The balancing item of the account is known as *net disposable income (B6N)*. This balancing item is exactly equal, in the case of corporations, to their *net saving (B8N)* because by definition corporations have no final consumption.

The capital account

We now come to the last of the accounts for non-financial corporations, namely the *capital account*. This account describes how saving is used by corporations for financing investment (GFCF) in non-financial assets and changes in their inventories. Hence, rather than "uses" on the left-hand side of the table we now have "changes in assets"; and "changes in liabilities and net worth" instead of "resources" on the right-hand side.

Table 7.6. **Australia: Capital account for non-financial corporations (S11)**
Billions of Australian dollars, 2012

Changes in assets		Changes in liabilities and net worth	
P51. Gross fixed capital formation	230.7	B8N. Net saving	45.4
P52. Changes in inventories	4.6	K1. Consumption of fixed capital	114.1
K2. Acquisitions less disposals of non-produced non-financial assets	-1.0	B8. Gross saving	159.4
B9. Net lending (+)/net borrowing (-)	-69.7	D9. Total net capital transfers	5.2

Source: Australian bureau of statistics (2013), Australian system of National Accounts: Table 18. Non-financial Corporations Capital Account, *www.abs.gov.au/AUSSTATS/abs@.nsf/DetailsPage/5204.02012-13?OpenDocument*.

StatLink ᵐˢᵖ *http://dx.doi.org/10.1787/888933144040*

As can be seen in the above table, Australian firms had net saving of 45.4 billion Australian dollars in 2012. However, it is necessary to reconstitute on the right-hand side of the table ("changes in liabilities and net worth") the *gross* saving (B8) by adding consumption of fixed capital (K1), in order to compare it with *gross* fixed capital formation on the left-hand side of the table.

If we had put *net* fixed capital formation on the left-hand side (under "changes in assets"), there would have been no need for this adjustment. However, it is the tradition to show gross fixed capital formation under changes in assets. According to these figures, there was a sum of 159.4 billion Australian dollars in gross saving that was used by firms to finance their fixed investment of 230.7 billion Australian dollars. Most of the shortfall was financed by a net borrowing of 69.7 billion Australian dollars. This explains why gross saving is sometimes referred to as "self-financing", in other words, the financing of investment using the firm's own resources. It is possible to calculate a "self-financing ratio" by dividing gross saving by gross fixed capital formation. This ratio expresses the amount (in % of the GFCF), which is financed by the saving generated by the firms themselves, without using, for example, credits from banks or the issuance of new shares or bonds.

Net capital transfers receivable (D9) include such things as building and equipment grants from general government to research laboratories. Capital transfers payable include contributions to local government by real estate developers towards the cost of the construction of roads on their subdivisions and contributions by coal mining companies towards the cost of constructing railway lines.

The balancing item of the capital account is the item **B9 net lending/net borrowing** – "net lending" when it is positive and "net borrowing" when it is negative. In the case of *non-financial* corporations, it is in fact usually negative. It is indeed common practice for non-financial corporations to call on the saving of households to finance investment they are unable to make out of their own resources. This is traditionally done through borrowing from the banks or the issuance of shares and bonds.

If one turns to the Australian *financial* accounts, the estimate for the net borrowing of *non-financial* corporations is 69.4 billion Australian dollar figure, nearly the same as the balancing item in the capital account. It is not uncommon however to see larger statistical discrepancies between the estimates of net lending/borrowing in the capital and financial accounts. In both accounts, net lending/borrowing is obtained as a balancing item, and so the statistical discrepancy reflects inconsistencies between the estimates relating to the "real" economy as portrayed in the capital account and the financial data in the financial account. As will be seen in Chapter 8, the financial accounts often use different data sources (mainly data from banks) than the non-financial accounts (corporate accounts).

3. From corporations to firms

We have now seen in some detail the accounts of corporations. In practice, however, macroeconomists are more interested in having at their disposal accounts for all enterprises, whether incorporated or not, since they are more interested in economic rather than legal criteria when carrying out their analyses. Unincorporated enterprises are producers like any others. Unfortunately, the national accounts are not currently capable of providing the full set of accounts for all firms, because unincorporated enterprises, by definition, do not have complete sets of accounts. However, some countries like France and the United States calculate partial accounts for all firms including unincorporated enterprises. In France, this grouping is known as "NFCs-UEs" (in French: "SNFEI"), standing for "non-financial corporations and unincorporated enterprises" ("sociétés non financières et enterprises individuelles"). This grouping excludes financial corporations. A similar sector in the United States is the "business sector", which also includes financial corporations (see Chapter 12). Some other countries (Germany, Italy) classify part of their unincorporated enterprises as "quasi-corporations" and include them in the non-financial corporation sector.

Who are these sole proprietorships with their unincorporated enterprises (UEs)? They are generally members of a household who manage family firms such as a retail store, a taxi company, a farm, a medical or legal firm, provided that they do not have corporate status. Farmers make up a substantial portion of the UEs, but self-employed doctors, lawyers and architects are another significant constituent group. Note that the national accounts do not go so far as to classify homeowner-occupiers as sole proprietorships. The imputed output of housing services and all the related transactions form part of the "pure" household sector. This is also the case for the non-imputed output of housing services when a household that owns another dwelling in addition to its own rents it out directly to tenants. Notwithstanding the fact that housing services are being produced by one unit for the consumption of another, these households are not regarded as sole proprietorships.

From an economic standpoint, the UEs are producers as much as corporations are. Statistically, however, it is impossible to distinguish certain transactions of UEs that are linked to their entrepreneurial activity from transactions relating to their functions as households. This explains why it is not possible to draw up a complete set of accounts for UEs, nor for "pure" households (i.e. excluding transactions related to the UEs' productive activities).

France nevertheless has a partial set of accounts for the UEs. All that is then needed is to add this to the accounts for the non-financial corporations (NFCs) to obtain a set of accounts for NFCs-UEs, i.e. for all non-financial market producers. This partial account makes it possible to calculate, for example, the gross profit share (or, if preferred, the net profit share) that was discussed earlier, but this time in a version extended to the UEs.

Table 7.7. **France: Comparison of the profit shares
of non-financial corporations and non-financial corporations plus
unincorporated enterprises**

As a percentage of value added

	2008	2009	2010	2011
Profit share of NFCs (S11)	31.5	29.1	30.1	28.6
Profit share of NFCs-UEs (S11 + S14A)	38.1	35.8	36.7	35.3

Source: Insee Databases (2013): Statistical indices and series: Macroeconomic Database: National Accounts *www.bdm.insee.fr/bdm2/index?request_locale=en.*

StatLink ⬛🖳 *http://dx.doi.org/10.1787/888933144055*

It can be seen that the profit share of NFCs-UEs is roughly seven percentage points higher than that of the NFCs. One might be tempted to deduce from this that unincorporated enterprises are distinctly better performers than corporations, since it is their inclusion that brings about this leap in the profit share. However, this is not the case. The profit share of NFCs-UEs is higher because, by definition, the "profits" of unincorporated enterprises include the implicit remuneration of the work performed by the sole proprietorships. This remuneration is a very high percentage (around 80%) of the profit, and this pushes up the overall profit share. Because of this, the analytical information content of this indicator is severely reduced. In fact, the balance of the generation of income account for the UEs is known as "mixed income" (carrying the code B3), whereas the balancing item of the generation of income account for corporations is known as the "operating surplus" (carrying the code B2). The use of the term "mixed income" reflects the notion that this form of operating profit is not comparable with that of corporations since it "mixes" the remuneration of the capital factor and the labour of the owner of the unincorporated enterprise. To arrive at an improved comparison of the profitability of corporations and that of unincorporated enterprises, sometimes an income is estimated for the labour input of the owner and the family, by using average labour income for employees. This income is subsequently subtracted from mixed income. When comparing the profit share of the non- financial corporation sector between countries, it is important to check that the classification of individual entrepreneurs is harmonised. Chapter 3 discusses this issue when comparing the profit share ratio between France, Germany and Italy. The inclusion of many "quasi-corporations" with many non-salaried individual entrepreneurs in the two latter countries introduces a measurement bias in the results.

Notes

1. This percentage will be substantially higher after the introduction of the new standards, the 2008 SNA. According to the new standards, R&D, which often is produced in-house, will also be considered as Gross Fixed Capital Formation (GFCF).

2. In the case of defined contribution pension schemes (see Chapter 6 for definition), this item equals the income earned on the investment of available funds and it is distributed to the holders of the pension schemes. In the case of defined benefit schemes, where the entitlements are related to the (past) salary of the pension holder, the investment income equals the discount rate used in calculating the net present value of the future benefits.

References

Australian bureau of statistics (2013a), Australian system of National Accounts: Table 17. Non-Financial Corporations Income Account, *www.abs.gov.au/AUSSTATS/abs@.nsf/DetailsPage/5204.02012-13?OpenDocument*.

Australian bureau of statistics (2013b): Australian system of National Accounts: Table 18. Non-financial Corporations Capital Account, *www.abs.gov.au/AUSSTATS/abs@.nsf/DetailsPage/5204.02012-13?OpenDocument*.

Insee Databases (2013), Statistical indices and series: Macroeconomic Database: National Accounts *www.bdm.insee.fr/bdm2/index?request_locale=en*.

OECD (2014), "Detailed National Accounts: Non-financial accounts by sectors, annual", OECD National Accounts Statistics (database), doi: *http://dx.doi.org/10.1787/data-00034-en*.

Key points

- An enterprise is an institutional unit whose objective is to produce market goods and services; in other words, to sell its products on the market at an economically significant price.

- One of the criteria used by national accountants to decide whether a price is economically significant is to calculate a sales/costs ratio. If this ratio is higher than 50%, the enterprise is regarded as being "market".

- The corporate sector is essentially made up of firms that are legally constituted as corporations and produce complete sets of accounts, unlike the unincorporated enterprises. The non-financial corporations sector excludes banks, insurance companies and other financial intermediaries, but includes the non-financial public enterprises owned and controlled by government.

- Some countries calculate accounts for the grouping consisting of corporations and unincorporated enterprises. This grouping is sometimes called the "business sector". However, it is not possible to calculate more than a partial account for this grouping, since by definition unincorporated enterprises do not have complete sets of accounts separate from those of their owners.

- The profit share is the principal indicator of performance as regards the profits of non-financial corporations in the national accounts. It is most often calculated in its "net" version, i.e. as the net operating surplus divided by the net value added (and multiplied by 100). Theoretically speaking, this net profit share (net of consumption of fixed capital) is analytically preferable to the gross profit share (gross operating surplus/gross value added), since it takes into account depreciation (i.e. consumption of fixed capital).

- The "self-financing ratio" measures the proportion of fixed investment financed by the saving generated by the firms themselves, as opposed to external financing (bank loans or the issuance of shares or bonds). It is calculated as gross saving divided by GFCF (and multiplied by 100).

Going further

Consumption of fixed capital, depreciation and amortisation

Consumption of fixed capital is defined in the SNA 2008 as "the decline, during the course of the accounting period, in the current value of the stock of fixed assets owned and used by a producer as a result of physical deterioration, normal obsolescence or normal accidental damage" (SNA 2008, paragraph 6.240). It also defines what economists refer to as depreciation. In the national accounts, therefore, the consumption of fixed capital can be regarded as a synonym for depreciation. Company accountants, on the other hand, use the term "amortisation", which covers the same concept but measures it in a slightly different way compared with the national accounts. This box explains the difference.

A key part of the definition quoted above is "decline ... in the current value". National accountants measure the consumption of fixed capital by applying a "depreciation coefficient" to the current value of each capital asset, that is to say to its current market price, whereas company accountants usually apply a depreciation coefficient to the value of the capital good at its original purchase price (they call this "historic cost"). When the prices of capital goods rise, the difference can therefore be very significant. This method of business accounting is partly explained by tax considerations. The rules binding company accountants do in fact authorise the re-evaluation of assets, but since this re-evaluation may be taxable, they generally avoid doing so, and their assets in most cases continue to be valued at their purchase price. The national accounts, which are not affected by tax rules, prefer to evaluate these items at their current market value.

Company accountants and national accountants both often make the assumption that capital goods lose their value in a constant proportion each year. This is known as "straight-line" depreciation. For example, if one considers that the service life of a certain capital asset is 10 years, it will be assumed that it loses 1/10 of its value each year. Now suppose that the asset is in its ninth year of life and that it cost 100 when it was purchased eight years ago. Suppose also that, as a result of inflation, the market price of this asset had been rising by 4% each year since it was purchased. In this situation:

- The accountant of the commercial firm calculates its depreciation in the ninth year of its life by taking $100 \div 10 = 10$.

- The national accountant calculates the consumption of fixed capital in the ninth year of its life as $[100 \times 1.04^8] \div 10 = 13.7$. In other words, s/he revalues the asset by the cumulative rate of inflation before calculating the depreciation.

There is an economic explanation for this difference. Because of inflation, the real utilisation cost of this asset during its ninth year is not 10, but 13.7, since this is the amount the firm has to set aside to replace this asset when it comes to the end of its productive life. There is another important difference between the two accounting systems, which is that company accountants apply the mortality rates for the asset that are most favourable to them from a tax standpoint, whereas the national accountants do their best to apply physical and economic laws. For example, if the tax authorities allow a truck to be depreciated in three years, the company accountants will do just that, while the national accountants will take the view that in fact a truck lasts 10 years and will depreciate it over this longer period. In the final analysis, national accountants cannot calculate the consumption of fixed capital simply by taking the sum of the depreciation declared by firms in their accounts. They have therefore designed their own method, which is known as the "perpetual inventory method" or PIM (see Chapter 8). Currently, this method is the best available for calculating the consumption of fixed capital, but it involves numerous assumptions regarding service lives and rates of depreciation. This probably explains why certain national accountants prefer to publish incomplete accounting balances (gross and not net) on the grounds that they are more reliable, instead of the net figures that are more correct but less reliable.

Profits and gross operating surplus: not to be confused

In the national accounts, the gross operating surplus is the portion of the income derived from production that is earned by the capital factor. It differs from the profit figure shown in the company accounts for several reasons. The following diagram (which remains approximate) shows the reconciliation of the two:

The first stage in this reconciliation consists of adding the consumption of fixed capital in order to obtain a gross accounting balance, in this case the gross operating surplus. Then we subtract the company accountants' measure of depreciation. It is then necessary to add the holding gains and losses from owning inventories, known as the "inventory valuation adjustment". For the

	net operating surplus (national accounts)
plus	consumption of fixed capital
=	gross operating surplus (national accounts)
minus	depreciation (company accounts)
plus	inventory appreciation (national accounts)
minus	conceptual or practical differences (treatment of intellectual property products, fraud, leasing arrangements
minus	property income paid excluding distributed income and reinvested earning on foreign direct investment (national accounts)
plus	property income received (national accounts)
plus	exceptional losses and profits, in particular capital gains and losses
=	pre-tax profit (company accounts)
minus	taxes on profits
=	**after-tax profit (company accounts)**

company accountants, this item is included in the profit calculation, whereas in the national accounts it is excluded from the measurement of output, and hence from the operating surplus. Next, it is necessary to adjust for certain other conceptual differences. For example, the national accountants treat most spending on intellectual property products as investment and not as intermediate consumption. This is done so that the relevant expenditure does not affect the operating surplus (except for depreciation), whereas it generally affects directly the calculation of company profits. Similarly, the national accountants adjust the figures supplied by firms to take into account the understatement of profit for reasons of fraud in certain sectors. Finally, leasing arrangements may be treated differently in the two accounting systems.

The next stage is to add property income received and deduct property income paid, the latter excluding distributed income and reinvested earnings on foreign direct investment. Profit as measured by company accountants is calculated taking these flows into account. Finally, company accounting rules permit certain "exceptional" transactions to be taken into consideration in calculating profits. For example, company profits can include the capital gains realised on the sale of subsidiaries or on currency transactions. Adding these exceptional elements can lead to substantial differences – in either direction – between the measurement of profits in the national accounts and in the company accounts.

Finally, and this is not the least of the practical differences, it must never be forgotten that the national accounts retrace only the operating profit of firms carrying out their activities on the economic territory. It is therefore impossible to compare the profits announced by the large multinational firms quoted on the stock markets with what is included in the national accounts, since the profits of the multinationals include those made by their overseas subsidiaries.

Insurance: are net premiums equal to the claims paid out?

The idea behind the modelling of transactions relating to non-life insurance in the national accounts can be summarised using the following simplified example. In this example, GP denotes gross premiums, in other words the sum of money appearing on your insurance invoice (for reasons of simplification, we ignore taxes such as VAT); S represents the insurance service (i.e. the output of non-life insurance in the national accounts, measured by the administrative expenses plus the operating profit of the insurance companies*); II represents investment income; and C represents claims payable. The net premiums, NP, are defined as equal to the gross premiums plus the investment income minus the insurance service, and this gives us the first equation: (1) $NP = GP + II - S$. The insurance service is measured by $GP + II - C$, i.e. the gross premiums plus the investment income minus the claims payable, giving us the second equation: (2) $S = GP + II - C$. Rearranging the two equations gives $NP = C$, so that the net premiums are equal to the claims. This "accounting identity" calls for two remarks.

First, the identity holds good only for the economy as a whole and not for individual institutional sectors, let alone individual customers. For example, in France in 2011, total net non-life insurance premiums amounted to EUR 36.0 billion and total claims to EUR 33.6 billion (the difference being explained by flows to and from the rest of the world). However, this does not imply that the net premiums paid by non-financial corporations are equal to the claims owed to non-financial corporations. It is quite possible that in that year they suffered fewer accidents of various kinds than other agents did. This is indeed what seems to have happened in France in 2011 since the net premiums of non-financial corporations were EUR 9.9 billion and their claims were only EUR 4.5 billion. However, such a situation is unlikely to last: if for structural reasons non-financial corporations have fewer expenses due to accidents than they pay out in premiums, it would be logical for the premiums to decline.

The second remark is that this equality is logically dubious. By what miracle should claims be identically equal to premiums when the insurance business is itself inherently unpredictable? Some years are catastrophic; others have relatively few claims. It is all a matter of probability – the theory that lies at the heart of the insurance profession. Obviously, the so-called law of averages operates in favour of certain regularity. But in practice the volatility of accidents, and hence of claims, means that premiums and claims are only rarely equal. In the national accounts, however, the miracle is

---

* See Chapter 4 for a more complete description of the output of insurance companies.

achieved in a simple manner: this volatile difference used to be allocated, by construct, to the output consisting of the insurance service S, as shown by equation (2). The counterpart of the accounting identity $NP = C$ therefore could potentially lead to substantial volatility of, and even negative values for the output of the insurance service. After long discussions among national accountants, it was proposed that this construct should be inverted by allocating the volatility, no longer to S, but to a transfer in the distribution of income account. The proposal for change was prompted by the fact that the current volatility of S was adversely affecting the interpretation of GDP. This reform has been introduced in the update of the SNA 2008.

Exercises for Chapter 7

Exercise 1. Accounting balances and ratios: from gross to net

This exercise is based on the French national accounts. It consists of recalculating the net accounting balances and ratios starting from the gross balances they provide. First question: find on the INSEE web site (*www.insee.fr*) the annual national accounts table that gives the consumption of fixed capital ("consommation de capital fixe") by non-financial corporations ("sociétés non financières") between 2009 and 2011. Second question: find on the INSEE web site the principal gross accounting balances for non-financial corporations over the same period (gross value added – "valeur ajoutée brute" – and gross operating surplus – "excédent brut d'exploitation"). Calculate the net balances. Deduce from these the gross and net profit ratios.

Exercise 2. To test the understanding of the accounts system

The following is a list of transactions made by an advertising firm. Place these various transactions correctly in the structure of accounts shown further below, and show that the firm's gross saving amounted to 620 K$ (1 K$ =1 000 $).

Revenue	K$
1. Sales to customers	4 500
2. Interest on bank account	30
3. Payment of claim for fire damage	10

Expenditure	K$
4. Paper, Ink and other office supplies used during the year	380
5. Rent paid for additional office space	150
6. Cost of electricity and telephones	60
7. CEO's remuneration	300
8. Gross staff wages and salaries	1 500
9. Employers' social security contributions on staff wages and salaries	800
10. Dividend paid to shareholders	420
11. Profits tax payable	180
13. Purchase of computers and software	240
14. Interest on the bank loan for the purchase of computers	40
15. Payment to the security company for the protection of buildings	70
16. Property tax on office buildings	20

Production account

Uses	Resources
P2. Intermediate consumption	P1. Output
	P11. Market
	P12 For own final uses

Generation of income account

Uses	Resources
DI. Compensation of employees:	B1. Gross value added
D11. Wages and salaries	
D121. Employers' actual social contributions	
D122. Employers' imputed social contributions	
D29. Other taxes on production	
D39. Other subsidies on production	
B2. Gross operating surplus	

Allocation of primary income account

Uses	Resources
D4. Property income:	B2. Gross operating surplus
D41. Interest	D4. Property income:
D421. Dividends	D41. Interest
D43. Reinvested earnings on direct foreign investment	D421. Dividends
D45. Rents on land and sub-soil assets	D43. Reinvested earnings on direct foreign investment
B5. Balance of primary incomes	D45. Rents on land and sub-soil assets

Secondary distribution of income account

Uses	Resources
D51. Taxes on income	B5. Balance of gross primary incomes
	D61. Social contributions:
D622. Private funded social benefits	D611 Actual social contributions
D71. Net non-life insurance premiums	D612. Imputed social contributions
D75. Miscellaneous current transfers	D72. Non-life insurance claims
B6. Gross disposable income	D75. Other current transfers 12

Use of disposable income account

Uses	Resources
B8. Gross saving	B6. Gross disposable income

Exercise 3. Some international comparisons for all corporations (including non-financial), year 2011

Using the below data, calculate three significant corporate ratios for each country: the net profit share $\left(\frac{NOS}{NVA}\right)$; the investment rate $\left(\frac{GFCF}{GVA}\right)$; and the self-financing ratio $\left(\frac{Grosssaving}{GFCF}\right)$. Be careful: the profit share you are being asked for is a net rate, whereas the investment rate and the self-financing ratio are gross rates. The results show a significantly higher profit share in Germany. Is that statistically significant?

	Germany	France	Spain
	M euros	M euros	M euros
Gross value added	2 334 890	1 793 759	959 762
Gross operating surplus and mixed income	1 019 420	665 557	445 104
Mixed income	229 000	121 699	153 136
Gross operating surplus	790 420	543 859	291 968
Saving, net	248 440	87 160	12 240
Consumption of fixed capital	391 070	279 212	168 394
GFCF	473 170	399 953	216 695
Profit share (net)			
Investment ratio			
Self-financing ratio			

Exercise 4. (Difficult) The calculation of the profit share for non-financial corporations

The data below are a slightly simplified representation of Table 27 of the "Informations Rapides", which is the main publication of the French quarterly national accounts (detailed results):

Breakdown of the gross profit share of non-financial corporations (%)

	2011	2012
Profit share (%)	35.7	35.1
Change in the profit share	-0.9	-0.6
Contributions to the change in the profit share		
Labour productivity (+)	1.1	0.2
Real compensation of employees (-)	0.8	0.2
Ratio price of GVA/price of Final consumption (+)	-0.8	-0.4
Other elements (+)	-0.5	-0.2

Explain how the change in the profit share can be expressed as a function of the change in labour productivity (expressed in terms of value added), growth in real compensation of employees, the ratio of the price of the gross value added to the price of final consumption, and other elements. For this purpose, start with the definition of the profit share and the equation GOS = GVA – CE – TNS, where GVA is the gross value added, GOS the gross operating surplus, CE the compensation of employees (including employers' social contributions) and TNS the taxes net of subsidies on production (from now on this last item will not be shown separately but will be included under "other elements"). Use the definition of labour productivity (value added in volume/employment) and real wage rate (the hourly compensation of employees divided by the price of final consumption). Based on these variables, comment on the change in the profit share in 2011 and 2012. Make the link with the economic principle governing wage bargaining, which says that real wage rates (including employers' social contributions) can increase by the amount of productivity gains.

Exercise 5 (Difficult). *Producer prices and production costs*

Table 26 of the "Informations Rapides" of the French quarterly national accounts (detailed results) includes the following table. Please note that in this table, different from the table in the previous Exercise 4, the percentage changes of the different cost elements of total unit cost are not expressed in terms of contributions to the total. The breakdown of the unit wage cost, however, is expressed as contributions to the total wage cost.

Change in production costs
In %

Non-financial corporations	2011	2012
Producer price	2.6	1.4
Total unit cost	3.4	1.7
Of which, intermediate consumption	4.2	1.1
Taxes related to production	18.8	9.6
Wage costs	1.1	2.6
Components of the unit wage cost		
Average wage per head (+)	2.7	1.9
Productivity[a] (-)	2.2	-0.5
Social contributions, employer (+)	0.6	0.1

a) Productivity is defined here in terms of output.

What is the implicit definition of total cost in this table? How can one deduce from it total unit cost? How does the analysis of total unit cost make it possible to understand the evolution in producer prices? Write down the formula for the relationship between total unit cost and its components. Write down the relationship between unit wage costs and its three component variables (average wage per head, productivity, and employers' social contributions). Justify the (+) and the (–). Why does the footnote relating to the productivity variable mention "in terms of output", whereas in the table for the previous exercise it mentioned "in terms of value added"?

The solutions to these exercises are available at:
http://dx.doi.org/10.1787/9789264214637-25-en

Chapter 8

The financial and balance sheet accounts

Financial accounts and balance sheet accounts in national accounts are the source of financial and non-financial stock data of households, and other institutional sectors (financial and non-financial corporations, and general government). These accounts make it possible to calculate not only the net worth of various groups at a given moment, but also to examine how this has evolved over time. This chapter describes the organization of these accounts.

Household final consumption accounts for 60% or more of GDP, so that a change of one or two percentage points in this aggregate can decide whether the economy does well or badly. The OECD economists therefore keep a close eye on the factors that influence household consumption. The most important of these is their disposable income during the period in question, but it is not the only one. Another variable influencing consumption is the change in household wealth.

1. The importance of household wealth for the analysis of the current economic situation

Households own financial and non-financial assets (the latter, primarily homes) comprising their wealth. When the value of these assets increases due, for example, to a rise in share prices, or a rise in housing prices above the rise of prices of other goods and services, households feel richer and hence are more inclined to save less and, therefore, spend more. It is wealth in the form of stocks that is most sensitive to these capital gains, or "holding gains" (see the appendix at the end of the chapter "Going further: Holding gains or losses and market prices in the national accounts"). These gains were particularly spectacular in the first half of the first decade of the 21st century thanks to rising prices of dwellings. They were unfortunately followed by as spectacular losses after the dwelling bubble exploded in the second part of the decade. This influence on household behaviour is known as the "wealth effect". It was particularly visible in the United States, where the dwelling price bubble was the most explosive.

The OECD regularly publishes indicators of the changes in household wealth. The following table, extracted from an OECD publication, deals with Canada, the United Kingdom and the United States.

The figures in Table 8.1 are expressed as percentages of **net disposable income,** making it possible to evaluate the wealth in terms of the number of years of annual income. For example, in Canada in 2010, households' net worth (synonym of "net wealth") was equivalent to 578.3% of their net annual disposable income, i.e., nearly six years' worth of income. The wealth comprises financial assets (bank accounts, savings accounts, stock market shares, other shares, bonds and other debt securities) and non-financial assets (land, housing, productive assets of sole proprietorships, etc.). But households also have debts (mortgages, consumer loans, etc.), and you are not

232

Table 8.1. **Household wealth and indebtedness**

As a percentage of net disposable income

	Canada			United Kingdom			United States		
	2000	2005	2010	2000	2005	2010	2000	2005	2010
Net wealth	531.1	561.7	578.3	770.9	832.1	825.6	590.7	659.6	536.3
Net financial wealth	254.0	227.5	218.0	380.5	303.3	298.4	360.5	353.0	325.3
Non-financial assets	277.1	334.2	360.3	390.5	528.7	527.3	230.1	306.6	211.0
Financial assets	373.1	363.5	377.3	498.4	467.4	464.8	460.9	484.0	448.0
of which: Equities	89.1	83.4	96.3	114.4	76.9	71.1	148.1	127.4	119.4
Liabilities	119.1	136.0	159.3	117.9	164.0	166.4	100.4	131.0	122.7
of which: Mortgages	73.6	83.2	99.8	86.0	122.6	..	67.5	97.9	90.5

Source: OECD (2013), "OECD Economic Outlook No. 93", OECD Economic Outlook: Statistics and Projections (database), doi: *http://dx.doi.org/10.1787/data-00655-en.*

StatLink ᴍᴧ▰ᴹ *http://dx.doi.org/10.1787/888933144065*

truly rich if you own substantial financial wealth but at the same time have considerable debts. This is why economists look at net worth, which is equal to total (financial and non-financial) assets minus total liabilities (all liabilities are financial). For example, the total financial and non-financial assets of Canadian households in 2010 came to 737.6% (377.3% + 360.3%), but, after deduction of liabilities equivalent to 159.3%, the net worth was only 578.3%, well below the figure in Table 8.1 for United Kingdom households but more than that of United States households.

Table 8.1 also illustrates the impact of the speculative housing bubble during the first decade of the century on household wealth. In the United States, the value of non-financial assets held by households rose from 230.1% in 2000 to 306.6% in 2005 of net disposable income in just five years. To some extent, this increase was due to an increase in the volume of dwellings bought by households, but mainly it was caused by a rise in dwelling prices. However, the 2007 downturn of housing prices wiped out almost half the potential gains accrued, and unrealized holding gains were just as rapidly replaced by unrealized holding losses, leading to a low level of non-financial assets held by American households, 211.0%, in 2010. Dwelling prices are less volatile than stock markets, but have their ups and downs as well. This would matter less were it not for the impact on economic growth, notably via the "wealth effect". Unfortunately, the downturn on housing prices in the United States not only directly affected household consumption but led to a crash of big financial institutions which had wrongly invested in fragile financial instruments (the so-called "subprimes"). This crash led to the largest recession in 2008 and 2009 since World War II.

The financial transactions accounts, which are generally called simply financial accounts (and sometimes flow of funds) and the balance sheet accounts (which are sometimes called asset and liability accounts) in the national accounts constitute the source for the household data we have just commented on. However, financial and balance sheet accounts exist not only for households, but also for all institutional sectors (financial and non-financial corporations, and general government) and, partly, for the rest of the world. These accounts make it possible to calculate not only the net worth of various groups of agents (i.e., the institutional sectors) at a given moment, but also how this has evolved over time. This chapter describes the organization of these accounts.

2. The principle of quadruple-entry bookkeeping

Preceding chapters have shown how the national accounts record transactions relating to production, consumption and distribution between the various institutional sectors. At the end of all these transactions, economic agents are either in a borrower situation, meaning that they have spent more than they have received, or in a lender situation, meaning that they have spent less than they have received. The financial accounts show how the borrower sectors obtain the financial resources they need, and how the lender sectors allocate their surpluses. In general, non-financial corporations are globally borrowers while households are globally lenders.* "Globally", means that the status of a borrower or lender applies to the sector as a whole, and not to each unit comprising the sector (for example, the great majority of poor households are not lenders).

We shall see here, in a section in which anyone who has worked on company accounts will recognize some familiar conventions (the so-called "double entry system"), that each transaction is recorded twice: once as a transaction related to production, consumption, etc., and once as a monetary transaction– national accountants would say once as a **non-financial transaction** and once as a **financial transaction**. This system shows the high degree of integration within national accounts.

In our money-based societies, every transaction has as a counterpart movement of funds (except for barter transactions, which are recorded solely as non-financial transactions). National accountants say that *each non-financial transaction has a financial "counterpart"*. For example, household H buys a television set for USD 300. This will be recorded as consumption of USD 300 in the form of a non-financial transaction. Because of this purchase, the household's bank balance is reduced by USD 300, which is reflected in a financial transaction, i.e., it is recorded in the financial accounts. Every

---

* In countries where the housing bubble of 2005-10 was the most explosive (United States, Spain and Ireland) households were investing so much in dwellings that they became globally, but temporarily, borrowers.

transaction by an agent therefore gives rise to two entries: one in the non-financial accounts; the other in the financial accounts, as shown in the summary T-account below.

Accounts of household H

Non-financial transactions		Financial transactions	
Uses	Resources	Uses	Resources
Consumption 300		Reduction in bank deposits 300	

We shall now record the same transaction, but this time from the point of view of corporation C, which sold the television set to household H. As with the household, there are two entries, but for the corporation both entries are under "resources": one as an output among non-financial transactions; and one as an increase in the company's bank balance among financial transactions.

Accounts of corporation C

Non-financial transactions		Financial transactions	
Uses	Resources	Uses	Resources
	Output 300		Increase in bank deposit 300

This means that, in total, a single transaction is recorded four times in the national accounts, hence the term quadruple-entry bookkeeping referred to in this section. Put another way, two entries are made for each of the two sectors involved in a transaction.

In practice, the financial accounts are somewhat more complicated than we have just shown. For one thing, continuing with the above example, instead of recording movements in funds under uses or resources depending on whether they correspond to an increase or decrease in a bank balance, all the transactions on the bank accounts are entered on the same side of the T-account.

Moreover, the equivalent of the "uses" column is renamed "changes in assets" (denoted by Δ Assets) and the equivalent "resources" column is renamed "changes in liabilities" (denoted by Δ Liabilities). Using these terms, our earlier example then gives the following entries:

Accounts of household H

Non-financial transactions		Financial transactions	
Uses	Resources	Δ Assets	Δ Liabilities
Consumption 300		Bank balance -300	

Accounts of corporation C

Non-financial transactions		Financial transactions	
Uses	Resources	Δ Assets	Δ Liabilities
	Output 300	Bank balance +300	

It will be seen that this leads to the existence in the financial accounts of transactions carrying a negative sign. For instance, the reduction of USD 300 in the household's bank balance is recorded as -300 under changes in assets. This complicates things somewhat, but remains easily understandable, since a negative number indicates a decrease in the financial asset in question – in this case a decline in the bank balance. Since a given period will see numerous movements in bank accounts, some positive and some negative, the financial account will record only the algebraic (net) sum of all these movements taken together.

On the liability side, we find the debts. To complicate our example slightly more, as illustrated below, if our household H had taken out a loan of USD 300 to pay for its television set, we would find on the "changes in liabilities" side a debt increase of USD 300, matched by an increase in the bank balance of the household. Note that it is quite possible to find a negative number among the changes in liabilities. For example, if a household repays a debt, this will be recorded as a negative number in the right-hand column, which reflects the "changes in liabilities" (for a more comprehensive example, see the appendix at the end of the chapter "Going further: a more complete example of entries in the financial accounts"). A final change in presentation involves placing the financial accounts of each agent one below the other and not side-by-side.

Accounts of household H		Accounts of corporation C	
Non-financial transactions		Non-financial transactions	
Uses	Resources	Uses	Resources
Consumption 300			Output 300

Accounts of household H		Accounts of corporation C	
Financial transactions		Financial transactions	
Δ Assets	Δ Liabilities	Δ Assets	Δ Liabilities
Bank balance (money obtained from the loan) +300 (money paid for the TV) -300	Loan taken out +300	Bank balance +300	

The T-accounts make it easier to visualize all the accounting relationships involved in the quadruple entry. We will call them "accounting identities". The *first accounting identity* is the consolidation, or cancelling out, along the row of the non-financial transactions, with the consumption of USD 300 under uses matched by output of USD 300 under resources. In contrast to the financial accounts, there are no figures with negative signs in the non-financial accounts (although there are exceptions). However, it is valid to place a "virtual" negative sign on a transaction in the uses column and a "virtual" positive sign on a transaction in the resources column. Thus, one can place a negative sign on the consumption of USD 300 and a positive sign on the output of USD 300. This gives (-300 + 300 = 0), so the accounting identity is respected.

If, for the moment, we forget the complication introduced by a loan taken out by households, the *second accounting* identity is the cancelling out along the row of the financial transactions, with the -$300 in household H's bank balance matched by +$300 in company C's bank balance: (-300 + 300 = 0).

To better visualize these two accounting relationships, one can introduce a crucial balancing item providing the link between the non-financial and the financial transactions. This is **net lending (+)/net borrowing (-)**, carrying the code **B9.**

The net lending/net borrowing is the balance of all the non-financial transactions. Once agents have produced their output, been paid for their work, consumed, paid their taxes, received their benefits, etc., they have either underspent their receipts, in which case they have "financing capacity" (i.e., they have generated "net lending"), or overspent their receipts, in which case they need to borrow, incurring "financing requirements" (i.e., they have incurred a "net borrowing" situation). This balancing item, like all similar balancing items in the non-financial accounts, is conventionally entered in the uses column and is calculated as the sum of the resources minus the sum of the uses. If the result is positive, there is net lending; if it is negative there is net borrowing. For the sake of simplicity in the national accounts, "net lending/net borrowing" is presented as a single item; a positive sign is attached to financing capacity (net lending) and a negative sign to financing requirements (net borrowing). The following table shows the accounts of the above example including the balancing item B9.

B9 is the book balance of all the non-financial transactions and, at the same time, the balance of all the financial transactions. We accordingly find the same number at the bottom of the financial transactions account, but in this case it is conventionally placed in the right-hand column and is calculated as the sum of the changes in assets minus the sum of the changes in liabilities. From the point of view of the financial accounts, this balancing

Accounts of household H		Accounts of corporation C	
Non-financial transactions		Non-financial transactions	
Uses	Resources	Uses	Resources
Consumption 300			Output 300
B9 Net lending/ net −300 borrowing		B9 Net lending/ net +300 borrowing	

Financial transactions		Financial transactions	
Δ Assets	Δ Liabilities	Δ Assets	Δ Liabilities
Bank balance −300		Bank balance +300	
	B9 Net lending/ net −300 borrowing		B9 Net lending/ net +300 borrowing

item can be interpreted as a change in financial net worth (in net financial wealth). If an agent is in a net lending situation, this means that, other things being equal (i.e. if movements in the price of assets and other changes in volume are not considered), he or she has become financially richer during the period. Note that this can be due to several different factors. The agent may either have increased his/her claims on other agents or reduced his debts, or performed a mixture of both. Conversely, if an agent is in a net borrowing situation, his/her financial net worth has decreased during the period, everything else being equal.

The *final accounting identity* results from the (theoretically) strict accounting identity between the balance on the financial accounts and the balance on the non-financial accounts. By definition, these two "B9s" are equal. For each of the two agents – corporation and household – this equality is respected in our example in this section. Unfortunately, however, it is not respected in the actual national accounts tables. This is not because there are exceptions to the general rule but because the statistical sources used for the calculation of the non-financial accounts are different from those used for the financial accounts. The resulting divergence in B9 measurements is known as a "statistical discrepancy", and its existence explains why the B9 of the non-financial accounts is sometimes coded "B9A" and that of the financial accounts "B9B" so as to differentiate them. The general government sector has at times no statistical discrepancy between B9A and B9B, thanks partly to the quality and consistency of the information available for the accounts of this sector but also, in Europe, to the need to produce the "cleanest" accounts possible, given that they are closely monitored by the European Commission (see Chapter 9). In the general government case, therefore, B9A is often equal or very nearly equal to B9B.

It is essential to have a firm grasp of these **three accounting identities** to be able to record in a convincing manner certain very complex operations (see Exercises 2 and 3 at the end of this chapter). An important corollary of these three accounting identities – or theorems – is that in a closed economy (one that has no relations with the rest of the world) the sum of the net lending and net borrowing for all sectors is zero by definition. In other words, one agent's net lending is necessarily another agent's net borrowing, as one can see in Box 8.1, "Saving and investment". In an open economy, the sum of the net lending and net borrowing of resident agents is equal to the net lending or net borrowing of the rest of the world, but carries the opposite sign.

Box 8.1. **Saving and investment**

The basic Keynesian model taught in elementary macroeconomics classes is: Y = C + I and R = Y. These equations are to be read as follows: demand Y is equal to consumption C plus investment I; income R is equal to output Y, which is itself equal to demand. From this is derived the well-known equation:

Saving = R – C = I

stating the basic rule that saving equals investment. If one assumes that firms do not self-finance any of their investment and that households do not invest, this is tantamount to restating our "theorem" that the sum of net lending(+)/net borrowing(-) is zero in a closed economy. In practice, households save and in this way are generally net lenders. Firms, for their part, have to find funding for their investment. Under the simplified conditions presented here, households' net lending exactly covers, by definition, firms' net borrowing. This is a reformulation of the basic Keynesian model and illustrates the convergence that exists between it and the national accounts model.

It is strongly recommended that Exercise 2 be done after a first reading of this chapter. In addition to providing an illustration of these accounting identities, it will demonstrate that some transactions are purely financial, in the sense that they involve no non-financial offsetting entries. For example, if a household sells shares, only the two movements in financial assets are recorded, with no corresponding entry in the non-financial accounts.

3. Financial assets and liabilities

In our very simple example, we have introduced only one type of financial asset (the bank account) and only two agents. In reality, there is a very wide variety of claims and debt and also a wide variety of institutional sectors. In particular, there is considerable detail in the financial accounts regarding the different categories of financial institutions. The complete list of these financial subsectors is given in Box 10.2 of Chapter 10.

The entire scope of the information provided by the financial accounts can be seen by referring to the box **"Integrated system of financial accounts"** in the appendix "Going further" toward the end of this chapter. However, before going into all these details, it is useful to start with a simplified presentation of the financial accounts, to show that things are not as complicated as they look in the integrated system.

Simplified presentation of the financial accounts

	Financial assets Δ		Liabilities Δ	
	Financial institutions (FI)	Non-financial agents (NFA)	Financial institutions (FI)	Non-financial agents (NFA)
Deposits		W	W	
Loans	X			X
Interbank financing	Y		Y	
Securities	Z1	Z2	Z3	Z4

In this simplified presentation, we have indicated by capital letters the cells in the table where the bulk of the transactions and the major accounting identities are to be found. As the presentation shows, the financial accounts trace out the assets and liabilities (and the changes in these) taking place between the *financial institutions sector* (mainly banks) and the *non-financial sectors* (households, non-financial corporations, general government). The principal financial assets are shown in the left-hand column: *deposits* (including current accounts), *loans* (i.e. bank loans to corporations and households), *interbank financing* (all the transactions between banks that are necessary for the financial system to function properly – see Box 8.2 below) and *securities* (bonds and shares).

For example, the deposits (W) are assets for the non-financial sectors and liabilities for the financial institutions, and the total of the one is equal to the total of the other. The loans (X) are mainly assets for the financial institutions and liabilities for the non-financial sectors, and again the two totals are equal. The amounts involved in interbank refinancing (Y) are often astronomical, and, while they are in fact internal to (and typical of) the financial institutions sector, with roughly the same amounts recorded as assets and liabilities, they were partly at the origin of the 2007-08 financial crisis. Only the securities (Z) are recorded on both the assets and liabilities sides for virtually all the institutional sectors and in the sector rest of the world. The exception is the household sector, since households do not issue securities. As with the identities for other lines, total securities issued (Z3 + Z4) equals total securities acquired (Z1 + Z2).

Box 8.2. **Could the financial accounts have been used to forecast the financial crisis of 2007-08?**

Ninety-nine percent of macroeconomists and supervisory experts were not able to forecast the upcoming financial crisis of 2007-2008, which started in the United States with the so-called "subprime" crisis. Subprimes were home mortgages that were distributed without ensuring that the benefiters would be able to repay, and which were bundled into financial assets (asset backed securities) sold in the financial markets with excellent ratings, while they were toxic. Could one have seen the thunderstorm gaining strength if they had looked more closely at the financial accounts? When looking a posteriori to a graph such as the one in the next page, which shows the new long-term loans (essentially home mortgages) undertaken by United States households during the last two decades, expressed in terms of personal income, one sees clearly the curb reaching previously unexplored heights just before the crisis. Perhaps economists should have looked better at financial accounts. However, it is easy to see the problem a posteriori, when we see the drop in the curb after the crisis. It was more difficult before, in particular because financial accounts do not give direct information on the level of risk associated with the financial instrument. It was easy to see that home mortgages were exploding. It was difficult to see that they were toxic. As discussed in Chapter 13, financial accounts are not sufficiently detailed, in particular regarding financial derivatives (the United States Federal Reserve unfortunately does not publish any data on financial derivatives in its "flow of funds") which were at the centre of the crisis. Following the crisis, the G20 and international organisations started to develop financial data more prone to a risk analysis. Will it avoid the next financial crisis?

There are in fact many more columns and rows in the table of financial transactions in the national accounts system than those included in the simplified table cited above. In particular, various financial assets are broken down by their degree of "liquidity" (a financial term measuring the rapidity and facility with which an asset can be transformed into cash or another generally accepted means of payment: a bank current account is highly liquid, but a share is less liquid because it first has to be sold, requiring payment of a commission). The following is the list of the principal financial assets recorded in the national accounts. The list of financial liabilities is identical to

Figure 8.1. **United States: Household loans in terms of personal income**

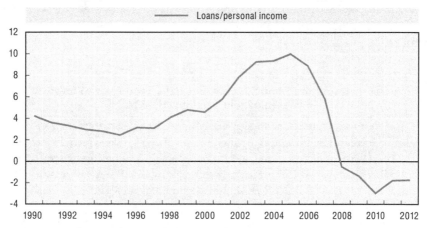

Source: Bureau of Economic Analysis (2013), National Income and Product Accounts Tables, *www.bea.gov/iTable/iTable.cfm?ReqID=9&step=1#reqid=9&step=3&isuri=1&904=2012&903=58&906=a&905= 1990&910=x&911=0* and OECD (2014), "Financial Accounts: Non-consolidated flows, annual", OECD National Accounts Statistics (database), doi: *http://dx.doi.org/10.1787/data-00023-en.*

StatLink 🔗 *http://dx.doi.org/10.1787/888933144077*

the financial assets, since one sector's or agent's financial asset is necessarily another sector's or agent's liability (see Box 8.3 "Tricks of the trade: how to distinguish a financial asset from a non-financial asset").

Box 8.3. **Tricks of the trade: how to distinguish a financial asset from a non-financial asset**

A financial asset for one agent always is a corresponding liability for another agent. For example, a bank account is an asset for a household and a liability for the bank holding it. Banknotes are assets for those who own them and a liability for the central bank that issues them. A loan is an asset for the lender and a liability for the borrower, and so on. Non-financial assets, on the other hand, have no identifiable counterpart. If a household owns a dwelling, this appears among its assets, but it is no one's liability. A firm owns a machine that appears among its assets but no other agent has a corresponding liability.

The list of financial assets is as follows using the new SNA 2008/ESA 2010 classification (*in parenthesis the old classification of SNA 1993/ESA 1995 is shown, but only when different to the new one*):

F1 – *Monetary gold and SDRs*. This item usually only concerns central banks. It reflects the gold held as a monetary reserve by a central bank plus

Special Drawing Rights (SDRs). SDRs are special assets created by the International Monetary Fund and held by central banks. There are three exceptions: in the United Kingdom, F1 is recorded for the sector S1311 (central government), while in the United States and Japan, it is split between S121 (central bank) and S1311 (central government).

F2 – *Currency and deposits.* This item includes "currency", code F21 (which is an asset for the holders and a liability for the issuers, mainly central banks). It also includes "transferable deposits", code F22, which includes demand bank accounts, as well as "other deposits" (F29). Item F2 does not exactly correspond to the so-called monetary aggregates (see section "Going further: financial accounts and money supply: the example of the euro area" at the end of this chapter).

F3 – *Debt securities (SNA 1993: Securities other than shares).* In SNA 1993, this item was broken down into two sub-items: F33 "securities other than shares, except financial derivatives" and F34 "financial derivatives". In SNA 2008, financial derivatives are not classified under this item but as F71 (see below). Thus, in SNA 2008, this item only contains debt securities, and is split into two sub-items: short-term (F31) and long-term securities (F32) and includes, in particular, the securities issued by the public treasury to finance the public deficit. It also includes all other bonds issued by non-financial corporations and financial institutions.

F4 – *Loans.* This item contains all the financial assets that are created when creditors lend money directly to debtors. This item includes consumer loans, housing loans and loans to all kinds of businesses. Like item F3, item F4 is broken down into two sub-items: short-term loans (for less than one year) and long-term loans (for more than one year). This breakdown has its limitations. For one thing, loans are sometimes renegotiable. For another, a long-term loan nearing the end of its life becomes a short-term loan.

F5 – *Equity and investment fund shares (SNA 1993: Shares and other equity).* This item includes shares (F51) in both quoted and unquoted companies and shares in investment funds (F52). How to value unquoted shares is the Achilles' heel of the financial accounts. It is in fact very difficult to estimate what their market price would be, since by definition there is no market for unlisted shares. Note, moreover, that shares are shown as liabilities of non-financial corporations and financial institutions, even though they are not a debt of these sectors but rather form part of their "own funds". Shares in investment funds (F52) are shares held indirectly, through portfolios managed by banks and other financial institutions (including property portfolios). This item is increasingly important, since households apparently prefer this type of product to direct holding of shares and bonds.

F6 – *Insurance, pension and standardized guarantee scheme (SNA 1993: Insurance technical reserves)*. In the SNA 1993, this item was broken down between F61 "net equity of households in life insurance reserves and in pension fund reserves" and F62 "prepayments of premiums and reserves for claims". In terms of holdings, item F61 represented the cumulative value of the savings invested by households in life insurance contracts and in capitalization pension funds. The value of these assets is attributed to households in the national accounts, despite the fact that these assets in company accounting appear in the balance sheets of the companies managing these funds. This attribution is a correct representation of economic reality, since the savings belong to the households and not to the companies managing them. Indeed, at some stage, these sums will be returned to the households in the form of annuities or retirement pensions. The implicit debts of the "distribution" (or "transfer") pension plans, also known as "pay-as-you-go" (often social security or civil service pension plans, at least in some European countries) are not recorded in the national accounts. For the time being, the institutional differences among countries regarding pension plans (capitalization versus pay-as-you-go) generate very significant differences in the financial accounts, making international comparisons difficult. In particular, vested pension commitments (in other words, future pension rights) in countries with mainly capitalization systems are recorded as households' assets, while the value of future pension rights in countries with pay-as-you-go public systems (like France, Germany, Italy and Spain) are not recorded. This difficulty in international comparisons should be resolved by the compilation by all OECD member states of a supplementary table, in which all pension obligations would be estimated, including social security. Item F62 represents the prepayments of accident insurance premiums and outstanding claims on insurance companies.

In the SNA 2008, this item is called "Insurance, pension and standardized guarantee schemes". The old F62 is now called F61 ("Non-life insurance technical provisions"). The old F61, is broken down into four sub-categories (F62 to F65), and a new category "F66 Provisions for calls under standardized guarantees" has been created. The latter was not recognized as a financial asset/liability in the old SNA.

F7 – *Financial derivatives and employee stock options (SNA 1993: F34)*. This is a very large item but is almost exclusively concerned with interbank refinancing, except for the very small category of employee stock options (F72). The description of financial derivatives (F71) is somewhat too technical for this manual.

F8 – *Other accounts receivable/payable (SNA 1993: F7)*. This item contains two sub-items: F81 (SNA 1993: F71) "trade credits and advances" and F89 (SNA 1993: F79) "other accounts receivable/payable". The first of these is a substantial item, since it includes credits related to commercial transactions (in France, for example, payments between firms for goods and services are frequently on a 60-days basis, meaning that the seller agrees to deliver the product while accepting payment 60 days later). The second sub-item includes, in particular, all the implicit credits relating to wages and salaries, taxes, rents, etc. The national accounts record transactions on the basis of "accrual accounting", as do company accounts. This means that a transaction must be recorded in such a way that the accounts reflect at any moment the value of agents' entitlements and obligations. For example, even if an employee's salary is paid two or three months late, the salary will be entered in the month during which the work was carried out, because this is when an obligation to pay by the employer was generated. Since the salary is entered but has not been paid, there is a claim by the employee on the firm, which is entered in sub-item F89. A similar entry will be made for tax due to the government but not yet paid.

4. The link between financial flows and financial stocks

As was pointed out at the beginning of this chapter, the purpose of complete financial accounts is mainly to provide figures on the net worth – i.e. assets *minus* liabilities, also known as net wealth – of institutional sectors. The balance, or stock, of assets and liabilities is recorded at a given moment in time. In the national accounts, this is usually 31 December, but many countries and the European Central Bank also publish quarterly financial accounts. Take the example of a UK household H, which on 31 December of year A, has £2 000 in a bank account, owns £13 500 of shares and £23 000 of bonds, while its short-term debts amount to £3 500 (consumer credit) and its long-term debts to £7 500 (mortgages).

Stocks of assets and liabilities at 31/12/A

Financial assets	
F2 Currency and deposits	2 000
F5 Shares	13 500
F3 Securities other than shares	23 000
Liabilities	
F41 Short-term loans	3 500
F42 Long-term loans	7 500

Starting with this situation at 31/12/A, let us suppose that the household to which we have been referring performs the following series of financial transactions during year A + 1. It spends £35 000 on consumption, receives £37 000 in wages and salaries, sells £6 500 of shares and repays £1 500 of its short-term debt and £2 500 of its long-term debt. These transactions (i.e. these financial *flows*) will be traced out in the financial accounts as movements between two consecutive financial balances (i.e. between two financial *stocks*).

Financial accounts for the year A + 1

Δ financial assets (net acquisition of financial assets)	During A + 1
F2 Currency and deposits	-35 000
	+37 000
	+6 500
	-1 500
	-2 500
	=4 500
F5 Shares	-6 500

Δ liabilities (net incurrence of liabilities)	During A + 1
F41 Short-term loans	-1 500
F42 Long-term loans	-2 500

Financial transactions are recorded at the prices actually paid, i.e. in current pounds sterling. In the case of transactions using payment instruments denominated in other currencies (euros, dollars, yen, etc.) the currency rates prevalent on the day of the transaction are applied and in the case of transactions in shares and bonds, whose market prices are subject to change, the actual prices at the time of sale or purchase are applied.

One would be forgiven for thinking that the situation at 31/12/A + 1 would therefore be equal to the situation at 31/12/A plus the movements carried out during year A + 1. However, we at least have to allow for the impact of changes in asset prices. Applying the general principles of the national accounts, financial (and non-financial) stocks of assets and liabilities are valued at the market prices ruling on the day the accounts are drawn up, usually on the 31 December for the annual accounts and the last day of the calendar quarter for the quarterly accounts. But market prices of shares and bonds change (for example, the value of a bond changes in inverse proportion to changes in interest rates – see the appendix "Going further: The valuation of assets and its relationship to economic theory"). The value of an asset held by an agent can therefore change between 31/12/A and 31/12/A + 1, even in the absence of any transactions, simply through the operation of price changes on the market, leading to holding gains in the case of upward movements and holding losses in the case of downward movements.

Returning to the example of our household, let us suppose that the average price of the shares it owns falls by 20% between 31/12/A and 31/12/A + 1. One can also suppose that it was in anticipation of this fall that the household sold a substantial portion of its shares (let us assume that this took place at the very beginning of the year, before the price fall, so as to simplify matters). The household will therefore have suffered a holding loss of 20% on the remaining £7 000 held in shares, i.e. a loss of £1 400. Let us at the same time suppose that the bond portfolio of the household consists of 6% Treasury bonds and that during the year the market rate of interest on Treasury bonds fell to 4%. In this case, the market value of the 6% bonds will have risen (see Exercise 4 for the calculation of bond values). Let us suppose that this produced a holding gain of £3 200. All these changes in the price of assets are recorded in a special account known as the "revaluation account". Because in our example on the asset side the cash holdings (or on the liability side the loans) are not subject to revaluation, no revaluations are required for these items.

Revaluation account for year A + 1

Δ Financial assets subject to revaluation	During A + 1
F5 Shares	-1 400
F3 Securities other than shares	+3 200

We are now in a position to find the value of the financial holdings at the end of period A + 1, which equals the initial balance (stock) at end of year A (or at the beginning of year A + 1), *plus* the transactions in assets or liabilities during the year *plus* the revaluations. For example, the amount of shares at 31/12/A + 1 is equal to £13 500 (balance at 31/12/A) *minus* £6 500 (sale of shares) *minus* £1 400 (holding losses on the remaining shares in the portfolio), which gives £5 600.

	Financial assets and liabilities 31/12/A	Financial transactions During A + 1	Revaluations During A + 1	Financial assets and liabilities 31/12/A + 1
Assets				
F2 Currency and deposits	2 000	4 500		6 500
F5 Shares	13 500	-6 500	-1 400	5 600
F3 Securities other than shares	23 000		+3 200	26 200
Liabilities				
F41 Short-term loans	3 500	-1 500		2 000
F42 Long-term loans	7 500	-2 500		5 000

This example presents the complete information available for households in the financial accounts (with the exception of a special account called "other changes in volume" mentioned below). The complete financial accounts (integrated system of financial accounts) show the financial transactions, revaluation accounts, the other changes in volume accounts (not included in this example) and the financial net worth accounts (also called "balance sheets" or "financial assets and liabilities accounts", which comprise the balances (stocks) for the various items) for all the institutional sectors – households, non-financial corporations, financial institutions, general government, and NPISHs. Taken together, the revaluation and other changes in volume accounts are termed "reconciliation accounts" because, together with transactions, they "reconcile" the assets and liabilities at the beginning of the period with those at the end of the period. As might be expected, these accounts are particularly detailed for the financial corporations, which play a critical role in the management of financial relations among the various sectors and constitute the prime statistical source for the financial accounts.

The complete financial accounts are in three parts. First, there are the financial transactions, which are brought together in the financial transactions account. Second, the revaluation accounts as well as the accounts reflecting the other changes in the volume of financial assets (i.e., the reconciliation accounts) and, finally, the financial wealth accounts, showing the positions or balances (stocks). This financial wealth constitutes the financial component of the net worth accounts described in the last section of this chapter. An example of the integrated system comprising the aforementioned accounts is given in the paragraph "Integrated system of financial accounts" in the appendix "Going further" at the end of this chapter. This section reproduces a synthesis of the "Financial Accounts of the Spanish Economy" published by the Bank of Spain showing the financial wealth at the beginning of 2012, the flows affecting it throughout 2012, (i.e., the financial transactions, revaluations and other changes in volume) and the financial wealth at the end of 2012 resulting from these changes. All these accounts refer to the total of the economy and the rest of the world and to each of the resident sectors comprising the total economy, i.e. non-financial corporations, financial institutions, general government and households and NPISHs. For simplification, the section does not cover non-financial corporations and general government.

Taken together, these tables show for each institutional sector the details of the financial counterpart of its net lending/net borrowing and the composition of its net worth. Conversely, for a given financial asset – shares, for example – issued by one sector or by all of them, it is possible to know the net issue flows during the period and the purchasing sectors, and finally, in the financial net worth of the economy overall, the total value of the outstanding shares issued in the economy and, at the end of a given period (in this case the year 2012), the sectors that have issued these shares and those holding them in portfolio. The financial accounts began to be drawn up annually, referring in principle to the financial institutions sector (central banks, banks, other financial intermediaries – see the box "Data sources:

Statistical sources for the financial accounts" in the appendix "Going further" at the end of this chapter). The financial accounts published by the financial institutions are the basic source for the financial accounts of all the sectors.

5. The non-financial assets

The net worth of the various agents, and especially of households, is not made up solely of *financial* assets and liabilities but also includes *non-financial* assets such as housing. For the household sector, non-financial assets include dwellings and in some countries assets in the form of housing are greater than households' financial assets. Many households prefer to put their savings into "bricks and mortar". Households' non-financial assets also include the plant, equipment and the software owned by individual entrepreneurs (who are classified in the household sector).

The national accounts list a wide variety of non-financial assets: buildings and other structures; machinery and other equipment; inventories; valuables; land; mineral deposits; non-cultivated biological resources; reserves of water whose ownership can be established and transferred; and certain intangible assets (software, patents, licenses, assignable contracts, research and development). One curious feature is that the national accounts distinguish between the value of land and the structures built on this land, although in practice the two are indivisible.

However, the definition of assets in the SNA is restricted to instruments "*functioning as a store of value over which ownership rights are enforced by institutional units, individually or collectively, and from which economic benefits may be derived by their owners by holding them or using them over a period of time.*" This definition excludes, for example, the so-called human capital, as discussed in the section "Limitations of the national accounts: The exclusions from the balance sheet accounts" in the appendix "Going further" at the end of this chapter.

The value of non-financial assets (also called **capital stock**) is usually estimated by the perpetual inventory method (PIM). The PIM method is based on data for past GFCF transactions in volume and applies the simple principle that today's stock is equal to what was previously invested minus what has since been used up. Applying assumptions regarding physical deterioration and decommissioning for any other reason, this method is therefore based solely on very long series of GFCF that are, in principle, available to the national accountants. Each annual investment is an addition to the stock, while each decommissioning (retirement from the stock of capital) or element of physical deterioration (consumption of fixed capital) is a deduction.

Using this method, it is possible to calculate the gross (or net) stock of fixed capital at the end of period n, with GC(n) being equal to the gross (or net) stock of fixed capital at the end of the previous period $GC(n-1)$ plus the GFCF in period n, $GFCF(n)$, minus the decommissioned items $DEC(n)$ (or, respectively, the consumption of fixed capital $CFC(n)$). This gives, for the gross capital stock: $GC(n) = GC(n-1) + GFCF(n) - DEC(n)$ and for the net capital stock: $NC(n) = NC(n-1) + GFCF(n) - CFC(n)$. Measured in this way, the net capital stock is the market value of the stock of fixed assets and is a major component of the net worth (or net wealth) of the nation and of the institutional sectors that own these assets. The gross capital stock does not have any clear economic meaning: it has been sometimes used in estimates of the production function (see introduction to Chapter 4) but most economists now use measures of capital services for this purpose rather than the capital stock whether on a net or gross basis (OECD, 2001).

By developing these formulae, it can be seen that the stock of capital is a function of past investment, decommissioning and physical deterioration of capital equipment. If the series for past GFCF is sufficiently long, the initial GC or NC is no longer of great importance, since at the end of a certain amount of time all the initial assets will have been retired from the capital stock. Everything depends, however, on the estimations of $DEC(n)$ and of $CFC(n)$, which are themselves based on assumptions relating to the average service lives of different kinds of assets, "mortality functions" (which for intangible assets perhaps should be called "obsolescence functions"), which describe the distribution of decommissionings around these averages, and physical deterioration (also known as "wear and tear"). OECD countries use several different types of mortality functions. Many European countries use a log-normal mortality function while other OECD countries prefer Weibull or Winfrey functions. Physical deterioration is usually assumed to be a "straight-line," meaning that it occurs uniformly over the lifetime of the asset, although some countries, including the United States, assume that it occurs at a constant rate. Estimates of the average service lives of different kinds of assets are clearly very important in applying the PIM. In certain countries, these parameters are derived from a survey of enterprises. The following are examples in the case of France: it has been estimated that IT hardware has an average service life of five years; transport equipment between seven and 15 years; a building 25 years and public infrastructure 60 years. On the basis of these assumptions, one obtains "discard rates" D_i such that. $DEC(n) = \Sigma_i\, GFCF(n-i) \times D_i$. The rates of consumption of fixed capital C_i are calculated as a linear smoothing of these discard rates, and this gives $CFC(n) = \Sigma_i\, GFCF(n-i) \times C_i$. Taken together, this makes it possible to calculate the stocks of gross capital $GC(n)$ and net capital $NC(n)$ in volume. The same formulae are then used, but with the introduction of price indexes, to obtain the stock of capital and the consumption of fixed capital at current prices.

6. The balance sheet accounts

The balance sheet accounts are a synthesis of the tables of (financial and non-financial) assets and liabilities for the various institutional sectors and the rest of the world. They make it possible to see in a single table all the assets and liabilities of each sector and hence measure the total net worth of macroeconomic agents at a given date (generally December 31). The estimates are made at market prices and hence provide the best measure of this wealth at this date (even though it is potential because unrealized). The estimation of this wealth is nevertheless limited to the items that the national accountants consider as eligible to be considered as assets or liabilities (see the table "Limitations of the national accounts: exclusions from the balance sheet accounts" in the appendix "Going further" at the end of this chapter).

The following is a summary model of the balance sheet accounts that we shall use to introduce the definition of "net worth" (or "net wealth"), which is the most all-embracing heading in the national accounts.

Simplified balance sheet account at 31/12/A for any sector

Assets		Liabilities	
Non-financial assets	NFA	Net worth (including shares and other equity)	C = A-L
Financial assets	FA	Liabilities (excluding shares and other equity)	L
Total	A = NFA + FA	Total	A

As the table shows, the net worth of an institutional sector is equal to the total assets A (financial assets FA and non-financial assets NFA) minus total liabilities L, excluding shares and other equity appearing under liabilities as they are not debt but form part of the own funds of the companies. Indeed, in the case of non-financial corporations and financial institutions, the net worth includes shares because the recording of shares in the liabilities column is by convention and does not mean that the non-financial corporations and financial institutions owe these sums to anyone. In other words, shares are not debt of the companies as by their nature, holders of shares (households and non-financial corporations and financial institutions) cannot demand that issuers redeem the shares as long as these entities continue to operate. Since households have no shares on the liability side of their accounts, the net worth in their case is equal to assets minus total liabilities (with equity liabilities being null).

One sometimes hears mention of *financial* net worth (or *financial* net wealth). This is a net worth figure but limited in scope to financial assets and liabilities and taking no account of non-financial assets. This is a somewhat narrow concept, since non-financial assets play just as important a role as financial assets in agents' behaviour.

The tables in the balance sheet accounts make it possible to explain how the net worth is created, in other words the way in which the stock of net worth at the end of a given period is arrived at from the stock of net worth at the end of the previous period. Changes in stocks can be due to several factors:

- Consumption of fixed capital: this measures the physical depreciation and the obsolescence of the non-financial assets.

- Actual changes in non-financial and financial assets: these are made up of gross capital formation in the case of non-financial assets, and for financial assets, of the financial transactions described earlier.

- Revaluations: they measure the holding gains or losses during the period that have affected assets and liabilities held by the sector under review. There are positive and negative revaluations of financial and non-financial assets.

- Other changes in volume: this account covers exceptional transactions, generally of non-economic origin, that can affect the wealth of institutional sectors and the rest of the world. For example, the destruction of buildings as the result of a natural catastrophe or a war is recorded negatively in this item; the discovery of new exploitable oil reserves will also be recorded there but this time positively. An example of a change in volume of a financial asset is the write-down of a receivable due to the insolvency of the borrower. This item is also the place where the effects of changes in the sectoral classification of certain units will be recorded.

Taken together, these changes lead to the table shown at the end of the next section.

7. The complete sequence of accounts of an institutional sector

We are now in a position to visualize the entire set of accounts of an institutional sector (non-financial corporations or financial institutions, for example) right through from the production account to the balance sheet account, using the simplified diagram set out below, which includes all its financial and non-financial transactions.

Note the organization of the accounts in "T" form, with the first block of tables, comprising the non-financial accounts (right through from the production account to the capital account) showing uses on the left and resources on the right, while the second block, comprising the financial account, showing "net acquisitions of financial assets" (or "changes in financial assets") on the left and "net incurrence of liabilities" (or "changes in liabilities") on the right.

The second table shows the link between the balance sheet (stocks) at the end of the prior period (column 1) and the balance sheet (stocks) at the end of the current period (column 7). Columns 2 through 6 show the changes (flows) for the current period; these are the capital flows (columns 2 and 3), financial flows (column 4), and changes in stocks deriving from the reconciliation accounts (columns 5 and 6), which do not derive from transactions. The "X" in the table indicates the cells that may include data.

Accounts of the institutional sectors

	Uses			Resources	
1. Non-financial accounts					
Production account	P2.	Intermediate consumption	P1.	Output	
	B1	Value added, gross			
Generation of income account	D1.	Compensation of employees	B1	Value added, gross	
	D29.	Other taxes on production (minus subsidies)			
	K1.	Consumption of fixed capital			
	B2N	Operating surplus, net			
Distribution of income account	D4.	Property income	B2N.	Operating surplus	
	D5.	Current taxes on income and wealth			
	D6.	Social benefits (paid by employers)	D6.	Social contributions (received by employers)	
	D7.	Current transfers	D7.	Current transfers	
	B8N	Saving, net			
Capital account	P5.	Gross fixed capital formation	B8N	Saving, net	
	K1.	Consumption of fixed capital (with a minus sign)	D9.	Capital transfers	
	B9A	Net lending/ net borrowing			
		Net acquisitions of financial assets (Changes in financial assets)		Net incurrence of liabilities (Changes in liabilities)	
2. Financial accounts					
			F1.	Monetary gold and SDRs[a]	
	F2.	Currency and deposits	F2.	Currency and deposits	
	F3.	Debt securities	F3.	Debt securities	
	F4.	Loans	F4.	Loans	
	F5.	Equity and investment fund shares	F5.	Equity and investment fund shares	
	F6.	Insurance, pension and standardised guarantee schemes	F6.	Insurance, pension and standardised guarantee schemes	
	F7.	Financial derivatives and employee stock options	F7.	Financial derivatives and employee stock options	
	F8.	Other accounts receivable/payable	F8.	Other accounts receivable/payable	
			B9.B	Net lending/net borrowing	

a) "Monetary" gold and SDRs will appear only in the accounts as assets of the central bank or similar institutions and the offsetting entries appear with the opposite sign in the assets of the rest of the world

Link between the balance sheets at the beginning and the end of the period

	Stock as of 12/31 of the prior year	Minus Consumption of fixed capital	Plus Gross fixed capital formation	Plus Financial transactions	Plus Revaluations	Plus Other changes in volume	= Stock as of 12/31 of the current year
	1	2	3	4	5	6	7 = 1 - 2 + 3 + 4 + 5 + 6
Financial assets	X			X	X	X	X
Non-financial assets	X	X	X		X	X	X
Liabilities in form of shares	X			X	X	X	X
Liabilities (excluding shares)	X			X	X	X	X
Net worth (including shares)	X						X

References

Banco de España (2014), Cuentas Financieras de la Economía Española, *www.bde.es/webbde/en/estadis/ccff/cfcap2.html*.

Bureau of Economic Analysis (2013), National Income and Product Accounts Tables, *www.bea.gov/iTable/iTable.cfm?ReqID=9&step=1#reqid=9&step=3&isuri=1&904=2012&903=58&906=a&905=1990&910=x&911=0*.

OECD (2013), "OECD Economic Outlook No. 93", OECD Economic Outlook: Statistics and Projections (database), doi: *http://dx.doi.org/10.1787/data-00655-en*.

OECD (2013a), "Detailed National Accounts: Non-financial accounts by sectors, annual", OECD National Accounts Statistics (database), doi: *http://dx.doi.org/10.1787/data-00034-en*.

OECD (2013b), "Financial Accounts: Non-consolidated flows, annual", OECD National Accounts Statistics (database), doi: *http://dx.doi.org/10.1787/data-00023-en*.

OECD (2001), "Measurement of Capital Stocks, Consumption of Fixed Capital and Capital Services", OECD, Paris, 2001.

SNA 2008, European Commission, International Monetary Fund, Organisation for Economic Co-operation and Development, United Nations, World Bank, New York, 2009, System of National Accounts 2008, *http://unstats.un.org/unsd/nationalaccount/docs/SNA2008.pdf*.

Key points

- Generally speaking, in the national accounts a transaction by an agent is recorded twice: once in the non-financial accounts and once in the financial accounts. However, when the transactions are purely financial, they are recorded twice in the financial accounts, and in this case without any impact on net lending/net borrowing.

- Since a transaction involves two agents, it is therefore recorded four times, i.e. two entries in the accounts for each agent.

- The complete financial accounts trace out first the flows, and then the stocks of agents' financial assets and liabilities and the reconciliation accounts. The accounting balance of the financial flows is item B9B "net lending/net borrowing"; the accounting balance of the financial stocks is the financial net worth (also known as financial wealth).

- If an agent is in a net lending position, his financial net worth (assuming there have been no revaluations and other asset or liability volume changes) has risen during the period. Conversely, if an agent is in a net borrowing position, his financial net worth (again, assuming there have been no revaluations and other asset or liability volume changes) has diminished during the period.

- The item B9B is in theory equal, by definition, to the accounting balance of the non-financial accounts, i.e. item B9A. In practice, there is a difference between the two, called statistical discrepancy.

- Theorem: in a closed economy, the sum of the B9 items for various agents is zero.

- The balance sheet accounts give an estimate of the net worth (net wealth) of the institutional sectors at a given date.

- Stocks of financial and non-financial assets and liabilities are valued at market prices (the prices prevalent on the day the accounts are drawn up – usually 31/12/A). Transactions involving financial and non-financial assets and liabilities are valued at the prices prevalent on the date of the transaction.

- The difference between the amount of the financial and non-financial stocks at the beginning and end of a period derives from the transactions, revaluations and other changes in volume of assets and liabilities executed during the period.

- The net worth of an institutional sector is equal to total financial and non-financial assets minus liabilities (excluding shares and other equity, in the case of non-financial corporations and financial institutions). This is the broadest measure of the net wealth of institutional sectors at a given date.

Going further

Holding gains or losses and market prices in the national accounts

The prices of the assets held by households and corporations vary over time. Share prices can rise and fall on the stock market, just as prices of buildings and dwellings vary in response to the law of supply and demand and the current economic climate. When the prices of assets held by economic agents rise, the agents concerned have a holding gain; when they fall they have a holding loss. A distinction is sometimes made between "unrealized" gains and losses and "realized" gains and losses. A typical unrealized gain or loss occurs when the price of a share held by an agent changes but when the agent has not yet sold his holding. By contrast, realized gains (or losses) result from the sale of the shares. The agent has then received the proceeds of the holding gain (which is in most cases subject to tax). His unrealized gain has then become a realized gain. However, national accountants do not measure realized holding gains and are only interested in the unrealized holding gains, partly because economic agents feel richer when the prices of their assets rise, whether they sell them or not. In any case, the realized holding gains are difficult to measure.

The prices at which assets (and liabilities) are valued in the national accounts are the prices on the day in question (generally December 31). This is the rule for both financial and non-financial assets and liabilities. The difference between the opening value (January 1) and the closing value twelve months later (December 31) therefore includes the holding gains and losses. These are recorded in the national accounts, and the data can be used by economists to calculate the "wealth effect". However, these changes in value are not recorded in the income account but in a special "revaluation account" that comes after the income account in the sequence of accounts. As a consequence, these holding gains and losses, whether unrealized or realized, do not affect the measurement of agents' income in the national accounts, in contrast to the practice adopted for company accounts. In the national accounts, agents' incomes come almost entirely from output and from the redistribution of the proceeds of this output, and not from holding gains/ losses. This convention has its advantages, as it avoids introducing into the measurement of income an element that is volatile and may be only potential.

It also has disadvantages since agents modify their behaviour in light of holding gains/losses. In fact, as agents see it, there is no real difference between a realized capital gain and income from labour, apart from the fact that a realized capital gain is less predictable (although some salaries and entrepreneurial income can also be difficult to predict). Moreover, there is a certain contradiction in the national accounts in that the tax on realized capital gains is deducted from disposable income, whereas the capital gain on which the tax is based is not itself part of this disposable income.

The valuation in the national accounts of assets and liabilities at market prices is also open to discussion. In fact, this "wealth" may be only potential. For example, the mere suggestion that someone holding a large portfolio of shares in a firm might dispose of his holdings can lead to a fall in the price of the shares capable of reducing this same holder's potential realized holding gain. Much the same is true of the sale of property by a large institutional investor (an insurance company or a bank). For this reason, company accountants are more cautious than national accountants and apply the principle of valuation at the purchase price (except in the case of some quoted shares, for which the potential holding gain is practically certain to become a real gain). This caution leads to difficulty in interpreting the exact amount of assets and liabilities in company accounts. These totals do not reflect economic reality since they add together assets or liabilities valued at very different dates. This difference between the company accounts and the national accounts makes it difficult to use company balance sheets in the calculation of the balance sheet accounts of the national accounts. However, it is possible that the two sets of accounts could better coincide upon the application of the principle of "fair value" in company accounts. The application of "fair value" is equivalent to valuing companies' assets and liabilities similarly to the national accounts. This principle is being recommended for some assets and liabilities by the International Accounting Standards Board (IASB), the international accounting standard setter organization for listed companies.

A final detail regarding valuation prices for financial assets is that they exclude taxes, fees and expenses, unlike the prices of non-financial assets. In both cases, the fees and expenses correspond to payment for a service. In the case of financial assets, the service is explicitly consumed as such; in the case of non-financial assets, it is consumed in the form of a capital good, since it is included in the price.

A more complete example of entries in the financial accounts

An example can be used to illustrate the additional information coming from the presentation of financial transactions in terms of "changes in assets/

changes in liabilities" in the national accounts compared to the simplistic presentation in terms of "uses/resources". Suppose that an agent (for example, a bank) in a given period borrows 100, repays 20 on a previous borrowing, lends 50 and is repaid 10 on loans made earlier.

With simplistic uses/resources recording, this would give:

Resources: 110 = (100 + 10)

Uses: 70 = (20 + 50)

The bank receives 100 through borrowing and 10 from the repayment of the loan, resulting in resources of 110. It pays out 20 in loan repayment and lends 50, resulting in uses equal to 70.

But the recording in the national accounts will be as follows:

Change in assets: 40 = (50 − 10)

Change in liabilities: 80 = (100 − 20)

How do we interpret these figures in the national accounts? To obtain information on the situation of the bank in terms of assets and liabilities (which is what interests us for purposes of the financial and balance sheet accounts), the key is to note that the agent has increased his assets by lending 50 and has reduced them by 10 through the partial repayment of a previously extended loan. In addition, he has increased his liabilities by 100 (the amount of the loan he received) and decreased them by 20 as a result of the repayment of a previous loan.

Only the figures in the national accounts give real information regarding the situation in terms of assets and liabilities, in other words on the change in the agent's net worth (net wealth), which has here decreased by 40, as the change in liabilities (80) is 40 more than the change in assets (40). This is in contrast to the simplistic analysis in terms of uses/resources, which merely records the agent's cash position.

Financial accounts and money supply: the example of the euro area

One often hears of "the money supply", defined more or less broadly as the aggregates known as M1, M2 or M3. These "M" aggregates correspond to progressively broader definitions of money. Currently, in the euro area, only the money supply of the area as a whole has any economic significance, not that of each of the countries comprising it. (Some central banks in the euro area continue to publish a figure for money supply, but this only shows their country's contribution to the euro-area money supply, but the trend of national contributions is not taken into account in monetary policy decisions). The European Central Bank (ECB) follows the "M" aggregates closely, using principally a measure of type "M3", even though since 2003 this has been of secondary importance for the ECB compared with the inflation indicator.

However, if M3 increases too rapidly, the ECB may take it into account in its interest rate decisions.

There is obviously a relationship between the financial accounts and the money supply aggregate and its counterparts. Starting with the simplified diagram of the financial accounts shown in the main text of this chapter, the extraction of the column "financial institutions" gives the following:

Simplified balance sheet of financial institutions (FI)

	Assets	Liabilities
	Financial institutions (FI)	Financial institutions (FI)
Deposits		W
Loans	X	
Interbank financing	Y	Y
Securities	ZI	Z3

Knowing that interbank financing is roughly equal on the assets and liabilities sides, this row can be eliminated. Furthermore, it is assumed that the securities in the liabilities column are there only by convention, and so the preference is to show them in the assets column, with a negative sign, under the term "stable resources". We then have the following table:

Money supply and its counterparts

	Assets	Liabilities
	Financial institutions (FI)	Financial institutions (FI)
Deposits		W
Loans	X	
Securities	ZI	
Stable resources	-Z3	

The money supply is then equal to total deposits W on the liability side of financial institutions. Its counterparts are the three items in the assets column: loans plus securities minus stable resources (securities on the liability side for financial institutions). The precise definitions of the money supply depend on the breadth of the definition of deposits. The following, in decreasing order of liquidity, are the definitions of M1, M2 and M3, according to the content of the items included in W:

M1 = Currency in circulation (F21) + sight deposit (F22)

M2 = M1 + deposit repayable on up to three months' notice (including the products classified in F29) + term deposit with maturity of up to two years.

M3 = M2 + repurchase agreements + holdings in monetary mutual funds + securities other than shares and participations for up to two years issued by monetary financial institutions in the euro zone.

Certain items in M2 and M3 have definitions that do not match categories in the financial accounts (notably the reference to maturities of less than two years). It is therefore not easy for anyone who is not an expert to make the precise reconciliation between the financial accounts and the monetary aggregates.

Data sources: the statistical sources for the financial accounts

This section illustrates the sources of financial accounts using the case of Canada as an example. The statistical sources for the Canadian financial accounts consist mainly of the financial balance sheets of banks, statistical surveys of other types of financial institutions and non-financial corporations, as well as administrative and survey data on governments and their agencies. Data on non-residents are a rearrangement of the balance of payments and international investment position accounts. Data on households are largely derived as counterpart entries from the data of all other sectors, in particular from financial institutions. The role of the financial accounts is to analyse for coherence and integrate data coming from various sources to produce comprehensive, accurate and reliable estimates of transactions and positions (stocks). Data from the "chartered" (commercial) banks form an integral part of the data in the financial accounts. Chartered bank data arise from a tri-party arrangement (central bank, regulator of financial institutions and Statistics Canada) whereby the banks registered in Canada submit to Statistics Canada on a quarterly basis income statement and balance sheet data along with supplementary information. The supplementary information provides crucial data on deposit-taking and lending activities with the various units (sectors/industries/agents) in the economy. For example, counterpart household borrowing/debt estimates (the bulk of these funds provided by chartered banks) are mainly constructed from banking loan asset detail. A periodic review of bank reporting is currently underway. Comprehensive surveys of other types of financial institutions are also conducted by Statistics Canada mainly as part of the quarterly enterprise survey program in the economic statistics field. Near-banks (by sub-industry), life insurance business (by segment), investment funds, sales finance companies, consumer loan companies, asset securitization fund managers, holding companies, financial holding companies and other financial entities are all part of these surveys.

Questionnaires are sufficiently detailed to provide considerable asset breakdowns and to provide for reliable counterpart entry estimates in non-financial sectors (borrowing and deposits) – in particular, in the household sector. For example, the survey on investment funds permits calculation of the mutual fund assets of households. Non-financial corporations' estimates are derived from quarterly enterprise surveys. While only total non-financial corporations are published in the financial accounts, the survey covers all the activities of companies in considerable detail. Detailed quarterly surveys of pension funds are conducted as part of the social statistics program at Statistics Canada, and they make up an important share of institutional investors' assets. The net pension assets of these surveyed plans provide the bulk of the employer-sponsored pension plan assets in the household sector accounts. Government sector data (federal, provincial and local) are compiled from the annual audited Public Accounts as well as from sub-annual administrative sources and survey data. Government business enterprises data are based principally on quarterly surveys. Detailed databases on issues/positions in securities (i.e. shares, corporate and government bonds) are also maintained as part of the supporting detail in the financial accounts. Comprehensive coverage of issues of securities and their details form the basis of these databases, which are used to supplement the survey-based information.

Financial transactions' asset-side information is mainly derived from adjusted (for capital gains, foreign currency adjustments, etc.) balance sheet survey data, discussed above. Adjustments are, to a significant extent, based on specific surveys of revaluations of assets and liabilities by instrument. In addition to asset-side transactions, the balance of payments group also makes use of a database derived from depositories' information on new purchases of securities.

The household sector accounts are constructed using indirect methods. Estimates are based largely on counterpart information from financial institutions for major asset holdings (deposits, pension fund reserves, investment fund shares, insurance technical reserves and bonds) and for liabilities. However, selected assets are calculated using residual derivation. In particular, this is the case for marketable securities. While holdings of marketable debt instruments are not significant in the household sector, marketable shareholdings are, and, since they are obtained using residual derivation, depend on the quality of the information recorded elsewhere in the system. Non-marketable (unlisted) shareholdings are also obtained using residual derivation. Direct household surveys are just starting to be used in the context of financial accounts.

In many countries, as in Canada, financial accounts are compiled based on banking statistics regarding the financing of the economy, whereas the non-financial accounts are based on the statistics of non-financial corporations. Therefore, it is hardly surprising that the two B9 balances, B9A and B9B, do not coincide in practice, and that a row showing a statistical discrepancy between the two has to be introduced. In many European countries, one exception to this rule is that the banking sources and the administrative sources based on which the general government accounts are drawn up can be reconciled, to the point that the statistical discrepancy is small in this sector's accounts. Lastly, in financial accounts, the data available in some countries for the drafting of the financial accounts refer only to outstanding assets/liabilities, i.e., to balances or stocks. In this case, flow data have to be calculated by difference, imputing when necessary a valuation change in the assets/liabilities (see Exercise 6).

The valuation of assets and its relationship to economic theory

In the national accounts, an economic asset is defined as a tangible or intangible good on which right of ownership is exercised and whose holding or use procures economic advantages for the owner.

In economic theory, the value of such an asset is equal to the "present value" of the future income it will bring in for its holder. Suppose that the asset brings in a sum of St each year (t representing the year) until year T. Then, if all the conditions of perfect information and perfect competition are met, the market price of the asset is equal to $\Sigma S_t \div (1 + r_t)^t$, summed from 1 to T, where r_t denotes the discount rate, in other words agents' preference for the present (an interest rate containing no risk premium). This method could in theory have been used to calculate asset values in the national accounts, but it is difficult to apply in practice and so other methods are used. Even so, the calculation of present values is useful in helping to understand certain entries in the national accounts.

Take the case of a bond purchased at 1 000 and bringing in 10% a year, or 100, for five years. Its value is equal to the sum of the present values of each annual flow, in other words to the annual flow divided by the discount rate raised to the power of the number of periods. It can be verified that this value is equal to 1 000, the purchase price of the bond.

Period t (1)	Annual flow (2)	Discount rate or interest rate $[(1 + 10\%)]^t$ (3)	Present value (column (2) divided by column (3)) (4)
1	100	1.1	90.90909
2	100	1.21	82.64463
3	100	1.331	75.13148
4	100	1.4641	68.30135
5	1 100	1.61051	683.0135
		Sum of the present values	1 000

Let us now suppose that interest rates fall on the capital markets. For example, suppose that at the end of Period 3 they fall suddenly to 5%. The value of the bond calculated using present values will rise simultaneously to 1 136.162 as shown in the following table. It is not surprising that it is at this new value that the markets find equilibrium. This is because the bond brings in 10%, twice the return on a newly issued bond. It is therefore normal that its price on the secondary bond market should rise. The national accounts record the increase (or the decrease, in the event of a rise in interest rates) in the value of the bond in its revaluation accounts as a holding gain (or loss). Exercise 4 illustrates this case, extending it to the even more complex cases of bonds issued below par or to zero coupon bonds.

Period t	Annual flow	Discount rate or interest rate $[(1 + 5\%)]^t$	Present value
3	100	1.05	95.2381
4	100	1.1025	90.70295
5	1 100	1.157625	950.2214
		Sum of present values	1 136.162

The irrefutable logic of the calculation based on the sum of present values has numerous applications in national accounts. Let us suppose that an agent, for example a central government, undertakes to pay St per year for 10 years in the form of retirement benefits in return for the receipt in the current year of a sum A, which can be regarded as an advance payment of pension contributions Exercise 3 shows that recording this transaction in the national accounts necessarily requires an interest element.

Limitations of the national accounts: The exclusions from the balance sheet accounts

A very broad definition of investment as "expenditure made today that will provide income tomorrow" could have led to the use of an extensive notion of assets. But the national accounts have not gone as far as this, so the following assets that meet this broad definition are excluded from the national accounts: 1) human capital, which can be defined as the ongoing expenditure on the training of individuals; 2) natural capital, which can be defined as the value of non-mineral natural resources (naturally-occurring water, air, etc.); 3) public monuments (the Château de Versailles in France, Stonehenge in England, the Roman Forum in Italy, The Alhambra in Granada, Spain, Machu Pichu in Peru, the monuments of the Plaza del Zócalo in Mexico, etc.); 4) household durable goods, which are conventionally recorded as consumption although their service life is longer than one year; 5) pension rights in pay-as-you- go plans; 6) certain intangible assets such as trademarks, customer goodwill, etc. It is to be noted that the national accounts have extended recently, with the SNA 2008/ESA 2010, the borderline of asset recognition to research and development (R&D) and large weapon systems. On the liability side, conditional financial liabilities such as debt guarantees or provisions recorded by companies in their books are not included as liabilities in the national accounts. For example, the debt of public-sector enterprises guaranteed by the State is not recorded as a liability for central government in the national accounts.

In recent years, economic research has paid considerable attention to the idea of measuring human capital. This involves attaching a market value to each member of the population, especially as a function of his/her education. Studies on the application of this principle have calculated the economic value of academic training as the present value of the additional salaries that can be expected during a person's lifetime as a result of obtaining a higher diploma. The 2008 SNA (§ 1.54) explains why it would be difficult to include this value in the national accounts:

"It is often proposed that expenditures on staff training and education should be classified as gross fixed capital formation as a form of investment in human capital. The acquisition of knowledge, skills and qualifications increases the productive potential of the individuals concerned and is a source of future economic benefit to them. However, while knowledge, skills and qualifications are clearly assets in a broad sense of the term, they cannot be equated with fixed assets as understood in the SNA. They are acquired through learning, studying and practicing, activities that cannot be undertaken by anyone else on behalf of the student and thus the acquisition of knowledge is not a process of production even though the instruction conveyed by education services is."

Education assets are embodied in individuals as persons. They cannot be transferred to others and cannot be shown in the balance sheets of the enterprises in which the individuals work (except in rare cases when certain highly skilled individuals are under contract to work for particular employees for specified periods). This last sentence explains why certain football players are considered assets in the accounts of most of the major football clubs. It is clearly the clubs' contracts with the players that are the assets and not the players themselves.

Integrated system of financial accounts

The Bank of Spain publishes an integrated system of financial accounts. It comprises the financial net worth (financial balance sheet) accounts, financial transactions accounts, financial asset revaluation accounts, the other changes in volume of financial assets accounts for the entire economy, the rest of the world and the various resident sectors. Tables 8.2, 8.3 and 8.4 below have been prepared based on the publication of the Bank of Spain on the financial accounts of the Spanish economy (Banco de España, 2014). They include a summary of the financial balances at the beginning and end of 2012 and the other accounts cited for the year 2012. The codes of these tables correspond to old SNA 93 codes.

A reading of these tables (in which, for reasons of space, the presentation of accounts has been simplified) can give an idea of how all the accounts are interrelated and their analytical value. In reading them one should bear in mind that when the tables refer generically to "Financial assets" and to "Liabilities" they refer to: i) the financial stock of assets and liabilities (that are shown in columns 1 and 5 of the three tables and comprise the balance sheet accounts); ii) the net acquisitions of financial assets and net incurrence of liabilities (column 2, extracted from the financial accounts); iii) the financial asset revaluation accounts (column 3), and iv) the other changes in volume of financial assets accounts (column 4). In Tables 8.3 and 8.4, the accounts of financial institutions are not consolidated. We have not shown, for simplification the other sectors.

Table 8.2 shows the set of accounts for the Total economy and the Rest of the world. The accounts of the Total economy are consolidated, which means that all internal transactions among resident sectors have been eliminated. The rest of the world account shown in this table is consolidated by definition since it only includes the country's relationships with the rest of the world. On this table, one can verify that, once the total economy account is consolidated, the assets of the Total economy (excluding monetary gold and SDRs) are equal, by definition, to the liabilities of the Rest of the world, as well as conversely, the assets detained by the Rest of the world on Spain are equal to the liabilities versus the Rest of the world of Spain.

Each financial asset has a counterpart liability, except in the specific case of monetary gold which, by convention, is only a financial asset. Table 8.2 shows that identity between the various assets in the economy (whose total at the beginning of 2012, after deducting 14.2 billion, the amount of the monetary gold and SDR entry, is 1 343.9 billion) and the various liabilities for the rest of the world (actually totalling 1 343.9 billion at the beginning of 2012). In the case of monetary gold and SDRs, the sum of the assets for the entire economy (the above-mentioned 14.2 billion) plus the sum of the assets for the rest of the world (-14.2 billion) is equal to zero, since the established convention for these financial assets is that they are the only assets that do not have a counterpart liability. Therefore, transactions with gold and SDRs always imply a change in ownership of these financial assets. Table 8.2 also shows (see book balances) that the Spanish economy had net worth vis-à-vis the rest of the world of -917.8 and -927.0 billion euros at the beginning and end of 2012, respectively.

One can see that based on the initial position, the debtor position increased over the year for transactions (-6.7) as well as for revaluations (-5.8) and decreased for other changes in volume (3.3).

Table 8.3 shows loans constitute the principal asset of financial institutions (with the balance outstanding being EUR 2 025.8 billion at the beginning of 2012, with 72.9 billion in loans having been redeemed over the period). Meanwhile, currency and deposits are shown in the portfolio (i.e., in assets) and are particularly significant in the households sector and NPISHs (balance outstanding of EUR 855.4 billion at the beginning of 2012). Shares are also among the principal assets for households and NPISHs (balance outstanding of EUR 512.8 billion at the beginning of 2012) and financial institutions (380.4 billion).

On the liabilities side (Table 8.4) the principal liabilities of financial companies are currency and deposits (EUR 2 817.6 billion at the beginning of 2012). Other significant liabilities of financial companies are securities other than shares and loans (EUR 1 047.3 and 437.3 billion respectively) while the liabilities of households and NPISHs are mainly loans (EUR 874.3 billion).

Finally, one must bear in mind that the Spanish accounts, which may be accessed at *www.bde.es*, include the following features: 1) they are quarterly, and the annual accounts are derived from the quarterly accounts, in which the net worth figures correspond to those for the last quarter of the year and the flows (transactions, revaluations and other changes in volume) correspond to the sum of the quarterly data; 2) they are published on dates included in a preannounced schedule that is followed faithfully; 3) they present breakdowns for the sectors (by subsectors and sometimes by agents); for example, comprehensive accounts are prepared for all general governments and also for the central government, autonomous communities, local governments and social security administrations, and 4) they present breakdowns for instruments: a) by nature; for example, the entry shares and participations is broken down into listed shares, unlisted shares, other equity, except investment funds, participations in investment funds and shares issued by investment companies, and b) by counterpart sectors ("whom to whom" principle), such that, for example, one can see what portion of shares and participations held by households and NPISHs were issued by the rest of the world, non-financial companies and financial institutions.

Table 8.2. **Spain: Link between the balance sheet at the beginning and end of year 2012**

Financial assets, book balances and liabilities (billion euros)

| | Codes | Financial equity at the beginning of the period | Financial transactions account | Other changes in financial assets | | Financial equity at the end of the period |
				Revaluation account	Other changes in volume account	
		1	2	3	4	5 = 1 plus 2 to 4
Total Economy (consolidated)	**S1**	**1 358.1**	**17.7**	**-9.1**	**3.3**	**1 370.2**
Monetary gold and SDRs	F/FA.1	14.2	0.0	0.3		14.6
Currency and deposits	F/FA.2	256.8	6.5	-0.3	0.0	263.0
Securities other than shares	F/FA.3	283.3	-12.7	4.0		274.5
Loans	F/FA.4	197.9	19.3	-0.4	-0.3	216.5
Shares and other equity	F/FA.5	550.2	4.2	-12.7		541.6
Insurance technical reserves	F/FA.6	5.3	0.4			5.7
Other accounts receivable/payable	F/FA.7	50.6	0.1	3.6		54.3
Rest of the World	**S2**	**2 261.7**	**24.4**	**-3.6**	**0.0**	**2 282.6**
Monetary gold and SDRs	F/FA.1	-14.2	0.0	-0.3		-14.6
Currency and deposits	F/FA.2	642.4	5.9	-0.4		648.0
Securities other than shares	F/FA.3	680.5	-57.9	10.7		633.3
Loans	F/FA.4	382.1	42.3	-4.5		419.9
Shares and other equity	F/FA.5	521.7	35.4	-9.1	0.0	548.1
Insurance technical reserves	F/FA.6	4.6	0.0			4.7
Other accounts receivable/payable	F/FA.7	44.6	-1.3			43.3
Total Economy (consolidated)	**S1**	**1 358.1**	**17.7**	**-9.1**	**3.3**	**1 370.2**
1. Book Balances	**(FA- L)**	**-917.8**	**-6.7**	**-5.8**	**3.3**	**-927.0**
Net equity at the beginning of the period	BE.90	-917.8				
Financing capacity/requirements	B9.		-6.7			
Revaluations	BE.10.3			-5.8		
Other changes in volume	BE.10.2				3.3	
Net equity at the end of the period	BE.90					-927.0
2. Total Liabilities	**F/FA**	**2 275.9**	**24.4**	**-3.3**		**2 297.3**
Currency and deposits	F/FA.2	642.4	5.9	-0.4		648.0
Securities other than shares	F/FA.3	680.5	-57.9	10.7		633.3
Loans	F/FA.4	382.1	42.3	-4.5		419.9
Shares and other equity	F/FA.5	521.7	35.4	-9.1	0.0	548.1
Insurance technical reserves	F/FA.6	4.6	0.0			4.7
Other accounts payable.	F/FA.7	44.6	-1.3			43.3
Rest of the World	**S2**	**2 261.7**	**24.4**	**-3.6**	**0.0**	**2 282.6**
1. Book Balances	**(FA- L)**	**917.8**	**6.7**	**5.8**	**-3.3**	**927.0**
Net equity at the beginning of the period	BE.90	917.8				
Financing capacity/requirements	B9.		6.7			
Revaluations	BE.10.3			5.8		
Other changes in volume	BE.10.2				-3.3	
Net equity at the end of the period	BE.90					927.0

Table 8.2. **Spain: Link between the balance sheet at the beginning and end of year 2012** (cont.)

Financial assets, book balances and liabilities (billion euros)

	Codes	Financial equity at the beginning of the period	Financial transactions account	Other changes in financial assets		Financial equity at the end of the period
				Revaluation account	Other changes in volume account	
	Codes	1	2	3	4	5 = 1 plus 2 to 4
2. Total Liabilities	F/FA	1 343.9	17.7	-9.4	3.3	1 355.6
Currency and deposits	F/FA.2	256.8	6.5	-0.3	0.0	263.0
Securities other than shares	F/FA.3	283.3	-12.7	4.0	-	274.5
Loans	F/FA.4	197.9	19.3	-0.4	-0.3	216.5
Shares and other equity	F/FA.5	550.2	4.2	-12.7	-	541.6
Insurance technical reserves	F/FA.6	5.3	0.4	-	-	5.7
Other accounts payable.	F/FA.7	50.6	0.1	3.6	-	54.3

Source: Banco de España (2014): Financial Accounts of the Spanish Economy, *www.bde.es/webbde/en/estadis/ccff/cfcap2.html*

StatLink ⬛ *http://dx.doi.org/10.1787/888933144088*

Table 8.3. **Spain: Link between the balance sheet at the beginning and end of year 2012**

Resident sectors (financial institutions are not consolidated)

Financial assets (billion euros)

	Codes	Financial equity at the beginning of the period	Financial transactions account	Other changes in financial assets		Financial equity at the end of the period
				Revaluation account	Other changes in volume account	
	Codes	1	2	4	5	6 = 1 to 5
Financial Institutions	**S12**	**4 924.8**	**206.6**	**14.5**	**-50.9**	**5 094.9**
Monetary gold and SDRs	F/FA.1	14.2	0.0	0.3	-	14.6
Currency and deposits	F/FA.2	1 264.0	123.7	-0.5	-7.5	1 379.8
Securities other than shares	F/FA.3	1 139.0	147.9	19.6	-1.2	1 305.2
Loans	F/FA.4	2 025.8	-72.9	-0.5	-39.7	1 912.8
Shares and other equity	F/FA.5	380.4	2.1	-4.5	-1.5	376.4
Insurance technical reserves	F/FA.6	17.0	0.7	-	-	17.8
Other accounts receivable	F/FA.7	84.4	5.0	-	-1.0	88.4
Households and NPISHs	**S14+S15**	**1 764.6**	**-6.7**	**38.6**	**-1.2**	**1 795.2**
Currency and deposits	F/FA.2	855.4	3.3	-	-	858.7
Securities other than shares	F/FA.3	69.8	-15.9	-	5.2	59.2
Loans	F/FA.4	-	-	-	-	-
Shares and other equity	F/FA.5	512.8	8.3	26.7	-1.2	546.6
Insurance technical reserves	F/FA.6	263.9	1.0	6.6	-	271.5
Other accounts receivable	F/FA.7	62.7	-3.5	-	-	59.3

Source: Banco de España (2014): Financial Accounts of the Spanish Economy, *www.bde.es/webbde/en/estadis/ccff/cfcap2.html*

StatLink ⬛ *http://dx.doi.org/10.1787/888933144093*

Table 8.4. **Spain: Link between the balance sheet at the beginning and end of year 2012**

Resident sectors (financial institutions are not consolidated)

Book balances and liabilities (billion euros)

		Financial equity at the beginning of the period	Financial transactions account	Other changes in financial assets		Financial equity at the end of the period
				Revaluation account	Other changes in volume account	
	Codes	1	2	4	5	6 = 1 to 5
Financial institutions (1+2)	**S.12**	**4 924.8**	**206.6**	**14.5**	**-50.9**	**5 094.9**
1. Book balances	(FA- L)	151.3	66.1	-21.4	-39.7	156.4
Net equity at the beginning of the period	BE.90	151.3	-	-	-	-
Financing capacity/requirements	B9.	-	66.1	-	-	-
Revaluations	BE.10.3	-	-	-21.4	-	-
Other changes in volume	BE.10.2	-	-	-	-39.7	-
Net equity at the end of the period	BE.90	-	-	-	-	156.4
2. Total liabilities	F/FA	4 773.4	140.4	35.8	-11.2	4 938.5
Currency and deposits	F/FA.2	2 817.6	132.9	-1.0	-7.5	2 942.1
Securities other than shares	F/FA.3	1 047.3	13.9	27.4	-2.6	1 086.1
Loans	F/FA.4	104.0	-8.9	-	-	95.1
Shares and other equity	F/FA.5	437.3	1.3	2.8	-0.7	440.7
Insurance technical reserves	F/FA.6	311.0	1.8	6.6	-	319.4
Other accounts payable	F/FA.7	56.2	-0.6	-0.5	-	55.1
Households and NPISHs (1+2)	**S14*+S15**	**1 764.6**	**-6.7**	**38.6**	**-1.2**	**1 795.2**
1. Book balances	(FA- L)	827.9	21.7	39.1	5.2	893.8
Net equity at the beginning of the period	BE.90	827.9				
Financing capacity/requirements	B9.		21.7			
Revaluations	BE.10.3			39.1		
Other changes in volume	BE.10.2				5.2	
Net equity at the end of the period	BE.90					893.8
2. Total liabilities	F/FA	936.8	-28.4	-0.6	-6.4	901.4
Loans	F/FA.4	874.3	-35.5	-0.6	-1.4	836.8
Other accounts payable	F/FA.7	62.5	7.1	-5.0		64.6

Source: Banco de España (2014): Financial Accounts of the Spanish Economy, *www.bde.es/webbde/en/estadis/ccff/cfcap2.html.*

StatLink ⬛ *http://dx.doi.org/10.1787/888933144103*

Exercises for Chapter 8

Exercise 1. Say whether the following affirmations are true or false

In the national accounts: (a) a holding gain adds to agents' income; (b) a holding loss reduces agents' income; (c) a transaction is generally recorded four times; (d) every non-financial transaction has a counterpart recorded as a financial transaction; (e) every financial transaction has a counterpart recorded in the non-financial accounts; (f) the price of an asset remains constant, at its purchase price; (g) human capital is included in the evaluation of national accounts wealth; (h) in a closed economy, the sum of the balancing items B9 is zero; (i) repayment of a loan leads to an increase in recorded assets; (j) the difference between the net values at 31 December in the current year and 31 December in the previous year is explained entirely by the balancing item B9 of the agents concerned.

Exercise 2. Quadruple entry

Household H is employed by corporation C, a producer/supermarket. To simplify the entries, it will be assumed that all the household's economic relations are with this one corporation. H receives a salary of 40 000 from the corporation and consumes 30 000 in products from the corporation. With the remaining 10 000, the household buys further shares in the corporation for 2 000, and with the remaining 8 000 it pays off part of the debt contracted with the employer the previous year, amounting to 15 000. The corporation pays H a dividend of 200, and H pays the corporation interest on its debt, amounting to 300. Lastly, the corporation grants H another loan of 9 000. Draw up the financial and non-financial T-accounts. Check the accounting identities. Would the recording of the credit of 9 000 to H have been the same if the corporation had been a bank? Among these transactions, find one that is purely financial, and demonstrate that it has no impact on B9 and hence no impact on net worth.

Exercise 3 (difficult). Application of accrual accounting

Let us suppose that an agent, the central government in this case, undertakes to pay retirement benefits amounting to S for a period of T years, in return for the payment by households in year 0 of a sum A, which can be assimilated to a contribution. The aim of the exercise is to record this transaction in the national accounts on an accrual basis.

Question 1: show the relationship between A and the series of payments S, using the calculation of the present value.

Question 2: record the initial transaction and the series of payments S using the T-shaped financial accounts without the introduction of interest.

Question 3: calculate the residual debt of central government at the end of the first period of payment of benefits and show that it is different from the present value of this residual debt. Deduce from this that it is necessary to record interest. Draw up all the corresponding T-shaped accounts. Draw a parallel with a loan. Justify the fact that the B9 of central government is negative. Conclude from this that if interest is recorded the transaction will be neutral as regards agents' wealth.

Exercise 4. Calculation of the value of a bond

This exercise is a direct application of the discussion of the value of an asset in economic theory in the section Going further. The market rate of interest is 4%. Let there be a Treasury bond of USD 1 500 issued in 2004 and carrying a coupon of USD 60 per year for 10 years.

Question 1: verify that the bond was issued at the market rate and that the issue price of this bond corresponds to the present value of the future income from it.

Question 2: suppose that, in 2007, the interest rate for these same Treasury bonds increases to 6%. What will be the new price of the bond on the secondary market? How will the national accounts record this difference in price for the bondholder and for the issuer of the bond? Comment.

Question 3: return to question 1. Let us suppose that the government issues the same bond at a price of USD 1 250. How should the difference versus the market price be treated in the national accounts?

Question 4: let us suppose that the government issues this bond in the form of a zero-coupon bond, putting it on sale at a price of USD 1 014. How should this case be treated in the national accounts?

Exercise 5. Treatment of debt cancellation

Using the principles of quadruple entry, record the transaction by which the Spanish government cancels a debt of 1 000 that it had granted to a corporation that had not paid its taxes. Draw up a simplified financial T-account for the two agents before the transaction, and then describe the transaction in terms of flows. Identify the impact on the B9s of central government and the firm. Justify this economically. Deduce from the accounting identity of the non-financial and financial B9s that it is imperative to enter a counterpart in the non-financial transactions (D99, a capital transfer).

Draw conclusions for the impact on the central government resulting from a debt cancellation granted by Spain to a developing country. Discuss.

Exercise 6. Calculations of flows using stocks at market value

The sources for the financial accounts are largely bank balance sheets. The difference from one year to another in these balance sheets ($S^t - S^{t-1}$) can be used to calculate the flow (F), but as we have seen, it is necessary to make a distinction between a flow and a revaluation. Each of these two elements has to be estimated, using simple assumptions. This exercise will illustrate the calculation. The starting point is the following equation:

$S^t - S^{t-1} + \upsilon S^{t-1} + F + \dfrac{\upsilon}{2}F$, where υ denotes the change in price between t–1 and

t. This equation expresses the fact that the stock at the end of the period S^t is equal to the stock at the beginning of the period S^{t-1} plus the revaluation of the stock held at the beginning of the period υS^{t-1} plus the transaction (F) plus the

revaluation for the transaction $\dfrac{\upsilon}{2}F$. The assumption is made that transaction

F takes place in the middle of the period, hence the term $\dfrac{\upsilon}{2}$.

Use this equation to calculate F in the following case of loans denominated in US\$. We suppose

S^{t-1} (in euros) = 1 000; S^t = 1 500; $\dfrac{US\$}{euro}$ exchange rate in $t - 1 = 1$;

$\dfrac{US\$}{euro}$ exchange rate in t = 0.8.

The solutions to these exercises are available at:
http://dx.doi.org/10.1787/9789264214637-26-en

Chapter 9

The general government account

This chapter first describes general government accounts and outlines the composition of general government. Next, it explains how to calculate the four major public finance indicators: general government deficit, general government debt, general government expenditure, and taxes and compulsory social contributions.

O ECD *Economic Surveys* on individual member countries always contain in-depth analysis of fiscal data, and they sometimes criticise government fiscal policy. Here are some extracts from the March 2013 report on France:

"Since the late 1970s, the general government budget has always been in deficit, resulting in a trend increase in the public debt-to-GDP ratio. Hitting announced budget targets over the last three years has enhanced France's fiscal credibility, as reflected in the low interest rates on its public debt. The public debt-to-GDP ratio (Maastricht definition) is projected by the OECD to have risen from 57% in 2001 to 91% in 2012 before it reaches nearly 96% of GDP in 2014. Cutting public indebtedness substantially is crucial for ensuring macroeconomic stability and underpinning long-term growth. The public spending ratio would stabilise in 2013 at the same level as in 2011 and 2012, i.e. 56.3%. It should then gradually decline to 53.1% by 2017. However, specific measures for reducing spending have not yet been decided. Tax hikes may also be more attractive than spending cuts in the short run because they trigger less social resistance that might unnerve financial markets. But in the medium run, spending cuts are thought to hurt economic growth less than tax hikes, perhaps because they reflect a stronger and more lasting commitment. In light of already high taxes in France, placing too much reliance on tax hikes for fiscal consolidation could thus prove risky in the medium term." (OECD, 2013).

As shown in Table 9.1 below (published by INSEE, the French statistical office), the French public deficit was 7.5% of GDP in 2009, but was reduced to 4.8% in 2012, still considerably above the 3% ceiling set by the Maastricht Treaty for EU member countries. In addition, French public debt widely exceeded the other Maastricht ceiling of 60% of GDP in 2009 and rose further between 2010 and 2012. These results are due to the continuing upward drift in public spending (56.6% of GDP in 2012), while compulsory levies (taxes and social contributions), the main source of revenue for general government, continue to increase as a percentage of GDP (45.0% in 2012). The OECD economists also use an indicator called "*structural deficit*" to better understand the underlying trend in fiscal policies (see Box 9.1: "The cyclically adjusted financial balance").

All the indicators cited above come directly from the national accounts published by INSEE for the general government sector. This is not surprising. Because the central government is the major macroeconomic agent, it is normal to use macroeconomic accounts for analysing its policy. But it is the Maastricht Treaty criteria, which are based on definitions contained in the national accounts, that intensified the use of national accounts by EU member countries to analyse their public finances (see the appendix of this chapter "Going further: The Maastricht criteria"). Since then, compilation of the government accounts has become a very significant part of the work of European national accountants, to the point that national accounts in Europe can be dubbed as accounts for GDP plus "S13-B9" (which is the code for the surplus/deficit of the general government). Macroeconomists should gain thorough knowledge of these definitions or risk talking nonsense.

Table 9.1. **The French general government account**
Percentage of GDP

	2009	2010	2011	2012
General Government Deficit[a]	-7.5	-7.1	-5.3	-4.8
General Government Debt[a]	79.2	82.4	85.8	90.2
General Government Expenditure	56.8	56.6	55.9	56.6
Taxes and compulsory social contributions	42.1	42.5	43.7	45.0

a) According to the Maastricht Criteria
Source: Insee Databases (2013): Statistical indices and series: Macroeconomic Database: National Accounts www.bdm.insee.fr/bdm2/index?request_locale=en.

StatLink ⟐ http://dx.doi.org/10.1787/888933144116

We start this chapter by describing the general government account via a simplified diagram. Then, we outline the composition of general government, and we end with how to calculate the four major public-finance indicators shown above in Table 9.1.

Box 9.1. **The cyclically adjusted financial balance (or "structural deficit")**

General government spending and revenues are often highly sensitive to economic developments. Tax revenues tend to decline during economic downturns as income and consumption slow down, while at the same time public spending may increase as more people become unemployed and qualified for social assistance or unemployment benefits. On the other hand, during upturns, public finances improve as tax revenues boom and the number of those receiving social benefits usually declines. These fluctuations in tax revenue and public expenditure– in the absence of any discretionary change in policy – make it difficult to assess whether the fiscal stance is expansionary, neutral or restrictive for a given period, and to judge whether fiscal balances are sustainable in the long run.

> **Box 9.1. The cyclically adjusted financial balance (or "structural deficit")** *(cont.)*
>
> To respond to these key questions, economists have developed the concept of cyclically adjusted fiscal balances– often called "structural balances" or "structural deficits" when negative – by untangling structural and cyclical components of the general government balances of the national accounts. To derive these cyclically adjusted fiscal balances, one has to: (1) define what would be the potential (or structural) output of a country (see Chapter 4); and (2) estimate how tax revenue and public spending react when the actual output deviates from its potential during the economic cycle. Girouard and André (2005) provide a detailed view on the methodology used at the OECD. One should note that some one-off factors may make comparisons of cyclically adjusted public finance data across time and countries dubious if not corrected for. Examples include the transfer of future pension liabilities from a public enterprise to the general government sector accompanied by a transfer of existing pension fund assets from the enterprise to the general government sector. Under SNA 93, this improved the cyclically adjusted balance at the time of the transfer but result in deterioration in the longer-term. Thus the economists in the EU Commission and in OECD remove not only the impact of the economic cycle, but also the impact of these "one-offs". However, the definition of a one-off remains itself fuzzy.

1. A simplified diagram for general government

General government (GG) constitutes a very important **institutional sector,** including central government, local authorities and the social security funds. In federal countries (such as Germany) state authorities (called "Länder" in Germany) are also included. The official code for general government in the national accounts is "S13". Put simply, this sector has two functions: the production of non-market services (education, health care, defence, policing, etc.) and the redistribution of income (social benefits, subsidies). To finance the cost of these functions, general government levies taxes and social contributions. Part of these resources is used to pay public employees' salaries, as well as the intermediate consumption and investment needed to produce non-market services supplied free of charge. The rest is redistributed in the form of social benefits or subsidies.

National accountants use a common accounting framework for all the institutional sectors, be they private companies or government. However, it is worth remembering that government agencies are structured differently than firms. For one thing, government services have no selling prices, since they are free of charge. For another, most general government agencies are not aiming to make an operating profit. Economists in fact use different aggregates depending on whether they are looking at firms or at general government: in the case of firms, they look mainly at the profit ratio (net operating surplus/ value added), while for general government they look mainly at **net lending/ net borrowing** (which is coded as "B9").

Box 9.2. **Why is such importance attached to item B9?**

For general government, B9 (net lending/borrowing) is equal to revenue minus expenditure. A negative B9 shows the existence of a public deficit or "net borrowing", which, as it names indicates shows that the government has to borrow to finance it. General government must strive not to spend more than it earns, on a structural basis. In general, net borrowing leads to an increase in the public debt and hence in the interest charges that have to be borne by future generations. A positive B9 means the existence of net lending, or a "surplus", enabling the government to reduce its debt. B9 is one of the main criteria in the Maastricht Treaty (see Going further at the end of the chapter). As a result, European countries pay a lot of attention to this balance.

Several non-European countries – for example, the United States – prefer to use a different balance, namely net saving (B8N). The disadvantage of the B9 aggregate is that it can become negative as a result of investment by government, which, in most cases, is positive in nature because it can contribute to future output. Net saving (B8N) has the advantage of being unaffected by a particular amount of investment in a given period, reflecting solely current operations, namely current revenue and current expenditure (including consumption of fixed capital). The rule that countries using this balance B8N impose on themselves is that current revenue should, on average, cover current expenditure, allowing that investment can be financed through borrowing. This is often referred to as the "golden rule".

The following simplified picture of the general government account illustrates how national accounts manage to bring the specific "non-market" operations of general government into the common framework. As in the case of the other institutional sectors, the account is in traditional "T" form, with "Uses" on the left and "Resources" on the right. The shaded areas of the account represent the monetary flows actually recorded (in other words, the revenues and expenditures) which are: taxes and social contributions under "resources"; employee compensation, intermediate consumption, subsidies, social benefits, interest on the public debt and GFCF under "uses". At the bottom of this shaded section, there is a row showing the balance representing net borrowing/net lending. All these amounts are calculated at current prices.

We now have to add to this framework items that are not based on monetary transactions (since prices are zero). This invented (or "imputed") portion is shown in italics in the un-shaded areas. In the top right-hand corner of the account, as resources, we see **output of non-market services** defined as equal to total costs (compensation plus intermediate consumption plus consumption of fixed capital – see Chapter 4). As a result, the profit – or to be more precise, the net operating surplus (NOS) – is zero, which should come as no surprise when dealing with non-profit institutions. This non-market output is provided to households and firms, but it is not recorded as consumption by these sectors but as consumption by the government itself. Thus, to counterbalance this "imputed" output of general-government resources, the "Uses" section of general government includes an entry for final consumption by general government, which equals non-market output (simplifying somewhat – see Box 9.4. "Definition of final consumption expenditure of general government" further down the chapter).

General government account: simplified diagram

The shaded areas show monetary flows, the un-shaded areas imputed flows

Uses	Resources
	Output of non-market services
Compensation of employees	
Intermediate consumption	
Consumption of fixed capital	*Profit =NOS =0*
Subsidies	Taxes
Social benefits	
Debt interest	
	Social contribution
Final consumption equal (with some simplification) to output of non-market services	
GFCF	
Net lending/ net borrowing	

It is very important to note that "final consumption by general government" is an accounting convention. General government does not actually consume its output. Households and firms consume that output as public services. However, because there are no observable monetary transactions (the services are free of charge), national accountants have given up on the idea of attributing this consumption specifically to households or to firms, and they have attributed it to general government itself. Note also, however, that the addition of the "imputed" items (output of non-market services and final consumption) makes no difference to the bottom line of the account (i.e. net lending/net borrowing), because the addition to resources is exactly offset by the addition to uses. In the end, net lending/net borrowing remains equal to the difference between actual revenue and expenditure.

There are exceptions to the rule that only actual flows affect the calculation of net lending/net borrowing. For example, when a government writes off debt owed by a developing country, no payment is made, but the amount is still recorded as a capital transfer expenditure in the national accounts, and thus affects net lending/borrowing.

To conclude, note that the simplified diagram of the government account presents four major quasi-principles: (1) the important balance is net lending/net borrowing, which is the difference between actual revenue and expenditure, (2) non-market output by definition equals total costs; (3) the net operating surplus of general government is zero; (4) by convention, general government consumes what it produces.

2. Detailed structure of the general government account

A complete set of accounts for France in 2011 (including the financial accounts and balance sheets) is shown on the following two pages. These accounts illustrate how the general government accounts are integrated into the national accounts, from production to balance sheet. In contrast to the earlier T-shaped model, with uses on the left and resources on the right, we have in this case shown the uses below the resources. However, this is merely a matter of presentation and does not affect the analysis.

As is typical, each account ends with a balance, which is coded with an initial capital B (for example, "B1 Value added, gross") shown under uses in the upper part of the account and under resources in the lower part. For example, the balance of the production account is gross value added, which is then shown again under resources in the generation of income account. Certain intermediate balances (disposable income, for example) are shown even though they have little meaning in the case of general government and are only rarely commented on by economists. By contrast, the final balance, "B9 net lending/net borrowing" is highly significant. Certain secondary transactions are grouped together under miscellaneous, because they are marginal and of interest only to specialists.

Let us start by taking the upper part of the accounts. The output of general government consists essentially of **non-market output** (EUR 376.8 billion in 2011), whose definition and evaluation have been explained in the diagram and in Chapter 4.

The official title of this entry is "Other non-market output", but we have simplified this in the text and in the diagram.

But there is also a certain amount of market output, and output for own final use (together amounting to EUR 59.4 billion). The former consists of sales by general government (publications, sales of medicines by hospitals, exports of warships from naval shipyards, sales of water supply by communal syndicates). Output for own final use consists mainly of the costs of producing in-house software.

After deducting from total output intermediate consumption of EUR 109.6 billion (which represents all the current operating costs of functioning, such as paper, telephone, rentals, etc.), general government shows gross value added of EUR 326.7 billion, equivalent to 16.3% of GDP (see Box 9.3: "Limitations and pitfalls"). Most of the expenditure in the generation of income account consists of compensation of civil servants (EUR 262.7 billion), which includes actual and imputed social contributions (see Chapter 6). The imputed contributions are fairly high for general government because, in France, the state is itself the manager of the pension system for its employees and therefore does not pay employers' contributions. This item therefore has to be imputed in order to evaluate the actual cost of employing civil servants.

Table 9.2. **Non-financial accounts of general government**

France, 2011

	Production Account	
	Total resources	
P11_P12	Market output and output for own final use	59.4
P13	Non-market output	376.8
	Total uses	
P2	Intermediate consumption	109.6
B1G	Gross domestic product/ Gross value added	326.7
K1	Consumption of fixed capital	53.8
B1N	Net domestic product/ Net value added	272.9
	Generation of income account	
	Total resources	
B1N	Net domestic product/ Net value added	272.9
	Total uses	
D1	Compensation of employees	262.7
	Miscellaneous	6.3
B2N	Net operating surplus	3.8

Table 9.2. **Non-financial accounts of general government** (cont.)
France, 2011

	Allocation of primary income account	
	Total resources	
B2N	Net operating surplus	3.8
D2	Taxes on production and imports, receivable	305.2
	Miscellaneous	-13.4
	Total uses	
D41	Interest	52.6
B5N	Net national income/ Net balance of primary incomes	242.9
	Secondary distribution of income account	
	Total resources	
B5N	Net national income/ Net balance of primary incomes	242.9
D5	Current taxes on income, wealth etc.	224.6
D61	Social contributions	375.6
D7	Other current transfers	14.3
	Total uses	
D5	Current taxes on income, wealth etc., payable	0.1
D62	Social benefits other than social transfers in kind	388.7
D631	Social transfers in kind (via market producers)	122.0
D7	Other current transfers	64.9
B6N	Net disposable income	403.7
	Use of income account	
	Total resources	
B6N	Net disposable income	403.7
	Total uses	
P3	Final consumption expenditure	490.0
P31	– Individual consumption expenditure	320.5
P32	– Collective consumption expenditure	169.5
B8N	Net saving	-86.2
	Capital account	
	Total resources	
B8N	Net saving	-86.2
	Net capital transfers	-9.1
	Total uses	
P5	Gross capital formation	62.5
	– GFCF	62.7
	– other	-0.2
K1	Consumption of fixed capital	53.8
P5N	Net capital formation	8.7
B9	Net lending (+)/Net borrowing (-)	-105.9

StatLink ⟶ http://dx.doi.org/10.1787/888933144124

Table 9.2. **Financial accounts of general government**
France, 2011

	Financial account	
	Changes in liabilities (flows of transactions)	133.3
F2	Currency and deposits	7.1
F3	Securities other than shares	125.1
F4	Loans	-9.6
F5	Shares and other equity	
F6	Insurance technical reserves	
F7	Other accounts payable	10.8
	Changes in assets (flows of transactions)	27.5
F1	Monetary gold and SDRs	
F2	Currency and deposits	15.9
F3	Securities other than shares	-4.7
F4	Loans	7.0
F5	Shares and other equity	-4.8
F6	Insurance technical reserves	0.0
F7	Other accounts receivable	14.1

StatLink ⬛⬛ http://dx.doi.org/10.1787/888933144124

Balance sheet of general government, 2011

	Value at beginning of 2011	Transactions	Consumption of fixed capital	Revaluation	Other volume changes and adjustments	Value at end of 2011
Non-financial assets	1 693.8	63.0	53.6	54.6	5.6	1 763.4
Financial assets (consolidated)	921.4	31.4		-30.0	-1.1	921.7
Financial liabilities (consolidated)	2 030.9	135.3		11.6	0.1	2 177.8
Net worth	584.3	-40.9	53.6	13.1	4.4	507.2

Source: Insee Databases (2013): Statistical indices and series: Macroeconomic Database: National Accounts *www.bdm.insee.fr/bdm2/index?request_locale=en*; and OECD (2014), "General Government Accounts: Main aggregates", OECD National Accounts Statistics (database), doi: *http://dx.doi.org/ 10.1787/data-00020-en* and OECD (2014), "Financial Accounts: Consolidated flows, annual", OECD National Accounts Statistics (database), doi: *http://dx.doi.org/10.1787/data-00022-en*.

StatLink ⬛⬛ http://dx.doi.org/10.1787/888933144124

The net operating surplus, which measures profit, is equal to EUR 3.8 billion, which is practically zero at this level of macro accounts. This is something of a surprise, since it was stated earlier that the profit of general government was zero by definition. The fact is that the diagram was an oversimplification, since small parts of the government sector operate as market enterprises (for example, certain water-supply units), so they record

> ### Box 9.3. **Limitations and pitfalls of percentages of GDP**
>
> All the main public-finance indicators are normally expressed as percentages of GDP, in other words, the amounts in current prices divided by GDP at current prices and then multiplied by 100. This permits international comparisons, such as comparing countries' deficits (expressed in billion euros or dollars or any other currency), which would otherwise have little meaning, since for the same absolute level of deficit a large country is much more capable of financing its shortfall than a small country with correspondingly smaller taxation and borrowing potential. Presentation as a percentage of GDP is applied to all public finance indicators and especially to total government expenditure and total fiscal burden, which is the sum of taxes and compulsory social contributions. These two latter indicators are widely used to measure the importance of the government's role in the economy, which in France is quite large (largest among the OECD countries). However, this approach is open to criticism. GDP is the sum of the values added. Strictly speaking, therefore, the importance of government activity in relation to GDP should be measured as the contribution of its value added to GDP, that is, 16.3% in the case of France. But even using this more rigorous yardstick, France would still have one of the largest ratios of government activity to GDP in the OECD.

operating profits or losses. The amounts remain very small, however, and it should be remembered that, as a matter of principle, **the net operating surplus of general government is zero**. One might even call this one of the fundamental equations of the national accounts.

Then we have the two major accounts "allocation of primary income and secondary distribution of income."

The differentiation between the two accounts ("primary" and "secondary") is somewhat artificial and should not be considered an important feature.

In them are resources commonly called "indirect taxes" but known in the national accounts as **"taxes on production and imports"** (EUR 305.2 billion), most of which in the case of France consist of VAT (Value-Added Tax) and the TIPP (internal tax on petroleum products). Among uses, note the size of the item for interest on the public debt (EUR 52.6 billion). Note also, further down, the substantial sum derived from so-called direct taxes, known in the national accounts as **"taxes on income and wealth"** (EUR 224.6), which include income tax and corporate profits tax, as well as numerous other taxes, including, the wealth tax in the case of France. The resources also include the substantial amount of social contributions received by the social security funds (EUR 375.6), which are subsequently redistributed to households. Note that social security funds are not financed exclusively through social contributions but also through more general taxes, and sometimes through borrowing. Taxes and social contributions are measured on an "accrual basis" (see box "Accrual accounting and government accounts" at the end of this chapter).

The analysis of social benefits in the national accounts is somewhat complicated. The classification distinguishes **social benefits other than social transfers in kind** (D62) and **social transfers in kind** (D631). A large part of the payments to households by social security and other social insurance or social assistance units (pensions, maternity allowances, family allowances, death benefits, etc.) is recorded under D62. It is this part (EUR 388.7 billion) that appears as a use in the general government account under "social benefits" (and as a resource in the household account). However, another substantial part (EUR 122.0 billion) is classified under D631. This includes repayments from the health sector of social security – medicines, medical visits and costs of transporting patients – payment of household and medical assistance in the home and housing allowances. Somewhat strangely, these are not shown as social benefits received by households but as "social transfers in kind", in a subsidiary account called "adjusted disposable income", and they are counted as final consumption expenditure of general government, and not as consumed by households.

This explains why the sum recorded as **(P3) final consumption expenditure of general government** (EUR 490.0 billion) is higher than the non-market output (EUR 376.8 billion), contrary to what was shown in the simplified diagram. The fact is that, as explained in the previous paragraph, the major part of the **social transfers in kind**, the part corresponding to purchases by general government of goods and services produced by market producers and supplied to households, is recorded as final consumption expenditure by general government and not as social benefits. To complicate matters even more, the national accounts record a small portion of the sales by general government under "partial payments" by households. In the case of France, these consist mainly of daily hospital fees, which in fact represent a very small fraction of hospitalisation costs. This part of the consumption expenditure of general government has to be removed, since it is recorded directly under household consumption. Thus, the formula that precisely defines the final consumption expenditure of general government is therefore more complicated than the one in the simplified diagram and is shown in Box 9.4:

> **Box 9.4. Definition of final consumption expenditure of general government**
>
> P3/S13 Final consumption expenditure of general government = P13/S13 Non-market output − P131/S13 Partial payments by households + [D6311 + D63121 + D63131]/S13 Social transfers in kind corresponding to purchases of products supplied to households via market producers. This gives, in billion euros: 376.8 − 8.9 + 122.0 = 490.0. Unfortunately, the last two figures in the bracket are not shown in the main table published by INSEE for general government and one has to go to the subsidiary accounts to find them.

Final consumption expenditure of general government is itself split into **individual consumption expenditure** (EUR 320.5) and **collective consumption expenditure** (EUR 169.5). The former includes expenditure by general government that can be unmistakably attributed to households, consisting essentially of spending on healthcare and education. The latter covers all other expenditure, i.e. that part of which it cannot be said with certainty who the consumers are, households or enterprises. These are collective expenditure items, such as general administration, defence, policing, etc. It was shown in Chapters 3 and 5 that by adding together individual consumption expenditure and household expenditure, one obtained **households' actual final consumption**, a concept used for international comparisons, in particular.

It will be seen from looking at other rows in the account that the column "uses" include net capital formation of general government, which is equal to GCF (EUR 62.5 billion) *minus* consumption of fixed capital (EUR 53.8 billion). Finally, there is the now familiar item **net lending/net borrowing of general government (B9A)**, which in 2011 was a negative EUR 105.9 billion, representing net borrowing or, in common terms, a public deficit. This balance is the most important Maastricht criteria. It closes the sequence of accounts known as the **non-financial accounts** of general government.

The non-financial accounts are then followed by the financial accounts, showing how general government has financed the deficit. As can be seen on the side of "changes in liabilities" (see Chapter 8 for definitions), this was done mainly by issuing securities – i.e. Treasury bonds, called in France BTF (short-term), BTAN (medium-term) or OAT (long-term) – for a sum of EUR 125.1 billion. We shall not comment here on the smaller financial transactions of the government, but it is worthwhile to comment on the "balance of transactions in financial assets and liabilities", which is another name for net lending/net borrowing (in fact, it has a similar code: B9B). It will be seen that, unlike the household and enterprise accounts, the B9B balance is exactly equal to the B9A balance, demonstrating the higher quality of the general government account compared to business or households accounts (see box "Sources" at the end of this chapter).

As can be seen in the row entitled "financial liabilities" on the balance sheets, the substantial issuance of Treasury bonds has contributed to a rise in the public debt (EUR 135.3 billion). The amount of public debt, as defined in the national accounts (which differs from the definition of public debt according to the Maastricht treaty) is EUR 2 177.8 billion. INSEE estimates that the total assets of general government at current prices amount to EUR 2 685.0 billion, of which EUR 1 763.4 billion is non-financial assets (land, buildings, other construction) and EUR 921.7 billion of financial assets (essentially listed or non-listed shares in public-sector enterprises). It is interesting to note that the net worth of the general government estimated by INSEE actually increased during 2011, while at the same time the government has very significantly increased its debt. These messages are contradictory: the first is positive, the second negative. The positive message should be considered with caution, because the increase in the net worth is essentially due to the estimated re-evaluations of the non-financial assets of the government (+54.6). This probably corresponds to estimated holding gains on government buildings. But these estimates are very approximate, and because it is probably difficult to sell some of the government buildings, this is only "potential" revenue.

3. What is the scope of the general government?

The figures shown in the national accounts for the totality of general government clearly depend on the scope of this sector. It is obvious that parts of the administration, like the Finance Ministry or the Education Ministry, are included. In fact, all the units financed through the budget discussed in Parliament are included. But there are many entities, particularly in France, that are commonly said to be "on the border" between public and private. In the national accounts, one says that they are on the frontier "between the market and non-market sectors". For example, are the French public utility Électricité de France (EDF) and the French Post Office, both of which have long exercised a public monopoly, part of general government? Does a university or a secondary school form part of general government? Since the net lending/net borrowing of general government is equal to the sum of the net lending/net borrowing of the bodies included in it, knowing which entities are part of general government is essential to reliable calculation of the public deficit and, above all, a calculation that is internationally comparable.

National accountants pay particular attention to the decision-making process in deciding which **institutional units** form part of general government. Institutional unit means an economic decision-making centre, characterised by autonomous decision-making in carrying out its principal function, and a complete set of accounts. Autonomy in decision making is judged by the unit's ability to make commitments, take on debts and award contracts in its own name. If a unit does not have these characteristics, it has to be included in the institutional unit that makes these decisions for it.

The general government sector is comprised of institutional units whose main activity is either to produce non-market goods and services or to redistribute income and national wealth. Non-market producers are those that provide services – and sometimes goods – free of charge, or at prices that are **not economically significant.** This original concept plays an important role in determining whether a unit is inside or outside the general government. The international system of national accounts defines prices that are not economically significant as "prices which do not have a significant influence on the amounts the producers are willing to supply, or on the amounts purchasers wish to buy". In practice, many countries interpret this criterion as meaning "prices that cover less than half the cost of production". Take the case of EDF, the large French electricity enterprise. EDF is indisputably an institutional unit (having a complete set of accounts), but it does not produce non-market goods and services, since electricity is sold at economically significant prices (prices cover costs: EDF makes, most often, a profit). Like the other large French public enterprises, (Railways, Post Office) EDF is thus included in the enterprise sector, not the general government. Now take the case of a statistical office like INSEE. It is not an institutional unit because it has very limited financial autonomy and cannot contract significant debts in its own name. It is therefore included as part of its supervisory institutional unit, the Finance Ministry, which is itself included in the unit known as central government. INSEE therefore forms part of general government via the central government unit under which it comes. On the basis of these general principles, national accountants have developed a decision-making tree containing three even more precise questions (see Box 9.5 below).

> ### Box 9.5. **The decision-making tree regarding inclusion in general government**
>
> The tree is made up of three interlinked questions:
>
> First question: Is the unit an institutional unit? If so, go on to the next question; if not, it is included in the institutional unit it comes under (as we saw in the example of the statistical office discussed earlier in the text).
>
> Second question: Is it public? Meaning: is it controlled by a unit that is itself part of general government? If so, go on to the next question; if not, it does not form part of general government.
>
> Third question: Does it produce non-market goods and services? This criterion here is whether goods and services are sold at "prices that are not economically significant", a concept that in practice is often measured by whether sales regularly represent less than 50% of the production costs. If so, it is classified in general government.
>
> Let us apply the decision-making process above to a farm. Is it an institutional unit? Yes. Is it controlled by a part of general government? No. Farms, therefore, however much they receive in the way of subsidies in France, do not form part of general government. Now take the case of "Réseau Ferré de France", the public enterprise that manages the railway infrastructure in France (while the SNCF manages transport on that infrastructure). It is an institutional unit. It is controlled by general government (its managers are appointed by central government). However, its sales (tolls paid by SNCF) cover slightly more than 50% of its costs. It is therefore not part of general government.* Even using this tree, however, there remain problematical cases, such as that of financial units, because measuring their sales presents practical problems.
>
> * The reform of SNCF/RFF introduced in June 2014 might interfere with this conclusion.

Table 9.3. shows the general government sector in the case of France (figures in brackets show the total expenditure of each element, in order to give an idea of its importance[1]). As can be seen, the general government sector is itself broken down into three sub-sectors: central government (S1311), local government (S1313) and social security funds (S1314).

The international classification contains four subsectors, including S1312, which consists of the "states" level in the case of a federation. For example, in Germany, the subsector S1312 consists of the "Länder".

Central government in the narrow sense of "the State" is the largest unit of general government, and its expenditure and revenue constitute the largest part of the overall general government account (expenditure amounting to EUR 414.6 billion). Central government in France also includes the accounts of almost 800 organisations collectively known as "various central government agencies". These are institutional and quasi-institutional units meeting the criteria set out above. They include the universities, all the specialised higher-educational schools, the CEA (Atomic Energy Commissariat) and the CNRS (National Centre for Scientific Research). This clearly shows the importance of the public sector in France in education and research.

Table 9.3. **Composition of the French general government sector**

General government (S13) (Total expenditure in 2011: EUR 1 118.5 bn)	Central government (S1311)	State (S13111) (Total expenditure in 2011: EUR 414.6 bn)	General budget Special Treasury accounts Ancillary budgets Treasury operations
		Various central government agencies (S13112) (Total expenditure in 2011: EUR 79.5 bn)	Comprises roughly 800 bodies of varying legal status, in many cases public establishments of an administrative nature, reflecting the tradition of State centralisation and intervention in France, especially in the fields of higher education, research and cultural activities.
	Local government (S1313) (Total expenditure in 2011: EUR 235.31bn)	Local authorities (S13131) (Total expenditure in 2011: EUR 215.7 bn)	"Communes", "départements", régions, inter-communal syndicates, urban communities and non-market "régies" (semi-official enterprises).
		Various local government agencies (S13132) (Total expenditure in 2011: EUR 34.1 bn)	Non-market units that are part of communes or locally financed; Chambers of commerce; secondary schools, etc.
	Social security funds (S1314) (Total expenditure in 2011: EUR 532.1 bn)	Social insurance funds (S13141) (Total expenditure in 2011: EUR 508.2 bn)	General social security system; special funds; other supplementary pension funds for employees and independent workers
		Bodies controlled by social insurance (S13142) (Total expenditure in 2011: EUR 84.6 bn)	Public hospitals; other bodies

Source: Insee Databases (2013): Statistical indices and series: Macroeconomic Database: National Accounts www.bdm.insee.fr/bdm2/index?request_locale=en.

StatLink 🖳 http://dx.doi.org/10.1787/888933144135

The local authorities comprise the regions (22 in number in 2014), the "departements" (101) and the "communes" (around 36 000) together with the numerous and varied bodies attached to them. Lastly, the social security funds include the major funds for employees and independent workers (CNAM: sickness, CNAF: family, CNAVTS: retirement), UNEDIC (unemployment insurance), the supplementary pension schemes (AGIRC, ARRCO), and, the largest item, the public hospitals – or more precisely, the hospitals participating in the public hospital service.

4. The principal public-finance indicators

These are the four indicators shown in the table at the beginning of this chapter: (1) the public deficit; (2) the public debt; (3) public expenditure; (4) total taxes and social contributions. They are usually shown as percentages of GDP (in other words divided by GDP at current prices and then multiplied by 100). In the case of the EU countries, the first two indicators are among the Maastricht criteria that are reported (or "notified") to the European Commission. The other two are not central to the national accounts but derived from them. They do not form part of the Maastricht criteria.

Public deficit: item B9A "net lending/net borrowing of general government". When the item is negative, it is a public deficit and when positive, a public surplus.

Public debt: the amount of public debt on the balance sheets of general government. In the case of EU countries, the "notified" (or Maastricht-reported) public debt is appreciably different from debt as it appears in the national accounts, for three reasons. First, the notified debt is consolidated, meaning that debts owed by one general government unit to another are cancelled out, for example, the debt of central government vis-à-vis local authorities. Second, the notified debt is valued at face value and not at market prices as is done in the national accounts. Finally, the notified debt includes only part of the debt, excluding that relating to pension liabilities, the still unpaid accrued interest and certain very short-term debt (commercial borrowing and advances). Exercise 8, at the end of this chapter, shows the reconciliation of the two definitions.

Public expenditure: this is total actual expenditure, meaning monetary payments by general government.[2] This indicator is widely used to measure the size of the role played by general government in the national economy. French governments of both main political tendencies have always regarded it as an important indicator and tried to reduce it.

Total taxes and social contributions: this indicator has much in common with the previous one, but it is measured by general government revenue and not expenditure. As its name indicates, it reflects the taxes and actual contributions (in other words, not including imputed contributions) that households and firms must pay to various parts of general government. The figure is very high for France by comparison with other countries (see Table 9.4), and all governments have tried to reduce it.

In France, this indicator is called "prélèvements obligatoires" translated as "compulsory levies".

It should be stressed that, for EU countries, the figures include taxes paid to the EU institutions (including the European Community portion of Value-Added Tax). For this reason, it is more accurate to refer to taxes and social contributions *payable to general government and EU Institutions.*

Table 9.4. **Taxes and compulsory contributions**
Percentage of GDP, 2010

France	42.9
Germany	36.1
Italy	42.9
Sweden	45.5
United States	24.8
OECD – Total	**33.8**

Source: OECD (2012), "Economy-wide regulation", OECD Product Market Regulation Statistics (database), doi: *10.1787/data-00593-en.*

StatLink ᘯᵫᵽᔤ *http://dx.doi.org/10.1787/888933144143*

Notes

1. The sum of the lower parts is sometimes larger than the higher level. This is because, moving up one level, the consolidation of certain cross-transactions means that they cancel each other out. For example, certain transfers between central government and local authorities are counted as expenditure by central government but not by general government, since this expenditure appears elsewhere as revenue for local authorities that are part of general government.

2. In principle only, because in practice it includes some amounts that are not actually paid, such as imputed contributions (included in compensation of employees) or gross fixed capital formation in the form of software produced for own account. Moreover, this amount includes (somewhat bizarrely) certain "negative expenditures", such as the proceeds from the sales of mobile telecommunications licences.

References

Girouard, N. and C. André (2005), "Measuring Cyclically-adjusted Budget Balances for OECD Countries", OECD *Economics Department Working Papers*, No. 434, OECD Publishing, doi: *http://dx.doi.org/10.1787/787626008442.*

Insee Databases (2013): Statistical indices and series: Macroeconomic Database: National Accounts *www.bdm.insee.fr/bdm2/index?request_locale=en.*

OECD (2014), "Financial Accounts: Consolidated flows, annual", OECD National Accounts Statistics (database), doi: *http://dx.doi.org/10.1787/data-00022-en*.

OECD (2014), "General Government Accounts: Main aggregates", OECD National Accounts Statistics (database), doi: *http://dx.doi.org/10.1787/data-00020-en*.

OECD (2013), *OECD Economic Surveys: France 2013*, OECD Publishing, doi: *http://dx.doi.org/10.1787/eco_surveys-fra-2013-en*.

OECD (2012), "Economy-wide regulation", OECD Product Market Regulation Statistics (database), doi: *http://dx.doi.org/10.1787/data-00593-en*.

Key points

- The general government sector consists of institutional units producing non-market goods and services or carrying out transactions that redistribute income or national wealth.

- Non-market output is the sum of the costs involved: intermediate consumption, compensation of employees, consumption of fixed capital.

- The net operating surplus of general government is, by definition, basically zero.

- In the national accounts, accounting convention requires that the non-market output of general government be accounted for as if it were consumed by general government itself.

- The consumption expenditure of general government is equal to the non-market output (minus partial payments) plus the social benefits in kind purchased by general government for the benefit of households.

- The public deficit is measured by item B9 "net lending/net borrowing" of general government. If this is negative, it means a deficit; if it is positive, a surplus.

- Total taxes and social contributions consist of taxes and actual social contributions paid by households and firms to general government, and in the case of the EU countries, to the European institutions.

Going further

The Maastricht criteria

When the European countries decided to introduce the euro as a common currency, it was necessary to reach agreement on fiscal policy in order to prevent bad fiscal management in one country from affecting the others. If one country allows deficits to build up and thus increases its public debt at the expense of future generations, it can destabilise the whole euro zone as the financial markets will push interest rates to unsustainable levels, thus necessitating the rescue of the country. Despite all the constraints of Maastricht criteria, this is what happened in 2009 in Greece, and since this year the whole Euro zone is struggling against the domino effect of this initial catastrophe. This has led the EU Commission to strengthen the constraints and to extend its analysis to the competitiveness imbalances in the Euro zone. These imbalances were hidden by the existence of a single currency. Returning to statistical measurement, policy makers continue to impose fiscal rules on all EU governments, via the so-called "Maastricht Treaty". Because the national accounts provided the best internationally comparable accounting framework, the Maastricht Treaty outlined criteria based on the definitions in the national accounts. On 1 April and 1 October each year, performance in relation to these criteria is "notified" to the European Commission. The first of these criteria is the notified public deficit, measured by item S13-B9 in the national accounts. This must be less than 3% of GDP. The second criterion is the notified public debt (see definition in the text) which has to be less than 60% of GDP. Since the introduction of these criteria, Eurostat has put considerable effort into recommending comparable treatment among countries, even in the most difficult cases. The financial prowess of government Treasuries is in fact just as great as that of other big players in the financial markets. In the end, the relevance, comparability and transparency of public accounts have benefited considerably from the use of national accounts.

The two Maastricht criteria on the deficit and debt levels are in fact linked, since a deficit can be expected to lead to an increase in debt. In fact, at the origin, there was a mechanical link between the thresholds of 3% and 60%: 3% of deficit is the amount that stabilises the debt at 60% of GDP, assuming

296

that nominal GDP increases by 5% (which was more or less the case in the 1990s). Some economists criticise the Maastricht criteria on the grounds that they should take the economic situation into account. They think it is absurd to ask a country in the throes of a recession to cut expenditure in order to meet the criterion; at time when tax revenue is declining, this would tend to intensify the recession. The European Commission is therefore moving toward an interpretation based more on longer-term trends, by setting a target for a reduction of the structural deficit, in other words the deficit adjusted for the impact of the economic cycle. (The structural deficit is explained in the box "Cyclically Adjusted Financial Balance"). At the same time, it is interesting to note that the debt criterion appears to go somewhat against the fundamentals of capital management theory, because it focuses on "gross debt", not taking into account assets held. Capital management theory prefers "net debt", which equals liabilities minus assets. This is because for a given amount of gross debt, the diagnosis for two countries can differ widely depending on their assets.

For example, one country may have no assets, while another has considerable shareholdings. By selling these shares, the second government can reduce its debt, which is not true of the first. In practice, however, the assets of general government are difficult to measure and some of these assets are not easy to sell. This probably explains why the Maastricht Treaty refers only to gross debt and not net debt. However, this can result in certain paradoxes (see Exercise 7).

Data Sources: How are the figures obtained?

The general government accounts are the most precise of the national accounts. For this sector, unlike the situation for households and firms, national accountants have all the accounts of the institutional units making up the sector and not just a statistical sample. The compilation method used for general government therefore becomes less statistical and more accounting oriented. In France, the accounts of central government, the social security system and the thousands of local entities are transmitted to the "Direction de la Comptabilité Publique" (Public Accounts Directorate) in the Finance Ministry. Here, a special service consisting of some 30 people transforms the thousands of accounts and budget headings into the aggregates used in the national accounts, following the very detailed directives supplied by INSEE. The compilation method nevertheless remains statistical for the initial estimates, at a time when not all the accounts, especially those of the social security, are yet available. For 2012, for example, INSEE published its initial estimates of the accounts of general government on the 27 March 2013. These initial estimates are to be subsequently revised.

There are two fortunate consequences of the excellence of government-accounts data: (1) In many countries, there is little to no need to reconcile the balances of the non-financial accounts and the financial accounts (B9A and B9B, respectively) for the general government (i.e. the so-called "statistical discrepancy" is very small). (2) National accountants can use government data to improve the compilation of accounts for the other sectors. For example, since they include comprehensive data for social contributions received by general government, and since these necessarily correspond to the social contributions paid, the figures can be used to improve the enterprise account, which is not exhaustive in this respect. Because of this, national accountants say that the general government account acts as a "pilot" account.

Tricks of the trade: Above and below the line

For the non-specialist in public finances, analysing the accounts of numerous public entities is a nightmare when it comes to adding together (or "consolidating") several of these. This is because of the numerous flows between these entities, making it easy to get lost in the complexity of relationships, with the result that mistakes can be made in calculating the overall deficit. The national accounts provide a simple benchmark that can even be expressed mathematically: the net lending/net borrowing item is an additive variable. In other words, the overall net lending/net borrowing for a group of units is precisely equal to the sum of their individual net lending/net borrowing. It is therefore easy for national accountants to measure the impact of the reclassification of a government unit. The net lending/net borrowing of this unit can be added to that of general government as a whole, without needing to know anything about its complex relations with others.

Reference is sometimes made to "above-the-line" and "below-the-line" accounting. What do these obtuse terms mean? Are they used to hide something? No. These expressions are sometimes used by national accountants to describe whether a given operation will have an impact on the deficit. The "line" in question is item B9A, the net borrowing/net lending of the capital account. An operation is classified as "above" this line (corresponding to its actual location in the sequence of accounts) if B9A is affected, and "below" this line if there is no impact. Let us take an example. Central government can obtain cash (to buy back part of its debt, for example) either by selling shares or by selling property. If it sells shares, the operation is below the line (national accountants also say that it is "entirely financial"). This is because shares constitute a financial asset; financial assets are included in the financial account, i.e. below the line, and the money obtained is also a financial asset, treated similarly. The situation is quite different if the government sells property. The money obtained is again shown below the line, but the sale of the property is shown above the line, with the result that the public deficit is correspondingly reduced. Exercise 6 explains this case, which is interesting in that it highlights one of the limitations of the definition of the public deficit. Why should the impact be different between a financial disposal (of shares) and a non-financial disposal (of property)? The answer is that it is based on a convention, and like any convention, the definition of the deficit has advantages and disadvantages.

Accrual accounting in general government accounts

National accounts are drawn up on what is known as the **accrual basis** (for more on accrual accounting, see appendix "Going further (3)" in Chapter 10). Here we shall merely describe the implications for the general government account. Accrual accounting is a basic accounting practice in the private sector, but it has not so far been completely accepted for public accounting except in a few countries. In France, while the social security institutions have adopted it, this is not yet true of the State Budget, which to a great extent remains on a "cash" basis, especially for income. However, in the recent years, France has developed an accrual system for the State (so-called "comptabilité generale d'exercice"). However, because these accounts are recent, INSEE, the French statistical office continues to use the cash accounts, thus recording the tax payments received and not the tax due. It is therefore obliged to transform the budgetary data in certain cases, notably for VAT (Value-Added Tax). In practice, VAT generated and collected by firms during a given month is received by the government only six weeks later. INSEE therefore brings forward the VAT recovery by these six weeks (see Exercise 9 at the end of this chapter). For certain other taxes, INSEE records tax assessments instead of tax payments and therefore has to introduce an adjustment item called "assessed but unlikely to be collected" (see Exercise 5). INSEE is also obliged to make significant modifications in the amount of interest paid by government in order better conform to the accrual concept. For example, some government bonds are "zero-coupon", meaning that interest is not paid annually but in a lump sum at the end of the bond's maturity. INSEE spreads out the interest over the life of the bond in order to give a truer account of government's actual annual charges.

Exercises for Chapter 9

Exercise 1. Updating the first table

The figures in this chapter are extracted from the old SNA 93 system of accounts. Go to the INSEE web site, *www.insee.fr*. Using the pages devoted to the annual national accounts for general government, find the amounts in million euros in recent years for the following: general government net lending/borrowing (B9A); the public debt; public expenditure; taxes and compulsory contributions. Also find GDP at current prices. Using these figures, update the four indicators in Table 9.1 of this chapter and adapt them to the new SNA 2008.

Exercise 2. MCQ: Are the following propositions true or false?

a) The "deficit" is the same as "net lending".

b) All output of general government is non-market.

c) Social benefits are financed out of social contributions.

d) The convention in the national accounts is that general government consumes its non-market output.

e) B9A is the official code of the net lending/net borrowing item.

f) The sum of the B9A items of the institutional units making up general government is less than the B9A of general government.

g) In France, the state monopoly generating electricity (EDF) is an institutional unit forming part of general government.

h) Non-market output is sold at economically significant prices.

i) The gross operating surplus of general government is zero.

Exercise 3. Identifying general government expenditure in the general government account (a tricky exercise)

The following table shows INSEE's calculation of total French general government expenditure in 2011. On the basis of this model, find the principal elements of this calculation (those in bold type), using the full set of general government accounts included in the text and other information. Explain why total final consumption expenditure of general government is not included in the expenditure figure, despite being the largest "use" item of general government. Explain why the consumption of fixed capital is not included.

Table of government expenditure
2011

Intermediate consumption (P2)	**109.6**
Compensation of employees (D1)	**262.7**
of which: Employers' imputed social contributions (D122)	39.1
Other taxes on production (D29)	9.5
Property income excluding interest (D4 except D41)	0.1
Current taxes on income, wealth, etc. (D5)	0.1
Interest (D41)	52.6
Social benefits other than social transfers in kind (D62)	**388.7**
Social transfers benefits in kind of market goods and services (D63 – part)	**122.0**
Subsidies (D3)	29.5
Other current transfers (D7)	64.9
Capital transfers (D9 except D995)	14.5
Gross fixed capital formation (P51)	**62.7**
Other net acquisitions of non-financial assets (P52, P53, K2)	**1.6**
Total expenditures	1 118.5

Source: Insee Databases (2013): Statistical indices and series: Macroeconomic Database: National Accounts *www.bdm.insee.fr/bdm2/index?request_locale=en.*

Exercise 4. Moving from expenditure to revenue

Total expenditure was shown in the previous exercise (EUR 1 118.5 billion). How can the figure for revenue be very easily obtained from the general government account?

Exercise 5. Moving from revenue to compulsory levies (a tricky exercise)

Compulsory levies are the sums raised by government from households and firms in the form of taxes and compulsory social contributions. They therefore correspond to government revenue. This exercise consists of attempting to move from the general government revenue (shown below) to total compulsory levies in the case of France, using subsidiary information. Use two principles: (1) do not include imputed social contributions; (2) include taxes paid to the European institutions. The result you are looking for is EUR 875.4 billion.

Revenue of general government

2011

Market output and residual sales (P11)	58.0
Output for own final use (P12)	1.4
Partial payments of households (P13 – partly)	8.9
Other subsidies on production (D39)	3.1
Interest (D41)	3.6
Property income excluding interest (D4 except D41)	12.6
Taxes on production and imports (D2)	305.2
Current taxes on income, wealth, etc. (D5)	224.6
Capital taxes (D91)	10.3
Social contributions (D61)*	375.6
Taxes and social contributions assessed but unlikely to be collected (D995)	-6.2
Other current transfers (D7 except D73)	14.3
Capital transfers (D9 except D91, D995)	1.2
Total receipts	1 012.7
For information:	
* *of which:* Imputed social contributions (D612)	39.1
Actual compulsory levies received by institutions of the European Union	5.0

Source: Source Insee Databases (2013): Statistical indices and series: Macroeconomic Database: National Accounts *www.bdm.insee.fr/bdm2/index?request_locale=en.*

Exercise 6. Deficit and debt as recorded in the T-shaped accounts

The object of this exercise is to illustrate the difference between "above the line" and "below the line" transactions. This exercise is training in the use of T-shaped accounts, which are an excellent instrument that any national accountant should use before replying to what is a difficult question.

Let us first suppose that the State sells shares worth EUR 10 billion in order to pay off part of its debt. Show that this has no impact on the deficit, by completing the non-financial and financial T-shaped accounts below.

Non-financial account of general government

Uses	Resources
	B9A Net lending/net borrowing

Financial account of general government

Changes in assets	Changes in liabilities
Currency and deposits	Currency and deposits
Securities other than shares	Securities other than shares
Shares and other equity	
	B9B Balance on the financial account

Show, using the same accounts, that the sale of property for EUR 10 billion, again for the purpose of reducing the debt, has an impact on B9A. Draw conclusions.

Exercise 7. (A follow-up to 6, but slightly more complicated)

The object of this exercise is to complete the T-shaped tables below with the following information. The government sells property for EUR 5 billion and equities for EUR 3 billion, issues long-term Treasury notes for EUR 30 billion and buys in short-term Treasury notes for EUR 10 billion. By how much will its deficit be reduced? How will its debt change? Recapitulate the variation in general government net worth.

Non-financial account of general government

Uses	Resources
GFCF	
	B9A Net lending/net borrowing

Financial account of general government

Changes in assets	Changes in liabilities
Currency and deposits	Currency and deposits
Short-term securities	Short-term securities
Long-term securities	Long-term securities
Shares and other equity	
	B9B Balance of the financial account

Exercise 8. Calculation of tax revenue on an accrual basis

The following table shows a quarterly series for the receipts of VAT (Value-Added Tax) by the Treasury. Calculate the amount of VAT as recorded in the national accounts for the year, remembering that it is assumed that there is a lag of six weeks between the generation of the VAT (the purchases by households) and receipt by the Treasury. Suppose that the government raises the VAT rate by 2 percentage points at the beginning of November. Show why the series on an accrual basis is more useful in macroeconomic terms than the series on a cash basis.

Q1	Q2	Q3	Q4	Q1	Q2
15 420	16 658	14 548	16 510	18 540	19 870

The solutions to these exercises are available at:
http://dx.doi.org/10.1787/9789264214637-27-en

Chapter 10

The input-output table and integrated economic accounts

National accounts constitute one of the rare cases in which statisticians provide tables that are (almost) completely consistent, and it is this that gives national accounts their potency. This chapter explores how these consistent tables come to be, focusing on supply-and-use tables, aggregate supply and final uses tables, the intermediate use table, and the input-output table. It concludes by considering calculations of GDP and also examines integrated economic accounts.

According to Edmond Malinvaud, one of the most distinguished contemporary French economists, the national accounts are "the presentation, in a rigorous accounting framework, of all the quantitative information relating to the nation's economic activity" (Malinvaud, 1973). Here, the importance of the words "rigorous accounting framework" must be stressed. In fact, any macroeconomist carries in his head a simplified model of the economy in which everything made by someone is used by someone else, anything exported by someone is imported by someone else, anything saved by someone is invested by someone else, and so on.

However, basic statistics are not presented in a "rigorous accounting framework". They never precisely tie in together. For example, for a given product, the figures for total output are not going to correspond to the figures for total use. The reason for this is simply that output statistics are compiled differently from those of use: the statistical questionnaires are not addressed to the same people; the classifications are different; statisticians apply different methods; and so on. Some people have even ironically formulated a "theorem" that states if two statisticians are given the same set of data, the aggregate results they provide will necessarily be different!

For these reasons, macroeconomists appreciate that national accounts constitute one of the rare cases in which statisticians provide tables that are (almost) completely consistent.

"Almost" because there nevertheless remain certain inconsistencies known as "statistical discrepancies" that will be discussed later in this chapter. Some of these we already saw in Chapter 8 as the difference between the "B9s" in the non-financial accounts and the "B9s" in the financial accounts.

The totals are equal to the sum of the parts, the resources are equal to the uses, and so on. The simple model carried by macroeconomists in their heads is therefore given concrete shape, and it is this that gives national accounts their potency.

Even so, it has to be remembered that there are no miracles in statistics. To obtain consistent tables, national accountants have been obliged to cut here, to re-evaluate there – often arbitrarily – even though they use the best possible methods. The high level of consistency among tables in the national accounts (to within a few million of the national currency) should not be allowed to mask what is still only limited accuracy (see Chapter 11). Some statisticians take the view, however, that it is the attempt to achieve consistency in the statistics that is one of the driving-forces for better quality. This consistency is obtained by using several global tables that we consider in this chapter.

1. The supply-and-use tables (SUTs)

In the national accounts, the first set of global tables is known as the "supply-and-use tables" (SUTs). A table of this kind applies to each product of the classification, for instance software. The equilibrium for this product can be stated as follows:

Equation 1:

Output + Imports = Supply = Uses = Intermediate consumption + Final consumption + GFCF + Changes in inventories + Exports.

First, let us interpret this equation in terms of *numbers*. The equation then signifies that the *number* of software programmes produced plus the *number* of software programmes imported is *necessarily* equal to the sum of the *numbers* of software programmes purchased by the user firms. The software is either for: (1) intermediate consumption (the small "disposable" programmes); (2) investment (the large professional programmes); (3) consumption by households (games software, in particular); (4) stocked as inventories by the software-producing firms in the form of work in progress; or (5) it is exported.

This is an absolute equality: the resources (another name for "supply") are *necessarily* equal to the uses, by definition. This explains why national accountants also refer to this equation as an **accounting identity**. They make constant use of it, mainly to derive one item based on results for the others. For example, suppose there were no statistics concerning changes in inventories of software programmes. No matter: if statistics are available for the other items, the "change in inventories" item can be obtained by making intelligent use of the accounting identity and deriving it as the balance of the other items:

Change in inventories = Supply − Intermediate consumption − Final consumption − GFCF − Exports

In this way, we kill two birds with one stone: we obtain an estimate of the changes in inventories, and at the same time we verify the accounting identity. This example was not chosen at random because in certain countries, like France, this is the way changes in inventories are obtained. Incidentally, this illustrates a paradox of the national accounts, namely that those compiling them are not necessarily anxious to have statistics on every single item in the supply-and-use tables. For one thing, it is certain that in this case the statistics will not spontaneously "tie up". It will be necessary to choose which of the figures to trim, and this is no easy exercise.

Therefore, it should not be thought that the accounting identity method is perfect. If changes in inventories are calculated as the balance between resources and other uses, all the errors of evaluation in any of these items will find their way into the change in inventories, with possibly pernicious results. It is therefore better in this case to have direct statistics in order to make corrections "by hand" of the supply-use balance. As can be seen, while in theory the equilibrium between resources and uses is indisputable, its verification in practice forms part of the "art" of the national accountant. The following box explains the statistical sources of the SUTs.

Box 10.1. **Sources for the supply-and-use tables**

Chapters 1, 3 and 4 have already described the sources for each of the items in the supply and use tables in the case of France. We shall therefore give here only a brief reminder of what these are, still in the case of France. Market output is derived principally from sales statistics. Figures for merchandise imports and exports are taken from customs figures. Imports and exports of services mainly come from the Balance of Payments statistics of the Banque de France. Non-market output and consumption by general government come from the public accounts.

The allocation of uses on the "domestic market" (defined as output + imports – exports) depends on the nature of the product. When the product is an investment, the use will be GFCF. When it is not an investment good, it is either household consumption or intermediate consumption. The nature of the product generally makes it possible to decide whether the sales constitute solely or mainly household consumption, or, by contrast, intermediate consumption. However, in cases where the nature of the product is not a sufficient criterion, bold assumptions have to be made to allocate the sales between final consumption and intermediate consumption. It is the intermediate consumption that is the most difficult to identify. This is because systematic surveys of firms – making it possible to know the nature of their purchases – are no longer done in France. Many of the cells in the intermediate consumption matrix are therefore estimated on the basis of information regarding the past. This is why INSEE, the French statistical office, is reluctant to publish intermediate use tables at detailed level. The changes in inventories are sometimes calculated as the difference between other items.

> Box 10.1. **Sources for the supply-and-use tables** (*cont.*)
>
> The estimates are compiled, product by product, at the 332 level of the product classification, meaning that there are 332 SUTs. These are then aggregated and compared with the global estimates derived from statistical processing of the company accounts transmitted by firms to the tax authorities. The art of the national accountant then lies in matching the global estimates and the detailed estimates to obtain the high degree of consistency shown by tables in the national accounts. This operation is known as "arbitration" (see Chapter 11).

Interpreting the accounting identity in terms of the *number* of software programmes was clearly simplistic. In practice, SUTs are drawn up in monetary terms, i.e. the amount of software programmes bought or sold *in millions of national currency* – in other words, the quantities multiplied by the prices. When these prices are those of the current period, one speaks of a supply-and-use table at current prices; when they are valued at the prices of a different period (often the previous year), one speaks of a supply-and-use table at constant prices. We saw in Chapter 2 the importance of constant-price data in the national accounts, since they are fundamental to the calculation of GDP growth in volume.

In both cases, whether at current prices or constant prices, the accounting identity still holds.

The accounting identity holds only in volume based on constant prices.
It does not hold using chain-linked volumes, which lead to
non-additivity (see Chapter 2).

However, the introduction of prices complicates the equilibrium somewhat, because the different transactions are not carried out at the same prices. The following is a more complete version of the full supply-use equilibrium, this time expressed in monetary aggregates:

Equation 2:

Output + Imports + non-deductible VAT + Other taxes on products – Subsidies on products + Trade margins + Transport margins = Supply = Uses = Intermediate consumption + Final consumption + GFCF + Changes in inventories + Exports.

Analysis of the complete equation

Compare this second equation with the first. It is in the resources that the differences are to be found. The additions include non-deductible VAT (see the section "Going further: the treatment of VAT in the national accounts"), other taxes (minus subsidies) on products, trade and transport margins. Why these additions? The answer is because of the conventions used to evaluate the price of each transaction. The most important of these conventions are as follows:

- On the resources side: a unit of output is evaluated at the **"basic price"**, defined as the amount the producer can obtain from the production of this unit. This definition therefore excludes taxes on products invoiced by the producers but then passed on to the government. Imports are valued "cif", in other words, at the price paid for them at the frontier, including cost, insurance and freight (i.e. transport) from the country of origin to the importing country's frontier.

- On the uses side: all domestic uses are valued at their **market price**, also known as the **purchase price**, including non-deductible Value-Added Tax (VAT) and other taxes as well as transport and trade margins. Exports are valued "fob" (free on board), meaning the price paid by the customer to have the merchandise loaded on a ship (or a plane or a truck) at the frontier of the exporting country.

It can therefore be seen that the difference between prices applied to resources and prices applied to uses includes the taxes payable on the products. VAT is one of the most important taxes, but there are also certain country specific taxes on petroleum products, alcohol or cigarettes. In addition to taxes, prices on the resources side include the corresponding subsidies (treated as negative taxes) and the trade and transport margins. For a better understanding, here are some examples:

- *Taxes on products.* An oil company produces motor fuel. Its basic price per litre is the proceeds received as refiner, say 20 cents. The purchase price to the consumer will be its market price, which is the refiner's receipts, *plus* VAT and the specific petroleum-products tax payable to the government on this litre. These taxes amount to 80 cents, meaning that the pump price is 100 cents. The supply-use equilibrium is therefore (per litre): 20(*basic price*) + 80(*taxes on products*) = 100(*price to the consumer*). The taxes are not counted in the basic price, since the producer merely collects them for passing on to government.

- *Trade margins.* First, note that by convention national accounts do not consider retail and wholesale services to be consumed directly. Instead, the national accounts register the consumption of retail and wholesale services as the trade margins included in the cost of the products bought.

Take the example of computers. Producers are unlikely to sell these directly to households (with some exceptions related to Internet sales). Instead, they sell through a supermarket or another type of retailer. Suppose that the producer sells a computer to the supermarket for 1 000 euros. The supermarket will add its mark-up, say 500 (to cover inventory charges, publicity, etc. and its profit margin). It also has to add VAT of 225 (assuming a VAT rate of 15%). The supply-use equilibrium of the "computer" product will therefore be: 1 000(*basic price of the producer*) + 500(*trade margin*) + 225(*VAT*) = 1 725(*price to the consumer*).

● An alternative presentation would have been to establish the equilibrium for computers excluding trade margins, as follows: 1 000(*basic price*) + 150(*VAT*) = 1 150(*price to the consumer excluding trade margins*), and *in parallel* an equilibrium for the "distribution" product: 500(*basic price for the commercial service*) + 75(*VAT*) = 575(*price to the consumer for the commercial service*). This presentation, which is highly artificial, has not been adopted by the national accountants, so that in the end the accounts show no specific consumption of commercial services. And yet there has indeed been output of retail and wholesale services, equal to the sum of the trade margins. To resolve this contradiction, national accountants add a negative column in the input-output table, which reflects a conventional cancelling out of the output of distribution. We shall come back to this point later in this chapter.

The complete equation in constant prices

The above examples are at current prices. However, Equation 2 can be applied in exactly the same way using prices from a different period, for example the previous year. It can then be used to calculate changes in volume.

The following is a (simplified) balance for year A, at current prices, for a given product, in quantities, prices and monetary aggregates. It can be verified that the monetary aggregates are equal to the unit prices multiplied by the quantities.

	Output	Imports	Trade margins	VAT	Total Resources	Final consumption	GFCF	Exports	Total Uses
Quantity	35 900	18 800			48 700	42 150	854	5 696	48 700
Unit price	15 000	15 000				18 940	16 000	16 000	
Value in millions	538.5	192.0	48.7	123.9	903.1	798.3	13.7	91.1	903.1

The following is the balance, also at current prices, for the following year, A + 1.

	Output	Imports	Trade margins	VAT	Total Resources	Final consumption	GFCF	Exports	Total Uses
Quantity	42 000	14 100			56 100	43 580	950	11 570	56 100
Unit price	15 500	15 500				19 538	16 500	16 500	
Value in millions	651.0	218.6	56.1	132.4	1058.1	851.5	15.7	190.9	1 058.1

The following is the resource-use balance for year A + 1, at year A's prices (in constant prices), obtained by replacing the prices of year A + 1 by the prices of year A.

	Output	Imports	Trade margins	VAT	Total Resources	Final consumption	GFCF	Exports	Total Uses
Quantity	42 000	14 100			56 100	43 580	950	11 570	56 100
Unit price	15 000	15 000				18 940	16 000	16 000	
Value in millions	630.0	211.5	56.1	128.1	1 025.7	825.4	15.2	185.1	1 025.7

The last row of this table therefore shows the "volumes", at the previous year's prices. All that is then needed to obtain the growth in volume is to divide these volumes for year A + 1 by the corresponding values at current prices for year A. For example, the growth in household consumption *in volume* between year A and year A + 1 is 825.4/798.3 = 1.0344, i.e an increase of 3.4%.

Special mention should be made of the significance of in-volume figures for VAT and trade margins. These two items (VAT and trade margins) are elements of prices, so how is it possible to speak of volume in their case? This is another example of a national accounting convention one simply has to get used to. The volume of VAT is defined as the monetary amount obtained by applying the growth rate in volume of the use item on which VAT is received to the VAT at current prices of the previous year. In our example, therefore, the VAT in volume for year A + 1, i.e. 128.1, is obtained by applying the growth rate of 3.4% to 123.9, which is the value of VAT in year A. Why 3.4%? Because this is the increase in volume of household consumption, the item on which the VAT is paid. Similarly, the trade margins in volume for year A + 1 are obtained by multiplying the growth rate in volume of each of the items of demand concerned by the trade margin to the corresponding value of the trade margin in year A.

Although already quite complicated, the above example has deliberately been kept simple in comparison with actual practice. Our main purpose is to illustrate the supply-use balance as an essential building block in national accounts calculations, at both current and constant prices.

2. The aggregate supply and final uses tables

There are as many supply and use tables as there are product categories in the national accounts. In the case of France, for example, 332 detailed SUTs are calculated each year at both current prices and previous year's prices. These detailed tables are then summed up to obtain more aggregated tables.

At aggregate level, the supply-and-use tables are broken down into three parts: the resources table; the intermediate uses table; and the final uses table (final uses being all uses other than intermediate). It has to be recognised, however, that not all countries use this presentation in their national accounts. The following elements are therefore not strictly capable of being generalised to all the OECD countries. They nevertheless make it possible to highlight certain practical presentation problems.

The resources table constitutes the left-hand part of the supply and use table.

In the US, the resource table is called the "make" table.

Below is a version for France based on the highly aggregated so-called E level classification, consisting of 17 product groups. Tables at less aggregated levels would be too large for a single page. This Table 10.1 is to be read as if each SUT had been placed one above the other. For example, the first row shows resources for agricultural products (item AZ in the classification), the third shows food products (item C1, Food products, beverages and tobacco). For each item, one finds the resource headings set out in Equation 2 of the current chapter: output, imports, margins, taxes, subsidies.

The section "Going further" explains the rows for the cif-fob adjustment (PCAFAB) and the territorial adjustment (PCHTR).

Table 10.2 below shows final uses and is the counterpart of the previous table (Table 10.1). For each product category, it shows each type of final use.

Table 10.1. **France: Supply table**

Billion euros, 2011[a]

		Output of products	Imports	Cif-fob Adjustment	Trade margins	Transport margins	Total taxes on products	Of which, VAT	Subsidies on products	Total resources
AZ	Agriculture, forestry, and fisheries	76	12	0	23	2	2	2	-1	113
DE	Mining and quarrying; energy; water supply; waste management and remediation activities	159	61	0	1	3	14	7	-4	236
C1	Manufacture of food, beverages and tobacco	165	35	0	74	7	29	13	0	310
C2	Manufacture of coke and refined petroleum products	51	28	0	10	2	35	10	0	126
C3	Manufacture of electrical, electronic and computer equipment - Manufacture of machinery	91	105	0	45	4	7	7	0	252
C4	Manufacture of transport equipment	126	70	0	26	1	13	13	0	236
C5	Total institutional sectors - Manufacture of other industrial products	364	199	0	140	16	28	26	0	746
FZ	Construction	271	0	0	0	0	23	21	0	293
GZ	Trade, Repair of motor vehicles and motorcycles	369	3	0	-325	0	2	2	0	50
HZ	Transportation and storage	181	27	-16	0	-36	4	3	-9	151
IZ	Accommodation and food service activities	89	0	0	0	0	4	4	0	93
JZ	Information and communication	184	9	0	5	1	12	10	0	209
KZ	Financial and insurance activities	190	6	0	0	0	14	3	0	209
LZ	Real estate	293	0	0	0	0	3	3	0	296
MN	Scientific and technical activities; administrative and support service activities	446	26	0	0	0	25	13	0	496
OQ	Public administration, education, health and social work	508	0	0	0	0	1	1	0	509
RU	Other service activities	94	2	0	0	0	7	3	0	103
PCHTR	Products consumed outside national territory	0	32	0	0	0	0	0	0	32
PCAFAB	CIF/FOB adjustment	0	-16	16	0	0	0	0	0	0
	Total	3 656	598	0	0	0	223	141	-15	4 461

a) The sums of the columns and the rows may not correspond to the totals shown because of rounding.

Source: Insee (2014), Comptes de la nation, TES et TEE, www.insee.fr/fr/themes/theme.asp?theme=16&sous_theme=5.5

StatLink 🔗 http://dx.doi.org/10.1787/888933144159

Table 10.2. **France, Final uses table**

Billion euros, 2011[a]

		Final consumption expenditure Households	Final consumption expenditure general government	Final consumption expenditure NPISH	Total final consumption expenditure	Total GFCF	Valuables	Changes in inventories	Total GCF	Exportations	Total final uses
AZ	Agriculture, forestry, and fisheries	32	0	0	32	1	0	2	3	16	51
DE	Mining and quarrying; energy; water supply; waste management and remediation activities	46	0	0	46	0	0	1	1	12	59
C1	Manufacture of food, beverages and tobacco	167	0	0	168	0	0	1	1	41	210
C2	Manufacture of coke and refined petroleum products	51	0	0	51	0	0	0	0	15	67
C3	Manufacture of electrical, electronic and computer equipment – Manufacture of machinery	34	0	0	35	35	0	1	36	82	153
C4	Manufacture of transport equipment	67	0	0	67	31	0	4	35	83	185
C5	Total institutional sectors – Manufacture of other industrial products	147	30	0	177	34	1	5	39	172	388
FZ	Construction	13	0	0	13	210	0	0	210	0	224
GZ	Trade, Repair of motor vehicles and motorcycles	15	0	0	15	0	0	0	0	12	27
HZ	Transportation and storage	35	3	0	38	0	0	0	0	20	58
IZ	Accommodation and food service activities	79	1	0	79	0	0	0	0	0	79
JZ	Information and communication	50	1	0	50	39	0	0	39	7	96
KZ	Financial and insurance activities	56	0	0	56	0	0	0	0	10	66
LZ	Real estate	206	15	0	221	7	0	0	7	0	228
MN	Scientific and technical activities; administrative and support service activities	24	11	0	35	40	0	0	40	25	100
OQ	Public administration, education, health and social work	57	409	24	490	0	0	0	0	1	490
RU	Other service activities	43	20	18	80	3	0	0	3	2	85
PCHTR	Products consumed outside national territory	-7	0	0	-7	0	0	0	0	39	32
PCAFAB	CIF/FOB adjustment	0	0	0	0	0	0	0	0	0	0
TOTAL	Total	1 114	490	41	1 645	400	1	15	415	538	2 599

a) The sums of the columns and the rows may not correspond to the totals shown because of rounding.

Source: Insee (2014), Comptes de la nation, TES et TEE, www.insee.fr/fr/themes/theme.asp?theme=16&sous_theme=5.5

StatLink ᵐᵖᵈ http://dx.doi.org/10.1787/888933144165

3. Intermediate use table (IUT)

In addition to these two tables – the product supply table and the product final uses table – national accounts break out "intermediate consumption" for a given product into a variable number of intermediate consumption figures by **industry**. An industry is defined as the aggregation of firms, or parts of firms, making a given product.

For a better understanding, let us take a fictitious and simplified supply-use balance for the electricity category. In this case, we have *Output* (250)+ Imports (15) = Intermediate consumption (142) + Final consumption (97) + Exports (26). National accountants distribute the amount of 142 for intermediate consumption among detailed industries, recording, for example, 12 for the consumption of electricity by the automobile industry, 9 for the textile industry, 26 for the aluminium industry, and so on.

In this way, a matrix known as the intermediate use table (IUT) is compiled, showing consumption *by products* in the rows, and intermediate consumption *by industry* in the columns. Table 10.3 below is an illustration in the case of France using the E-level classification (17 products/17 industries) for 2011.

Table 10.3 is to be read as follows: First, along the rows, we find intermediate consumption of a given product by different industries. For example, the row C2 Coke and refined petroleum products shows that the French AZ industry (Agriculture, forestry and fisheries), shown in the first column, had intermediate consumption of coke and refined petroleum products amounting to 4 billion euros; the C1 industry (Manufacture of food, beverages and tobacco products) consumed 1 billion euros (the third column); and the HZ industry (Transportation and storage) consumed 15 billion, and so on. Total intermediate consumption of coke and refined petroleum products amounted to 60 billion euros, the total of all the figures in this row.

Looking at the columns on Table 10.3, one can see the intermediate consumption of all product types for any given industry. In the case of "C2 Manufacture of coke and refined petroleum", it can be seen that in 2011 its intermediate consumption of Mining and quarrying; energy, water supply, waste management and remediation products amounted to 37 billion, its consumption of transportation and storage services to 1 billion, its consumption of Other industrial products to 2 billion, etc. Its total intermediate consumption amounted to 49 billion euros.

Be sure to note the difference between reading the rows, which show figures for a single product category, and the columns, which show a single industry. It is essential not to confuse the two, even if the items in the classification have the same name. In our example, the Agriculture product category and the Agriculture industry are both labelled AZ, and yet one

316

Table 10.3. **France: Intermediate uses table**
Billion euros, 2011[a]

Industries		AZ	DE	C1	C2	C3	C4	C5	FZ	GZ	HZ	IZ	JZ	KZ	LZ	MN	OQ	RU	TOTAL
AZ	Agriculture, forestry, and fisheries	17	0	40	0	0	0	3	0	0	0	1	0	0	0	0	0	0	**62**
DE	Mining and quarrying; energy; water supply; waste management and remediation activities	2	66	5	37	1	1	26	4	5	2	2	4	1	2	4	11	2	**176**
C1	Manufacture of food, beverages and tobacco	9	0	39	0	0	0	5	1	3	1	26	1	0	0	4	8	2	**99**
C2	Manufacture of coke and refined petroleum products	4	1	1	4	0	0	8	4	11	15	1	2	0	0	4	2	1	**60**
C3	Manufacture of electrical, electronic and computer equipment – Manufacture of machinery	2	3	1	1	20	19	14	14	5	2	0	6	0	0	7	3	2	**99**
C4	Manufacture of transport equipment	0	0	0	0	1	35	1	0	4	2	0	0	0	0	2	5	0	**51**
C5	Manufacture of other industrial products	13	13	11	2	25	31	135	56	12	4	1	12	2	1	13	21	5	**358**
FZ	Construction	0	4	0	1	1	1	2	39	1	1	0	2	1	4	4	7	1	**70**
GZ	Distributive trades – Repair of motor vehicles and motorcycles	0	0	1	0	1	1	2	1	11	2	0	1	0	0	1	1	0	**23**
HZ	Transportation and storage	0	1	2	1	1	1	5	2	22	35	1	4	2	1	8	8	2	**92**
IZ	Accommodation and food service activities	0	0	0	0	0	0	1	0	3	1	1	1	1	0	2	3	1	**14**
JZ	Information and communication	0	2	2	0	2	1	5	3	14	3	1	32	13	2	22	8	3	**113**
KZ	Financial and insurance activities	2	2	3	0	1	1	5	5	14	7	2	5	53	18	15	6	2	**143**
LZ	Real estate	0	0	1	0	1	1	3	1	16	3	2	4	8	10	14	4	1	**68**
MN	Scientific and technical activities; administrative and support service activities	3	11	15	2	12	15	38	28	44	17	5	20	21	11	111	35	8	**396**
OQ	Public administration, education, health and social work	0	0	0	0	0	1	1	1	1	2	0	1	1	0	2	7	0	**19**
RU	Other service activities	0	0	1	0	0	1	1	1	2	1	0	1	1	1	3	1	4	**17**
PCHTR	Products consumed outside national territory	0	0	0	0	0	0	0	0	0	0	0	0	0	0	0	0	0	**0**
PCAFAB	CIF/FOB adjustment	0	0	0	0	0	0	0	0	0	0	0	0	0	0	0	0	0	**0**
TOTAL	**Total**	**52**	**105**	**122**	**49**	**67**	**109**	**254**	**159**	**169**	**96**	**44**	**97**	**104**	**52**	**216**	**131**	**36**	**1 862**

a) The sums of the columns and the rows may not correspond to the totals shown because of rounding.

Source: Insee (2014), Comptes de la nation, TES et TEE, *www.insee.fr/fr/themes/theme.asp?theme=16&sous_theme=5.5.*

StatLink ᴍᴙᴘ *http://dx.doi.org/10.1787/888933144173*

consists of agriculture products and the other of the firms producing these agriculture products. The similarities and differences between product and industry classifications are explained in the appendix "Going further".

4. The input-output table

We can now synthesize the three tables we have just looked at, plus two more. The resulting vast **input-output (IO) table** encompasses what might be called **goods and services accounts**. (This is in contrast to the "institutional sector accounts" that are part of the "integrated economic accounts" presented in Section 7 of this chapter). The organisation of the IO table is shown below. In the middle, we have the intermediate use table; on the left is the product supply table, and on the right is the product final uses table.

Table 10.4. **Input output table**

Product supply table	Intermediate use table	Final uses table
	Production account by industry	
	Generation of income account by industry	

Underneath the intermediate use table there are two accounts that we have not yet looked at in this chapter: the production account by industry; and the allocation of income account by industry (see Table 10.5). These two accounts give for each industry its output, its intermediate consumption and, finally, its value-added, as well as the breakdown of the value-added between compensation of employees and gross operating surplus (or mixed income). All these concepts were examined in Chapters 6, 7 and 9, which focused on the accounts of households, firms and general government. In fact, these tables constitute a breakdown by industry of these accounts.

The input-output (IO) presentation, made up of these five tables, gives both a global and a detailed view of all the economic relationships involving products and industries. To get an idea of the wealth of data in the national accounts, note that the IO table of France is calculated at 139 products and 139 industries. On its own, the French input-output table therefore contains 19 321 cells (139 x 139) for each of 20 years.

However, INSEE does not publish all the detailed tables. Resources and final uses are available at the G level (88 products), but the input-output table is available only at the F level (38 products). Unfortunately, even at the most aggregated level, IO would not fit in a page of this book, so we cannot illustrate it here. However, Exercise 1 at the end of this chapter proposes the compilation of an IO table using copy-and-paste. The reader is advised to re-read the preceding paragraphs with a complete IO table of this kind in front of him or her. This will show the high internal consistency of the goods and services accounts much more clearly than any verbal description.

Table 10.5. **France: Production and generation of income account by industry**

		AZ	DE	C1	C2	C3	C4	C5	FZ	GZ	HZ	IZ	JZ	KZ	LZ	MN	OQ	RU	TOTAL
	Production account by industry																		
P2	Intermediate consumption	52	105	122	49	67	109	254	159	169	96	44	97	104	52	216	131	36	**1 862**
B1	Value added	34	44	32	2	23	17	109	111	200	85	44	85	86	237	221	403	61	**1 794**
P1	Output by industry	86	149	154	51	91	126	364	270	369	180	88	182	190	289	437	534	96	**3 656**
	Generation of income account by industry																		
		AZ	DE	C1	C2	C3	C4	C5	FZ	GZ	HZ	IZ	JZ	KZ	LZ	MN	OQ	RU	**TOTAL**
B1	Value added	34	44	32	2	23	17	109	111	200	85	44	85	86	237	221	403	61	**1 794**
D1	Compensation of employees	8	20	21	1	19	15	77	68	126	58	30	54	51	14	154	307	44	**1 064**
B2 or B3	Gross operating surplus or mixed income	34	23	9	1	3	1	27	40	68	22	13	29	29	201	61	90	17	**666**
D29	Other taxes on production	1	3	2	0	1	1	6	4	8	5	2	3	6	23	8	11	2	**87**
D39	Operating subsidies	-9	-1	0	0	0	0	0	0	-1	-1	0	-1	0	0	-2	-4	-1	**-23**

a) The sums of the columns and the rows may not correspond to the totals shown because of rounding
Source: Insee (2014), Comptes de la nation, TES et TEE, *www.insee.fr/fr/themes/theme.asp?theme=16&sous_theme=5.5.*
StatLink ⧉ *http://dx.doi.org/10.1787/888933144184*

5. The use of the input-output table for economic analysis

What impact will the construction of a new high-speed rail link have on various branches of the national or regional economy? For the construction of the high-speed track, the civil engineering firm will need steel for the rails, electric pylons and also pre-stressed concrete for the bridges and other major construction works. The result will be to increase demand for the products of the steel and concrete industries. But this is not all. The firm will also need to buy new excavators and cranes and the production of these will in turn also require more steel. The steel industry will therefore see demand for its products rise substantially and, since it consumes coal and electricity, demand for the products of these other industries will also increase, and so on.

This is one type of question for which the input-output table can be useful, once one accepts the fairly bold assumptions of a linear production function and, in particular, the fundamental assumption that the "technical coefficients" remain fixed (Malinvaud, 1973). The "technical coefficients" for industry are the ratios obtained by dividing the value of each of the various products consumed by an industry by the output of that industry.

"Accounting coefficient" would be a better term than "technical coefficient", since what we have are monetary amounts and not quantities. However, the term "technical coefficient" is generally used.

These technical coefficients can be denoted by a_{ji}, where j is the intermediate-consumption product and i is the industry (a_{ji} is therefore "the technical coefficient" of industry i for product j).

It is assumed, in this simplified universe, that the classifications by product and by industry are identical, in other words that the i and the j belong to the same universe, with i and j running from 1 to n. The a_{ji} are equal to X_{ji}/x_i, where X_{ji} is the intermediate consumption of product j by industry I, and x_i is the output of industry i. They are called "technical coefficients" because they are meant to represent a given production technique: for example, making one tonne of steel requires 5 tonnes of coal, 3 tonnes of iron, 10 megawatts of electricity, etc. The ratio between the value of the five tonnes of coal and the value of the resulting tonne of steel constitutes a coefficient that is representative of this production technique and is assumed to be fixed in volume. For the limitations of these assumptions, see Going further: "Relationship with economic theory".

Using these notations, and adding a variable y_j to represent final (not intermediate) demand for product j, a simplified supply-use balance can be written as follows:

$$x_j = X_{j1} + X_{j2} + ... + X_{jn} + y_j \qquad (3)$$

The above indicates that the output of product j is equal to the sum of the intermediate consumption of product j by the various industries 1 to n, plus the final demand for this same product j.

As $a_{ji} = X_{ji} \div x_i$, equation 3 can be written:

$$x_j = a_{j1} x_1 + a_{j2} x_2 + ... + a_{jn} x_n + y_j \qquad (4)$$

Using a matrix notation, and denoting by [A] the square matrix of the coefficients $[a_{ji}]$, by [x] the output column vector $[x_j]$ and by [y] the final demand vector $[y_j]$, we have:

$$[x] = [A] \times [x] + [y] \qquad (5)$$

Reorganising and denoting the diagonal unit matrix by I, and expressing [x] as a function of the remainder, we find:

$$[x] = [I - A]^{-1} \times [y] \qquad (6)$$

In other words, output is equal to the inverse of matrix [I – A] multiplied by the final demand vector. If one makes the bold assumption that the technical coefficients are fixed, this equation also holds for a variation Δy in demand. We then have:

$$[\Delta x] = [I - A]^{-1} \times [\Delta y] \tag{7}$$

and Δx is therefore the value of change in output necessitated by the variation Δy in demand.

The answer to our initial question regarding the impact of a high-speed train link is therefore obtained by a calculation of this kind. One sets a value Δy_j on the variation in final demand necessitated by this project and applies equation 7. Exercise 4 at the end of this chapter is based on a similar simulation.

6. From the sum of the values added to GDP

Table 10.5, presented earlier, represents the production account by industry and gives the gross value added of each of these industries. We explained in Chapter 1 that GDP is the aggregate of output (free of double counting) obtained from the *sum of the gross values added*. We call this value *GDP output approach*. The total column in the "gross value added" row of the production account in Table 10.5 gives a value of 1794. Is this the value of GDP for France?

The answer is no, because the national accountants have chosen to arrange matters so that GDP corresponds *also* to the sum of final uses; in other words, the *GDP output approach* must equal the *GDP expenditure approach*. However, we have seen that both the value added and output approaches to calculating GDP use basic prices, while the final uses approach uses purchase prices, including taxes on products, net of subsidies on products.

This explains why the exact definition of GDP is not the sum of the values added, but the sum of the values added *plus* the taxes on products (D21), *minus* the subsidies on products (D31).

The US is an exception regarding this rule. Value added in the NIPA accounts (see Chapter 12) is valued at market price, not at basic price.

This price adjustment makes it possible to bring the GDP output approach and final uses approach into equality.

Table 10.6 below shows the reconciliation between the output approach for calculating GDP and the expenditure approach, in this case using the case of Korea for 2012. For information, the table shows both estimates under SNA 1993 and SNA 2008 (Korea has published its SNA 2008 estimates a few weeks before the publication of the present manual). Let's use the SNA 1993 column for further comments, but would we have used the SNA 2008 ones, the conclusions would not change, even if the data are different. The first part of the table clearly shows the addition to value added at basic prices of taxes on products minus subsidies on products (D21 – D31). It is this adjustment that makes it possible to obtain the value of GDP at market prices (as it is often called), and this also equals the figure obtained using the expenditure approach.

Table 10.6. **Korea: Gross Domestic Product: the three approaches**

2012, Billions of won, current prices, SNA 1993 and SNA 2008

		SNA 1993	SNA 2008
	Gross domestic product (output approach)	**1272459.5**	**1377456.6**
B1	Gross value added at basic prices, excluding FISIM	1145970.9	1251455.2
D21_D31	+ Taxes less subsidies on products	126488.6	126001.5
	Gross domestic product (expenditure approach)	**1272459.5**	**1377456.6**
P3	Final consumption expenditure	882232.5	911938.1
P5	+ Gross capital formation	350616.8	427028.6
P6	+ Exports of goods and services	718967.0	776062.5
P7	– Imports of goods and services	679786.1	737572.5
	+ Statistical discrepancy	429.3	-0.1
	Gross domestic product (income approach)	**1272459.5**	**1377456.6**
D1	Compensation of employees	583377.0	599308.5
B2_B3	+ Gross operating surplus and gross mixed income	548480.5	636915.0
D2_D3	+ Taxes less subsidies on production and imports	140602.0	141233.3
D29_D39	of which: Other taxes less subsidies on products	14113.4	15231.9
D21_D31	of which: Taxes less subsidies on products	126488.6	126001.4
	+ Statistical discrepancy	0	0

Source: OECD (2013), "Aggregate National Accounts: Gross domestic product", OECD National Accounts Statistics (database), http://dx.doi.org/10.1787/data-00001-en.and OECD calculations from Bank of Korea source.

StatLink 🖳 http://dx.doi.org/10.1787/888933144199

Table 10.6 also illustrates the equality of these two approaches with the "income approach", which is also based on the input-output table. The three GDPs are indeed equal, whether in SNA 1993 or SNA 2008. The generation of income account by industry shown earlier (Table 10.5) gives, for each industry, the breakdown of value added between the two factors of production – labour ("Compensation of employees", coded as D1) and capital ("Gross operating surplus and mixed income", coded as B2/B3) – plus D29_D39 "Other taxes on production" (D29) net of "Other subsidies on production" (D39).

This breakdown is also found in Table 10.6. Indeed, the gross value added at basic prices used to calculate the output-approach GDP (1 272 459.5) is equal to the sum of: "D1 Compensation of employees" or 583 377.0; plus "B2/B3 Gross operating surplus and mixed income", or 548 480.5; plus "D29-D39 Other taxes on production", net of subsidies, or 14 113.4. These "other" taxes and subsidies (D29 and D39) should not be confused with taxes and subsidies on products (D21 or D31). D29 and D39 are specific taxes and subsidies, generally for small amounts, not applied to products but to the production process. An example is taxes on the wage bill. The income-approach GDP can also be obtained as the sum of the compensation of factors of production plus all taxes on production, and it can be expressed using the codes as: D1 + B2/B3 + D2 – D3. We already saw this three-pronged approach to GDP in Chapter 1. Exercise 2 illustrates these calculations.

Table 10.6 also contains a typical "statistical discrepancy". Korea's GDP using the expenditure approach is equal to the GDPs obtained by the output and income approaches only if an additional 429.3 (in SNA 1993; in SNA 2008, it is, by chance, very small for 2012), called the "statistical discrepancy", is added to the various elements of demand. The reason is that Korea's national accounts are derived from two distinct statistical sources. The figures for both the output and income accounts come from the database consisting of the company accounts sent to the tax authorities, whereas the elements of demand (consumption, GFCF) come from surveys.

As a consequence, Korea's GDP obtained using the expenditure approach differs slightly from that obtained using the other approaches. Because the Korean national accountants found no satisfactory method of spreading this difference between the other items, they decided to show it separately in its own right. This practice of maintaining certain "statistical discrepancy" items between the different approaches to GDP has been adopted by several other OECD countries (the United States, in particular). Other countries, by contrast, eliminate these differences by various methods and do not show discrepancies that arise from the different ways of measuring GDP. This difference of methodology between countries does not imply that the statistical sources for the first group of countries are less reliable than for the second group. It is more a practical question and a presentational choice.

These statistical discrepancies are contrary to the "rigorous accounting framework" espoused by Edmond Malinvaud, but it is reasonable to leave a certain amount of latitude in the national accounts tables. As Alan Greenspan, former Chairman of the US Federal Reserve, used to say: showing statistical discrepancies has the advantage of reminding users that national accounts are far from being 100% reliable. Greenspan even added that the analysis of these discrepancies could itself be a source of information. In fact, some observers have shown a correlation between the value of the statistical discrepancies and the business cycle.

The three approaches to GDP reflect valuation of GDP at market prices as opposed to valuation "at factor cost". In the factor-cost approach, now abandoned, value added was calculated at the prices remunerating each of the factors of production, labour and capital. No taxes were taken into account. Some regret the abandonment of GDP at factor cost as an aggregate indicator of output. Indeed, from the point of view of the producer, taxes on products have no great influence on production decisions. But this has not prevented most economists and national accountant from using GDP at market prices as the main indicator of output, because it is highly practical to have GDP equal to the sum of final uses. However, some consider that this practice has led to some double counting in GDP (see in Going further: "Limitations of the national accounts").

If instead of using the sum of the *gross* values added, one had used the values added *net* of the consumption of fixed capital, one would then have had NDP, standing for Net Domestic Product. This aggregate is unfortunately little used despite being conceptually more correct than GDP, for both the production and income approaches. However, NDP is less robust statistically because of the difficulty of calculating the consumption of fixed capital.

7. The integrated economic account (IEA)

We have just looked at the input-output table, the internally consistent table for the presentation of the goods and services accounts. The second major internally consistent table is known as the integrated economic account (IEA). This provides a synthesis of the entire institutional sector accounts (see box "Institutional units and institutional sectors"). The IEA table is much too large to be shown on a page of this book. In fact, it spreads over two pages, with the uses on the left and resources on the right, columns for the institutional sectors and rows for the transactions. It can be summarised by saying that it constitutes the juxtaposition of the accounts of households, corporations and general government presented in Chapters 6, 7 and 9. In addition to these sectors, the IEA table shows the account of the whole national economy and the account of the rest of the world (we shall be returning later to these two accounts). The advantage of the IEA account is that it provides an immediate and consistent vision of all the transactions concerning a given operation. One of the important rules of national accounts as depicted in the IEA is **accrual accounting** (see appendix "Going further").

Let us take, among the 60 or so rows in the integrated economic account (IEA) for Denmark, the row for "interest" (D41). In the IEA, this is a single row, with the left side showing the amounts as uses, and the right side showing the amounts as resources. But for space reasons, in Table 10.7 we show the resources below the uses (even though in the actual table they are side by side).

Box 10.2. **Institutional units and institutional sectors**

The basic economic unit in the national accounts is known as the **institutional unit.** It is defined as "an elementary economic decision-making centre characterised by uniformity of behaviour and decision-making autonomy in the exercise of its principal function". A household is an institutional unit in the sense that it is within the household that decisions are made regarding the modalities of its principal function, i.e., consumption. For a "legal person" (i.e. a corporate body and not a "physical person") to be an institutional unit it must, among other things, have a complete set of accounts. If the unit in question does not have complete accounts, it is considered as forming part of the larger unit that contains it. For example, the French statistical office (INSEE) is not an institutional unit, because it is a directorate of the Finance Ministry, which is itself part of general government. General government has complete accounts but INSEE does not.

The **institutional sectors** are groupings of institutional units. They are six in number: households (S14); non-financial corporations (S11); financial corporations (S12); general government (S13); non-profit institutions serving households (S15); and the rest of the world (S2). The rest of the world is not really an institutional sector since it comprises only that part of the accounts of non-resident units that relates to transactions with resident units. The notion of residence was explained in Chapter 4. The definition of most of the institutional sectors was set out in Chapters 5, 6, 7 and 9, except for financial corporations.

The **financial corporations** are the institutional units specialising in financial intermediation (banks) and in insurance. The financial corporation sector (S12) comprises the central bank, the commercial banks, specialised financial corporations, mutual funds (also called UCITS in Europe – undertakings for collective investment in transferable securities), financial auxiliaries, which comprise certain portfolio management companies, insurance companies and pension funds.

Here is how to read the table: The first sub-table shows the "uses", i.e. the interest *paid* by the institutional sectors. The first group in the column is entitled "National economy" and labelled S1. This is the institutional sector, consisting of the sum of the four *resident* institutional sectors, as opposed to the "Rest of the world", consisting of *non-residents*. The four resident sectors are the non-financial corporations, the financial corporations, general government, households and non-profit institutions serving households. The figure of 305.5 billion DKK for interest is therefore the total amount of interest paid by each of the domestic sectors, i.e.: 47.1 + 141.1 + 37.5 + 79.8, these figures all appearing in the same row.

The equality between S1 and the sum of the resident sectors is
a consequence of the national accounts not being "consolidated"
(see appendix "Going further").

Following this, the next column indicates the interest paid to Denmark by the rest of the world, amounting to 62.1 billion DKK. In all, 367.6 billion of interest is paid by the various sectors.

Table 10.7. **Extract from the integrated economic account for Denmark, row "D41 interest"**

Billions of Danish kroner, 2011

		Uses					
		S1: National economy	S11: Non-financial corporations	S12: Financial corporations	S13: General government	S14_S15: Households and NPISH	S2: Rest of the world	Total
D. 41	Interest	305.5	47.1	141.1	37.5	79.8	62.1	367.6

	Resources						
Total	S2: Rest of the world	S14_S15: Households and NPISH	S13: General government	S12: Financial corporations	S11: Non-financial corporations	S1: National economy	
367.6	56.9	19.9	23.7	245.1	21.9	310.7	Interest

Source: OECD (2014), "Detailed National Accounts: Non-financial accounts by sectors, annual", OECD National Accounts Statistics (database), doi: *http://dx.doi.org/10.1787/data-00034-en.*

StatLink ᵃˢᵐ *http://dx.doi.org/10.1787/888933144200*

The second sub-table ("resources") shows the interest *received*, broken down by institutional sectors. Obviously the total interest received, 367.6 billion, is equal to the total interest paid, in conformity with the principle of consistency of the national accounts. Going along the row, one finds the sums received by each institutional sector.

This table is interesting because it makes it possible to visualise how the interest flows are broken down among agents. It nevertheless has two limitations. The first is that it is not consolidated (see appendix "Going further"), so it is important not to misinterpret the figures. The large sum of interest paid by the financial corporations does not signify that this interest is paid to other institutional sectors – far from it. Most of the interest paid by financial corporations is to other financial corporations, as a result of the complexity of modern financial systems.

The second limitation, linked to the first, is that these tables fail to show what national accountants call the "who-to-whom" element. For example, the table does not show "to whom" the financial corporations pay the 245.1 billion. Most probably, as has just been said, it is paid largely to other financial corporations, but also to households and non-financial corporations. However, these amounts are not known. Only a "who-to-whom" matrix could answer this question. The statistical offices have this type of information for certain transactions but do not generally publish them.

8. The transition from GDP to national income

It would be redundant to comment on all the rows in the integrated economic account (IEA) since the accounts for the main institutional sectors have already been described, one by one, in Chapters 6, 7 and 9. Here we shall only comment on the accounts of the S1 "National economy" sector, which is interesting in that it includes major aggregates such as Gross National Income, Gross Disposable Income, national saving and the nation's net lending/net borrowing.

Gross national income

Since GDP equals the sum of the values added plus taxes on products net of subsidies, it has an important place in the production account of sector S1, an extract of which is shown for Korea in Table 10.8 (in SNA 1993, but the conclusions would be the same in SNA 2008). The second important aggregate in this account is Gross National Income (GNI), or Net National Income (NNI), if the consumption of fixed capital is subtracted. This aggregate (GNI) used to be called Gross National Product, but too many people confused it with Gross Domestic Product, and it was therefore given a new – and more suitable – name.

Gross Domestic Product is the economic wealth produced during a certain period by economic agents within the economic territory. Gross National Income is the sum of the primary incomes of the economic agents resident in the territory during a certain period. In the case of Korea, the difference between the two appears clearly in the first part of Table 10.8 below. In order to derive GNI from GDP, the following steps are necessary:

1. start with GDP (1 272 459.5 in 2012);

2. add the primary incomes received from the rest of the world (+25 156.6). These primary incomes consist of wages and salaries, property income (interest, dividends) and taxes and subsidies;

3. deduct the primary incomes paid to the rest of the world (-18 069.7);

4. to finally obtain the GNI (1 279 546.4).

Table 10.8.   **Korea: The transition from GDP to GNI and other major aggregates**

Billions of won, current prices, 2012, SNA 1993

B1_G	Gross domestic product	1 272 459.5
D1_D4	+ Primary incomes receivable from the rest of the world	25 156.6
D1_D4	- Primary incomes payable to the rest of the world	18 069.7
B5_G	Gross national income at market prices	1 279 546.4
K1	- Consumption of fixed capital	164 262.5
B5_N	Net national income at market prices	1 115 283.9
D5_D7	+ Current transfers receivable from the rest of the world	17 891.8
D5_D7	- Current transfers payable to the rest of the world	21 009.1
B6_N	Net national disposable income	1 112 166.6
P3	- Final consumption expenditures	882 232.5
B8_N	Saving, net	229 934.2
D9	+ Net capital transfers from the rest of the world	802.5
P5	- Gross capital formation	350 616.8
K2	- Acquisitions less disposals of non-financial non-produced assets	122.9
K1	+ Consumption of fixed capital	164 262.5
B9	Net lending/net borrowing	44 259.6

Source: OECD (2013), "Aggregate National Accounts: Disposable income and net lending/borrowing", OECD National Accounts Statistics (database), *http://dx.doi.org/10.1787/data-00002-en*.

StatLink ᵃᵐᵉ⁵ᵃ *http://dx.doi.org/10.1787/888933144216*

The above makes it easier to interpret GNI. It is the totality of the primary incomes received by economic agents resident in the territory, regardless of whether these incomes are obtained in the territory or not. In addition to the income derived from production within the territory (already included in GDP), there are the incomes derived from production outside the territory (not included in GDP). This explains the addition of the compensation of employees received from the rest of the world, in all likelihood the wages and salaries of workers resident in Korea but working in neighbouring countries. Conversely, it is necessary to deduct the wages and salaries of workers who are non-resident in Korea but who have come to work there. The same operation is carried out for trans-border flows involving the two other forms of primary income, namely property income and taxes and subsidies on production. And the final result is GNI, which (unlike GDP) is an *income-based* concept and not a *production-based* concept, since it includes income derived from production abroad (and hence not recorded in its totality) and excludes the value of output repaid to foreign factors of production. Hence, the word "Income" instead of "Product" is used in its name. This being said, in the case of Korea the difference between the GDP and GNI is very small. We saw in Chapter 1 that it is greater for a country such as Luxembourg because of the importance of trans-border workers in relation to the country's economy.

GNI is an important aggregate for European Union (EU) countries because it is one of the main indicators used to allocate the budget and the operating costs of the EU institutions among member countries.

Given GNI, it is possible to calculate Net National Income (NNI) by subtracting the consumption of fixed capital.

The rest of Table 10.8 outlines the transition from NNI to **National saving**. Similar additions and deductions for transactions with the rest of the world are made in order to obtain Net Disposable National Income, from which is deducted total final consumption expenditure in order to obtain National saving, which itself equals the sum of the savings of the different institutional sectors. Finally, one arrives at the **Nation's net lending/net borrowing**, essentially by deducting capital formation. It can be seen from Table 10.8 that in 2012 Korea had net lending of 44 259.6 billion won. In other words, Korea had no need of foreign financing for its investment. On the contrary, Korea globally provided more financing to foreign countries than foreigners did to Korea.

References

Ahmad, N. and A. Wyckoff (2003), "Carbon Dioxide Emissions Embodied in International Trade of Goods", *OECD Science, Technology and Industry Working Papers*, No. 2003/15, OECD Publishing, doi: *http://dx.doi.org/10.1787/421482436815*.

Insee (2014), Comptes de la nation, TES et TEE, *www.insee.fr/fr/themes/theme.asp?theme=16&sous_theme=5.5*.

Malinvaud, E. (1973), " Initiation à la Comptabilité Nationale ", INSEE.

OECD (2013a), "Aggregate National Accounts: Gross domestic product", OECD National Accounts Statistics (database), *http://dx.doi.org/10.1787/data-00001-en*.

OECD (2013b), "Aggregate National Accounts: Disposable income and net lending/ borrowing", OECD National Accounts Statistics (database), *http://dx.doi.org/10.1787/data-00002-en*.

Key points

- The balances depicted in the supply-and-use tables (SUTs) for products constitute the basic accounting identity for the goods and services accounts. They compare resources (output, imports) with uses (intermediate consumption and final uses). They are calculated at current prices and in volume.

- Output is valued at basic prices. Uses are valued at market prices.

- Trade and transport margins as well as taxes (net of subsidies) are all included in the calculation of resources for products in the supply-and-use table.

- The input-output (IO) table consists of the juxtaposition of the supply-and-use balances (resources table and final uses table) and the matrix of intermediate consumption. This matrix shows in its columns the various intermediate consumptions for a given industry.

- The input-output table also includes the production accounts and the generation of income accounts for industries.

- The input-output table is available at current prices and in volume.

- When value added is calculated at basic prices (which is generally the case), the Gross Domestic Product is the sum of the values added of the industries plus taxes on products net of subsidies.

- Gross National Income (GNI) is the new name for Gross National Product, which must not be confused with Gross Domestic Product. GNI equals the sum of the primary incomes of economic agents resident in the territory, regardless of whether these incomes were obtained within the territory or not. GNI does not include the primary incomes generated in the territory by non-resident agents.

- The Integrated Economic Account is a reorganised grouping of the accounts of the institutional sectors. It shows the amounts of uses and resources of each institutional sector for all transactions. It is calculated only at current prices.

Going further

The treatment of VAT in the national accounts

In many countries, the VAT (Value-Added Tax) is one of the main taxes on products. It is collected in stages by firms for the benefit of government. The principle is as follows. All market producers (including distributors) are obligated to invoice a certain additional VAT percentage on the prices of the goods and services they sell. VAT is identified separately on the invoices of the seller firms so that the buyer firms know how much VAT they have paid. Firms pay to the government only the difference between the VAT they have collected on their sales and the VAT they have paid on their purchases. Hence the description "value-added": the tax relates to the difference between output (sales) and intermediate consumption and investment, a notion that therefore comes close to that of value added in the national accounts. VAT is not invoiced at all on exports. It is applied to imports, however.

Due to this construction, VAT is an economically more rational tax than the old taxes based on sales, which could show an increase, for example, simply if a new intermediary joined the chain from producer to consumer. This cannot happen with VAT. The success of this tax, which is now applied in more than 100 countries, lies also in the fact that it is less open to fraud than traditional taxes. This is because buyer firms have an interest in seeing that the seller firms record VAT correctly, since they are able to claim reimbursement.

The term "deductible VAT" is applied to the VAT payable on firms' intermediate consumption or gross fixed capital formation, since these amounts are deductible from the VAT owed by the firm to government as a result of its sales. Conversely, the term "non-deductible VAT" applies to the VAT that the buyer cannot deduct from his own VAT debt to the state. By definition, therefore, the VAT paid by households is totally non-deductible, since households are final consumers of the goods. On the other hand, also by definition, virtually all the VAT paid by firms on their purchases is deductible. There remain, however, special cases in which firms cannot entirely deduct the VAT on their purchases and are accordingly liable for a small portion of non-deductible VAT.

In the national accounts system, only the non-deductible VAT is recorded. It would have been too complicated, and in the end would have been of little use for the purposes of analysis, to trace the flows of deductible VAT. This decision has three consequences. First, in the national accounts, the VAT paid on household consumption appears in the accounts in its entirety because it is totally non-deductible. By contrast, however, firms' intermediate consumption and investment are subject, in the national accounts, only to a very small amount of VAT, since most of the VAT on these flows is deductible. Lastly, VAT is recorded not as having been received by government from individual firms but as a global receipt from "the total economy".

The brief example given below shows both the actual mechanism for the recovery of VAT and its recording in the national accounts (considering a VAT rate of 20%).

● Actual VAT mechanism: firm A makes a sale of 120 to firm B, including 20 of VAT, which firm A pays back to the government. Firm B makes a sale of 270 to the final consumer, including 45 of VAT. It therefore pays the government (45 – 20) = 25. In total, the government receives 45 in the form of non-deductible VAT.

● Corresponding treatment in the national accounts: firm A is recorded as making a sale of 100 to firm B (and not 120, as in reality). The 20 of VAT is not recorded because it is deductible. Firm B makes a sale to the final consumer of 270, including 45 of VAT. This amount of 45 is recorded in its totality, being non-deductible. Moreover, it is recorded as being received by the government not from firm B, but from the total economy.

As can be seen, the treatment in the national accounts does not correspond to the monetary flows. However, the result is the same from the point of view of the government's receipts of VAT. Better still, this presentation is more suited to macroeconomic analysis, because it means that virtually the total amount of VAT in the national accounts is shown as affecting household consumption. The system therefore marks a return to economic reality that might be otherwise masked. The payers of the VAT received by government are the final consumers, or households, and not the firms, which merely collect the tax.

Note that in Europe a small portion of the VAT is paid into the European budget. In practice, this portion is received by the government and then transferred to the European budget. Under the current system the national accounts (ESA 1995) it is treated as being paid directly to the European institutions. Under the new system (ESA 2010), it will be treated as received by government and transferred to the EU institutions.

Industries, products and specific operations in the input-output table

This section explains certain additional notions that are indispensable for a full understanding of the tables making up the input-output table, using the example of France.

The classification of industries is almost the mirror image of the classification of products. In fact, an industry is defined as the totality of firms, or parts of firms, that produce a given product. For a full understanding of the relationship between the two, the best thing is to go to the INSEE website: *www.insee.fr/fr/methodes/default.asp?page=nomenclatures/naf2008/naf2008.htm.*

INSEE presents its classifications as being simultaneously products and industries. From the above website, let us consider a classification at level G, titled "C21 Pharmaceutical industry." This is itself contained within level F under "C Manufacturing industry" and in turn contains another subhead within the level H titled "C21.1 manufacturing of basic pharmaceutical products". The terminology used in this last case, including the word "manufacture", seems to suggest that it is an industry. But it is important not to go wrong on this point, since it can also be interpreted as the output of this industry, in this case medicines. It therefore represents simultaneously the activity (industry) and its result (the medicines produced). The principle that has to be kept in mind is that the output of industry X is (virtually) equal, by definition, to the output of product X. The word "virtually" is necessary because the national accounts are somewhat more complicated, and this equality does not hold for certain industries. It would take too long to go into the details here.

There is, however, one case where an industry exists but there is no corresponding product. This is "trade" (retail and wholesale trade). In the national accounts there is indeed output of trade services (measured by the trade margin) but there is no "trade" product, since, as explained in the main text, the trade margin is included in the purchase price of the product being sold. For this reason, the product supply table for France (Table 10.1) contains a row "GZ Trade, Repair of motor vehicles and motorcycles" with 369 in the output column, but this amount is cancelled out slightly further down by the purely conventional introduction of a negative margin of -325. The two amounts are not exactly equal, since the GZ item in fact contains other sub-headings than pure trade, but the idea is there: there is an output of trade, but no trade product. Although there is not the same dichotomy in the case of transport (for which there is both an industry and a product), a similar conventional cancelling out is applied relating to transport margins on final uses. This explains the figure of -36 appearing in the "transport margins" column for the "HZ Transportation and storage" product in Table 10.1.

Two other rows in the French input-output table deserve additional explanation. These are the last two rows of Tables 10.1 and 10.2: "Products consumed outside national territory" and "cif-fob adjustment". The first concerns products consumed outside the territory, in practice tourism expenditure (see Chapter 5). Spending by French tourists abroad is conventionally recorded as an import of services (worth 32) in the product supply table (Table 10.1). Spending by foreign tourists in France is recorded as exports (worth 39) in the final uses table (Table 10.2). The difference between the two (-7) is recorded in the final uses table, in the same row and in the column "household final consumption expenditure". This sum will be added to the other consumption expenditure* in order to obtain, at the bottom of this column, the total household final consumption expenditure of households residing in France. This is because the other product rows in Table 10.2 include purchases by foreign tourists and these therefore have to be deducted to obtain consumption by residents. Conversely, the other product rows do not contain consumption by French tourists abroad and this has to be added in order to obtain their total consumption. This dual operation is carried out in the input-output table with the help of this row.

The cif-fob adjustment also pertains to relations with the rest of the world. As we saw in the main text, imports of goods are calculated cif, i.e. including cost, insurance and freight to the frontier. However, this price includes transport services from the exporting country's frontier to the French frontier. To give a more precise image of the imports of services, it was decided to show the total of imports at fob (free on board) prices, which exclude these transport costs, and to show the imported transport charges in total in the "transport" row. This explains the subtraction of 16 billion euros in the cell at the intersection of the "imports of goods" column and the "cif-fob adjustment" row in Table 10.1. If the transport service is carried out by a resident transporter, the output of this service will be included in the output of the "HZ Transportation and storage" industry. If it is carried out by a non-resident transporter, it will be included in imports of transport services. In either case, these amounts have to be deducted from the transport product row, since there is no use corresponding to these resources. This explains the entry for the same amount of -16 billion in the cell at the intersection of the "cif-fob adjustment" column and the transport row in Table 10.1. As for the cell at the intersection of the "cif-fob adjustment" column and the "cif-fob adjustment"

---

* This value is in fact negative in the case of France and so it would be more correct to say that it is subtracted. It is negative because spending by foreign tourists in France is greater than spending by French tourists abroad. This situation is also described by saying that the tourism balance is positive

row in Table 10.1, this is purely conventional and serves only to ensure that the row totals and the column totals for this specific operation cancel out. This cif-fob adjustment is quite complicated but has no overall impact. Its sole purpose is to give a clearer picture of the total aggregate imports of goods and services.

Limitations of the national accounts: Is there double counting in GDP?

GDP is equal to the sum of the components of final demand, each expressed at their purchase price, including taxes on products such as VAT. At the same time, GDP contains an estimate of the value of the output (and consumption) of non-market services, partly financed by these taxes. In so doing, are we not counting these taxes twice over?

The following simplified example will make it easier to understand the problem. Let us take an elementary economy in which there are only two products, manufactured goods and education. In this economy, the manufactured goods are subject to VAT at 20% and the proceeds are used by the authorities to purchase the services of teachers who provide free education services to households. It is assumed that there is no intermediate consumption in the economy.

A simplified economy financing education by VAT on manufactured goods

	Output = Value added	VAT	Final consumption
Manufactured goods	100	20	120
Education	20		20
GDP	140		140

The national accountants calculate GDP using the production approach: sum of values added + VAT, resulting in (120 + 20) = 140. This result matches that of the expenditure approach, since the addition of all the components of final demand, reduced in this case to consumption, does in fact give 140. But is there not something strange about including a VAT of 20 in the value of final consumption of manufactured goods and also counting this 20 in the consumption of education, although the latter is in fact free? Moreover, is it correct to speak of GDP at market prices when the consumption of education services is valued at a price that is not the one observed on the market, since education is free?

In order to understand the implications of the problem, let us suppose that the authorities decide to abolish VAT and to have the teachers paid directly by households. In addition, it will be assumed that nothing else happens either to volume or to prices. Following this change, we then obtain a GDP of 120 at current prices, representing a drop of 20.

Abolition of VAT, replaced by direct purchase of educational services

	Output = Value added	VAT	Final consumption
Manufactured goods	100		100
Education	20		20
GDP	120		120

This decline is somewhat strange. Seen from the producers' viewpoint, the value of their output has not changed; seen from the consumers' viewpoint, the value of their overall consumption has not changed. There has indeed been a decline in the prices of manufactured goods, thanks to the abolition of VAT, but this decline was offset by the rise in prices of educational services, which were previously free and now have to be paid for. The overall decline in GDP of 20 is therefore difficult to interpret.

The conclusion is that unfortunately the present definition of "GDP at market prices" is impacted by such institutional changes. There is not a double counting but a weakness of the GDP definition. Should this be cause for concern? Not fundamentally, since the changes in volume will be unaffected. GDP in volume at the previous year's prices will still equal 140 following the institutional change. The consumption in volume of manufactured goods will also equal 140, since the prices applied are those of the previous period. In total, volume growth will be zero, which is intellectually satisfactory. As regards spatial comparison with another country, if (as is desirable) purchasing power parity (PPP) is applied, the problem will also be solved, since PPPs are calculated after tax and so will automatically correct for any "double counting".

It remains true that direct comparisons of GDP at current prices should not be made in the absence of PPP adjustment, although this is something one sees very often. Also, it is not clear how to interpret the movement of the GDP price index when going to no VAT (the implicit deflator of GDP will decrease, while it should remain constant). Nevertheless, there is no other definition of GDP that makes it possible to verify that GDP = output = income = expenditure. One question could be: is this equation purely theoretical due to the wedge introduced by taxes?

Relationship with economic theory: Wassily Léontieff and the use of input-output tables

The first input-output tables were developed by an American economist of Russian descent, Wassily Léontieff. In the 1930s, he published an input-output table for the United States for the years 1919 and 1926 and used it to describe the structure of the American economy. However, it was in his native country, which had by then become the Soviet Union, that the most extensive use of the table was made. Gosplan, the Soviet Planning Ministry, drew up a five-year plan which set targets for the availability of consumer and capital goods and used input-output tables to evaluate the output needed to reach these targets. Each industry was accordingly given production targets that it was obligated to meet. Other countries like India, Egypt, China, Vietnam and Cuba adopted similar methods.

France and the Netherlands also had their five-year plans, but the purpose of these was not to impose targets on industries but rather to provide benchmarks and incentives. France and the Netherlands are market economies in which industries are not told what to produce. The five-year plans have now totally disappeared. At the same time, use of input-output tables to estimate the output needed to meet a given demand has become rarer but has not completely disappeared.

The assumption of fixed technical coefficients is a limitation of the method, except in the short term. Indeed, relative price movements between intermediate goods are not taken into account while they can generate technical changes that call this assumption into question. Moreover, long-period analysis of technical coefficients shows that they change substantially over time. Indeed, one of the major trends in recent decades has been industrial firms' increasing externalisation of entire portions of their production systems ("outsourcing"). For example, firms have drastically reduced their internal IT services to buy the IT services of specialised outside firms, regarded as giving better value for the money. This same phenomenon has occurred in the case of financial auditing, cleaning services and security, among others. Lastly, more and more industrial firms have been calling on the services of temporary agency staff (seen as being more flexible) even for their core productive activities. In all these cases, this outsourcing increases the intermediate consumption of industrial firms without correspondingly increasing their output. The result is a slow but inexorable increase in technical coefficients.

Although the use of input-output tables for economic analysis has been tending to diminish, there are certain examples to the contrary. The OECD has published an interesting study using this technique in an economic/environmental framework (Ahmad and al., 2003). The international Kyoto protocol on the environment sets targets for reductions in emissions of CO_2 (the principal "greenhouse gas") for the industrial countries. Most of the signatories have made progress towards these targets. However, this may not correspond to a genuine reduction in the emissions of CO_2 attributable to a country.

The problem is that the Kyoto protocol focuses on emissions within a country's borders, whereas globalisation means relocation of industries from the rich countries to the poor countries, reducing the emissions of the former but increasing the emissions of the latter, especially as they tend to use inefficient production techniques. In total, CO_2 emissions are higher than before. The OECD study dealt with emissions of CO_2 that are attributable not to the production of the rich countries, but to their consumption. For this purpose, it used input-output tables to determine which industries are involved in meeting certain types of consumption, including industries located in other countries. The study concluded that the emissions of CO_2 attributable to the consumption of the rich countries were 5% greater than the emissions due to their domestic production.

Accrual accounting

The so-called accrual basis is applied throughout the national accounts, and it is based on the same method used in company accounts. The principle is as follows: a transaction must be recorded in accordance with the amount and the timing of the creation of the claim (for the creditor) or of the obligation (for the debtor). For example, sales from firm A to firm B will be recorded at the time of change of ownership, in other words, when the sales contract is signed, without waiting for the payment of the money corresponding to the sale. In the period between the time of sale and the time when the money is transferred, the accounts will show a credit by the seller in favour of the buyer. This is the general principle applied in theory to all the series in the national accounts.

There is a dual justification for adopting this principle. First, if one considers that one aim of the national accounts is to show the wealth of economic agents at the end of the period, it is nothing less than indispensable. An agent's wealth at the end of the period must include as positive items all the unconditional claims on other agents (for example, if the sales contracts have been signed and the product delivered, the seller has an unconditional claim on the buyer) and, as negative items, the obligations contracted vis-à-vis other agents (for instance, even if he has not yet paid the government the taxes for the period, he still owes them). Second, its application permits better analytical correspondence among the variations of the macroeconomic series. For example, if the government raises the VAT rate in December of a given year, the repercussions on VAT receipts will be felt in the first quarter of the following year, given the time lag between the payment of VAT by agents and the receipt of these monies by government. However, it would be analytically incorrect to record the rise in VAT only in the following year, whereas some consumption at the new rate has already taken place in the current year. In accountants' jargon, it is said that the VAT receipts have to be "adjusted" in order to attach them to the period when the flow was generated (at the time when, for example, a household purchases a product).

In practice, things are not so simple. On the one hand, the national accountants use company accounts, for which this rule is primordial. One might therefore think that the rule is respected. However, this is not totally the case, since in many countries one of the largest macroeconomic agents, i.e. government, does not systematically apply this rule. Quite rightly, the national accountants consider that for certain transactions (e.g. taxes) government statistics are better than those derived from aggregating the company accounts. The national accounts, which are bound to be internally consistent, therefore replace the accrual-basis tax data supplied by firms with the government statistics, which are better in terms of coverage but worse with respect to the accrual basis. This is finally done by shifting the timing of the VAT receipts of the government in order to bring them more into line with the timing of the generation of the tax.

Another practical difficulty needs to be pointed out, namely the difficulty experienced by the national accountants in applying this principle without taking into account "provisions". A firm always has to deal with bad payers. While it will therefore record all its claims on its purchasers, it will also, by precaution, set aside a "provision" to cover non-payment and this will be recorded in its income statement. But the national accounts do not allow for the recording of these provisions, which, by definition constitute a view taken by one agent of other agents, entailing a lack of symmetry. The national accounts, for the purpose of internal consistency, record only what is symmetrical. This is a contradiction that needs to be resolved.

What does "consolidation" mean?

There are two ways of aggregating institutional accounts. The first is simply to add them together, as do most national accounts systems. The second is to add them together but to eliminate the transactions between individual institutional units involved in the aggregation. This method is known as "consolidation". When consolidation has been carried out, there remain only the transactions between the aggregate grouping created and the units located outside this grouping. For example, in the extract from the integrated economic account concerning interest discussed in the main text (see Table 10.7), if the total for the national economy (S1) had been calculated by consolidation, the figure would have been much smaller than DKK 305.5 billion, because most of the interest is paid by resident units to other resident units, and so takes place within S1.

It is fairly easy to find a consolidated figure for S1. This is because if one eliminates transactions between resident sectors all that is left, in principle, are the transactions with non-resident sectors, and there is only one such sector, i.e. the rest of the world (S2). The "consolidated S1" figures therefore correspond to the counterpart of the figure for S2, and so the consolidated interest paid by "S1 National Economy" is necessarily equal to the interest received by "S2 Rest of the World", i.e. DKK 56.9 billion. Note that two sectors are already consolidated. These are the rest of the world and households. The rest of the world by definition because the national accounts for a country take no interest in transactions that are internal to other countries or to transactions between other countries; households by statistical necessity because their accounts are obtained by difference since virtually no direct information is available regarding households. Because they are obtained by difference, household accounts are consolidated out of necessity. However, as it is very difficult to consolidate aggregate business accounts, they are most often not consolidated in the national accounts.

Note also that the items obtained as balancing items in the accounts (value added, operating surplus, saving, net lending/net borrowing) are generally invariant, whether there is consolidation or not. This is because they result from the difference between resources and uses. If the resources consist of transactions internal to the sector, the uses must necessarily include them also.

Exercises for Chapter 10

Exercise 1. Reconstitution of an input-output table using "copy and paste"

The aim of this exercise is to compile a life-size input-output table at level E of the French classification (17 products/industries). Go to the INSEE website (insee.fr), find the annual national accounts, and then look for "Synthesis tables" and then "input-output table" ("tableau des entrées et sorties"). This will give you the product supply table ("tableau des ressources en produits"), the final use table ("tableau des emplois finals par produits"), the intermediate use table ("tableau des entrées intermédiaires") and, underneath, the production accounts ("comptes de production") and the generation of income accounts ("comptes d'exploitation") by industry ("branche"). Print out these tables separately. Using copy and paste, reassemble them so as to obtain the picture of the input-output table given in Section 4 of this chapter. Be careful to ensure that both the rows and the columns correspond. Read again Sections 1 to 4 of this chapter with this new set of tables in front of you. For those courageous enough, the INSEE site makes it possible to perform the same manipulation at level F (38 products). The result is a very large table. Imagine how big it would be at level G (88 products)!

Exercise 2. Reconstitution of the accounts of institutional sectors

Take the case of an economy with three institutional sectors: households (including NPISHs), corporations (financial and non-financial) and general government.

Various sources have been used and processed according to the definitions in the national accounts, with the following result:

	Corporations	General government	Households
Expenditure			
Interest	162	35	20
Employers' social contributions	129	53	11
Dividends	60		
Other taxes minus subsidies on production	54	2	2
Operating surplus	?	?	65
Gross wages and salaries	431	87	51

	Corporations	General government	Households
Withdrawals from income of quasi-corporations	24		
Current taxes on income, wealth, etc.	34		178
Other property income	25		
Income from land and sub-soil assets	31	7	27
Final consumption expenditure		368	1 031
Social security reimbursements		57	
Benefits		162	
Other current transfers	57	159	73
Social benefits other than social transfers in kind	43	289	
Adjustment for the change pension entitlements	11		
Resources			
Value added (at basic prices)	780	158	561
Social contributions	54	268	
Dividends	28	5	13
Taxes minus subsidies on products		133	
Other current transfers	59	109	72
Income from land and sub-soil assets	44		21
Other property income	16		23
Interest	139	14	56
Withdrawals from income of quasi-corporations		13	44

In addition, the balance of payments supplies the following data:

Debit (resources of the rest of the world)	
Gross wages and salaries	2
Interest	21
Dividends	14
Other current transfers	59
Withdrawals from income of quasi-corporations (located within the economy)	3
Credit (uses of the rest of the world)	
Gross wages and salaries	6
Other property income	14
Interest	13
Withdrawals from income of quasi-corporations (located in other countries)	36
Other current transfers	10

This exercise consists of completing the accounts for the three institutional sectors shown on the following pages.

Here are certain indications that will be useful for the exercise:

1. the data shown in the first table above are not complete, and additional figures will have to be reconstituted;

2. the wages and salaries shown in the balance of payments table are by their nature paid to, or received, by the rest of the world, and the remainder are paid to households;

3. social benefits are by definition received by households;

4. social contributions received by corporations and general government are paid by households;

5. the adjustment for the change in pension entitlements applies to households, by definition;

6. households' adjusted disposable income is equal to disposable income plus social transfers in kind (Social Security reimbursements, other benefits in kind).

Households

Generation of income account	
Uses	Resources
Compensation of employees	Value added
gross wages and salaries	
employers' social contributions	
Other taxes on production, less subsidies	
Operating surplus	
Mixed income	

Allocation of primary income account	
Uses	Resources
	Gross operating surplus and mixed income
	Compensation of employees
	gross wages and salaries
	employers' social contributions
Property income	Property income
interest	interest
income from land and subsoil assets	dividends
	withdrawals from income of quasi-corporations
Balance of primary incomes	income from land and subsoil assets
	other property income

Secondary distribution of income account	
Uses	Resources
Current taxes on income, wealth, etc.	Balance of primary incomes
Social contributions	Social benefits other than social transfers in kind
Other current transfers	Other current transfers
Disposable income	

Households (cont.)

Use of income account

Uses	Resources
	Disposable income
Final consumption expenditure	Adjustment for the change in pension entitlements
Saving	

Use of adjusted income account

Uses	Resources
	Adjusted disposable income
Actual consumption	Adjustment for the change in pension entitlements
Saving	

Corporations

Generation of income account

Uses	Resources
Compensation of employees	Value added
gross wages and salaries	
employers' social contributions	
Other taxes on production, less subsidies	
Operating surplus	

Allocation of primary income account

Uses	Resources
Property income	Operating surplus
interest	
dividends	Property income
withdrawals from income of quasi-corporations	interest
other property income	dividends
	income from land and sub-soil assets
	other property income
Balance of primary incomes	

Secondary distribution of income account

Uses	Resources
Current taxes on income, wealth, etc.	Balance of primary incomes
Social benefits other than social transfers in kind	Social contributions
Other current transfers	Other current transfers
Disposable income	

Use of income account

Uses	Resources
Adjustment for the change in pension entitlements	Disposable income
Saving	

General government

Generation of income account

Uses	Resources

Compensation of employees
    gross wages and salaries
    employers' social contributions
Other taxes on production, less subsidies
Operating surplus
	Value added

Allocation of primary income account

Uses	Resources

Property income
    interest
    income from land and sub-soil assets
    other property income
 	
Balance of primary incomes
	Operating surplus
	
	Taxes minus subsidies on production and imports
	    taxes minus subsidies on products
	    other taxes minus subsidies on production
	Property income
	    interest
	    dividends
	    withdrawals from income of quasi-corporations
	    other property income

Secondary distribution of income account

Uses	Resources
  Social benefits other than social transfers in kind Other current transfers Disposable income	Balance of primary incomes Current taxes on income, wealth, etc. Social contributions Other current transfers

Use of income account

Uses	Resources
Final consumption expenditure Saving	Disposable income

Use of adjusted income account

Uses	Resources
Actual consumption Saving	Adjusted disposable income

Exercise 3. Creating an integrated economic account

Use the accounts of the three institutional sectors in the previous exercise to complete the integrated economic account in the following three pages:

Integrated economic account (extract) (1/3)

Total	Rest of the world	Total economy	Corpora-tions	General govern-ment	House-holds	Production account	Corpora-tions	General govern-ment	House-holds	Total economy	Rest of the world	Total
						Imports					499	499
540	540					Exports						
						Output	1 708	410	1 264	3 382		3382
1 883		1 883	928	252	703	Intermediate consumption						
						Taxes minus subsidies on products				133		133
1 632		1 632	780	158	561	Value-added/GDP						
-41	-41					Trade balance (goods and services)						
						Generation of income account)						
						Value added						
						Compensation of employees						
						Gross wages and salaries						
						Employer's social contribution						
						Taxes *minus* subsidies						
						On products						
						Other taxes						
						Operating surplus						
						Mixed income						

Integrated economic account (extract) (2/3)

Total	Rest of the world	Total economy	Corpora-tions	General govern-ment	House-holds	Allocation of primary income account	Corpora-tions	General govern-ment	House-holds	Total economy	Rest of the world	Total
						Operating surplus/ mixed income						
						Compensation of employees						
						Gross wages and salaries						

Integrated economic account (extract) (2/3) *(cont.)*

Total	Rest of the world	Total economy	Corpora-tions	General govern-ment	House-holds	Allocation of primary income account	Corpora-tions	General govern-ment	House-holds	Total economy	Rest of the world	Total
						Employer's social contribution						
						Taxes *minus* subsidies						
						On products						
						Other taxes on production						
						Property income						
						interest						
						dividends						
						income from quasi-corporations						
						income from land and sub-soil assets						
						other property income						
						Balance of primary incomes/National Income						

Integrated economic account (extract) (3/3)

Total	Rest of the world	Total economy	Corpora-tions	General govern-ment	House-holds	Secondary distribution of income account	Corpora-tions	General govern-ment	House-holds	Total economy	Rest of the world	Total
						Balance of primary incomes						
						Current taxes on income, wealth, etc.						
						Social contributions						
						Other social benefits						
						Other current transfers						
						Disposable income						
						Use of income account						
						Disposable income						
						Final expenditure						
						Change in pension entitlements						
						Saving						
						Current-account balance						

Exercise 4. Use of the input-output table in a so-called Léontieff model

Take the following input-output table, consisting of: [M] the intermediate consumption matrix; [Y] the vector of final demand for intermediate goods, capital goods and consumer goods; and, lastly [X], the vector of output from the industries producing these same goods (in order, intermediate goods, capital goods and consumer goods).

	[M]			[Y]
Intermediate products	5	20	20	5
Capital goods	5	10	12	33
Consumer products	10	6	15	89
[X]	50	60	120	
	Intermediate products	Capital goods	Consumer goods	

Given the above figures, and with the help of the equations in Section 5 of this chapter, do the following:

1. calculate the matrix [A] of technical coefficients;

2. use Equation 7 to calculate the impact on [X] of an increase of 20 in final demand for consumer goods (say, as a result of a tax cut by the government).

The solutions to these exercises are available at:
http://dx.doi.org/10.1787/9789264214637-28-en

Chapter 11

The national accounts machinery: Compilation and reporting

This chapter looks at the "machinery" of national accounts. It explains how national accounts are compiled and describes the main consequences of this process for the user of national accounts. It first discusses quarterly accounts then examines the relationship between quarterly national accounts and annual national accounts. Finally, it turns to ordinary revisions and comprehensive revisions in the national accounts. It uses France as the example country, but the lessons drawn are applicable for other countries as well.

P revious chapters concentrated on the definitions of the variables in the national accounts. This chapter is quite different; its aim is to explain how national accounts are compiled *in practice* and to describe the main consequences of this process for the user. We will start by discussing the quarterly accounts; then we will examine the relationship between quarterly national accounts and annual national accounts. Finally, we will look at ordinary revisions and comprehensive revisions in the national accounts. The example used will be France, but the lessons to be learned apply also to other countries.

1. The quarterly national accounts

In the United States or the United Kingdom, the national accounts have been from the start almost entirely quarterly. In France and in many other countries, they have been essentially annual for a long time but are becoming increasingly quarterly, thanks to the progress made in the collection and processing of statistics. It is therefore essential for the macroeconomist to be well-informed regarding the timing, format and publication of quarterly national accounts.

Why have quarterly accounts?

One of the crucial objectives of macroeconomic statistics is to help the authorities make the right decisions at the right moment. It would not be appropriate to launch a policy boosting the economy when the upswing has already started, or conversely to "cool down" the economy when it is already entering recession. It is therefore desirable to have the most refined possible information regarding the economic cycle and its turning points. In this context, the annual national accounts, which in the French case are published in May of the following year, arrive far too late. Moreover, exclusive reliance on annual averages can in fact be misleading about the true state of the economy (see Exercise 1 at the end of this chapter). Hence, it is important to compile accounts that are more timely than annual ones. The present situation regarding the resources available and the reliability of statistics limits this effort to extend quarterly accounts compilation, but some countries such as Canada calculate GDP monthly.

The quarterly national accounts constitute the central instrument for short-term economic analysis at the OECD. The first pages of *Economic Outlook No. 93* dated May 2013 open with the following graph and the attached comment:

"The global economic recovery has continued to proceed in fits and starts, especially in the OECD area, with quarterly output growth fluctuating around a modest positive rate. The pace of the recovery has also continued to diverge across the major OECD economies and within the euro area, reflecting inter alia cross-country differences in macroeconomic and structural policies, as well as other factors affecting financial conditions." (OECD, 2013a).

Figure 11.1. Quarterly real GDP: Canada, Euro area, Japan and USA
2008 Q1 = 100

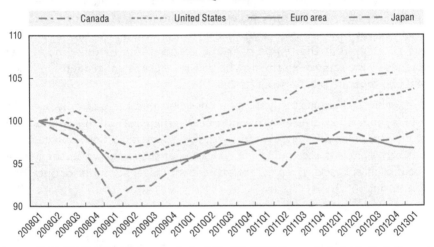

Source: OECD (2013), "OECD Economic Outlook No. 93", OECD Economic Outlook: Statistics and Projections (database), doi: http://dx.doi.org/10.1787/data-00655-en.
StatLink http://dx.doi.org/10.1787/888933144222

Quarterly accounts are much used by forecasters, whether in the Finance Ministry helping in the preparation of the government budget or in private research institutions such as those connected to the large banks, or in international organisations such as OECD. Thanks to the quarterly accounts, these economists are in a position to update their forecasts for the coming year as quarterly information becomes available for the current year.

A good forecast is, above all, one that is based on the most recent past figures.

In France, the quarterly accounts are also used in connection with the six-month forecasts made by INSEE's Short-Term Economic Forecasts Department. These are presented in the regular publications entitled *Conjoncture en France*, which contain numerous quarterly figures accompanied by comments regarding average year-on-year changes or statistical carryover (see Box 11.1: "Annualisation and various growth indicators"). The French INSEE is in fact one of the few statistical institutes in the world that makes forecasts.

Specific features of the quarterly accounts

In certain countries such as the United States or the United Kingdom, the user of the national accounts sees no real difference between the annual accounts and the quarterly accounts. Both countries developed the national accounts *simultaneously* on a quarterly and on an annual basis from the start. In France and certain other countries, the quarterly accounts were developed much later than the annual accounts (in the mid-1970s for France, as compared with the 1950s or even earlier for the US and the UK). It is in fact only recently that the teams of INSEE accountants involved have been attached to the same department. This means that the user could think there were two separate sets of publications.

However, there is *strictly* no difference between the quarterly accounts and the annual accounts as regards the basic principles and the definitions of the variables. The difference is merely that the size of the flows shown in the quarterly accounts are roughly one quarter of those shown in the annual accounts (as is logical, given that one calendar quarter accounts for only three months out of 12).

This does not apply to the quarterly accounts published for example in the United States, which are "annualised", and thus multiplied by 4 (see Box 11.1: "Annualisation and various growth indicators").

Conversely, the annual flows are equal (in theory, as we will see later) to the sum of the flows for the four quarters.

Box 11.1. Annualisation and various growth indicators

The most important use made of the national accounts is to forecast the following year in order to provide the macroeconomic framework for the government budget. The prime aim is to evaluate the growth of GDP in volume for the following year, on an "annual average" basis. This expression signifies that one is trying to evaluate the variation between GDP in calendar year Y and GDP in year $Y + 1$, i.e. $(Y + 1)/Y$. The information given in the quarterly accounts generally shows quarterly changes, i.e., $(Q + 1)/Q$. The further one moves into the year, the more information there is on recent quarters thanks to the quarterly accounts, and the closer one comes to the prime aim of forecasting annual average growth.

> **Box 11.1. Annualisation and various growth indicators** *(cont.)*
>
> Certain national accountants (Canada, Japan, Mexico, United States) usually express quarterly figures "at annual level", meaning that quarterly levels are multiplied by four. They also express quarterly changes "at annualised rate", which amounts to raising them to the power of 4. The advantage of this method is to place the quarterly growth rate on a slope that uses the same measurement framework as for the annual data. This practice has not however been generalised to the other countries. This practice is indeed not without problems as it is based on the assumption that the observed changes for the quarter are going to continue, which is by no means certain. Thus some short-term analysts prefer to use "year-on-year changes" and/or "the statistical carryover" in order to give indications regarding the annual growth rate. Year-on-year changes consist of calculating the change for the current period (quarter, in this case) since the corresponding period of the previous year (Q/Q-4). The "statistical carryover" consists of calculating an annual average for the current calendar year on the assumption that the remaining quarters are at the same level as the last known quarter. The further one moves into the year, the closer the statistical carryover comes to the future annual average, the two becoming equal when the fourth quarter is known. Exercise 1 at the end of this chapter provides an opportunity to work with these notions. One of the indispensable conclusions to be drawn is that one should be careful to avoid the trap of comparing an American growth figure (raised to the power of 4) with a French or European figure that is not. To make valid comparisons, either one takes the fourth root of the American growth or one raises the European figure to the power of 4.

The aim of the quarterly accounts is to provide at the earliest possible moment reliable figures for the changes in the major macroeconomic aggregates. Thus, the quarterly accounts are simplified compared with the annual accounts and are presented slightly differently. In France, for example, quarterly accounts are calculated using a classification consisting of 38 items, and the accounts made available to the users are based on a 17-item classification. The detailed analyses of structural changes in the economy are left to the annual accounts, which are calculated for a 332-item classification and published for a 88-item classification. On the same lines, the detail of the transactions in the accounts for institutional sectors is not as great in the quarterly accounts as in the annual accounts. This enables INSEE to reduce the workload entailed by the more frequent calculation of quarterly accounts which are calculated twice per quarter, as shown in the following table. This frequency of calculation is made possible by highly effective estimation procedures using rapidly available indicators (see Going further: "Sources and methods used for the French quarterly accounts").

Table 11.1. **France: Calendar for the publication of the accounts for quarter Q**

Q + 45 days	Q + 90 days
First results	Detailed results
GDP + goods and services accounts + certain elements of the income approach of GDP.	Revised GDP + revised goods and services accounts + fairly complete accounts for institutional sectors

GDP and a complete set of goods and services accounts are published at Q + 45 days, at the time of the publication of the "first results", and is then accompanied by some limited elements regarding profits and the total wage bill. The first revision takes place at Q + 90 days in the form of "detailed results", this time including fairly complete accounts for institutional sectors. As a result, figures are published quarterly for the household saving ratio or the corporate profit ratio at Q + 90 days. A similar calendar applies for other countries (see Table 11.2). For completeness, mention should also be made of the existence in some countries of a monthly series of national accounts. In France, it is limited to "household expenditure on consumption of manufactured goods". This monthly national accounts series makes it possible to know, roughly 23 days after the end of the month, the change in consumption expenditure – limited to manufactured goods, admittedly. However, since changes in total consumption are closely linked to consumption of manufactured goods, this indicator is useful for the short-term analysts.

Despite the fact that the definitions of the variables are the same in the two sets of accounts, it turns out in practice that the sums of the four quarters from the quarterly accounts are not equal to the corresponding annual figures, because the French quarterly accounts are "working-day adjusted" (wda). To be more precise, the French quarterly national accounts are now calculated "wda-sa" meaning that they are adjusted both for the number of working days and for seasonal variations.[1] In statisticians' terminology and in this context, "wda" and "sa" are in opposition to the unadjusted figures. The **working-day adjustment** consists of calculating the quarterly accounts as if each quarter contained the same number of working days. This means that changes in GDP are not affected by differences in the numbers of working days in each quarter. The adjustment gives a better indication of the actual ongoing tendency in the economy and leads to smoother quarterly variations than shown in the unadjusted figures. Many countries make this adjustment (see Table 11.2).

The difficulty created in some countries (France, Italy and Germany) by the working-day adjustment is that the sum of the four quarters no longer equals *by definition* the unadjusted figures for the year because there are often differences in the number of working days between one year and the next, partly because of leap years, but it is not the most important factor. More important, for example, is the fact that public holidays fall on week-ends in some years, but on working days in other. The difference can be quite significant, as in the case of the year 2004 compared with 2003 (see Box 11.2: "Calendar effects: the years 2003 and 2004"). Does this not suggest that all national accounts, including annual accounts, should be calculated after adjustment for the number of working days? Economists are divided on this point because, while adjusted data is more useful to analyse the trend, some major economic aggregates are unadjusted. For example, the government budget that is voted by Parliament is unadjusted (i.e. is not working-day-adjusted). The best solution would be to have a choice between the two, as is given in the case of France where there are two sets of accounts: one (wda) consisting of the quarterly accounts and one (unadjusted) for the annual accounts. In order to obtain the annual accounts on a wda basis, one merely has to add up the four quarters from the quarterly accounts; to have the unadjusted annual figures all that is needed is to take the figures in the annual accounts. In some other countries, such as the US, wda is conducted for quarters but the data are then benchmarked to the unadjusted annual figures, or the annual data are obtained by the sum of the quarters so that, at the end, there is no difference between the sum of the four quarters and the annual figure.

Box 11.2. Calendar effects: the years 2003 and 2004

In France, the years 2003 and 2004 were very special from the point of view of the calendar. The number of working days in 2003, at 252, was in fact slightly below the average of 253. The year 2004 was exceptional with 255 working days, a figure not seen since 1976. The impact of this greater number of working days on the annual change in GDP, everything else remaining equal, is estimated to have been 0.2/0.3 of a percentage point, which is by no means negligible. It is nevertheless smaller than the simple ratio of the numbers of working days: $255 \div 252 = +1.2\%$. This is because INSEE's estimate of the impact of the number of working days attaches different weights to individual days of the week, especially for the months of July and August, and the "catching-up" that takes place between different months. The estimation method used is econometric. The unadjusted monthly figures are projected on variables representing the different types of days of the week (number of working Mondays, non-worked Tuesdays, etc.) and the number of Sundays.

The other calendar adjustment of the quarterly accounts is the **seasonal adjustment**. This consists in eliminating, by means of complex statistical processes based on moving averages, the changes from one quarter to the next that are due simply to seasonal effects. For example, the output of transport services rises systematically and steeply before Christmas and the summer holidays. It is therefore better to eliminate the impact of this seasonal effect in order to know whether holidaymakers actually consumed more or less in the quarter in question than in the previous quarter. Unlike the working-day adjustment, things are so arranged that the sum of the quarterly seasonal adjustments for the year as a whole is zero. In other words, the sum of the quarterly seasonally adjusted figures is equal to the unadjusted figure for the year.

Table 11.2. **Some features of quarterly national accounts for selected OECD countries**

	First estimate (Q + 60 means published 60 days after end of quarter)	Second estimate	Third estimate	Working Day Adjustment (in italics countries for which the sum of four quarters do not equal the annual value)	Mean absolute revision of quarterly GDP growth[b] (in %)
Australia	Q + 60			Yes	0.38
Canada	Q + 60			Yes	0.23
France	Q + 45	Q + 90		*Yes*	0.27
Germany	Q + 44	Q + 54		*Yes*	0.34
Italy	Q + 44	Q + 70		*Yes*	0.24
Japan	Q + 44	Q + 70		Yes	0.65
Korea	Q + 26	Q + 66[a]		Yes	0.62
United Kingdom	Q + 25	Q + 56	Q + 86	Yes	0.18
United States	Q + 30	Q + 60	Q + 90	Yes	0.29

a) Q + 80 for the fourth quarter.
b) In terms of quarterly rates (i.e. Q/Q-1), absolute rates, first estimate versus three years after (see the "Revision Database" on the OECD Web site). This is different from what appears in the US tables of revision published for the accounts of the United States, in which all quarterly growth rates are systematically "annualised" (see Box 11.1: "Annualisation and various growth indicators").

2. The annual national accounts

If all one needs are the major economic aggregates, one needs to look no further than the series and publications of the quarterly accounts. However, if one wants detailed results, it is necessary to consult the series and publications of the annual national accounts. In particular, the very important general government account is still, for some OECD countries, available only on an annual basis, as are the financial accounts and the balance sheet accounts. However, there is a sustained effort by OECD countries to expand the number of tables compiled quarterly. It is therefore possible than soon, general government accounts will be available quarterly for all OECD countries.

In France, like in all OECD countries, there are major dates for publications. The main publication for the annual accounts is the report entitled *The French Economy* (Insee, 2014), published in June and providing indispensable analysis of the recent economic evolution. This publication goes hand-in-hand with the publication on the INSEE Web site of a set of tables giving details for institutional sectors accounts, external flows of goods and services, gross fixed capital formation by products and institutional sectors, final consumption expenditure and population and employment.

The annual accounts are the backbone of the whole system of national accounts. They are based mainly on four sources: (1) the aggregation of company accounts (in France, INSEE receives and processes each year the accounts of more than 2 million corporations and unincorporated enterprises); (2) the complete accounts of all general government, consisting of central government and the attached agencies, local authorities and all the Social Security bodies (around 120 000 organizations in all in France); (3) the detailed accounts of the financial institutions that are supervised by the central bank (Banque de France) whose statistical directorate is, as in all countries, the main collaborator of the National Statistical Office for production of the national accounts; (4) the balance of payments (generally published by the central bank), which makes it possible to trace relations with the rest of the world.

Much of these data, however, are available only after a certain time-lag, generating a specific calendar of compilation and publication. In what follows, Y will refer to the year for which new accounts are calculated. In France, each year, in May of year Y + 1, new annual accounts are published containing new data for year Y (the so-called "provisional" accounts), for year Y – 1 (the so-called "semi-final" accounts) and for year Y – 2 (the so-called "final" accounts). The mechanism used for the annual accounts therefore implies two systematic revisions for each set of published accounts, revisions that obviously, by definition, have an impact on the quarterly accounts. For example, the annual GDP for year Y will be published in May Y + 1 as "provisional", in May Y + 2 as "semi-final" and in May Y + 3 as "final" (as we shall see later, the term "final" is in fact inappropriate). This sequencing is explained mainly by the delays in obtaining data from the principal source mentioned earlier, namely company accounts. Other countries may have some difference in the timing and terminology, but basically the system is similar to that of France.

In France, the "provisional" accounts are mainly the combination of the quarterly accounts for the goods and services accounts *plus* the complete accounts for the general government *plus* the financial accounts. At the time these provisional accounts are published, INSEE has not yet received any company accounts and has to wait until Q4 of year Y + 1 before receiving and processing a first substantial set of corporate accounts (for roughly 400 000 large firms), but still excluding the bulk of smallest firms. This information can thus only be processed to be published in May of the next year, on the occasion of the publication of the next year's provisional accounts. Finally, the totality of corporate accounts (for roughly 2 500 000 firms) is received and processed by INSEE only in Q4 of year Y + 2. Table 11.3 below recapitulates this sequence. In the end, it is necessary to wait two years and five months for national accounts that have "digested" the totality of the available statistical sources used for the national accounts for calendar year Y.

Table 11.3. **France: Sequencing of the calculations of the annual accounts for year Y**

May Y + 1	May Y + 2	May Y + 3
Provisional accounts Accounts at the F level (38 headings). Complete accounts for institutional sectors.	Semi-final accounts Revised accounts at the G level (88 headings corresponding to divisions of NACE). Complete revised accounts for institutional sectors.	Final accounts Re-revised accounts at the G level. Complete revised accounts for institutional sectors.
Source: quarterly accounts, general government accounts, financial corporations accounts	*Source:* first version of corporate accounts, with a partial coverage for the smallest firms. Complete revised version of the general government accounts	*Source:* complete version of the corporate accounts, with a full coverage of the smallest firms

3. The revisions to the national accounts and their precision

As we have just seen for France (and the situation is similar in other countries), the complete sources for the national accounts are available only in Q4 of year Y + 2. If they had to wait as long as this for this information, short-term macroeconomic analysts would have no use for the national accounts. This explains the complex sequencing of successive quarterly and annual accounts, the aim being to provide the most reliable information possible as rapidly as possible. However, the price paid for this rapidity is the need to revise the initial figures. Some macroeconomists complain about revisions to the national accounts. However, it is not possible to "have one's cake" in the form of reliability and at the same time "eat it" in the form of rapidity. Nor should one be fooled: the countries that performed little or no revision were the Soviet bloc countries, where statisticians, for political reasons, were forbidden to make revisions. This did not mean that the national accounts were reliable – quite the contrary. On the other hand, major revisions are obviously not a good thing. The professionalism of national accountants is judged by their capacity to combine a high degree of reliability with satisfactory rapidity.

When does a figure for quarterly GDP growth become "final"? The somewhat surprising answer is "never". As an illustration, this is the sequence of events that in France covers the repeated revision of the quarterly GDP change: (1) first publication at Q plus 45 days; (2) first revision at the time of the "detailed results" at Q + 90 (source: availability of new indicators); (3) minor revisions due to changes in the seasonal adjustment coefficients[2] occur at the time of publication for the following quarters; (4) major revision in May in the following year due to benchmarking on the semi-final annual accounts; (5) significant revision in May in the following year due to the benchmarking on final annual accounts; (6) later still, possible minor revisions due to changes in the seasonal adjustment coefficients, etc.

Clearly, the most significant revision is the first one, followed in May of the following year at the time of the benchmarking of the unadjusted quarterly accounts on the annual accounts. The other revisions are very small. Even so, the user of the national accounts, if he or she wants to be really up-to-date, must study each publication to find the whole new series and not be content with adding the latest figure to an already existing series. Today, thanks to computer processing and the Internet, downloading an entire series costs no more than downloading the last figure, so no one can complain about this state of affairs. French policy regarding revision is an extreme case. Some other countries make revisions less systematically.

Numerous studies have addressed the question of the scale and sign of the revisions. In France, it is thought that the average revision of the GDP growth rate in volume for a given quarter (i.e., $Q \div (Q - 1)$) is 0.3% in absolute value. In other words, there is a 90% chance that the revision in the quarterly growth rate (after a few years have passed) is between +0.6% and -0.6% compared with the initial published figure. This range is comparable to that for the American quarterly accounts (see Table 11.2). Some other OECD countries make slightly larger revisions, on average. As regards the annual accounts, the following chart illustrates a sequence of revisions between the provisional accounts and the final accounts for France. On average, over this period the average revision amounted to 0.4% (in absolute value). As can be seen, there are no earth-shaking revisions, but on occasion the annual revision has amounted to as much as 1.0% (for example, in 1988, a year of strong recovery), which is quite significant. Some observers have seen signs that the initial figures in the national accounts are understated in years of recovery and overstated in years of recession, because the sources used in the first estimates exclude small businesses that are more affected by the business cycle than large businesses.

Figure 11.2. **France: Comparisons of estimates of annual growth for the "provisional" and "final" accounts**

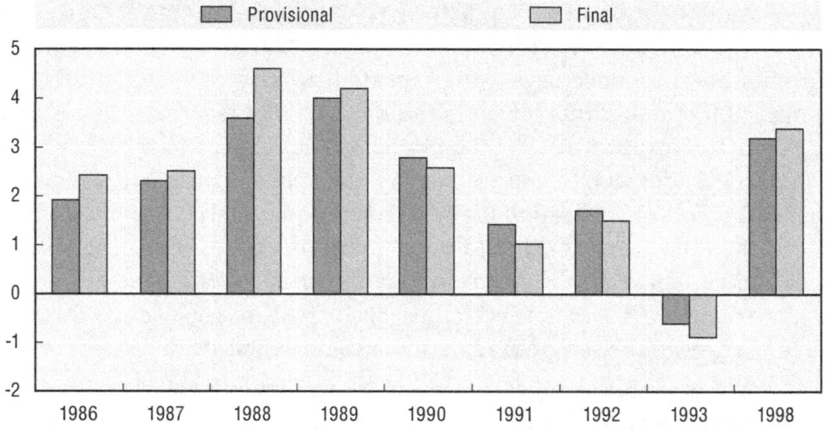

Source: INSEE.

StatLink ⬛⬛⬛ http://dx.doi.org/10.1787/

The various revisions to the GDP *growth rate* listed above show that the national accounts cannot claim to be absolutely precise. It would in fact be by no means wrong to conclude from the previous paragraphs that the initial estimates of the quarterly GDP growth rate for France should probably be presented in the form of a range of ± 0.5% of the estimated figure (and even greater amplitude for the other detailed items in the accounts, especially GFCF). American quarterly accounts are indeed presented with an accompanying note presenting this type of range for the main aggregates.

As explained in a previous footnote, US quarterly growth rates are systematically annualized in US publications (see Box 11.1: "Annualisation and various growth indicators"), so the range of deviation published in the US quarterly accounts may (wrongly) appear much larger than for France or other countries.

It would be good to know the precision attached to the *level* of GDP. Unfortunately there is no way of knowing this. While it is fully possible to calculate scientifically the precision of an extrapolation of a sample survey to the total population, it is impossible to do so for the national accounts, whose sources are a blend of surveys and comprehensive databases that are then the subject of "arbitration" vis-à-vis many other sources.

"Arbitration" is a key word in the machinery of annual national accounts. In France, there are two ways of estimating GDP: the approach based on output and final uses and the income-based approach. It is therefore necessary to "arbitrate" between the two resulting values. This is an operation that INSEE is trying to make increasingly scientific. Some countries, like the United States, do not perform arbitration, and there are therefore officially two GDPs and a statistical discrepancy between the two.

Another consideration is that, as we saw in Chapter 4, the national accounts attempt to take into account the "underground economy", but the calculations to do this are inevitably tainted with substantial error. In the end, the "real" level of GDP could well differ from the published figure by several percentage points, although probably less than 5% in France. Just as there is no need to react to all the accusations levelled at statisticians, it is equally necessary to recognise the limitations of the national accounts, and in particular, recognise that changes are better known than absolute levels. Thus, as was explained in Chapter 3, international comparisons based on the levels (of GDP or other variables) are to be treated more cautiously than comparisons between variations in national aggregates. Moreover, in all countries, preference is given to changes over levels when there is a choice in the matter. This means that, if an error is discovered in a recent figure in the national accounts, but for technical reasons it is not possible to correct all the past series, national accountants will not correct this recent figure, since it would introduce bias into the changes. Instead, they will maintain the error in absolute level in order to preserve the changes until the following comprehensive revision. National accountants in France give this approach the somewhat bizarre title of "constant error computation".

4. Comprehensive revisions

In addition to the revisions described above, which might be qualified as ordinary, national accountants from time to time make "comprehensive revisions", also called "base changes" or "benchmark years", and these involve much more substantial overhauls of the system. For all OECD countries, a major comprehensive revision has or will occur with the implementation of the new SNA 2008. Already, in mid 2014, this new manual has been implemented in the USA, Australia, Canada, Mexico, Israel and Korea. In Europe, the corresponding manual is the ESA 2010, which has been implemented by law in September 2014 in all EU member states. For an overview of the changes implied by the implementation of SNA 2008/ESA 2010, see Chapter 14.

In addition to this exceptional change in the global framework, there are regular "base changes". In France, INSEE has recently decided to carry out base changes approximately every five years. The penultimate took place in 2011, and the most recent has taken place in May 2014 on the occasion of the introduction of ESA 2010 (see Box 11.3: "France: recent base changes"). A base change involves four distinct operations: (1) the absolute levels for the year known as the "base year" are re-estimated using statistical sources that are not available every year (population or economic census, housing surveys, etc.) and corrected for past errors; (2) changes of a conventional nature are introduced in conformity with the evolution of the international standards for national accounts; (3) the reference year for chained prices is modified; (4) all past data are re-estimated using past changes, corrected as needed for benchmarking on the new level of the base year. The latter operation, known as "retropolation" or "back-calculation", is quite costly in terms of resources.

A base change, and, moreover, a change in the global framework, therefore leads to fairly generalised modification of all the series, often accompanied by changes in classifications. The macroeconomists using these series need a certain amount of time to update their databases and re-estimate their models. The principal difficulty from their point of view is that statistical offices do not always immediately provide the long time-series, because of the difficulty of "retropolation".

Box 11.3. France: recent base changes

In France, the penultimate base change (the so-called base 2005) was introduced in May 2011 and implemented a revised statistical classification of economic activities (NACE rev. 2). There were also modifications in absolute levels, notably of GDP (-0,8%), related to a better evaluation of the activity of households and NPISH, a revised estimation of the Non-Observed Economy (NOE), and the integration of a new framework for structural business statistics (Esane). All the volume series were presented on the 2005 base year (instead of on the 2000 base year in the preceding base). The most recent base change (base 2010) has taken place in May 2014 and has taken into account the new ESA 2010. Significant changes have been be introduced, such as the recording of R&D and military hardware spending as GFCF or a new description of foreign trade (goods for processing, merchanting, see Chapter 14).

---

5. Other datasets related to the national accounts

For reasons of space, we can only describe in this manual the central national accounts framework. However, numerous other datasets gravitate around this framework and use broadly the same definitions as the national accounts, while at the same time adjusting them for their own special purposes. They are known as "satellite accounts". Below is a listing of satellite accounts that exist in France, including the agencies that compile them:

- Regional accounts or GDP by region. Most OECD countries calculate regional accounts. In Europe, these accounts are used by the European Commission as the basis for the allocation of structural funds; in Canada, they are used to allocate VAT.

- Housing accounts – data published by the statistical service of the Ministry of Equipment and Housing.

- Health accounts – statistical service of the Health Ministry.

- Social welfare accounts – statistical service of the Health Ministry.

- National defence accounts – statistical service of the Defence Ministry.

- Education accounts – statistical service of the Education Ministry.

- Research accounts – statistical service of the Research Ministry.

- Environment accounts – IFEN (French Institute for the Environment).

These accounts are not necessarily available every year. In countries other than France, the range of satellite accounts differs from country to country. Most countries compile health, tourism and environment satellite accounts. Some researchers (such as in the US) publish a household satellite account, which includes an estimate for unpaid domestic services produced by household members.

Notes

1. In the methodology used for the French quarterly accounts (see Going further: "The sources and methods used for the French quarterly accounts"), it is the indicators that are adjusted, first for the number of working days and then for seasonal variations. The calibration (see a definition of this term later in the same box) is then applied to each type of indicator: unadjusted, sa, wda-sa. There are thus three sets of quarterly accounts: the unadjusted accounts; the seasonally adjusted accounts; and the wda-sa accounts. The quarterly calibration residuals are the same in the three cases. The wda-sa accounts are the ones appearing in the principal publication and subjected to comment. The unadjusted figures are available on request.

2. The "seasonal adjustment coefficients" are the coefficients applied to the unadjusted quarterly series to eliminate seasonal variations. In the methodology

used for the French quarterly accounts, these coefficients are re-estimated every quarter, leading to slight revisions, even affecting quarters going back as far as the 1970s, although to an almost imperceptible degree.

References

Insee (2014), L'économie française, *www.insee.fr/fr/publications-et-services/sommaire.asp?ref_id=ECOFRA14*.

Insee Databases (2013), Statistical indices and series: Macroeconomic Database: National Accounts *www.bdm.insee.fr/bdm2/index?request_locale=en*.

OECD (2013a), *OECD Economic Outlook*, Vol. 2013/1, OECD Publishing, Paris, doi: *http://dx.doi.org/10.1787/eco_outlook-v2013-1-en*.

OECD (2013b), "OECD Economic Outlook No. 93", OECD Economic Outlook: Statistics and Projections (database), doi: *http://dx.doi.org/10.1787/data-00655-en*.

Key points

- The quarterly national accounts constitute the most important source of data for macroeconomists.

- Most OECD countries publish quarterly growth as the simple growth ratio based on Q/Q-1. Some countries, however, "annualise" this figure. The OECD often uses annualised figures. Another indicator of growth is the year-on-year change which is the variation between the current quarter and the corresponding quarter of the previous year $(Q \div (Q - 4))$.

- Most quarterly accounts are seasonally adjusted ("sa"); in addition, some are working-day adjusted ("wda"). In this case, the sum of the four quarters may not equal to the corresponding annual accounts.

- The national accounts are subject to regular revisions. It is therefore necessary to use the whole of the newly published series and not be content with the latest published figure.

- In France, revisions to the growth rates in the national accounts average around 0.3% in absolute value for the quarterly accounts $(Q \div (Q - 1))$ and 0.5% for the annual accounts $(Y \div (Y - 1))$. The scale of revisions in other countries is slightly different.

Going further

Sources and methods used for the French quarterly accounts

In all countries, the full wealth of annual statistical data is not available on a quarterly basis. For example, there is no substantial quarterly database for company accounts, which are on an annual basis and often are one of the principal sources for the annual accounts. Instead, the quarterly accounts use monthly or quarterly "indicators" whose annual changes are similar to the change of the corresponding figures in the national accounts. For example, France's INSEE publishes monthly production indices, derived from small-scale surveys of a sample of firms. The quarterly accountants use the changes in this indicator to deduce movements in the figures for the quarterly accounts, basing themselves on the pre-existing structure of the annual accounts (i.e. the quarterly accounts are not themselves capable of providing levels, so they rely for this purpose on the annual accounts).

Many countries use indicators in a simple way: they simply use the change of the indicator to extrapolate the quarterly account. In France, and in some other OECD countries, a more sophisticated statistical method has been developed for using indicators to derive quarterly accounts. This is known as "benchmarking" or also "calibration/fitting" ("étalonnage/calage" in French). Calibration consists of estimating an econometric model that relates the annual value of the indicator to the annual series in the national accounts. Once the coefficients of this model have been estimated, the assumption is made that the same coefficients (divided by four) can be applied on a quarterly basis and this provides the basis for the calculation of the so-called "non-fitted" quarterly accounts. The annual sum of these quarterly accounts is not equal to the annual account, since there is no reason why the annual residuals estimated by the econometric method should be zero. Thus, there is an additional step to the calculation, known as "fitting", which consists of interpolating the sum of the annual residuals in a relatively "smooth" manner (one talks of "quarterly smoothing") in order to obtain a series of quarterly residuals which, combined with the non-fitted series, produce a quarterly so-called "fitted" series. These are equal by definition to the annual accounts series (ignoring at this stage the adjustment for the number of working days). Exercise 3 gives a highly simplified example of calibration/fitting. Because of the sophistication of the method used for the French quarterly accounts, some people consider that the quarterly accounts are more in the nature of an econometric model. Fortunately, this is not true. If this were indeed the case, there would be confusion between statistical calculations and modelling. There are in fact no "behavioural" relationships in the calculation of the French quarterly accounts. The calibration/fitting relationship is purely statistical, linking two time series that are intended to measure roughly the same thing.

In France, the principal indicators for the quarterly accounts are as follows: for output, the industrial production indices and the sales indices derived from processing VAT declarations; for consumption, a variety of sources derived from panels of distributors (business surveys by the Banque de France) or from administrative data (for example, new vehicle registrations in the case of car consumption); for exports and imports, the sources are the same as for the annual accounts, and since customs figures are available monthly the calibration is of excellent quality; investment (GFCF) is estimated either from sales sources or from indicators of availability on the domestic market (output + imports – exports). In France, contrary to some other countries that have better surveys, there is no direct source for variations in inventories and they are estimated as a balancing item in the supply-use balance. The price indicators are the major price indices compiled by INSEE (consumer price indices or producer price indices), which are available either monthly or quarterly. In this case, too, the sources are the same as for the annual accounts and calibration is therefore almost perfect.

Values added for institutional sectors are obtained by difference between output and intermediate consumption. Wages and salaries in the market sector are estimated using statistics of hours worked combined with hourly wage rates. Recently, the French quarterly accountants have introduced a direct quarterly indicator of the wage bill paid by general government. Taxes, social contributions and social benefits are for the most part available on a quarterly basis. The gross operating surplus is obtained as the difference between resources and uses, and not from a direct survey of profits, as in some other countries. Relations with the rest of the world are obtained through the balance of payments, which is available monthly. For certain items, no quarterly indicator is available. In this case, quarterly interpolation within the annual series is carried out by an automatic method known as quarterly smoothing; therefore, the quarterly accounts do not provide any real information regarding the within-year pattern of the series. In 2014, INSEE will publish a quarterly net lending/borrowing for the government sector, as a European Directive imposes to all EU member states to publish their quarterly government deficit/surplus

Box 11.4. **Resources of national accounts departments**

Good statistics are the result of a complex process which needs appropriate human resources. For example, INSEE, the French statistical office, employs 5 500 staff. National account departments constitute only a very small part of this: only around 120 are directly employed to process the national accounts in France. In Japan, the staff for national accounts is even less: around 50. This is explained by the fact that national accountants do not directly organize surveys and/or other basic statistics, which are resource-costly. They use statistical or administrative data that are already processed by other statistical units and transform these data into the definitions of the national accounts. Thus, in fact, the total cost for processing national accounts is much more than the cost of the staff directly devoted to its compilation. Still, when compared to the resources devoted to company accounts, those devoted to national accounts appear low. Some may consider that it is already sufficiently costly for statistics. Others consider that, in the context of the increasing importance of national accounts, in particular for the monitoring of public finance, the resources directly devoted to national accounts remain insufficient.

Exercises for Chapter 11

Exercise 1. Quarterly versus Annual Results

Calculate the annual averages for years A and B of the series for quarterly GDP in volume as shown in the following table. Make a graph for the quarters, including points for the annual averages. Illustrate the difference between the change in the annual averages and the within-year economic situations.

A Q1	600.00
A Q2	420.00
A Q3	300.00
A Q4	150.00
B Q1	180.00
B Q2	250.00
B Q3	380.00
B Q4	450.00

Exercise 2. Annualisation, year-on-year changes, statistical carryover

The table below shows the quarterly series for French GDP in volume for the years 2010, 2011 and 2012. Question 1: calculate the annual GDP for the years 2010 and 2011. Question 2: show the quarterly absolute levels in 2010 "at annual level". Question 3: calculate the 2010 annual average on the basis of these figures and find the GDP for 2010. Question 4: calculate the annual average change between 2010 and 2011. Question 5: calculate the quarterly change between Q3 2012 and Q2 2012. Question 6: Express this change at "annualised rate". Question 7: calculate the year-on-year change for Q3 2012. Question 8: calculate the statistical carryover in Q3 2012. Comment on all these results.

Table 11.4. **GDP at constant 2005 prices**
Volumes chained at previous year's prices

	2010	2011	2012
Q1	439.22	451.30	453.03
Q2	441.82	451.04	451.50
Q3	444.09	452.11	452.21
Q4	446.33	452.91	

Source: Insee.

Exercise 3. Calibration/fitting: the French method for calculating the quarterly accounts

This exercise consists of breaking down the stages of the "calibration/ fitting" method used for the French quarterly accounts and described in the box "The sources and methods used for the French quarterly accounts". Note that the statistical methods used in this exercise are ultra-simplified compared with the methods used by INSEE or other countries that also use this type of methods, but the exercise at least makes it possible to understand the underlying principles.

The tables below show a series for the quarterly indicator (QI) and the corresponding annual item in the national accounts (AA). Stage 1: calculate annual averages AI for the indicator series. Stage 2: draw a graph showing the point cloud for the abscissa AI and the ordinate AA. Verify that the straight-line regression equation $AA = a \times AI + b$ is an acceptable approximation. Stage 3: estimate, by the least squares method, the parameters a and b for the model $AA = a \times Ai + b$. Stage 4: calculate the non-fitted quarterly series (QA) by applying the same model to the quarterly absolute figure $QA = \frac{a}{4} \times QI + \frac{b}{4}$ and calculate the annual residuals. Stage 5: deduce from this the quarterly residuals (by simply dividing by 4). Stage 6: calculate the calibrated/fitted QA series. This constitutes the final quarterly accounts series.

Quarterly indicator QI (over five years)

	Y1	Y2	Y3	Y4	Y5
Q1	105.2	103.9	111.5	117.6	116.3
Q2	106.7	105.9	117.2	118.1	115.8
Q3	104.3	107.8	117.3	119.1	114.2
Q4	104.2	109.6	117.5	117.4	112.0

Annual accounts series AA (over the same five years)

Y1	Y2	Y3	Y4	Y5
6658.1	6813.2	7435.4	7455.9	7302.4

The solutions to these exercises are available at:
http://dx.doi.org/10.1787/9789264214637-29-en

Chapter 12

The national income and product accounts of the United States

This chapter focuses on the United States and its National Income and Product Accounts, otherwise known as NIPA. It first presents the history of NIPAs from the 1930s through to today. It looks at the NIPA summary account tables, and at other NIPA tables, and it explains how NIPAs are disseminated. Next, it considers the other sets of national, industry, regional, and international accounts produced by the Bureau of Economic Analysis (BEA) and integrated with the NIPAs, as well as programmes that provide source data used for the preparation of the NIPAs. Finally, the chapter discusses the importance of the BEA's advance quarterly GDP estimate and explains the methodology used to prepare it.

During the global economic recession, the US economy as measured by real GDP declined 4.3 percent from its peak in the fourth quarter of 2007 to its trough in the second quarter of 2009. Subsequently, real GDP began to grow again. From the second quarter of 2009 through the fourth quarter of 2013, real GDP growth averaged 2.4% per quarter (at an annual rate), and in the last quarter of 2013, real GDP reached a level that was 6.5% higher than its level six years earlier, before the recession began.

Estimates presented in this chapter reflect the official GDP estimates available on January 31, 2014. For a definition of "annual rates", see Chapter 11.

Because real GDP increased at annual rates of 4.1% in the third quarter and 3.2% in the fourth quarter, at the end of 2013 forecasters were generally optimistic about the outlook for growth in 2014.

In its forecast published in the November 2013 *OECD Economic Outlook*, the OECD observed that fiscal contraction, low consumer and business confidence had constrained growth in 2013, but it assumed that those constraints would likely diminish during 2014 (OECD, 2013). Debt deleveraging and increases in asset prices were expected to boost growth in consumption and investment and contribute to gradual labour market recovery. These factors were reflected in the OECD forecasts of 2.9% US real GDP growth for 2014 and 3.4% for 2015. OECD forecast of real GDP growth for the four quarters ending in the fourth quarter of 2014 was 3.2%, and for the four quarters ending in the fourth quarter of 2015 was 3.5%.

This November 2013 OECD forecast was slightly more optimistic than the median forecast from a survey of US forecasters published in December 2013. In the United States, the National Association for Business Economics (NABE) has regularly published projections of economic activity since 1965 based on projections from a survey of a panel of expert forecasters.[1] According to the survey, released on December 9, 2013, annual growth for 2014 was projected to be 2.5%, and growth for the four quarters ending in the fourth quarter of 2014 was projected to be 2.8% (NABE, 2013).

Thus, in late 2013 many forecasters, both at the OECD and in the United States, predicted that the US economy will continue to grow over the next years. Forecasts are, of course, prone to error. Reading this manual after 2015, the reader will be in a good position to judge whether the forecasts were right. In any case, all these projections are primarily based on the GDP and related measures from the US national income and product accounts, or NIPAs, which are the US non-financial national accounts. The NIPAs are used by the executive and the legislative branches of government to prepare budget estimates and projections, by the central bank (the Federal Reserve Board) to set interest and exchange rates, by international organisations and by the private sector to track and develop financial and investment strategies.

1. Background

The history of the NIPAs can be traced to the Great Depression of the 1930s, which highlighted the lack of comprehensive national economic data. To address this need, the Department of Commerce commissioned future Nobel laureate Simon Kuznets of the National Bureau of Economic Research (NBER) to develop a set of national income statistics. Kuznets co-ordinated the work of researchers at the NBER and a small staff of economists within the Commerce Department's Bureau of Foreign and Domestic Commerce. The first set of estimates was presented in a report to Congress in 1934, *National Income, 1929-32*, and beginning in 1935 the Bureau published annual updates to these series. By the late 1930s estimates were expanded to include income by state and a monthly income series.

To support World War II planning efforts, annual estimates of gross national product (GNP) by final expenditures were introduced in 1942, complementing the estimates of national income. By 1943, the main elements had been compiled for a set of accounts consisting of a consolidated production account at current and constant prices, sector income and outlay accounts, and a consolidated saving-investment account. These accounts were used for the analysis of wartime production goals and the development of anti-inflation policies. The NIPAs were formally introduced by the Office of Business Economics (OBE), an office created by the Commerce Department in 1945, with the publication of *National Income Supplement to the Survey of Current Business, 1947*.

Over the next three decades, the OBE extended the US accounts and improved their accuracy through the development of official input-output tables, capital stock estimates, more detailed and timely state and local personal income estimates, and improved measures of prices and inflation-adjusted (real) output. On the other hand, during that period the US largely chose not to adopt the emerging international standards (*System of National Accounts 1953* and *SNA 1968* – see Chapter 14) and retained the accounting structure that had been introduced in 1947.

In the 1980s, the Bureau of Economic Analysis (BEA), which was formed in 1972 as the successor agency to OBE, expanded the information on international trade in services in the International Transactions Accounts and the NIPAs. To improve the measurement of real output, BEA worked with the IBM Corporation to develop quality adjusted price and output measures for computers. BEA also dealt with rising concerns about the underground economy's impact on US economic statistics by revamping how it adjusted tax-return information used to prepare the NIPAs.

BEA actively participated in the 1993 revision of the SNA and announced that it planned to move toward the SNA.[2] Since the early 1990s, BEA has made many changes that have brought the NIPA measures of GDP, investment, and saving more closely in line with SNA 1993, and then SNA 2008. In 1991 BEA recognised GDP as the featured measure of US output, and in 1996 it adopted a chain-type Fisher index formula for measuring changes in real GDP and prices. In 1999 BEA recognised investment in software. In 2003, BEA adopted the reference rate approach for measuring the implicit financial services that borrowers and depositors receive from banks and renamed or revised the summary accounts to improve conformity with the SNA classification of transactions. In addition, BEA expanded the NIPA framework, as expressed in a series of summary accounts, from five to seven accounts, and made several changes to sector definitions to improve consistency with the SNA, as well as with BEA input-output (IO) accounts, the Federal Reserve Board (FRB) financial accounts, and the Bureau of Labour Statistics (BLS) productivity statistics. BEA also began to present industry estimates on the basis of the new North American industry classification system (NAICS), adopted in 1997 by the United States, Canada and Mexico.

Although these changes to the NIPAs have increased the consistency of both the NIPAs and the SNA, a few differences remain. As BEA continues to work toward improving consistency with the SNA, most of these differences are likely to eventually go away, though in a few cases special presentations of the accounts will be retained in order to address the needs of the US users. An overview of these differences is provided at the end of this chapter in section "Going further: Differences between the NIPAs and SNA". Several differences occur only in terminology and not in substance. For example, the NIPA name for household final consumption expenditures is Personal Consumption Expenditures (PCEs).

Most of the US economic accounts are prepared by BEA, a statistical agency located in the Department of Commerce. In addition to the NIPAs, BEA prepares estimates of the US International Transactions Accounts (ITAs), which provide US transactions and balances with the rest of the world and include current, capital and financial accounts, and the international investment position. The Federal Reserve Board (FRB) prepares the Financial

Accounts of the United States (FAUS), formerly known as the flow of funds accounts, which provide capital accounts, financial accounts, and balance sheets for sectors. BEA and FRB jointly prepare the Integrated Macroeconomic Accounts (IMAs), which combine NIPA, financial accounts, and balance sheet data in an SNA-style presentation. Productivity estimates are prepared by the BLS, a statistical agency located in the Department of Labour. Although both the financial accounts and the productivity estimates are prepared separately from the NIPAs, there is close co-ordination between BEA and the other agencies.

BEA describes its mission as providing timely, relevant and accurate economic accounts data in an objective and cost-effective manner. It also works to promote a better understanding of the US economy in the publication of its accounts.[3]

Although the NIPAs are BEA's main project, BEA has extended its estimates to cover a wide range of economic activities. In addition to the NIPAs, BEA now prepares national, regional, industry and international accounts, providing information on such key issues as economic growth, regional economic development, inter-industry relationships and the US position in the global economy.

To produce these programmes, BEA collects data from other statistical agencies as well as from businesses. These data come from over 400 surveys and other data collections sponsored by other federal statistical agencies, from aggregate tax data, administrative and regulatory sources, and private trade sources. BEA also conducts its own surveys, mostly on direct investment and on international trade in services.

To ensure that the accounts continue to provide appropriate measures for a changing economy, BEA staff engages in research and collaborates with researchers in other government agencies. BEA also participates in research conferences and workshops through organisations such as of the Conference on Research in Income and Wealth and the International Association for Research in Income and Wealth. BEA obtains more direct input through a BEA Advisory Committee and through participation with the Census Bureau and BLS in the Federal Economic Statistics Advisory Committee. Both committees, which consist of economists and statisticians from academia and business, meet regularly to provide advice and recommendations on agency policy.

2. NIPA Tables

The NIPAs consist of the NIPA summary accounts (see Tables 12.1 and 12.2) and other NIPA tables. The summary accounts provide a simplified presentation of the most important aggregates in the NIPAs and illustrate the accounting relationships among the accounts. The other nearly 300 regularly published NIPA tables provide monthly, quarterly and annual detailed estimates, including key measures not presented in the summary accounts. NIPA estimates are regularly published on BEA website and in the *Survey of Current Business*; supplemental estimates, including underlying detail, are also made available on BEA website.[4] As with most countries, the frequency, timeliness, coverage and presentation of the US national accounts largely reflect the availability of reliable source data and the needs of data users.

Table 12.1. **Summary national income and product accounts, 2012**

Billions of US dollars, current prices

Account 1. Domestic Income and Product Account

Line			Line		
1	Compensation of employees, paid	8 620.0	15	Personal consumption expenditures (3-3)	11 149.6
2	Wages and salaries	6 935.1	16	Goods	3 769.7
3	Domestic (3-12)	6 920.5	17	Durable goods	1 202.7
4	Rest of the world (5-11)	14.6	18	Nondurable goods	2 567.0
5	Supplements to wages and salaries (3-14)	1 684.9	19	Services	7 379.9
6	Taxes on production and imports (4-15)	1 122.9	20	Gross private domestic investment	2 475.2
7	Less: Subsidies (4-8)	57.3	21	Fixed investment (6-2)	2 409.1
8	Net operating surplus	4 033.2	22	Non-residential	1 970.0
9	Private enterprises (2-19)	4 060.9	23	Structures	437.3
10	Current surplus of government enterprises (4-25)	-27.7	24	Equipment	907.6
11	Consumption of fixed capital (6-14)	2 542.9	25	Intellectual property products	625
			26	Residential	439.2
12	**Gross domestic income**	**16 261.6**	27	Change in private inventories (6-4)	66.1
			28	Net exports of goods and services	-547.2
13	Statistical discrepancy (6-20)	-17	29	Exports (5-1)	2 195.9
			30	Imports (5-9)	2 743.1
			31	Government consumption expenditures and gross investment (4-1 plus 6-3)	3 167.0
			32	Federal	1 295.7
			33	National defense	817.1
			34	Nondefense	478.6
			35	State and local	1 871.3
14	**Gross domestic product**	**16 244.6**	**36**	**Gross domestic product**	**16 244.6**

Account 2. Private Enterprise Income Account

Line			Line		
1	Income payments on assets	2 654.2	19	Net operating surplus, private enterprises (1-9)	4 060.90
2	Interest and miscellaneous payments (2-21 and 3-20 and 4-20 and 5-13)	2 407.2	20	Income receipts on assets	2 475.80
3	Dividend payments to the rest of the world (5-14)	141.1	21	Interest (2-2 and 3-4 and 4-7 and 5-5)	1 809.90
4	Reinvested earnings on foreign direct investment in the United States (5-15)	105.9	22	Dividend receipts from the rest of the world (5-6)	297.9

Table 12.1. **Summary national income and product accounts, 2012** (cont.)

Billions of US dollars, current prices

5	Business current transfer payments (net)	106.9	23	Reinvested earnings on US direct investment abroad (5-7)	368.1
6	To persons (net) (3-24)	41.4			
7	To government (net) (4-23)	70.6			
8	To the rest of the world (net) (5-19)	-5.1			
9	Proprietors' income with inventory valuation and capital consumption adjustments (3-17)	1 224.9			
10	Rental income of persons with capital consumption adjustment (3-18)	541.2			
11	Corporate profits with inventory valuation and capital consumption adjustments	2 009.5			
12	Taxes on corporate income	434.8			
13	To government (4-16)	402.4			
14	To the rest of the world (5-19)	32.4			
15	Profits after tax with inventory valuation and capital consumption adjustments	1 574.7			
16	Net dividends (3-21 plus 4-21)	770.3			
17	Undistributed corporate profits with inventory valuation and capital consumption adjustments (6-12)	804.3			
18	**Uses of private enterprises income**	**6 536.7**	**24**	**Sources of private enterprises income**	**6 536.70**

Account 3. Personal Income and Outlay Account

Line			Line		
1	Personal current taxes (4-14)	1 498.0	10	Compensation of employees, received	8 611.6
2	Personal outlays	11 558.4	11	Wage and salary disbursements	6 926.8
3	Personal consumption expenditures (1-15)	11 149.6	12	Domestic (1-3)	6 920.5
4	Personal interest payments (2-21 and 3-20 and 4-20 and 5-13)	248.4	13	Rest of the world (5-3)	6.3
5	Personal current transfer payments	160.4	14	Supplements to wages and salaries (1-5)	1 684.9
6	To government (4-24)	88.5	15	Employer contributions for employee pension and insurance funds	1 170.6
7	To the rest of the world (net) (5-17)	71.9	16	Employer contributions for government social insurance	514.3
8	Personal saving (6-11)	687.4	17	Proprietors' income with inventory valuation and capital consumption adjustments (2-9)	1 224.9
			18	Rental income of persons with capital consumption adjustment (2-10)	541.2
			19	Personal income receipts on assets	1 958.5
			20	Personal interest income (2-2 plus 3-4 plus 4-7 plus 5-5 less 2-21 less 4-20 less 5-13)	1 211.6
			21	Personal dividend income (2-16 less 4-21)	746.9
			22	Personal current transfer receipts	2 358.3
			23	Government social benefits (4-4)	2 316.8
			24	From business (net) (2-6)	41.4
			25	Less: Contributions for government social insurance, domestic (4-18)	950.7
9	**Personal taxes, outlays and saving**	**13 743.8**	**26**	**Personal income**	**13 743.8**

Table 12.1. **Summary national income and product accounts, 2012** (*cont.*)

Billions of US dollars, current prices

Account 4. Government Receipts and Expenditures Account

Line			Line		
1	Consumption expenditures (1-31)	2 548.0	13	Current tax receipts	3 041.2
2	Current transfer payments	2 384.7	14	Personal current taxes (3-1)	1 498.0
3	Government social benefits	2 334.8	15	Taxes on production and imports (1-6)	1 122.9
4	To persons (3-23)	2 316.8	16	Taxes on corporate income (2-13)	402.4
5	To the rest of the world (5-18)	18	17	Taxes from the rest of the world (5-18)	17.8
6	Other current transfer payments to the rest of the world (net) (5-18)	49.9	18	Contributions for government social insurance (3-25 and 5-18)	955.3
7	Interest payments (2-21 and 3-20 and 4-20 and 5-13)	631.6	19	Income receipts on assets	131.4
8	Subsidies (1-7)	57.3	20	Interest and miscellaneous receipts (2-2 and 3-4 and 4-7 and 5-5)	107.9
9	Net government saving (6-13)	-1 362.3	21	Dividends (2-16 less 3-21)	23.4
10	Federal	-1 109.7	22	Current transfer receipts	159.1
11	State and local	-252.7	23	From business (net) (2-7)	70.6
			24	From persons (3-6)	88.5
			25	Current surplus of government enterprises (1-10)	-27.7
12	**Government current expenditures and saving**	**4 259.2**	**26**	**Government current receipts**	**4 259.2**

Account 5. Foreign transaction current account

Line			Line		
1	Exports of goods and services (1-29)	2 195.9	9	Imports of goods and services (1-30)	2 743.1
2	Income receipts from the rest of the world	818.6	10	Income payments to the rest of the world	565.7
3	Wage and salary receipts (3-13)	6.3	11	Wage and salary payments (1-4)	14.6
4	Income receipts on assets	812.3	12	Income payments on assets	551.1
5	Interest (2-21 and 3-20 and 4-20)	146.3	13	Interest (2-2 and 3-4 and 4-7)	304.1
6	Dividends (2-22)	297.9	14	Dividends (2-3)	141.1
7	Reinvested earnings on US direct investment abroad (2-23)	368.1	15	Reinvested earnings on foreign direct investment in the United States (2-4)	105.9
			16	Current taxes and transfer payments to the rest of the world (net)	144.6
			17	From persons (net)(3-7)	71.9
			18	From government (net) (3-25 plus 4-5 plus 4-6 less 4-17 less 4-18)	45.4
			19	From business (net) (2-8 plus 2-14)	27.3
			20	Balance on current account, national income and product accounts (7-1)	-439
8	**Current receipts from the rest of the world**	**3 014.5**	**21**	**Current payments to the rest of the world and balance on current account**	**3 014.5**

Account 6. Domestic Capital Account

Line			Line		
1	Gross domestic investment	3 094.2	10	Net saving	129.4
2	Private fixed investment (1-21)	2 409.1	11	Personal saving (3-8)	687.4
3	Government fixed investment (1-31)	619	12	Undistributed corporate profits with inventory valuation and capital consumption adjustments (2-17)	804.3
4	Change in private inventories (1-27)	66.1	13	Net government saving (4-9)	-1 362.3

Table 12.1. **Summary national income and product accounts, 2012** (cont.)

Billions of US dollars, current prices

5	Capital account transactions (net)	-6.6	14	Plus: Consumption of fixed capital (1-11)	2 542.9
6	Transfer payments for catastrophic losses (7-3)	7.7	15	Private	2 049.3
7	Other capital account transactions (7-4)	-14.2	16	Government	493.6
8	Net lending or net borrowing (-), national income and product accounts (7-5)	-432.4	17	General government	434.2
			18	Government enterprises	59.4
			19	Equals: Gross saving	2 672.2
			20	Statistical discrepancy (1-13)	-17
9	**Gross domestic investment, capital accounts transactions and net lending**	**2 655.2**	21	**Gross saving and statistical discrepancy**	**2 655.2**

Account 7. Foreign Transactions Capital Account

Line			Line		
			2	Capital account transactions (net)	-6.6
			3	Transfer payments for catastrophic losses (6-6)	7.7
			4	Other capital account transactions (6-7)	-14.2
			5	Net lending or net borrowing (-), national income and product accounts (6-8)	-432.4
1	**Balance on current account, national income and product accounts (5-20)**	**-439**	6	**Capital account transactions (net) and net lending, national income and product accounts**	**-439**

The seven NIPA summary accounts presented above cover the transactions that are grouped in the SNA as the production account, the distribution and use of income accounts, and the capital accounts. Relative to the SNA (see Table 12.2), the NIPA domestic income and product account (Summary account 1) provides estimates of GDP by final expenditure component and is similar to the SNA production account for the total economy. NIPA Summary Account 1 also provides information about the income earned in the production of GDP; in the SNA, these items are included in the generation of income account. The NIPA personal income and outlay account (Summary account 3) and the government current receipts and expenditures account (Summary Account 4), and part of the private enterprise income account (Summary account 2) roughly correspond to the remaining SNA distribution and use of income accounts for the domestic sectors (Summary account 2 actually corresponds most closely to the SNA entrepreneurial income account). The NIPA domestic capital account (Summary account 6) corresponds to the SNA capital account for the total economy. Both the NIPAs and SNA include a current account and a capital account for the rest-of-the world sector (Summary accounts 5 and 7). The major entries in the NIPA summary accounts are described below for each account.[5]

Table 12.2. **NIPA Summary accounts**

Transactions		Domestic Accounts		Rest of the World
		Economic Sectors		
	Business	Government	Personal	
Production		Domestic income and product (Summary Account 1)		Foreign transactions current account
Income and outlay	Private enterprise income (Summary Account 2)	Government current receipts and expenditures (Summary Account 4)	Personal income and outlay (Summary Account 3)	(Summary Account 5)
Saving and investment		Domestic capital account (Summary Account 6)		Foreign transactions capital account (Summary Account 7)

"1-36" means line 36 of Summary Account 1.

Account 1, the domestic income and product account, shows the consolidated production of all sectors of the economy as the sum of goods and services sold to final users on the right side and the income generated by that production on the left side. GDP, (1-36) the featured measure of US output, is the market value of the goods and services produced by labour and property located in the United States. GDP is measured by the sum of goods and services produced in the US and sold to final users (the "expenditure" or "final demand" approach). The NIPAs use "Gross domestic income" (GDI) (1-12) to refer to the measure of GDP based on the income approach, that is, the costs incurred and the incomes earned in the production of GDP.[6] Although, in theory, GDP should equal GDI, in practice they differ because their components are estimated using largely independent and less-than-perfect source data. In the US accounts, this difference, the "statistical discrepancy," is not allocated among various GDP or GDI components, but is recorded as an "income" component. The section "Going further: Statistical Discrepancies in the NIPAs", provides additional information.

Account 2, the private enterprise income account, provides additional information on the sources and uses of income by private enterprises, which explains for most of the output in the US economy. This account shows sources of private enterprise income (2-24) on the right side of the account and uses of private enterprise income (2-18) on the left side. It can be thought of as a consolidation of the accounts for non-financial corporations, financial corporations, and unincorporated businesses, including owner-occupied housing. Public (government) enterprises are not included in this account, however, because complete estimates on sources and uses of income of public quasi-corporations are not currently available. The IMAs present separate, SNA-style accounts for non-financial corporations, financial corporations, and unincorporated businesses.

Accounts 3, 4 and 5 show the receipts and expenditures of the other major sectors of the US economy. Account 3 is the personal income and outlay account and covers the NIPA personal sector, which is made up of households and non-profit institutions serving households. It shows "personal income" (3-26) on the right side and the disposition of this income in terms of personal taxes, outlays and saving on the left side. Account 4, the government receipts and expenditures account, shows government current receipts (4-27) on the right side and government current expenditures and net saving (4-13) on the left side. Account 5, the foreign transactions current account, shows current payments to the rest of the world and balance on current account (5-21) on the right side, and current receipts from the rest of the world and balance (5-8) on the left.

Account 6 is the domestic capital account and provides information on the saving and investment of the domestic sectors of the economy. Account 7 is the foreign transactions capital account and provides information on capital transactions with the rest of the world. Account 6 shows the gross saving and the statistical discrepancy (6-20) on the right side and gross domestic investment, capital account transactions and net lending (6-7) on the left side. Net lending or net borrowing (–), national income and product accounts (6-8) is equal to the balance on current account (5-20) less capital account transactions (6-5). Account 7 shows on the right side the sum of two entries from Account 6, capital account transactions to the rest of the world (net) and net lending or net borrowing (–), national income and product accounts. Capital account transactions consist of capital transfers and acquisition less disposals of non-produced assets. The left side shows the balance on current account, national income and product accounts (7-1).

All of the NIPA tables, with the most recent estimates, are available on the BEA website. There are about 100 tables with monthly or quarterly estimates. The remaining tables either show annual estimates of additional detail than is shown quarterly, data on special topics, such as employment and hours worked, or comparisons of source data with NIPA aggregates. Several NIPA tables feature supplemental measures that have no counterparts in the seven NIPA summary accounts. Information about these measures, which also are shown in BEA news releases, is provided in Box 12.1.

Box 12.1. **Featured Measures of NIPA Tables**

Gross domestic purchases is the market value of goods and services purchased by US residents, regardless of where those goods and services were produced. It is GDP minus net exports of goods and services; equivalently, it is the sum of PCE, gross private domestic investment and government consumption expenditures and gross investment. The SNA refers to this aggregate as domestic final expenditures. BEA uses gross domestic purchases for its featured measure of price change because it excludes prices paid by foreigners for US exports and includes prices of imports. *Final sales to domestic purchasers* is gross domestic purchases minus the change in private inventories. Some analysts refer to this measure as **"domestic demand"** or **"final domestic demand"**. *Final sales of domestic product* is GDP *minus* change in private inventories; equivalently, it is the sum of PCE, gross private fixed investment, government consumption expenditures and gross investment, and net exports of goods and services. Gross national product is the market value of the goods and services produced by labour and property supplied by US residents. In the SNA, this measure is called gross national income (GNI). In the NIPAs, GNI is based on the income approach and GNP is based on the expenditure approach, so they differ by the statistical discrepancy. *Personal saving as a percentage of disposable personal income*, frequently referred to as **"the personal saving rate"**, is the ratio of personal saving to disposable personal income. *Gross saving as a percentage of gross national income*, sometimes referred to as **"the national saving rate"**, is calculated as the ratio of gross saving (the sum of gross private saving and gross government saving) to GNI.

3. Dissemination of NIPAs

Each month, BEA releases quarterly estimates of most NIPA tables and monthly estimates of personal income and outlays. The quarterly GDP estimates are released through a news release on the following schedule: "advance" estimates are released near the end of the first month after the end of the quarter; as more detailed and more comprehensive data become available, "second" and "third" estimates are released near the end of the second and third months, respectively.[7] The three sets of quarterly GDP estimates – the advance, second and third – are referred to by BEA as the "current" estimates.[8]

For the advance release, estimates of GNI, GDI, national income, net operating surplus, corporate profits and net interest payments are not prepared. Except for fourth-quarter estimates, the initial estimates for these series are released with the second GDP estimates, and the revised estimates are released with the third GDP estimates. For the fourth quarter, these estimates are released only with the third GDP estimates. The monthly personal income and outlays estimates are released in another news release, usually one business day following the release of the quarterly estimates and one month after the end of the reference month.

When the quarterly GDP are released, estimates for preceding quarters or months are generally not revised except as follows. At the time of the release of the second quarterly GDP estimate, revisions to the preceding quarter (and corresponding months) are made to private wages and salaries and related income components to reflect newly available comprehensive source data on wages and salaries. (See Section 5: "Compilation of quarterly gross domestic product".) Revisions to monthly personal income and outlays are made to the months of the same quarters that are revised in the quarterly GDP estimates. Each July, an annual NIPA revision is usually carried out, and revisions are made to the months and quarters of at least the three most recent years. These revisions are timed to incorporate newly available major annual source data. Lastly, at about five-year intervals, comprehensive revisions are carried out. These revisions incorporate the benchmark I-O (Input-Output) accounts that are prepared at five-year intervals, as well as conceptual changes (such as updates to SNA), other improvements in statistical methodology, and changes in the tables that present the estimates. The conceptual changes to the accounts are generally carried back as far as necessary and feasible, in some cases leading to revisions back to 1929.

News releases are prepared for the quarterly GDP and monthly personal income and outlays releases. At 8:30 in the morning of each release date, the news release is posted on BEA website and printed copies are given to representatives of the media at the Commerce Department's main office in Washington, DC. For GDP, the release is accompanied by a technical note, which provides information about BEA assumptions for key missing source data and provides information about methodologies used to prepare the newly released estimates.

Later that same morning and in the following several days, additional information is posted on BEA website. The posting usually starts with updating the 106 NIPA tables that will appear in the next issue of the *Survey of Current Business*. The tables are available as "interactive tables" that allow the user to specify options such as frequency and date ranges, as well as in several other formats, such as "pdf." Each month's *Survey* also includes an article, "GDP and the Economy," which provides an analysis of the most recent estimates.

The remaining NIPA tables mostly provide annual estimates and usually are published each year in the August issue of the *Survey* at the time of an annual or comprehensive NIPA revision.

In addition, after each monthly estimate, BEA posts to its website what it calls "supplemental estimates". These estimates include monthly and quarterly detail not included in the NIPA tables, additional information on BEA assumptions for missing source data in the latest advance GDP estimates, and SNA-related NIPA data. The additional (underlying) NIPA detail consists primarily of estimates used by BEA to prepare the monthly and quarterly NIPA estimates that BEA considers less reliable as individual series. The information on "Key source data and assumptions" for the first (advance) estimate of each quarter provides the key source data and assumptions used by BEA in preparing the quarterly estimates of GDP and its major expenditure components, including information on more monthly source data series than are provided in the technical note.

The information on SNA-related estimates consists of two entries. The first is "Estimates prepared by BEA for international comparisons based on the System of National Accounts". These estimates are SNA-based estimates prepared annually, usually several weeks after the release of revised annual NIPA data in late July. The estimates are prepared in response to a questionnaire used by the OECD and are slightly different from the official NIPA estimates published by BEA to improve comparability with the accounts of other countries. The second set of SNA-related estimates appears as "Gross Domestic Product by final expenditure category (International Style)". These tables present quarterly NIPA final expenditure data in a format that is more consistent with accounts and presentations used by the OECD. The estimates show final consumption expenditures (government and personal consumption expenditures) and gross domestic investment (government gross investment and gross private domestic investment).

The IMAs are posted on BEA website once each quarter, a few days after the FRB releases the FAUS. The FRB also posts the IMAs on its own website, *www.federalreserve.gov*.

4. Other NIPA-related programmes

In addition to the NIPAs, BEA produces other sets of national, industry, regional, and international accounts that are integrated with the NIPAs, as well as programmes that provide source data used for the preparation of the NIPAs. The following discussion, summarised in Figure 12.1, covers the programmes that produce these estimates, which are the ITAs, the benchmark I-O accounts, fixed assets and the annual industry accounts programme. Detailed information on each of the programmes is available on BEA website.

Figure 12.1. **Integration of US national accounts**

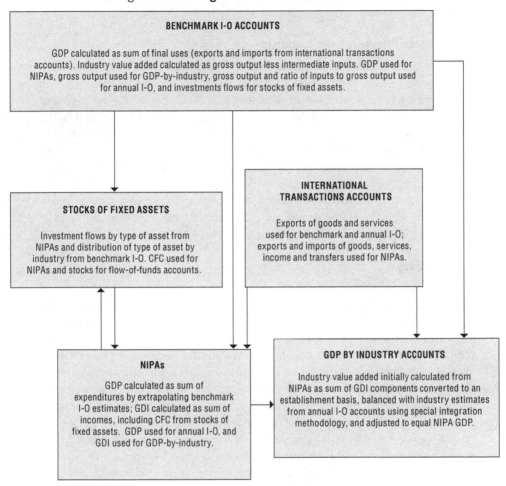

International transactions accounts (ITA)

The ITAs provide monthly estimates of international trade in goods and services (prepared jointly by BEA and the Census Bureau) and quarterly and annual estimates of the US international transactions accounts. The ITAs are revised annually, with the revised estimates published in the July issue of the *Survey*. The current account, which measures receipts and payments on goods, services, income, and unilateral current transfers, provides the basis for all foreign transactions in the NIPAs as well as in the benchmark and annual I-O accounts. NIPA Table 4.3 presents an annual reconciliation of differences between the two accounts. Quarterly, an abbreviated reconciliation is published in the *Survey* in Appendix A, under "Additional Information About the NIPA Estimates".

Benchmark input-output accounts

The SNA includes an integrated set of supply-and-use tables that balance industry output for each commodity with its final uses (see Chapter 10). BEA benchmark I-O accounts provide detailed "make" (supply) and "use" tables at five-year intervals corresponding with the economic census. In contrast to the SNA, which recommends the valuation of resources at basic prices and the valuation of uses at market prices, in BEA accounts both resources and uses are valued at market prices. The make and use tables provide benchmark estimates of gross output and intermediate inputs that are consistent with the annual industry accounts and benchmark estimates of final uses that are consistent with the NIPAs. Benchmark I-O accounts for 2002 were released in 2007 and the accounts for 2007 were released in 2013.

Fixed assets

BEA prepares annual estimates of the net stocks of equipment, of structures, and of intellectual property products owned by business and by government.[9] The estimates are presented at current cost and as real estimates, expressed both as chain-type quantity indexes and chained dollars. The accounts include estimates of depreciation (that is, consumption of fixed capital) and investment, and also include estimates of historical-cost private net stocks and depreciation for making comparisons with business accounts. Detailed estimates are provided for net stocks, depreciation, and investment by industry and by asset type. The estimates of net stocks and depreciation are derived using the perpetual inventory method, which is based on investment flows and a geometric depreciation formula; the gross investment flows used for these calculations are from the NIPAs. The depreciation estimates are used for the NIPA estimates of consumption of fixed capital, which are used to derive net income, saving, and investment.

Annual industry accounts

In 2004, BEA introduced integrated annual industry accounts, which consist of GDP-by-industry and annual I-O accounts. The integration provides detailed, consistent information on the structure of the US economy, including the annual contributions of private industries and government to GDP and the annual flow of goods and services used in the production processes of industries and going to the final uses that comprise GDP.[10] It should be noted that when BEA annual industry accounts are balanced, they do not provide an independent measure of GDP; they use the NIPA GDP measure that is based on the expenditure approach. Except in benchmark years, when measures of output and final demand are fully reconciled in the benchmark I-O accounts, BEA does not use the production approach to determine GDP because the source data on intermediate inputs are not available on a timely basis and are less reliable than the source data used for the expenditure approach. As in the benchmark I-O accounts, BEA estimates of value added by industry are calculated at market prices rather than at basic prices, as called for by the SNA. The different definitions of value added by industry are discussed in the section, "Going further: Alternative methods of valuation of output and value added: Basic Prices and Market Prices".

5. Compilation of quarterly gross domestic product

As reported in the previous section, BEA prepares a series of current estimates of GDP for each quarter. The first (advance) estimate is published at the end of the first month after the quarter ends, the second estimate is published at the end of the second month, and the third estimate is published at the end of the third month. Additional estimates of each quarter are published as part of an annual revision (usually at the end of each July) or a comprehensive revision (every five years).

Although the advance quarterly GDP estimate is based on a combination of preliminary survey results and BEA projections of missing months of survey data, both of which are revised in subsequent GDP estimates, it is the advance estimate that attracts the most attention by users. This focus reflects the timeliness of the advance estimates (one of the most timely of OECD countries), the transparency of the processes used by BEA to prepare the estimates and their history of reliability. For example, a key to the transparency of the quarterly GDP estimates is the public availability of the source data and estimating procedures used by BEA to prepare these estimates. BEA provides this transparency with the following: 1) annual publication in the *Survey* of the source data and estimating methods for the major NIPA components; 2) public announcement, preferably in advance, of any changes of source data or estimating methods, including special adjustments; 3) publication of BEA assumptions for missing source data for key indicator series at the time of the release of the advance estimate; and 4) publication of the underlying detail used to prepare the current quarterly GDP estimates.

As for the reliability of the advance and two other current quarterly GDP estimates, these estimates have a long history of reliability, defined as whether the GDP estimates present a consistent, general picture of the economy. This history, which is based on published studies of reliability, have found that the advance estimates have consistently indicated whether growth is positive or negative, accelerating or decelerating, high or low relative to the trend and where the economy is in relation to the business cycle.[11] A 2011 study shows that the quarterly estimates correctly indicate the direction of change of real GDP 97% of the time, its acceleration or deceleration 72% of the time, and correctly indicate whether real GDP growth is above, near or below trend growth more than 80% of the time. Other results of these studies are summarised in a special section of the advance quarterly GDP news release as shown in the section below, "Revisions to GDP".

Revisions to GDP

In the news release for the advance quarterly GDP estimates, BEA provides summary information on revisions by comparing successive estimates of current-dollar and real GDP. Based on data for 1983-2010, from the advance estimate to the preliminary estimate (one month later), the average revision to real GDP without regard to sign is 0.5 percentage point in terms of annual rate; from the advance estimate to the third estimate (two months later), it is 0.7 percentage point, and from the advance estimate to the latest estimate, it is 1.3 percentage points. The larger average revisions to the latest estimate reflect the fact that comprehensive revisions include major conceptual improvements to the NIPAs, such as the introduction of chain indexes and the capitalisation of software and research and development.

The current quarterly GDP estimates are developed from aggregating individual estimates of the expenditure components of GDP. These individual quarterly estimates are prepared by the extrapolation of estimates of the previous quarter using, for example, direct indicators from monthly or quarterly surveys and indirect indicators, such as past trends. Specific information on these source data is provided in the next section of this chapter. The extrapolation procedure used is designed to prepare estimates based on the "best change method" from the previous quarterly estimates. Using this method, estimates for the most recent quarter are determined by calculating the change (usually in percentage terms) in the indicator series and multiplying that change with the published value for the previous quarter.[12] This calculation means that if the level of an indicator series has been revised, the revised "best level" is not reflected in the current estimate. Instead, best levels are not reflected until the time of an annual or comprehensive revision. Incorporating the source data on a best-change basis provides accurate measures of the change in GDP although resulting in levels of the estimates that are not fully consistent with the source data. In general, BEA incorporates source data on a best-change basis in order to preserve accurate estimates of growth and consistent time series.[13]

The process for all quarterly GDP estimates starts with a group of BEA specialists who prepare estimates for specific components. This estimation process takes place over a two-week period set to coincide with the availability of key source data. The specialists work with the standard methodologies, obtain the source data and apply the appropriate estimating methodology that, depending on the quarterly estimate that is being prepared, may include developing judgmental assumptions for missing source data. The estimates are made using seasonally adjusted values of the source data whenever available in order to ensure comparability between the source data and the GDP estimates. If seasonally adjusted source data are not available, the specialists apply seasonal adjustments to the source data before extrapolating it. The specialists also review the source data for changes that would affect consistency, such as a new survey methodology, reliability (such as a high no response rate) or relevance for estimating the GDP component for a particular period, such as a natural disaster. Based on this review, the specialist determines if any special adjustments are needed. For example, the survey for wages and salaries measures average weekly hours only for the middle week of the month. If this middle week is not representative of the entire month because of severe weather that occurred later in the month, the specialist would recommend that an adjustment is needed.

The estimates recommended by the specialists are then subject to a two-step review process. The first review is conducted by a special review team of senior economists who work with the specialists. This team reviews all of the recommended estimates to make sure that the assumptions for missing source data for all components have been made in a consistent manner, that adjustments have been made where needed, and that economic relationships between components, such as between inventory change and sales, are consistent with the state of economic activity depicted by the overall GDP estimate. Frequently, this review results in specialists revising their initial estimates. This review takes place over a three- to four-day period and ends two days before the publication of the GDP estimate. The team concludes its work by preparing a complete set of NIPA estimates for presentation for the second review step. This second review is conducted by BEA senior staff the day before the estimates are published. They conduct a high-level review of the impact of assumptions for key source data on the major aggregates and compare the proposed GDP estimates to alternative measures of output, such as hours worked, industrial production, or private sector forecasts of GDP growth. The senior staff review seldom results in changes to the estimates proposed by the review team, but the review does prepare them to respond to questions from users about the implications of the estimates.

Although the steps in the estimation process are the same for each of the three current GDP estimates, there are some important differences in the processes depending on the estimate. For the advance estimate, many of the monthly key source data series are available only for the first two months of the quarter, which are usually subject to revision in subsequent months. As a result, the specialists and two groups that review the estimates focus on the assumptions for missing source data, based on historical information and on likely revisions to the available source data. For series for which there are data for all three months of the quarter, differences between the source data and the corresponding NIPA component are reviewed for anomalies. For example, such a review would be made of differences between the Consumer Price Index (CPI) and the PCE measures of price change.[14]

For the second and third estimates, more source data become available to replace the specialists' assumptions for missing data, and for the first three quarters of the year, direct estimates of corporate profits are also available. Consequently, the review of the specialists estimates shifts from the assumptions for missing source data to the revisions from the incorporation of new and revised source data. The availability of direct estimates of corporate profits also shifts the focus of the review to the specialists' assumptions for missing source data for profits of certain industries. The most important difference between the review of the advance and the second GDP estimates is that the availability of corporate profits provides an estimate of GDI and the statistical discrepancy. Because large changes in the statistical discrepancy indicate problems in the source data, when there are such changes, the review team in particular looks at the reliability of the NIPA components to determine if adjustments are needed. For the third GDP estimate, there is even less missing source data and fewer assumptions to review. In addition, the specialists and review team look at past revisions to source data to determine any patterns of future revision that might warrant additional adjustments.

As in other OECD countries, one of the major purposes of BEA release process is to insure the integrity of these estimates.[15] This process consists of steps to ensure that the estimates have been prepared without any interference or influence by persons outside of BEA and that the estimates to be published are not given to anyone not authorised to have them. In particular, considering the importance given in the financial markets, for example, to the advance estimate of the US quarterly GDP, pre-release access to confidential information by people trading in the bond and stock market would give these traders an unfair advantage and infringe on the proper functioning of these and related markets. To preclude any outside influence or interference, BEA has put into place the following restrictions: 1) strict adherence to the release of data according to an announced schedule; 2) access to data prior to release is limited to certain BEA staff with a need to know; 3) under *Statistical Policy Directive 3* issued by the President's Office of Management and Budget, access by policy officials is limited to the provision of the data to the Council of Economic Advisers on the afternoon before the data are released; and 4) physical and computer security restricts access to those with a need to know.

A key security feature of the BEA process is reflected in the conduct of the senior management review of the proposed GDP estimates. This meeting, known as the "lock-up" meeting, is conducted the day before release, has limited attendance, and is conducted in a physically secure location at BEA headquarters. Once the attendees of these meetings have been provided the proposed estimates, they may not be in contact with anyone outside BEA and are allowed only limited and monitored access to BEA staff for the duration of the meeting. Meetings usually begin shortly after noon and continue until the estimates are final and the news release and supporting materials are completed and delivered to the Council of Economic Advisers. This delivery usually is made in the late afternoon by a member of the review team.

There is no additional distribution of the news release or the estimates until the next morning. If requested by policy officials of the Department of Commerce, BEA will provide these officials with a briefing on the estimates an hour before release under the condition that these officials remain at the briefing with no contact with anyone else until release time. The news media are also provided the estimates a half hour before release in a secure room that prevents contact with anyone outside the room until release time; the room is equipped with computers for the media to prepare their stories and telephone lines for representatives of the broadcast media to record their stories at release time.

6. Methodologies for preparing quarterly GDP

BEA publishes detailed and summary methodologies – both the source data and the estimating methods – used to prepare GDP and other NIPA components. Detailed methodologies are published in *Concepts and Methods of the U.S. National Income and Product Accounts* and in separate methodology papers. Because improvements to these methodologies are regularly incorporated as part of each annual and comprehensive revision, BEA includes descriptions of changes in methodology in annual *Survey of Current Business* articles about the revisions and also publishes a separate annual article in the *Survey* that provides summary information on the methodologies for the components of GDP and GDI.[16] The methodologies used for the calculation of the advance quarterly estimate is the last step of a process that begins with the incorporation of the most recent benchmark I-O account into a comprehensive revision. First, revised annual estimates are calculated by extrapolating forward the estimates of NIPA components for the newly incorporated I-O benchmark.[17] Second, quarterly estimates are calculated by interpolating these new annual estimates. Third, quarterly estimates up to the most recent period are calculated by extrapolating forward the last interpolated quarterly estimate. Finally, the advance quarterly estimate for the latest quarter is calculated by extrapolation. For annual revisions, the calculation of revised annual and quarterly estimates follows the same sequence, but only covers the years open for revision (generally, the most recent three years).

This section provides information on the methodologies used to prepare the selected components of the advance quarterly estimates of current-dollar and real GDP. In Section 2, three aspects of the NIPAs were noted: current-dollar GDP is measured using the expenditure approach; the measure based on the income approach is called GDI, which differs from GDP by the statistical discrepancy; finally estimates of value added by industry are not based on a separate production approach, but are controlled to GDP from the expenditure approach. Thus, the discussion of the methodologies used for GDP is limited to the components that are the elements of final expenditures (household final expenditures, government final consumption, gross capital formation, and exports *minus* imports).

For both quarterly and annual real GDP, the methodologies focus on the calculation of the detailed expenditures components of real GDP. These component estimates of prices and quantities are aggregated to GDP and its major components, using an index number aggregation formula. BEA uses a Fisher index formula allowing for changes effects in relative prices and in the composition of output over time. As a result, the quantity or price changes are not affected by the substitution bias that is associated with changes in quantities and prices calculated using a fixed-weighted (Laspeyres) formula. Annual changes in quantities and prices are calculated that incorporate weights from two adjacent years. Quarterly changes in quantities and prices are calculated using a Fisher formula that incorporates weights from two adjacent quarters, and quarterly indexes are adjusted for consistency to the annual indexes before percent changes are calculated.

The chained-dollar values for the detailed GDP components will not necessarily sum to the chained-dollar estimate of GDP (or to any intermediate aggregate) because the relative prices that are used as weights differ from those of the reference year. A measure of the effect of such differences is provided by a "residual" line – the difference between the chained-dollar value of the main aggregate in the table and the sum of the most detailed components in the table. For periods close to the reference year, when the relative prices that are used as weights have usually not changed much, the residuals tend to be small, but for periods further from the reference year, the residuals tend to be larger. The non-additivity of the chained-dollar estimates makes them less useful for analyses of contributions to growth (see Chapter 2); consequently, BEA provides tables of "contributions to percent change" that can be used as exact measures of the contributions of individual components.

For the current-dollar NIPA estimates, the 14 components of final demand covered in this section have been selected as representative of the estimating methods used by BEA and of the availability of source data for the advance GDP estimate. In its annual presentation of summary methodologies, BEA shows source data and estimating method for components grouped by estimation method for the complete NIPA calculation and revision process. The presentations cover about 50 groupings of GDP components and 40 groupings of GDI components.

Availability of source data

BEA uses a wide range of monthly, quarterly and annual source data as well as indicator series to extrapolate from benchmark-year estimates. These data come from statistical agencies, federal tax returns, federal government regulatory programmes, and private trade sources, and they vary greatly in their publication and revision practices.

The timely availability of the source data determines their use in the calculation of the estimates. For most components, source data are not available for all the months of the quarter at the time of an advance GDP estimate, thus BEA calculates trend-based data for the missing source data, some of which are quarterly and some of which are monthly. For most components, these trend-based estimates are replaced by indicator series in successive revisions. For example, for an advance GDP estimate, about 46% of GDP is calculated using quarterly indicators or monthly indicators that are available for all three months of a quarter, 30% is calculated using two months of the indicator series and one month of trend-based data, and 24% is calculated using only trend-based data.[18] For the third quarterly estimate of GDP, which is published two months later, about 90% of GDP is calculated from indicator series, about 9% from only trend-based data, and less than 1% from a combination of indicator series and trend-based data. A few new indicator series, such as the Census Bureau's quarterly services survey and monthly data on electricity consumption, become available for the second and third quarterly GDP estimates.

To allow users to assess the validity of the trend-based data, which are usually based on the judgment of the BEA specialists, BEA provides users with the "assumptions for missing source data", and publishes the most important of these assumptions at the time of the GDP news release.

Estimating methods

BEA selects the estimating method for a component depending on the availability and reliability of the source data and the extent to which these source data meet NIPA definitions. Among the estimating methods that BEA uses to calculate the current-dollar estimates are the following: the commodity-flow method; the retail control method; the perpetual inventory method; and the fiscal year analysis method. The commodity-flow method starts with estimates of domestic output, adjusts the output for imports, exports and inventory change, and allocates the result to purchases by households, business and government. The complete commodity-flow method is used for most expenditure components of the benchmark I-O accounts; an abbreviated form of this method is used to prepare annual and quarterly NIPA estimates for components for which the necessary source data are available.[19] The retail control method uses retail store sales data, adjusted to reflect sales to households, to estimate annual and quarterly household purchases of specific products. The perpetual inventory method, which cumulates flows to derive stocks, is used to calculate estimates of the stock of fixed assets, which is used to estimate annual and quarterly estimates of consumption of fixed capital. The fiscal year analysis method is used to estimate annual estimates of consumption expenditures and gross investment by the federal government. The estimates of expenditures are calculated based on analysis of detailed outlays data from budget documents. BEA adjusts these budget outlays to NIPA definitions and allocates them to the appropriate NIPA component, such as consumption expenditures or transfer payments. The fiscal year analysis also provides a set of control totals for quarterly NIPA estimates.

For the estimates of real GDP, BEA uses three methods: deflation, quantity extrapolation and direct valuation. The most widely used method is the deflation method in which a quantity index is calculated by dividing the current-dollar index by an appropriate price index. In the quantity extrapolation method, quantity indexes are used to extrapolate from the base-year value. In the direct valuation method, quantity indexes are calculated by multiplying the base-year price by actual quantity data for the index period. In all three methods, quantity indexes are converted into real or chained-dollar GDP by multiplying the index number by the base year current-dollar value.

Methodologies for selected components of current-dollar GDP

Table 1 of the November 2013 *Survey of Current Business* summary methodology article shows the methodologies for about 50 groups of GDP components. The components selected below illustrate the various combinations of estimating methods and source data used for the annual estimates, other than a benchmark year, and for the advance quarterly GDP estimates. The first 13 components are listed in sequence by the number of months of source data available for the advance estimate. For the first four components, key source data are available for the advance estimate for all three months of the quarter. For the fifth through the tenth components, key source data are available for only two months of the quarter. For components 11-13, the advance quarterly estimate is based primarily on trend-based data calculated by BEA. The last component, investment in software, illustrates the use of different source data for the quarterly and annual estimates.

1. *PCE for most durable and nondurable goods.* Both the annual and quarterly estimates of these PCE components are calculated using the retail control method. For all but the most recent year, annual estimates are based on estimates of retail store sales from the Census Bureau annual retail trade survey. For the most recent year, the annual estimate is based on the Census monthly survey of retail trade. For the advance quarterly estimate, all three months of survey results are available and subject to further revision.

2. *PCE for gasoline and oil.* Both the annual and quarterly estimates of this component are calculated as the product of physical quantities purchased and the average retail price. For the advance quarterly estimate, all three months of gallons consumed and average retail price are available and subject to further revision.

3. *New autos and light trucks (both PCE and private fixed investment).* Both the annual and quarterly estimates for these components are calculated as the product of quantity purchased and an average price. Unit sales, information on allocating sales among consumers and other purchasers, and average list price, are available from trade sources. For the advance estimate, all three months of unit sales and price data and two months of data to allocate sales among consumers and other purchasers are available.

4. *State and local government compensation of employees.* Annual estimates for wages and salaries are from BLS tabulations from the quarterly census of employment and wages (QCEW). For the other components of compensation, employer contributions for government social insurance are from federal agencies administering these programmes; employer contributions for employee pension and insurance funds are from actuarial reports from state pension plans, from trade sources, from the Centers for Medicare and Medicaid Services, and from Census annual surveys of state and local governments. For the advance estimate of wages and salaries, BEA combines three months of BLS employment data with quarterly earnings data from the BLS employment cost index. The monthly

employment data are subject to further revision. For other components, BEA calculates trend-based estimates.

5. *Fixed investment for most types of new structures.* Both annual and quarterly estimates are from monthly the Census surveys of the value of construction put in place. For advance quarterly estimates, two months of source data are available from the Census monthly construction survey and are subject to further revision.

6. *Private fixed investment in equipment except motor vehicles.* For the annual estimates for all but the most recent year, estimates are calculated using the abbreviated commodity-flow method using shipments from annual Census survey of manufactures, adjusted for exports and imports from the Census foreign-trade data. For the most recent year and the advance quarterly estimate, an abbreviated commodity flow method calculated from shipments from Census monthly survey of manufactures is used. For the advance estimate, two months of monthly shipments, exports and imports data are available and subject to further revision.

7. *Exports and imports of goods and services.* This GDP component is estimated by BEA as part of the preparation of the ITAs. For both annual and quarterly estimates of goods, estimates are calculated using monthly Census foreign trade data, with adjustments by BEA for coverage and valuation to convert the data to a balance-of-payments and NIPA basis. For the advance estimate, two months of foreign trade data are available and are subject to further revision. For services, annual estimates for government transactions are based on reports by federal agencies, and for most other services are based on annual and quarterly BEA surveys. For the advance quarterly estimates, BEA calculates trend-based estimates for both goods and services for the third month.

8. *Federal government consumption expenditures and gross investment for most types of spending.* For spending except for structures, software, R&D, consumption of fixed capital, and financial services furnished without payment (FISIM), BEA uses the fiscal year analysis method. Within a control total established by this analysis, estimates of military wages are based on data from the *Budget of the United States* and estimates of civilian wages and benefits are based on data from federal agencies. Estimates of employer contributions for social insurance programmes are from the Department of the Treasury's monthly report on outlays and receipts and from other federal agencies. Estimates of employer contributions for employee pension and insurance funds are from actuarial reports from the various federal pension plans and from other federal agencies. For the advance estimate, compensation estimates are based on three months of employment data from the Department of Defense and BLS. Other

components are based on the control totals from the fiscal year analysis and three months of data from the monthly Department of the Treasury report and reports from other federal agencies. Estimates for structures are explained above in item 5 above; software, R&D, and consumption of fixed capital are explained below.

9. *Federal and state and local government consumption of fixed capital.* Both annual and quarterly estimates are based on perpetual-inventory calculations at current cost, based on gross investment and on investment prices.

10. *Space rent for owner-occupied dwellings and rent for tenant-occupied dwellings.* For all but the most recent year, estimates are based on data on housing stock and average annual rent. The housing stock is based on data from the Census Bureau biennial housing survey and the current population survey. The average annual rent for owner-occupied dwellings reflects growth based on data from BEA fixed asset accounts and the BLS CPI for owners' equivalent rent; the average annual rent for tenant-occupied dwellings reflects data from the biennial housing survey and the BLS CPI for rent of primary residence. Estimates for the most recent year are based on the Census monthly survey number of new, private housing units completed and the BLS CPI for rent. For the advance quarterly estimate, three months of the CPI is available and the number of units is estimated using trend-based data.

11. *State and local government consumption and investment except consumption of fixed capital, compensation, intellectual property products and FISIM.* For all years except the two most recent years, final estimates are based on total expenditures from Census annual surveys of state and local governments. Estimates for the most recent two years and the advance quarterly estimate are trend-based data except for structures, which are based on Census surveys of the value of construction put in place.

12. *PCE for physicians, dentists, medical laboratories, and all other professional medical services, except home health care.* For all years, expenses of non-profit professional services and receipts for the other services adjusted for government consumption are from the Census service annual survey. Estimates for the advance and second estimates are based primarily on trend-based data, and the third estimate is based on data from Census quarterly services survey.

13. *Private and government investment in research and development.* Investment in research and development (R&D) includes both purchased and own-account investment and is estimated by measuring the production costs associated with spending on R&D. Current-dollar investment values are derived mostly from data on R&D spending from business and government surveys from the National Science Foundation (NSF). Adjustments for

coverage and scope differences are made, including accounting for imported and exported R&D; including R&D expenditures not captured in the NSF data in certain years – such as social science R&D – to align BEA measures of R&D with the SNA; converting depreciation for structures and equipment used to produce R&D to an economic cost, rather than historical cost, basis; reconciling NSF data with data from the Census Bureau's economic censuses; removing expenditures on software R&D that BEA already includes in a separate software investment category; and in certain cases, converting measures for purchased R&D from a cost-basis to a purchase-basis. For years when NSF data is unavailable, estimates are extrapolated using data on R&D expenses from company financial statements, federal budget data, and data on wages and salaries paid by the R&D industry. The advance estimates are based on BLS current employment statistics, which are replaced by data from company financial reports for the second and third estimates.

14. *Private and government investment in software.* Investment in software is estimated in two parts: purchased software and own-account software. For years except for the most recent year, purchased software is calculated using the abbreviated commodity flow method based primarily on industry receipts from the Census service annual survey and Census foreign trade data. For the most recent year, industry receipts data are from the Census quarterly services survey. The advance and second estimates are based on receipts from company reports and the third estimate is based on the quarterly services survey. For all years, annual estimates for own-account software are based on annual production costs derived from BLS employment data from the quarterly census of employment and wages (QCEW). The advance estimates of own-account software are based on BLS monthly current employment statistics, which are available for all three months.

Methodologies for real GDP estimates

Unlike the source data used to calculate current-dollar GDP estimates, the source data used to calculate deflators for real GDP for the advance estimate are generally available all three months of the quarter, are less likely to be subject to revision, and are not replaced by annual source data. Consequently, quarterly, annual and benchmark-year estimates are almost all calculated using the same source data and estimating method.

For the deflation method, which is most widely used, price indexes are primarily available from the BLS price index programmes – the CPI, PPI and international price indexes (IPI). Elements of the CPI and PPI are used not only for components of PCE and fixed investment, but also for components of government consumption and investment where more appropriate indexes are not available. Elements of the IPI are used for exports and imports of goods and services and for other components where explicit estimates of imports are used to calculate the corresponding current-dollar estimate. For components for which the BLS indexes do not provide complete coverage, such as investment in structures, BEA uses cost indexes from private trade sources or special quality-adjusted price indexes prepared by the Census Bureau. For the expenditures of non-profit institutions, such as educational and religious and welfare, BEA uses its own input cost indexes or cost indexes from other sources. For national defence and related non-defence consumption and investment expenditures, BEA has developed an extensive set of specially designed price indexes.[20] For R&D, price change is measured using an input-cost approach with a multi-factor productivity adjustment.

GDP components for which BEA uses the quantity extrapolation method include: FISIM; brokerage charges; most types of insurance; mining exploration, shafts and wells; and compensation of employees of federal and state and local government. Components for which BEA uses the direct valuation method include net purchases of used motor vehicles, inventory change for utilities, government consumption of fixed capital and some defence expenditures for goods and services.[21]

Notes

1. NABE is a professional association of more than 2 500 members who use economics in their work.

2. "New International Guidelines in Economic Accounting", *Survey of Current Business,* February 1993, p. 42.

3. The accounts and the supporting information, including the monthly online journal the *Survey of Current Business,* are available free of charge on its website at *www.bea.gov.*

4. The monthly *Survey of Current Business,* BEA official journal, is no longer available in printed format, but is available for download free of charge on BEA website *www.bea.gov/scb/date_guide.asp.*

5. For information on the individual lines of the summary accounts see "A Guide to the National Income and Product Accounts of the United States" on BEA website.

6. In contrast, the SNA uses "real gross domestic income" to refer to the purchasing power of the total incomes generated by domestic production—that is, a measure of GDP that adjusts for trading gains and losses due to changes in the terms of trade.

7. BEA and other statistical agencies that prepare selected economic indicators, including GDP and personal income and outlays, are required each September to publish the release dates for the next year.

8. The quarterly estimates of the FAUS are released by the FRB early in the third month after the end of the quarter. Annual revisions are usually released in

September. Quarterly estimates of productivity are released by BLS a week after the advance and second GDP estimates.

9. This program also provides estimates of the net stock of durable goods purchased by households. Estimates for 2003-12 were published in "Fixed Assets and Consumer Durable Goods" in the October 2013 issue of the *Survey of Current Business*; estimates for earlier years are posted on BEA website *www.bea.gov/scb/date_guide.asp*.

10. For a description of the balancing program used to accomplish the integration, see Strassner and al, 2013; Rassier and al, 2007.

11. For additional details on BEA studies of reliability see Fixler and al., 2011.

12. Some other countries, such as France, use econometric methods for estimating the best change of the quarterly entry (see Chapter 11).

13. For additional information, see Chapter 4 of *Concepts and Methods of the U.S. National Income and Product Accounts*, November 2012, available on the BEA website, *www.bea.gov*.

14. For an explanation of the differences between the CPI and the PCE price index, see McCully and al., 2007.

15. As required by *Statistical Policy Directive Number 3*, all release dates for key economic indicators, which include quarterly GDP and several other BEA reports, are set in the fall of the preceding year and made available to the public at that time. This advance publication schedule is designed to prevent policy makers from an early release of "good" news and from delaying the release of "bad" news.

16. The most recent summary appeared in "Updated Summary of NIPA Methodologies" in the November 2013 *Survey of Current Business* (BEA, 2013).

17. Estimates for periods between benchmark I-O accounts are calculated by a similar interpolation process.

18. These percentages are from Chapter 3 of *Concepts and Methods of the U.S. National Income and Product Accounts*, November 2012, available on the BEA website, *www.bea.gov*.

19. See Horowitz and Planting.

20. For additional information on these special indexes, see "MP-5, Government Transactions", on the BEA website.

21. Table 2 in the summary methodologies article in the November 2013 *Survey* (BEA, 2013) provides a detailed list of the estimating methods and source data used to prepare real GDP.

References

Aruoba, S. Boragan, Diebold, Francis X., Nalewaik, Jeremy, Schorfheide, Frank, and Song, Dongho, Song, (2012), "Improving GDP Measurement: A Forecast Combination Perspective," in Chen, X. and Swanson, N., eds., *Recent Advances and Future Directions in Causality, Prediction, and Specification Analysis: Essays in Honor of Halbert L. White Jr.* Springer, pp. 1-25.

BEA (1993), *Survey of Current Business, www.bea.gov/scb/date_guide.asp*.

Fixler, D. J., Greenaway-McGrevy, R. and Grimm, B. T., "Revisions to GDP, GDI, and Their Major Components" in the July 2011 *Survey of Current Business*.

Guo, J. and Planting, M. A., "Integrating U.S. Input-Output Tables with SNA: Valuations and Extensions," presented at the International Association for Research in Income and Wealth, August 2006.

Horowitz, K. J., and Planting, M. A., *Concepts and Methods of the Input-Output Accounts* on BEA website, *www.bea.gov*.

Landefeld, J. S., "Comment" in *Brookings Papers on Economic Activity*, Spring 2010.

McCully, C. P., Moyer, B. C., and Stewart, K. J., "Comparing the Consumer Price Index and the Personal Consumption Expenditures Price Index" in the November 2007 *Survey of Current Business*.

Mead, C. I., Moses, K. E. and Moulton, B. R., "The NIPAs and the System of National Accounts", December 2004 *Survey of Current Business*.

Mead, C. I., McCully, C. P., and Reinsdorf, M. B., "Income and Outlays of Households and Nonprofit Institutions Serving Households" in the April 2003 *Survey*.

Nalewaik, Jeremy J., "The Income- and Expenditure-Side Estimates of U.S. Output Growth," *Brookings Papers on Economic Activity*, Spring 2010.

National Association for Business Economics, 2013, *NABE Outlook*, December 2013, available on the NABE website at *www.nabe.com*.

OECD (2013), *OECD Economic Outlook*, Vol. 2013/2, OECD Publishing, Paris, doi: *http://dx.doi.org/10.1787/eco_outlook-v2013-2-en*.

Rassier, Dylan G., Howells, Thomas F., Morgan, Edward T., Empey, Nicholas R., and Roesch, Conrad E., "Integrating the 2002 Benchmark Input-Output Accounts and the 2002 Annual Industry Accounts," in the December 2007 *Survey of Current Business*. *www.bea.gov/scb/date_guide.asp*.

Strassner, E. H. and D. B.Wasshausen, "Preview of the 2013 Comprehensive Revision of the Industry Economic Accounts," in the June 2013 *Survey of Current Business*.

Going further

Differences between the NIPA and SNA

For several reasons, the US has not adopted all of the guidelines for national accounting set forth in the 2008 version of the SNA, although users should not overestimate the impact of these differences. Major aggregates such as GDP are calculated in accordance with almost all SNA guidelines. Over the last 20 years BEA has taken many steps to improve consistency with the SNA while still endeavouring to retain the long, consistent time series that NIPA users have come to expect.

The remaining discrepancies with SNA guidelines are largely in the areas of the institutional sector accounts, the presentation of the accounts, and in the valuation of industry output in the industry accounts. The goal of improving NIPA consistency with the SNA remains part of BEA mission of producing "accurate, relevant and timely statistics, of responding to customers and of meeting the challenges of a changing economy.[1]"

This section identifies some of the more important differences between the NIPAs and SNA 2008.[2] It reviews the differences that affect: 1) the level of total GDP and its expenditure components; 2) valuation; 3) definitions of the sectors; and 4) the presentation of the accounts. Of course, in addition to differences in accounting concepts and presentation, national accounts can also differ across countries because of differences in source data and methodology, such as differences in the use of quality adjusted price indexes (see Chapter 3), but this section will not discuss statistical or methodological differences.

The only major conceptual difference between the NIPA and SNA in the scope of GDP is that cultivated assets, such as orchards and dairy cattle, are treated in the SNA as investment, while in the NIPAs, they are currently treated as intermediate consumption. However, BEA has research underway to develop estimates for these assets and is likely to recognise cultivated assets in a future revision. Other differences that previously existed, such as the treatment of expenditures for military weapon systems as investment in the NIPAs, have been harmonised with the 2008 SNA update and subsequent NIPA comprehensive revisions. As in other countries, there are some also other differences from the SNA guidelines that exist because of gaps in information.

For example, illegal production, such as prostitution or the cultivation or manufacture of illegal drugs, in theory should be included according to the SNA, but currently is excluded from the NIPAs due to lack of source data. Another example is that the NIPAs do not include government inventories in its measure of the change in inventories. Because little information is available on government inventories, the NIPAs count goods acquired by governments as intermediate consumption when purchased rather than when used.

Both the NIPAs and the SNA value total GDP at market (or purchasers') prices. However, for the valuation of sector and industry output, the SNA recommends valuation at basic prices. For the NIPAs and for its I-O and the GDP-by-industry accounts, BEA uses market prices. Consequently, the NIPAs include taxes on products and exclude subsidies for calculating value added of industries; using the SNA, taxes on products are excluded and subsidies on products are included. This difference is quite important for users. It means that for the US national accounts, GDP is equal to the sum of the value added at market prices of the different industries, while for other OECD countries it is equal to the sum of the value added at basic prices *plus* taxes less subsidies on products. The use of basic prices would facilitate international comparisons because taxes vary significantly across countries. Market price valuation causes very significant additions to the output of trade industries in the US, thus rendering international comparisons of industry statistics and resulting productivity calculations difficult to determine.

Recently, BEA has been conducting research on changing from market prices to basic prices for valuing its I-O accounts.[3] According to the data provided to the OECD, in 2011 taxes less subsidies on products accounted for about 7% of the published US GDP. However, there is a significantly larger impact on trade industries, where much of the taxes are allocated. If the United States were to adopt the use of basic prices, value added in both wholesale and retail trade would be reduced by about 20%, thus reducing the share of GDP accounted for by service-producing industries.

The NIPAs have two groupings for the institutional sector. For production, the NIPAs focus on three major sectors: business, households and institutions, and general government. The business sector includes all private entities that are organised for profit, including unincorporated enterprises, and other units (such as government enterprises) that are primarily engaged in producing goods and services for sale at a price that is intended to cover the costs of production. Thus, the business sector in the NIPAs differs from the corporations sector of the SNA in that it includes unincorporated enterprises that are, in principle, classified in the SNA in the household sector. The business sector in the NIPAs also excludes non-profit institutions serving households. This NIPA presentation has the advantage of providing a measure of the output of the whole of the market production, a measure used as the numerator in the calculation of labour and multifactor productivity. Several other countries also compile such a grouping (see Chapter 7). The households and institutions sector consists of household activities that are not engaged in market production (specifically, the services of owner-occupied housing and the labour of domestic workers) and of production by NPISHs. The general government sector consists of all government agencies other than those classified as government enterprises. Also, the NIPAs do not base the distinction between market and non-market producers strictly on the 50 percent rule that is used to determine economically significant prices in many countries. In the NIPAs, government producers and non-profit institutions providing services to households that rely on a mix of donations and sales for their funding are generally treated as non-market producers, even when the value of their sales exceeds half the production costs.

For measuring income, outlays and saving in the NIPAs, the institutions are grouped into three major sectors: personal, government and corporate. The personal sector includes the income that is earned by, or transferred to, households and NPISHs as well as net income of businesses that are owned by households, including owner-occupied housing. The personal sector is thus close to the combination of the SNA household and NPISH sector, since it includes the income of unincorporated enterprises. In addition, the NIPAs include an annual table that shows NPISH income and outlays separately from household income and outlays.[4] The NIPA government sector includes general government and government enterprises, while the SNA government sector excludes government enterprises. This treatment reflects the fact that the source data available for state and local governments in the US generally consolidates government enterprises with general government agencies. The NIPA corporate sector consists of businesses organised for profit that are legally organised as corporations and that are required to file corporate tax returns. It differs from the SNA non-financial and financial corporations sectors by not including government enterprises and unincorporated businesses that operate like corporations. Although the NIPAs do not give emphasis to the distinction between financial and non-financial corporations, data are available for both categories of corporations.

In addition to the substantive differences described above, there are also several differences in presentation between the two systems. It is important to understand that these differences in presentation can easily be overcome by reorganising the different tables. Indeed, both the IMAs as well as the annual accounts that BEA provides to the OECD are based on a more traditional SNA-style presentation. For its main NIPA presentation, BEA uses seven summary accounts to illustrate the major accounting relationships. The section of this chapter "Presentation of NIPAs and related tables" includes a discussion of the major presentational differences between the organisation of these NIPA summary accounts and the SNA production, distribution and use of the income account, and capital accounts.

In particular, the presentation of GDP by type of expenditure in the NIPAs and the SNA slightly differ. The NIPAs show GDP as the sum of four main components: personal consumption expenditures; gross private domestic investment; net exports of goods and services; and government consumption expenditures and gross investment. The SNA groups these same components differently, as the sum of final consumption expenditures, gross capital formation (GCF), and exports of goods and services *minus* imports of goods and services. The SNA final consumption expenditures are the sum of final consumption expenditures by households, NPISHs and government. As noted above, GCF is presented as consisting of three items: gross fixed capital formation; change in inventories; and acquisitions less disposals of valuables.[5]

The NIPAs include also some differences in terminology such as "gross national product" which is the NIPA name for "gross national income" in the SNA, and also several aggregates that are not in the SNA, such as corporate profits, and personal income (Box 12.1 in the main text "Featured measures of NIPA tables" discusses several aggregates not found in the SNA). Similar measures of disposable income appear in both the NIPAs and the SNA. However, these measures – NIPA disposable personal income and SNA household disposable income – differ not only because this NIPA measure includes NPISHs but also in the way the two measures are calculated. NIPA disposable personal income includes all sources of personal income, less contributions for social insurance and personal taxes and includes interest and other transfers paid by persons. In contrast, household disposable income excludes interest and other transfers paid by households. Also, NIPA disposable personal income includes pension fund contributions but does not include pension benefits, whereas HDI excludes pension fund contributions and includes pension benefits. Despite these differences in disposable incomes, the NIPA and SNA measures of saving are comparable. The NIPAs treat interest paid by persons and personal transfer payments as a type of outlay, and the SNA includes an adjustment for pensions (called "D8 Adjustment for net equity of households in pension funds") so that both systems' saving figures reflect households as the owners of pension funds.

The NIPA and SNA classification systems used to present industries and types of products also differ. For example, the industry detail shown in the NIPAs is based on the North American Industry Classification System (NAICS), which is used by Canada, Mexico and the US; SNA presentations are based on the International Standard Industrial Classification of All Economic Activities (ISIC).

Another difference in the presentation of the NIPAs and some other countries' presentations relates to the use of balancing items in the two systems. As noted in the section "Going further: Statistical discrepancies in the NIPAs", GDI (gross domestic income), which is the NIPA name for what is called the "income approach of GDP" in this book (the sum of incomes), does not equal GDP, which is calculated as the sum of expenditures, because the components are measured independently. The difference between GDP and GDI in the NIPAs is called the statistical discrepancy and is shown as a type of income. Not all other OECD countries incorporate such an entry either because one or more expenditure or income types are calculated as a residual, or because they allocate such discrepancies to other components. In the US, the term GDP is strictly associated with the expenditure approach.

Finally, it is very important to remind international users of national accounts that all quarterly changes in the NIPAs are presented at an annual rate. Many other OECD countries simply use quarterly rates.

As noted elsewhere in this chapter, BEA prepares a special set of annual NIPA estimates for international organisations, such as the OECD, that are more consistent with the SNA. These estimates are included in the OECD's annual national accounts database.

Statistical discrepancies in the NIPA

In the NIPAs, the difference between gross domestic income (GDI), which is measured as the sum of incomes earned in production, and gross domestic product (GDP), which is measured as the sum of final expenditures, is called the "statistical discrepancy". This is not the only statistical discrepancy in the national accounts. There are also the statistical discrepancies for each sector between the net lending/borrowing obtained from the non-financial accounts and the financial accounts. However, this section focuses on the statistical discrepancy between GDP and GDI. In theory, GDI should equal GDP, but in practice they differ because their components are estimated using largely independent and less-than-perfect source data.

In NIPA summary account 1 (see Table 12.1), the statistical discrepancy is recorded as a type of income. This placement reflects BEA view that GDP is a more reliable measure of output than GDI and that it has not developed a satisfactory methodology for allocating the discrepancy among GDP or GDI components.[6] Both of these views are explained below.

In the mid-1990s, there was considerable public debate about the growth of the US economy because growth measured by real GDI had increased faster that growth measured by real GDP.[7] The debate subsided for a while, but later was rekindled when Jeremy Nalewaik and others conducted research that suggests that GDI may be more reliable than GDP.[8]

BEA view that GDP is more reliable than GDI is based on its analysis of the source data underlying the two aggregates.[9] For the initial quarterly estimates, there are direct extrapolators for most major expenditure components. The GDP estimates are missing direct source data for several components of consumer spending for services, for residential improvements and for most state and local government spending. For GDI, direct source data are missing for most employer contributions to employee pension and insurance funds, and for most of the net operating surplus of private enterprises. In addition, past trends in these components indicate that it is more difficult to make reliable assumptions about the missing data for the components of GDI than for GDP.

For annual estimates, more comprehensive source data are available for almost all components, albeit with a lag. Most of the annual source data used for estimating GDP are based on complete annual enumerations, such as federal government budget data, or are regularly benchmarked to complete enumerations, such as the economic censuses and census of governments done every five years and are incorporated in BEA benchmark I-O accounts. For GDI, only the annual tabulations of wages and salaries from employment tax returns and federal government budget data are complete enumerations, and for most of the remaining components of GDI, the annual source data are tabulations of samples of income tax returns. Furthermore, in using tax and administrative data to prepare annual estimates of GDI, BEA needs to make significant adjustments to account for differences in concepts and accounting practices between the national accounts and the tax or administrative data. The source data for GDP are largely collected from surveys that are designed, in part, for use in the compilation of GDP.

BEA has continued to work to reduce the size of the statistical discrepancy, but it is highly unlikely that it can be eliminated completely, largely because of sampling and non-response errors and coverage limitations in the underlying source data, as well as the need for BEA to make adjustments for NIPA definitions based on incomplete information. Many users have expressed the need to continue to publish both measures so that they can draw their own conclusions as to the accuracy of the two estimates. In response, BEA has added additional information on GDI to the news releases for quarterly GDP.

Notes

1. For additional information, see Mead and al, 2004. Since this article was published, however, the 2008 update of the SNA was completed and BEA has undertaken two comprehensive revisions, so some of the information is now out of date.

2. The differences discussed in this section are based primarily on the December 2004 *Survey* article and on a June 2003 Statistics Canada research paper, "Measurement of Output, Value Added, and GDP in Canada and the United States", posted on the Statistics Canada website.

3. See Guo and al, 2006.

4. For additional information, see Mead and al, 2003.

5. The NIPAs do not include a separate account for valuables, but do include adjustments to prevent, for example, exports and imports of nonmonetary gold that is held as a valuable from affecting GDP.

6. For the NIPA table that shows gross value added by broad sector (Table 1.3.5), BEA eliminates the discrepancy by calculating the value added of the business sector as a residual. For the data that BEA provides to the OECD on an SNA basis, BEA does not eliminate the discrepancy. For the GDP-by-industry accounts, which are based on the industry distribution of GDI, BEA allocates the discrepancy to industries so that the sum of industry value added equals GDP.

7. BEA estimates real GDI using the GDP deflator; the estimates are shown in NIPA Table 1.7.6.

8. See Nalewaik and al, 2010 and Aruoba and al, 2012.

9. See Landefeld, 2010.

Chapter 13

The 2007-2009 financial crisis and recession: Reflections in the national accounts

This chapter describes the financial crisis and recession as reflected in the national accounts of OECD countries. It first summarises how the 2008-09 recession affected GDP and other major national accounts data, including the financial accounts and balance sheets, focusing on the experience of the OECD in aggregate and of the G7 countries. Next, the chapter considers how the rate of recovery has differed across countries since 2009. It then looks back at the period leading up to the recession and at how some of the imbalances were reflected in national accounts. The chapter concludes by considering the data gaps in accounts that were exposed by the crisis: what relevant information would policy makers have liked to have had, but which national accounts were unable to provide? It also discusses some of the steps that are being taken to address these gaps.

During 2000 through 2006, real estate prices in the United States and a number of other OECD countries increased rapidly in what is now widely considered to have been a bubble. Prices peaked in the United States and began falling, which placed stress on debt that was secured by home mortgages (see Figure 13.1). The use of "subprime" mortgages – that is, mortgages made to US borrowers who were considered especially risky – grew rapidly during the period, but in 2006 the rate of serious delinquencies (the share of subprime mortgages that were in foreclosure or with more than 90 days overdue) began to rise sharply. By the first half of 2007, news reports were warning that subprime mortgages could be a threat to the markets and policy makers were discussing possible regulatory responses.[1] However, few macroeconomists were able to forecast the consequences for the financial system and the global economy of this heightened level of risk. In August 2007, events reached the crisis stage when BNP Paribas, one of the largest banks in the world, announced that it would halt redemptions on three investment funds due to subprime loan losses in the United States. With financial markets that are now totally interlinked, investors throughout the world began trying to withdraw funds, freezing the markets. Both the US Federal Reserve and the European Central Bank expanded lending to counteract the liquidity shortage.[2]

In September 2007, Northern Rock, the United Kingdom's fifth-largest mortgage lender, was facing a run on deposits until the Bank of England provided a liquidity injection, and in February it was taken into state ownership. In March 2008, Bear Stearns, a leading US investment bank, was facing bankruptcy until the Treasury and Federal Reserve arranged for it to be sold to JP Morgan Chase, using a USD 30 billion loan guarantee from the Fed. Meanwhile, most OECD countries began falling into recession as GDP started to decline in the first half of 2008.

In July 2008, another US financial institution, IndyMac Bank, failed. On September 7, Fannie Mae and Freddie Mac, the two largest US guarantors of securitised mortgage instruments, were placed in government conservatorship. On September 15, Lehman Brothers, the fourth largest investment bank in the United States, filed for bankruptcy. The next day, AIG, one of the largest insurance companies in the world, was kept afloat with the announcement of a loan of up to USD 85 billion from the Federal Reserve. These events set off a worldwide financial panic. The so-called "shadow

Figure 13.1. **United States house price indexes (2000 Q1-2013 Q3)**
2000 Q1 = 100

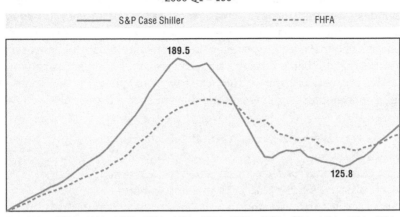

Note: The S&P Case-Shiller US national composite home price index is a proprietary index that includes all types of mortgages and weights transactions according to value. The FHFA index is the Federal Housing Finance Agency's all-transactions house price index. It is based on repeat mortgage transactions on single-family properties whose mortgages have been purchased or securitised by Fannie Mae or Freddie Mac; it excludes houses financed by "non-conforming" mortgages, such as jumbo and subprime mortgages, which tend to have more volatile prices than houses financed by conforming mortgages.
Source: FRED (Federal Reserve Economic Data), Federal Reserve Bank of St. Louis, http://research.stlouisfed.org/.   StatLink ⟶ http://dx.doi.org/10.1787/888933144236

banking" system, which had grown to rival the traditional commercial banks, faced a run as investors endeavored to withdraw funds and flee to safety. The TED spread – the difference between interbank rates and short-term US Treasury rates – spiked, reflecting much heightened levels of credit risk.

Over the next few weeks, governments and central banks throughout the world took extraordinary actions to try to restore liquidity and confidence. Meanwhile, GDP throughout most of Europe, North America, and Japan plunged. Economic activity in most countries reached a trough in the first half of 2009, and since then the recovery has generally been slow and erratic, particularly in the Euro area, where the original crisis was aggravated by a crisis of confidence in Euro-area government bonds, first in Greece, followed by Ireland, Portugal, Spain and other countries.

This chapter describes the financial crisis and recession as reflected in the national accounts of the 34 advanced economies that are members of the OECD. It will provide a summary of how the 2008-09 recession affected GDP and other major national accounts data, including the financial accounts and balance sheets, with the primary focus being on the experience of the OECD in aggregate and of the G7 countries, though specific experiences of several other countries will also be mentioned. Next the chapter provides a summary of the period of recovery since 2009 and of the differences between countries in the rate of recovery. It will next discuss the period leading up to the recession and how some of the imbalances were reflected in the accounts. The chapter concludes with a discussion of some of the data gaps that were exposed by the crisis – relevant information that policy makers would like to have had, but which the national accounts were unable to provide. It also discusses some of the steps that are being taken to address these measurement gaps with the objective of trying to avoid in the future what happened in this crisis – the inability of economists to forecast and prevent such a major crisis.

In 2008, the OECD countries represented 69% of the world's GDP based on exchange rates, or 55% of the world's GDP based on purchasing power parities, according to the IMF's World Economic Outlook database from October 2013. In turn, the G7 countries – United States, Japan, Germany, France, United Kingdom, Italy, and Canada – represented 77% of the OECD's GDP based on exchange rates, or 76% of the OECD's GDP based on purchasing power parities.

On the other hand, this chapter does not attempt to provide an accounting of the explanations for the financial crisis, nor does it provide an analysis of the policies that were used or might have been used either to avert the crisis or to speed the recovery. Many books have already been written on these subjects, and doubtless more will be written in years to come.[3] Although there is much interest in the policy implications of the financial crisis, analysis of the implication is beyond the scope of this chapter.

1. The Great Recession

The Great Recession of 2008-09 was the most severe global economic downturn since the Great Depression of the 1930s. Most of the advanced economies that are represented in the OECD fell into recession during this period, with large declines in economic activity as measured by real GDP. Changes in nominal GDP and various price deflators can help us understand the relative importance of changes in aggregate demand and aggregate supply. Furthermore, the effects of the recession were reflected in many of the other balances that are included in the quarterly national accounts, such as in the measures of disposable income, saving, and net lending, as well as in the national and institutional sector balance sheets.

Real GDP

Over the four quarters from the first quarter of 2008 to the first quarter of 2009, real GDP of the OECD countries in aggregate decreased 4.9% (see Table 13.1 and Figure 13.2).[4] The recession was initially relatively mild, with

Table 13.1. **Peak quarter, trough quarter, and cumulative change in real GDP, OECD Countries, During the Great Recession**

Country	Peak	Trough	Change in real GDP	Number of quarters to surpass pre-crisis peak
Austria	Q1 2008	Q2 2009	-5.1%	13
Belgium	Q2 2008	Q1 2009	-4.3%	11
Canada	Q3 2008	Q2 2009	-4.2%	9
Chile	Q1 2008	Q1 2009	-3.1%	7
Czech Republic	Q3 2008	Q2 2009	-5.6%	*
Denmark	Q2 2008	Q2 2009	-8.0%	*
Estonia	Q4 2007	Q3 2009	-20.0%	*
Finland	Q4 2007	Q2 2009	-10.4%	*
France	Q1 2008	Q2 2009	-4.4%	*
Germany	Q1 2008	Q1 2009	-6.8%	12
Hungary	Q1 2008	Q3 2009	-8.5%	*
Iceland	Q3 2007	Q2 2010	-12.8%	*
Ireland	Q4 2007	Q4 2009	-11.5%	*
Israel	Q3 2008	Q1 2009	-0.9%	4
Italy	Q3 2007	Q2 2009	-7.2%	*
Japan	Q1 2008	Q1 2009	-9.2%	*
Korea	Q3 2008	Q4 2008	-4.6%	4
Luxembourg	Q1 2008	Q1 2009	-9.4%	*
Mexico	Q2 2008	Q2 2009	-6.7%	9
Netherlands	Q1 2008	Q2 2009	-5.0%	*
New Zealand	Q4 2007	Q1 2009	-2.6%	8
Norway	Q4 2007	Q2 2009	-3.4%	17
Poland	Q3 2008	Q4 2008	-0.4%	3
Portugal	Q4 2007	Q1 2009	-4.2%	*
Slovak Republic	Q4 2008	Q1 2009	-8.5%	10
Slovenia	Q2 2008	Q4 2009	-9.7%	*
Spain	Q1 2008	Q4 2009	-5.0%	*
Sweden	Q4 2007	Q1 2009	-7.6%	12
Switzerland	Q3 2008	Q2 2009	-3.3%	8
Turkey	Q1 2008	Q1 2009	-13.3%	9
United Kingdom	Q1 2008	Q3 2009	-7.2%	*
United States	Q4 2007	Q2 2009	-4.3%	14
Euro area (17 countries)	Q1 2008	Q2 2009	-5.7%	*
OECD – Total	**Q1 2008**	**Q1 2009**	**-4.9%**	**14**

* As of Q3 2013, the pre-crisis peak in real GDP had not been surpassed.

Source: OECD (2012), "Quarterly National Accounts", OECD National Accounts Statistics (database), doi: http://dx.doi.org/10.1787/data-00017-en.

Figure 13.2. **Real GDP for OECD – Total and G7 Countries (2005 Q1-2013 Q3)**

2008 Q1 = 100

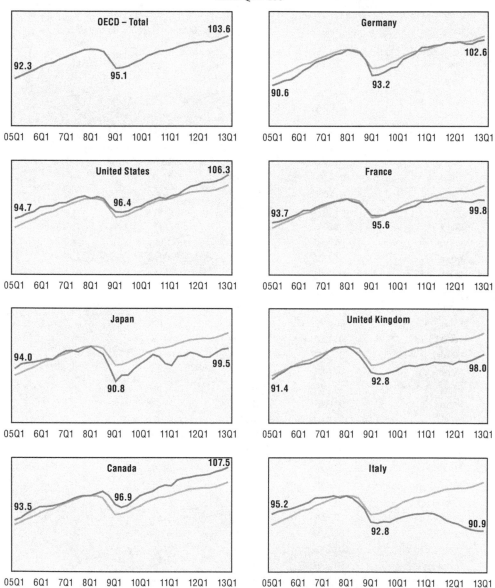

Source: OECD (2012), "Quarterly National Accounts", OECD National Accounts Statistics (database), doi: http://dx.doi.org/10.1787/data-00017-en.

StatLink http://dx.doi.org/10.1787/888933144240

OECD total real GDP declining only 0.1% in the second quarter of 2008. But the pace of the descent accelerated in the third quarter to 0.5%, and in the fourth quarter, following the bankruptcy of Lehman Brothers and the ensuing financial panic, GDP fell an additional 2.2%. In the first quarter of 2009, real GDP fell another 2.3% as it reached its cyclical trough.

Although there were some differences among the OECD countries in the timing and duration of the recession, the sharp decreases in the fourth quarter of 2008 and the first quarter of 2009 were synchronous among almost all of advanced economies. The real GDP of the United States reached its cyclical peak in the fourth quarter of 2007; it then decreased 0.7% in the first quarter of 2008, before rebounding with an increase of 0.5% in the second quarter. GDP turned down again in the third quarter, decreasing 0.5%, then fell 2.2% in the fourth quarter, 1.4% in the first quarter of 2009, and another 0.1% in the second quarter of 2009. In all, the Great Recession lasted six quarters in the United States and real GDP declined 4.3%.

In Europe, the declines in real GDP were even more severe. Among the OECD countries in Europe, GDP in aggregate decreased 5.7% from the first quarter of 2008 to the first quarter of 2009. Germany's GDP fell 6.8%, and France's GDP fell 4.4%. The decline in Italy's GDP began somewhat earlier, and it fell a cumulative 7.2% by the second quarter of 2009. The UK GDP also fell 7.2%. In many European countries, the level of pre-crisis peak was still not recovered in Q3 2013, 20 quarters after the first impact of the crisis.

The impact of the Great Recession was especially severe in Japan, where real GDP fell 9.2%. In Canada, on the other hand, the recession began relatively late, as the economy had been bolstered in the first half of 2008 by strong commodities prices. From the third quarter of 2008 through the second quarter of 2009, however, Canada's real GDP decreased 4.2%.

Similar patterns appeared among most of the OECD countries outside of the G7, though several countries experienced especially deep downturns. Estonia's GDP fell 20.0%. In Iceland, where the financial crisis led to the collapse of country's three largest commercial banks, the recession began earlier and lasted longer than in the other OECD countries; Iceland's GDP reached its trough in the second quarter of 2010, 12.8% below its cyclical peak. Ireland's GDP fell 11.5% from the fourth quarter of 2007 to the fourth quarter of 2009.

At the other end of the spectrum, a few OECD countries managed to avoid the worst effects of the global recession and did not experience the two consecutive quarters of decline in real GDP that typically denotes a recession. Poland's GDP fell in only one quarter, the fourth quarter of 2008, and only by 0.4%. The only quarterly decrease in Australia's GDP during the Great Recession occurred in the same quarter, a fall of 0.9%.[5] The GDP of Korea also only fell for one quarter, again the fourth quarter of 2008, though by a substantially larger amount, 4.6%. The GDP of the Slovak Republic also fell in a single quarter, the first quarter of 2009, but with a drop of 8.5% it can hardly be considered to have avoided the effects of the global recession. Finally, though the GDP of Israel experienced two quarters of decrease from the third quarter of 2008 to the first quarter of 2009, the cumulative decline was a relatively mild 0.9%.

In the emerging markets outside of the OECD, the impact of the Great Recession was more varied. A number of countries experienced downturns at the same time as the advanced countries. For example, South Africa's GDP decreased 2.7% over three quarters, Brazil's GDP decreased 5.4% over two quarters, and the GDP of the Russian Federation decreased 10.7% over four quarters. On the other hand, emerging markets in Asia appear to have been more insulated from the recession, with India experiencing only one quarter of decline, -1.9%, and Indonesia's GDP never declined. For China, we lack seasonally adjusted quarterly GDP measures for that period, but the annual GDP measures and other available data suggest that China's economy also continued to grow throughout the period.

Turning to the major components of GDP expenditures, most OECD countries experienced a similar pattern of change. For the OECD in total, real private (that is, households and non-profit institutions serving households) final consumption expenditures decreased 2.7% over the recession – a decrease that was smaller than the overall decrease in GDP, but nevertheless a major contributor to the drop in demand, due to the large share of private final consumption expenditures in final demand (see Figure 13.3). The decreases were more pronounced in gross fixed capital formation (including construction of new dwellings), which began falling in the first quarter and had decreased 15.1% over seven quarters when it reached its trough in the third quarter of 2009. In contrast, the decline in aggregate exports of the OECD countries lasted only three quarters, from the second quarter of 2008 to the first quarter of 2009, but the total decrease was very large, 15.2%. The decline in aggregate imports lasted a little longer; from the first quarter of 2008 to the second quarter of 2009, imports of goods and services fell 16.9%. In contrast, countercyclical fiscal policy contributed to growth in real general government final consumption expenditures, which increased 2.9% in OECD countries during the recession. Only later, during the recovery phase, would general government final consumption expenditures begin to decline as austerity measures were adopted. As described in Box 13.1, fiscal policy is reflected in several components of GDP, and not only in general government final consumption expenditures.

The national accounts also provide information on value added by industry. The downturn was concentrated in manufacturing and in the associated goods distribution industries of wholesale and retail trade and transportation. For example, for the European Union, the volume index for manufacturing gross value added fell 16.3% from 2007 to 2009; in the United States, it fell 11.5%. The construction industry in the United States,

Figure 13.3. **Real GDP by final expenditure category, OECD-Total
(2005 Q1-2013 Q3)**

2008 Q1 = 100

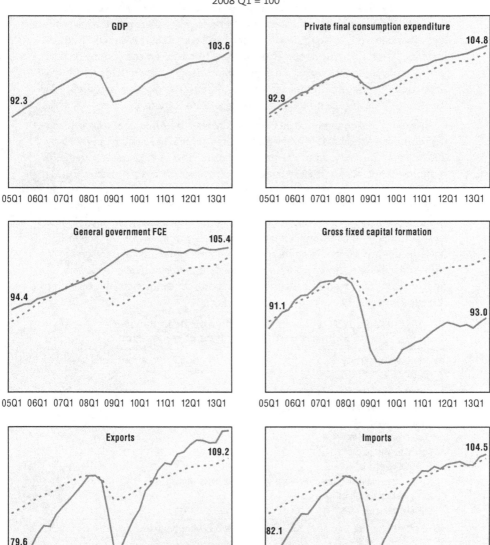

Source: OECD (2012), "Quarterly National Accounts", OECD National Accounts Statistics (database), doi: http://dx.doi.org/
10.1787/data-00017-en.   StatLink ⬛🔗 http://dx.doi.org/10.1787/888933144252

Box 13.1. Countercyclical fiscal policy in the national accounts

Countercyclical fiscal policy consists of increases in general government expenditures or reductions in taxes or other revenues that are intended to boost aggregate demand. Although government can boost demand directly through increases in final consumption expenditures, more often the countercyclical policy aims to boost household final consumption expenditures through reductions in taxes or increases in social benefits, or gross fixed capital formation through subsidies, capital transfers, or reductions in taxes.

An example of countercyclical fiscal policy was the American Recovery and Reinvestment Act of 2009 in the United States, which was enacted in February 2009. The estimated cost of the act in terms of increased expenditures and reduced receipts was USD 825.4 billion, with most of the costs occurring during the first three years. After accounting of the effects of the act through the first quarter of 2013, about 26% of the costs to the government came in the form of reduced taxes and other receipts, and about 74% came in the form of additional expenditures. The additional expenditures were primarily for social benefits (such as unemployment benefits and refundable tax credits) and for grants to state and local government; only 7.3% was spent by the federal government on final consumption or gross fixed capital formation that enters GDP expenditures directly (see Table 13.2).

Table 13.2. Share of Costs the American Recovery and Reinvestment Act, by type of transaction

Federal Government Transaction	Percent of total cost of act
Receipts (reductions)	25.7%
Current taxes on income, wealth, etc. (households)	23.1
Current taxes on income, wealth, etc. (corporations)	2.5
Expenditures (additions)	74.3
Final consumption expenditures	5.1
Current transfer payments	54.7
Social benefits	25.0
Other current transfers (primarily grants to state & local government)	29.8
Gross fixed capital formation	2.2
Capital transfer payments	10.0

Source: US Bureau of Economic Analysis, Federal recovery programs and BEA statistics, www.bea.gov/recovery/.

experienced a long, steep decline that began before the recession, with real gross value added falling 28.5% from 2005 to 2010. Also, finance and insurance activity in the United States was adversely impacted by the drop off in mortgage activity and by the financial crisis, falling 15.2% from 2006 to 2008, before rebounding in 2009.[6] (See Box 13.2)

Box 13.2. **How the financial crisis affected measures of financial services**

In Chapter 4, the section "Going Further: FISIM" describes how banks and other financial intermediaries provide services to their customers that are not invoiced directly. Although banks usually charge fees, their fees do not fully cover the cost of the services that they provide. A portion of the services that banks provide are paid for indirectly by charging a higher average rate of interest on the funds that they lend than the average rate of interest that they pay to depositors. The margin between these two rates of interest is another source of funds, in addition to fees, which can be used to pay for the provision of services and is known as financial intermediation services indirectly measured (FISIM). As described in Chapter 4, the cost of these services is assigned to depositors and to borrowers based on the differences between the depositor and borrower rates and a reference interest rate.

During the financial crisis, the first impact was an increase in the loans and other financial assets that were classified as nonperforming (that is, loans whose payments of interest or principal are past due by 90 days or more) or that defaulted. Nonperforming loans do not appear directly on the SNA balance sheets, though it recommends that they be recorded as memorandum items. In cases in which mortgages or other loans that were securitised, the market value of those securities fell during the crisis, which was reflected on the SNA balance sheets as a revaluation.

As the crisis proceeded, investors engaged in a "flight to quality," withdrawing funds from investments that were regarded as risky – causing their interest rates to rise – and moving their funds into the investments that were regarded as safe, such as Treasury securities or government-insured deposit accounts – causing their interest rates to fall. In terms of the national accounts measure of FISIM, there were several effects moving in different directions. In the case of the United States, for example, both the reference interest rate and the rate paid to depositors declined as part of the flight to quality. Rates charged on loans increased relative to the reference rate, but much of that increase represented charges that were required to offset the increased risk of default, which is not recognised as a cost of production in the SNA. Consequently, the US national accounts have decided to make an adjustment to their FISIM calculations to remove the effects of changes in expected defaults.[1] The FISIM estimates for the United States indicate that the value (in current prices) of both depositor and borrower services declined during the financial crisis, though the value of depositor services recovered relatively quickly[2] (see Chapter 4 for more).

1. See Hood, 2013.
2. The value of depositor services is presented on line 44, and the value of borrower services on line 96, of national income and product accounts table 7.11, Bureau of Economic Analysis website.

Aggregate demand and supply

Economists often explain recessions in terms of shifts in aggregate demand and aggregate supply. Although these are theoretical concepts, the measures in the national accounts can be used to represent these concepts in actual economic data.

Aggregate demand represents the relationship between the aggregate volume of goods and services that are demanded by final users and the aggregate price level. It is generally drawn as a downward sloping curve in which the volume of output demanded increases as the aggregate price level falls. The aggregate demand curve can shift in response to changes monetary or fiscal policy.[7]

Changes in aggregate demand will be reflected in changes in nominal GDP (which is the product of real GDP and the GDP price deflator), so the movements in nominal GDP are often taken to be an approximate indicator of aggregate demand. Figure 13.4 shows changes in the nominal GDP for the United States and the Euro area, both areas showing a sharp downward shift during the Great Recession. After the Great Recession, nominal GDP in the United States resumed growing, though it never exhibited accelerated growth to allow it to catch up to the previous trend line. In the Euro area, nominal GDP experienced a second slowdown beginning in 2011 and is now far below its pre-recession trend. Nominal GDP of most OECD countries fell in 2009, though notable exceptions included Australia, Israel, Korea, and Poland – countries that also managed to avoid the sustained effects of the recession. Decreases in aggregate demand, as measured by nominal GDP, appear to have been a major contributor to the recession in most countries.

Figure 13.4. **GDP in current prices, national currency, for United States and Euro Area Countries (2005 Q1-2013 Q3)**

2008 Q1 = 100

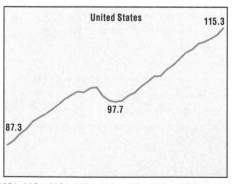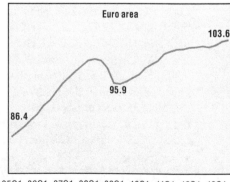

05Q1 06Q1 07Q1 08Q1 09Q1 10Q1 11Q1 12Q1 13Q1   05Q1 06Q1 07Q1 08Q1 09Q1 10Q1 11Q1 12Q1 13Q1

Source: OECD (2012), "Quarterly National Accounts", OECD National Accounts Statistics (database), doi: *http://dx.doi.org/10.1787/data-00017-en.*

StatLink ⬛⬛⬛ http://dx.doi.org/10.1787/888933144265

On the other hand, changes in aggregate supply – that is, a shift in the level of potential GDP – may be harder to characterise with national accounts data. In some cases, they may be associated with "stagflation" – that is, a decline in real GDP associated with acceleration in inflation. Because there are many factors that could cause the level of potential GDP to change, such as productivity shocks, changes in the terms of trade, or the deadweight losses associated with changes in taxes or regulations, it may not be possible to easily identify all changes in aggregate supply.

Although more difficult to measure, aggregate supply factors may have also contributed. In particular, the global prices of oil and other commodities increased sharply in the first half of 2008. This is because, despite the recession in OECD countries, the global demand for commodities remained high as the emerging part of the world – countries such as China, India, and Indonesia – continued to boom. The disconnect between the global situation of OECD countries and the outlook of big emerging countries is one of the important new features of the global economy. For countries that import commodities, these price increases contributed to consumer inflation and to deterioration in the terms of trade. For example, in the United States, the price index for private final consumption expenditure increased 4.0% from the third quarter of 2007 to the third quarter of 2008, whereas the GDP price index increased only 2.2% (see Figure 13.5). Over the same period, the terms of trade index (the ratio of the export price index to the import price index) fell from 100.0 to 92.5.[8] The increase in energy prices may have depressed consumer spending on other goods and services and increased the costs of manufacturing and other activities.[9] On the

Figure 13.5. **GDP Deflator and Private Final Consumption Expenditure Deflator, United States (2006 Q1-2010 Q3)**
2008 Q1 = 100

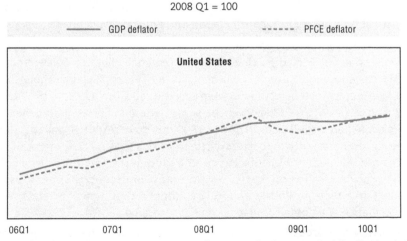

Source: OECD (2012), "Quarterly National Accounts", *OECD National Accounts Statistics* (database), doi: http://dx.doi.org/10.1787/data-00017-en.   StatLink ᴍᴍᴘ http://dx.doi.org/10.1787/888933144277

other hand, for countries that export commodities, the increase in commodity prices boosted their terms of trade and helped delay some of the adverse impacts of the financial crisis, though commodity prices ultimately dropped sharply in the fourth quarter as the effects of the Great Recession extended globally.

Saving, net lending or borrowing, and balance sheets

The effects of the global financial crisis and the Great Recession are apparent not only in the measures of production and income, but also in the effects on saving, net lending or borrowing, and on balance sheets. The recession has led to renewed interest by economists in the relationships between balance sheets and economic activity.[10]

In the United Kingdom and the United States, the rapid growth in real estate prices during the "housing bubble" from 2001 to 2006 was associated with lower household saving and growth in household debt. For example, by 2007 net saving of households and NPISH was 3.2% of net disposable income in the United States and even negative, -3.7% of net disposable income, in the United Kingdom. Denmark and Ireland, which also experienced real estate bubbles, also exhibited negative household net saving in 2007. By 2009, illustrating the major change in prospects for the future, the household saving rates in these countries had increased – by more than 3 percentage points in the United States (to 6.4%), by nearly 6 percentage points in the United Kingdom (to 2.3%), by 4 percentage points in Denmark, and by 12 percentage points in Ireland. The increase in household net saving was reflected in weakness in the household consumption component of GDP final expenditures for these countries.

These effects on net saving were less pronounced in countries that had not participated in the boom in real estate prices. There was essentially no increase in the household saving rate in Germany or Italy, and increases of only about one percentage point in Japan and France.

The notable increase in saving in the United Kingdom and the United States was also reflected on the household balance sheet as deleveraging – that is, as reductions in household debt. In the United Kingdom, household debt as a percentage of net disposable income fell from 179.8 to 167.9 from 2007 to 2009 (See Figure 13.6). Over the same period, the household debt ratio in the United States fell from 142.8 to 133.3. This downturn in household debt, however, was primarily associated with countries that had experienced the real estate bubble. As shown in Figure 13.6, during the Great Recessions the household debt ratios of Japan and Germany continued their downward trends, while those of France and Italy continued their upward trends, with little evidence of a notable impact from the recession.

During the Great Recession, the net lending of general government decreased (or net borrowing increased) for almost all OECD countries. Of

Figure 13.6. **Debt of Households as a Percentage of Net Disposable Income, Selected Countries (2001-12)**

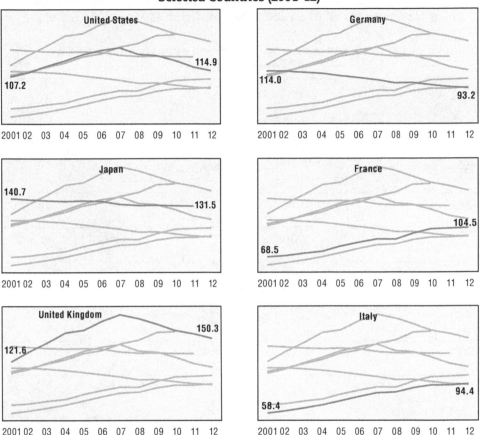

Source: OECD (2014), "National Accounts at a Glance: National Accounts at a Glance", OECD National Accounts Statistics (database), doi: http://dx.doi.org/10.1787/data-00369-en.

StatLink ᴍᴇᴅ http://dx.doi.org/10.1787/888933144281

course, there were many recession-related economic factors that would have automatically contributed to this decrease in the fiscal balance, such as the reduction in tax receipts as economic activity and incomes declined and the automatic increases in expenditures for various social benefits, such as unemployment insurance. Furthermore, a number of countries undertook expansionary fiscal programmes, such as the American Recovery and Reinvestment Act of 2009 in the United States and various car scrappage ("cash for clunkers") programmes in various OECD countries. From 2007 to 2009, net borrowing as a percentage of GDP increased by 9 percentage points (from 3.6% to 12.7%) in the United States, by 8 percentage points in the United Kingdom, by 6 percentage points in Japan, and by more than 4 percentage points in the Euro area.

Along with the reduction in net lending (or increase in net borrowing), from 2007 to 2009 the debt of general government as a percentage of GDP increased in almost all OECD countries, (see Figure 13.7). In some cases, the

Figure 13.7. **Debt of General Government as a Percentage of GDP, G7 Countries (2002-12)**

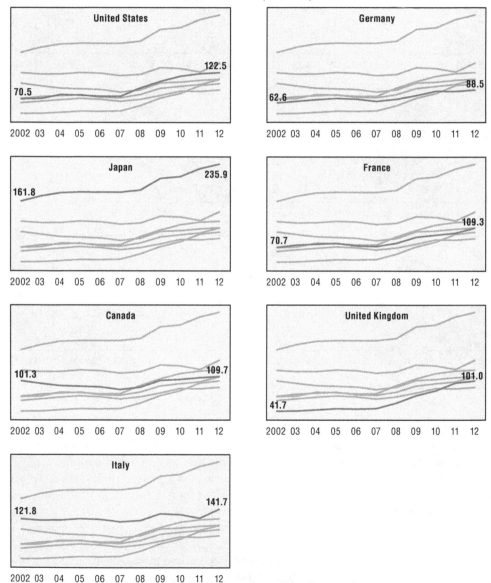

Source: OECD (2014), "National Accounts at a Glance: National Accounts at a Glance", OECD National Accounts Statistics (database), doi: http://dx.doi.org/10.1787/data-00369-en.

StatLink 🔗 http://dx.doi.org/10.1787/888933144296

increases in the general government debt ratio during the recession were quite large – for example, from 2007 to 2009 the US ratio increased 29 percentage points (from 75.8% to 105.0%), and the UK ratio increased 25 percentage points (from 47.0% to 72.1%). Many other countries also had increases in the debt ratio of 10 percentage points or more. Box 13.3 explains the difficulty in comparing levels of government debt between OECD countries.

Box 13.3. **Measuring and comparing public debt**

Public debt as a percentage of GDP is a headline indicator. But there are many ways (i.e. conventions) to measure the numerator of this ratio. All of them will more or less show the same "story" of the debt increasing more than GDP during the recent period, similarly to what is shown by Figure 13.7. Thus, in terms of changes in debt, all measurement conventions will tend to give the same message. But Figure 13.7 can also be used to compare debt levels between countries. This is where the convention chosen can dramatically change the picture. Some conventions do not allow good international comparability. Figure 13.7 is one of them despite the fact that it reflects total liabilities of general government as reported in OECD statistical databases.

Consolidation

Generally, the public debt of the general government is shown consolidated. This means that if one unit of the government owes debt to another unit of the government, this is not counted in the overall public debt. Indeed, this debt is internal to the government. This convention is widely implemented and Figure 13.7 shows consolidated debt for all countries, except Japan, which does not transmit consolidated figures to the OECD. Thus while comparability with respect to consolidation is ensured for other countries, it is not the case for Japan which levels of debt are systematically overestimated in Figure 13.7 compared to other countries (by between 8% in 2002 to 17% in 2012).

Netting assets

Figure 13.7 shows gross debt. This means it reflects all the liabilities owed by the general government without taking into account the assets that the government may dispose of. For example, government may issue bonds on the financial markets in order to lend to banks. In this case, this borrowing increases the gross debt, but one could consider that it does not increase the net debt, as the government has an asset (the loan to the banks) which is the counterpart of the bonds. Most common figures of public debt are gross ones (in particular the Maastricht debt), but the OECD also publishes a figure of net debt, which is equal to the gross debt minus all financial assets owned by the general government. This reduces the level of public debt, and may change the relative level of public debt between countries. Economists are split between those in favour of monitoring gross debt and those in favour of monitoring net debt.

Box 13.3. **Measuring and comparing public debt** (cont.)

Coverage of debt instruments

Figure 13.7 shows the widest convention for measuring public debt. It reflects the total of all gross liabilities of the general government as recorded in the national accounts. This covers liabilities in: currency and deposits (F2), bonds (F3-which constitute the core of public debt), loans (F4), pension liabilities (F6), and payables (F8*). The international comparability of this measure is problematic, essentially because of the recording of pension liabilities of government employees. In non-European OECD countries, such as the United States, Australia or Canada, national accounts include an estimate of the obligation of the government in terms of the future pensions of its employees. In EU countries, the national accounts do not include this amount. This is a very substantial amount, representing around 14% of GDP in Canada in 2012, and 20% in the United States In terms of level of debt, the convention used in Figure 13.7 is therefore fraught with non-comparability as it includes these amounts for Canada and United States, but not for France, Germany, Italy, Japan and UK, even though there are such pension obligations in these countries, but which are not recorded in the national accounts.

Maastricht convention

In the EU, the Stability and Growth Pact, a cornerstone of the fiscal monitoring of EU member states, uses a convention which is even more restrictive. The financial instruments that are included are only F2 (currency and deposits), F3 (bonds) and F4 (loans). This excludes F8 (payables) in addition to the exclusion of F6 (pension liabilities) already discussed above. The Maastricht debt uses also a valuation of debt at so-called "face" value, while other valuations are at "nominal" value (which means including interest accrued but not paid) or even, which is the theory in national accounts, at "market value" (bonds are revalued as if they were exchanged on secondary markets). However, only few countries apply thoroughly the valuation at market value for public debt in their national accounts.

Table 13.3 gives an indication on the impact of these differing conventions on the level of debt for a sample of three countries. As can be seen, the order of ranking in terms of debt level changes dramatically depending on the convention used. In particular, the situation of Canada appears much better when using more comparable data. In fact, OECD's Economic Outlook does not publish the data corresponding to Figure 13.7, as it is considered not comparable enough.

* F7 in SNA 1993

Source: OECD (2014), "Financial Balance Sheets: Consolidated stocks, annual", OECD National Accounts Statistics (database), doi: http://dx.doi.org/10.1787/data-00024-en.

Box 13.3. **Measuring and comparing public debt** (cont.)

Table 13.3. **Effects of different conventions on level of debt**

2012, in percentage of GDP	United States	Canada	France
(1) Gross total liabilities (Figure 13.7)	122.5	109.7	109.3
(2) Gross debt excluding pension liabilities (line 1 – F6)	102.1	96.1	109.3
(3) Maastricht debt (line 2 – F8; at face value)[*]	94.2	72.9	90.2
(4) Net debt excluding pension liabilities (line 2 – financial assets)	80.0	43.6	70.3

[*] Estimate by OECD for USA and Canada.

Source: OECD (2014), National Accounts at a Glance: National Accounts at a Glance, OECD National Accounts Statistics (database), doi: http://dx.doi.org/10.1787/data-00369-en

2. Slow economic recovery

After reaching a trough in the first half of 2009, the advanced economies began growing again, but in most countries the growth was slow and erratic (see the final column of Table 13.1). Over the 4½ years from the trough of the Great Recession through the third quarter of 2013, real GDP of the OECD in aggregate increased 9.0%, or at an average annual rate of 1.9%.

In many European countries, the recovery from the Great Recession was interrupted by economic downturns due to the sovereign debt crisis and the related banking crisis in the Euro area. For example, the Euro area experienced a gradual recovery over the first two years after the trough, and its real GDP had increased 4.0% by the third quarter of 2011. Then much of Europe entered another recession, with GDP for the Euro area decreasing 1.5% over the next six quarters. After the first quarter of 2013, Euro area GDP resumed gradual growth.

Aggregate averages, however, hide a great deal of variation in the experiences of various countries; within the Euro area, there have been large differences between countries. Greece, at the center of the Euro area crisis, has, unfortunately, experienced the largest and most continuous recession in the world, with an estimated 25% decrease in real GDP between the last quarter of 2007 and the last quarter of 2013. Portugal's GDP began declining again in the fourth quarter of 2010 and had decreased 7.0% by the first quarter of 2013. Rather than recovering from the Great Recession, from the trough in 2009 through the fourth quarter of 2013, Portugal's real GDP decreased 2.8%. Italy's GDP began to decline in the third quarter of 2011, and by the third quarter of 2013 it had decreased 4.9%. As of the fourth quarter of 2013, Italy's real GDP was 2.0% below its 2009 trough. Spain's GDP began declining in the second quarter of 2011 and fell 3.3% by the second quarter of 2013. From the 2009 trough through the fourth quarter of 2013, Spain's GDP had decreased 2.3%.

At the other end of the spectrum within Europe, over 19 quarters from the end of the Great Recession, Poland's GDP grew 14.2%, a 2.8% annual rate, and the Slovak Republic's GDP grew 13.4%, a 2.7% annual rate. The largest economy of the Euro area, Germany, also experienced relatively solid growth, with its real GDP growing 10.5%, a 2.1% annual rate. On the other hand, France's GDP grew only 4.6% (a 1.0% annual rate), and GDP of the Netherlands grew only 2.0% (a 0.4% annual rate). The United Kingdom, which is not part of the Euro area, also experienced a downturn for three quarters in 2011-2012 and overall modest growth since the 2009 trough of 6.3% (a 1.5% annual rate).

In North America, the recovery proceeded at a slow, but relatively steady pace. US GDP increased 11.2% since the 2009 trough, a 2.4% annual rate, and experienced only one quarter of decrease (in the first quarter of 2011). Canada's GDP increased at a 2.5% annual rate, and Mexico's increased at a 3.8% annual rate. In Northeast Asia, Japan's GDP experienced two periods of downturn, a drop of 2.4% over the first two quarters of 2011, and another decline of 1.3% over the first three quarters of 2012. Overall, Japan's GDP grew 9.9% (a 2.0% annual rate) from its trough in 2009 through the fourth quarter of 2013. Korea, on the other hand, experienced relatively uninterrupted growth of 21.8%, a 4.0% annual rate.

In terms of GDP final expenditures, growth in exports was the main driver of recovery in most OECD countries. Contrary to what happened after the depression of 1929, policy makers did not fall into the trap of anti-globalisation policies. For the OECD countries in aggregate, real exports increased 28.7% from the trough of the recession in the first quarter of 2009 through the third quarter of 2013, a 5.8% average annual growth rate (see Figure 13.3). Imports increased 22.8%, a 4.7% growth rate, over the same span. In contrast to most economic recoveries, however, the recovery in gross fixed capital formation was unusually weak. Since the 2009 trough in GDP, real gross fixed capital formation increased only 6.3%, a 1.4% annual rate, and remained 7.0% below its level in the first quarter of 2008, when GDP for the OECD countries was at its pre-recession peak. Private final consumption expenditure grew, but more slowly than GDP (7.6%, a 1.6% annual rate) as consumers in several countries continued to deleverage. General government final consumption expenditure grew during the first four quarters of the recovery, but after the second quarter of 2010 it began to contract as many countries began to institute austerity measures in response to the expansion in general government debt. By the third quarter of 2013, general government final consumption expenditure was only 2.4% above its level at the trough of the Great Recession.

Government debt and deficit were perhaps the mostly hotly debated economic policy issues during the recovery. Despite austerity measures that included cuts in social benefits and tax increases, government debt continued to rise in many OECD countries as slow economic growth constrained the recovery in government receipts. From 2009 to 2012, debt as a percentage of GDP increased in all of the G7 countries by amounts ranging from 29 percentage points in the United Kingdom to 8 percentage points in Canada (see Figure 13.7).

3. Prelude to the financial crisis

We've seen that the national accounts provide us with a statistical account of the Great Recession and the subsequent slow recovery. To what extent do the national accounts also provide us with an account of the imbalances that led to the global financial crisis? This turns out to be a question of some interest, as analysts have noted that the national accounts had both successes and failures in identifying the critical imbalances.

This is an opportunity to remind users of national accounts that it is unfortunately not possible to find a housing price index directly from the national accounts tables. Indeed, while revaluations include the impact of the change in the price of old dwellings on the value of households assets, it does not include information on the volume of the stock of old dwellings. It would be interesting for national accounts users that such a housing price index is included in the standard national accounts tables.

The real estate bubble that affected the United States was visible in the balance sheets of the US integrated macroeconomic accounts, as seen in Figure 13.8. From 2001 to 2006, real estate assets owned by households increased 67.6%.[11] The increase primarily reflected revaluation due to rising real estate prices, though housing construction also contributed to the increase. The effects of the subsequent crash in real estate prices are also apparent, with the value of household real estate assets dropping 27.4% from 2006 to 2011. The increase in household leverage is also apparent, as US households became net borrowers during the years of the real estate boom. This was also the case in Ireland and Spain, two other countries strongly affected by a housing bubble.

Although in principle, the national accounts should be able to tell similar stories for all of the countries that experienced a real estate bubble, in practice we are limited by the lack of complete nonfinancial balance sheets for many countries. In a 2009 report to the G20 finance ministers and central bank

Figure 13.8. **Real estate assets of households and NPISH, United States (2001-12)**

Billion of US dollars

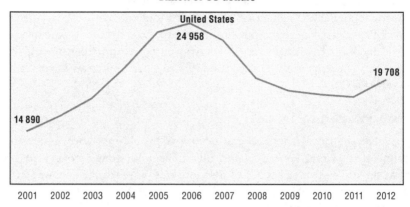

Source: Integrated Macroeconomic accounts of the United States, table S.3.a, from Bureau of Economic Analysis, www.bea.gov/national/sna.htm.

StatLink ▉▉▉ http://dx.doi.org/10.1787/888933144309

governors, the IMF staff and Financial Stability Board Secretariat concluded, "The crisis has weaknesses in the availability of some sectoral and other financial economic databases." It recommended "a strategy to promote the compilation and dissemination of the [balance sheet approach], flow of funds, and sectoral data more generally."[12]

In 2009, Michael Palumbo and Jonathan Parker wrote an interesting critique of the effectiveness of the US integrated macroeconomic accounts in identifying macroeconomic imbalances in the years leading up to the financial crisis.[13] While they found that the SNA data correctly identified the increased leverage and borrowing of the household sector, primarily with mortgages, they also found that the rise in the aggregate home loan-to-value ratio was relatively small. From other sources, they were aware that many mortgages were initiated with little down payment and extremely high leverage, but this effect was not apparent in the home loan-to-value ratio because rising real estate prices greatly boosted the denominator of this aggregate ratio. However, as Takashi Yamashita pointed out, another measure of growth in leverage can be constructed from the flow data, the ratio of the household sector's net incurrence of mortgage debt to gross residential fixed capital formation, which is shown for the United States in Figure 13.9.[14] If mortgage debt was incurred to purchase newly constructed dwellings, this ratio would indicate the typical mortgage share of financing of new home purchases. However, in the United States much mortgage debt is incurred through refinancing, and refinancing often allows the homeowner to take cash out (that is, refinance with a larger mortgage than the previous one, with

Figure 13.9. **Ratio of net incurrence of mortgages to residential gross fixed capital formation, Households and NPISH, United States (1998-2007)**

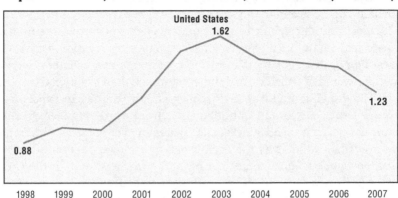

Source: Integrated Macroeconomic accounts of the United States, table S.3.a, from Bureau of Economic Analysis, *www.bea.gov/national/sna.htm.*

StatLink ⟨ᵐˢᴾᴬ http://dx.doi.org/10.1787/888933144312

the difference reflecting a cash payment to the homeowner). Cash-out refinancing can thus be used to fund household consumption expenditures and was regarded as a contributor to the high levels of household consumption and low levels of saving during the housing bubble. This ratio moved above 1.0 in 2001 and remained above 1.4 during the real estate bubble of 2002 through 2006, as cash-out mortgage re-financing allowed consumers to increase spending and reduce their saving. The unusually high level of this ratio was indicative of the high level of exposure of mortgage borrowers to volatility in real estate prices. It peaked in 2003, as gross residential fixed capital formation (the denominator of the ratio) grew rapidly during the last years of the real estate bubble.

The inability of the national accounts to identify subsets of households that were highly leveraged or otherwise under financial duress has led to efforts to develop data on the distribution of income and of consumption that are consistent with the more aggregated national accounts data. The Commission on the Measurement of Economic Performance and Social Progress, chaired by Joseph Stiglitz, Amartya Sen, and Jean-Paul Fitoussi, recommended giving more prominence to the distribution of income, consumption, and wealth, and the OECD has formed an Expert Group on Disparities in National Accounts. This was also one of the recommendations by the IMF and the Financial Stability Board in their report to the G20 finance ministers on data gaps.

Palumbo and Parker were also critical of the capability of the US integrated macroeconomic accounts to identify the financial sector's "rise in exposure to the housing market as well as increases in leverage, balance sheet complexity, maturity mismatch, and counterparty risk-taking," factors that they saw as critical in the spreading of the real estate market shocks to financial institutions and to the real economy.[15] In particular, they noted that two factors made it difficult to see the increased exposure of the financial sector to real estate price shocks. First, the SNA's aggregation across asset classes did not distinguish different types of bonds and collateralised debt obligations, some of which carried much more risk than traditional corporate bonds. The growing importance of securitization resulted in exposures to mortgage debt that couldn't be identified from aggregate SNA financial account and balance sheet data. Second, aggregation of financial corporations made it difficult to identify the high levels of leverage of certain financial institutions, such as investment banks, broker/dealers, and, in the United States, government-sponsored enterprises such as Fannie Mae and Freddie Mac. Because the financial corporations sector mixes high leverage institutions with other institutions that carry very little leverage, such as mutual funds, pension funds, and insurance companies, the financial sector as a whole showed only a modest increase in balance sheet leverage during the credit boom.

To some extent, the issue of excessive aggregation is already addressed within the SNA through its ability to disaggregate into smaller subsectors and financial instruments. Furthermore, the data gaps initiative of the IMF and the Financial Stability Board includes several concrete recommendations to better monitor risk and share information. Nevertheless, aggregated information will probably always face the criticism that the process of aggregation hides or disguises important risks, which implies that macroeconomic statistics will never fully substitute for the monitoring of institution and asset-specific risks. The measurement community, however, continues to conduct research on developing improved measures of risk and integrating that information with the national accounts.[16]

Another set of imbalances that has received considerable attention is the external balances, as summarised by the current and financial accounts. For several countries that experienced housing bubbles, including the United States, Spain, and Ireland, the countries became significant net borrowers prior to the Great Recession. We should also note, however, that some countries that fared poorly did not experience large swings in the current or financial account balances, and that other countries that fared relatively well, such as Poland, were net borrowers during that period.

In conclusion, although the national accounts were not able to capture all of the imbalances that developed during the 2000s prior to the financial crisis and the Great Recession, they were very useful for identifying a number of the most important imbalances. Furthermore, continuing work such as the G20 data gaps initiative and other efforts to add distributional and risk information to the national accounting framework should lead to improved performance in the future. Furthermore, in tracking the economic activity, income, saving, and balance sheets during and after the Great Recession, the national accounts were indispensable.

Notes

1. See Isidore, 2007 and Bernanke, 2007.

2. See Federal Reserve Bank of St. Louis, 2008 and Johnson, 2008.

3. For example, Schiller, 2008; Reinhart and Rogoff, 2009; Lowenstein, 2010; Johnson and Kwok, 2010; Lewis, 2011; Rajan, 2011; Gorton, 2012.

4. Except where specifically noted otherwise, the source of all of the statistical data cited in this chapter is the OECD Stat Extracts database, and in most cases they reflect the data that were available on February 24, 2014.

5. Source: Australian bureau of statistics (2013): Australian system of National Accounts, *www.abs.gov.au/AUSSTATS/abs@.nsf/DetailsPage/5204.02012-13?OpenDocument*.

6. The data cited in this paragraph are from the national accounts databases shown on the Eurostat and Bureau of Economic Analysis websites.

7. See, for example, Mankiw (2003), pp. 242-245.

8. Source: National accounts database, NIPA Table 1.8.6, Bureau of Economic Analysis website.

9. For example, see Hamilton, 2009: 215-261.

10. For example, see Mian and al, 2010: 74-11 6 and Dynan, 2012: 299-34 4.

11. Source: Integrated macroeconomic accounts of the United States, table S.3.a, Bureau of Economic Analysis website.

12. See IMF and al., 2009.

13. See Palumbo and al. 2009: 80-86 ; Eichner and al. 2010.

14. See Yamashita, 2013.

15. See Palumbo and al. 2009b. 80-86.

16. See Hulten and al., forthcoming.

References

Australian bureau of statistics (2013): Australian system of National Accounts, *www.abs.gov.au/AUSSTATS/abs@.nsf/DetailsPage/5204.02012-13?OpenDocument*.

Bernanke, B. S (2007), "The Subprime Mortgage Market", speech given at Federal Reserve Bank of Chicago's 43rd Annual Conference on Bank Structure and Competition (May 17).

Dynan, K. E. (2012), "Is a Household Debt Overhang Holding Back Consumption?" Brookings Papers on Economic Activity (Spring).

Eichner, M. J., Donald, L.K, and. Palumbo, M. G, "Financial Statistics for the United States and the Crisis: What Did They Get Right, What Did They Miss, and How Should They Change?" paper presented at Fifth ECB Conference on Central Bank Statistics, Frankfurt, April 22-12 , 2010.

Federal Reserve Bank of St. Louis (2008), "The Financial Crisis: A Timeline of Events and Policy Actions"; Martin Neal Baily, Robert E. Litan.

FRED (Federal Reserve Economic Data), Federal Reserve Bank of St. Louis, *http://research.stlouisfed.org/*.

Gorton, G. B. (2012), Misunderstanding Financial Crises: Why We Don't See Them Coming, Oxford University Press, New York.

Hamilton, J. D. (2009), "Causes and Consequences of the Oil Shock of 2007-08", Brookings Papers on Economic Activity (Spring).

Hood, K. K. (2013), "Measuring the Services of Commercial Banks in the National Income and Product Accounts: Changes in Concepts and Methods in the 2013 Comprehensive Revision", Survey of Current Business, 93, No. 2 (February), 8-19.

Hulten, C., Palumbo, M. and Reinsdorf, M. (forthcoming), Wealth, Financial Intermediation, and the Real Economy, NBER Book Series, Studies in Income and Wealth, conference held November 12-13 , 2010.

IMF staff and the Financial Stability Board Secretariat (2009), "The Financial Crisis and Information Gaps", Report to the G20 finance ministers and central bank governors (October 29).

Integrated Macroeconomic accounts of the United States, table S.3.a, from Bureau of Economic Analysis, *www.bea.gov/national/sna.htm.*

Isidore, C. (2007), "Subprime Woes: How Far, How Wide?" CNNMoney (March 5).

Johnson, M.S (2008), "The Origins of the Financial Crisis", Brookings Institution, Fixing Finance Series – Paper 3 (November).

Johnson, S.and Kwok, J. (2010), 13 Bankers: The Wall Street Takeover and the Next Financial Meltdown, Vintage Books, New York.

Lewis, M. (2011), The Big Short: Inside the Doomsday Machine, W.W. Norton & Company, New York.

Lowenstein, R. (2010), The End of Wall Street, Penguin Press, New York.

Mankiw, N. G. (2003), Macroeconomics, Worth Publishers, New York.

Mian Atif and Sufi Amir (2010), "Household Leverage and the Recession of 2007-2009", IMF Economic Review, 51, No. 1 (April).

OECD (2012a), "Quarterly National Accounts", OECD National Accounts Statistics (database), doi: *http://dx.doi.org/10.1787/data-00017-en.*

OECD (2010b), "National Accounts at a Glance: National Accounts at a Glance", OECD National Accounts Statistics (database), doi: *http://dx.doi.org/10.1787/data-00369-en.*

OECD (2010c), "Financial Balance Sheets: Consolidated stocks, annual", OECD National Accounts Statistics (database), doi: *http://dx.doi.org/10.1787/data-00024-en.*

Palumbo, M. G. and Jonathan A. Parker (2009), "The Integrated Financial and Real System of National Accounts for the United States: Does It Presage the Financial Crisis?", American Economic Review: Papers & Proceedings, 99, No. 2; *www.aeaweb.org/articles.php?doi=10.1257/aer.99.2.80.*

Rajan Raghuram G. (2011), Fault Lines: How Hidden Fractures Still Threaten the World Economy, Princeton University Press, Princeton.

Reinhart, C.M. and Rogoff, K.S. (2009), This Time Is Different: Eight Centuries of Financial Folly, Princeton University Press, Princeton.

Shiller, R. (2008), The Subprime Solution: How Today's Global Financial Crisis Happened and What to Do about It, Princeton University Press, Princeton.

US Bureau of Economic Analysis, "Federal recovery programs and BEA statistics", *www.bea.gov/recovery/*.

Yamashita, T. (2013), "A Guide to the Integrated Macroeconomic Accounts", Survey of Current Business, 93, No. 4 (April), 12-26.

Chapter 14

International systems
of national accounts:
Past and future

This chapter presents the history of systems of national accounts, from the 17th century to today. After a look at the earliest accounts, it offers in-depth analysis of the 1953, 1968, 1993 and 2008 systems of national accounts (SNAs). It also looks at the 1995 and 2010 European System of Accounts (ESA). For both, it clearly explains what aspects of SNAs and ESAs have evolved across the years, with helpful boxes outlining the changes in each iteration, in particular the latest one (SNA 2008/ESA 2010).

There are four relatively recent studies of the history of national accounts. The preface to the 1993 *System of National Accounts* describes the development of the 1953, 1968 and 1993 versions of the SNA. André Vanoli, the French expert in national accounts, provides an impressive overview in *A History of National Accounts* (Vanoli, 2005). Angus Maddison in the introduction of *The World Economy: Historical Statistics* (OECD, 2003), describes the very earliest attempts to measure national income. A very entertaining history of national accounts, linking it to the early development of bookkeeping and business accounting in the golden age of Venice merchants, is provided in *Double Entry* (Gleeson-White, 2011). Maddison is the main source for the next section.

1. From the very beginnings…

Historically, wars and threats of war have provided the main impetus for the development of national accounts. They were seen as a quantitative framework for devising policies to mobilise a nation's resources to fight wars or to repair the subsequent damage. The first national accounts were developed in the 17th Century by William Petty. His *Verbum Sapienta* (1665) presented a set of national accounts for England and Wales designed for resource mobilisation during the second Anglo-Dutch war from 1664 to 1667. In 1694, Charles Davenant published a crude set of national accounts in *Essay upon Ways and Means of Supplying the War* (war of the League of Augsburg from 1668 to 1697), and this encouraged his friend Gregory King to produce a more detailed set of economic and demographic accounts in *Natural and Physical Observations and Conclusions on the State and Condition of England* (1696). In 1707, Sebastien le Prestre de Vauban published estimates of French national income in *La dîme royale*. Vauban's interest in the topic came from his experience in mobilising resources for the construction of military forts on the northern and eastern borders of France.

2. …to the first modern accounts

Jumping ahead a few centuries to the modern era, the first official national income statistics were published in the United States (1934) by Simon Kuznets (Nobel Price 1971) and in the United Kingdom (1941) by Richard Stone (Nobel Prize 1984). The impetus was again to provide quantitative frameworks for war-time resource mobilisation and peacetime reconstruction.

In 1947, Richard Stone wrote a report, *Definition and measurement of the national income and related totals,* for the Sub-Committee on National Income Statistics of the League of Nations Committee of Statistical Experts. This was the first step toward an international accounting system. Stone was subsequently invited by the Organisation for European Economic Co-operation (OEEC, later to become the OECD) to develop a system of national accounts that could be used by its member countries to monitor post-war reconstruction under the Marshall Plan. The Marshall Plan, named after a United States Secretary of State, was an extensive programme of financial aid from the United States and Canada to the European countries that had been devastated by World War II. The result of Stone's work, *A Standardised System of National Accounts* published by the OEEC in 1952, can fairly be described as the first international system. The following year, the United Nations published a revised version of the OEEC system as *A System of National Accounts and Supporting Tables.* This is referred to below as the 1953 SNA.

3. The 1953 SNA

The principal author of the 1953 SNA – Richard Stone – noted that attempts to quantify the national economy had hitherto followed four separate paths:

1. measuring the national income;

2. constructing input-output tables;

3. flow-of-funds analysis; and

4. compiling balance sheets.

Stone saw the four approaches as being closely related and hoped that eventually they could be combined into a single system. The 1953 SNA, however, confined itself to the first of these. Another limitation noted by the authors was that there were no tables at constant prices, and this was identified as another area for future development.

The 1953 SNA consists of a simple set of six accounts: final expenditure on the GDP; national income; domestic capital formation; disposable income and net borrowing of households and government; and the external account. These accounts were supplemented by a set of standard tables that countries were to use in reporting national accounts statistics to the United Nations. In addition to establishing the basic accounting relationships – which have essentially remained in place to the present time – the 1953 SNA was notable for having finally resolved a number of issues that were still under debate at that time. For example:

● Production was defined to include two important types of own-use production: subsistence farm production and housing services produced by owner-occupiers. Other services produced for consumption within the household – cooking, cleaning and child rearing – were, however, excluded from the production boundary.

- No distinction was made between legal and illegal production. Provided goods or services were being traded between willing producers and willing buyers, the activities concerned were deemed to be productive. Despite this early recommendation, it is interesting to note that not all OECD countries include full estimates of illegal production in the GDP.

- Governments were treated as producers, but because the services they produce are not sold, their output was to be measured as the total of the costs of production – compensation of employees, intermediate consumption and consumption of fixed capital. The same approach was to be used for non-profit institutions. However, this feature was not implemented in all countries immediately. For example, France included government in its accounts only in 1976.

- Capital formation was defined as expenditure on physical objects – buildings, machinery, roads – that would provide productive services over a number of years. Other types of expenditure that could also be expected to produce a stream of future services but which had no *physical* embodiment, advertising and research and development, for example, were treated as current consumption. Expenditure on education, or investment in human capital as it is sometimes termed, was also excluded from capital formation "because human beings are not capital assets".

In the decade that followed publication of the 1953 SNA, about 60 countries began to publish some kind of national accounts on a regular basis. Many OECD countries were able to complete all the supporting tables of the 1953 SNA, but other countries published only estimates of GDP obtained by adding up the value added of different industries with a summary breakdown by final expenditure. Even these simple national accounts proved useful for monitoring economic developments and for fiscal and monetary policy. Equally important, the national accounts were increasingly used as a framework for organising other economic statistics, such as indices of industrial output, price statistics, retail sales and labour force data. The definitions and classifications of the 1953 SNA were applied to these related areas.

4. The 1968 SNA

By the early 1960s, there was a consensus among national accountants that it was time to revise the 1953 SNA to take into account developments in input-output tables (in France and the Netherlands, for example), in flow of funds statistics (in the United Kingdom) and in balance sheets (in the United

States). In addition, most OECD countries had been developing accounts at constant prices and had also started publishing much greater detail than suggested in the 1953 system.

There had also been a shift in economic policymaking. Starting from using the national accounts to understand what had happened in the recent past and to forecast what could be expected in the near term, policymakers became increasingly drawn to the idea of actively planning the future course of the economy. Detailed five-year plans were being drawn up in India and Egypt, for example, while a looser form of "indicative planning" was being implemented by France and other western European countries. The new system was designed to support this growing interest in economic planning.

The 1953 SNA was described in 46 pages, and the accounts were shown on 2 pages, whereas the 1968 SNA (titled *A System of National Accounts*, United Nations, 1968) required 250 pages and the accounts alone filled 12 pages. This is because the 1968 SNA not only provided a more in-depth description of the various transactions and their sources as well as extra detail – such as input-output tables and balance sheets – but also a number of innovations (see Box 14.1). However, it did not change the accounting identities, the size of the production boundary or the distinction between capital formation and current expenditure, all of which were inherited from the earlier system.

Box 14.1. **What was new in the 1968 SNA?**

- All entities participating in monetary transactions were assigned to **institutional sectors**. In the 1953 SNA, only households and government had been explicitly identified. In the 1968 System, corporations were split into financial and non-financial sectors, and non-profit institutions were identified as a separate sector.

- The accounts for institutional sectors were expanded to include: a production account; an income and outlay account with saving as the balancing item; a capital finance account with net lending as the balancing item; and a financial account showing the acquisition of financial assets and incurrence of liabilities.

- Distinction was made between **market** and **non-market producers**. The former (termed "industries") sold goods and services at a profit, while the latter (termed "other producers"), typically government and non-profit institutions, provided services and sometimes goods for free, or at nominal prices. A similar distinction was made between "commodities" (sold at a profit) and "other goods and services".

Box 14.1. **What was new in the 1968 SNA?** *(cont.)*

- A full chapter was devoted to "The System as a Basis for Quantity and Price Comparisons" – i.e. national accounts at **constant prices**. Although it gave some practical guidance for national accountants and price statisticians, the discussion was mainly theoretical. One important contribution was to identify the limits to constant price measurement. Final expenditures can be converted to constant prices by deflating them with the relevant price indices. And value added can be expressed in constant prices by the ingenious method (apparently invented by the Irish statistical office) of deflating gross output and intermediate consumption by their own price indices and deriving constant price value added as the difference between them. Both of these statistics can be expressed in constant prices because the underlying flows can be decomposed into price and quantity components. Other entries in the accounts – compensation of employees, property income, taxes, operating surplus, etc. – cannot be broken down in this way. They can be expressed in constant purchasing power – how much of a fixed basket of goods can this year's salary buy compared to last year – but constant purchasing power is a different concept from constant prices.

- The 1968 SNA was a major step toward integrating the four approaches to national economic measurement that Stone had identified in 1953. **Input-output** tables were integrated into the production accounts; the financial accounts included a **flow of funds** table showing both parties to transactions in various financial instruments; and the links were explained (partially) between the opening and closing **balance sheets** and the transactions recorded in the accounts during the year.

---

5. The 1993 SNA

The 1968 SNA represented a major step forward in macroeconomic measurement, but no system could possibly remain relevant for all time. Economies evolve and international accounting systems must adapt to reflect new realities. The decision to revise the 1968 SNA was made in the early 1980s, largely as a result of discussions at the annual meetings organised by the OECD for national accountants from member countries, and at the biennial conferences of the International Association for Research in Income and Wealth. The archives of the meetings of the OECD are available on the Web site of the OECD.

The 1953 SNA had been written by a committee of five and the 1968 SNA by a group of about fifteen. For the 1993 SNA, it was decided to involve a much wider group of experts and more than 50 statisticians and economists were involved in the revision process. A wider group of international agencies also took part. The two earlier versions had been published by the United Nations alone, but the 1993 SNA was a joint publication of the OECD, Eurostat, the World Bank, the International Monetary Fund and the United Nations. Other international agencies were also consulted, including the International Labour Office, United Nations regional commissions and the Commonwealth of Independent States.

While the revision was already under way, the internationalist aspirations of the 1993 SNA received a further boost from the fall of the Berlin Wall. The Soviet bloc countries had previously used their own system of national accounts – the *Material Product System* – but in the early 1990s, these countries announced that they would switch to the SNA. China, Mongolia and Vietnam followed suit. At the present time, only two countries have not formally adopted the 1993 SNA as the basis for their official national accounts – Cuba and North Korea.

An important feature of the 1993 SNA is that it is consistent with other international data systems, such as the OECD Guidelines on Foreign Direct Investment, the IMF's manuals on Balance of Payments and Government Finance Statistics. Clearly, this is a considerable advantage to both the users of these data and to national statistical offices. The 1993 SNA is also much more explicit in dealing with issues that had been known to create difficulties for many countries, such as: insurance transactions; imputed bank-service charges (financial intermediation services indirectly measured, or "FISIM", as they are now termed); financial versus operating leasing; and consumption of fixed capital. In addition, there are separate chapters on satellite accounts and on social accounting matrices, or "SAMs". All this of course had a cost in terms of page inflation, and the 1993 SNA has over 700 pages. Box 14.2 identifies the main innovations.

Box 14.2. **What was new in the 1993 SNA?**

- **Balance sheets** are fully incorporated into the system. Linking the opening and closing stocks of assets with the flow transactions during the year requires not only a revaluation account (as had been introduced in the 1968 SNA) but an additional account that records changes in the volume of assets. These may arise from new discoveries of mineral reserves, natural growth of cultivated forest and catastrophic losses due to earthquakes or tempests, depletion of oil reserves, and so on. The awkwardly named "Other Changes in the Volume of Assets Account", to distinguish these changes from volume changes due to investments for example, was introduced to record these events.

Box 14.2. **What was new in the 1993 SNA?** *(cont.)*

- The four accounts for institutional sectors of the 1968 SNA were expanded to a total of sixteen. Much of the increase came from a fragmentation of the 1968 SNA accounts. The 1968 income and outlay accounts were split into six separate accounts in order to identify new balancing items that were thought relevant for economic analysis.

- In the previous systems, government was shown as consuming its entire output. In the 1993 SNA, an important distinction is made between government services that are provided to households on an individual basis – health and education for example – and those that are provided on a collective basis to the community at large – security and defence, for example. While government pays for production of both collective and individual services, households can be regarded as the true consumers of the latter. A new concept, actual individual consumption of households, was introduced. This is the value of the individual services provided by government plus the goods and services that households buy with their own money.

- Volume estimates are given much more consideration. Recent developments in price index theory were used to show that the best measures of price inflation are obtained by using chained Fisher indices, with chained Laspeyres indices as a second best.

- The asset boundary was enlarged to include expenditures on software, mineral exploration, artistic originals and valuables. In earlier systems, software expenditure (generally insignificant before the 1970s) was treated as a current cost. But in the 1993 SNA, all software expenditures – off-the-shelf programmes, software written in-house and custom-designed software purchased from specialised companies – are treated as capital formation. Mining companies have usually treated exploration expenditures (money spent on looking for new deposits) as a capital outlay, and this same approach was adopted in the 1993 SNA. Note that the costs of exploration, whether anything is found or not, are treated as capital expenditures. Artistic originals relate to the production of the original films, sound recordings, manuscripts, etc. that give rise to future income earnings, for example in the form of royalties. Valuables are precious objects, such as paintings, antiques, jewellery and precious metals that are bought as "stores of value". In the earlier systems, most of these expenditures on valuables would have been included in household consumption expenditure

6. The 1995 ESA

In the 1960s, the fledgling Europe Union realised that it needed harmonised national accounts statistics for its member states. The first such system was published in 1970 as the *European System of Accounts,* and a revised version came out in 1979. This was then replaced by the *European System of Accounts 1995,* or 1995 ESA, which is the European version of the 1993 SNA.

The 1995 ESA is 99% consistent with the 1993 SNA and gives more precise guidelines on some border-line issues that were deliberately left open in the 1993 SNA. For example, in the 1993 SNA the distinction between "market" and "non-market" producers depends on whether they sell their output at "economically significant prices". In the 1995 ESA a non-market producer is one whose output is sold at prices that cover less than 50% of the cost of production. All that has happened here is that the 1995 ESA has defined an "economically significant price" as one that covers more than 50% of the production costs. These more precise guidelines are necessary because national accounts statistics are used by the European Commission to allocate regional development funds, calculate the contribution to the European budget, to monitor the sustainability of public finance (Maastricht criteria) and, more recently, macroeconomic imbalances.

The administrative use of national accounts in Europe has at the same time boosted the harmonisation and use of these statistics, but it has also made their production more rigid. The 1995 ESA is embedded in EU legislation so that international harmonisation of national accounts is a legal requirement for EU member states, as well as for countries that have applied for future membership. The 1993 SNA was designed to have sufficient flexibility so that it could be applied by countries with very different economic systems and at various stages of economic development. The 1993 SNA is therefore somewhat less effective than the 1995 ESA in ensuring international comparability.

7. The 2008 SNA

In 2009, it was decided to replace the 1993 SNA by the 2008 SNA. At the end of 2014, most OECD-countries had implemented the revised standards. Chile, Japan and Turkey having plans to implement the 2008 SNA by 2015, were the exceptions. Looking at the differences between the 1993 SNA and the 2008 SNA, the main ones relate to an improved accounting for assets and liabilities, the inclusion of all kinds of new developments in the financial sector, issues related to the increasing globalisation of the economy, and better descriptions of government finance and the informal sector. Box 14.1 illustrates the change for France. The page inflation, mentioned above under the section on the 1993 SNA, could be stopped, although only by using a two column format and putting more words on a page! With the completion of the 2008 SNA, more than 50 changes to the 1993 SNA had been introduced. The major changes include:

- *Treating Research and development (R&D) as an asset.* After decades of discussion, it has been decided to record R&D expenditures as GFCF (Gross Fixed Capital Formation) and not current costs, despite the difficulties associated with this change. One of the difficulties is that in most countries business accounting standards do not recommend the same (R&D is treated as current expenditure). As a consequence, it is more difficult to obtain satisfactory data. On the other hand however, many countries have a long history of collecting data on R&D according to the so-called Frascati Manual, which has proved to be an invaluable source of information. This change has increased the level of GDP, but hardly affected the level of NDP.

- *Treating expenditure on large military weapons as assets.* The new SNA also records large military weapons – warships, ballistic missiles and tanks, etc. – as fixed capital assets. This also raised the level of GDP, not because of the change in classification of these amounts from final expenditure to GFCF, but because a consumption of fixed capital is recorded and is added to the measure of government consumption.

- *The treatment of goods for processing.* The 1993 SNA treated goods that were sent abroad for processing and then returned to the country from where they were dispatched as undergoing an effective change in ownership. The goods were therefore recorded in exports and imports. The 2008 SNA on the other hand recommends that imports and exports are recorded on a strict change of ownership basis. This can have a substantial impact on the distinction between trade in goods and trade in services, especially for countries that are heavily involved in processing of goods. More generally, the 2008 SNA has also triggered substantial discussions on the treatment of global production arrangements, e.g. how to account for so-called "factory-less producers".

- The valuation of government output and output for own final use. As explained in Chapter 4, the 1993 SNA was criticised for underestimating the cost of the government's use of capital because it did not add to capital consumption an estimated return on capital in order to reflect the full cost of "capital services". Unfortunately however, no agreement could be reached on the inclusion of a return on capital for government fixed assets. On the other hand, it was agreed to include such a return on capital for market-producers (households and corporations), when measuring output for own final use.

- *Extending the measurement of pension liabilities.* The 1993 SNA only recorded pension liabilities for funded plans. The new SNA extended this to all private employer pension schemes regardless of whether they are funded or unfunded, whereas in the case of government schemes for their own employees and social security plans some flexibility in the recording is allowed. To arrive at internationally comparable data for government related schemes, it has also been decided to introduce a "supplementary table", in which all pension schemes, whether funded or not, are accounted for. This extension could have a major impact on the measurement of the government debt, because unfunded retirement plans for government employees involve heavy liabilities in some countries. Another change, which for some countries can have a substantial impact on government deficit, relates to the recording of large one-off payments by public corporations to government, to compensate government for taking over pension liabilities of the relevant corporations. Whereas the recording of these payments was not that clear in the 1993 SNA, and in Europe it was decided to treat them as capital transfers, the relevant transactions have to be treated as purely financial transactions, not affecting government deficit, in the 2008 SNA.

● *Smoothing the measurement of non-life insurance output.* In the 1993 SNA, the gross output of non-life insurance companies was essentially measured as the difference between premiums and claims. The terrorist attack of 11 September 2001 highlighted a problem with this approach that has troubled national accountants in several countries – namely, the sharp fluctuations in output, even becoming negative, that can occur when claims are unexpectedly large in a given year. In the 2008 SNA, it has been agreed to deduct *expected* rather than *actual* claims in measuring output.

● *Including share options as part of compensation of employees.* During the stock market bubble of the late 1990s, employees in many hi-tech companies accepted low salaries in return for the chance to buy their company's shares at bargain prices. The logic of the 1993 SNA required share options to be treated as financial transactions, and are therefore excluded from the compensation of employees. However, the employees receiving share options clearly regard them as part of their "compensation package". Thus, share options are included in compensation of employees in the new SNA.

● *Allocating holding companies to the financial corporations sector.* The 1993 SNA recommended that holding companies were to be assigned to the institutional sector in which the main activity of the group of subsidiaries was concentrated. According to the 2008 SNA, these holdings should always be allocated to the financial corporations sector.

Together with the revision of the SNA, the *European System of Accounts (ESA) 1995* has also been revised and replaced by the *ESA 2010* to keep the consistency between the worldwide set of standards and its European equivalent.

Box 14.3 illustrates the impact of the implementation of SNA 2008/ESA 2010 in the case of France.

In conclusion, the SNA is a system of statistics that is being constantly updated, more and more widely used, and evolving in parallel with new economic developments. One interesting feature is that the measurement of GDP has systematically been modified under the different SNAs into a broader concept, thus extending progressively the production frontier, and inflating GDP. This has once more happened with the SNA 2008, with the capitalisation of R&D and military weapon systems. It is probable that this process will continue. For example, the concept of human capital, which is not incorporated in the asset boundary of the 2008 SNA, will become more and more relevant to OECD economies in the future. Its incorporation in the national accounts would once more enlarge the production boundary. But this will not happen tomorrow...

Box 14.3. Revisions of the national accounts for France due to implementation of SNA 2008/ESA 2010

France published its new data based on SNA 2008/ESA 2010 in May 2014. As in all OECD member states, the result of the implementation of the new SNA 2008/ESA 2010 for France was an increase of the level of GDP, by 3.2% (61.8 bn euros), compared to the previous estimate. This number refers to the year 2010. However, as the change is structural, in the sense that GDP is more or less systematically revised upwards by the same percentage, it is representative. One consequence of this "level change" is that the growth of GDP is globally unaffected. Not all of this change is due to the new SNA. Part of this change is due to a revision from new sources for business statistics and other factors (inclusion of Mayotte island), for an amount of 0.8 percentage points (15.4 bn euros). Strictly speaking the impact of the conceptual changes in SNA 2008/ESA 2010 on GDP is therefore limited to 2.4% (46.4 bn euros). Table 14.1 below illustrates the change for some other variables. One interesting impact is that all ratios using GDP as a denominator structurally decrease, simply because of the increase of GDP. This is particularly the case of the ratio of public debt, which decreases by 1.5 p.p. This is less than the increase of GDP (+3.2%), because some reclassifications contributed to increase the public debt (the numerator).

Table 14.1. **SNA 2008/ESA 2010 revisions of national accounts. France. May 2014**

	2010 level revision in %	New level for 2010	Source of revision
GDP	+3.2%	1 998.5 bn EUR	Capitalisation of R&D (+41.5 bn), weapon systems (+3.3) and databases (1.2). New statistical sources on businesses.
GNI	+3.2%	2 039.3 bn EUR	Capitalisation of R&D (+41.5 bn), weapon systems (+3.3) and databases (1.2). New statistical sources on businesses.
Profit share of non-financial corporations	+1.5 pp	31.6%	Capitalisation of R&D and databases. New statistical sources on businesses.
Share of manufacturing in total value added.	+0.7 pp	13.5%	Capitalisation of R&D and databases. New statistical sources on businesses.
Total exports	+5.2%	520.5 bn EUR	Goods for processing (-9.9); New statistical source (+30).
Total imports	+3.7%	558.1 bn EUR	Goods for processing (-8.6); New statistical source (+30).
GFCF	+16.9%	441.1 bn EUR	Capitalisation of R&D (+41.5 bn), weapon systems (+3.3) and databases (1.2). New statistical sources on businesses.
Public deficit/GDP	-0.3 pp	6.8%	Variable impact depending on year due to new treatment of transfers of pension obligations and tax credits.
Public debt/GDP	-1.5 pp	80.8%	GDP increase (-3.1 pp); reclassifications (+1.6 pp)

Source: INSEE (2014), les comptes nationaux passent en base 2010, www.insee.fr/fr/themes/comptes-nationaux/ default.asp?page=base_2010/methodologie/methodo-b2010.htm.

References

Gleeson-White (2011), Double Entry: How the merchants of Venice shaped the modern world – and how their invention could make or break the planet, ASIN: B005ZLZJ46.

INSEE (2014), les comptes nationaux passent en base 2010, www.insee.fr/fr/themes/ comptes-nationaux/default.asp?page=base_2010/methodologie/methodo-b2010.htm.

Maddison, A. (2003), The World Economy: Historical Statistics, Development Centre Studies, OECD Publishing, doi: http://dx.doi.org/10.1787/9789264104143-en.

SNA 1993, Commission of the European Communities, International Monetary Fund, Organisation for Economic Co-operation and Development, United Nations, World Bank (1993), System of National Accounts 1993, Brussels/Luxembourg, New York, Paris, Washington, DC, http://unstats.un.org/unsd/nationalaccount/docs/1993sna.pdf.

SNA 2008, European Commission, International Monetary Fund, Organisation for Economic Co-operation and Development, United Nations, World Bank (2009), System of National Accounts 2008, New York, http://unstats.un.org/unsd/ nationalaccount/docs/SNA2008.pdf.

Vanoli (2005), A History of national accounts, IOS Press, ISBN-10: 1586034693, ISBN-13: 978-1586034696.

Chapter 15

GDP as a welfare metric:
The "beyond GDP" agenda

This chapter discusses the limitations of GDP for measuring "welfare" and "well-being". It illustrates the recent development of "better life" indicators, both inside and outside the national accounts framework, which allow to measure these two complex concepts, but so important for the society.

The concept of "welfare" (i.e. economic well being) has been typically understood by economists and statisticians as people's command over commodities. This concept describes the "opulence" of a person (i.e. how well-off he or she is), as opposed to a broader notion of "well-being" (i.e. how well the person is), which encompasses aspects only indirectly related to people's possessions, such as political or social rights, or the range of attributes that shape their life (i.e. their health and education. In this chapter, we will distinguish these two basic notions: "welfare" and "well-being".

While, as argued in earlier chapters of this manual, GDP is primarily a measure of economic production, it is linked to welfare in various ways. At the most basic level, conventional economic theory posits that, under perfect information and when consumers' preferences satisfy relatively simple properties, market prices are equal to changes in the utility that people draw from different commodities consumed: it follows that household final consumption, a big chunk of GDP, is linked to the welfare of households and that, for a consumer with given preferences, higher money income corresponds to commodity-bundles on a higher indifference curve, which implies higher welfare for the person being considered.

Despite being *related* to welfare, the national accounts focus on measuring economic activity rather than welfare *per se*. Historically, the roots of modern national accounts, as developed in the 1930s and the 1940s, were in Keynesian macroeconomics and in the need for policy-makers to manage the war effort and reconstruction, to secure full employment and high tax revenues and, more generally, to assure the management of the economic system within the limits of its productive capacity. The reference manual of national accounts, the SNA 2008 (see Chapter 14), makes *"no claim that GDP should be taken as a measure of welfare and indeed there are several conventions in the SNA that argue against the welfare interpretation of the accounts"*.

Conceptually, GDP is only a partial measure of welfare for many reasons. These include:

- The differences between the concept of economic production – "domestic", i.e. by residents and non-resident units within the territory of a country, and "gross", i.e. with no deduction of the output that needs to be set aside to replace the capital stock used in production – and that of net income ("the maximum value which (a man) can consume during a week, and still expect to be as well off at the end of the week as he was at the beginning", in the definition provided by John Hicks in 1939), which is the concept most directly linked to the welfare of individuals.

- The fact that GDP only informs about total (or per capita) aggregates, rather than on distribution of that aggregate among different people or households. The distinction between aggregate and individual-level amounts is important from a welfare perspective as, even when assuming that the welfare of a person is adequately described by its income, *any* assessment of "social welfare" (i.e. of the welfare of a community as a whole) requires normative judgments on distribution, as the marginal utility of income differs among people (i.e. a one dollar gain will increase the welfare of a poor person by more than a one dollar loss reduce the welfare of a rich one).

- The fact that some of the production activities that fall inside the national accounts production boundary increase GDP even when, from a welfare perspective, they are simply offsetting some of the "disamenities" associated to higher economic growth (e.g. the consumption flows related to people's commuting to work) or the consequences of human- and natural disasters. Conversely, people's welfare is enhanced by both production flows that fall beyond the national accounts boundary (e.g. services produced by households for their own use) as well as by non-market activities (e.g. leisure) that cannot be conceived as "production".

- Conceptually, the market prices that are used to weigh the various quantities of commodities in GDP reflect the value to consumers of the last unit consumed. While this approach has roots in consumer theory, it neglects the full amount that consumers would be willing to pay for the total quantity of the good considered (i.e. it fails to represent the full value of all units consumed before the last one), which is the concept more directly related to people's welfare.

- There may be externalities and other departures from market equilibrium, which imply that market prices cannot always be interpreted as reflecting the relative worth (at the margin) of different goods and services produced and consumed. In other cases, no markets may exist for both inputs used in production (i.e. common pool resources) and for welfare-enhancing assets that are affected by human activities (e.g. the climate system).

- Finally, a static measure of welfare does not say much on whether this level can last over time. "Sustainability" requires considering how economic activities are impacting on different types of capital stocks that either enter the production process (when the focus in on the sustainability of GDP growth) or, more generally, that are important for the welfare of people and of the planet in the future. This concern is especially important when recognising the importance of limited resources (i.e. non-reproduced natural capital), whose services cannot be provided by other types of (produced) resources.

All of the above arguments are well recognised by professional economists and statisticians. They are, however, typically lost in the media and in political discussions, where GDP is taken as a general metric of "success", losing sight of the extent to which GDP is an empirical construct rather than a "fact" and of the arguments and reasoning that led to its construction (Coyle, 2014). While already discussed in the 1970s (Nordhaus and al, 1973), the limits of GDP as a welfare metrics were given recently high visibility by the recommendations of an international commission established in 2008 by French President Nicolas Sarkozy on the measurement of economic performance and social progress, whose key recommendations are summarised in Box 15.1. In fact, most of the statistical initiatives undertaken in recent years to improve the measurement of welfare, quality of life and sustainability can be traced down, directly or indirectly, to these recommendations.

Prominent among these initiatives are those launched by the OECD in the context of its "Better Life Initiative" (www.oecd.org/statistics/ betterlifeinitiativemeasuringwell-beingandprogress.htm) and those undertaken by the European Statistical System in the context of the "Sponsorship Group on Measuring Progress, Well-being and Sustainable Development".

The first five recommendations should not be seen as unconditionally rejecting the existing national accounts variables but giving better visibility to some parts of national accounts that remain still not visible enough and developing new dimensions of existing national accounts aggregates, in order to enrich their welfare measurement potential. The last five recommendations are related to developing measures related to the measurement of "well-being" beyond economic elements.

This chapter describes some of the approaches that have been proposed or implemented within the system of economic accounts to derive measures that are more reflective of people's welfare. First, the chapter describes those (household level) measures of welfare that are already available within the system of national accounts. Second, the chapter reviews some of the approaches that have been used to move beyond the nationals accounts, thus "beyond the average" (i.e. to account for inequalities in economic conditions between people with different characteristics), "beyond the market" (i.e. to accounts for flows and stocks that are not exchanged through markets), and beyond the "here and now" (i.e. to account for sustainability). Finally, the

Box 15.1. **The recommendations of the Commission on the Measurement of Economic Performance and Social Progress**

- *Recommendation 1: When evaluating material well-being, look at income and consumption rather than production*, as conflating GDP and economic well-being can lead to misleading indications about how well-off people are and entail the wrong policy decisions.

- *Recommendation 2: Emphasise the household perspective*, as citizens' material living standards are better followed through measures of household income and consumption.

- *Recommendation 3: Consider income and consumption jointly with wealth*, which requires information on balance sheets and proper valuation of these stocks.

- *Recommendation 4: Give more prominence to the distribution of income, consumption and wealth*, which requires that measures of average income, consumption and wealth should be accompanied by indicators of their distribution.

- *Recommendation 5: Broaden income measures to non-market activities*, such as the services people received from other family members as well as leisure time.

- *Recommendation 6: Quality of life depends on people's objective conditions and capabilities*, such as people's health, education, personal activities and environmental conditions but also their social connections, political voice and insecurity.

- *Recommendation 7: Quality-of-life indicators in all the dimensions covered should assess inequalities in a comprehensive way*, taking into account linkages and correlations.

- *Recommendation 8: Surveys should be designed to assess the links between various quality of-life domains for each person*, and this information should be used when designing policies.

- *Recommendation 9: Statistical offices should provide the information needed to aggregate across quality-of-life dimensions*, allowing the construction of different indexes.

- *Recommendation 10: Measures of both objective and subjective well-being provide key information about people's quality of life*, and Statistical offices should incorporate questions to capture people's life evaluations, hedonic experiences and priorities in their own survey.

- *Recommendation 11: Sustainability assessment requires a well-identified dashboard of indicators*, whose elements should be interpretable as variations of some underlying "stocks".

- *Recommendation 12: The environmental aspects of sustainability deserve a separate follow-up based on a well-chosen set of physical indicators.*

Source: Stiglitz, Sen and Fitoussi (2009).

chapter considers some of the approaches that are being used by economists and statisticians to measure the broader notion of people's well-being (i.e. what people do and who they are, beyond the commodities that they possess). These statistical indicators are new and still work-in-progress, compared to the "old" national accounts variables described in the previous chapters. However, as shown in this chapter, they have recently moved out of the first stage of development, the experimental/research stage, to the second stage, that of being regularly produced, in particular by the OECD.

1. Better welfare measures within the national accounts

1.1. Household-level measures

GDP is just one measure within a full-fledged set of accounts referring to the economic system as a whole. Within this set of accounts, better proxies of economic well-being than GDP do exist. These are those measures that specifically refer to households (rather than to the economy as a whole), as individuals and households are the natural basis for all welfare evaluations. As explained in Chapter 5, the national accounts allows tracking down how the *primary income* generated through economic production (both monetary and imputed flows) leads to the *disposable income* available to households. As the notion of welfare refers to people, these household-level accounts provide the starting point for deriving measures that bear a closer relation to the concept of welfare. Measures of household disposable income (i.e. the income that is left after deducting taxes and compulsory social security contributions paid by households) and of consumption expenditures (i.e. the value of consumption goods and services purchased by a household to meet its needs) are important because they may evolve differently from GDP, both over the business cycle and in the medium-term (Figure 15.1), for example due to changes in fiscal policies or in wage and profit shares. Depending on their purposes, these household measures may be corrected for population size, which may be achieved through measures expressed per capita, per household or per consumption units.[1]

Two further types of adjustments can be applied to SNA measures for the household sector to deliver metrics that bear a closer relation to the concept of "welfare".

● The first is to adjust household gross disposable income for the amount that should be set aside in order to offset for the wearing out of capital used in production. This adjustment, which in the case of households mainly relates to depreciation of the housing stock, is needed to bring the national accounts-measure of gross household income closer to the Hicksian income definition, i.e. *net household disposable income*.

Figure 15.1. **Trends in per capita GDP
and gross household disposable income (HDI)**

Indexes, United States 1990 = 100 and Euro area 2007 = 100

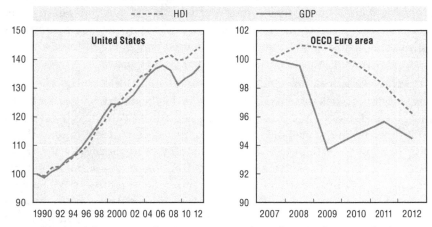

Source: OECD (2013), "Aggregate National Accounts: Gross domestic product", OECD National Accounts Statistics (database), *http://dx.doi.org/10.1787/data-00001-en;* and OECD (2014), "Detailed National Accounts: Non-financial accounts by sectors, annual", OECD National Accounts Statistics (database), doi: *http://dx.doi.org/10.1787/data-00034-en.*

StatLink ᵃⁱᵍᵖ *http://dx.doi.org/10.1787/888933144328*

- The second adjustment is to add to the monetary flows pertaining to households (e.g. the money income that they receive and their consumption expenditures) the imputed value of the in-kind services that household receive from governments and from non-profit institutions serving households. This adjustment leads to average measures of *household net adjusted disposable income* and *household actual consumption* (see Chapter 5). The in-kind services added to derive these measures are those that benefit individual consumers (e.g. education) rather than the collective services that benefit all households or the economy as a whole (e.g. defence). Although, from a welfare perspective, these individual services should be valued at the price of equivalent services purchased on the market, they are typically valued at their production costs; this implies that changes in the volume of *household net adjusted disposable income* and *household actual consumption* will be under-estimated when the quality of these in-kind services (or the productivity with which they are produced) improves over time.

Both concepts (net adjusted household disposable income and actual household consumption) provide valid measures of the *flow* of household economic well-being, and several initiatives have been undertaken by statistical offices in recent years to enhance their use as well as the frequency and timeliness of their production. But the *stock* of household net worth (i.e.

the differences between household assets, both financial and non-financial, and their liabilities, see Chapter 8) also matter for people's welfare, both in itself (i.e. households with a higher net worth are better off than those with the same income and consumption but with lower stock of wealth) and because changes in the value of stocks are affected by flows (e.g. capital or withholding gains/losses) that are not counted as income in the SNA, and which may be very large in periods of changing asset prices.

While these SNA household-level measures provide a starting point to assess welfare, much remains to be done to make them more widely available, and several factors limit their use. First, not all OECD countries currently compile complete household sector accounts. Second, even among those countries that do so, there are differences in terms of frequency (e.g. few OECD countries compile these data quarterly), timeliness (e.g. annual sectoral accounts are typically available 1 or 2 years after the release of the first estimate of GDP) and scope (some countries do not distinguish between households and non-profit institutions serving them, or rely on different definition of quasi-corporate enterprises or of individual government services). Even larger differences characterise the compilation of household balance sheets.

1.2. Incorporating information on disparities among households within national accounts

One limit of the national accounts from the perspective of informing on welfare is that they do not provide any information on the distribution of household economic resources between units with different characteristics. This is an important limit because *any* assessment of social welfare requires normative judgments about the distribution of economic resources. From this perspective, the choice of looking only at total or average (e.g. per capita) amounts does not avoid normative choices but rather implies that units within a community are "weighted" by the amount of their income (i.e. the richer you are, the higher your weight when deriving average measure), a objectionable choice from most normative perspectives.

Beyond conceptual reasons, integrating information about inequalities into economic accounts is also important for several practical reasons:

● First is the trend towards wider inequalities in the distribution of household income that has been observed in most OECD countries since the mid-1980s (OECD, 2011). These inequalities imply that, while rates of income growth were relatively uniform across the distribution in most OECD countries from the mid-1950s until the early 1980s (making it plausible for macroeconomists to ignore inequality, and to adhere to the assumption of a single "representative agent"), this is less plausible today as benefits at the top failed to "trickle down" to everyone else.

- Second is the fact that average measures of household income and consumption obtained from micro-sources (typically household surveys, administrative records, and various ways to integrate the two) have been increasing at lower pace that national account measures of the same items. While this may reflect both a decline in the propensity of richer households to participate in surveys used to assess the distribution of economic resources (possibly linked to an increase in their income relative to that of the rest of the population) and the growing importance in the national accounts totals of items that are not recorded in micro-sources (e.g. imputations for life-insurance policy holders, or of the services from owner occupied housing), it implies that a growing share of household economic resources will be missed by survey data.

- Third is the fact that developments over recent decades have also been characterised, in several OECD countries, by different trends in the inequality of household income, household consumption, and household wealth. These differences underscore the importance of looking at inequalities in the distribution of economic resources jointly rather than assuming that they will always mirror each other.

All these factors motivate the efforts by statistical offices and individual researchers to better integrate macro- and micro-data on household economic resources, overcoming a long-standing separation between the two types of approaches. In particular, work pursued by the OECD/Eurostat Expert Group on Disparities in the National Accounts, which operated from 2012 to 2014 and that is now being further pursued within OECD setting, had two critical goals.

The first goal was to comprehensively assess the size of the differences between micro- and macro-based measures of different types of household economic resources. These differences may reflect differences in the scope and definitions of the two sources (e.g. that one specific type of household income is included in macro statistics but excluded from micro-ones) and differences in the actual measures of the same aggregate from the two sources (i.e. even when the same type of income in considered by both sources). Differences between micro- and macro-sources partly reflect the different traditions and research questions pursued two stream of work, and they relate to:

- Differences in the scope of the two types of measures. Micro sources typically exclude households living in collective living quarters (such hotels or lodging houses) or institutions (such as military barracks) as well as people living in remote or scarcely populated areas, which are instead included in macro-statistics for the household sector.

- Differences in the range of items included. Macro-sources include several imputed items (such as imputed rents, capital income attributed to insurance policy holders, or financial services indirectly measured) that are not always included in micro-sources as individual respondents are not well placed to report about them.

- Differences in research questions. Micro-statistics are typically used to highlight differences in how economic resources are distributed at a point in time, while macro-measures aim to describe changes that occur over time, which requires a consistent set of measures for prices and volumes, and highly-consistent measures over time.

- Finally, even when the same type of economic resource is covered by both SNA and micro-data, the actual measure of their overall size may differ. This is because national accounts data, as a set of consistent accounts, make extensive use of (counterpart) information from other institutional sectors (e.g. on the size of household financial assets and liabilities held by financial intermediaries), while surveys typically rely only in the information provided by respondents.

Figure 15.2 shows that average gap (across a sample of OECD countries in the mid-2000s) between national accounts and micro-measures of household adjusted disposable income, household consumption, and household net worth, based on the estimates provided by Fesseau at al. (2013a). This study shows that:

- In the case of household adjusted disposable income, the average gap (across a sample of 20 OECD countries) is around 40%. This difference narrows to less than 20% when the comparison is limited to those items that fall within the scope of both national accounts and micro-data. However, the gap varies significantly across countries, ranging from 5% in Japan to 57% in Mexico. The match between macro and micro total is "good" (i.e. in a range between 80 and 120%) in more than $\frac{4}{5}$ of the countries for "wages and salaries" and "actual employers social security contributions", but only in $\frac{2}{3}$ of countries for "taxes on income" and "receipts of social benefits in cash"; conversely the alignment is much lower for "income and other property income received" (with a good match in only $\frac{1}{3}$ of the countries) and, to an even larger degree, for "income from self-employment" and from "leased dwellings" (with a good match in less than $\frac{1}{4}$ of the countries).

- In the case of household actual consumption expenditure, the average gap (across 21 OECD countries) is slightly above 40%. This difference narrows to less than 30% when the comparison is based on items "adjusted" to reflect differences in scope between the two sources, and ranges between a minimum of 16% in Australia and a maximum of 62% in Mexico. In general, the match between micro and macro totals is "good" for the largest expenditure components (food, housing and transport) but considerably lower for "alcohol beverages and tobacco" and for "miscellaneous goods and services".

● In the case of household wealth, the size of the gap between the two types of sources is marginally higher (when taking into account differences in scope and definitions) than for household income and consumption, although in this case the evidence is limited to only 7 OECD countries. The range of the gap across countries is similar to those reported for household income and consumption.

Figure 15.2. **Average gap between SNA and micro-measures of different types of household economic resources**

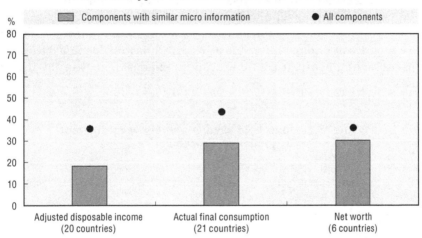

Notes: The chart shows average gap between SNA-based and micro-based measures of various types of household economic resources when including all components from either SNA or surveys (circles) and when including only components that are included in both SNA and surveys (histograms).
Source: Data drawn from Fesseau et al. (2013a).

The second element of the work undertaken by the OECD/Eurostat task force was to bring together information on disparities in the distribution of different types of economic resources, while trying to adhere as strictly as possible to the definition and total amounts that are available through the national accounts. This exercise, performed by experts from 16 OECD countries based on detailed information from macro and micro sources in their country, led to experimental estimates of disparities in household income and consumption in a year in the early or late 2000s for different types of households (by income quintile, by main income source and by household type) based on common choices on units of analysis (i.e. individual or households), criteria for grouping households with different characteristics, and type of micro-sources to use in the exercise (Fesseau et al. 2013b).

While the size of the income disparities highlighted by this exercise was, in general, quite close to those shown by the micro-sources that are typically used in OECD countries, one pattern highlighted by this exercise – which is typically missed by analysis that look separately at inequalities in household income and consumption – was the prevalence of negative savings rates at the bottom and middle of the distribution in all OECD countries; in other terms, savings are highly concentrated at the top of the income distribution, while households at the bottom and middle of the distribution are typically dissaving. While this may partly reflect methodological features of the exercise (i.e. inconsistencies between micro sources, and the neglect of infra-household transfers), it also suggests that, in many countries, low- and middle-income household may have run into debt to support their living standards in the period (characterised by wider income inequalities and stagnant median income) before the 2007 crisis, a feature identified by many analysts as an important contributor to the financial crisis in the United States.

Figure 15.3. **Household saving rates between different groups of households**

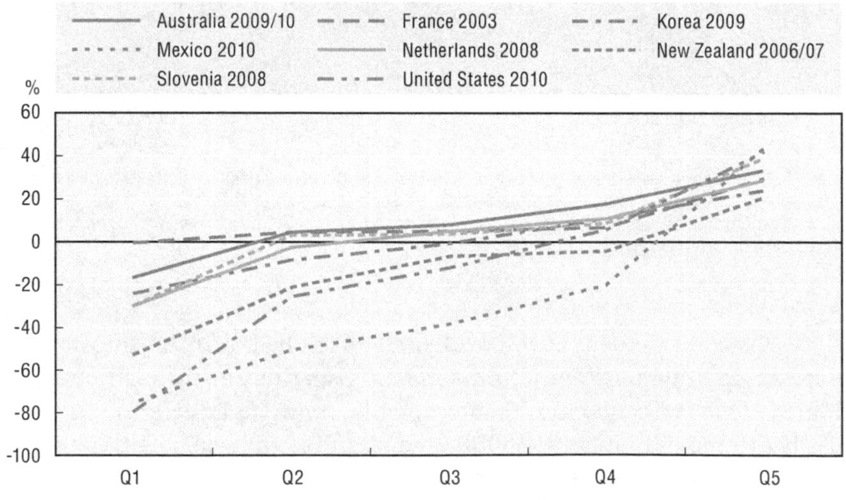

Source: Fesseau at al. (2013b).

2. Welfare measures beyond the national accounts

Devising better measures of people's economic well-being may also require moving beyond the national accounts boundaries and conventions. From a national accounts perspective, some of these extensions are, conceptually, less problematic than others. This is the case of those production activities that are not included within the SNA production boundary or of commercial natural resources exchanged in markets. Other extensions, such as those related to non-production activities or to the support functions provided by nature, raise however more controversial issues, and imply more significant departures from the SNA framework.

2.1. Accounting for production flows outside the national accounts

Production activities are conventionally defined as those whose output could have been produced by someone else hired for that purpose (the "third party criterion"). But there are production activities that, while satisfying this criterion, fall outside the national accounts production boundary because of the practical difficulties in measuring them. This applies in particular to households' production of services for their own use. While both household production of goods for own use (e.g. from subsistence agriculture) and the production of services from owner-occupied dwellings are part of GDP, this does not apply to services produced by households such as cooking, caring, or the inputs provided by parents to the development of their children. The exclusion is important both for welfare comparisons across countries at a point in time (e.g. women in some countries provide much more of these services than in others) and for interpreting changes in welfare over time (when production shifts from households to markets, the national accounts will count the additional market production but not deduct the lower production of household services, hence over-estimating welfare growth).

Relying on an input-based approach to value non-market household services, Ahmad and Koh (2011) concluded that considering these services would lower the welfare-gap for all OECD countries relative to the United States (the country where household final consumption expenditure per capita is highest, with this gap narrowing from 70% to 50% (depending on the valuation method used) in Turkey (the OECD country where household consumption of these services is highest, Figure 15.4). Estimates by the same authors also suggest that, when assuming no change in the productivity of these services, the decline in the volume of production of household non-market services observed over the past four decades in the five OECD countries where time-series data on time use are available would imply that the growth rate for this "enlarged" GDP (i.e. including these non-market services) would be around 40% lower than that for GDP alone.

Figure 15.4. **Gap relative to the United States in the volume of total household consumption per capita**

Index, US = 100

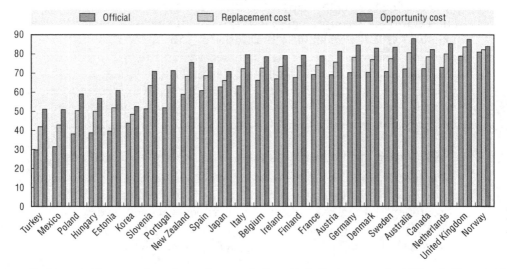

Note. Total household consumption refers to the sum of adjusted individual consumption (AIC) and of household production of non-market services. The approach used by the study valued both the labour-inputs entering the production of these household services (based on data from national Time Use Surveys) and the capital services (based on estimates of the stock of household consumer durables). Labour-costs were valued based on either replacement costs (based on an average post-tax hourly wage, representative for the broad range of activities covered by the production of these non-market services) or opportunity costs (based on the average post-tax hourly wage across the whole economy). The series labelled as 'official' refers to the SNA measure of AIC per capita.
Source: Ahmad and Koh (2011).

2.2. Accounting for non-production flows

Other activities that do not represent economic production (i.e. they do not satisfy the third-party criterion) are also important for people's welfare, as they imply higher consumption possibilities. This is the case of leisure, i.e. the time that people spend in activities that are unrelated to production and to maintaining people's physical integrity (such as sleeping and eating). This implies that, when workers gain higher income through longer working hours or lower holidays (rather than a higher wage rate, for a given number of hours worked) something that is not measured by the national accounts (i.e. leisure time) is "lost" to workers as their income rises. As both levels and trends in working time differ across countries, any adjustment that attributes a positive value to leisure-time (as compared to the zero value implicit in conventional economic accounts) is bound to have a significant impact on a broader measure of economic well-being.[2]

As argued by Stiglitz, Sen and Fitoussi (2009): "Consuming
the same bundle of goods and services but working for 1500 hours
a year instead of 2000 hours a year implies an increase in one's
standard of living".

Providing a monetary estimate of leisure time raises difficult issues when measuring both quantities and prices. Concerning the first, while information on the time that people devote to various activities can be derived through Time Use Surveys, these are typically undertaken very infrequently, and their comparability across countries is limited. The boundary between leisure-time and other types of time-use (e.g. time spent with children) for the same individual is also partly arbitrary; and similarly, when comparing people in various situations, the free-time of an unemployed will have a different nature than the same amount of time available to a person with a well-paid job. Concerning valuation, placing a monetary value on leisure time, so that it can be compared with the economic benefits from higher consumption of market goods and services, is more challenging than valuing the time spent on household production of goods and services, as market-equivalent measures do not exist.

While no international consensus exists on how to address these challenges, monetary estimates of leisure time, and of its impact on a broader measure of well-being, have been produced in the past. While earlier approaches measured the total value of leisure time, more recent ones have confined themselves to valuing the impact of *changes* in leisure over time, with valuation based on different measures of opportunity costs. Boarini et al. (2006) estimated that, for a variety of valuation methods, adjusting GDP for the leisure time of workers would raise the living standards of a several European countries (the Netherlands and Denmark) above US levels. Also, while most European countries would significantly narrow their gap relative to the US, these gaps would widen in countries (such as Mexico and Korea) where working time exceeds US levels.

2.3. Accounting for differences among consumption goods

The standard approach to consumer theory assumes that the people's preferences are given and independent of those of others, and that the marginal benefits of different unit of additional consumption goods are equal. All these assumptions contribute to the view that "higher consumption implies higher welfare", an assumption which is implicitly reflected in the National Accounts methodology. In reality, the nature of the commodities consumed may impact on consumers' welfare in a variety of ways. For instance, beyond the private goods considered by conventional economic theory, there are *positional goods* (i.e. goods whose utility is negatively affected by the consumption of others) and *status goods* (i.e. goods delineated by style, fashion and brand), where higher expenditures will not lead to higher economic well-being for the community as a whole. In addition to that, there are goods that are *inherently in short supply*, such as housing located close to specific amenities, where relative rather than absolute income is what matters for access to them; as well as *public goods* (which are non-rival and non-excludable) and *common pool resources* (which are rival but non excludable), both of which will tend to be underprovided in market settings. For all these types of goods the conventional evaluation provided by National Accounts (i.e. the use of market prices) fails to measure the real impact of their consumption on people's welfare.

Finally there are some goods that can be considered as "regrettables", such as expenditures related to congestion, litigation and security, or to limit the consequences of environmental externalities, which are undertaken only to offset some of the consequences of a previous event that reduced people's well-being. In this case, some economic activities that increase GDP simply correct for the dis-amenities of economic growth (e.g. urbanisation) or for the decline of natural capital (e.g. expenditures to reduce pollution) or social capital (e.g. expenditures to increase home security in neighbourhoods with higher crime). While all these expenditures are treated as "final consumption" in the national accounts, different normative choices (i.e. reclassifying these flows as "intermediate" rather than "final" consumption) would lead to a different assessment and measurement of economic well-being. A further consideration with respect to these expenditures on "regrettables" is that, while they may be welfare-enhancing in a given situation (e.g. spending on legal services improves welfare after litigation has occurred), in reality they simply remedy the effects of some type of assert depletion that was not accounted for in the national accounts, which is the subject of the next section.

2.4. Accounting for capital stocks: sustainability

In a world with limited non-renewable resources, higher GDP today may come at the expense of lower welfare in the future. This trade-off is at the core of the discussion on "sustainability". Much of the drive for the discussion of sustainability, and for the engagement of the statistical community in it, has been spurred by concerns linked to finite natural resources and environmental limits. While the System of National Accounts provide measures of the consumption of fixed capital (which, when deducted from GDP, lead to measure of "net" domestic product), this consumption is only a partial measure of how much capital is being used up in economic production (and, *a fortiori*, of how much of the capital stocks that matter for other well-being outcomes are being depleted by economic processes). The canonical definition of sustainable development provided by the Brundtland report in 1987 defined it as development that *"meets the needs of the present without compromising the ability of future generations to meet their needs"*. To this definition, Martin Wietzman added the insights that a measure of "net" national product (corrected for the depreciation of all types of resources that contribute to it) can be thought of as the maximum rate of consumption that could be maintained indefinitely into the future.

Part of the discussion on sustainability is driven by concerns on the state of natural resources. The national accounts include in GDP the output generated by commercial natural resources (e.g. timber), as well as expenditures for exploration and maintenance, but excludes the depletion of the underlying stocks. Similarly, the national accounts includes expenditures for restoring habitats damaged by oil spills or other types of natural or human-made disasters but not the damage that occurred in the first place. While restoring habitats does improve people's well-being once the damage has occurred, it may still leave people well-being lower than before the damage occurred, and this despite higher GDP. This suggests that, from a sustainability perspective, the problem of GDP as a welfare metric is not the inclusion of defensive expenditures related to the environment, but rather the omission of economic-related impacts on (non-produced) natural capital.

Natural capital consists of a wide range of assets, ranging from tradable items such as minerals and timber, through to oceans and the atmosphere. A distinction can be made between "environmental assets", which are individual components of the environment (such as fish or oil resources), and "ecosystems", which refer to the joint functioning of different environmental assets (such as soil, forests, aquatic environments and the atmosphere). A further distinction, within environmental assets, is that between renewable and non-renewable resources. Non-renewable resources are exhaustible, in that natural stocks cannot be regenerated after exploitation, and include items such as metals and other minerals, land, coal, oil and gas. Renewable assets are those that after exploitation can, in principle, regenerate through a process of growth or replenishment – provided certain conditions, such as not violating "critical" stock levels, are met. These renewable assets include timber from managed forests, wool from farmed sheep, and fish from sustainably managed stocks.

The increased availability of statistics on environmental assets and flows has led to the development of accounts to track, in an integrated and consistent way, the different elements of the environment and the ways they are related to the economy. In 2012, the United Nations Statistical Commission published a new System of Environmental and Economic Accounting (SEEA), and adopted the central framework of this system as an international standard. The SEEA proposes a framework for measuring environmental assets in both physical and monetary units. Elements of the SEEA central framework are currently being implemented in many countries around the world, typically focusing on specific elements of the overall framework. Starting from 2015, the OECD will be collecting a set "core tables" for comparative purposes, initially focusing on emissions to air and natural resources, and with the goal to extend productivity measures to account for natural resources used in economic production. Within the European Union, a first EU regulation on Environmental Accounts adopted in 2011 requires all member States to compile annual data on three modules: i) environmental taxes; ii) emissions to air of 14 substances by industries and households; and iii) economy-wide material flow accounts showing domestics extraction, imports and exports if some 40 materials, with a first data delivery taking places in 2013. A second EU regulation is in the process of being adopted, comprising three new modules on: i) expenditure on environmental protection; ii) environmental goods and services; and iii) physical energy flows, with first data delivery envisaged in 2017.

Other types of capital beyond natural and environmental resources matter for sustainability (in the same way that other outcomes beyond those relating to commodities matter for well-being). To account for the broad range of indicators needed to measure sustainable development, the Conference of European Statisticians (a body supported by the UN Economic Commission for Europe) issued in 2014 a set of recommendations on measuring sustainable development. This framework distinguished between the dimensions of "here and now" (i.e. measures of current well-being outcomes in a country at a given point in time), "later" (i.e. measures of capital stocks in a given country) and "elsewhere" (i.e. measures of the impacts of a given country on the flows and stocks prevailing elsewhere). This framework includes both measures of how economic activities in one country affect capital stocks beyond the territory of the country where production takes place and measures of other types of capital stocks beyond natural capital.

With respect to the first, "footprint" measures assess the impact of economic activities in one country on the stock of natural resources available in others or globally. These measures require a world input-output table providing information not just on the economic transactions taking place within a country but also on cross-border flows of goods and services, thereby informing on the unbundling of production and consumption activities that characterises globalisation. Footprint measures are most developed in the case of carbon emissions, as these emissions can be directly linked to the volume of energy inputs used in economic production. Experimental measures of such carbon footprint show that, over the period 1995 to 2005, demand-based carbon emissions by OECD countries increased at a rate about ¼ higher than production-based emissions (as these countries increasingly switched to import carbon-intensive goods and services from non-OECD countries), while the opposite patterns characterised emerging economies.

Figure 15.5. **Production-based and demand-based CO$_2$ emissions**
Rate of change per year, 1995-2005

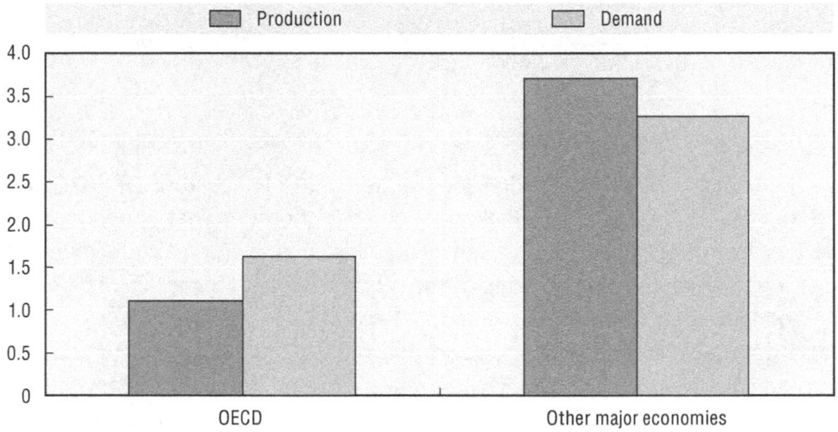

Source: OECD (2011b), *Towards Green Growth: Monitoring Progress – OECD Indicators*, OECD Publishing, Paris.
StatLink ⟨⟩ http://dx.doi.org/10.1787/888933144339

With respect to the second (i.e. other types of non-economic capital that matter for sustainability), human capital is a case in point. Human capital is not included in the national accounts asset boundary both because it is a stock that, while embedded in the person who invested in it, it is not "owned" and transferrable across units; and because the activities undertaken by the person who invested in it are not regarded as "production" (i.e. they could not have been delegated to a third party). Human capital also has other characteristics that set it apart from economic capital, in particular the fact it is enhanced (rather than depleted) by use. While physical measures of human capital exist for both its quantity (e.g. the number of people having attained different educational qualification, sometimes summarised through statistics on "mean years of schooling", or having participated to different types of vocational training) and its quality (e.g. test scores at school exams, or "pencil and papers" assessment of the competences of students and adults), they all have limits in terms of comparability across countries and programmes. Monetary measures of the stock of human capital exist, and are typically based on variants of either an output or an input based approach (Boarini et al., 2013); no consensus however exists on the best measurement approach to be used, and on the scope for integrating such measures within the national accounts. Despite such lack of consensus, considering the learning activities undertaken by individuals as a contribution towards human capital formation could have significant implications for the classification of those educational-related flows that are already included in the national accounts, and which are currently considered as a form of consumption rather than as an investment.

The OECD defines human capital as "the knowledge, skills, competencies and other attributes embodied in individuals or groups of individuals acquired during their life and used to produce goods, services or ideas in market circumstances" (Boarini and al., 2013).

3. Measuring well-being: the broader agenda on "Beyond GDP"

The notion of welfare addresses the question of "*how well-off people are* " and answers that question by looking at the commodities that people possess. The *broader* notion of well-being, however, addresses the question of "*how well people are*", which requires looking at the requirements of a *good life*. The notion of a good life is the focus of the broader "Beyond GDP" agenda. While there are many approaches to defining a good life, most of them do not reduce it to people's possessions alone. They encompass instead a diversity of aspects and attributes that cannot be traded on the market and that matter both at individual level (for instance health, friends, safety, etc.) and at society one (e.g. strengths of communities, social norms). This broader range of factors is simply not accounted for by GDP or any other measures within the national accounts.

Some authors have argued that, to the extent that GDP is highly correlated with non-monetary aspects of well-being, focusing on the former is all that is needed to get adequate measures of well-being. However evidence in support of this view is weak. Many non-monetary components of people's well-being move hand in hand with GDP only up to a given point (Figure 15.6 panel A and B). For instance, both life expectancy and life satisfaction (two critical dimensions of people's well-being) display a log-linear relationship with GDP; this implies that, on average, the gains of life expectancy and life satisfaction associated with additional units of GDP become increasingly smaller, but also that a given percentage change in GDP per capita brings the same gain in non-monetary dimensions of well-being whatever on the average income of the country considered. While a log-linear relationship is consistent with the standard microeconomics assumption (that marginal utility is decreasing in its components), it can also be interpreted as saying that, in high-income a countries, GDP is a weak proxy of people's well-being, and that the quality of this proxy worsens as a country's GDP increases. This is also true for all countries that lie outside the curvilinear relation highlighted by Figure 15.6. For instance Russia or Chile are characterised by large differences in well-being outcomes despite having a similar level of GDP per capita, implying that factors other than GDP are key drivers of the outcome considered.

Figure 15.6. **The relationship between life expectancy and life satisfaction**

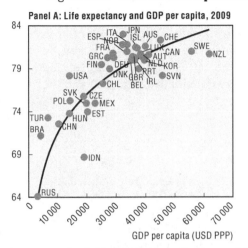

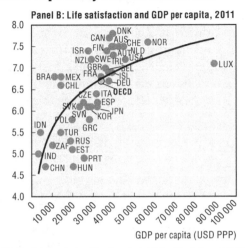

Source: OECD (2013), "OECD Health Data: Health status", OECD Health Statistics (database), doi: *http://dx.doi.org/10.1787/data-00540-en*, and OECD (2014), "Aggregate National Accounts: Gross domestic product", OECD National Accounts Statistics (database), doi: *http://dx.doi.org/10.1787/data-00001-en* and Gallup World Poll, *www.gallup.com/home.aspx?ref=b.*
StatLink ᴍᴇᴸ *http://dx.doi.org/10.1787/888933144347*

The relationship between life satisfaction and income has made the object of lot of research around the so-called "Easterlin Paradox". Richard Easterlin, a US economist, observed in the 1970s that economic growth (or growth in income) in the United States did not translate into higher subjective well-being (Easterlin, 1974). Some of the explanations put forward to explain the paradox include the relative income hypothesis (i.e. that individuals care only about changes in relative income positions, not about absolute changes of their income), the adaptation or treadmill hypothesis (i.e. that people modify their aspirations as they grow rich) and the saturation hypothesis (i.e. that income brings additional subjective well-being to the poor only).

3.1. Well-being as capabilities

As GDP alone is insufficient to measure people's well-being in all its complexity, many efforts have been undertaken to devise additional metrics of welfare. Most of these efforts have been inspired by the "capabilities" approach developed by Amartya Sen. This approach defines well-being in terms of the *opportunities to live a good life*. These opportunities (capabilities) are quantified by the set of alternative combinations of functionings (i.e. the various things that a person may value to do and be) that people can achieve. Development and progress require broadening people's opportunities set and escaping tragic choices where one has to give up health or education or dignity to secure material subsistence. Implicit in this view is the notion that the various aspects of the good life are valuable in themselves rather than just instrumentally to produce higher welfare.

The capabilities approach implies a multidimensional definition of well-being that includes both capabilities and achieved outcomes. Since both functionings and capabilities are important, this approach can be operationalised through a dashboard of indicators that assumes that all dimensions are important. The OECD Better Life Initiative (Box 15.2) and the OECD Better Life Index follow this route.

Box 15.2. **The OECD framework for measuring well-being**

The OECD well-being framework (Figure 15.7) is an attempt to operationalise the capabilities approach and making it measurable through well-being indicators that can be used by policy-makers and national statistical offices to monitor well-being conditions in the population and their evolution over time. Operationalising the framework requires firstly, to choose the list of functionings and capabilities that should be considered and, secondly, to identify the specific indicators measuring them. Concerning the first aspect, the OECD defines well-being in two main domains: material living conditions (i.e. "welfare" or "economic well-being") and quality of life. These two domains are further broken down into eleven *dimensions*, namely: i) income and wealth; ii) jobs and earnings; iii) housing; iv) health; v) work and life balance; vi) education; vii) social connections; viii) civic engagement; ix) environmental conditions; x) personal security; and xi) subjective well-being. These eleven dimensions are considered as universal, i.e. relevant to all societies. Indeed, while indicators measuring these dimensions may vary across countries and cultural contexts, the dimensions selected have a claim to be important for all countries around the world, irrespective of their level of socio-economic and human development.

Measuring each well-being dimensions raises specific issues and for many dimensions the available indicators are not of perfect quality (see OECD 2011 and 2013 for an in-depth discussion of these aspects). However, much statistical progress has been achieved over the past twenty years in measuring some of them (e.g. employment, health, skills, the environment). For others there is still a long way to go before indicators based on well-established international standards become universally available (e.g. social connection, governance, personal security). In general, well-being statistics suffer from limited time-comparability, lack of timeliness and insufficient level of detail (i.e. they are available at macro-level but not for different subgroups of the population).

Box 15.2. **The OECD framework for measuring well-being** (cont.)

Also, they are typically available only in physical terms, implying that they do not allow confronting trade-offs involving valuation. In some cases, comparable data are only available through non-official instruments, which however have other statistical limits.

Figure 15.7. **The OECD framework for measuring well-being**

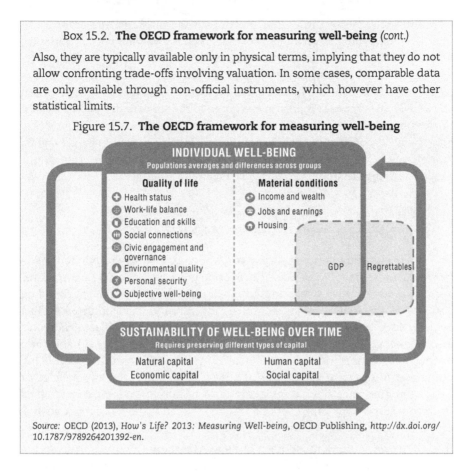

Source: OECD (2013), How's Life? 2013: Measuring Well-being, OECD Publishing, http://dx.doi.org/10.1787/9789264201392-en.

3.2. Measuring and understanding multidimensionality: Dashboard or Index?

As capabilities' approach considers all the outcomes as valuable in themselves, the most natural way to operationalise it is by adopting a dashboard of indicators that shows each outcome separately. While one shortcoming of dashboards is that they only allow partial ordering among states (i.e. they allow to tell whether one country is doing better in each of the dimensions *separately* but not whether a better performance is achieved *overall*), one advantage is that they describe the performance trends of the elementary components, an aspect which is very important from a policy perspective.

The alternative to the dashboard is represented by indices that combine the elementary indicators into a headline figure. *Composite indices* combine information at aggregate level and *synthetic indices* combine information at individual level. The advantage of composite/synthetic indices is that they simplify the reading of the data and take into account the joint correlation of outcomes, therefore indicating possible interrelationships among the components (synergies or trade-offs at aggregate level and concentration of advantages/disadvantages at individual level). One drawback of composite/ synthetic indices is that they may require arbitrary assumptions on various steps needed for their construction, i.e. the normalisation of indicators (when the individual components are not measured in the same units), and the choice of the functional forms used to combine together the various elements (e.g. substitutability or complementarity of the arguments), as well as their weights. Therefore it is very important that these assumptions are either grounded in economic theory and/or tested through sensitivity analysis.

The OECD Better Life Index avoids the problem by allowing users to choose their own individual weight to aggregate the many indicators.

The dichotomy between dashboard and composite/synthetic indices is however increasingly seen as unnecessary, as one can use composite/ synthetic indices when they bring value-added to the analysis but at the same time report more disaggregated information through dashboards as well as acknowledge the limitations of the composite/synthetic indices. There are also circumstances where composite/synthetic indices are more suitable than dashboards, for instance when the goal is not that of monitoring well-being but rather to evaluate the impact of policy on well-being. Many policies or public programmes have a wide range of effects on people's lives; it is therefore important that their *ex ante* or *ex post* appraisal comes with a judgement on their *overall* impact on people's well-being.

OECD work along these lines aims at assessing the impact of various types of policies on a composite measure of well-being that combines three of the well-being dimensions included in the Better Life Initiative framework through a monetary metric (see Box 15.3).

Box 15.3. **The OECD Inclusive Growth Framework**

In the OECD Inclusive Growth Measurement Framework, a composite index of well-being (called "Multidimensional living standards") is defined in terms of the income and selected non-income aspects of life achieved in a country, and by how these aspects are distributed across the population. The index is built through the following three steps:

- First, a measure of *income-based* living standards (captured for instance by consumption or real income) is computed at the individual level.

- Second, several other *non-income* dimensions are brought into the analysis and measured at the level of individuals or groups of individuals in order to combine them with measured income.

Box 15.3. **The OECD Inclusive Growth Framework** (*cont.*)

● Third, this broader living standard measure is aggregated across individuals to obtain an overall measure of multidimensional living standards.

The OECD framework follows the income-equivalent approach (Fleurbaey, 2009) to perform the second step. Equivalent income is the hypothetical income that would make an individual indifferent between her/his current situation in terms of non-income aspects of life and a benchmark situation (typically the best possible outcome in non-income dimensions). Equivalent income then replaces monetary income, and welfare comparisons between individuals, or over time, are similar to those undertaken in the standard case. The equivalent income approach requires monetising the benefits from non-income components. This monetisation depends first on a reference level to which individuals can compare their actual outcome (e.g. the number of years of life expectancy above or below a benchmark level of longevity). In a second step, individuals' distance to the benchmark, measured in non-monetary units, is monetised and expressed in terms of equivalent income. Figure 15.8 shows that, between 1995 and 2007, the monetary value of a measure of (multidimensional) living standards of the median household increased at a faster pace than both GDP per capita and household income, driven by gains in longevity and lower unemployment. Since the crisis of 2007-2009, (multidimensional) living standards fell by more than GDP in all OECD countries affected by the crisis, due to higher unemployment.

Figure 15.8. **Growth in Multidimensional Living Standards for the median household, 1995-2007**

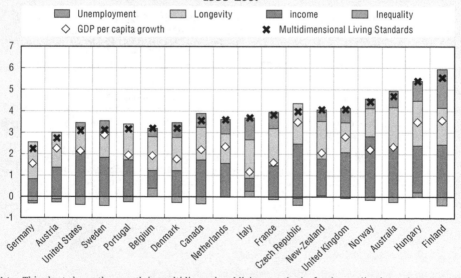

Note: This chart shows the growth in multidimensional living standards for the median house between 1995 and 2007. It also shows the components of multidimensional living standards growth, namely changes in income, longevity, unemployment and life expectancy.
Source: Boarini et al., 2014.

StatLink ᨆ᠊ᢧᨆᢅ *http://dx.doi.org/10.1787/888933144366*

Notes

1. Consumption units typically adjust the number of people belonging to the same household through factors ("equivalence scales") that reflect the sharing of resources that takes place within households. Computation of consumption units typically require information of how persons are grouped in different household, i.e. micro-level information. For a description of "equivalence scales", see: *www.oecd.org/eco/growth/OECD-Note-EquivalenceScales.pdf*.

2. OECD estimates of average annual hours worked per person in employment (referring to both full- and part-time workers) in 2012 ranged between 2,226 hours in Mexico and 1,381 Netherlands (i.e. a difference of around 40%). Since 1979, annual hours actually worked per person declined by 18% in France but by only 2% in the United States.

References

Ahmad, N. and S. Koh (2011), "Incorporating Estimates of Household Production of Non-Market Services into International Comparisons of Material Well-Being", OECD Statistics Working Papers, No. 2011/07, OECD Publishing, Paris, doi: *http://dx.doi.org/10.1787/5kg3h0jgk87g-en*.

Boarini R., Å. Johansson and M. M. d'Ercole (2006), "Alternative Measures of Well-Being", OECD Social, *Employment and Migration Working Papers*, No. 33, OECD Publishing, Paris, doi: *http://dx.doi.org/10.1787/713222332167* .

Boarini R, De Mello L., De Serres A., Martin F., Schreyer P. (2014), "OECD Framework on Inclusive Growth", *OECD Statistics Directorate Working Paper*, forthcoming, OECD Publishing, Paris

Boarini R., M. Mira d'Ercole and G. Liu (2012), "Approaches to Measuring the Stock of Human Capital: A Review of Country Practices", OECD Statistics Working Papers, No. 2012/04, OECD Publishing, Paris, doi: *http://dx.doi.org/10.1787/5k8zlm5bc3ns-en*.

Coyle D. (2014), "GDP: a brief but affectionate history", Princeton University Press, Princeton, New Jersey

Fesseau, M., F. Wolff and M. L. Mattonetti (2013a), "A Cross-country Comparison of Household Income, Consumption and Wealth between Micro Sources and National Accounts Aggregates", OECD Statistics Working Papers, No. 2013/03, OECD Publishing, Paris, doi: *http://dx.doi.org/10.1787/5k3wdjrnh7mv-en*.

Fesseau, M. and M. L. Mattonetti (2013b), "Distributional Measures Across Household Groups in a National Accounts Framework: Results from an Experimental Cross-country Exercise on Household Income, Consumption and Saving", OECD Statistics Working Papers, No. 2013/04, OECD Publishing, Paris, doi: *http://dx.doi.org/10.1787/5k3wdjqr775f-en*.

Fleurbaey M. (2009), "Beyond the GDP: The quest for measures of social welfare", Journal of Economic Literature, Vol. 47, No. 4, December, pp. 1029-1075, doi: 10.1257/jel.47.4.1029

Gallup World Poll, *www.gallup.com/home.aspx?ref=b*.

Nordhaus W. D. and J. Tobin (1973), "Is Growth Obsolete?" in *The Measurement of Economic and Social Performance, Studies in Income and Wealth*, National Bureau of Economic research, Vol. 38.

OECD (2014), "Detailed National Accounts: Non-financial accounts by sectors, annual", OECD National Accounts Statistics (database), doi: *http://dx.doi.org/10.1787/data-00034-en*.

OECD (2013a), "Aggregate National Accounts: Gross domestic product", OECD National Accounts Statistics (database), *http://dx.doi.org/10.1787/data-00001-en*.

OECD (2013b), "OECD Health Data: Health status", OECD Health Statistics (database), doi: *http://dx.doi.org/10.1787/data-00540-en*.

OECD (2013c), "Income Distribution", OECD Social and Welfare Statistics (database), doi: *http://dx.doi.org/10.1787/data-00654-en*.

OECD (2013d), How's Life? 2013: Measuring Well-being, OECD Publishing, doi: *http://dx.doi.org/10.1787/9789264201392-en*.

OECD (2011), How's Life?: Measuring Well-being, OECD Publishing, Paris, doi: *http://dx.doi.org/10.1787/9789264121164-en*.

Stiglitz J. E., A. Sen, and J-P Fitoussi (2009) *Report by the Commission on Measurement of Economic Performance and Social Progress*, available under *www.stiglitz-sen-fitoussi.fr/en/index.htm*.

Chapter 16

National accounts in a globalising world

This chapter illustrates the increasing trend of globalisation, whereby products are the result of processes taking place all around the world. It proposes a new statistical tool, TiVA, to better understand these interlinked international trade flows. It discusses how to maintain the quality of national accounts statistics in this more and more globalised world.

Globalisation is a centuries old phenomenon of growing interaction between national economies. In recent decades, this phenomenon has gained a new momentum, mainly because of political developments and progress in information and communication technology. The traditional interrelations between countries, e.g. in exchanging products and in closely connected financial markets, have grown considerably. At the same time there has been a deepening of globalisation through, for example, global production arrangements. Increasingly production processes extend over the whole world. Think of the production of an iPAD, where product innovation and development takes place in the United States, all kinds of semi-fabricates are produced in several countries and then assembled in China, after which they are traded all over the world, with advertising campaigns being developed in yet another country. The image in the next page shows some of the worldwide interrelationships in the production of a Boeing commercial airplane.

These developments have had a positive impact on worldwide income and productivity. However, the economic and financial crisis, which started in the United Sates in 2007 and rapidly spread to other parts of the world, also revealed major risks associated with the growing interconnectedness of national economies. The downturn in the US real estate market did not only affect the value of the portfolios of American corporations, but also directly, via investments in the US real estate market, or indirectly, via investments in related American corporations such as Fanny Mae, Freddy Mac and Lehman Brothers, corporations in the rest of the world. Another example is the Fukushima-disaster which did not only affect the Japanese economy, but also the economies of other countries which were entangled with the Japanese companies via all kinds of supply chains.

When looking at globalisation from a statistical perspective, one is confronted with a number of challenges, which can be grouped into four broad categories:

- The measurement of the phenomenon itself. How can we measure (the further development of) globalization? Which indicators capture the growing interdependence of national economies?

- The description of the behaviour of multinational enterprises, which are the driving force behind globalization. How do these enterprises behave, and why? What are the reasons behind the division of activities and the

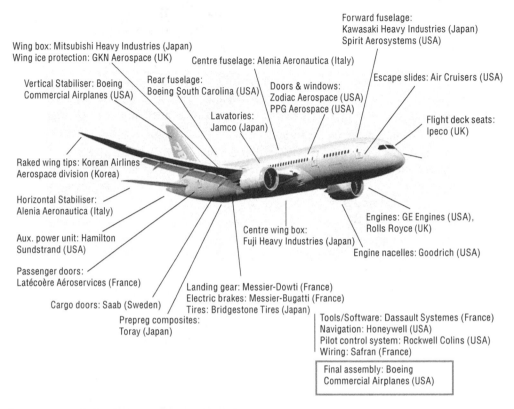

Forward fuselage:
Kawasaki Heavy Industries (Japan)
Spirit Aerosystems (USA)

Wing box: Mitsubishi Heavy Industries (Japan)
Wing ice protection: GKN Aerospace (UK)

Centre fuselage: Alenia Aeronautica (Italy)

Escape slides: Air Cruisers (USA)

Vertical Stabiliser: Boeing
Commercial Airplanes (USA)

Rear fuselage:
Boeing South Carolina (USA)

Doors & windows:
Zodiac Aerospace (USA),
PPG Aerospace (USA)

Lavatories:
Jamco (Japan)

Flight deck seats:
Ipeco (UK)

Raked wing tips: Korean Airlines
Aerospace division (Korea)

Horizontal Stabiliser:
Alenia Aeronautica (Italy)

Engines: GE Engines (USA),
Rolls Royce (UK)

Centre wing box:
Fuji Heavy Industries (Japan)

Aux. power unit: Hamilton
Sundstrand (USA)

Engine nacelles: Goodrich (USA)

Passenger doors:
Latécoère Aéroservices (France)

Landing gear: Messier-Dowti (France)
Electric brakes: Messier-Bugatti (France)
Tires: Bridgestone Tires (Japan)

Cargo doors: Saab (Sweden)

Prepreg composites:
Toray (Japan)

Tools/Software: Dassault Systemes (France)
Navigation: Honeywell (USA)
Pilot control system: Rockwell Colins (USA)
Wiring: Safran (France)

Final assembly: Boeing
Commercial Airplanes (USA)

Source: www.newairplane.com.

subsequent allocation of these activities to countries? What are the comparative advantages of national economies?

- The impact of globalisation on traditional indicators. Globalization can have a significant impact on all aspects of a society's development, economic, social and environmental. More (detailed) information to support further analysis and research is particularly important in the areas of significant impact.

- The impact of globalization on the compilation of traditional indicators. The increasing proportion of enterprises running their business on an international scale and the growing cross-border movement of people, financial capital, goods and services pose specific problems to compilers of national statistics, in particular national accounts.

While globalisation can pose problems for compilers of statistics, it is important to remember that macroeconomic policies still remain largely national based. Even in the Eurozone, it is only the monetary policy which is unique to the 19 countries of the zone together, not the budgetary policies which remain based on national economic developments. As such, the *national* accounts variables remain essential as they constitute the statistical framework on which the economic policies are based. In other words, the term *national* in national accounts does not become obsolete because of globalisation, it "simply" becomes more difficult to measure national accounts aggregates, and statisticians have to devise ways of maintaining their quality.

In this chapter, we will start with showing some examples of the growing globalisation. The chapter will subsequently dwell upon the role of multinational enterprises and the impact they may have on the interpretation of trade flows and the competitiveness of national economies, based on a new statistical tool, Trade in Value Added (TiVA). The chapter will conclude with addressing some of the measurement issues, especially when it comes to the compilation of national accounts.

1. Evidence of increasing globalisation

Globalisation is often thought of in terms of increasing imports and exports of goods and services, as a percentage of GDP. Although this certainly is not the only way in which the interconnectedness of national economies can be measured, it provides an immediate understanding of the phenomenon. In Figure 16.1, it shows that in the period 1995 to 2012, the average share of exports in OECD-countries has increased from 20.1% to 29.0%

Figure 16.1. **Average export share for OECD-countries**
Exports of goods and services. % of GDP

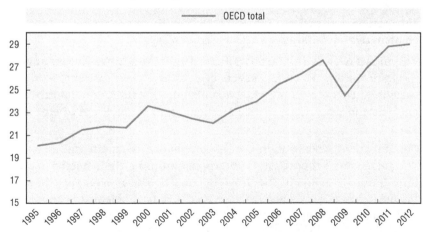

Source: OECD (2014), National Accounts at a Glance 2014, OECD Publishing, doi: http://dx.doi.org/10.1787/na_glance-2014-en.

StatLink ᐸᔑᒲ http://dx.doi.org/10.1787/888933144375

of GDP. In a small and open economy like Luxembourg, the share of exports goes well beyond 100% of GDP, with a top of 182% just before the financial crisis. But also countries like Belgium, Estonia, Hungary, Ireland, the Netherlands, and the Slovak Republic have high export shares of above 75% in recent years. Looking at the developments over time, it shows that the economic and financial crisis caused a major hick-up in the long-term developments, although the trend was quickly recovered with export shares in 2011 generally being higher than before the crisis.

Another indicator showing the growing interconnectedness between national economies is the share of Foreign Direct Investment (FDI), again as a percentage of GDP. FDI mainly relates to the financial investments made by multinational enterprises in setting up subsidiaries in other economies. Figure 16.2 shows the average position of outward FDI for OECD-countries over the period 1990-2013. One can observe similar developments as for the export shares. While the average position of OECD-countries was 9.7% in 1990, it has increased to 42.6% in 2013 in an almost continuous upward trend. In Luxembourg and Ireland, the levels of outward investment were well beyond 200%, closely followed by Belgium and Switzerland with level around 190% in recent years.

Figure 16.2. **Average Foreign Direct Investment share for OECD-countries**
% of GDP

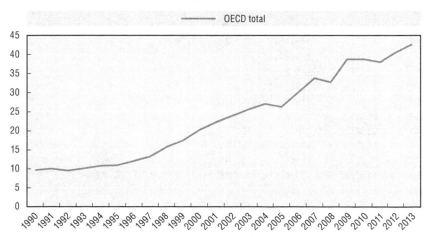

Source: OECD (2013), FDI series of BOP, *http://stats.oecd.org/Index.aspx?DataSetCode=FDI_BOP_IIP* and *www.oecd.org/investment/statistics.htm.*

StatLink 🔗 *http://dx.doi.org/10.1787/888933144407*

One can also look at the generation of domestic output and employment by enterprises which are directly controlled by foreign corporations. The following table presents some evidence for the Netherlands. It shows that the share of foreign controlled corporations in all non-financial corporate activities has increased substantially over the past period from 1995. The share of foreign controlled enterprises in value added has grown from 19.0% in 1995 to around 30% in 2009-11. For compensation of employees, the share has increased from 16.5% to around 25% in 2009-11. A particularly strong increase was noticeable in the early crisis years, suggesting that the foreign controlled corporations were more resilient against the economic downturn.

All of this clearly shows the growing interconnectedness of national economies. Similar examples can be found in the increasing number of daily transactions in financial capital worldwide. In the following section, more attention will be paid to multinational enterprises and the role they play.

Table 16.1. **Foreign controlled non-financial corporations in The Netherlands**

Value added and compensation of employees

	Value Added by foreign controlled corporation	Compensation of employees paid by foreign controlled enterprises	Value Added by non-financial corporations	Compensation of employees paid by non-financial corporations	Share in Value Added	Share in compensation of employees
1995	32 490	17 207	171 001	104 177	19.0%	16.5%
1996	34 175	18 033	179 451	109 181	19.0%	16.5%
1997	37 558	18 545	192 310	115 903	19.5%	16.0%
1998	41 317	21 188	204 671	125 214	20.2%	16.9%
1999	44 602	23 674	217 558	134 326	20.5%	17.6%
2000	49 246	25 358	237 147	144 303	20.8%	17.6%
2001	55 600	29 912	251 994	154 574	22.1%	19.4%
2002	61 780	32 296	263 024	161 243	23.5%	20.0%
2003	63 461	32 617	266 631	164 883	23.8%	19.8%
2004	68 858	35 949	273 709	168 539	25.2%	21.3%
2005	72 365	38 312	287 162	170 995	25.2%	22.4%
2006	78 791	39 889	304 212	179 049	25.9%	22.3%
2007	84 228	42 810	325 204	190 018	25.9%	22.5%
2008	82 997	42 238	339 872	201 020	24.4%	21.0%
2009	94 399	51 402	322 929	201 913	29.2%	25.5%
2010	100 335	51 874	327 892	201 801	30.6%	25.7%
2011	100 161	51 289	338 359	207 140	29.6%	24.8%

Source: CBS (2012), Internalisation Monitor 2012, www.cbs.nl/nl-NL/menu/themas/internationale-handel/publicaties/publicaties/archief/2012/2012-internationalisation-monitor-2012-pub.htm.

StatLink ⟐ http://dx.doi.org/10.1787/888933144385

2. A new statistical tool to measure the impact of globalisation: Trade in Value Added (TiVA)

Major players in the globalising world are the multinational enterprises. More and more enterprises are nowadays heavily involved in global production arrangements which often span the whole world. Production processes are fragmented and allocated to countries which provide the most efficient way to take care of the various stages in the production process. This directly affects in which countries value added and employment is generated, the developments in international cross-border trade flows and the ways in which these flows are to be interpreted, and what are to be considered the competitive advantages of a country in a globalised world. The world is increasingly interconnected and conventional approaches used to understand how national economies work can no longer rely solely on national statistics. Increasingly, in order to understand how economies work, and how to target and create industrial policies, targeting competitiveness for example, it is necessary to see the whole.

To address the issues related to globalisation, various initiatives have been developed to shed more light on this phenomenon and to improve the data and analysis needed to address the many economic policy questions countries are faced with. One of these initiatives is the so-called Trade in Value Added (TiVA), jointly developed by the OECD and the World Trade Organisation (WTO). The TiVA initiative addresses the double counting implicit in current gross flows of trade, and instead measures flows related to the value that is added (labour compensation, other taxes on production and operating surplus, or profits) by a country in the production of any good or service that is exported. The simple example below illustrates this. Country A exports USD 100 of goods, produced entirely within A, to country B that further processes them before exporting them to C where they are consumed. B adds value of USD 10 to the goods and so exports USD 110 to C. Conventional measures of trade show total global exports and imports of USD 210 but only USD 110 of value-added has been generated in their production. Conventional measures also show that C has a trade deficit of USD 110 with B, and no trade at all with A, despite the fact that A is the chief beneficiary of C's consumption.

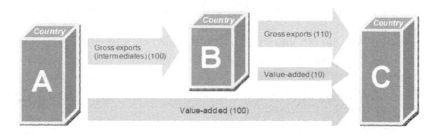

If instead one would track flows in value-added, one can recalculate C's trade deficit with B on the basis of the value-added it "purchases" from B as final demand, which reduces its deficit on this basis, to USD 10, and apply the same approach to A's value-added to show C running a deficit of USD 100 with A. Note that C's overall trade deficit with the world remains at USD 110. All that has changed is its bilateral positions. This simple illustration reveals how output in one country can be affected by consumers in another and by how much (for example C's consumers driving A's output) but it can also reveal many other important insights into global production arrangements. For example it shows that B's exports depend significantly on intermediate imports from A, and so reveals that protectionist measures on imports from A could harm its own exporters and hence competitiveness. Indeed, by providing information at the level of specific industries, it is possible to provide insights in other areas too, such as the contribution of the service sector to international trade. In this respect, Pascal Lamy, the Director General of the WTO, noted that "the statistical bias created by attributing commercial value to the last country of origin perverts the true economic dimension of the bilateral trade imbalances. This affects the political debate, and leads to misguided perceptions" (Financial times, 24 January 2011).

To disentangle these trade flows, and to arrive at estimates of the trade in value-added, the TiVA uses a global input-output table that brings together national input-output tables for national economies, combined with bilateral trade data on goods and services. In this context, it is important to understand that TiVA is not meant to adjust the main variables of the national accounts, such as value added or GDP, which remain free of any double-counting or biases. On the contrary, TiVA estimates are based on the system of national accounts as it is. TiVA simply gives an additional interpretation of gross trade flows. The following provides a number of examples of the key messages provided by this new presentation of international trade flows data.

Exports require imports

The data reveals that the import content of exports (the share of value added by the export of a given product that originates abroad) is significant in almost all countries. Figure 16.3 shows the reverse ratio (i.e., the domestic content of exports), as a percentage of total exports. Typically the larger a country the higher the domestic content, reflecting in part scale and cost. But a number of smaller economies also have relatively high domestic content in their exports, such as Australia, Chile, and Norway, reflecting their high share of exports of natural resource goods such as ores, oil and copper, which have not surprisingly a low foreign content. Geography also plays a role too, which helps to explain New Zealand's relatively high ratio, as well as its relatively high dependency on agricultural exports, which also have a relatively low

Figure 16.3. **Domestic content of exports**

Domestic Value-Added exports, % of total gross exports, 2009

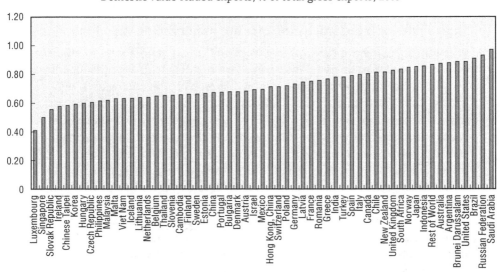

Source: OECD/WTO (2013), OECD-WTO: Statistics on Trade in Value Added, (database), doi: http://dx.doi.org/10.1787/data-00648-en.

StatLink ᴍ⃗ᴍ http://dx.doi.org/10.1787/888933144418

foreign content. For mid-size economies however, particularly those in Eastern Europe, the norm is for around only two thirds of the value of exports to reflect domestic content. Up to one-third reflects foreign content. More generally, the data reveal the existence of European, Asian and North American production hubs and also the significant dependency many countries have on imports to generate exports. In Mexico, with its maquilladores, and China with its processors/assemblers, about one-third of overall exports reflect foreign content.

Some care is needed in interpreting the results however: 2009 was an exceptional year, the year that signified perhaps the nadir of the economic and financial crisis, and which was partly characterised by an unprecedented slowdown in global trade since World War II. Illustrative data going back to 1995 suggests that international fragmentation of production (the import content of exports) had been steadily rising in most countries over recent decades, which continued over the period 2005-08, despite the slowdown that began to occur in many countries in 2008. But 2009 saw falls in the import content of exports, and, so, rises in the domestic content, suggesting that the greater the fragmentation of a good or service, the more likely it was to be affected by the synchronised slowdown in trade. In most countries therefore, the import content of overall exports in 2009 returned to around the ratios seen in 2005 but in China the data points to a steady fall in its foreign content over the period, suggesting developments that saw China begin to move up the value-added chain.

High shares of intermediate imports are used to serve export markets

The figures above reveal that exporting firms require access to efficient imports in order to be competitive, and, so, highlight the potential counter-productive effects of protectionist measures. But an alternative way of indicating the adverse effects of such policies can be seen when looking at the overall share of intermediate imports that are used to serve export markets. In most economies, around one-third of intermediate imports are destined for the export market. Not surprisingly, typically, the smaller the economy the higher the share, but even in the United States and Japan these shares are 15% and 20% respectively at the total economy level, with a higher incidence of intermediate imports in some highly integrated industries (Figure 16.4). In Japan for example nearly 40% of all intermediate imports of transport equipment end up in exports. In many other countries, the share of intermediate imports embodied in exports is significantly higher. In Hungary, for example two-thirds of all intermediate imports are destined for the export market after further processing, with the share reaching 90% for electronic intermediate imports. In China, Korea and Mexico around three-quarters of all intermediate imports of electronics are embodied in exports.

Figure 16.4. **Intermediate imports embodied in exports**
% of total intermediate imports, 2009

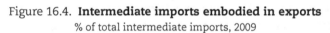

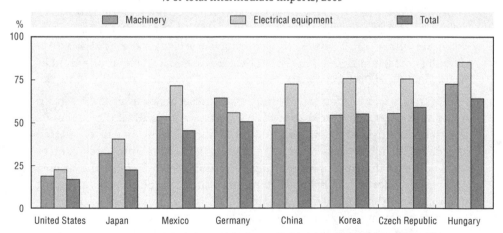

Source: OECD/WTO (2013), OECD-WTO: Statistics on Trade in Value Added, (database), doi: http://dx.doi.org/10.1787/data-00648-en.

StatLink ᵐˢᵖ http://dx.doi.org/10.1787/888933144425

Open and efficient services markets matter

Services comprise about two-thirds of GDP in most developed economies. However, based on gross terms, trade in services typically accounts for less than one-quarter of total trade in most countries. This partly reflects the fact that significant shares of services output are generally not (internationally) tradable, e.g. government services, many personal services and imputations such as those made in GDP calculations to reflect the rent homeowners are assumed to pay themselves. But it also reflects the fact that the service sector provides significant intermediate inputs to domestic goods manufacturers.

Accounting for the value added produced by the services sector in the production of goods shows that the service content of total gross exports is over 50% in most OECD economies, approaching two-thirds of the total in the United Kingdom (Figure 16.5). Canada, with significant exports of natural resources, which have typically low services content, has the lowest services content of its exports in the G7 but even here the share is close to 40%. Typically, emerging economies and other large exporters of natural assets, such as Norway, Chile and Australia, have the lowest shares of services. On the other hand, in India over half of the value of its gross exports originates in the service sector. Indonesia has the lowest share of the 40 countries in the database at around 20%.

Figure 16.5. **Services value added: % of total exports (2009)**

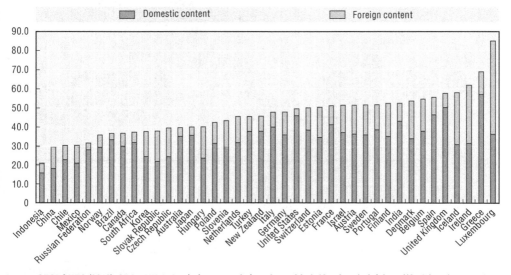

Source: OECD/WTO (2013), OECD-WTO: Statistics on Trade in Value Added, (database), doi: http://dx.doi.org/10.1787/data-00648-en.

StatLink ᗧᗧᗡ http://dx.doi.org/10.1787/888933144433

Part of the explanation for the difference between OECD countries and emerging economies reflects the relatively higher degree of (largely domestic) outsourcing of services by manufacturers in OECD countries in recent decades, suggesting that a similar process could lead to improvements in the competitiveness of emerging economy manufacturers. Figure 16.5 also reveals a not insignificant contribution to exports coming from foreign service providers.

Another, perhaps clearer way, of illustrating the importance of services to exports is to consider, the services content of specific exports in goods producing sectors. Figure 16.6 below, which takes an average of all 40 countries in the database, shows that services make a significant contribution (typically one-third) across all manufacturing sectors, with significant shares provided by both foreign and domestic service providers. For individual sectors in specific countries the importance of the service sector is often starker. In France, for example, the data reveals that over half of the domestic value-added generated in producing transport equipment originates in the French service sector.

Figure 16.6. **Services Value Added: % of total exports of goods, average of 40 countries (2009)**

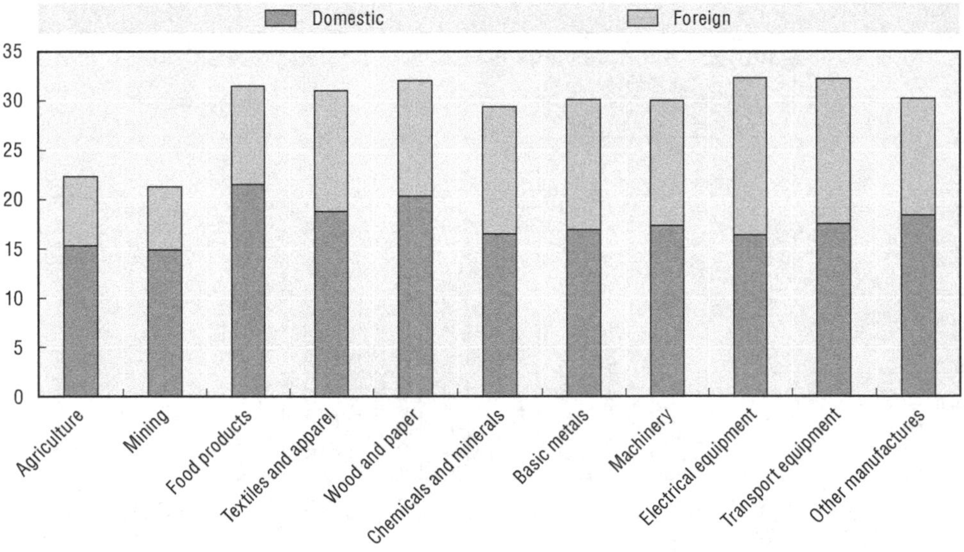

Source: OECD/WTO (2013), OECD-WTO: Statistics on Trade in Value Added, (database), doi: http://dx.doi.org/10.1787/data-00648-en

StatLink ᴍᴐ▬ http://dx.doi.org/10.1787/888933144440

What you see is not what you get: trade patterns change

Bilateral trade balance positions can change significantly when measured in value-added terms, although the total trade balance is unaffected. For example, China's bilateral trade surplus with the United States was over USD 40 billion (25%) smaller in TiVA terms in 2009 (and 30% smaller in 2005). This partly reflects the higher share of US value-added imports in Chinese final demand but also the fact that a significant share (one-third) of China's exports reflect foreign content which is the result of the "Factory Asia" phenomenon. The data illustrates that significant exports of value-added from Korea and Japan pass through China on their way to final consumers, resulting in significantly smaller Chinese trade deficits with these countries but also typically higher Japanese and Korean trade surpluses with other countries. Similarly the data show that Korea's significant trade deficit with Japan in gross terms almost disappears when measured in TiVA terms.

Figure 16.7. **Difference between China's value-added and gross trade balances**
USD billion, 2009

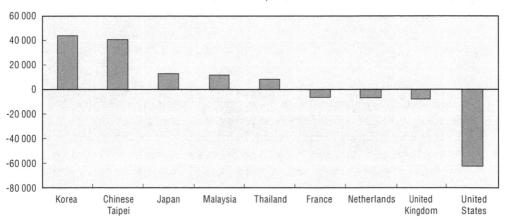

Source: OECD/WTO (2013), OECD-WTO: Statistics on Trade in Value Added, (database), doi: *http://dx.doi.org/10.1787/data-00648-en.*

StatLink ━━ *http://dx.doi.org/10.1787/888933144458*

In conclusion, one can state that competitive strengths of countries cannot simply be derived from the type of products countries typically export, as they may contain a high share of value added produced in other countries. In a globalising world, the competitive edge of a country may be much more related to certain types of activities in the global value chain.

3. Continuing to compile good national accounts in a globalising world

While TiVa is an important extension of the traditional national accounts, the activities of multinational enterprises may also raise concerns in relation to the quality of national accounts for national economies. The first and perhaps most prominent issue relates to the allocation of value added to national economies. Multinationals have substantial intra-firm transactions in goods and services which cross the borders of national economies. The valuation of these transactions, often referred to as "transfer pricing", has a direct impact on the allocation of value added and GDP. If, for example, a multinational from the USA arranges the production of its goods in China, and subsequently distributes them to another subsidiary in Europe, an artificially low price for the export from China to Europe will result in lower measured output, value added and profits in China, and higher values outside China, and vice-versa. Although such prices, according to most national tax legislations, have to be set at market-equivalent prices, there is room to manoeuvre, especially in the case the relevant goods contain high margins for reasons of knowledge content and/or brand reputation, or in the case the relevant goods are intermediate products which are not marketable as a consequence of which it is not possible to apply a true market-equivalent price.

Another issue may relate to the appropriate allocation of the use of services which are produced within a multinational enterprise. Especially the recording of the use of intangible assets may raise issues. Here, one can think of, for example, software that is produced in one location of the multinational but used throughout the enterprise. Another example relates to Research and Development (R&D), which according to SNA 2008 are also to be treated as gross fixed capital formation. Anecdotal evidence for a number of large Dutch multinationals shows that R&D-activities are heavily concentrated, a relatively high share taking place in the home country close to the headquarters of the multinational. These activities however may benefit the production of goods and services of the subsidiaries allocated in various countries. Nonetheless, one hardly observes any payments from the subsidiaries to the headquarters for the use or the outright purchase of R&D-capital, as a consequence of which value added and investments in the countries of the subsidiaries may be underestimated from an economic substance point of view.

Another issue is the establishment of brass plate companies, often referred to as Special Purpose Entities (SPEs), in certain countries, to reallocate the collection and distribution of royalties, license fees, or profits more generally, with the purpose of avoiding or minimising worldwide tax payments. For obvious reasons, some countries are very attractive for the establishment of such conduits. The use of them often gets front page news coverage, once they become publicly known and relate to well-known multinational enterprises.

The above examples of artificial and creative accounting can have an impact on the allocation of output, value added (GDP) and profits across the world. It goes without further saying that not having an adequate description of production processes in the various national economies, but reasons related to worldwide tax minimisation, will often govern decisions at the enterprise level, thus possibly hampering the adequacy of providing a good macroeconomic picture of national economies. To provide a more concrete example, Table 16.2 (extracted from Lipsey, 2010) provides an overview of the profit allocation of multinational enterprises with their headquarters in the United States. It shows that in some countries the ratio of profits to compensation of employees of subsidiaries is as high as 35-36 (Barbados and Bermuda). The Other Western Hemisphere as a total has a ratio which is close to 12. This is strikingly different from the worldwide average equalling 0.8. For European subsidiaries, the ratio is even lower, less than 0.6, although Ireland has a particularly high level of 6.6. However, the recent OECD initiative on Base Erosion and Profit Shifting (see Box 16.1) may, on the contrary, amend for this bias and have positive indirect impacts on the quality of national accounts.

Table 16.2. **Ratio of profit-type return to compensation of employees**

Majority-owned non-bank affiliates of US non-bank parents, 2005

All countries	0.840
Canada	0.848
Europe	0.579
Ireland	6.639
Netherlands	0.878
Switzerland	1.614
Latin America and other western hemisphere	1.555
Central and South America	0.978
Other western hemisphere	11.709
Barbados	34.967
Bermuda	36.062
British Islands, Caribean	8.833
Western hemisphere, n.e.c	6.347
Middle East	1.837
Asia Pacific	1.178
Hong-Kong	0.953
Singapore	2.978

Source: US department of Commerce, Bureau of Economic Analysis (November 2007)

StatLink 🔗 *http://dx.doi.org/10.1787/888933144394*

Box 16.1. **OECD-project on Base Erosion and Profit Shifting**

In an increasingly interconnected world, national tax laws have not kept pace with global corporations, fluid capital, and the digital economy, leaving gaps that can be exploited by companies who avoid taxation in their home countries by pushing activities abroad to low or no tax jurisdictions. This undermines the fairness and integrity of tax systems. The project, quickly known as BEPS (Base Erosion and Profit Shifting) looks at whether or not the current rules allow for the allocation of taxable profits to locations different from those where the actual business activity takes place, and what could be done to change this if they do.

Following the *Declaration on BEPS* adopted at the 2013 Ministerial Council Meeting and at the request of G20 Finance Ministers, in July 2013 the OECD launched an Action Plan on Base Erosion and Profit Shifting (BEPS), identifying 15 specific actions needed in order to equip governments with the domestic and international instruments to address this challenge. The plan recognises the importance of addressing the borderless digital economy, and will develop a new set of standards to prevent double non-taxation. This will require closer international co-operation, greater transparency, data and reporting requirements. To ensure that the actions can be implemented quickly, a multilateral instrument to amend bilateral tax treaties will be developed.

This Action Plan was fully endorsed by the G20 Finance Ministers and Central Bank Governors at their July 2013 meeting in Moscow as well as the G20 Heads of State at their meeting in Saint-Petersburg in September 2013. The actions outlined in the plan are aimed to be delivered within the coming 18 to 24 months. For the first time ever in tax matters, non-OECD/G20 countries are involved on an equal footing.

This initiative, while not directly linked to the compilation of statistics, may still have, indirectly, a positive impact on the quality of national accounts by amending some artificial accounting, and creating better statistical sources for multinational enterprises.

In the most recent standards for the compilation of national accounts, the SNA 2008, some of the above issues related to globalisation have also been addressed. In the latest standards, much more attention is paid on phenomena like merchanting and goods for processing, which are typical ways of arranging global production. The recording of both has been changed and clarified, as compared to the previous standard, SNA 1993 (see Chapter 14). Furthermore, a specific section is devoted to the existence of Special Purpose Entities and other captive institutions (SNA 2008, para. 4.55-4.67). However, at the moment of writing this publication, one has to recognise that we are only at the verge of fully understanding the implications of globalisation for the compilation of national accounts, although much progress has been made. For example, many national statistical offices nowadays have specific survey programmes to capture consistent data on multinationals. Further guidance has also been provided in the UNECE/ Eurostat/OECD (UNECE and al.). More specific considerations on the recording and measurement of global production arrangements will be provided in a Guide on Measuring Global Production to be completed at the end of 2014 or the beginning of 2015.

It should also be clear that it will not be possible to solve all of the issues mentioned in the above. The allocation of value added and profits for large multinationals being governed by tax considerations, rather than by arriving at an accurate understanding of production processes is a matter of fact, and for some part also reflects economic rationale. On the other hand, there are also millions of smaller firms that do not have these possibilities and, while this kind of issues may affect, at least to some extent, the measurement of the level of GDP, it will usually affect the estimation of economic growth to a lesser extent. Multifactor productivity analysis, the analysis of changes in the volume of output as compared to changes of the volume of all inputs including services provided by intangible capital, may also need to be treated with care, especially in cases of knowledge intensive industries with high shares of foreign controlled enterprises. The same is true, even to a larger extent, for analysis of value added and profits of foreign controlled enterprises.

Some have argued that it would be preferable to put more emphasis on Gross or Net National Income (GNI/NNI) than on GDP. GNI/NNI is indeed not affected by the allocation of value added and profits across countries, as all profits will anyhow end up in the country of residence of the multinational, via "reinvested earnings on foreign direct investment" (see Chapter 7). This idea may already be reality in smaller economies with high levels of activities by multinationals. In this respect, it can be noted that the budget allocation of most international organisations is already based on GNI rather than on GDP.

That being said, it clearly becomes more and more relevant to separately distinguish foreign controlled enterprises, or more generally internationally operating enterprises, from other enterprises in the description of the national economy. This is not only true for the detailed analysis of the production process in supply and supply tables, but also for the analysis of income and finance as described in the institutional sector accounts. By separately distinguishing these corporations, one could analyse the behaviour of international enterprises, which in a national setting by definition only describe parts of (substantially) larger entities. One would also arrive at an improved description of mainly domestically operating enterprises.

Having data on foreign controlled enterprises at the national level would potentially also allow for the compilation at an aggregate level of worldwide consolidated data on multinational enterprises, consistent with the description of the national economies, and enabling a detailed analysis of multinationals. It may also improve the consistent recording of (international) transactions of multinationals, which countries currently predominantly survey and record at the national level, without an international exchange of data for reasons of confidentiality at the individual enterprise level. A first step in this direction is the construction of internationally consistent national business registers, e.g. the Eurogroups Register, an initiative at the EU-level, which will allow for an appropriate and consistent disentanglement and allocation to countries of the sometimes very complex organisational structures of multinationals. All these and related initiatives will lead to a better understanding, capturing and analysis of economic developments in a globalising world.

References

CBS (2012), Internalisation Monitor 2012, *www.cbs.nl/nl-NL/menu/themas/internationale-handel/publicaties/publicaties/archief/2012/2012-internationalisation-monitor-2012-pub.htm.*

Lipsey, R. (2010), "Measuring the Location of Production in a World of Intangible Productive Assets, FDI and Intrafirm Trade", Review of Income and Wealth, Issue 56, Special Issue 1, June 2010.

OECD (2014), *National Accounts at a Glance 2014*, OECD Publishing, Paris, doi: *http://dx.doi.org/10.1787/na_glance-2014-en.*

OECD (2013), FDI series of BOP, *http://stats.oecd.org/Index.aspx?DataSetCode=FDI_BOP_IIP* and *www.oecd.org/investment/statistics.htm* and *www.oecd.org/investment/statistics.htm.*

OECD/WTO (2013), OECD-WTO: Statistics on Trade in Value Added, (database), doi: *http://dx.doi.org/10.1787/data-00648-en.*

SNA 2008, European Commission, International Monetary Fund, Organisation for Economic Co-operation and Development, United Nations, World Bank, New York, 2009, System of National Accounts 2008, *http://unstats.un.org/unsd/nationalaccount/docs/SNA2008.pdf.*

UNECE and al., UNECE/Eurostat/OECD, "Guide on the Impact of Globalisation on National Accounts"; see *www.unece.org/fileadmin/DAM/stats/publications/Guide_on_Impact_of_globalization_on_national_accounts__web_.pdf.*

Understanding National Accounts
Second Edition
© OECD 2014

Index

Glossary

Accounting identity: Chapter 10

An equality between national accounts variable which stands by definition.

For example, supply = use is an accounting identity.

Accrual accounting: Chapter 10

Accrual accounting records flows at the time economic value is created, transformed, exchanged, transferred or extinguished; this means that flows which imply a change of ownership are entered when ownership passes, services are recorded when provided, output is entered at the time products are created and intermediate consumption is recorded when materials and supplies are being used.

Actual consumption: Chapter 5

Actual individual consumption is measured by the total value of household final consumption expenditure, non-profit institutions serving households (NPISHs) final consumption expenditure and government expenditure on individual consumption goods and services.

Actual final consumption of households is the value of the consumption goods and services acquired by households, whether by purchase in general, or by transfer from government units or NPISHs, and used by them for the satisfaction of their needs and wants; it is derived from their final consumption expenditure by adding the value of social transfers in kind receivable.

Actual final consumption of general government is measured by the value of the collective (as opposed to individual) consumption services provided to the community, or large sections of the community, by general government; it is derived from their final consumption expenditure by subtracting the value of social transfers in kind payable.

There is no actual final consumption of non-profit institutions serving households (NPISHs) because, in practice, most of their services are individual in nature and so, for simplicity, all services provided by NPISHs are treated by convention as individual (as social transfers in kind).

Aggregate: Chapter 1

Data obtained by aggregation, as distinct from unit record data.

Apparent productivity: Chapter 4

Apparent labour productivity is defined as output or value added per person employed or per hour worked.

Balance sheet: Chapter 8

A balance sheet is a statement, drawn up at a particular point in time, of the values of assets owned and of liabilities outstanding. The balancing item is called net worth. In national accounts a balance sheet is drawn up for sectors, the total economy and, partly, the rest of the world. For a sector the balance sheet shows the value of all assets – produced, non-produced and financial – and liabilities and the sector's net worth. For the total economy the balance sheet provides as balancing item what is often referred to as national wealth: the sum of non-financial assets and net financial assets with respect to the rest of the world.

Basic price: Chapter 10

The basic price is the amount receivable by the producer from the purchaser for a unit of a good or service produced as output minus any tax payable, and plus any subsidy receivable, on that unit as a consequence of its production or sale; it excludes any transport charges invoiced separately by the producer.

Basic wage: Chapter 2

Wage rates measure the basic remuneration per time unit or unit of output.

Although the Resolutions of the 12th International Conference of Labour Statisticians (ICLS, 1973) does not contain a specific definition of "wages" as such, it recommends the compilation of wage rate statistics which should include basic wages, cost-of living allowances and other guaranteed and regularly paid allowances, but exclude overtime payments, bonuses and gratuities, family allowances and other social security payments made by employers. Ex gratia payments in kind, supplementary to normal wage rates, are also excluded.

Wage rate data should relate to an appropriate time period- hour, day, week or month.

Wage rates may be viewed from the perspective of a "price" of labour services.

Capital stock: *Chapter 8*

Gross capital stock is the value of all fixed assets still in use, at the actual or estimated current purchasers' prices for new assets of the same type, irrespective of the age of the assets.

Net capital stock is the sum of the written-down values of all the fixed assets still in use; it can also be described as the difference between gross capital stock and consumption of fixed capital.

Changes in inventories: *Chapter 1*

Changes in inventories (including work-in-progress) consist of changes in: (a) stocks of outputs that are still held by the units that produced them prior to their being further processed, sold, delivered to other units or used in other ways; and (b) stocks of products acquired from other units that are intended to be used for intermediate consumption or for resale without further processing; they are measured by the value of the entries into inventories less the value of withdrawals and the value of any recurrent losses of goods held in inventories.

Collective consumption expenditure: *Chapter 9*

Goods and services that are consumed simultaneously by a group of consumers or by the community as a whole: for example, defence services provided by the state.

Compensation of employees: *Chapter 1*

Compensation of employees is the total remuneration, in cash or in kind, payable by an enterprise to an employee in return for work done by the latter during the accounting period.

Compensation of employees has two main components:

a) Wages and salaries payable in cash or in kind;

b) The value of the social contributions payable by employers: these may be actual social contributions payable by employers to Social Security schemes or to private funded social insurance schemes to secure social benefits for their employees; or imputed social contributions by employers providing unfunded social benefits.

Constant prices: *Chapter 2*

Data is said to be "at constant prices of a given year" when it reflects values of flows or stocks of goods and services from which has been factored out changes in the prices of the goods and services concerned since the given year.; the term "at constant prices" commonly refers to series which use a volume fixed-base Laspeyres formula. More generally, "constant prices" is sometimes used as a synonym for "volume".

Consumption of fixed capital: Chapter 1

Consumption of fixed capital represents the reduction in the value of the fixed assets used in production during the accounting period resulting from physical deterioration, normal obsolescence or normal accidental damage.

Demand: Chapter 5

Final demand is the short term used by economists to qualify the sum of final consumption expenditures, investment expenditures and net exports.

Disposable income: Chapter 1

Disposable income is derived from the balance of primary incomes of an institutional unit or sector by adding all current transfers, except social transfers in kind, receivable by that unit or sector and subtracting all current transfers, except social transfers in kind, payable by that unit or sector; it is the balancing item in the Secondary Distribution of Income Account.

Domestic demand: Chapter 5

Final domestic demand is the short term used by economists to qualify the part of final demand that is domestic: final consumption expenditures + investment expenditures.

Economic territory: Chapter 5

The economic territory of a country consists of the geographic territory administered by a government within which persons, goods, and capital circulate freely. It includes: (a) the airspace, territorial waters, and continental shelf lying in international waters over which the country enjoys exclusive rights or over which it has, or claims to have, jurisdiction in respect of the right to fish or to exploit fuels or minerals below the sea bed; (b) territorial enclaves in the rest of the world; and (c) any free zones, or bonded warehouses or factories operated by offshore enterprises under customs control (these form part of the economic territory of the country in which they are physically located).

Economically significant: Chapter 9

Prices are said to be economically significant when they have a significant influence on the amounts the producers are willing to supply and on the amounts purchasers wish to buy.

External demand: Chapter 5

External demand is the short term used by economists to qualify net exports.

Final consumption expenditure: Chapter 9

Government final consumption expenditure consists of expenditure, including imputed expenditure, incurred by general government on both individual consumption goods and services and collective consumption services.

Household final consumption expenditure consists of the expenditure, including imputed expenditure, incurred by resident households on individual consumption goods and services, including those sold at prices that are not economically significant.

Final consumption expenditure of non-profit institutions serving households (NPISHs) consists of the expenditure, including imputed expenditure, incurred by resident NPISHs on individual consumption goods and services.

Final uses: Chapter 5

Short terminology used to qualify the sum of final consumption expenditures, gross capital formation and net exports.

Financial corporations: Chapter 10

Financial corporations consist of all resident corporations or quasi-corporations principally engaged in financial intermediation or in auxiliary financial activities which are closely related to financial intermediation.

Financial intermediation: Chapter 4

Financial intermediation is a productive activity in which an institutional unit incurs liabilities on its own account for the purpose of acquiring financial assets by engaging in financial transactions on the market; the role of financial intermediaries is to channel funds from lenders to borrowers by intermediating between them.

Financial intermediation services indirectly measured (FISIM): Chapter 4

Financial intermediation services indirectly measured (FISIM) is an indirect measure of the value of financial intermediation services provided but for which financial institutions do not charge explicitly.

Financial transaction: Chapter 8

Financial transactions between institutional units and between institutional units and the rest of the world cover all transactions involving change of ownership of financial assets, including the creation and liquidation of financial claims.

Flow of funds table: Chapter 8

Synonym for "financial accounts".

GDP deflator: Chapter 1

GDP at current prices divided by GDP in volume.

GDP in volume: Chapter 1

Gross Domestic Product (GDP) in volume often refers to GDP at constant prices which is obtained by expressing values in terms of a base period.

In theory, the price and quantity components of a value are identified and the price in the base period is substituted for that in the current period. Two main methods are adopted in practice.

The first, referred to as "quantity revaluation", is based on a methodology consistent with the above theory (i.e., by multiplying the current period quantity by the base period price).

The second, commonly referred to as "price deflation", involves dividing price indexes into the observed values to obtain the volume estimate. The price indexes used are built up from the prices of the major items contributing to each value.

General government: Chapter 1, 9

The general government sector consists of the totality of institutional units which, in addition to fulfilling their political responsibilities and their role of economic regulation, produce principally non-market services (possibly goods) for individual or collective consumption and redistribute income and wealth.

Goods: Chapter 4

Also called "merchandises". All products that are not services.

Goods and services accounts: Chapter 10

The goods and services account shows for the economy as a whole and for groups of products, the total resources in terms of output and imports, and the uses of goods and services in terms of intermediate consumption, final consumption, gross capital formation and exports.

Gross capital formation: Chapter 1

Gross capital formation is measured by the total value of the gross fixed capital formation, changes in inventories and acquisitions less disposals of valuables for a unit or sector.

Gross domestic product (GDP): Chapter 1

Gross domestic product is an aggregate measure of production equal to the sum of the gross values added of all resident institutional units engaged in production (plus any taxes, and minus any subsidies, on products not included in the value of their outputs). It is also equal to the sum of the final uses of goods and services measured in purchasers' prices, less the value of imports of goods and services. It is also equal to the the sum of primary incomes distributed by resident producer units.

Gross fixed capital formation: Chapter 1

Gross fixed capital formation is measured by the total value of producer's acquisitions, less disposals, of fixed assets during the accounting period plus certain additions to the value of non- produced assets (such as subsoil assets or major improvements in the quantity, quality or productivity of land) realised by the productive activity of institutional units.

Gross national income (GNI): Chapter 1

Gross national income (GNI) is GDP less net taxes on production and imports, less compensation of employees and property income payable to the rest of the world plus the corresponding items receivable from the rest of the world (in other words, GDP less primary incomes payable to non- resident units plus primary incomes receivable from non-resident units). (note that gross national income is identical to gross national product (GNP) in the old terminology of national accounts).

Gross national product (GNP): Chapter 1

See Gross national income (GNI).

Household: Chapter 1, 6

The concept of household is based on the arrangements made by persons, individually or in groups, for providing themselves with food or other essentials for living. A household is essentially a "family" in ordinary terms. A household may be either (a) a one-person household, that is to say, a person who makes provision for his or her own food or other essentials for living without combining with any other person to form part of a multi-person household or (b) a multi-person household, that is to say, a group of two or more persons living together who make common provision for food or other essentials for living. The persons in the group may pool their incomes and may, to a greater or lesser extent, have a common budget; they may be related or unrelated persons or constitute a combination of persons both related and unrelated.

A household may be located in a housing unit or in a set of collective living quarters such as a boarding house, a hotel or a camp, or may comprise the administrative personnel in an institution. The household may also be homeless.

Household final consumption expenditure: Chapter 1

Household final consumption expenditure consists of the expenditure, including imputed expenditure, incurred by resident households on individual consumption goods and services, including those sold at prices that are not economically significant.

Household saving ratio: Chapter 1

The household saving ratio is most often defined as net saving divided by the sum of net disposable income and the adjustment D8. A gross version exists: gross saving divided by the sum of gross disposable income and the adjustment D8.

Households' actual final consumption: Chapter 3

Actual final consumption of households is the value of the consumption goods and services acquired by households, whether by purchase in general, or by transfer from government units or NPISHs, and used by them for the satisfaction of their needs and wants; it is derived from their final consumption expenditure by adding the value of social transfers in kind receivable.

Imputed expenditures: Chapter 5

Some transactions which are desirable to include in the accounts are not exchanged for money and therefore cannot be directly measured; in such cases a conventional value is imputed to the corresponding expenditure (the conventions used vary from case to case and are described in the SNA as necessary).

Individual consumption expenditure: Chapter 3

Part of general government expenditure that can be attributed to households plus all expenditure of NPISHs.

Input-output table: Chapter 10

An input-output table is a means of presenting a detailed analysis of the process of production and the use of goods and services (products) and the income generated in that production.; they can be either in the form of (a) supply and use tables or (b) symmetric input-output tables.

Institutional sector: Chapter 9, 10

The SNA 08 states that Institutional units are grouped together to form institutional sectors, on the basis of their principal functions, behaviour, and objectives.

Institutional unit: Chapter 9, 10

An institutional unit may be defined as an economic entity that is capable, in its own right, of owning assets, incurring liabilities and engaging in economic activities and in transactions with other entities.

Intermediate consumption: Chapter 1

Intermediate consumption consists of the value of the goods and services consumed as inputs by a process of production, excluding fixed assets whose consumption is recorded as consumption of fixed capital; the goods or services may be either transformed or used up by the production process.

Market producers: Chapter 4

Market producers are producers that sell most or all of their output at prices that are economically significant.

Market price: Chapter 9

Market prices are the actual price agreed upon by the transactors. In the absence of market transactions, valuation is made according to costs incurred (non-market services produced by government) or by reference to market prices for analogous goods or services (services of owner-occupied dwellings).

Market sector: Chapter 4

Also called "business sector". The sector comprising all enterprises selling their output at economically significant prices.

Mixed income: Chapter 1

Mixed income is the surplus or deficit accruing from production by unincorporated enterprises owned by households; it implicitly contains an element of remuneration for work done by the owner, or other members of the household, that cannot be separately identified from the return to the owner as entrepreneur but it excludes the operating surplus coming from owner-occupied dwellings.

Net disposable income: Chapter 6

Gross disposable income minus consumption of fixed capital.

Net domestic product (NDP): Chapter 1

Net domestic product (NDP) is obtained by deducting the consumption of fixed capital from gross domestic product.

Net exports: Chapter 5

Difference between exports and imports of goods and services. Also referred to as net foreign balance or balance of imports and exports.

Net lending/net borrowing: Chapter 8

Net lending is the net amount a unit or a sector has available to finance, directly or indirectly, other units or other sectors.

It is the balancing item in the capital account and is defined as: (Net saving plus capital transfers receivable minus capital transfers payable) minus (the value of acquisitions less disposals of non-financial assets, less consumption of fixed capital).

Negative net lending may also be described as "net borrowing".

Net lending/net borrowing of general government: Chapter 1, 9

See "Net lending/net borrowing".

Net value added: Chapter 1

Net value added is the value of output less the values of both intermediate consumption and consumption of fixed capital.

Non-financial accounts: Chapter 8

The complete sequence of national accounts excluding financial accounts and balance sheet.

Non-financial corporations: Chapter 7

Non-financial corporations are corporations whose principal activity is the production of market goods or non-financial services.

Non-financial transaction: Chapter 8

A transaction not included in the financial accounts of the system of national accounts.

Non-market producers: Chapter 4, 9

Non-market producers are producers that provide most of their output to others for free or at prices which are not economically significant.

Non-market sector: Chapter 4

The sector comprising all non-market producers which are producers that provide most of their output to others free or at prices which are not economically significant.

Non-observed: Chapter 4

The groups of activities most likely to be non-observed are those that are underground, illegal, informal sector, or undertaken by households for their own final use. Activities may also be missed because of deficiencies in the basic statistical data collection programme.

Non-profit institutions serving households (NPISHs): Chapter 5

Non-profit institutions serving households (NPISHs) consist of NPIs which are not predominantly financed and controlled by government or by corporations and which provide goods or services to households free or at prices that are not economically significant.

Net operating surplus: Chapter 7

Gross operating surplus minus consumption of fixed capital.

Operating surplus: Chapter 7

The operating surplus measures the surplus or deficit accruing from production before taking account of any interest, rent or similar charges payable on financial or tangible non-produced assets borrowed or rented by the enterprise, or any interest, rent or similar receipts receivable on financial or tangible non-produced assets owned by the enterprise.

Note: for unincorporated enterprises owned by households, this component is called "mixed income".

Output: Chapter 4

Output consists of those goods or services that are produced within an establishment that become available for use outside that establishment, plus any goods and services produced for own final use.

Output gap: Chapter 4

An output gap refers to the difference between actual and potential gross domestic product (GDP) as a per cent of potential GDP.

Output of non-market services: Chapter 9

Other non-market output consists of goods and individual or collective services produced by non- profit institutions serving households (NPISHs) or government that are supplied free, or at prices that are not economically significant, to other institutional units or the community as a whole.

Such output is one of three broad categories of output in the System of National Accounts (SNA), with the others being market output and output produced for own final use.

Potential GDP: Chapter 4

Potential gross domestic product (GDP) is defined in the *OECD Economic Outlook* publication as the level of output that an economy can produce at a constant inflation rate. An economy can temporarily produce more than its potential level of output but the higher level comes at the cost of rising inflation. Potential output depends on the capital stock, the potential labour force (which depends on demographic factors and on participation rates), the non-accelerating inflation rate of unemployment (NAIRU), and the level of labour efficiency.

Production function: Chapter 4

Production function is the maximum set of output(s) that can be produced with a given set of inputs. Use of a production function implies technical efficiency.

Purchaser's price: Chapter 10

The purchaser's price is the amount paid by the purchaser, excluding any deductible VAT or similar deductible tax, in order to take delivery of a unit of a good or service at the time and place required by the purchaser; the purchaser's price of a good includes any transport charges paid separately by the purchaser to take delivery at the required time and place.

Purchasing power of household gross disposable income: Chapter 6

Household gross disposable income deflated by an appropriate price index, in general the implicit deflator of household final expenditure.

Purchasing power parities: Chapter 3

Purchasing power parities (PPPs) are the rates of currency conversion that equalise the purchasing power of different currencies by eliminating the differences in price levels between countries. In their simplest form, PPPs are simply price relatives which show the ratio of the prices in national currencies of the same good or service in different countries.

Residence: Chapter 5

A unit is said to be resident in a country when its "centre of economic" interest is situated in that country's economic territory.

Rest of the world: Chapter 1

The rest of the world refers to all non-resident institutional units that enter into transactions with resident units, or have other economic links with resident units. Included are certain institutional units that may be physically located within the geographic boundary of a country, for example, foreign enclaves such as embassies, consulates or military bases, and also international organisations.

Saving: Chapter 1, 6

Saving is disposable income less final consumption expenditure (or adjusted disposable income less actual final consumption), in both cases after taking account of an adjustment for pension funds; saving is an important aggregate which can be calculated for each institutional sector or for the whole economy.

Seasonal adjustment: Chapter 11

Seasonal adjustment is a statistical technique to remove the effects of seasonal calendar influences operating on a series. Seasonal effects usually reflect the influence of the seasons themselves either directly or through production series related to them, or social conventions.

Other types of calendar variation occur as a result of influences such as number of days in the calendar period, the accounting or recording practices adopted or the incidence of moving holidays (such as Easter).

Services: Chapter 4

Services are opposed to "goods" which embed the production in a physical object. Services are the result of a production activity that is not embedded in a physical object and rather directly changes the conditions of the consuming unit. Services cannot be traded separately from their production. By the time their production is completed they must have been provided to the consumers.

Social benefits in kind: Chapter 9

Social benefits in kind consist of (a) social security benefits, reimbursements, (b) other social security benefits in kind, (c) social assistance benefits in kind; they are equal to social transfers in kind excluding transfers of individual non-market goods and services.

Social benefits other than social transfers in kind: Chapter 9

Social benefits other than social transfers in kind consist of all social benefits except social transfers in kind.

They consist of:

a) all social benefits in cash – both social insurance and social assistance benefits – provided by government units, including social security funds, and NPISHs; and

b) all social insurance benefits provided under private funded and unfunded social insurance schemes, whether in cash or in kind.

Supply and use balance: Chapter 10

Supply and use tables are in the form of matrices that record how supplies of different kinds of goods and services originate from domestic industries and imports and how those supplies are allocated between various intermediate or final uses, including exports.

Taxes net of subsidies: Chapter 1

Taxes minus subsidies.

Taxes on income and wealth: Chapter 9

Most current taxes on income, wealth, etc. consist of taxes on the incomes of households or profits of corporations and taxes on wealth that are payable regularly every tax period (as distinct from capital taxes levied infrequently).

Taxes on production and imports: Chapter 9

Taxes on production and imports consist of taxes payable on goods and services when they are produced, delivered, sold, transferred or otherwise disposed of by their producers plus taxes and duties on imports that become payable when goods enter the economic territory by crossing the frontier or when services are delivered to resident units by non-resident units; they also include other taxes on production, which consist mainly of taxes on the ownership or use of land, buildings or other assets used in production or on the labour employed, or compensation of employees paid.

Terms of trade indices: Chapter 5

Terms of trade is the ratio of export and import prices.

Underground: Chapter 4

Underground production consists of activities that are productive in an economic sense and quite legal (provided certain standards or regulations are complied with), but which are deliberately concealed from public authorities for the following reasons:

a) to avoid the payment of income, value added or other taxes;

b) to avoid payment of social security contributions;

c) to avoid meeting certain legal standards such as minimum wages, maximum hours, safety or health standards, etc.;

d) to avoid complying with certain administrative procedures, such as completing statistical questionnaires or other administrative forms.

Value added: Chapter 1

Gross value added is the value of output less the value of intermediate consumption; it is a measure of the contribution to GDP made by an individual producer, industry or sector; gross value added is the source from which the primary incomes of the SNA are generated and is therefore carried forward into the primary distribution of income account.

Volume index: Chapter 2

A volume index is most commonly presented as a weighted average of the proportionate changes in the quantities of a specified set of goods or services between two periods of time; volume indices may also compare the relative levels of activity in different countries (e.g. those calculated using PPPs).

Working-day adjustment: Chapter 11

Working day or trading adjustments refer to the correction for differences in the number of working or trading days in a given month or quarter which differ from year to year which will impact upon the level of activity in that month or quarter for flow series or the sort/type of day for stock series.

In most countries working day adjustment and trading day adjustment are used as synonyms.

ORGANISATION FOR ECONOMIC CO-OPERATION AND DEVELOPMENT

The OECD is a unique forum where governments work together to address the economic, social and environmental challenges of globalisation. The OECD is also at the forefront of efforts to understand and to help governments respond to new developments and concerns, such as corporate governance, the information economy and the challenges of an ageing population. The Organisation provides a setting where governments can compare policy experiences, seek answers to common problems, identify good practice and work to co-ordinate domestic and international policies.

The OECD member countries are: Australia, Austria, Belgium, Canada, Chile, the Czech Republic, Denmark, Estonia, Finland, France, Germany, Greece, Hungary, Iceland, Ireland, Israel, Italy, Japan, Korea, Luxembourg, Mexico, the Netherlands, New Zealand, Norway, Poland, Portugal, the Slovak Republic, Slovenia, Spain, Sweden, Switzerland, Turkey, the United Kingdom and the United States. The European Union takes part in the work of the OECD.

OECD Publishing disseminates widely the results of the Organisation's statistics gathering and research on economic, social and environmental issues, as well as the conventions, guidelines and standards agreed by its members.

OECD PUBLISHING, 2, rue André-Pascal, 75775 PARIS CEDEX 16
(30 2014 05 1 P) ISBN 978-92-64-21462-0 – 2014-02

CPSIA information can be obtained
at www.ICGtesting.com
Printed in the USA
LVHW08s0211260818
588076LV00001B/2/P

9 789264 214620